AMERICAN SOCIOLOGY SERIES

Kimball Young, General Editor

AMERICAN SOCIOLOGY SERIES

Minorities in
American Society

CHARLES F. MARDEN

Assistant Professor of Sociology
Rutgers University, New Brunswick, N. J.

AMERICAN BOOK COMPANY

New York Cincinnati Chicago Boston Atlanta Dallas San Francisco

TO FREDA AND PHILIP

Ardent practitioners of the democratic way of life.

ACKNOWLEDGMENTS

The writer is greatly indebted to many people for their generous counsel in the preparation of this book. He wishes to acknowledge with deep appreciation the assistance rendered by several of his colleagues at Rutgers, the State University of New Jersey, for their critical reading of chapters as indicated below. Professor Edward McN. Burns read several chapters with particular attention to the first chapter and Chapter 14, concerned with religious minorities. Dr. Paul W. Massing gave counsel on the analytical and interpretative sections, especially Chapters 2 and 16, and also Chapter 15, dealing with Jewish-gentile relations. The chapter on race was read with critical comment by Professor Ashley M. F. Montagu, and the chapter dealing with the impact of immigration on American society by Professor L. Ethan Ellis.

Outside of the author's academic circle, grateful acknowledgment is tendered the following for their cooperation in giving expert advice on other portions of the book: Professor George I. Sanchez of the University of Texas for the chapter on Spanish-speaking Americans; Professor Joel V. Berreman of the University of Oregon for the chapter on the Chinese and Japanese; Dr. Ira DeA. Reid of Haverford College for the entire section on Negro-white relations; Professor John Collier of the College of the City of New York for the chapter on the American Indians; and Professor Edwin A. Burrows of the University of Connecticut for the section dealing with the peoples of Hawaii. The above mentioned have not in all cases read the final draft as it appears in publication and are not, in any event, responsible for any errors which may appear nor for any failure of the writer properly to interpret their numerous and invaluable suggestions.

The writer wishes also to express his gratitude to Professor Kimball

Young of Northwestern University, general editor of the American Sociology Series, to which this volume is added, for his encouragement and stimulating editorial criticism in the later stages of the preparation of the manuscript.

The timely assistance of Miss Hilda Wobber in the preparation of the index is acknowledged with thanks.

Finally, it is difficult, indeed, for the author to express adequately his gratitude to his wife, Freda Wobber Marden, for her part in the creation of this book. She has not only spent countless hours in helping prepare the text but has also contributed many creative suggestions and rewritten numerous passages. Beyond this, the author appreciates her willingness to subordinate other interests to make the completion of the book possible.

The lines quoted on page 326 are from *Indians of the Americas* by John Collier, published as a Mentor Book by The New American Library of World Literature, Inc., and in a clothbound edition by W. W. Norton and Company, Inc. Other source credits and permissions to quote appear in the footnotes accompanying the text.

FOREWORD

Throughout its history, American society has included in its membership many groups who have been considered as somehow alien, not quite belonging to the normative society: immigrants; colored people; and non-Christians. The study of these groups and their relation to the larger society about them has occupied the attention of social scientists throughout the 20th century. They were often studied particularistically, each group by itself or sometimes as classes of groups variously described as ethnics, races, or sects. Such study began to show that the position which each of the groups occupied in American society was in conceptual terms so similar that each could be denoted by the term "minority." Thus social science began to generalize about the characteristics of a minority and to describe typical stages in the process by which minorities became assimilated, that is, became accepted as bona fide Americans. Ultimately the study of the various groups in their relation to the norm-setting "native" group became a recognized special field of social science analysis and the various data and materials gathered from the study of particular groups began to be integrated as the sociology of minorities. The appearance in 1932 of Donald Young's textbook, *American Minority Peoples,* marks the acceptance of this new, more integrated approach. Our book, likewise designed as a text covering this same field, aims to carry on, and it is hoped, carry forward, this integrated standpoint.

In its approach to this field, the book differs in its emphasis from its predecessors by taking as its central unit, not minorities as such, but rather the relations, or the dynamic interaction, between the minority and its reciprocal, which we shall call the dominant. The term *minority* has only within the past decade become recognized as a formal concept. The term *dominant* has not been used in a conceptual sense. Minority, however, as it is defined, can have no meaning except in relation to its reciprocal. We are accustomed in our society to the term minority as designating a political party out of power, with the majority, in power, as its reciprocal. The characteristics of the

ix

intergroup relations with which we are concerned differ from that of majority-minority in this political usage. The structure of the relations we study are superordinate-subordinate in nature connoting superior and inferior statuses for the two groups in the larger, total society. Furthermore, this kind of social structure originates through the superior power possessed by the superordinate group and continues to be sustained by this power. Because of these characteristics we consider the word *dominant* the most appropriate term to designate the reciprocal of minority.

The interaction between the dominant and the minority has been in the American scene a dynamic process, following in general a sequence of development or stages leading toward assimilation. Therefore, in treating each specific intergroup situation, we trace the relations in a time sequence. This procedure helps to bring out more precisely the role of the dominant in this interactional process. While at the time of first contact with the dominant, the minority has differences which it brought with it, the impact of dominant discrimination begins to create other differences. In the case of the American Negroes where the original difference was physiognomic and cultural, derived from their aboriginal heritage, today the remaining group difference, aside from the physiognomic features, derives in considerable part, from the effect of systematic discrimination.

Insofar as an integrated approach to dominant-minority relations is valid, it follows that a general, over-all interpretation should be possible. This we attempt to provide at the conclusion, after having described in its specific content, each dominant-minority situation. While in such a general interpretation, minority differences and minority behavior are contributing factors, the conditions and circumstances which motivate the dominant group to discriminate provide the unifying basis for interpretation.

Finally, the phenomena with which we deal are widely considered to constitute a social problem. Although our primary aim is to provide a faithful description and objective interpretation of the dominant-minority structure and process, it seems to us somewhat unrealistic to ignore their problem aspects. Social problems cannot, however, be adequately treated without considering in each case the value system which is being employed. In this book wherever a "problem" aspect of dominant-minority relations is discussed without reference to any other specific value system, the reader may assume the "American Creed," as Myrdal has popularized the term, as our value frame of reference. In essence, this creed holds that all Americans irrespective of race, nationality origin, and religious affiliation have the right of equitable access to justice, freedom, and opportunity.

TABLE OF CONTENTS

TABLES

Table   Page

FIGURE

Figure   Page

CHARTS

Chart   Page

GRAPHS

Graph   Page

PART ONE

Introduction

In subsequent parts of this volume the main minority situations in the United States and its territories are delineated in detail. In this part, some general considerations pertinent to them all are introduced. In Chapter 1, we point out the significance to American society of the presence of minorities, with special emphasis upon its meaning in relation to the present situation of the United States in world affairs. Chapter 2 provides a general introduction to the sociology of dominant-minority relations, portraying their essential character and defining the terms as they are used in this book to describe and analyze this form of intergroup relations. Because "race consciousness" is a factor involved in many dominant-minority patterns and because "race" is a term about which so much confusion still prevails, it seems appropriate to provide a general orientation in Chapter 3 to the meaning of race as social science now views it in contrast to the myths about race which large segments of the public still believe.

CHAPTER 1

The Significance of Minorities
in American Society

FIRST NEGRO ADMITTED TO BAR ASSOCIATION—COLLEGE FRATERNITY ADMITS FIRST NEGRO MEMBER—SEGREGATION ENDED IN PUBLIC SCHOOL—PROPOSED BILL TO INDEMNIFY JAPANESE FOR WARTIME PROPERTY LOSSES—SUPREME COURT HOLDS RESTRICTIVE COVENANTS CANNOT BE ENFORCED BY LAW—MORE AID FOR NAVAJOS GRANTED—COURT BERATES YOUTH FOR ANTI-SEMITIC VANDALISM—PRESIDENT PUSHES ANTIDISCRIMINATION ON JOB BILL.

Headlines like these with the accompanying news accounts have been almost daily occurrences in the leading newspapers of the United States since the conclusion of World War II. Admittedly such headlines are selective. In the postwar period traditional discriminations against minorities have persisted in large measure. But such headlines represent a new tone in race relations. This is further reflected in the subjects of numerous magazine articles, in novels such as *Gentlemen's Agreement* and *Kingsblood Royal,* and in motion pictures such as *Pinky* and *Intruder in the Dust* and *The Lawless.* All this manifests an accelerated public interest in the condition of minorities. National self-consciousness about minorities is the most outstanding new fea-

3

ture of intergroup relations in the current American scene. Furthermore, the prevailing public sentiment seems to view the situations of the minorities as "problems" and to feel that as problems they require "solutions." Several states have established "good-will commissions"; a number of community groups have conducted audits of their discriminatory practices; many professional, civic, and other clubs have had speakers on race relations. In the midst of all this accentuated goodwill among the dominant elements, formal organizations representing the minorities have displayed a rising, although cautious, militancy. Finally, in regard to solutions, or steps toward them, the prevailing trend is in the democratic direction—toward the elimination of discrimination and segregation. Variations in public disagreement over solutions range about how much discrimination should be eliminated and how rapidly. Publicly, at least, few voices advocate tightening the barriers still further.

These heightened interests and activities concerning minorities are, in part, cumulative results of social forces long present in our society, particularly the dynamics of our domestic democracy. However, one detects in the current situation a growing note of urgency created by the rapidly changing international scene. The United States now occupies a position of peculiar responsibility in the efforts to organize world unity on democratic principles. In addition to its power and resources, the nation has a heritage and experience in democratic processes which qualify it in many ways for this role. But one of its serious limitations is its past and present treatment of its own minorities. On October 23, 1947, the National Association for the Advancement of Colored People presented to the Human Rights Commission of the United Nations a petition entitled "A Statement on the Denial of Human Rights to Minorities in the Case of Citizens of Negro Descent in the United States of America." It is doubtful whether many people in America would deny the substantial truth of the statements made therein. Nor would many people deny that much more could be added to document discrimination against Americans of other minority lineage. Here we face the anomalous situation of the champion of democracy indicted for its failure to practice democracy in its dealings with a substantial portion of its own citizens. It is this aspect of the situation which gives heightened urgency to the subject of minorities.

Along with this increased general public interest in minorities, there has developed an increased interest in the topic on the part of social scientists. It is pertinent to note that greater scientific interest in minorities comes at a time when American social science is approaching a new level of maturity, especially in its definition of research projects and its development of more precise procedures of social investigation. This conjunction of events is a fortunate circumstance since the phenomena of dominant-minority relations are highly complicated and in some ways peculiarly resistant to research procedures which yield valid results in other fields of investigation. For example, in opinion polling, significant differences are found in the answers to the same questions by Negro respondents when Negro interviewers are used rather than white. While social scientists as responsible citizens will undoubtedly play a part in determining the goals to be sought, their greater contribution will be to show how best to proceed toward whatever goals the public consensus may decide to strive for. Beyond any question, there has never been so much research devoted to the area of minorities in American life as in the past decade. Granted that vastly more knowledge is needed, the results already achieved which may help to guide social policy are indeed substantial.[1]

The purpose of this book is to present a comprehensive description of many of the most important minority problems which have arisen and still prevail in the United States; to analyze and interpret the relations of the dominant to minority groups within a sociological framework; to state the general principles which emerge from such a study; and finally, to indicate how our present knowledge may be brought to bear upon social policy respecting minorities. What is meant by "within a sociological framework" will be more fully developed in Chapter 2. At this point, however, we need but say that the central focus of the book is the interaction which takes place between the dominant and the minority, the discriminations imposed and maintained by the former, and the reactions generated by these discriminations as manifested by the latter.

In this opening chapter, a preview of the range and scope of our inquiry in this book will be indicated by (1) a brief historical summary of dominant-minority relations in the modern era; (2) a summary preview of minority situations in United States history; and (3) a preliminary statement of some of the major ways in which these intergroup relations have affected our national life, and the nature of the problems which they create.

THE EMERGENCE OF DOMINANT-MINORITY RELATIONS IN MODERN HISTORY

The dominance of some human beings over others is as old as recorded history. In modern history, however, there has emerged a distinctive form of dominant-minority relations, in which "race con-

[1] See bibliography for Ch. 17 for research findings applicable to social policy.

sciousness" has been a salient feature. During the past four hundred years, Europeans, in general, and western Europeans, in particular, have penetrated other continents, and in various ways have established hegemony over much of them. The United States came into being through just such a process and the people who founded it, mostly of British origin, were among the leaders in this European expansionism. While what happened in the United States is explainable in large measure by forces present in its own history, full explanation requires viewing America's minority situations as a part of the larger historical process. In order to set the record of events in the United States in its proper perspective, we need a brief account of the relations of Europeans to these other peoples during the course of this great expansion.

Four major patterns of dominant-minority relations have arisen in modern history: the political annexation pattern; the colonial pattern; the slave pattern; and the immigration pattern.

The annexation pattern. The first of these is what has been viewed in modern European history as the political problem of minorities. Through their wars upon neighbors, conquering European nations have annexed portions of their neighbors' lands and have imposed special discriminations upon the newly acquired subjects of a different national culture, designed to force the assimilation of the minorities to the dominant culture pattern. Alsace-Lorraine, alternately French and German; Poland, attempting to resist Russification under the Tsars; Magyar dominance over sundry Slavic folks in Hungary—all these are illustrations of situations in which minorities arise by means of political annexation.

The colonial pattern. The colonial pattern developed along several lines, all best illustrated by Great Britain, the greatest colonizer of all. The development of a great trading economy, subsequently strengthened by the Industrial Revolution and the rapid growth of its population, prompted the British to establish political control over various parts of the world and to dominate the economic life of these vast areas primarily in the interest of Great Britain. Where these areas were densely populated by native peoples, control was maintained by placating the upper class rulers, as in India, and applying military force when needed. According to Raymond Kennedy, the outstanding characteristics of this system have been the political and economic subordination of the native population; poor development of social services, especially education, for natives; and the color line, with its rigid social barriers between the white ruling class and the subject people.[2] Of these, the most important feature for the study of minorities is the last—the color line. Concerning this, Kennedy writes:

The colonial code that dictates complete social segregation of the races is rationalized either by the commonplace assertion that natives are ignorant or unclean or uninteresting; or by the claim that they do not desire whites to become familiar with them; or by the argument that informality, camaraderie and, most of all, intermarriage would weaken the prestige of the ruling class in the estimation of their subjects. . . .

The British colonial code draws the most rigid color line of all. Paradoxically, the greatest colonizers in the world are the most provincial in their attitudes towards strange groups and cultures. The British have been in contact for a longer time with more dark peoples than any other western nation, yet they hold aloof from their subjects to an unequalled degree. They refuse to associate freely or make friends with other races, and this exclusiveness has engendered a reciprocal feeling toward them on the part of their colonial peoples. The attitude of the latter varies from indifference to active dislike, but, except in isolated instances, it never approaches friendliness. Natives often express a grudging admiration for the moral rectitude, financial incorruptibility, and legalistic fairness of Britishers, especially government officials, in the colonies; but bonds of mutual friendship and affection are lacking. . . .

The British demonstrate by their attitudes and behavior that they do not wish the natives to develop any sense of belonging to British society, and the entire social ritual of the colonies symbolizes the separateness of rulers and ruled. Nowhere in the colonial world are the lines of caste drawn more rigidly: in clubs, residential areas, places of public accommodation, and informal cliques. Nowhere is the taboo on intermarriage stronger, and the penalty for infraction more drastic.[3]

Where the areas of British expansion were thinly populated, the British themselves often settled, pushing back and partly annihilating the native population to take over the area, as in North America, Australia, and New Zealand. The remaining remnants of these native populations have eventually become wards of the Anglo-Saxon commonwealths.

The dominant-minority pattern of South Africa represents a mixture of the two foregoing types of development. Here the British settled, defeated in war their Dutch rivals, and then joined them to establish a nation based on a pattern of interracial segregation with 20 per cent white dominant and 80 per cent black (and some Hindu) subordinate. Race relations in South Africa are at a highly unstable

[2] Raymond Kennedy, "The Colonial Crisis and the Future," in Ralph Linton, ed., *The Science of Man in the World Crisis* (New York: Columbia University Press, 1945) p. 311.
[3] *Ibid.*, pp. 318, 320. By permission of the publishers, Columbia University Press.

and critical point. The racial hierarchy includes the European-descended whites at the top, the native African Negroes at the bottom, with Indians and mixed bloods, called *colored* to distinguish them from the natives, in between. A rigid pattern of segregation and discrimination prevails. The system in recent years has been undergoing severe strain both from within and from without the Union. In spite of the severe limitations imposed upon the nonwhites, their acculturation to western ways has proceeded far enough for Simons to write, "It is civic status, and not culture, that is correlated with racial origins." [4] These minorities are becoming more active in pressing for improvement in welfare and rise in status. Over the past two decades, the dominant white group has met this challenge, on the one hand by substantial increase in social services, but on the other hand with further tightening social and civic discrimination.[5] In 1950, the present administration processed a so-called Group Area Bill, designed to divide the nation into racial compartments, in each of which land would be owned and occupied only by the members of a designated race.[6] Outside the Union, criticism of its racial policies has been increasing, in which India has taken the lead, often through the United Nations.

Colonization on the part of Latin nations went through the same historic period in a spirit which was more romantically adventurous, but also much less efficient, and very much less successful. Early in the process Spain and Portugal lost more of their colonial empires. In their relations with the native populations, the Mediterraneans have never drawn the color line so rigidly. They have exploited native populations, but in their personal relations they have never been so adamantly possessed of the idea of racial superiority. Intermarriage has been far more frequent. Latin America has had more a rigid class system than Anglo-Saxon America but it has never been so preoccupied with race as a determiner of superiority or inferiority. This difference is further reflected in the contrasting treatment of slavery to which we now turn.

The involuntary migrant slave pattern. The enslavement of African peoples and their forced immigration to newly established colonies is the third pattern—or perhaps an auxiliary pattern—of dominant-minority relations to be found in the modern era. The Anglo-Saxons ultimately restricted their slave trade to the Negro but pursued it

---

[4] H. J. Simons, "Race Relations and Policies in Southern and Eastern Africa," in Ralph Linton, ed., *Most of the World* (New York: Columbia University Press, 1949) p. 324.
[5] *Ibid.*, pp. 324-329.
[6] G. H. Archambault, "South Africa Is Pressing Race Segregation Problem," *The New York Times*, June 11, 1950, E 5.

with characteristic efficiency, leaving a traditional legacy, reinforced by the timely invention of the cotton gin, to the American nation, destined to generate a social problem of the utmost gravity. The Latins made slaves out of Indians and white men as well as Negroes. But from the start, their slave policy varied from that of the Anglo-Saxons. The Latins accorded slaves a status as human beings, established definite rules which limited the rights of masters, provided definite procedures by which freedom might be obtained, and once freed, accepted them as free men.[7] This contrast between the Anglo-Saxons and the Latins as to the significance attached to race is strikingly evident in the last of the four major patterns of dominant-minority relations, that created by immigration.

The voluntary immigrant pattern. The fourth pattern of dominant-minority relations arose in consequence of the voluntary immigration of peoples from nations other than those of the original colonists. In this instance, the scene narrows largely to the United States which we discuss later, and secondarily to South America. Canada, Australia, New Zealand, and South Africa restricted immigration largely to British peoples, thus preserving a large measure of cultural homogeneity at the expense of more rapid population growth and industrial expansion. Of immigration to Latin America in the 19th and 20th centuries, the total has amounted to probably not more than 11 or 12 million, and practically all of this has been to two countries, Brazil and Argentina.[8] Of all South American countries, Argentina has the highest proportion of white, or Caucasian, population. It also has had the largest amount of European immigration of any Latin American country, most of which occurred between 1857 and 1930. In 1914 about three-tenths of its 8,885,000 inhabitants were foreign born. The greatest number of these were Italians and Spaniards with a scattering of newcomers from many of the other European nations. The government of Argentina adopted a policy of positive encouragement of this immigration and, in general, it can be said that these newcomers did not suffer discrimination. On the contrary, Davie writes, "The foreign-born are in a better position than citizens, since they have all the advantages that the latter enjoy and are exempt from certain obligations, like military service, that weigh upon the citizens."[9] Immigration to Brazil, on the other hand, has not been so great. Between 1820 and 1930 official figures report a total of about 4.5 million. An important element of contrast in the Brazilian situation was

[7] Frank Tannenbaum, *Slave and Citizen* (New York: Alfred A. Knopf, Inc., 1947).
[8] Maurice R. Davie, *World Immigration* (New York: The Macmillan Company, 1947) p. 446.
[9] *Ibid.,* p. 448.

that its native population included large admixtures of Negro strains and some Indian strains. "An estimate in 1928 placed the whites at 51 per cent, Negroes at 14 per cent, Indians 2 per cent, mulattoes 22 per cent, and other mixed bloods 11 per cent." [10] Like Argentina, Brazil officially encouraged European immigration in which Italians and Portuguese participated in about equal numbers, with Spaniards third, and a scattering of other nationalities. Included among immigrants to Brazil were also about 50,000 Japanese. The immigrants settled largely in the southern portions of the nation. In recent years, Brazil has, however, drastically curtailed immigration.

In summary, immigration expanded the culturally pluralistic character of these two Latin-American nations without introducing new dominant-minority situations. This fact stands in contrast to the United States whose record is presently to follow.

MINORITY SITUATIONS IN THE UNITED STATES

A brief historical account of the manifold minority situations in the United States will serve to establish the pervasive character of dominant-minority relations throughout its prenational and national existence.

Indians. From the earliest settlements in the colonial period to 1871, the white people increasingly encroached on the land possessed by American Indians. Prior to 1871, the relations of the whites to the Indians were considered formally, if somewhat fictionally, contractual relations between sovereign political entities. Following this date, Indians have been official wards of the United States Government and are thus formally, as well as actually, a minority. During this wardship period, neither the welfare nor the status of the Indians improved prior to 1934 when a new deal for them was established through new policies, the results of which are yet to be adequately measured. In any event, the Indians are today our fastest growing minority.

Negroes. Importation of Negro slaves to the English colonies began in 1619. Thus the new nation, born in 1776, inherited a slave minority brutally forced into pitiful subservience. The issue of their status was an important factor in the Civil War, one of the bloodiest intersectional struggles in human history. In spite of their long residence in this country, Negroes occupy the lowest status of all the American minorities. The situations in the North and South differ so markedly as to require separate treatment. Viewing minority situations as problems, those of Negro-white relations are the most serious. With the

[10] *Ibid.*, p. 455.

possible exception of the natives of South Africa, Negroes in America constitute the most conspicuous minority to be found in any nation today.

European immigrants. Even before American Negroes moved from slavery to the status of a minority caste, there began a movement which was destined to change profoundly the character of the United States. This was the immigration from Europe. Large concentrated aggregates from various nations came to this country. Their ways of life differed markedly from those of the "natives" among whom they settled. First came the Irish, Scandinavians, and Germans; later the southern and eastern Europeans. The relation of these various peoples to the older residents followed a pattern of processes broadly and monotonously similar; beginning with indifference, antagonism, and conflict and ending with assimilation and acceptance. The Immigration Act of 1924 with its small quota system set the stage for the final act of this particular minority group drama.

Once the restriction of European immigration went into effect, an important era in United States history began to end. While there still remain many immigrants who will live out their days never fully assimilated to American life, their children and certainly their grandchildren have been, or are being, assimilated. This chapter in the history of our minority group relations, as we shall point out later, is ending as the result of indirect social forces rather than as a result of any direct and purposeful planning. Compared with the situation of other minorities, it is no longer a problem. A study of this immigration era would have historical significance only, except for two considerations. First, from an analysis of the era can be learned much that may be applied to the analysis of other minority situations. Second, as a consequence of World War II, the problem of displaced persons required a reconsideration of our present immigration policy. The lessons learned from the great immigration period have a bearing on this more recent phase of immigration to this country.

As a foretaste of this new world problem, our country received a group of immigrants fleeing from the Nazis in the late 1930's who came to be known as "refugees." Although their numbers were not large, their tendency to concentrate in the metropolitan areas of the Middle Atlantic coast created a minor stir of characteristic "native" reaction toward the new alien in these localities. However, as they were absorbed quickly into the economy of a nation with increasing employment and into the social structure of the various nationality groups which they represented, this particular "refugee" problem did not seem too serious.

Of far greater significance than the prewar "refugee" immigration has been the postwar problem of the displaced persons, the vast number of people in Europe who were displaced as a result of World War II. The resettlement of these people became an international responsibility ultimately assumed by a special agency of the United Nations. The United States as the most prosperous and among the less crowded nations faced a major share in this responsibility. After much delay, a bill authorizing the admission of 228,514 displaced persons was passed in 1948 to be supplemented by another authorizing the admission of an additional 172,230 in 1950. While the great mass of those who were DP's at the close of the war has now been permanently resettled, new inflows of political refugees to western Europe from behind the Iron Curtain portend the extension of the DP problem into an indefinite future. Thus far, the manner in which the United States has handled this problem reflects the old and the new ways. The specific qualifications of the Displaced Persons Act (1948) were regarded by some people as reflecting anti-Semitic and anti-Catholic attitudes. Yet the actual processing of displaced persons for immigration has been conducted with elaborate planning by government and private agencies with the result that the characteristic problems of immigrant adjustment to their new life have been largely nonexistent.

Oriental immigrants. Overlapping chronologically with European immigration was the migration of Chinese and Japanese who concentrated in visible numbers in West Coast communities. First, they were tolerated with condescension in the role of exploitable labor. However, as these people, particularly the Japanese, began to succeed in competition with native whites, further immigration was curtailed by governmental policy before it reached major proportions. Those who remained here were frozen into a fixed pattern of segregated minority status little altered until the drastic relocation of Japanese during World War II was effected by the Federal Government. This latter unique epoch in the history of American minorities, from any long range view a regrettable episode, reveals a certain ineptitude and immaturity in handling of minority group problems.

Mexicans. Following the cessation of unrestricted immigration of Europeans there began a large influx of Mexicans into the Southwest. Again the usual pattern of interaction between native Americans and immigrant peoples was repeated except that up to 1950 the process has not advanced beyond the point of accommodation. Mexicans in the United States have encountered more severe discrimination than any other immigrant group except the Orientals. Probably numbering well over 2 million, they constitute one of the larger minority groups. In the Southwest, likewise, dwell the Hispanos, descended from the people who inhabited the region prior to its invasion by "Anglos" and its subsequent annexation by the United States. Hispanos make up a substantial fraction of the population of New Mexico, living mostly by themselves in rural areas. While they are not accorded differential treatment by the Anglos, their economic and health conditions rank among the lowest to be found in the nation.

New Wards: Filipinos, Hawaiians, Puerto Ricans. For yet another general phase of our minority group history, one must go back to the turn of the century. America became a world power and added overseas territories to its domain. In the process of this expansion, the United States acquired new peoples, the Filipinos and the Puerto Ricans. Subsequently two distinct patterns of dominant-minority groups have resulted in regard to these minority wards of our 20th-century expansion. The political and economic emissaries of the dominant homeland group treated their new national compatriots as a minority group, although the upper classes of these areas were dealt with differently than the masses. The Filipinos who migrated to the States, being easily recognized as Orientals, encountered the differential treatment usually accorded minorities in major degree. The most recent minority situation arises out of a substantial influx of Puerto Ricans primarily to New York City, into what is now known as Spanish Harlem.

Hawaii presents a distinctive picture of a dominant-minority relation. At least, the general impression prevails that this small, although in population composition amazingly heterogeneous, island archipelago is a paradise of harmonious interracial relations. This impression, as we shall see, deserves some qualification, if attention is directed toward the relation of the Caucasian to the non-Caucasian groups.

Jews. Finally, one important minority-group problem remains, bearing on Jewish-gentile relationships. While Jews were European immigrants, and while to some extent their relations with natives followed the characteristic immigrant pattern, distinctive aspects arose growing out of the unique character of Jews as a dispersed people. Broadly speaking, Jews accommodated to American life more quickly than any other immigrant group except some of those of north European origin. Yet their complete assimilation in the United States is blocked by the persistence of strongly entrenched gentile attitudes and, to a degree, by their own cohesiveness and by their heavy concentration in metropolitan New York. Of all the minority group problems, gentile-Jewish relations are the most puzzling to explain and are not promising of easy solution. The ebbs and flows in gentile discrimination against Jews provide significant clues to the interpretation of the behavior of dominant groups.

THE SIZE OF AMERICA'S MINORITIES

The question, "How many persons under the political jurisdiction of the United States are to be considered as possessing minority status at the present time?" may be answered with only rough approximation. First, there arises the problem of agreement on the groups to be included. For example, are all southern and eastern European immigrants to be considered minorities? If so, are all persons in the country descended from such lineage, *e.g.*, are those of Greek descent to be counted? Second, for several groups generally considered minorities, no precise count of their numbers exists, as is the case with American Jews and with Puerto Ricans living on the mainland. The difficulties concerned with determining the numbers of each minority group will be considered in the appropriate chapters together with some of the estimates which have been advanced. Before presenting our estimate of the size of minority groups as of 1950, consideration is given to the estimate provided by Robert M. Mac-Iver[11] and that presented by Arnold and Caroline Rose[12]. While the actual figures arrived at in the two studies are now superseded by 1950 census data and by later estimates, the manner by which the authors proceeded to determine who should be counted is instructive. MacIver divides minorities into three gradients: The first he describes as the "sheer caste line," under which he places Negroes; Mexicans and other Latin Americans; Orientals, mostly Japanese and Chinese; and American Indians. The second gradient, which MacIver calls "the deep fissure line," marks off Jews. The third gradient, "the minor fissure line" separates the immigrants and their descendants from southern and eastern Europe from the rest of the population. Altogether, these groups totalled 37,000,000 on the basis of the 1940 census. MacIver, however, suggests that other considerations may well "expand the area of discrimination" beyond the persons heretofore specifically included. Under particular circumstances of time and place, Roman Catholics in general may undergo discrimination. "Furthermore, if there is a general prejudice against any group, *all* the members of that group . . . are likely to have the uneasy sense that

[11] Robert M. MacIver, *The More Perfect Union* (New York: Macmillan, 1948) pp. 25-26.
[12] Arnold and Caroline Rose, *America Divided* (New York: Alfred A. Knopf, Inc., 1948) pp. 60-61; and Table 1: "Size of Minority Groups in the United States, 1940–1947," p. 62.

they are not fully admitted to the membership of the community."[13] These considerations lead MacIver to conclude that from 40 to 50 million Americans may feel all or some of the time that they belong to minority groups.

Rose and Rose in their accounting of the size of America's minorities include all the non-Caucasian peoples; Mexicans of foreign birth and those born in the United States of such parentage; other Latin American groups; and the Jewish population. Based again on the 1940 census, the above listed groups total 20,567,528. For their grand total, however, these authors include all Roman Catholics. Subtracting those Catholics included among the groups first listed, there remain 23,090,311 Catholics to be added to the list. Their final total embraces 43,657,839 people. It is interesting to observe that both MacIver and Rose and Rose find the proportion of minority status persons to be between a quarter and a third of the national population.

In Table 1 are listed the groups which may more definitely be considered minorities with the latest estimates of their numbers. The total given in this table is an undercount. To it should be added many people of southern and eastern European ancestry and some non-Protestants not otherwise listed. For reasons which we develop in subsequent chapters, it seems to us too hazardous to attempt an estimate of the numbers of those groups which can now be considered minorities.

TABLE 1

Partial List of Minorities in Mainland United States
and Their Estimated Numbers in 1950

Negroes	14,984,000 [14]
Japanese	135,000 [15]
Chinese	90,000 [15]
Other Asiatics	60,000 [15]
American Indians	430,000 [15]
Mexicans	3,000,000 [16]
Americans of Jewish ancestry	4,000,000 [17]

[13] MacIver, op. cit., p. 26.
[14] Preliminary estimate of 1950 Census.
[15] Estimate of Non-white Population of Continental United States, By Race: 1940–47, Series P-25, No. 23. The figures given for 1947 were Japanese 131,000; Chinese 87,000; American Indians 402,000. The present writer has projected these figures conservatively to allow for increase in the three consecutive years, 1948, 1949, 1950.
[16] See Lyle Saunders, supra, p. 195.
[17] From American Jewish Year Book, Vol. 50, 1948–49, p. 694.

Table 1 likewise does not include any of the population of the territories of the United States where there are many groups whose status qualifies them for minority classification, as in Hawaii and Puerto Rico. Thus it can be stated with certainty that in 1950, close to 24 million people living under American jurisdiction possessed minority status, or 16 per cent of the population. It can be stated further with high degree of probability that there are several million others who actually possessed minority status.

PRELIMINARY CONSIDERATION OF THE SOCIAL PROBLEMS CREATED BY DOMINANT-MINORITY RELATIONS

In this closing section of the present chapter we shall give preliminary consideration to some of the effects produced by dominant-minority relations which in the view of substantial numbers of citizens are considered "social problems."

Recent approaches to the subject of social problems have taken the position that whether certain verifiable social facts constitute a problem or not depends on the value system of the viewer of the facts. For example, to many Americans, the segregation of Negroes is simply in the natural order of things; while to many others with broad ethical values, any group discrimination is a moral problem. Again, the definition of the problem varies among those with varying personal value systems. To a traditional white Southerner, the rising militancy of Negroes creates the problem of "how to keep them in their place"; while to the humanitarian liberal, the problem is "how best to cooperate with these minority efforts to advance toward their complete equality." The value system we shall adopt contains two beliefs: (1) that democracy is the most desirable form of social organization; and (2) that the welfare of the society as a whole, either the nation or the community, properly takes precedence over the welfare of any special groups within this whole. Whenever occasion arises in this book to treat the phenomena at hand as problems, these two beliefs may be taken as the writer's value system. In this preliminary consideration, attention focuses upon the main ways in which discrimination against minorities creates problems measured in terms of these values. Further relevant data to verify or qualify these problem aspects will be found in subsequent chapters.

The incidence of personal disorganization. The belief has been widely held by the dominant status group that the minority groups furnish a disproportionate share of delinquents, criminals, mentally diseased, and persons otherwise disorganized. In some specific instances, researches have verified these beliefs; in other instances, they have failed to do so. We shall have occasion to examine the facts in more detail as we take up particular minorities. In this preliminary consideration, we shall direct attention to the kinds of explanations given for higher indices of personal disorganization among minorities when they actually occur. Dominant people often attribute such behavior either to the racial or to the cultural inferiority of the minority groups. Social scientists find three classes of causes: (1) the inevitable strain which a people of different culture faces in adjusting to a new situation; (2) the influence of the environmental conditions associated with the spatial and economic position of the minority, i.e., living in slum areas; and (3) the frustrations and resentments growing out of discrimination itself. It is this last class of causes which is least generally recognized and which also most directly pertains to our interest. A Negro boy may steal because he is poor; he may also steal as a way of getting even with "white people." In the latter instance, the direct influence of minority status as a causal factor in delinquency is more evident. Whatever the incidence of personal disorganization among minorities is, part of it may be properly attributed to the impact of minority status upon personality.

Effective use of abilities. All minorities are discriminated against to some extent in the choice of their employment; some are discriminated against in training for specific occupations. It will be indicated that the range of mental capacities of all the minorities is broadly similar to those of the dominant groups. The tendency to place the job ceiling for minorities at any particular level results in an ineffective utilization of the potential capacities of the minority as a whole group. The significance of this cost in terms of wasted manpower was brought sharply to public attention during World War II in many occupational fields as, for example, the inability to use trained Negro nurses in white hospitals with severe personnel shortages.

Effect on national income. From the viewpoint which places national welfare above that of any special interests, it has been argued that minority discrimination retards the growth of national income. Roper, for example, points out that the average annual income of the Negro family in a recent year was $1,043 as compared with $3,062 as the average for whites.[18] He has calculated that if Negro incomes were raised to an average of the non-Negro incomes, the national income as a whole would rise by four billion dollars. While there is considerable oversimplification to this kind of argument, the general prosperity of the nation would rise appreciably if Negroes had equal access to both adequate training for and employment in occupations. As we

[18] Elmo Roper, "The Price Business Pays" in R. M. MacIver, ed., *Discrimination and National Welfare* (New York: Harper and Brothers, 1949) pp. 18, 19.

know, a number of factors conspire to make the Deep South the poorest economic region of the nation, but the poverty of their large Negro population is clearly one important reason. And discrimination is an important factor contributing to the poverty of the Negro.

Group tension and violence. Dominant-minority group situations especially in modern, rapidly changing societies inevitably create intergroup tensions which periodically produce violent conflict with attendant bloodshed and economic waste. Race riots in the North and lynching of individual Negroes as well as mass white attacks on Negro areas in the South occurred even in the 1940–1950 decade.

The tension and conflict growing out of dominant-minority relations are especially difficult to cope with by orderly processes in a society where the status of minority groups is not recognized by the laws of the society. Labor-employer relations also generate tension and violence, but the latter at least in our society is now infrequent due to the recognition by law of the status of the two groups as normal opposing forces with the rules of conflict defined with increasing explicitness. In the case of dominant-minority relations, however, in a democratic society, minority status cannot with good faith be recognized in legal procedures. The conflict thus generated is therefore peculiarly dangerous. Local laws in some regions have legalized discrimination, but in more and more cases the Supreme Court of the United States has declared these laws unconstitutional. Thus the nation is approaching a point where discrimination against minorities below the level of "social" discrimination cannot be successfully maintained except by lawless procedures.

Inconsistency in values. The status of minority groups in American society constitutes a basic ideological conflict which is viewed by many thoughtful people as a moral or ethical problem. Gunnar Myrdal, the Swedish social scientist, who has made a most incisive interpretation of Negro-white relations in the United States, makes the violation of the American Creed in our treatment of the Negroes a basic point:

From the point of view of the American Creed the status accorded the Negro in America represents nothing more and nothing less than a century-long lag of public morals. In principle the Negro problem was settled long ago; in practice the solution is not effectuated. The Negro in America has not been given the elemental civil and political rights of formal democracy, including a fair opportunity to earn his living, upon which a general accord was already won when the American Creed was first taking form. And this anachronism constitutes the contemporary "problem" both to the Negroes and to whites.[19]

[19] Gunnar Myrdal, *An American Dilemma* (New York: Harper and Brothers, 1944) p. 24. By permission.

Effect on international relations. The brief record of events presented above referred to the adverse reaction to Americans by the peoples and the governments of the lands which furnished so many immigrants, resulting from our characteristic "dominant" behavior. Illustrative of recent implications in this connection is the following account of an incident in the Pan-American conference at Lima in 1939 when the Cuban delegation proposed a resolution condemning race discrimination as contrary to the fundamental principles of hemisphere organization:

Debate upon this in commission was intensified, and far reaching. The anti-Nazi, of course, thought at once of discrimination against the Jews. The United States delegates, imbued with the German menace, argued along that line. Prevention of an anti-Semitic campaign was, to them, part of the whole program of inter-American defense.

The delegates of the other American republics, however, saw a wider, or perhaps more approximate, application. The American representative meeting in the particular commission was asked point-blank by an opponent of the resolution whether the United States could possibly accept the idea that race discrimination could be a matter of international concern—the implication being that the United States might find herself on the defensive, perhaps oftener than her sister republics. To Secretary Hull's everlasting credit he authorized an immediate statement that if the United States were found erring in this respect, it would be a matter of international concern, and the United States should accept an inquiry thus brought. Clearly the question related to discrimination against Negroes in some parts of our country; against Mexicans in others; possibly against Indians, and still others, and so forth.[20]

In a similar connection is a statement by Roger Baldwin.

In Japan in 1947 I heard repeated statements from high Japanese authorities, and former ambassadors to the United States, that the 1924 act did more than any other single factor to break the bonds of friendship with the American people and to set Japan on the road to anti-Americanism.[21]

Whatever the past costs in international relations as a result of American discrimination, the present and future costs should be calculated in terms of the handicap which discrimination imposes upon America's position in the United Nations and upon its policy of containing the sphere of influence of Soviet Russia. Because of the vital urgency of this topic, it is appropriate to review the past record and present trends of Soviet policy and practice in relation to minorities.

[20] Adolph Berle, "Race Discrimination and the Good Neighbor Policy," in MacIver, *Discrimination and National Welfare*, p. 93. By permission.
[21] Roger N. Baldwin, "Our Standing in the Orient," in MacIver, *ibid.*, p. 87. By permission. Roger N. Baldwin was for years director of American Civil Liberties Union.

SOVIET RUSSIA AND MINORITIES

Soviet Russia during the more than 30 years of its existence has acquired a reputation for being free from prejudice toward and discrimination against ethnic and racial groups. This reputation is a powerful ideological weapon in Russia's efforts to persuade the colored peoples of the world of the superiority of Communism. The power of this reputation is enhanced by the contrasting reputation acquired by the colonial western European nations and the United States. We shall therefore examine the circumstances through which Soviet prestige in its treatment of minorities has been acquired and give consideration to its validity and significance.

When the Soviets came into power in 1917, there were four main factors in the Russian situation relating to its minorities. First, the population of Russia was highly heterogeneous in its ethnic and racial composition. About one-half of the population was composed of the "Great Russians," and another fifth was made up of the closely related Ukranians.[22] These two groups and the so-called "White Russians," who composed about 3 per cent of the population, were considered Slavic peoples. The remainder of the population, roughly one-fifth, included nearly 200 groups sufficiently distinctive by ethnic designation to have a special identity. In racial appearance these groups varied widely over most of the Caucasoid range and included several Mongoloid groups as well as some Mongoloid admixture among the predominantly Caucasoid peoples. The religion of the majority of Russians was Orthodox Christian, but among the non-Slavic groups were some Mohammedans, and scattered in the predominantly Slavic areas lived close to 3 million Jews.

The second factor in the situation as the Bolsheviks took over was the presence among many of the regional groups of Russia of strong nationalist sentiments which had grown even stronger as the result of the policy of forced assimilation by the previous Tsarist regime. This process of Russification had discouraged or sometimes forbidden the use of non-Russian languages and had given preference in state service to Russians.

A third significant element was the presence of a strong anti-Semitic feeling in Russia, which had been actively supported by the Tsarist governments, particularly those of Alexander III and Nicholas II. Places where Jews might settle were limited and they were not permitted to buy land. Jews were generally excluded from state service

---

[22] William H. Chamberlin, *Soviet Russia* (Boston: Little Brown & Company, 1930) p. 211. Chap. 9, "The Babel Tower of Nationalities," summarizes the situation of minorities in Soviet Russia to about 1930.

and the number allowed to pursue higher education was restricted. Sporadically, pogroms were carried out with little or no government interference.

Finally, it is pertinent to note the absence in Russia of that kind of racial antagonism based upon the consciousness of color so highly developed among the British and American peoples. This may have been due, in part, to the historical circumstance that the expansion carried on under the Tsars had taken place contiguous to its own boundaries and had added to their population comparatively few non-Caucasoid peoples. Thus, the Soviets faced primarily two problems concerning minorities: regional resentment of "Great Russian" dominance and anti-Semitism.

In the formal organization of their new society, the Soviets aimed to remove all manifestations of ethnic and racial discrimination. Ethnic groups inhabiting an area were permitted to retain their identity by organizing into separate "republics" with their own local government and their own language. Hence, the various regional groups were made to feel that they were all equal to the others. Again, in contrast to the Tsarist policy, the new government permitted no legal discrimination against Jews and attempted to suppress the expression of latent anti-Semitic attitudes. That this was not wholly successful is indicated by Chamberlin.

. . . it is frequently complained that the lower organs of the party, the Union of Communist Youth, and the trade unions do not act with sufficient energy when cases of race persecution are brought to their attention. Complaints of this kind have increased during the last few years; this is probably due to the fact that the party and its junior organization, the Union of Communist Youth, have been increasing very rapidly in membership and have absorbed into their ranks, along with their new members, a certain quota of Russian popular prejudices. Of course, the position of the Jews, as regards personal safety, is far better than it was in the Tsarist days, when anti-Semitic organizations were allowed to organize openly and incite riots. But the elimination of anti-Semitism is still a hope of the future, rather than a present-day reality.[23]

This official policy of ethnic equality was made ultimately explicit in the Soviet Constitution of 1936.[24]

---

[23] *Ibid.*, pp. 228-229. By permission of author, W. H. Chamberlin.

[24] The Constitution of the Union of Soviet Socialist Republics, as published by the Cooperative Publishing Society of Foreign Workers in the USSR, Moscow, 1936, Article 123, reads as follows:

"The equality of the right of citizens of the U.S.S.R., irrespective of their nationality or race, in all spheres of economic, state, cultural, social, and political life, is an immutable law.

"Any direct or indirect restriction of these rights, or, conversely, any establishment of direct or indirect privileges for citizens on account of their race, or nationality, as well as any propagation of any racial or national exclusiveness or hatred and contempt, is punishable by law."

Whether or not the Soviets fully deserved their reputation for freedom from racial and ethnic tolerance, the belief in its validity helped to make some converts to communism among ethnic and racial minorities in countries outside the Union, including the United States.

The full meaning, however, of Soviet Russia's policy toward minorities cannot be understood without reference to certain other facts about the Soviet system which are of common knowledge. First, the Soviet Government has in fact been controlled by the Communist Party through totalitarian procedures bearing little relation to its outward form. As a consequence, civil liberties as we know them have not existed for anyone in Russia, and cultural freedom has been allowed expression only to the extent that it did not interfere with the government, i.e., with party decree. Relating this to the status of minorities we have therefore an interesting situation. In Soviet Russia, members of groups which were minorities in the old days have equal opportunity with all other Soviet citizens to cooperate in doing what they are told, and when they fail to do so are not accorded any differentially unequal punishment because of their group's identity. By contrast, minorities in the United States do not have equal opportunity to enjoy the far higher standard of living or to enjoy the far greater personal freedom characteristic of the United States in general. It does not seem at all improbable that, if absolute comparisons were to be made between the two nations, persons of minority status in the United States, with the probable exception of Negroes in the South, have more individual freedom than anyone in the Union of Soviet Socialist Republics and enjoy a generally higher standard of living than all but the elite of the Soviet Union's society.

A second important factor in the Soviet system, growing closely out of party control without any real limitations, is the opportunistic character of such control. Since in the pursuit of its aims the party-government is not necessarily restricted either to Marx's principles or to a constitution, it can reverse on short notice any former practice. The early established minority policy is a logical expression of the philosophy that all proletarians are equal. But it also served the exigencies of the situation which the Soviet regime faced. That, when and if circumstances so change that such a policy is less expedient, it can easily be changed is already indicated by several other current developments on the Soviet scene.

The first of such developments has to do with foreign forced labor. The Soviets during the war and afterward could make good use of cheap labor. German and Japanese prisoners of war were most suitable for this purpose. Therefore they are, six years after the war, still being exploited in this capacity.

The second development concerns the need for suppressing the nationalist sentiments in order to retain strict control. During World War II certain ethnic groups whose loyalty was questioned were accorded drastic treatment. Koestler relates incidents in which entire groups were deported to Arctic Siberia because their conduct proved "unreliable." [25] Constant alertness was exercised to suppress nationalist sentiment in the areas to the west, the Baltic nations and eastern Poland, which were incorporated into the Union as a consequence of the Second World War.

The third major development away from the principle of ethnic equality has been the increasing discrimination against Jews in the Soviet Union, to which several recent observers of the Soviet scene have called attention.[26] Among such comments are those of former ambassador, General Walter Bedell Smith, who records his observation of antagonism toward Jews and suggests some of the reasons for it.

Soviet law specifically prohibits any racial discrimination or anti-Semitism. A few Jews, such as Kagonovitch and Ehrenburg, hold high positions in the Soviet Union, and are always pointed to by the Kremlin to refute any implication of anti-Semitism. But during the past decade, it seems Jews have systematically been removed from influential positions in the Soviet Government and the diplomatic and armed services. Reliable reports attribute these removals to Soviet suspicion of Jews as persons who have a tradition of international culture and ties abroad, and who cannot be relied upon to conform to the increasingly tight ideological strait jacket demanded by the party under postwar conditions. From the Foreign Office alone, while I was in Moscow, Litvinov, Lozovsky, Maisky and less important but almost equally able Jewish officials were relieved or relegated to retirement or to positions of less importance.

During my stay in the Soviet Union, the only reported violence against Jews was in the Ukraine, where latent anti-Semitism had been inflamed by the racial theories of the Germans during the war. This, however, was the work of anti-Soviet Ukrainian nationalists, and the government acted promptly, employing stern measures in an effort to suppress these illegal acts. However, many Jews were killed in the Ukraine in small-scale "pogroms," and others felt unsafe in leaving their homes at night. There were reports, which I consider reliable, that this campaign became so widespread that the government has not been able to suppress it completely, and, as a result, many Ukrainian Jews migrated to the Asiatic Autonomous Jewish Oblast of Birobijan, which was founded in 1924 and which for a time held the attention of

[25] Arthur Koestler, "Babbitts of the Left," *Life*, May 3, 1948.
[26] See John Fischer, *Why They Behave Like Russians* (New York: Harper and Brothers, 1947) p. 109, and Cyrus Sulzberger, *The New York Times*, May 2, 1949.

world Jewry, attracting some immigrants and, during the 1920's and early 1930's, a fair amount of foreign financial aid. A more recently reported transfer of Jews from the western area of the Soviet Union to Birobijan would appear to have been carried out by the government for its own purposes.[27]

Summary and significance of Soviet Russian minority practice. In summary it may be said (1) that the Soviet regime made conspicuous efforts to establish ethnic and racial tolerance within the Union and acquired a reputation abroad to this effect; and (2) that more recent developments tend to bring that reputation into question. The significant point for the United States is that this Soviet reputation has been and still continues to be a strong ideological weapon for the Soviet regime in its efforts to win adherents to communism, particularly among the many peoples whom Americans look upon as "colored." An accurate description of the discrimination against minorities in the United States is highly persuasive for Soviet propaganda purposes without the need for the exaggeration which the Soviets will give to it.

Finally, the international repercussion from our treatment of minorities compels a redefinition of the problem by the American people. Some of the losses arising from dominant-minority relations fall heaviest on the particular regions where the problems are greater. The damage to the prestige of the United States is, however, a cost borne equally by all Americans. Local and regional communities where there are concentrations of minority peoples have frequently resented outside interference. Now that the problem of minorities in the United States is so clearly defined as a national problem, the pleas of local interests that it is their concern alone become untenable.

TOPICS FOR DISCUSSION AND PROJECTS

1. Collect from the files of any leading metropolitan newspapers all items, articles, and editorials, over a short period, pertaining to minorities. Analyze the contents around the topic, "How contemporary American publics view the minorities question."
2. In the family or neighborhood in which you were reared, what were the attitudes expressed toward peoples of different racial, religious, or nationality backgrounds?
3. If you have traveled abroad, cite any instances of the behavior of Americans observed in foreign lands indicative of their attitudes toward other peoples.
4. Prepare a 10-minute talk designed to convince a dominant status audience that discrimination is costly to them.
5. Cite any current events concerned with minorities having implications affecting America's position in international affairs.

[27] Walter Bedell Smith, *My Three Years in Moscow* (Philadelphia: J. B. Lippincott Company, 1950) pp. 275-276. By permission.

6. If you were an American representative in the United Nations, what would you say in reply to an attack by a Communist representative upon the treatment of minorities in the United States?

SUGGESTED READING

Brown, F. J. and Roucek, J. S. *One America*. New York: Prentice-Hall, Inc., 1945.
> *Contains in one volume a brief factual account of all the minorities of the continental United States. The tables in the Appendix are especially convenient for handy reference for the student of minorities.*

Comhaire, J. L. L. "Urban Legislation and Racial Legislation in South Africa," *American Sociological Review*, Vol. 15, No. 3, June 1950, pp. 392–397.
> *Discusses the difficulties of enforcing South Africa's racial legislation in urban areas of the Union.*

MacIver, R. M., ed. *Discrimination and National Welfare*. Harper and Brothers, 1949.
> *A number of authorities write of the many different ways in which discrimination affects the national welfare of the United States.*

Macrone, I. D. *Race Attitudes in South Africa*. Johannesburg: South African Institute of Race Relations, 1937.
> *The most comprehensive treatment of the relations between the white, mixed-blood, and nonwhite people of the Union.*

McWilliams, Carey. *Brothers Under the Skin*, rev. ed. Boston: Little, Brown & Company, 1951.
> *A popularly written account of all the "racial" minority peoples by perhaps the most prolific American writer on American minorities.*

Pierson, Donald. *Negroes in Brazil*. Chicago: University of Chicago Press, 1942.
> *A study of the status of Negroes and mixed Negro-white persons, in the city of Bahia.*

Record, Wilson. *The Negro and the Communist Party*. Chapel Hill: University of North Carolina Press, 1951.
> *A systematic study of the efforts of Communists in the United States to win American Negroes to their cause and an appraisal of the results, showing in general Negro resistance to these efforts.*

Stern, Bernhard J. "Soviet Policy on National Minorities," *American Sociological Review*, Vol. 9, June 1944, pp. 229–235.
> *A review of Soviet policy and practice in dealing with nationality minorities within its borders up to 1944.*

Wirth, Louis. "The Price of Prejudice," *Survey Graphic*, Vol. 36, No. 1, Jan. 1947, pp. 19–21.
> *Discusses the economic costs of racial segregation in the South.*

CHAPTER 2

Introduction to the Sociology
of Minorities

The purpose of this chapter is first to provide an introductory orientation of the particular field of dominant-minority relations to the general field of sociology. Secondly, we shall define the key terms needed in a description and an analysis of dominant-minority relations. All social relations may be described in two basic ways: from the structural viewpoint, that is, as a more-or-less fixed pattern of interacting relations; or as a changing pattern of relations. Attention first focuses upon dominant-minority relations as a structure of intergroup relations. Every society is at any given time differentiated in many ways. The type of differentiation which is our concern is a *status* differentiation. By status is meant the relative position, rank, or standing of a person in a group, or of a group in reference to some other group or groups. In terms of our subject, the status relation between groups is involved. Societies have other forms of status differentiations than those denoted by the relation between dominant and minority groups, notably age, sex, and class and caste differentiation. Following definition of the terms *dominant* and *minority* as they will be herein employed, their distinction from class and caste will be examined.

Minority and dominant defined. The term *minority* does not have a well-established place in the terminology of American sociology. Even the more recent general textbooks of sociology do not employ it as a definitive term, as a formal concept. In Europe "a minority" has most often connoted a folk or nationality which through the consequences

26

of war or diplomacy finds itself a part of a larger political unit where the dominant nationality discriminates in some ways against it. The Slovaks of Czechoslovakia and the Walloons of Belgium are examples. During its expansion period the United States has acquired minorities in the same way, although the situation, for example, of Puerto Ricans at home in relation to the mainlanders is not completely analagous to the relation of the Slovaks to Czechoslovakia.

In the United States, the demarcation of the area of intergroup relations with which we are to be concerned, and its treatment as a more or less integrated whole, began with the appearance of a book by Donald Young, entitled *American Minority Peoples*. In this pioneer text, the author observes, "There is, unfortunately, no word in the English language which can with philological propriety be applied to all these groups which are distinguished by biological features, alike national cultural traits, or a combination of both." [1] Subsequent to Young's publication, other writers have attempted to give the concept, minority, a more precise conceptual formulation. With the purpose of clarifying the meaning in which minority will be employed in this book, four recent definitions will be examined.

In a recent dictionary of sociological terms appears the following definition:

Group, minority. A subgroup within a larger group (ordinarily a society), bound together by some special ties of its own, usually race or nationality, but sometimes religion, or other cultural affiliations. Even in the common types of democracy, minority groups are precluded from expressing themselves in proportion to their numerical strength through the operation of the principle of majority rule.[2]

This definition would cover a wider range of groups than those with which we are concerned. Under it, for example, a political minority might well be included. Furthermore, it fails to state clearly the inferior status of a minority. Again, in attributing to the principle of majority rule the reason for the disproportionate influence of the minority, it fails to give due recognition to discrimination. Under the Southern system of Negro-white relations, the principle of majority rule is negated by an established system of white dominance. Finally, what is the special tie which binds Negro Americans together? It is not a distinctive culture nor Negroid physical traits, as such. The main bond between them is their common possession of inferior status, their common experience of discrimination.

[1] Donald Young, *American Minority Peoples* (New York: Harper and Brothers, 1932).
[2] *Dictionary of Sociology*, Henry P. Fairchild, ed. (New York: Philosophical Library, 1944) p. 134. By permission.

In contrast to the above definition is one by Louis Wirth, which defines a minority "as a group of people who, because of their physical or cultural characteristics, are singled out from others in the society in which they live for differential and unequal treatment, and who therefore regard themselves as objects of collective discrimination." [3] We consider Wirth as correct in assigning primary significance to discrimination or "differential and unequal treatment," and in assigning to secondary position the differences of the group. It is not so much the differences in themselves but what the dominant status group makes of the differences which counts. However, we feel that Wirth's statement puts too strongly the conscious and deliberate aspects of dominant behavior in his use of the wording "singles out." For example, many dominant status people who frequently tell humorous stories reflecting the stereotyped conception of a minority are quite unaware of the implications of their behavior as seen by the student of minorities. We should prefer the use of the words "receive" or "are accorded" instead of "singles out."

Going still further in defining the minority in terms of dominant behavior are Rose and Rose who write, "The mere fact of being generally hated because of religious, racial, or nationality background is what defines a minority group." [4] That hatred of certain minorities is a personality trait of *some* dominant status people cannot be denied. But to insist that the vast majority of dominant status people who consciously or unconsciously take the advantage over minorities accruing from their dominant status, do so out of hatred for the minority, puts an extreme interpretation on the matter.

The last definition we shall consider is that presented by Schermerhorn:

Minorities are subgroups within a culture which are distinguishable from the dominant group by reason of differences in physiognomy, language, customs, or culture patterns (including any combination of these factors). Such subgroups are regarded as inherently different and "not belonging" to the dominant group: for this reason they are consciously or unconsciously excluded from full participation in the life of the culture.[5]

In line with our prior comment, Schermerhorn's definition substantially fits our view. It indicates the difference and states objectively the role of discrimination.

[3] Louis Wirth, "The Problem of Minority Groups", in Ralph Linton, ed., *The Science of Man in the World Crisis* (New York: Columbia University Press, 1945) p. 47.
[4] Arnold and Caroline Rose, *America Divided* (New York: Alfred A. Knopf, Inc., 1948) p. 3.
[5] Robert S. Schermerhorn, *These Our People* (Boston: D. C. Heath & Company, 1949) p. 5. By permission.

Of the sources drawn upon in defining a minority, only the last essays to define the term *dominant group*. "When we speak of a dominant group we mean that group whose historical language, traditions, customs, and ideology are normative for the society; their eminence is enforced by the folkways or by law, and in time these elements attain the position of cultural presuppositions." [6] In a formal definition of the dominant, it would seem essential to give recognition to the aspect of discrimination which is explicit in the reciprocal. Thus we shall consider a dominant group as one whose distinctive culture or physiognomy is established as superior in the society and who treat differentially and unequally other groups in the society with different cultures or physiognomy.

Since our main focus of attention is upon the interaction of the two reciprocals, we proceed now to describe and analyze in general terms the characteristics of a dominant-minority situation.

CHARACTERISTICS OF DOMINANT-MINORITY SITUATIONS

Differential identifiability: "visibility." In order for a dominant-minority situation to exist, the two groups must possess one or more differences which are reciprocally perceptible by which the members of each respectively may be identified as belonging to their group. The traits which are perceived may be physiognomic ("racial") or cultural or both. Physiognomic traits are illustrated by the physical features of the Japanese or Chinese which distinguish them from the white, Caucasoid physical traits of the dominant population. Cultural features are illustrated by language, religion, mode of dress, or characteristic folk behavior, usually a combination of several features. The term "visibility" has been frequently used for this phenomenon. The differences involved are however sometimes perceptible by other senses than sight. For example, language involves audibility. In more subtle aspect, "Negroes" who are in appearance so completely Caucasoid in their visible features that they cannot be identified by sight are identifiable as Negroes by the general knowledge in the community of their Negro lineage or by the fact that they "choose" to acknowledge such lineage by associating with visible Negroes. In periods when dominant elements strongly desire to keep minorities in their place and when the latter's visibility is becoming too attenuated for the purpose, dominants have decreed the wearing of artificial insignia, as, for example, Nazi Germany in the case of Jews. Both because of its frequent usage in the literature of minorities and because it is a less awkward term than identifiability, the term *visibility* will be used to

[6] *Ibid.,* p. 6.

denote this characteristic, but it should be understood in this broader sense.

A remaining aspect of visibility which is frequently ignored in the discussion of minorities is what we shall call *associational visibility*. One frequently hears the questions asked in private conversation, "Is John a Negro?" or "Is Herbert a Jew?" Often the correct answer is determined only by finding out with what other persons the individual in question generally associates, particularly in his more intimate contacts. The writer has frequently not known whether or not certain students of his were Jewish until he learned of their fraternity affiliation. While as a means of identification, associational visibility is derivative from one or more of the other bases, it acquires significance through long practice.

When two peoples do differ from one another, each tends to stereotype the differences of the other into a sort of composite average. This stereotype comes to be the personal image which comes to the mind of the member of one group when the name of the other group is mentioned. As a result the conception of each of the other tends to ignore the wide range of variation which prevails in the other group. For example, to many American white people, all Japanese look very much alike. Dominant people often claim to perceive the traits in the stereotype when, in fact, they are not there. More significantly, as will be developed in Chapter 3, dominant people tend to attribute many other traits, mental and behavioral, to the minority on the assumption, largely invalid, that these additional traits are inevitably associated with the more visible ones. For example, the dominant reactions operates thus: A is visibly Jewish; in the stereotype Jews are aggressive; therefore A must be aggressive, whether I have seen any evidence of it in A's behavior or not.

Differential power. Minority status is imposed by one group upon another. The dominant group therefore must possess a greater power to impose the minority status upon another. The power may be any adequate combination of a number of elements, preponderant numbers, economic power, priorly acquired class status, and other elements.

Categorical discrimination against the minority. Discrimination, or as in the prior definition, differential and unequal treatment, by the dominant against the minority is an essential feature of the dominant-minority situation. In essence, the discrimination is categorical, that is, it applies against all members of the minority. Thus the eminent Negro scientist, Dr. George Washington Carver, was expected to conform to the rules of caste etiquette in Macon County, Alabama. At times dominant status people invite a particular temporary suspension of the prevailing discriminatory procedures in the case of a favored individual. But this breach comes at the invitation of the dominant who personally invites it as a friendly concession, not as a right.

Prejudice is frequently thought of as the psychological correlate of discrimination.[7] Applied to our subject, prejudice may be defined as an attitude unfavorable to or disparaging of a whole group and all the individual members of it based upon some elements of irrationality. In the case of such prejudiced people, their discrimination is the manifestation in action of their prejudice. Prejudice may, however, exist in the minds of people who have no opportunity to express it in discriminatory behavior. Likewise discrimination may be practiced without prejudice. The writer, for example, considers himself a discriminator against Negroes every time he conforms to the interracial etiquette of the Southern caste system, although he would deny that he is prejudiced against Negroes. There are motivations for discrimination other than prejudice. An illustrative instance would be gentile X who wants a promotion which gentile Y can bestow. Since Y is strongly prejudiced against Jews, X acts in an anti-Semitic manner to further ingratiate himself with Y. In subsequent analysis attention will focus primarily upon discrimination because it bears more directly upon minority status than does prejudice. However, the pattern of discrimination could not be sustained long by the nonprejudiced discriminators alone. It is the prejudiced discriminator who forms the hard core which does sustain the pattern.

Rationale for discrimination. The real reasons for the imposition of minority status upon a people are complex and varied as subsequent discussion will indicate. Reference here is to the fact that in all minority situations there develops a rationale for discrimination. This comprises the set of beliefs held generally by the dominant group, which are advanced to justify their discrimination. For instance, the belief that Negroes are inferior mentally is used to justify the need for white discipline of the Negro people; or the belief that Jews are so clannish as to be untrustworthy justifies their being kept out of certain positions. In the stereotyped beliefs about the minority, the domi-

---

[7] Prejudice may also be favorable toward some object. Dictionary definitions, however, indicate its more frequent use in the unfavorable sense. Some highly idealistic persons are "blind" to the faults of minority members or to certain tendencies in a group's behavior, which, however they may be accounted for, are in a sense undesirable by the prevailing standards of conduct. Therefore, the stereotype of the "saintly" minority is a handicap to the realistic understanding of intergroup relations.

nants include those elements connoting inferiority or undesirability for which there is some plausible evidence in the behavior of the minority, and ignore as far as possible any evidence casting doubt upon the uniformity of these stereotyped traits. As will be seen, two somewhat distinct types of stereotypes have developed. One refers to the mentally inferior, childlike, undisciplined, amoral personality type, best illustrated in the traditional white stereotype of the Negro. The other stereotype depicts an aggressive, overly ambitious, crafty, or cunning personality, the way in which the typical gentile dominant considers the Jew.

The "vicious circle." Once established, the dynamics of dominant-minority relations set in motion a continuous series of reciprocal stimuli and responses which has been frequently called in the literature of minorities the "vicious circle." Due to the circumstances in which contact takes place, the group destined to be a minority usually does possess behavior patterns which are in a practical, immediate sense "inferior." This provides some initial plausible justification for dominant discrimination. The discrimination, in turn, operates to make the members of the minority respond in ways which further strengthen the stereotype. To illustrate, Jewish immigrants, like other immigrants, tended to associate at the outset with other Jews. Gentiles came to consider them especially clannish. Gentiles also placed barriers to Jewish association with them. Thus the Jews were forced to associate more exclusively with each other. And then gentiles say, "See, the Jews are always sticking together, they don't want to assimilate."

The failure to understand how the vicious circle operates leads many well intentioned people astray in their interpretation of what they come to believe are the inevitable conclusions to be drawn from their "own observations." Merton provides an apt illustration. A Northern union member observes that many of the Southern Negroes coming into his industrial community take jobs at lower than prevailing wages and, further, that in strike times, the Negroes take jobs as strikebreakers. His observations thus appear to him as clear proof that Negroes are incapable of union discipline and ought not to be permitted to join unions. Merton comments:

> Our unionist fails to see, of course, that he and his kind have produced the very "facts" which he observes. For by defining the situation as one in which Negroes are held to be incorrigibly at odds with the principles of unionism and by excluding Negroes from unions, he invited a series of consequences which indeed made it difficult if not impossible for many Negroes to avoid the role of scab. . . . That Negroes were strikebreakers because they were excluded from unions (and from a large range of jobs) rather than excluded because they were strikebreakers can be seen from the

virtual disappearance of Negroes as scabs in industries where they have gained admission to unions in the last decades.[8]

Characteristic behavior patterns. A dominant-minority pattern of social relationship tends to produce characteristic attitudes and behavior patterns in the personalities of the members of the two groups. In this introductory orientation, attention is directed to two such polar pairs of attitudes and the behavior they evoke: the superiority complex of the dominant linked with the inferiority complex of the minority; and the "bullying" complex of the former coupled with the persecution complex of the latter. Turning to consider the two minority reciprocals, the inferiority complex refers to the tendency of persons long inured to minority status to accept the definition of themselves which the dominant group holds. It is illustrated by the Negro house servant whose mistress gives her a substantial cash present. After the Negro woman had quickly spent it on "trivialities," she reported to her mistress, "It don't do to give us colored folks much money because we just don't know how to take care of it." The other basic minority personality characteristic has frequently been called by some writers the "oppression" psychosis.[9] This refers to the attitude of the minority person that the status discriminations are unfair or unjust. While the intensity with which this feeling of inequitable treatment may often be severe enough to warrant the label "psychosis," the term persecution complex seems more appropriate to cover the milder manifestations which are more prevalent throughout the minority. On the behavioral side, this complex reveals itself in the unusual sensitivity of the minority person toward the often innocently meant behavior of dominant persons, for example, their reaction to humorous stories in which the stereotyped characterizations of the minorities are employed. This complex is further revealed in the interpretations given by minority individuals for their failure to achieve specific goals. The student of Italian lineage who is rejected for medical school, or the "light" Negro woman who fails to get a secretarial position, attribute their failure to dominant prejudice alone. While frequently such an interpretation is valid and sometimes it is not, our concern here is that the minority situation typically evokes the interpretation of discrimination.

Reciprocally, the situation structures in the personalities of dominant status people a superiority complex revealed in their relations

[8] Robert K. Merton, *Social Theory and Social Structure* (Glencoe, Ill.: Free Press, 1949) p. 182. By permission. Chapter 7, "The Self-fulfilling Prophecy," from which this illustration is drawn analyzes with penetrating insight the process by which "social beliefs father social reality."
[9] H. A. Miller, *Races, Nations, and Classes* (Philadelphia: J. B. Lippincott Company, 1924) Ch. 4.

with minority people. Among those dominants who feel secure in their status, the trait is revealed in behavior which is at various times, tolerating, condescending, supercilious, benevolent. On the other hand, persons of dominant status who feel less secure exhibit a tendency toward more aggressive behavior toward minorities, which may be given the informal designation "the bullying complex." It is manifested in overexaggeration of the etiquette of dominant-minority relations, and on occasion, in mental or physical abuse of minority persons who overstep, or appear to be overstepping, the established boundaries of segregation.

Minority and social class. One of the most difficult conceptual problems for students of minorities is the distinction between a social minority and a social class. Social class has been defined as "a stratum in society composed of families of equal standing. All persons of the same social level of prestige and esteem, who consider themselves to be social equals, form a relatively distinct social class".[10] Class is a status differentiation as is minority. The superordinate-subordinate pattern of interaction is present between classes as well as between dominants and minorities. The upper classes consider themselves superior to the lowers and "uppers" act discriminatingly, or at least deprecatingly, toward lowers and thus strive to maintain their higher ranking position.

A glance at the situation in any typical American community with ethnic or racial heterogenity will help to distinguish minority from class. In "Yankee City," a research team delineated a social class structure composed of three classes or six when subdivided:[11] upper upper, lower upper; upper middle, lower middle; upper lower, lower lower. In a figure, horizontal lines can be used to indicate the hierarchical gradations. Where do the various ethnic and racial groups fit into this scheme? For the ante-bellum South, one could perhaps simply draw in another horizontal segment below the lower-lower white class to represent the Negro slaves and call it a seventh class, which closely resembles a caste. That cannot be done to describe the pattern of Negro-white relations in the South today because there is a recognized Negro middle class.[12] To take, however, ethnic as distinct from racial

[10] *Dictionary of Sociology*, Henry P. Fairchild, ed. (New York: Philosophical Library, 1944) p. 278. By permission.
[11] See W. Lloyd Warner and Paul S. Lunt, *The Social Life of a Modern Community* (New Haven: Yale University Press, 1941) Ch. 5, "How The Several Classes Were Discovered," and p. 225, Table 7, "Class and Ethnic Groups." For comparison, see Robert S. and Helen M. Lynd, *Middletown in Transition* (New York: Harcourt, Brace & Company, Inc., 1937) pp. 458-459.
[12] See W. Lloyd Warner and Alison Davis, "A Comparative Study of American Caste," in E. T. Thompson, ed., *Race Relations and Race Problems* (Durham: Duke University Press, 1939).

minorities, in "Yankee City" it was found that in 1933 they distributed over several segments of the six-fold class structure. For example, some Italians are found as high as the lower middle class. They are thought of, however, as Italians and reacted to accordingly. Within each class level to which they rise, the ethnics are thought of as somehow not quite the same as the native members of the same class, that is, until as individuals they become assimilated. If one examines the status of ethnic minorities in the United States, the conclusion seems inescapable that it represents a combination of the horizontal and vertical principles of social differentiation. The test of the existence of a minority is to verify dominant behavior toward it within the same class. The way to express this distinction between class and minority in a figure is to take first the pyramid of the class structure of the dominants, superimpose the pyramid of the class structure of the minorities first exactly, and then to drop the latter less than a full horizontal segment to express the inferior position of each minority class segment to others within the class. The result is seen in Figure 1.

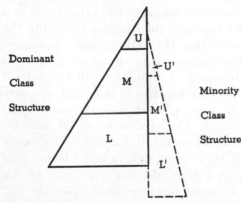

Dominant Class Structure

Minority Class Structure

U and U' = Upper Class

M and M' = Middle Class

L and L' = Lower Class

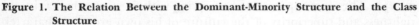

Figure 1. The Relation Between the Dominant-Minority Structure and the Class Structure

A further complication arises in that the determiners for class are sometimes different for the dominant and the minority. For example, a neighborhood grocer with a family operated store may be close to the top of the class structure of an ethnic minority, but a similarly occupied dominant might border between upper lower and lower middle in dominant class structure. To sum up, the main distinction between the term class and minority can be expressed by stating that in the former, people look up and down at each other, and in the latter, they look up and across, and down and across.

Minority and caste. For our purposes, it may be sufficient to point out that the term caste involves a situation in which the lines barring certain degrees of association between the groups are rigidly drawn. The prohibition of marriage across the caste line is the most adamant barrier of all, and if in spite of it, intermarriage does take place, the family thus formed is characteristically assigned the status of the lower caste. We shall see that the status of American minorities with marked racial visibility approximates caste.

DOMINANT-MINORITY RELATIONS AS A PROCESS OF CHANGE

We turn now to view dominant-minority relations as a process of change, to see how they arise in the first place, and how they change after they have become established.

How minorities arise. Cooperation and conflict are universal social processes occurring in some degree in all human relations. While dominant-minority relations involve some degree of cooperation, they are essentially opposing, antagonistic relations. In some instances there develop situations of a dominant-minority sort arising out of a prior homogeneous situation, for example, the situation created by the Mormons in the United States during the 19th century. But more often dominant-minority relations arise out of situations where two different peoples meet. Our discussion of minorities will be confined to those arising out of such contacts. When two or more different peoples come in contact within the same general area, the sociological stage is set for opposition to occur. The process by which man becomes a social and cultural animal makes it inevitable that some degree of antagonism will arise. In learning to be a social being, man becomes strongly loyal to his own kind, the *in-group*, and this in-group feeling is strengthened by some hostility toward possible *out-groups*. The in-group sentiment carries with it strong belief in the rightness and superiority of the culture of his own group, a characteristic of communal life which is called *ethnocentrism*. The eventual outcome of this opposition ranges from annihilation of one by the other to complete assimilation. Complete annihilation has seldom occurred. In our history, the nearest approach is in Indian-white relations. Even in this case, there are today almost as many Indians as there were in the area of the United States at any time. Complete assimilation has occurred, as in the case of North European immigrants in our country, but never without intervening stages of opposition. In between these two extremes we find accommodation: a pattern of interaction in which the two or more distinct peoples live together in the same area retaining much of their distinctiveness but establishing cooperative and differentiating procedures which permit at least the minimum of common life. Accommodation at any one time may be of the coordinate form where the status of the plural groups is broadly equal, as, for example, Switzerland as a national community. In its political expression, this form of accommodation is a federation. Another type of accommodation is a superordinate-subordinate form, where distinctiveness is retained, but one group maintains a superior status vis-a-vis the others. In this instance, all other groups within the community are minorities.

How the conflict occurring when peoples meet is resolved, depends upon three general forces: the relative power possessed by the opposing groups; the relative desire of the stronger group to use it; and the tenacity with which the weaker group cherishes its folk individuality.

What are the various elements of power influencing the outcome of intergroup contact? One is numbers. In the mainland of the United States all minority peoples are a numerical minority, although in certain counties of the South, Negroes outnumber whites. However, in South Africa, the non-European minorities outnumber the dominant Europeans four to one. Superiority in economic organization and technological capacity rank equally, if not preponderantly, in determining the issue.

While it has been suggested that some degree of opposition inevitably takes place when two peoples meet, all potentially stronger peoples do not manifest the same aggressiveness in the situation. Varying cultures generate varying attitudes toward strangers. Chinese culture has been less belligerent toward outsiders. Many Indian groups responded in friendly terms to the European invaders until they became disillusioned. In American culture, two important elements have been capitalism and political democracy. The dynamics of capitalism have favored the development of minorities in two ways: "minority status" is favorable to wage exploitation; and the individual economic insecurity and frenzied competition for higher economic and social status generate a large volume of frustration among the dominants which can in part be drained off in aggression toward conveniently available minorities. On the other hand, the dynamics of political democracy have pressed toward equality in status and the elimination of all discriminations. In the main, the extent of the problem of minorities in the United States is a result of the clashing of these two forces in our society.[13]

Finally the possible outcome of minority situations is partly affected by the tenacity with which the minority people wish to retain

[13] See Ch. 17 for fuller development.

intact their particular way of life. This is illustrated by peoples with a distinctive religious way of life who possess a strong desire to remain aloof from others, such as the Amish, the Mormons in their earlier history, and others. Of our major minorities, adherents to Judaism are considered as showing resistance to complete assimilation but the situation is complicated, as will be shown.[14]

How dominant-minority relations change. Arising out of interpeople contact, the patterns of dominant-minority relations are undergoing change even though they seem to be substantially frozen at certain levels at given times. Due to the varying situations of original contact, the pattern of change varies. For example, immigrant-native relations in the United States go through a series of developments which include: (*a*) the stage of initial contact, characterized by uncertainty as to status by both groups; (*b*) the opposition stage; (*c*) accommodation on a superordinate-subordinate, that is to say dominant-minority, basis; (*d*) the marginal stage when strides toward assimilation develop; (*e*) and finally the assimilation of the minority. The possibility that from intergroup conflict may emerge sociocultural pluralism on a coordinate status basis has already been mentioned. In the American experience this has not happened. There has never been a people with a sharply contrasting way of life, or with sharply contrasting racial characteristics which has not been a "minority people" in status. In the American scene at least, the process has ranged from maximum difference and discrimination to complete assimilation.

The trend in a dominant-minority process need not be consistently in one direction. The status of Jews in Germany underwent a sharp reversal under the Nazis. Broadly speaking, in America the long-time trend has been, however, in one direction, from minority inferior status toward equality in status. In particular communities the degree of discrimination increases as large numbers of the minority members enter over a short period of the time until a new equilibrium of accommodation is established. Again, severe economic depressions frequently increase the degree, for example, of occupational discrimination. Special circumstances such as a particularly heinous crime committed by a person of minority status may raise to great intensity discriminatory behavior by the dominants. Conversely, a heroic act by a minority member may lessen momentarily the intensity of discrimination. These are, however, in the nature of short-run changes not necessarily affecting the basic trend.

Change in welfare vs. change in status. In attempting to measure change in a dominant-minority relation, it is important to distinguish

[14] See Ch. 15.

between the sort of change which will be called change in *welfare,* or social conditions, from change in *status.* The building, for example, of a new modern apartment house to be rented to Negroes only improves the welfare of Negroes but not their status as a minority. The admission of Negroes, on the other hand, or their final acceptance as real neighbors, into a predominantly white residential area is a change in status, whether their new homes are physically better or not. While it is frequently true that improvement in the social conditions of a minority, especially better educational opportunity, indirectly contributes to raising of status, these two sorts of change should be kept distinct in the measurement of trend. The failure to make this distinction has led to much confusion.

DEFINITION OF OTHER KEY TERMS

In the analysis of dominant-minority relations, four terms are so frequently used that it is essential that the definitions to which this book will adhere should be at the outset clearly stated. These are *accommodation, acculturation, assimilation,* and *amalgamation.* These four terms are formal concepts in general sociology, and at the present time a fair consensus among American sociologists exists as to their definition. Representative of this general agreement are the definitions given by Kimball Young.[15] Three of the definitions given by Young are adopted for this book. For the fourth, we employ a different definition.

Accommodation. Used in two senses: As a condition, a state of equilibrium between individuals or groups in which certain working arrangements have been agreed upon or accepted. As a process, the social adjustment between individuals or groups, aimed at the more or less temporary suspension of conflict. Also called "antagonistic cooperation."

Acculturation. The merging of two or more cultures, ranging from accommodative arrangements to full assimilation or synthesis of cultures. The entire sequence of processes involved in the contact and subsequent intermixture of the traits and patterns of two or more cultures.

It is the distinction between acculturation and assimilation in which the greatest conceptual difficulty arises. We shall see that in the American scene, some groups whose descendants are acculturated are still "socially segregated" on the basis of certain criteria of visibility, notably "racial" visibility. Such groups are treated as if they do not quite belong to the larger common life, and the members of such groups feel as if they are not wholly accepted. In the usual definitions of assimilation, this sense of being one people, of belonging together, is not

[15] Kimball Young, *Sociology, A Study of Society and Culture,* rev. ed. (New York: American Book Company, 1949). See Glossary, p. 615.

made explicit.[16] For example in this instance, Young's definition of assimilation reads: "the fusion of divergent habits, attitudes, and ideas of two or more groups and societies into a common set of habits, attitudes, and ideas." While it is possible that the word "common" in the above definition implies the sense of group identity which we consider essential to an adequate definition of assimilation, we prefer the following definition, which is more explicit on this point.

Assimilation. The fusion of two or more groups into one group; the interpenetration of divergent habits, attitudes, ideas, and social relationships into a common unity.

Complete assimilation of two ethnic groups may be said to have been accomplished when cultural distinctions, including distinctions in social status, based upon ethnic or physiognomic ancestry cease to exist.

Amalgamation. The biological union of previously distinct racial or subracial groups.

Amalgamation is not to be confused with either assimilation or acculturation. While the process of assimilation operates to encourage increasing intermarriage and thus promote amalgamation, the latter refers to the biological process.

CLASSIFICATION OF MINORITIES

We have described above the structure and process of dominant-minority relations in general terms and now turn to classify some of the main variations. Classification presents the difficulty that many dimensions might be employed, i.e., in terms of the original mode of contact, in terms of the varieties and forms of discrimination, and on the basis of the types of visibility involved. As the study of minorities proceeds, classifications employing these manifold dimensions will no doubt develop.

As one example of a single-dimension classification Wirth classifies minorities in terms of the "major goals toward which the ideas, the sentiments, and the actions of minority groups are directed." [17] Minorities in this sense are grouped into the following four types: (1) *Pluralistic.* Here the minority is one which seeks toleration for its differences. In the United States, Jews, at least those who wish to retain Judaism, are an example. (2) *Assimilationist.* Here the mi-

[16] The use of the term "integration" in discussing the increasing interrelationship of Negroes with white people illustrates dissatisfaction with the commonly accepted definitions of assimilation. As long as Negroes or any other group are otherwise acculturated to the normative American culture but live to a large extent within a separate social structure, they can hardly be considered assimilated.
[17] *Op. cit.,* pp. 354-364.

ority wishes to lose its identity and be completely accepted. In general this appears to be the desire of American Negroes. (3) *Secessionist*. In this instance, the minority wishes to retain its identity and to be entirely free of its present dominant rulers. The Irish, Polish, and many other European nationalist movements resulting in independent statehood at the close of the first World War are examples of secessionist minorities. (4) *Militant*. This type of minority has set domination over others as its goal. The actions of the Sudeten Germans during the Nazi rise to power afford an illustration.

Kinds of visibility. The plan of organization of this book is based upon a classification of minority situations in terms of the type of visibility involved. Further consideration of the subject of classification will be limited to this type. American minorities have been most often distinguished by referring to them as ethnic or nationality, religious, or racial groups. While this appears a simple form of classification, its application to the American scene faces the difficulty that most of our minorities possess more than one type of visibility. The Japanese immigrants, for example, differed in their ethnic culture generally, had a distinctive physiognomy, and were preponderantly non-Christian. Perhaps only two minority groups can easily be fitted into a simple visibility scheme: the immigrants from the north of Europe who differ in ethnic culture without basic religious difference; and contemporary American Negroes who are distinguished almost solely by their physiognomic features. However, a useful clue to arranging minorities into a classification based upon visibility may be found by considering the ways in which the dominant status group has reacted to the visibilities involved.

Proceeding in this manner, it can be observed that the dominant groups conceived of minority groups in three ways: as "foreigners," as "colored," and as nonbelievers in the faith of the dominant group. While in most specific situations, the dominants look upon the minority in some combination of these three ways, in each case it seems possible to accord priority to one. For example, although the great majority of Italians are known to be Catholics, it is that entire configuration of cultural elements which compose the Italian "ethos," which identifies them most prominently. Again, in the case of the Japanese, while they are often thought of as foreigners, it is their physiognomic visibility which comes first to the mind of the person of dominant status when the word *Japanese* is mentioned. Furthermore, the leading element in the consciousness of the dominant in his conception of the Japanese is color. In spite of the fact that color is one of the less accurate traits to employ in racial classifications of mankind, it is consciousness of color which looms largest in the white man's concept of the other peoples of the earth. Wherever color difference is associated with other differences in the United States, it has always taken precedence over other factors in retarding assimilation.

Throughout human history, in-groups have looked upon out-groups as infidels, pagans, or heathens because from the point of view of the in-groups, the out-groups did not possess the "true" religion. Within the range of American minorities, the dominant sense of superiority over others for being non-Protestant or, in other contexts, non-Christian, is evidenced in such often used phrases as "papists," "the heathen Chinee," or "Christ-killers." While consciousness of religious difference does not appear as the primary factor in the dominant American attitudes toward most of the minorities, it is nevertheless the primary basis of anti-Catholicism, cutting across other minority situations, and has been at times an important element in anti-Semitism.

The general order in which the minorities are presented in Parts II, III, and V follows the three-fold division in visibilities indicated in the discussion just preceding. In Part IV, we depart from this general plan to use one additional classification in order to emphasize the special situation of those minorities who have been acquired by the United States through political expansion. While the peoples involved were culturally, and in some cases racially, different from normative Americans, they have also been thought of as "wards" and dealt with in a special way by their new governing authority.

In referring to the many groups who constitute our subject matter, it seems essential at times to use the adjective *ethnic,* a term widely used in sociological literature even though its precise meaning is not always clear. This word is sometimes employed to designate a group which was originally associated with a particular area and which therefore shared a common cultural heritage, for example, a tribe or a nation. Often the term is applied to a group with common racial features. In this book, the term will be used in the former sense. When it is employed in connection with groups which are distinguishable by both cultural and physiognomic traits, the context will be emphasizing the cultural ethos of the group. Although the ethnic groups to which we refer are generally minorities, it should be borne in mind that the dominant American group is an ethnic group as well.

Classification of the areas of discrimination. Discrimination against minorities is expressed in many areas of social life, sometimes in practically all areas simultaneously. We shall need qualifying adjectives for convenience in distinguishing certain broad areas of discrimination from one another. The classification to be followed in this connection is as follows:

Occupational Discrimination. This signifies the categorical denial of employment to a member of a given minority in certain occupations or social status levels of occupations. Denial of membership in unions and in occupational and professional associations also belong here, even though "social" aspects are involved.

Civic Discrimination. This covers the area of denial to minorities of equal participation in government, as the denial of the right to vote or to hold office; and also the discriminatory administration of justice, as illustrated by lynching or by those more subtle situations where the formalities of legal justice in fact miscarry due to the prejudice of its administrators.

Public Discrimination. This refers to the denial to minorities of equal access to and equal treatment in such public places as restaurants, hospitals, transportation facilities, and places of recreation.

Residential Discrimination. Under this is included the ways in which persons or families of minority status are denied the right to rent or buy living quarters for which they are prepared to pay the price which would be asked of persons of dominant status. Restrictive covenants, the asking of exorbitant prices and rents, falsification of the facts as to the availability for rent or sale of a premise are examples.

"Social" Discrimination. In a sense all discrimination is "social." But for the purpose at hand, "social" discrimination is restricted to those areas of social intercourse connoting close degrees of intimacy on planes of equality. Laws or other practices restricting marriage between dominant and minority persons fall under this heading. Likewise, all those practices which deny admission to formal or informal groups whose primary purposes are either sociable or prestige defining, illustrate "social" discrimination. Now that the limits have been defined in which the term "social" as qualifying discrimination will be used, the quotation marks will be hereafter omitted.

TOPICS FOR DISCUSSION AND PROJECTS

1. Develop with illustrations the point made on page 32 that minority persons tend to be "in a practical, immediate sense inferior" in some ways to the dominant group.
2. Give any illustrations you can recall from your experience in association with minority persons which indicate sensitivity to their minority status.
3. Are the students on your campus with minority group identification discriminated against in any way? If you think they are not, cultivate the friendship of one or more of them. Do not try talking about minorities with them until you have really earned their confidence. At this point, bring up the question above and see what they think about it.
4. Considering the threefold classification of minorities given in this chapter

under the heading of "visibility," where would you place people living in America from the following backgrounds: Turkish, Armenian, Hindu, Mexican, Puerto Rican?

5. Consider further the problem posed concerning the definitions of the terms acculturation and assimilation in this chapter. Do you agree or not with the writer that in the treatment of minorities the more usual definitions found in sociology textbooks are inadequate?

SUGGESTED READING

Cox, Oliver C. "Race and Caste—a Distinction", *American Journal of Sociology*, Vol. 50, 1945, p. 368.

> *The writer criticizes the use of the term "caste" to describe the relations between white and Negro in this country.*

Locke, Alain, and Stern, Bernhard J. *When Peoples Meet*. New York: American Educational Fellowship, rev. ed., 1946.

> *Selected excerpts from a wide variety of sources. Part III "The Ways of Dominant Peoples" and Part IV "The Ways of Submerged Peoples" are especially pertinent to this chapter.*

The Main Types and Causes of Discrimination. United Nations Publications.

> *Chapter 5 defines and classifies the various forms of discrimination, as they emerged from the deliberations of the Commission on Human Rights, United Nations.*

Rose, Arnold M., ed. *Race Prejudice and Discrimination*. New York: Alfred A. Knopf, Inc., 1951.

> *A valuable collection of readings in intergroup relations, many of which are drawn from sources not usually available.*

Rose, Arnold, and Rose, Caroline. *America Divided—Minority Group Relations in the United States*. New York: Alfred A. Knopf, 1948.

> *Chapter 1, "Minority Problems as Social Problems", defines the nature of the minority problem in terms of intergroup hatred.*

Schermerhorn, R. A. *These Our People: Minorities in American Culture*. Boston: D. C. Heath & Company, 1949.

> *Chapter 1, "Why Are Minorities a Problem?" deals with the concepts of dominant-minority relations and classification of minority groups.*

Warner, Lloyd W. "American Caste and Class," *American Journal of Sociology*, Vol. 42, Sept. 1936, pp. 234–237.

> *First statement of the author's distinction between class and caste in American race relations.*

Wirth, Louis. "The Problem of Minority Groups" in Ralph Linton, ed., *The Science of Man in the World Crisis*. New York: Columbia University Press, 1945, pp. 347–372.

> *Excellent statement of the problem in worldwide terms.*

Young, Donald. *American Minority Peoples*. New York: Harper and Brothers, 1932.

> *Chapter 1, "Racial Prejudices," and Chapter 27, "The Prospect," contain the main generalizations and interpretations in this text.*

CHAPTER 3

Race: Myth and Science

The basis of visibility or indentifiability, a necessary prerequisite for minority status, which is most frequently employed in dominant-minority relations is "race." The term is placed here in quotation marks because the meaning and significance of it in the popular thinking and behavior of dominants are so vastly at variance with current scientific thinking that one contemporary anthropologist has suggested, that in general usage at least, the term be discarded altogether.[1]

That the set of beliefs about race which have become established in popular sentiment may well constitute, as Montagu's title suggests, "man's most dangerous myth" was anticipated in the 1880's by a French pro-Aryan writer, Vacher de Lapouge, when he wrote, "I am convinced that in the next century millions of men will cut each other's throats because of one or two degrees more or less of cephalic index." [2] While the two great wars which have ensued since de Lapouge made this prophecy have not been based primarily on race antagonism, the idea of race was employed in the propaganda, for example, in the stereotype of "the Hun" in World War I, and in that of "the Jap" in World War II. Because these beliefs about race are so powerful a stimulus to social conflict, it is of the utmost importance that the student of social relations learn what race really is and how significant—or as will be shown, how insignificant—it really is.

[1] M. F. Ashley Montagu, *Man's Most Dangerous Myth: The Fallacy of Race* (New York: Columbia University Press, 1945) p. 12.
[2] Vacher de Lapouge, cited by Ruth Benedict, in *Race: Science and Politics*, rev. ed. (New York: Viking Press, Inc., 1945) p. 3.

To the student of dominant-minority relations in particular, understanding of the myth and reality of race is indispensable. For whatever the significance of racialist thinking in international relations in the past and for the future, already for two centuries it has performed yeoman service in bolstering the dominance of white Europeans over the colored peoples. As will be shown later, the beliefs about race arose after white subordination of colored peoples began. They gave to the dominant whites plausible intellectual and moral justification for the accomplished pattern of relations which was highly disadvantageous to the "colored."

The ensuing discussion of the science and myth about race will (1) begin by stating briefly the main tenets of the doctrine of racialism, (2) follow with a presentation of the contemporary scientific conclusions concerning race, and (3) conclude with tracing the history of the doctrine of racialism in relation to the main historical social forces in which the doctrine was nourished.

THE DOCTRINE OF RACIALISM

Race is the primary determiner of differences between peoples. The doctrine of racialism expounds the thesis that the main determiner of all the differences between peoples is their racial heredity. Differences in such elements of culture as language, religion, government, and art are assumed to be the result of racial differences. Likewise differences in folk personalities, that is, so-called tribal or national traits of a people, are associated with racial heredity as, for example, the practical drive of Englishmen in contrast to the mysticism of Hindus.

The races are unequal: the dominant is superior. Closely related to the first tenet is the belief that the races are unequal in general and specific abilities. Since the doctrine arose among Europeans, particularly among "Nordic," "Aryan," or "Teutonic" writers, it held that the white race was superior to the colored and among whites, the so-called "Nordic," or "Teutons," or "Aryans" were superior to other white peoples. Illustrative of this view are the following statements:

"The white race originally possessed the monopoly of beauty, intelligence, and strength." [3]

"It was Teutonic blood alone that formed the impelling force and the informing power. . . . It is a definite species of mankind which constitutes the physical and moral basis of our north European culture. The less Teuton a land the more uncivilized it is." [4]

[3] Arthur de Gobineau, *The Inequality of Human Races,* trans. by Adrian Collins (New York: G. P. Putnam's Sons, 1915) p. 209.
[4] Houston Stewart Chamberlain, *The Foundations of the Nineteenth Century,* translated from the German by John Lees (London: John Lane, The Bodley Head, Ltd., 1912) Vol. 2, p. 187.

"I do not think it would be an exaggeration to say that in respect of mental gifts the Nordic race marches in the van of mankind." [5]

"The civilization has been developed and history has been made chiefly by the white race." [6]

Since Europeans in general, and Teutons, in particular, are Christians, the problem existing for the racialist writers by the birth of the Messiah in Palestine was resolved by one such writer in this conclusion: "The probability that Christ was no Jew, that he had not a drop of genuinely Jewish blood in His veins, is so great that it is almost equivalent to certainty." [7]

The crossing of races is biologically deleterious. Arthur de Gobineau wrote, "By its [the white race's] union with other varieties, hybrids were created, which were beautiful without strength, strong without intelligence, or if intelligent both weak and ugly." [8] This illustrates an important aspect of racialism—that mating across race lines produces inferior people, monstrosities, as some racialists have put it.

One of the most strongly entrenched popular superstitions is the belief that interbreeding, or crossing, between "races" results in inferior offspring and that the greater part of such crossings lead to degeneration of the stock. The commonly employed stereotype has it that the half-caste inherits all the bad and none of the good qualities of the parental stocks. These bad qualities the half-breed is said to transmit to his offspring so that there is produced a very gradual and very definite mental and physical deterioration within the group, finally resulting in complete infertility.[9]

If the tenet of white, or in other contexts, "Nordic" or "Aryan," superiority is believed, it logically follows that race crossing would produce offspring inferior to the superior mate. Why, however, the results should be worse even than a mating of two inferiors, as many racialists imply, requires ingenious biological reasoning. The belief in this aspect of hybrid degeneration requires starting from a further premise, that races and subraces are fixed entities established at the beginning and meant either by God's will or nature's to remain that way.

In summary, then, the main ideas in the racialist doctrine are: (1) that cultural and personality differences between folk or national groups are primarily determined by racial heredity; (2) that the races are unequal, the white, or, in other cases, the "Aryan," "Teuton," or "Nordic," being superior in abilities which count most

---

[5] Baur, Fischer, and Lenz, *Human Heredity*, trans. by Eden and Cedar Paul (New York: The Macmillan Company, 1931) p. 655.
[6] Hutton Webster, *World History* (Boston: D. C. Heath & Company, 1923) p. 20.
[7] Houston S. Chamberlain, *op. cit.*, Vol. 1, pp. 211-212.
[8] Arthur de Gobineau, *op. cit.*, p. 209.
[9] Ashley Montagu, *op. cit.*, p. 100. By permission.

in progress; (3) that race crossing is deleterious per se; and (4) that the races are substantially fixed entities, and were meant to remain such in the cosmic plan. Some of the arguments advanced by the racialist writers or prevailing in the popular mind in defense of these basic ideas will be presented in relation to the scientific views about race.

SCIENCE AND RACE

Scientific knowledge and opinion about race have undergone much change, especially in the last few decades. At the present time, there is a common core of consensus, however, concerning race about which the various disciplines involved—anthropology, biology, psychology, and sociology—substantially agree.

The major stocks of mankind. Starting from the readily observable fact that the native peoples of Europe, Asia, Africa, and possibly aboriginal Australia, show in a general way marked differences in their physical characteristics, anthropologists have measured carefully representative samples of the population in these continental areas. By this process they have been able to determine that in a general way mankind can be classified into major racial types. Chart 1 presents one such classification. An examination of it shows how difficult it is to find many external features which are absolutely distinctive. The characteristics of any one race extend over a considerable range which frequently overlaps if not with both the other two, at least with one of them. While, for example, blue eyes are found only among whites, there are many whites whose eye color is as brown as that of many yellow people. Again, while in head form the yellow and black races are more clearly differentiated, the white race runs the whole gamut of human variation. Or consider the trait of hair in the chart. In hair form, while wavy hair is found only among whites, many other whites have straight hair as do almost all yellows. In this one of four aspects of hair, the black race with its frizzly hair is distinctive. In hair texture, and in the amount of bodily hair, the white stock is reasonably distinctive from the other two, but they in turn cannot be distinguished from each other. Consideration of such facts as these make it easy to understand why there is no one universally accepted classification of the stocks of mankind. Since any classification employing several traits will differentiate in a fairly distinctive way Caucasians, Mongoloids, and Negroids, classifications based upon these three types are currently most used, even though in terms of them several small stocks, particularly in the Australian region, cannot be placed.

Within each of the main racial stocks, physical anthropoligists have been able to delineate more or less clearly definable subvarieties.

CHART 1

Physical Characteristics of the Three Stocks of Mankind[10]

Trait	White	Yellow	Black
Skin color	Pale reddish white to olive brown	Saffron to yellow-brown; some reddish brown	Brown to brown-black; some yellow-brown
Stature	Medium to tall	Medium tall to medium short	Tall to very short
Head form	Long to broad and short; medium high to very high	Predominantly broad; height medium	Predominantly long; height low to medium
Face	Narrow to medium broad; tends to high; no prognathism	Medium broad to very broad; malars "high" and flat; tends to medium high	Medium broad to narrow; tends to medium high; strong prognathism
Hair	Head hair: color light blond to dark brown; texture fine to medium; form straight to wavy. Body hair: moderate to profuse	Head hair: color brown to brown-black; texture coarse; form straight. Body hair: sparse	Head hair: color brown-black; texture, coarse; form light curl to woolly or frizzly. Body hair: slight
Eye	Color light blue to dark brown; lateral eye fold occasional	Color brown to dark brown; medial epicanthic fold very common	Color brown to brown-black; vertical eye fold common
Nose	Bridge usually high; form narrow to medium broad	Bridge usually low to medium; form medium broad	Bridge usually low; form medium broad to very broad
Body build	Linear to lateral; slender to rugged	Tends to be lateral; some linearity evident	Tends to lateral and muscular, but some linearity evident

[10] Wilton Krogman, "The Concept of Race," in Ralph Linton, ed., *The Science of Man in the World Crisis* (New York: Columbia University Press, 1945) p. 50. By permission.

Drawing upon E. A. Hooton's detailed material, Kimball Young has summarized the features of these substocks and indicated their habitats.

The subraces of the white race are: (1) *Mediterranean,* found around the whole Mediterranean basin and through migration in the New World, tend to be of medium or stocky build; long-headed; brunet in skin color, with dark straight or wavy hair, and dark eyes. (2) *Keltic,* found mostly in Ireland, Wales, Scotland, and parts of England, and in this country and the British Dominions through migration, tend to be tall and slender; long-headed; from light-brunet to fair in skin color, with dark or reddish straight hair, and blue or gray eyes. (3) *Nordic,* in Scandinavia, Britain, the Baltic area, and through migration here and in the British Dominions, tend to be tall and slender; long-headed; with fair skin, straight or wavy blond hair, and blue eyes. (4) *Alpine,* chiefly in central Europe, some in the Balkans, the Baltic area, and the Near East, and in the United States through migration, tend to be from medium to stocky in build; broad-headed; brunet in skin color, with dark straight or wavy hair, and dark eyes. (5) *East Baltic,* in Finland, the Baltic area, Poland, north Germany, and in this country now, tend to be from medium to short-stocky in build; variable in head form; fair in skin color, with blond or brown straight or wavy hair, and gray or blue eyes. In addition there are two "composite" subraces: (6) *Armenoid,* of Turkey and the Near East, some in central Europe and the Balkans, and in the United States through migration, are usually stocky in build and have from long to medium head form; olive or swarthy skin; dark wavy hair, and dark-brown or medium-brown eyes. (7) *Dinaric,* found chiefly in Yugoslavia and the Dinaric Alps, and in this country through migration, tend to be stockier in build than the Armenoid but are like them in head form and usually have brunet skin, wavy brown hair, and brown eyes. (8) Also, the *Ainu* of northern Japan, now almost extinct, are usually considered a subrace of the white.

The subraces of the black race are: (1) *African* or *Forest* Negro, found in Africa south of the Sahara, in the Upper Nile region, and sporadically in east Africa, and the New World today, tend to be variable in body build; long-headed; from black to dark-brown in skin color; with black woolly or frizzy hair, and dark-brown or black eyes. (2) *Nilotic,* found in the Sudan and scattered among New World Negroes, tend to be taller and slender and to have black or bluish-black skin; otherwise they are similar to the Forest Negro. (3) *Negrito,* (the pygmies of the Congo, Malaya, and New Guinea) are very short; thick-set in build; medium in head form; with dirty-yellowish or brown color skin, black woolly hair, and from dark-brown to black eyes. All three subraces are characterized by broad noses.

The subraces of the yellow race are: (1) *Classic Mongoloid,* found in Siberia, the Amur region in north China, sometimes in Mongolia and Tibet, tend to be medium in build; broad in head form; from yellow to yellow-brown in skin color, with black, straight coarse hair, and from medium-brown to dark-brown eyes with Mongolian fold. (2) *Arctic Mongoloid,* in arctic regions of northeast Asia and North America, usually have a small but variable build and medium head form; otherwise they are much like the Classic Mongoloid, except that the Mongolian eyefold is incomplete. (3) *American Indian* of the New World, probably a composite but chiefly Mongoloid, are quite variable in build; also variable in head form; with yellow-brown or red-brown skin, usually black straight hair, and from dark-brown to black eyes, with Mongolian fold lacking. Then there is (4) a composite of *Mongoloid, Indonesian,* and *Malayan,* found in South China, Burma, Indochina, Japan, Malay, Thailand, the Philippines and East Indies, who are usually short in build; quite variable in head form; with dark yellow-brown skin, black straight hair as a rule, and from medium-brown to dark-brown eyes.[11]

Race: a changing phenomenon. Among the reasons why it is difficult to classify races is the fact that throughout human history peoples have migrated considerably and with this migration has frequently taken place some miscegenation. Far from being a fixed entity, race has been a dynamic, changing phenomenon.

To begin with, mankind apparently started out as one race. Since *Homo sapiens* evolved thousands of years prior to written history, it is not possible to know the racial features of prehistoric man with any exactitude. However, contemporary anthropology generally accepts on the basis of the piecemeal fossil evidence and the logic of evolutionary and genetic principles a monogenetic rather than a polygenetic theory of man's origin. Montagu has put it:

Concerning the origin of the living varieties of man we can say little more than that there is every reason to believe that a single stock gave rise to all of them. All varieties of man belong to the same species and have the same remote ancestry. This is a conclusion to which all the relevant evidence of comparative anatomy, palaeontology, serology, and genetics points. On genetic grounds alone, it is virtually impossible to conceive of the varieties of man as having originated separately as distinct lines from different anthropoid ancestors.[12]

Long before written history, the major differentiation of mankind into the main racial varieties occurred as a result of migration; of natural selection affecting the survival of certain variations; and of the limitations of variation through the relative isolation of the major varieties in their chosen continental habitats. Subsequently limiting their further migration largely to their own continental domain the main varieties "perfected," so to speak, their basic type. Subsequently continental migrations alternating with long periods of endogamous mating created and recreated loosely definable subtypes.

[11] Kimball Young, *Sociology, A Study of Society and Culture,* rev. ed. (New York: American Book Company, 1949) pp. 160-162.
[12] Montagu, *op. cit.,* p. 46. By permission.

The American Indian illustrates the process of subtype development. The ancestors of our Indians came from Asia and possessed general Mongoloid features. Natural selection and thousands of years of isolation limiting the range of variability to that present in the original migrating groups, perfected a distinctive Indian type.

While throughout the entire historic period mixing has occurred across the main divisions, in the past few centuries the wandering and mixing of peoples has created many new subtypes, involving combinations of traits from the main racial divisions. As examples may be cited the Pitcairn Islanders of *Mutiny on the Bounty* fame; and the American Negro.[13] The present Hawaiian situation where the various ethnic groups are intermarrying with increasing freedom is one of the most interesting examples of racial changes.

From the foregoing it can be seen that race is a highly unstable phenomenon. The racial variability of *Homo sapiens* has undergone more or less continuous modification. This changing nature of race makes the idea of a "pure" race meaningless. The greatest homogeneity in racial traits is found among small groups of people long isolated from the main currents of civilization, and whose cultures for that very reason are primitive or "backward."

In the sense then of the foregoing discussion there is such a thing as race difference among men. It should be clearly understood that all that this means is that these "races" are verifiable in terms of external, measurable physical characteristics which are known to be primarily determined by genetic processes. Such a process of classification tells us nothing about their respective abilities or throws any light at all upon the validity of the racialist doctrine. Anthropologists have investigated the possibilities that along with these racial features there might be differences in genetically determined general abilities and specific capacities which could explain the differences in their cultures and the relative superiority or inferiority in their civilizational status. To the results of such investigation attention is now focused.

Race and culture. Frequently one hears people speak of the Latin race or races, or of the French race, or perchance of the Mohammedan race. The use of such adjectives carries the implication that race and culture are correlated and that if one is by heredity a member of a given race, he is bound to manifest his raciality in corresponding forms of culture. The problem of the relation of race to culture is one aspect of the larger problem of the relation of heredity to environment, a subject which has provoked an enormous amount of con-

[13] See Ch. 8 for the racial features of Negroes in the United States.

troversy and also prompted volumes of research.[14] The racialist writers are one special group of biological determinists. In essence they hold that what determines the differences in the cultures of ethnic groups is the distinctive genetic racial heredity of each. One such group of writers was the "Aryan" school. Philological research revealed similarities in the languages of the Persians and Indians and those of the western Indo-Europeans, the Greeks, Romans, Teutons, Celts, and Slavs. Concluding that this meant that all languages derived from a common source, these writers posited a primitive Aryan tribe from which all the later Aryans descended. Considering these languages superior, and assuming without question that language and race are related, this school expounded the theory of the "superior Aryan race." It would take us too far afield to summarize the criticisms of the Aryan theories.[15] But the wide variation in both racial characteristics, as determined by anthropologists, and the cultures among the alleged Aryan peoples indicate that they have little scientific foundation.

To persons living in the United States, it is clear enough that people of any racial ancestry may acquire perfect English speech with the normative accent, even one peculiar to a region. The writer recalls the interesting experience of visiting a migrant labor camp where Jamaican Negroes were being housed for the harvest season and hearing them speak the king's English, in contrast to the Southern dialect typical of the majority of American Negroes. While there are areas where a high degree of racial homogeneity and similarity of language coincide, situations like the one just described indicate that no causal connection between race and language exists.

Race and nationality. The tendency to identify race and nation is perhaps the most widely held of all beliefs relating race to culture. Here again, there are instances in which a high degree of racial homogeneity parallels a fairly distinctive culture, as for example, in modern Japan. Ironically enough, however, it is in Europe, the very region where racialist theories were most earnestly expounded, where the lack of correlation between race and national culture is most clearly illustrated. This is notably true of Germany, France, and England, where Nordic, Alpine, and Mediterranean traits have been shown to be harmoniously blended in the citizenry of each nation. Dominian writes, "Northern France is perhaps more Teutonic than southern Germany, while eastern Germany is, in many places, more Slavic than

---

[14] All introductory sociology textbooks discuss the subject of heredity and environment. One of the clearest brief expositions of the topic may be found in R. M. MacIver and C. H. Page, *Society: An Introductory Analysis* (New York: Rinehart & Co., Inc., 1949) pp. 80-97.
[15] See the bibliography at the end of this chapter for material on Aryan theories and other aspects of race and culture.

Russia." [16] Hankins points out that within Germany, "A relative purity of Germanic elements along the Baltic and North Seas (but mixed even there with Slavic Poles and Wends) gradually gives way to the southward to an increasing complexity in which Alpine and Mediterranean elements increase." [17]

Since the English were racially mongrelized within the broad Caucasian limits, it follows that the old American stock was correspondingly a mongrel mixture of European varieties. In a study of Americans descended from this English stock, Hrdlicka showed that they ranged widely in skin color, hair color, and eye color with intermediates predominating over either the alleged Nordic type with fair skin, blue eyes, and blond hair, or the swarthy complexioned, brunet Mediterranean type. Altogether, the measurements indicate extensive hybridization in the old American stock.[18]

Beyond all this, the exhaustive study of the nature of culture and its processes which has gone on for the past few decades indicates that it is the common experience of living together that develops cultural similarities, irrespective of race. Thus American Negroes, whose lineal continuity with the American scene is almost as old as that of the English, were more Americanized in the cultural sense at the turn of the century than any of the recent white immigrant groups. An American Negro school child would have just as much difficulty acculturating himself to a central African tribe as any white child, except, of course, as differential reactions of the Africans to whiteness might place greater obstacles in the way of the acculturation of the white child.

Race and physiology. Comparative studies of the physiology of samples of racial groups have in some cases shown significant differences, and in other cases have failed to do so. No differences have been established in respiration and circulation.[19] Orientals show lower blood pressure and lower basal metabolism in comparison with whites.[20] Likewise there are differences in group odor.[21] While persons from different groups claim that the body odor of other groups is unpleasant, in view of the amount of miscegenation which has taken place, reactions to these differences are largely a matter of conditioning.

[16] Leon Dominian, *Frontiers of Language and Nationality* (New York: Henry Holt & Company, Inc., 1917) pp. 3-4.
[17] F. H. Hankins, *The Racial Basis of Civilization* (New York: Alfred A. Knopf, Inc., 1926) p. 286.
[18] Ales Hrdlicka, *Old Americans* (Baltimore: The Williams & Wilkins Company, 1925) Ch. 3.
[19] Otto Klineberg, *Race Differences* (New York: Harper and Brothers, 1935) p. 111.
[20] *Ibid.,* pp. 112-117.
[21] *Ibid.,* pp. 128-131.

Differences in immunity to disease would be important to the survival of races especially when the members of a group are transplanted to other than their accustomed environment. It is said, for example, that the peoples of north Europe are more susceptible to whooping cough and more resistant to goiter and cretinism, whereas the peoples of southern Europe succumb more often to the last two mentioned ailments but resist pulmonary diseases. While the rates for various specific diseases vary among racial groups, the environmental influences vary so widely that whether racial genetics have anything to do with the differences is not established. Admitting that these problems require much more explanation, Krogman concludes that science does not know "any genetico-racial biological differences in the organs which will conduce to, or inhibit, organic breakdowns under the onslaught of disease." [22]

The finding of some physiological differences between racial groups by no means establishes a genetic cause for them. General group differences in such matters as diet, modes of life, and other environmental factors are involved in interpreting these differences. In summary, Klineberg writes:

"There are interesting and significant group differences in physiological activity, but there is no adequate proof that these are determined by heredity. The studies of blood pressure in particular show the extent to which these organic functions may be affected by cultural and environmental factors, and they throw considerable doubt upon a racial interpretation." [23]

In short, what science now knows about race differences suggests that the stocks of mankind vary more in their visible physical characteristics than they do in their invisible physical traits. As a final illustration we refer to "blood", about which so much superstition has developed. The four types of human blood, designated by the labels O, A, B, and AB are inherited. But whites, Negroes, and Mongols have all these blood types.[24] Blood plasma derived from various racial groups was utilized for the wounded in World War II irrespective of their race, with no effect upon the personality or physiology of the recipients.

Race crossing. Random observation of people in large metropolitan areas of the United States will readily reveal persons of hybrid features of the main races of mankind whose external features are well pro-

[22] Wilton Krogman, "What We Do Not Know about Race," *The Scientific Monthly*, Vol. 57, Aug. 1943, p. 103.
[23] Klineberg, *op. cit.*, p. 131. By permission.
[24] Ruth Benedict and Gene Weltfish, "The Races of Mankind" in Benedict, *op. cit.*, pp. 174-175.

portioned and handsome. If an occasional "ugly" looking hybrid is noted, the same can be found in an occasional person who is not a hybrid. What science has to say about the effects of race crossing may be approached by first considering some conclusions drawn from specific studies of particular interracial crossings:[25]

Polynesian-White Crossing: The hybrid descendants of English mutineers and Tahitian women are taller than the average Englishmen or Tahitian, are more vigorous, and healthy, and mentally they are perfectly alert. The physical type of the descendants is in every way perfectly harmonious, with white characteristics predominating.

Australian-White Crossing: All unprejudiced observers agree that the offspring of aboriginal-white crossings in Australia represent an excellent physical type and that both the aborigines and the hybrids are possessed of considerable mental ability.

In Hawaii: Here are literally hundreds of varieties of mixed types, involving native Hawaiians (Polynesians), Japanese, Filipinos, Koreans, Chinese, and whites of many nationalities. The descendants of mixed Hawaiian unions have a much higher fertility rate than other ethnic groups and in height, weight, and other physical characteristics they tend to be intermediate between their Hawaiian and non-Hawaiian forebears.

Indian-White Mixtures: Boas showed that the "half-blood" Indian was taller and more fertile than the parental Indian and white stocks. Krogman concludes that Seminole Indians of Oklahoma, who are the descendants of a mixture of runaway Creek Indians, Negro slaves, and whites, are on the whole good physical types, and often beautiful. There is not the slightest evidence of degeneration of disharmony in development.

Upon this matter of race crossing, the verdict of biological and anthropological science is clear and unequivocal. Race crossing per se has no deleterious biological consequences. On the contrary, and most disconcerting to the exponents of racism, the preponderance of evidence points to at least an initial biological superiority of the progeny of the first hybrid generation over that of the respective racial parental generation. The phenomenon of "hybrid vigor" well known in plant and animal biology is indicated in many human interracial crossings. Of this the biologist Jennings writes:

In view of the immense number of genes carried by individuals of each race, and their separate history up to the time of the cross, the relatively few defects that have arisen are almost certain to affect genes of different pairs in the two. Hence when the races cross, the individuals produced will receive a normal gene from one parent or the other in most of their gene pairs; and

[25] The examples given are taken from Montagu, *op. cit.*, Ch. 8.

since the normal gene usually manifests its effect, the offspring of the cross will have fewer gene defects than either of the parents.[26]

Thus the offspring of diverse races may be expected to be superior in vigor, and presumably in other characteristics. . . . Data on this point are not abundant, but it is probable that hybrid vigor is an important and advantageous feature of race crosses in man.[27]

Biological considerations are, of course, not the only considerations involved in the matter of race crossing. For example, most white parents in the United States would attempt to dissuade their children from marrying a colored person by pointing out, among other reasons, that the children of such marriage would be accorded minority status. But this has nothing to do with biology. The merits or demerits of race crossing may be argued at the social level, but those who argue against it will find no sanction from biological science.

Race: equality or inequality. In the attempt to answer the question whether or not the different races vary significantly in their general capacities for civilizational development, researches have been pursued along three main lines: the evolutionary approach; the cultural achievement approach; and the psychological testing approach. The first and second approaches having been exhausted with substantially negative conclusions will be treated briefly; the third merits fuller treatment.

The Evolutionary Approach. The hypothesis upon which this approach to the question of race inequality was based was that the three main races of man evolved not only independently but at widely separated intervals, and that the earlier the evolution the more inferior and less highly developed the race was. Fossil remains of men have been discovered whose skeletal structure indicates probable inferiority to *Homo sapiens* in cultural capacity—the Java man (*Pithecanthropus erectus*) and the Peking man (*Sinanthropus pekinensis*), for example. The highest developed living species below man is the ape—thought to be in collateral, but not in the direct, line of evolution toward man. The results of comparing the three main races of man with apes have been summarized by Hankins as follows:

Human evolution has, however, not been in a straight line from the ape with the different races arranged in a hierarchical series with the Nordic at the top and the poor Australian at the bottom. There have been many turnings, bifurcations, and even reversions. All races are consequently simian in some traits but wholly nonsimian in others. The Negro, for example, is more

[26] H. S. Jennings, *The Biological Basis of Human Nature* (New York: W. W. Norton & Company, Inc., 1930) p. 280. By permission.
[27] H. S. Jennings, "The Laws of Heredity and Our Present Knowledge of Human Genetics on the Material Side" in H. S. Jennings et al., *Scientific Aspects of the Race Problem* (New York: Longmans, Green & Company, 1941) p. 71.

simian than either Mongolian or Caucasian in facial angle, largeness of jaw, recession of forehead, breadth of nose, and shortness of hair. He is farthest of the three races from the apes in hair texture, hairlessness of body, and fullness and redness of lips. The white races are most simian in the quantity of body hair, while the yellow races are closest to the apes in coarseness and length of hair.[28]

Cultural Superiority. To support the claim to white Nordic superiority, it has often been argued that the higher levels of civilization achieved by Europeans in general and north Europeans in particular, and the corresponding lesser civilizational advance of the Asiatic peoples, and even more particularly of the aboriginal African people, is evidence of the racial superiority of the Nordics. Let us disregard the question of the absolute superiority of European civilization over others and agree that during the last few centuries the center of greatest scientific advance and economic improvement has been in Europe, and subsequently North America. However, a thousand years ago, the centers of civilizational advance were in the Mediterranean countries; still earlier the Oriental civilizations were more advanced than European, and great civilizations had developed in north Africa, far more advanced than those of the north Europeans at that time. If it is primarily racial qualities which determine the degree of civilizational advance, why have the white peoples not been consistently in the van? Furthermore, the "Nordic over other whites" superiority part of the thesis involves the assumption that the populations of the various parts of Europe were racially homogeneous, an assumption which, as was pointed out above, is now repudiated.

The contemporary record of many colored peoples further challenges the hypothesis that level of cultural achievement is determined by race. The rise of Japan from a semifeudal civilization to a world power, capable among other things of defeating Russia in a modern war, within a period of fifty years fails to strengthen the conviction of innate white superiority. Against the further argument that Japan merely copies the discoveries and inventions of the West may be placed the actual new contributions of Japanese scientists and scholars to world science. Likewise, the many contributions of Negroes in the United States to our present technological level, as for example, the discoveries of George W. Carver belie the alleged monopoly of white people over hereditary capacity at the higher levels.

The Mental Test Approach. Modern psychological science has developed numerous tests designed to measure differences in mental responses and other psychological responses such as vision, mechanical

[28] F. H. Hankins, *The Study of Society* (New York: The Macmillan Company, 1935) pp. 121-122. By permission.

dexterity, and other aptitudes. Among these the most pertinent to the question of racial superiority and inferiority are the general intelligence tests. While one of the aims in developing mental testing was to devise tests which accurately determine the potential, innate ability of the persons tested irrespective of their relative environmental advantages and disadvantages, it is generally conceded that no test yet devised has succeeded in achieving this ideal. In fact, the more the interactional aspects of heredity and environment are studied, the more one may well doubt that such a scientific goal can ever be reached.[29]

In the United States an extensive amount of intelligence testing has been done comparing the scores of our various ethnic and racial groups. The greatest volume of material of this sort has been accumulated with comparative reference to Negroes and non-Negroes in the American population. The general results of these tests show: (1) an average higher score for the white sample; (2) a greater proportion of the white sample in the higher score brackets; and (3) an extensive overlapping of the distribution of the scores of both groups. There seems little doubt that the white population taken as whole in comparison with the Negro population as whole has a proportionally greater amount of developed, and therefore practically effective, abilities. However, analyses of these tests and others designed for the particular purpose provide strong indications that scores on the tests used were greatly influenced by environmental factors, by differential advantage and disadvantage.[30] Northern Negroes, for example, show up better than Southern Negroes, as Table 2 illustrates. Since this might

TABLE 2

Northern and Southern Negroes, Army Results, 1918[31]

(Percentages in Each Category)

	NUMBER	D—	D	C—	C	C+	B	A
Northern Negroes	8,163	19.6	27.6	22.1	21.4	6.7	2.3	0.6
Southern Negroes	14,994	55.7	26.4	9.8	6.2	1.4	0.4	0.1

be due to selection, that is, possibly the northward migrating Negroes tend to be those with greater intelligence, Klineberg made a special study involving the test scores of 3181 Negro ten and twelve-year-olds in Harlem schools. His conclusions were: "The results vary slightly in the different studies, but almost without exception they agree in show-

[29] See MacIver and Page, *op. cit.*, pp. 80-97, concerning this point.
[30] All the following general results are taken from Otto Klineberg, ed., *Characteristics of the American Negro* (New York: Harper and Brothers, 1944) in which he summarizes the materials in this field.
[31] *Ibid.*, p. 36. By permission.

ing that the lowest scores are obtained by the groups which have most recently arrived from the South. There is a close, though by no means perfect, relationship between test score and length of residence in New York City." [32] This suggests strongly that improvement in educational and cultural conditions brings with it improvement in test scores. This conclusion is further strengthened by the fact that the scores in the First World War army tests showed Negroes in certain northern states having higher median scores to whites in certain southern states, as Table 3 shows.

TABLE 3

Southern Whites and Northern Negroes, by States, Army Results, 1918 [33]

Whites		Negroes	
STATE	MEDIAN SCORE	STATE	MEDIAN SCORE
Mississippi	41.25	Pennsylvania	42.00
Kentucky	41.50	New York	45.00
Arkansas	41.55	Illinois	47.35
Georgia	42.12	Ohio	49.50

The results obtained by comparing all the various ethnic and racial differences are difficult indeed to explain on any racial genetic basis. Table 4 has arranged the results by ethnic groups. The ethnic groups presented are of course not all "racial" groups but enough of

TABLE 4

Summary Table of Ethnic Differences in I.Q. [34]

ETHNIC GROUP	NUMBER OF STUDIES	I.Q. RANGE	MEDIAN I.Q.
American Control Groups	18	85-108	102
Jews	7	95-106	103
Germans	6	93-105	100.5
English and Scotch	5	93-105	99
Japanese	9	81-114	99
Chinese	11	87-107	98
American Negroes	27	58-105	86
Italians	16	79- 96	85
Portuguese	6	83- 96	84
Mexicans	9	78-101	83.5
American Indians	11	65-100	80.5

[32] *Ibid.*, p. 44. By permission.
[33] *Ibid.*, p. 36. By permission.
[34] *Ibid.*, p. 35. By permission.

them are to be pertinent to the question. Reading down the list, the sharp break in range of scores occurs between Chinese and American Negroes. On racial grounds it is hard to explain the high position of Chinese and Japanese substantially equal to English and Scotch on the one hand; and the position of Portuguese and Italians in the low group, below that of American Negroes. Or again, what racial interpretation can be made of the position of American Indians at the very bottom of the list, when their racial kinship to the high ranking Chinese and Japanese is closer than to any other of the low-ranking groups, except possibly the Mexicans who have a substantial Indian admixture? The present status of the scientific position on the inferiority and superiority of races as indicated by intelligence testing is summarized by Klineberg as follows:

Because of the various difficulties inherent in the interpretation of test scores, there has been observed among psychologists something of a movement away from the former position that the mental inferiority of certain "races" had been proved by means of the tests. Probably few psychologists would now accept the statement made by Ferguson that "psychological study of the Negro indicates that he will never be the mental equal of the white race." Most psychologists working in the field at the present time appear to regard the mental test, and psychological methods in general, as incapable of leading to a definitive statement in this regard. In 1934 Thompson reported on the basis of a questionnaire circulated in 1929–1930:

"Competent scholars in the field of racial differences are almost unanimous in the opinion that, up to the present time, race superiority and inferiority have not been experimentally demonstrated—only 4 per cent of the respondents indicate that the first viewpoint which accepts the fact of race superiority and inferiority is valid."

As one more example of a change of attitude in this field we may cite a recent statement by Odum, that among the errors of sociology is the "assumption that races are inherently different rather than group products of differentials due to the cumulative power of folk-regional and cultural environment." 35

Summarizing this subject of the comparative mental abilities of the major races, the most certain conclusion is that there exists no valid proof that the three major races are unequal in the ranges or average of their innate mental capacities. On the basis of such methods as science has at its disposal, a wide range of mental abilities within each race is indicated. From a scientific point of view, the question of racial equality-inequality will never be settled except when studied in a single society where the three racial groups live together and where cultural opportunity and social status are not influenced by racial considerations. From a practical point of view, those who wish to apply such

35 *Ibid.,* pp. 95-96. By permission.

science as we have to social policy, as for example in the field of occupational guidance and employment, would best act on the reasonable assumption of race similarity in mental abilities.

THE SOCIAL SIGNIFICANCE OF THE RACIALIST DOCTRINE

If, as the case appears, there is almost no objective evidence to support any of the tenets in the doctrine of racism, how do we account for its development and persistence? Before taking up the main aspects of these questions, passing attention should be given to the fact that the kind of scientific evidence which has caused a complete discarding of the doctrine in the scientific world has not been in existence for so very many years. The persistence of the doctrine is in part related to the lag in discovery, and to the still remaining lag in the dissemination of the 20th century findings of science and race.

Much light upon why the racist myth arose and diffused among white men in general and north Europeans in particular can be obtained by examining the history of the doctrine and in considering some societal circumstances connected with its history.

Racialism: a corrollary of European expansion. A number of recent writers insist that the racialist myth, or doctrine, set forth above arose not earlier than the 18th century.

In the long history of the world men have given many reasons for killing each other in war: envy of another people's good bottom land or of their herds, ambition of chiefs and kings, different religious beliefs, high spirits, revenge. But in all these wars the skulls of the victims on both sides were generally too similar to be distinguished. Nor had the war leaders incited their followers by referring to the shapes of their heads. They might call them the heathen, the barbarians, the heretics, the slayers of women and children, but never our enemy Cephalic Index 82.

It was left for high European civilization to advance such a reason for war and persecution and to invoke it in practice. In other words, racism[36] is a creation of our own time.[37]

Prior to the sixteenth century the world was not race conscious and there was no incentive for it to become so.[38]

When we examine the scientific literature of the seventeenth century with a view to discovering what beliefs were held concerning the variety of man, we find that it was universally believed that mankind was comprised of a

[36] The use of the word "racism" in place of "racialism" is becoming increasingly common. It might serve a useful purpose to retain the more traditional term for the literary apologia for the phenomena concerned and to use the newer term to refer to the behavior manifesting this point of view. We shall, however, use the two terms synonomously.
[37] Benedict, *op cit.*, pp. 3-4. By permission.
[38] Ralph Linton, *The Study of Man* (New York: Appleton-Century-Crofts, Inc., 1936) p. 46.

single species and that it represented a unitary whole. . . . Physical differences were, of course, known to exist between groups of mankind, but what was unfamiliar was the notion that the differences exhibited by such peoples represented anything fundamental.[39]

In all of the three modes of dynamic social conflict arising in the 17th century, "racism" became involved. The first was class conflict. Racialism was invoked by the nobles of France to justify their position as superior to the masses and later by European aristocrats, generally to maintain their position as the "hereditary," and therefore for all time, superiors of the proletariat.[40]

Racialism becomes a support of nationalistic rivalries by adding to the cult of nationalism the idea that "our nation is a superior race" to the enemy nation. "Race as a factor in history . . . came into being as a concomitant of the nationalism upon which the political, economic, and cultural structure of modern civilization rests," Snyder writes.[41] But most pertinent to our interest, racism became a strong support of slavery and imperialism. In the process of establishing their economic hegemony over most of the world and in developing less settled areas under this domination to their own greatest advantage, white Europeans, particularly the English—whose tradition in this respect became American—developed a castelike relation to the "natives" of their colonies and also to the forcefully imported slaves under an even more indisputably inferior status. In fact, it seems clear that in actual time sequence, the white men first exploited native labor and brought in slaves, and subsequently expounded a theory of the inferiority of the "colored" peoples to support the *de facto* status.[42] Montagu develops this position. "Their different physical appearance provided a convenient peg upon which to hang the argument that this represented the external sign of more profound ineradicable mental and moral inferiorities." [43] Benedict puts the same idea in these summary sentences.

Racism did not get its currency in modern thought until it was applied to conflicts within Europe—first to class conflicts and then to national. But it is possible to wonder whether the doctrine would have been proposed at all as explaining these latter conflicts—where, as we have seen, the dogma is so inept—if the basis for it had not been laid in the violent experience of racial prejudice on the frontier.[44]

[39] Montagu, *op. cit.,* p. 16. By permission.
[40] Benedict, *op. cit.,* p. 112.
[41] L. L. Snyder, *Race: a History of Modern Ethnic Theories* (Chicago: Alliance Book Corporation, 1939) p. 48.
[42] See Ch. 8 in this connection for the development of philosophical justification of slavery in the United States long after the first slaves were imported.
[43] Montagu, *op. cit.,* p. 19.
[44] Benedict, *op. cit.,* p. 111. By permission.

In summary, the doctrine of racism appears to have developed in relation to the colored races as an ideological and moral justification for a system already established and highly useful to white dominants. It has been continued for the same reason. The fact that at the time of contact the native races were sufficiently colored to be identified and also were in level of civilization actually inferior (in terms of the standards of white civilization) offered plausible demonstration of the white man's allegation of their inferiority. Once systems of dominant-minority relations become established with the doctrine of white supremacy to reinforce them, two vicious circles were set in motion: the perpetual conditioning of subsequent generations of white children to accept the racist doctrine; and the impact of the system upon the minority to keep them in large measure inferior in their developed capacities.

Racialism: an adjunct of nationalistic movements. The potential power of racism in stimulating group conflict can be further illustrated by its application to two 20th century phenomena: the Japanese pan-Asiatic movement and the rise of the Hitler Reich. While it would be oversimplification to explain the aggressive policy pursued by Japan in the 20th century wholly on the basis of their own notion of race superiority, that this notion was prevalent and served a useful purpose in developing morale for aggressive political policies should not be overlooked. According to the Japanese scholar, Hirata, "from the fact of the divine descent of the Japanese people proceeds their unmeasurable superiority to the natives of other countries in courage and intelligence." [45] While like all tribes and nations, Japanese were always ethnocentric, the development of distinct "racial pride" as part of the cultural paraphernalia essential to whip up national enthusiasm for military, imperialistic expansion was a part of the great borrowing of Western ideas and knowledge which characterized modern Japan.

In the Nazi ideology, racialism was a dominant theme. The Nazi philosophers expounded the notion that the development of a pan-Nordic (German) state was the only bulwark against chaos. First of all the German nation itself must be further purified particularly from the deteriorating effect of the Jewish "race." Goebbels once observed, "Many intellectuals are trying to help the Jews with the ancient phrase, 'the Jew is also a man.' Yes, he is a man, but what sort of a man? The flea is also an animal." [46] In practice, Nazis subjected Jews to incredibly inhuman persecution. Once the German Nordic "race" itself was thus purified, the rest of the "race" was to be incorporated into a pan-German state, and Germans scattered in other

[45] Willard Price, "Japan's Divine Mission," *The New Republic*, Nov. 17, 1937.
[46] *Time*, July 8, 1935, p. 21.

parts of the world, notably the United States were to be encouraged to retain their racial purity and to foster Nazi ideas.[47]

Racialism in the United States. The doctrine of racialism is widely prevalent in the thinking of large segments of the population of the United States. How these racialist beliefs and attitudes serve to support dominant discrimination against minorities will be indicated repeatedly as we proceed to consider the stories of each minority group separately. At this point we shall limit our treatment of racialism in the United States to its literary expression. Writings of a racialist character directed specifically at showing the inferiority of the Negro and thus attempting to give moral justification to slavery arose in the South in the decades prior to the Civil War. (See Ch. 8.) It was, however, in the second and third decades of the 20th century that the racialist thesis found its greatest literary expression by the apostles of the Nordic movement, beginning with the publication by Madison Grant in 1916 of *The Passing of the Great Race*.[48] Borrowing heavily from the European Nordic protagonists, Grant applied its implication for the United States. He considered the "melting pot" thesis anathema and warned the "native" Americans, i.e., Nordics, to protect their heritage from being destroyed by new non-Nordic elements resulting from the later immigration. The same general thesis gained more academic respectability through the writings of Henry Fairfield Osborn, a professional paleontologist. Osborn belonged to the school of scientists who considered heredity far more determinative for human events than environment. He further believed that the Nordic racial group was superior to the Alpine and Mediterranean elements, and thus saw the gradual dying out of Nordic hereditary traits as the greatest single danger to the future of the country. Lothrop Stoddard, like Grant a lawyer, developed the same theme with an alarmist orientation. In his later work, Stoddard broadened out from the Nordic theme to encompass the doctrine of white supremacy over colored peoples, which supremacy he saw endangered by the trend of events. The title of one of his best known works, *The Rising Tide of Color Against White World Supremacy*, clearly indicates the burden of his theme.[49]

It is significant to observe that this period in which the Nordic movement was receiving its greatest literary development coincides with the enactment of restrictive legislation against European immigration, beginning 1921. (See Ch. 5.) While it is impossible to

[47] See Snyder, *op. cit.*, for racialism in the Third Reich.
[48] Madison Grant, *The Passing of the Great Race* (New York: Charles Scribner's Sons, 1916).
[49] See Snyder, *op. cit.*, Ch. 14, "Racialism Invades the United States."

determine what effect these writings may have had upon legislation, it is clear that the high quotas accorded the allegedly "Nordic" countries and the low quotas allotted to the "non-Nordic" nations harmonized with the beliefs of these pro-Nordic writers.

The popularity of these pseudoscientific Nordic proponents stimulated vigorous research and writing which was ultimately to demolish, as far as intellectual circles were concerned, not only Nordic doctrine but also all other expressions of racialism. From this exploration has emerged the scientific view of race presented earlier in the chapter. Racialism at the present time has no standing in American academic circles. Furthermore, the current antiracialist viewpoint is being widely diffused throughout the population, particularly through the formal educational program. If the elimination of minority discrimination depended solely upon "debunking" in rational terms the racialist doctrine, such discrimination should disappear in a generation. But as the history of racialism suggests, belief in its doctrine does not rest solely upon inadequate knowledge of its objective error but partly in the desire of the dominant to believe it.

TOPICS FOR DISCUSSION AND PROJECTS

1. Consult other "racial" classifications of mankind and compare them with that given on page 49.
2. Suggest as many reasons as you can why the comparative scores of two racial groups on mental tests may not reflect their true relative mental abilities.
3. Read Hitler's *Mein Kampf*, Chapter 11, "Nation and Race," and write a critical evaluation of it from the contemporary scientific view of race.
4. Interview a number of your fellow students, presenting them with a list of ethnic or racial minorities. Ask them from which groups they would under no circumstances select a marriage partner. Ask them why, and interpret the reasons given in the light of this chapter.
5. The term *race* is frequently used incorrectly in written and oral speech. As a term project, collect as many such uses as possible. Classify your material and give a summary interpretation of your findings.

SUGGESTED READING

Boyden, William C. *Genetics and the Races of Man*. Boston: D. C. Heath & Company, 1950.
> *A comprehensive treatment of physical anthropology based on genetic analysis.*

Count, E. W., ed. *This Is Race*. New York: Henry Schuman, Inc., 1950.
> *An anthology of the literature expounding scientific concepts of race from the 18th century to 1950.*

Howells, William W. *Mankind So Far*. New York: Doubleday & Company, Inc., 1944.

A professional anthropologist provides a popularly written account of animal evolution; the evolution of Homo sapiens; and the differentiation of Homo sapiens into races.

Klineberg, Otto. "Racial Psychology," in Ralph Linton, ed. *The Science of Man in the World Crisis*. New York: Columbia University Press, 1945, pp. 63–77.
   Critical examination of the belief that races have innate psychological differences.

Krogman, Wilton Marion. "The Concept of Race," in Ralph Linton, ed. *The Science of Man in the World Crisis*. New York: Columbia University Press, 1945, pp. 38–62.
   An exposition of the contemporary views about race in American social science.

Montagu, M. F. Ashley. *Statement on Race*. New York, Henry Schuman, Inc., 1951.
   An expanded and annotated account of the statement on race issued by United Nations Educational, Social, and Cultural Organization (UNESCO).

Snyder, L. L. *Race*. New York: Alliance Book Corporation, 1939.
   An excellent summary of the role of racialism in nationalist movements in modern times.

PART TWO

"Native"-Foreigner Relations

The first category of minority situations to be considered involves the relations of those Americans with native status to the many European immigrant groups who entered the country in large numbers beginning with the Irish immigration. Because the differences which made them visible were primarily cultural, each immigrant group moved up in turn in minority status and the process involved appears to lead to their full assimilation. In minor degree the physiognomic appearance of some of these European peoples presented enough variation from the host group so that the latter sometimes reacted to the foreigners with an element of race consciousness. But as the cultural visibility of these immigrant groups disappeared, any remaining sense of "color" consciousness in the mental complex of the dominants toward them tended to disappear as well. Because the assimilation of all these groups, except the Jewish group, has either occurred or appears to be largely a matter of time, we consider them all as a type in Chapter 4.

From time to time, however, the question is publicly debated: "Should we revise our immigration laws to permit a larger number of European immigrants to enter the country?" Therefore we consider in Chapter 5 the effects of our previous experience with immigration and further consider the implications of the changing international situation upon the question.

In Chapter 6, we describe the situation arising from the immigration of those Spanish-speaking people who migrated from Mexico in large numbers beginning about 1920. In terms of plan of the organization of this book, the most significant difference in this group is the presence of a greater measure of physiognomic visibility than in the case of the European groups which, in addition to other circumstances involved in their relations to the "Anglos," has retarded their assimilation.

The Immigrant Pattern:
European Nationalities

The background. The young nation of the United States in 1820 was composed largely of people who were Anglo-Saxon in their lineage with a substantially common culture woven around three main elements: political democracy, private economic enterprise, and Protestantism with a strong Puritan tinge. Scattered in its population were other north European people in insufficient numbers to disturb its homogeneity. While the Dutch in the Middle Atlantic States retained a certain distinctiveness, they easily became assimilated. Perhaps only in Louisiana where people of French descent were concentrated did the culture, involving Catholicism, have a distinctly variant ethnic flavor. This young America was made up largely of small towns and rural communities in which the close solidarity of primary groups prevailed. Class distinctions were not pronounced except in the few larger cities and in the South where the plantation system was built upon slave labor. A vast frontier of enormous resources beckoned for exploitation and settlement. The one large group of different people were the Negro slaves (and some free Negroes) who in 1820 constituted approximately 18 per cent of the population. This was the social setting in which the great drama of immigration was to begin and continue for a hundred years influencing in so many ways the subsequent development of the new nation.

The flow of European immigration. During the next 129 years, from 1820 to 1948, over 38 million immigrants came into the United States. Graph 1 shows the total immigration by decades.

GRAPH 1

Total Immigration to the United States by Decades[1]

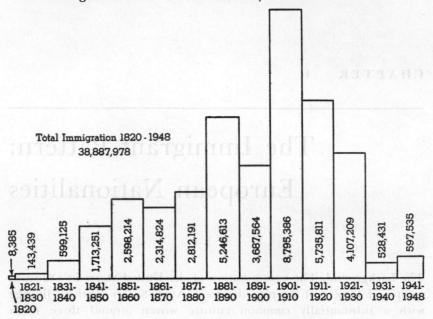

Total Immigration 1820-1948
38,887,978

| | 8,385 | 143,439 | 599,125 | 1,713,251 | 2,598,214 | 2,314,824 | 2,812,191 | 5,246,613 | 3,687,564 | 8,795,386 | 5,735,811 | 4,107,209 | 528,431 | 597,535 |

| 1820 | 1821-1830 | 1831-1840 | 1841-1850 | 1851-1860 | 1861-1870 | 1871-1880 | 1881-1890 | 1891-1900 | 1901-1910 | 1911-1920 | 1921-1930 | 1931-1940 | 1941-1948 |

The broad sweep is upward to 1910. Actually the peak of the immigration wave was the 10-year period, 1905–1914, during which time the average annual influx was slightly over a million a year. The First World War interrupted the flow of immigrants. From 1920 to 1924 immigration from Europe averaged around half a million a year. The adoption of restrictive legislation in 1924 marks the end of the great European immigration era. From 1925 to 1930 the annual immigration was about 300,000 a year, approximately half of it being admitted each year under quota, and about half under non-quota provisions.[2] In no year between 1931 and 1948 did the total amount of immigration equal the total allotted under the quota system. As a result of the depression of 1929, immigration dropped off in the 30's so that for the years 1932 to 1935 inclusive, emigration back to Europe exceeded immigration from it to the United States.[3]

The great bulk of this immigration came from Europe as Table 5 shows:

[1] *Annual Report of the Immigration and Naturalization Service,* U. S. Department of Justice, Philadelphia, for the fiscal year ending June 30, 1948, Table 1.
[2] See p. 105 for provisions of Immigration Act of 1924.
[3] Maurice R. Davie, *What Shall We Do About Immigration?* Public Affairs Committee, Inc. (Pamphlet No. 115) New York, 1946, p. 15.

TABLE 5

Immigration to the United States by Continents[4]

1820–1948

Europe	32,917,632
Asia	940,102
America	4,662,745
Africa	31,583

While every area of Europe over the period, 1820 to 1948, furnished some immigrants, the leading sources are indicated in Table 6.

TABLE 6

Total Immigration to the United States 1820 to 1948 from Specified Nations of Europe[5]

Germany	6,064,653
Italy	4,752,735
Ireland	4,605,091
Great Britain	4,352,788
Austria & Hungary	4,150,252
Russia	3,343,865
Sweden	1,223,083
Norway	810,217
Greece	436,668
Poland	419,957
Denmark	338,085

One of the most significant facts about immigration was the shift around 1880 in the principal sources of immigration from northern Europe to southern and eastern Europe. The north European immigration is frequently referred to as the "old," while the southern and eastern European immigration is called the "new." An indication of this shift is seen in Table 7 where the peak years for immigration from specified nations is indicated. It is interesting to observe that the peaks in immigration from the other countries of North America follow the cessation of the great European immigration. Over half of the 3,104,920 immigrating to this country from Canada between 1820 and 1947 ar-

[4] From United States Immigration and Naturalization Service, *Annual Report*, 1948, Table 4.
[5] *Ibid.*, Table 4. Polish immigration from 1899–1919 was included with that of Austria-Hungary, Germany, and Russia. For this reason the total number of immigrants of Polish ethnic background is far greater than their number in the table indicates. The total number of people of Polish lineage in the United States today is estimated between 4,000,000 and 5,000,000.

rived between 1911 and 1930. Similarly over four-fifths of the Mexican immigration came in the same two decades, over half of it in the twenties.

TABLE 7

Peak Decades for Immigration from Specified European Nations[6]

1851–1860	1881–1890	1901–1910	1911–1920
Ireland	Germany	Italy	Greece
	Sweden	Austria-Hungary	Portugal
	Denmark	Russia	
	Switzerland	Bulgaria	
	Netherlands		

Immigration from Asia, as officially counted over the period 1820–1947, totaled only 929,363 substantially divided between the Chinese immigration, concentrating between 1850 and 1883, and the Japanese immigration, concentrating in the 1890–1920 period.

The reasons why the vast multitude of Europeans came to the United States are well known to the student of American and European history.[7] While religious and political discrimination at home prompted the migration of certain selected groups and individuals, the consensus of those studying the subject leaves little doubt that the desire for economic improvement was the main motivating factor. The majority of Armenians, persecuted by the Mohammedan Turks for their Christianity, were refugees from persecution. Numerically greater were the large number of Russian and Polish Jews who fled from the many discriminations against them. Political dissatisfactions played a part in Irish immigration and in the case of many liberal minded Germans. However, the generally distressing economic conditions of Europe plus the greater economic opportunity in the United States constituted the central motive for this immigration.

As a result of this great influx, the United States is frequently thought of as a land of "foreigners." The term "foreigner" can be used purely statistically to mean those born abroad. Actually it has more meaning sociologically speaking when applied to people who are looked upon by natives as being foreigners. Individual English immigrants were scarcely thought of as foreigners from the first. Most Americans born to German immigrant parents are not thought of as foreigners; whereas many grandchildren of Italian immigrants are still thought of in terms of being alien. At this point, however, concern is

[6] *Ibid.*
[7] A summary of the factors involved is contained in W. C. Smith, *Americans in the Making* (New York: Appleton-Century-Crofts, Inc., 1939) Chs. I-III.

with census figures. Nearly 35 million were born in this country of foreign or mixed parentage. The number of foreign born is declining rapidly. From 1920 to 1950 their percentage dropped from 13.2 per cent of our total population to 6.7 per cent. Under the conditions prevailing in 1940, Davie estimates that the foreign born will fall to about six million in 1960, and to barely two million in 1980.[8] The United States is rapidly ceasing to be a land of foreigners.

NATIVE-IMMIGRANT RELATIONS

To what extent did the relations between these diverse European peoples and the natives assume a dominant-minority pattern and to what extent are any of these peoples minorities still?

The northern Europeans. Whether or not every body of foreigners who settled in thousands of American communities experienced a period of minority status would require much historical research to verify. Particularly would this be the case concerning the north European peoples. However, since for the most part their descendants are now assimilated—witness the Stassens and the Eisenhowers—interest in their possible earlier minority status would be largely historical. In a general way, their more rapid acculturation and social acceptance was facilitated by many favorable circumstances. They were less visibly different in a racial sense. Their cultures had more affinity to the dominant Anglo-Saxon culture. They were largely Protestant; were more experienced in democratic political practices; and possessed a heritage of independent agricultural occupation. They tended to settle beyond the areas of thick settlement, establishing new settlements of their own. While this semi-isolation enabled them to retain much of their Old World culture, it also provided opportunity for them to make their own adjustment to American life with a minimum of friction with the native population. That they were "looked down on" and "poked fun at" is illustrated by the following jingle quoted by Smith, directed at members of an immigrant group in Minnesota:

> Swedie, Swedie, stuck in the straw,
> Can't say nuthin' but 'Yaw, yaw, yaw.'[9]

But with the acquisition of the English language, without an accent in their children's cases, these north Europeans became accepted Americans.

A recent study of a community of about 10,000 population in the "North Prairie Region," called Jonesville, finds a Norwegian group

[8] Davie, *op. cit.,* p. 6.
[9] W. C. Smith, *op. cit.,* p. 149, f.n. 28.

still sufficiently ethnically distinctive to require separate treatment in the general description of the life of the community.[10] The authors, however, consider this situation atypical rather than characteristic for Norse descended people in the region in general. During the three or four generations of their sojourn in Jonesville, many of the Norse have lost their identity with the ethnic group. In the late 1940's, the visible group was composed of those Norse whose social mobility had been the least. The fact that they had been unable to rise in social status appears to have caused them to develop strong in-group morale by retaining a distinctive set of values which in this instance revolves around Lutheran sectarianism more than around Norse culture in general.

The Irish. The considerable number of Irish people who came to the colonies in the 18th century appear not to have been thought of as a distinct people apart from the rest, except for a brief time when they arrived in large numbers. According to Reilly, "Between 1714 and 1720 fifty-four ships arrived in Boston with Irish immigrants . . . In 1720 there were so many Irish in Massachusetts that the general court ordered that 'certain Irish families recently arrived from Ireland be warned to move off.' " [11]

The Irish, however, who migrated in great numbers beginning with the 1830 decade experienced a period of minority status. They were Catholic and anti-British. They were rural people who settled largely in cities and towns. They entered the lower occupational ranks of unskilled work, thus starting with lower class status at a time when class distinction was becoming more important.

Adams indicates that the native Americans looked down on the Irish for their whiskey drinking and their fighting, and then goes on to say, "But when these were combined, as they frequently were after 1830, with religious disputes, the Irish Catholics discovered themselves in a new and unhappy situation . . . they had become outcasts in a Protestant country, objects of positive antipathy among large groups of American workingmen and of cold suspicion on the part of their masters." [12] A Massachusetts source characterizes the Irish in these terms: "They are improvident, worrying little about the future, not extravagant but wasteful, drink too much and therefore are insecure in employment and poor, and given to having children with reckless regularity." An elderly gentleman born of Irish immigrant

[10] W. Lloyd Warner et. al., *Democracy in Jonesville* (New York: Harper and Brothers, 1949) Ch. 11.
[11] A. J. Reilly in F. J. Brown and J. S. Roucek, *One America* (New York, Prentice-Hall, 1946) p. 45.
[12] William F. Adams, *Ireland and Irish Emigration to the New World* (New Haven: Yale University Press, 1932) p. 339. By permission.

parentage and brought up around Boston replied when he heard the above characterization read to him: "You've hit something! I tell you, they treated us worse than niggers [sic]. I can remember my father, walking the streets of Boston, with the signs out everywhere. 'No Irish need apply'." [13]

The minority status of the Irish in the 19th century arises from the fact that they were the first non-English group to arrive in eastern United States, and that they were Catholic. The subsequent position of the Irish in American society has been largely affected by the special role they have to play in the development of Catholicism in the United States. For this reason further discussion of the position of the Irish in the 20th century is reserved for consideration in Chapter 14 where the subject of religious difference in minority situations is considered in detail.

In summary, it is clear that in general those Americans descended from the earlier immigrant groups have by now become so far assimilated that their ethnic origin has little significance in affecting their status in American society. It is interesting to note that in spite of a very substantial and continuous immigration from England from 1851 to 1930 one finds little reference to English immigrant colonies. This indicates that English immigrants as individuals or families were immediately absorbed into the native groups and accorded dominant status. For the Scandinavians and the Germans, the process of assimilation took somewhat longer, but except for a few isolated instances has been now completed.[14] The assimilation of the Irish has taken the longest of the earlier European immigrant groups. It appears that any sense of distinctiveness which they now possess which would affect their status derives from their special position as the leaders of American Catholicism.

We turn to consider the relations of the newer immigrant groups from southern and eastern Europe to native Americans. It should be noted that the composition of the population now to be considered "native," has been considerably broadened as a result of the assimilation of the earlier immigrant groups. The original cultural and ethnic base upon which dominant status rested involved British Protestant descent. With the possible exception of those who remained Catholic,

[13] Ruth D. Tuck, *Not With the Fist,* (New York: Harcourt, Brace & Company, Inc., 1946) p. 39. Dr. Tuck quoted the sentences cited to an audience in the Southwest for the purpose of indicating that the dominants have the same stereotyped conception of all minorities.

[14] During World War I, many German families with foreign born members suffered discrimination in the form of ostracism and verbal persecution. During World War II, the antagonism toward German people was more discriminating. Only such Germanic people who were, or who were thought to be, Nazi sympathizers received differential treatment.

Americans descended from the northern and western Europeans
were at the turn of the century rapidly being considered native, and
therefore dominant status Americans.

The later immigration: southern and eastern Europeans. As defined
in the thinking of the native population, immigration became a
"problem" in the years which followed the great mass immigration
from southern and eastern Europe, the volume of which was indicated
above. While the earlier immigration had a more pronounced influence upon the rural and frontier America, this later immigration was
primarily an urban phenomenon. The relations of the native population to these later immigrants developed into a characteristic pattern
which has been delineated in sociological texts for the past two decades. The rest of this chapter will be devoted to describing and analyzing this pattern. We shall start with a close-up view of these relations
in cities small enough to have permitted study of the total pattern of
ethnic relations; follow with some consideration of the contrasts between the metropolis and rural areas; and conclude with a detailed
delineation of the typical stages in the native-immigrant process of
interaction.

  Burlington, Vermont.[15] Burlington, the metropolis of the state, is a small
city of about 25,000 people, situated on the eastern shore of Lake Champlain.
It has a number of small factories and mills and otherwise is a small commercial and political center. Anderson decided to take the foreign born themselves
and their children as her criterion of membership in an ethnic group. Defined
thus in 1930, 40 per cent of Burlington's population were "foreigners," or as
the writer refers to them most frequently, "new comers." Of these newcomers,
the French-Canadian totaled nearly 5000, more than all the rest put together;
English-speaking Canadians slightly exceeded the 1200 mark; and the Irish fell
slightly short of it. Next were about 750 Russians and Poles, most of whom
were Jewish. The 457 English, 392 Italians, and 309 Germans were numerous
enough to be thought of as ethnic elements. A scattering membership from
29 other nationalities was to be found.

  Anderson describes the city as dominated by the Yankees who were, however, being challenged in leadership by the Irish. The Irish tended to
champion the cause of all the immigrant groups. The latter tended to accept
Irish leadership, although they frequently resented Irish officiousness. The
French-Canadians were unaggressive, docile, and slow to rise in economic
and social status. While cherishing their distinctive culture, they failed to
stick together on civic issues. The Jews[16] of Burlington presented the same

[15] Reprinted by permission of the publishers from Elin Anderson, *We Americans*,
(Cambridge, Mass.: Harvard University Press, 1937). The account given here is the
present writer's adaption of various portions of Anderson's book.
[16] Because of the special aspects of native-Jewish relations, fuller discussion of the
data derived from this and other community studies is reserved for a separate
treatment. See Ch. 15.

picture as elsewhere where found in sufficient numbers, successful in economic life but living in their separate social structure. The Germans still retained a fair degree of distinctiveness notwithstanding their more favorable assimilability. The Italians of Burlington being few in number showed less strong ethnic coherence than is found among Italians in other American cities.

The community life of Burlington in 1934 was greatly affected by a consciousness of ethnic difference and the corresponding cleavages in its social life associated with this sense of difference. In spatial distribution, three of the six wards, those less desirable to live in, were largely inhabited by newcomers; two were identifiable as largely Yankee wards. More than half of the French-Canadians, of the Germans, and of the Irish lived in the "foreign" wards with the latter showing the greatest dispersion. The class and occupational structure divided largely, although not precisely, along ethnic lines with the French-Canadians in the lower class, predominantly employed in factory and mill work; the Irish having moved up in social class and found increasingly employed in clerical and professional positions; and the Yankees with higher social prestige and employed in the higher ranking occupations.

The social life of most people in Burlington tended to revolve around those of similar ethnic origin. In formal associational life, for example, about 70 per cent of the Jewish, French-Canadian, and Italian men belonged only to organizations with membership exclusively from their own ethnic background. With the women in each group, the proportion of intraethnic associational exclusiveness was well over 80 per cent. Indications of the attitudes of the ethnics toward their own and toward other groups in the city was revealed in the preferences expressed for neighbors. As further choices, the newcomers rated Old Americans first, Irish second, and at the other extremes, Negroes and Chinese (of which there were a few) last. Consistently, the Old Americans gave English-Canadians as their second preference. Somewhat inconsistently, however, two-thirds of all the people interviewed indicated that "the preservation of nationality neighborhoods was of no interest to them." Only among the Old Americans and the French Canadians was there an emphatic minority expressing a desire to live apart from others. Granting that various circumstances conspire to make it natural, sociologically speaking, for this social distinctiveness in the earlier years, Anderson was impressed with "the persistence of a formal pattern of separation after the reasons for its existence have disappeared." She discovered that the members of each group were conscious of a strong pressure to remain in their group, manifested by criticism of those who sought friendships among other ethnic groups. The second and third generations among all groups were more strongly affirmative than the foreign born to the question, "One is criticized if one mixes freely with people of other nationalities in the community."

The movement outward from ethnic affiliation was influenced by religion. After their numbers became greater, French-Canadian Catholic parishes were organized distinct from those of the Irish. In the second and third generations, increasing numbers of the French-Canadians affiliated with the traditionally Irish parishes. Anderson came to the conclusion that with the decline in the strength of distinctive ethnic cleavage through the great fusion of the separate Catholic elements, the line of cleavage in community life between Catholics and Protestants as a whole became more pronounced, expressing itself in contrasting approaches to many community problems.

Yankee City. In 1941 the first of a series of several detailed studies of "Yankee City" was published.[17] Subsequently another volume on the ethnic groups of the city appeared. The basic interest of the research was to test the validity of the class system as the main integrating factor in American community life. Included in the material accumulated was probably the most definitive set of data on ethnic groups yet to have been gathered for any one city.

Yankee City—thus anonymously labeled because it has "a living tradition inherited from generations of Yankee forebears"—is situated on a harbor at the mouth of a large river within the orbit of metropolitan Boston. Its population was at the time of the study in the early 1930's about 17,000. About one-fourth of its working population was employed in the shoe industry. Other small factories, commerce, and the clamming industry completed its economic activities.

In basic ethnic composition, the population of Yankee City was 54 per cent "native" and 46 per cent "ethnic." By ethnic is meant any person who (a) either considers himself or is considered by others as a member of an ethnic group, or (b) who participated in the activities of the group. Since the research team was able to appraise the status of nearly every individual in the city, we have here a more accurate count than is usually available. This procedure eliminates in the counting a few individuals of a minority group origin who came before the mass influx of their compatriots and were therefore considered natives. It also counts as ethnics, persons of these various origins irrespective of generation who remained definable as ethnics in the terms adopted. The relations between these diverse ethnics in Yankee City are summarized as follows:[18]

The "natives" of Yankee City number 9030, or 54 per cent of the population. They comprise mainly the descendants of colonial British stock. Included, however, as natives are a few descendants from French Hugenot stock and German Jews who settled in the city early in its history. Also included are more recent immigrants from the British sources. "Predominant in number, this native group dominates the economic, political, and social structures of the community."

The 7646 individuals in Yankee City who are labeled as ethnics constituted in 1933, 46 per cent of the total population. About half of these

[17]William Lloyd Warner and P. S. Lunt, *The Social Life of a Modern Community* (New Haven: Yale University Press, 1941).
[18] The writer's condensed adaptation of Warner and Lunt, *op. cit.*, pp. 213-217. By permission.

were Irish who were the first large group of immigrants to enter, beginning around 1840. While speaking English like the Yankees, they differed in being Catholic and having a rural and agricultural background, in a city whose economic life was geared to shipbuilding and maritime commerce.

The French-Canadians came next around the 1880 period. They became more distinctive than the Irish, a group apart with high internal solidarity centering around their Catholicism, the French language, and a strong solidarity of family life. Next in order was the influx of Polish Jews beginning around 1903 which, added to a few German Jews who had come in earlier, formed a Jewish aggregate of 397 persons. The Jews differed from the rest in language, religion, and in family and cultural tradition. Being, however, from urban occupational backgrounds, the Jews maintained their original occupational pattern where the other ethnics had abandoned their original callings. Italian influx into Yankee City came about the same time as that of the Jews. Since, however, their numbers were few, 284 in 1933, they had not been organized in separate parishes from the Irish. They were, moreover, split into antagonistic north and south Italian subgroups. The Armenian group at the time of the study was only slightly less than the Italian, 246. They had come into the city around 1900 and were more than other ethnic groups employed in one industry, shoe manufacture. This Armenian subcommunity lacked integration because it was split along religious lines between Congregational Protestants and eastern Orthodox communicants.

While the greatest movement of Greeks into Yankee City occurred in the 1920's, their number increased so that in 1933 they were the fourth largest ethnic group, totaling 412. About two-thirds were employed in factory work. Others were confectioners, restaurant owners, barbers, etc. Their cultural accommodation centered around their separate Greek Orthodox Church with its parochial culture, their patriarchal type family, and their coffee houses. Still more recent arrivals were the Poles and Russians. The Poles themselves had come to number 677, thus being the third largest ethnic group. First they worked in the textile factories, but following the decline of the textile industry found employment in other factories. Interestingly enough in view of the antagonism between Poles and Russians in Europe, the Yankee City researchers found "close and amicable relations exist between them in Yankee City." This arose from the knowledge of each other's language, from frequent and informal meetings in their local provision stores, and from the smallness of the Russian group.

The Metropolis. No such over-all community studies of the interaction between native and the manifold ethnic peoples in America's great metropolises are available, even though it is well known that it was in them that the great drama of the immigration era, now reaching its final scenes, was acted out in all its colorful blend of comedy and tragedy. In some eastern cities the proportion of people who would qualify as ethnics under our definition comprised a substantial majority of the population. Illustrative of the principle of ecological segregation, the great city had many distinctive ethnic and racial areas, each comprising a little world of its own, Little Sicily, Yorkville, Spanish Harlem, Chinatown, etc. Many journalistic accounts of the life of the ethnic subcommunities have been written, and a few serious sociological studies have been made,[19] but altogether too little study of the reactions, behavior, and attitudes of the dominant group toward these peoples has been undertaken. One of the systematic studies describing different ethnic communities in some detail, their interrelationship with each other, and with at least the native population nearest to them, is a study of Greenwich Village in the early 1930's.[20]

Greenwich Village. The Village is located on the lower west side of Manhattan roughly bounded on the south by Houston Street, on the east by Sixth Avenue, on the north by 11th Street and again 14th Street, on the west by the Hudson river. In 1930, three years before this study was made, the population was around 38,000. In ethnic terms these people divide first into "Villagers" and "local" people. The former refers to persons of more native American origin with a bohemian way of life, artists, writers, and other people who wish to bask, at least during their early adult years, in an "emancipated" atmosphere. These people and their doings, and the night clubs and foreign restaurants which they and sightseers patronize, make up what is known to the outside world as Greenwich Village. In numbers, however, these Villagers comprised in 1933 only a small part of the population. At least four-fifths were people of more recent immigrant origin, called in the study "local" people. Of these, the largest element was Italian, next the Irish, a scattering of Jews, a small colony of Spanish, and a noticeable number of Germans.

The Villagers and the local people lived in two distinct social worlds. Virtually little personal contact took place between the two groups. Their respective values and the corresponding behavior patterns and forms of social organization presented a striking contrast and resulted in lack of understanding, mutual mistrust, and occasional antagonism. The Villagers were careless about money; the local people were frugal and hard bargaining in money matters. The "experimental" approach to love relations and the equality accorded women by the Villagers were in sharp contrast to the patriarchal, Catholic conception of family life held by the local people.

The social life of the local people in turn was divided very largely on ethnic lines. The Irish, by virtue of longer residence in the area possessed higher social status, but were being pressed by the increasingly larger Italian group. The tendency for the Irish to send their children to parochial schools and the Italians, to public schools further isolated them. The earlier intermingling of children was frequently arrested at the adolescence ages. While a sufficient amount of intermarriages had taken place between Irish

[19] Among ethnic area studies are Louis Wirth, *The Ghetto* (Chicago: University of Chicago Press, 1928), sections of Harvey W. Zorbaugh, *Gold Coast and Slum* (University of Chicago Press, 1929) and William F. Whyte, *Street Corner Society* (Chicago: University of Chicago Press, 1943).

[20] Caroline F. Ware, *Greenwich Village* (Boston: Houghton Mifflin Company, 1935).

and Italians to be a source of comment among the local people, the two groups remained substantially apart. As for the Spanish, Dr. Ware writes:

"The Irish considered the Spanish dirty as well as dangerous, regarding them, even more than the Italians, as foreigners and lumping together all Spanish-speaking peoples of various complexions—Cubans, Filipinos, Mexicans—as 'niggers'. . . .

"The Italians had practically no contact with the Spanish . . . [but] were much more ready to say a good word for them than were the Irish. . . . Although most [Spanish] had been in this country for more than ten years, few of those interviewed could speak English.

"The only two groups in the locality which had really shown social amalgamation had been the Irish and Germans." [21]

Immigrants in rural America. As the earlier European immigration was, except for the Irish, primarily a movement to rural America, so the later immigration was primarily an urban phenomenon. Reflecting the assimilation of these earlier rural immigrants is the absence in general texts on contemporary rural American society of much treatment of European ethnic groups. One of the most comprehensive studies directed to this topic was that of Brunner published in 1929.[22] This study aimed to ascertain the degree of assimilation of immigrant farmers and their children and was based on a survey of 70 rural communities. The main conclusion reached was that in more than two-thirds of the communities under survey the immigrant groups "were progressing more or less surely along a well chartered course leading toward complete assimilation into the life of rural America." [23] In the one-third of the communities where the process of assimilation had been slow, Brunner finds three main circumstances which retarded the process: (1) situations where the immigrant group were especially remote from their native neighbors; (2) situations "where the issue of the [first] World War and of the right of self-determination for formerly subject peoples" had been permitted to disturb neighborly relations; (3) a few situations in which "settlements of north Europeans, especially Germans, remained aloof and unassimilated, from choice." [24] Another significant finding in this survey was that where the foreign settlement was mixed, or polyglot, adjustment to the life of the American rural community was more rapid than in the case of a one-nationality settlement. In these mixed situations, on the one hand less native opposition was encountered, and on the other, the lack of a common cultural background and language forced upon the

[21] The writer's adaptation of material in *ibid.*, drawn from Chs. 4, 5. The quotation is from p. 141. By permission.
[22] Edmund deS. Brunner, *Immigrant Farmers and Their Children* (Garden City, L. I. Doubleday & Company, Inc., 1929).
[23] *Ibid.*, p. 115.
[24] *Ibid.*, p. 115.

immigrants a more rapid process of "self-Americanization . . ." [25]
Among the later immigrant groups, the Czechs and the Poles were
the two groups making the largest number of rural settlements. About
one-half of all Czech immigrants engaged in farming on farms owned
by Czechs. While the rural setting encouraged their carrying on for a
longer period many of the traditional aspects of their homeland culture, it also gave a greater stability than is found among the city groups.
The Polish farmers more often entered agriculture via the farm laborer route. Many subsequently bought abandoned or run-down farms
and by arduous efforts made them self-sustaining. As with the Czechs,
the rural milieu provided for greater stability in Polish group life,
although the assimilation of Polish farmers has not proceeded as far
as with other immigrant groups.[26]

THE PATTERN OF NATIVE-IMMIGRANT INTERACTION

From the urban studies such as those cited above emerges a characteristic pattern of interaction between each immigrant minority
and the dominant natives within any community. While this pattern
is a continuous process, it may be divided for convenience into four
stages: (a) the initial stage, (b) the accommodation stage, (c) the marginal stage, and (d) the final assimilation stage.

The initial stage. Detailed studies describing the relations of a new
immigrant minority with the dominant natives during the earliest
years comparable with studies of later stages are lacking. Smith[27] assembles autobiographic materials from scattered individual immigrants,
which describes their first experiences in the new land. On the
basis of such impressions he indicates the ways in which these experiences led to considerable initial disorganization. The typical immigrant looked forward to living in the United States with high hopes—
hopes which, temporarily at least, were considerably shattered by his
first experiences. Harsh treatment by immigration officials, disappointment in slum living conditions, the unfriendliness of the natives
with whom he came in contact, and the hurry and bustle of American
city life were bewildering and disillusioning. His ignorance of American ways led to his frequent exploitation not only by natives but also

[25] *Ibid.*, p. 106.
[26] See R. A. Schermerhorn, *These Our People* (Boston: D. C. Heath & Company,
1949), for the general facts and bibliographical sources on Poles in American agriculture, pp. 281-283; and for Czechs in rural areas, pp. 300-303.
[27] W. C. Smith, *op. cit.*, Chs. 4, 5, 6. Interesting documentary material on the demoralization of some immigrants in their early days in this country may be found
in Robert E. Park and Herbert A. Miller, *Old World Traits Transplanted* (New
York: Harper and Brothers, 1921) Chs. 3, 4.

by other more sophisticated immigrants. His culture, especially his inability to speak or comprehend the English language, made his adjustment to the practical affairs of life, such as obtaining employment and obeying the law, difficult. But even more disorganizing was the realization that his cherished ways of life were not only practically inadequate but that they were considered inferior and queer by the natives. For many immigrants at least, their situation at the start represented a loss in status. A report of the Immigration Commission in 1911 stated that "the present-day immigration from Europe to the United States is for the most part drawn from country districts and smaller towns and villages and is composed largely of the peasantry and the unskilled laboring classes . . . [but it] represents the stronger and better elements of the particular class from which it is drawn." [28] While it should be pointed out that class lines were rigid in the Europe he came from, nevertheless the position of a peasant in a peasant society carried with it more sense of self-respect and security than the position of a poorly paid "greenhorn" in our society. Whatever his status in Europe when he came and to whatever status he might finally arise, the immigrant was usually relegated at the start to the bottom of the Caucasian status ladder.[29] For all these reasons the typical immigrant in an initial period underwent temporary disorganization. Objective measurements of the disorganization of the immigrant population as reflected in indices of crime, mental disease, etc., have always been inconclusive. Earlier sweeping generalizations about the pathologies of "foreigners" may be disregarded as the product of untutored reflections of the biased dominant mentality. At this point, however, where the very first months or years are being considered rather than the immigrant's whole life in the new land, it can be scarcely doubted that the total impact of this early situation was for the moment disorganizing. That in so many of the indices of social pathology, the foreign born population fails to show any disproportionate contribution to the total national figures is in no small part due to the characteristic pattern of group accommodation which was unvaryingly established.

In this initial stage, the reaction of the bulk of the native population to the immigrants was largely one of disinterested aloofness. Except for those natives who were concerned with the newcomers in their impersonal functions of workers and customers, the immigrants were ignored. As the numbers of the immigrants began to in-

[28] United States Immigration Commission, *Abstract of Report on "Emigration Conditions in Europe,"* 1911, pp. 11, 12.
[29] Certain well-to-do individual Europeans of considerable means or definitely upper class status are, of course, exceptions. If they possessed some reasonably verifiable title of nobility, upper-class Americans tended to fawn upon them.

crease in the community, however, the native community began to be more conscious of their presence. In various ways these newcomers began to raise problems for the community. Often immigrants broke laws through their ignorance or misunderstanding of American regulations, for example, in the fields of sanitation or health. Due to their low economic status, in periods of economic depression some required relief. Their increasing numbers and their tendency toward large families were sensed by the natives as a potential force threatening to upset the political and economic balance of the community. Thus native disinterested aloofness gave way to more positive expressions of antagonism. Occasional violence broke out between natives and foreigners living close together, although few instances of large scale riots occurred, comparable to those arising where racial differences were involved.

The accommodation stage—the ethnic subcommunity. In every American community into which any considerable number of a particular nationality came, the immigrant group accommodated itself to the new situation by establishing a distinctive subcommunal structure in a more or less spatially compact section of the city. Three types of social forces account for the formation of these ethnic communities, or colonies as they are sometimes called. First, the general ecological processes characteristic of American city development were operative. These tend to sort out all kinds of "likes." [30] Since the immigrants were typically poor, their initial residence was within the low rent, least desirable areas of the city, in the slums or interstitial areas, as the ecologists describe them. Second, the cultural likeness, especially the sharing of a common language, of the members of a nationality group made them feel more at ease with others of their ethnic kind. Third, the distant, unfriendly, and often antagonistic attitudes of the dominant status natives reinforced the natural tendency of like to associate with like. Illustrative of this accommodation stage is the Italian community in Greenwich Village in the early 1930's.

The Italian community of Greenwich Village. As background for understanding this Italian community, Ware writes:

The culture which the Italian peasant brought with him to America was closely rooted in the soil, and centered in the family which was patriarchal in form and integral with the land. It rested on oral tradition rather than literacy. It accorded a place of dignity to manual skill and fine craftsmanship. It took for granted the Catholic faith, but accepted religious indifference as well as piety. It contained a body of superstitions revolving about the "evil eye" and the use of occult powers. It contained no element of community participation or social organization beyond the family group. Although this

[30] See bibliography at end of the chapter for sources describing the ecological processes and their application to ethnic settlements in American cities.

pattern had been substantially modified before emigration among some emigrants especially those who had lived in cities in Italy and some of those from the north who were more literate, most of those who came to America brought with them this pattern intact.[31]

The formal social organization of the Italian community was composed mainly of the family, the church, and numerous associations combining mutual aid and sociability formed on the basis of the part of Italy from which the people had come. The family was highly patriarchal, with women extremely subordinate and seclusive. Women stayed home, had children, took care of the house and family, and did little else. Children were expected to obey their parents and to work to support their parents. Daughters were peculiarly guarded. Any interest shown in them by males was interpreted as warranting marriage promptly. The formal allegiance of Italians to the Catholic church was unquestionable, although in the particular area under study the Church faced handicaps. The most important disadvantage was the higher prestige enjoyed by the Irish Catholics. According to Dr. Ware:

> In its effort to make and hold a place for itself in the changing community, the Italian church pursued three principal courses. It abandoned those characteristic Italian religious practices which marked it in the eyes of the younger generation as "foreign," while at the same time it retained enough of the atmosphere of a characteristically Italian church to make the older generation feel that it belonged to them; it sought to attain prestige and to give evidence of being able to meet an American situation in American terms by the construction of an imposing church building conspicuously "up-to-date" in its fittings; and it adopted the institutional programs which the Irish churches scorned, in an effort to bring members within the fold and to compete with the social agencies and the Protestant missions of the locality.[32]

Informal social relations were almost wholly restricted to relatives and to people from the same province. Both the narrow provincial tie and social class distinctions, where north Italians considered themselves superior, cut across the solidarity of the Italian community.

The Italian people had almost no contact with the natives of New York City. The only natives in Greenwich Village were indeed a most variant type of "natives"—the bohemian variant. Contacts between local people and Villagers (bohemian natives) were few and far between. When contact did occur, it was more likely to be a matter of conflict rather than of cooperation—frequently through hooliganism on the part of young Italians.

Immediate consciousness of minority status was borne in upon the Italians more by their subordinate position to the majority Irish than

[31] Ware, *op. cit.*, p. 173. By permission.
[32] *Ibid.*, pp. 311-312. By permission.

in regard to any natives.[33] "The Italians questioned found it much easier to state what they disliked about the Irish than to name anything which they liked." [34] The vehemence of this Italian attitude may be interpreted as evidence of the actually higher social position of the Irish. It was the sense of being looked upon as inferior which made for the solidarity of the Italian community. "Consciousness of being Italian was a defense reaction against . . . being treated as a 'Wop'—rather than a positive manifestation of group solidarity." [35]

In broad outline, the local Italian community which Ware describes typifies the process of accommodation of most of the new immigrant groups in our cities. With the exception of Jewish immigrants, the majority of the other immigrant groups were likewise peasant folk faced with the necessity of adaptation not only to a new national milieu but also to a city environment. With most of them, too, the patriarchal family and the Catholic Church—Roman or Greek—were the major institutional foci and, in informal life, kin relatives and literal neighbors furnished most of their sociability. Unlike the Italians, other immigrant communities reproduced their characteristic public institutions such as the Greek coffee house, the German *Turnverein,* etc.

Adaptive institutions. Because their old ways were so unsuited to the new situation, the immigrant communities perforce had to create some new adaptive institutions. Because the problem of economic crisis in certain families could not be adequately cared for by neighborly aid, mutual aid societies, providing benefits for various exigencies, were established by many ethnic groups embracing only their own kind. Again, although considerably insulated in their ethnic structure, the immigrant group needed some mechanism to protect their special interests in the larger community, and to help them express their citizenship in political and civic life. Thus, each immigrant group developed "Polish-American," "Hungarian-American," etc., associations to give expression to and to cultivate still further this new civic experience. For almost every large immigrant group in America, there arose newspapers printed in their own language, some with national and others with local circulation. Such papers printed news of activities in the old country and have been considered therefore as retarding assimilation. On the other hand, for those many immigrants

[33] This is the first of many instances subsequently to appear indicating a hierarchy among minorities and the presence of dominant-minority relations between minority groups.
[34] Ware, *op. cit.,* p. 131.
[35] *Ibid.,* p. 169.

who could not read English, the newspapers brought a wider knowledge of American public affairs and the native cultural values.

First bridges toward assimilation. As several writers have phrased it, the typical immigrant learned only something of the "public culture" of the native America, almost nothing of its "private culture." Through their business contacts in the market places and as applicants for jobs, these newcomers began to absorb the acquisitive drive and to develop increasing cunning in the pursuit of wealth. Their training in citizenship was acquired under the tutelage of the ward boss in the typical Tammany manner. The success of urban political machines, sometimes corrupt, in capturing the political allegiance of immigrant folks lies in no small part to their adeptness in making politics personal to the immigrant. The party which actually performed personal favors, a bit of relief here, fixing up matters when they got into trouble with the law, etc., coupled with a friendly interest in the immigrants as persons, elicited favorable response where the more impersonalized and abstract approach to civic life by the so-called "good government" forces, whose advocates scarcely could get themselves on a plane of friendship with the immigrant, failed.

Another bridge built between the immigrant and the native communities was the settlement house. This institution, which grew out of the efforts of socially conscious natives to go to the immigrants, live among them, and provide them with recreational, artistic, and educational opportunities, had limited success. Except in unusual instances, such as Hull House in Chicago, the inability of the native settlement house worker and the immigrant mutually to comprehend each other meant that the settlement house became peripheral to and not the center of the immigrant community. True, in the case of many an individual child of the immigrant the settlement house, through warm relationships established with a staff member, was an important avenue to his passing out of the immigrant community into the main stream of American life. But, on the whole, a large gulf remained between the settlement "natives" and the mass of the ethnic folks.

While the school was a more important factor in the assimilation of the native born children of the immigrants, it deserves mention in relation to the immigrant generation. Many cities set up night-school programs for the instruction of adult immigrants, with the curricula stressing the English and civics necessary for naturalization. The influence of the school on the adult immigrant, however, has been largely indirectly mediated through their children. For example, Galitzi says of the Roumanians: "The children learning the English language become the carriers of the new language and new ideas into the Roumanian home. They interpret to their parents the American standards of health, economic efficiency, civic duties, and fair play." [36]

In spite of his adaptive institutions, and these narrow bridges of contact with the dominant natives, the typical immigrant became accommodated but not assimilated to American life. The pattern of subcommunal segregation described above retarded assimilation but, given the situation as it was, it was a logical and necessary response. Mass immigration was encouraged and tolerated because the rapidly growing industrial society greatly needed cheap labor. Yet, for the most part, the immigrant was not desired as a neighbor, a friend, or a competitor by the dominant natives. Segregation suited perfectly the natives' attitudes, and arose in part in response to them. Equally well did it fit the need of the immigrant for a sense of self-respect, for expressing his accustomed mode of life, and for social security—the sense of really belonging.

The marginal stage: the second generation. The term "marginal" is employed as a formal concept in sociology to denote the position of the person who occupies an intermediate position between two cultural worlds. While in some instances, individual immigrants themselves reached this position, the full force of this difficult social situation was seen typically in the generations of children born in the United States to immigrant parents, beginning usually when they commenced school and later as their contacts outside the ethnic group increased. A vivid illustration of the marginal individual is given by Pauline V. Young.

You see, we young people live in two worlds, and learn the ways of both worlds—the ways of our parents and the ways of the big world. Sometimes we get mixed up and we fight, we fight our parents and we fight the big world. Sometimes I feel I am not much of an American. I was raised by Russians, I understand Russians, I like Russians. At other times, I think that I am not much of a Russian; except to my parents, I never speak Russian, and all my friends are Americans. Well, I am American, we live in America— why shouldn't we take their ways? When my parents object to my American friends, I say: "I work with them. I do everything with them; why shouldn't I go out with them?" Then they come back at me and say: "Why don't you sleep with them?" They think they would disgust me with Americans, but I get mad and say: "Well, I will!" and they have nothing more to say.

I almost always have a good comeback. I say: "This isn't Russia. When you go to Russia, you can be Russians; but you can't be Russians in America." I have learned American ways. I can't go against my friends and do the Russian way. . . .

[36] Christine A. Galitzi, *A Study of Assimilation Among the Roumanians in the United States* (New York: Columbia University Press, 1929) p. 228.

Many times I get mad, and then I leave the house. You see, I don't want to hurt my parents and still I want to live like I see is right—that is, right according to American ways. They can't see it my way, and I can't see it their way.[37]

Like all parents, immigrant parents conditioned their children to their accustomed social heritage. As a result of their school experience, and the other outside stimuli which their growing knowledge of the English language opened to them, the children desired to become Americanized. The children began to perceive that the culture of their parents was not American as defined by the outside dominant native world. Furthermore, the immigrant children learned that the ways of their parents were defined as inferior and that they, too, were socially rejected because of their background. For a time at least, typical immigrant children underwent extraordinarily difficult periods of inner conflict. In mass terms this inner conflict yielded its toll in overt delinquency or in neurotic disturbances or both. On the one hand, the children love and revere their parents and yet must rebel against their authority in order to try to become American as they imperfectly understood what being American was. On the other hand, the children's desire to be recognized as American by those more native than himself was only partly successful. In this extremely insecure position, the dominant native community either as an organized civic entity or in terms of personal efforts by dominant individuals did virtually nothing constructive to aid those "longing to be Americans," except to provide them free public education. While in the long run, it was to be this free education that assimilated the descendants of immigrants, in the short run, the school fell far short of solving the emotional problems of these culturally marginal young people. Smith's appraisal of the school's impact in this connection epitomizes the dominant attitude toward the immigrant minorities:

On the basis of the available data, we are forced to the conclusion that the American school, although well intentioned, has not dealt wisely with the children of immigrants. Unknowingly it has been actually ruthless in ignoring and belittling the cultural heritages of the diverse elements in our population while glorifying the dominant civilization, thereby bringing about permanent and often tragic estrangements. The school should have paid some attention to counteracting the various influences in the community which tend to produce conflicts between the two generations.[38]

Small wonder it was that so many immigrant children, particularly boys, went through a period in which their lives were ordered by the

[37] Pauline V. Young, *The Pilgrims of Russian Town* (Chicago: University of Chicago Press, 1932) pp. 114-115. By permission. The entire case from which these excerpts are taken is to be found on pp. 114-118.
[38] W. C. Smith, *op. cit.,* p. 303. By permission.

"code of the street," established by themselves in the disorderly environment of the city slum, a code which was neither that of their parents nor of the dominant "native" community. High lights of this code were "get what you can any way you can"; "exploit before you get exploited"; "trust your own gang, but distrust all others." [39]

In conclusion, it can be seen that the marginal stage is primarily a phenomenon of disorganization in contrast to the accommodation stage. The accommodation stage that takes place is essentially a process of organization where new situations are met by developing a new social organization compounded of Old World features and new adaptive features. In the marginal stage, this accommodative structure deteriorates to a point where it fails to function effectively to control the behavior of the group. The disorganizing aspects are further reflected in the higher incidence of personal disorganization, in juvenile delinquency and young adult crime, in sexual delinquency affecting the marginal young women of the ethnic groups, and in the mental conflicts related to the insecurity accruing from an insecure position in the American status system. But as its name implies, the marginal stage has been for the successive ethnic groups a prelude to ultimate assimilation. Many of the native born of foreign parentage move through this disorganizing stage to successful adjustment. For some of the more talented of the immigrant children, the very conflicts attendant to marginal position act as a spur to outstanding success.[40]

The assimilation stage. Like "the old immigration wave," most of the southern and eastern European immigrant peoples have become, or are in the process of becoming completely assimilated, that is to say acculturated and accepted socially without reference to their ethnic origin. As a typical example of how assimilation takes place, the case of Stanley is pertinent.

Stanley becomes a native. Paul Stanley through the aid of his athletic prowess had graduated from college and gone to law school while supporting himself working in the law office of a local lawyer of upper middle class (native) status.

Paul's father and mother had come from Poland when they were children. They had both worked in the shoe factory and gone to an "Americanization school" to improve their English. They were proud of their home which

[39] For penetrating studies of the native born of southern immigrant parents in American cities, see Ware, op. cit., F. M. Thrasher, The Gang (Chicago: University of Chicago Press, 1936) and W. F. Whyte, Street Corner Society (Chicago: University of Chicago Press, 1943).
[40] Cf. Paul H. Landis, Social Policies in the Making (Boston: D. C. Heath & Company, 1947) pp. 153-154. Landis suggests, for example, that one reason accounting for the fact that many of America's famous anthropologists are Jews arises out of their own personal experience as "marginal" men, stimulating their interest and capacity to analyze scientifically intercultural relations.

they owned outright, kept well painted, and landscaped with cast off tires, a border of half buried beer cans, and a well tended garden and lawn. They looked down on their less ambitious neighbors and also the Riverbrookers (lower-lower class people) with "native" status.

Mr. Stanley was very fond and proud of his son, Paul, for whom education had opened the door to greater social heights. Their first serious rift came when Paul became interested in Annie Tylor, a Riverbrooker girl; Paul wanted to marry her and eventually did, much to the disappointment of his parents. Annie's family were a typical ne'er-do-well low-class family known to the truant officer. Annie herself was the most ambitious and respectable of the lot and had in school managed to be accepted in "better class" cliques of girls. Because of all the in-law complications, Annie and Paul ran away to get married, causing a split in Annie's family who said she had married a "damn foreigner" and a Catholic fellow. Following their marriage, the new Stanleys drew away from both sets of parents who were not after all the kinds of parents they wanted their new friends to meet. Their new home was in a nonethnic neighborhood.

After graduating from law school Paul had been invited to join the Caribous, mostly made up of Yankees with only a few Poles. Within a year after his marriage, Paul became a member of the Antlers (higher social rating than the Caribous) and played bridge there several nights a week. He began to neglect his Caribou contacts. The Stanleys were now in a social clique made up of Yankee lower-middle class folks but were not, of course, ever invited to dinner at the home of the still higher class Antlers whom Paul knew at the club, or ever called upon by the nice ladies of Hill Street—upper class. "And anyway," they said, "we're going to see to it that our children have every advantage." [41]

It will be seen that Stanley's assimilation involved: a repudiation of his parent's ways of life; marriage into the native group, even though in this particular instance to a girl of lower-lower class status; admission into associations with "native" membership; and an increasing number of intimate friendships with others than those of Polish backgrounds. In short, Stanley in becoming an American moves both outward from his own ethnic affiliations and upward in class status.

The Yankee City studies provide four measures of the changes in status of the ethnics, all in the direction of increasing assimilation: residential mobility; occupational mobility; social class mobility; and membership in formal associations. In residential mobility, for example, the French Canadian residential index in 1893 was 1.67[42]; by 1933 it had risen to 2.43. The Poles coming much later had an index of 1.25 in 1923 and had risen only to 1.40 in 1933. Similarly in oc-

[41] Warner and Lunt, *op. cit.* Their account as given on pages 188-193 is adapted by the present writer.
[42] Zones and occupations were ranked from 1,2,3, etc. from low to high. Thus if all members of an ethnic group were in zone 1, the lowest ranking zone, the ranking of the group would be 1.00.

cupational status the Irish had risen from 1.62 (1850) to 2.52 (1933), while French Canadians rose from 1.95 (1893) to 2.23 in 1933. While class ratings are not provided similarly, an index of upward mobility is seen by comparing the status of the generations as of 1933. To take just two groups:

TABLE 8

Social Class Mobility of Specified Ethnics by Generation[43]

French Canadians

	LOWER LOWER	UPPER LOWER	LOWER MIDDLE	UPPER MIDDLE
Foreign born	46.0	40.9	11.8	1.2
Their grandchildren	40.0	37.9	21.0	1.1

Italians

	LOWER LOWER	UPPER LOWER	LOWER MIDDLE	UPPER MIDDLE
Foreign born	59.1	39.9	1.0	
Their children	35.0	35.8	28.3	0.9

A fourth measure of assimilation is to be found in the degree to which the ethnics become members of formal associations which include other ethnics or natives. Table 9 is adapted from Yankee City data and gives the situation as of 1933.

TABLE 9

The Membership of 357 Yankee City Associations— Native or Ethnic Background[44]

		NUMBER OF ASSOCIATIONS
Exclusively Native		54
Native mixed with Ethnics		258
Native with Irish only	58	
Native with Jewish only	3	
Native with one or more Ethnics	197	
Mixed ethnics—no natives		8
Exclusively one ethnic group		37

[43] W. Lloyd Warner and Leo Srole, *The Social Systems of American Ethnic Groups* (New Haven: Yale Univ. Press, 1945) p. 73. By permission.
[44] Since the research workers in Yankee City were interested more in status mobility as an index of assimilation, they did not present their material on ethnic membership in associations in the most useful form at this point. For our purpose the data has been assembled from their data, pp. 339-346, particularly fn. 10 on p. 341 of Warner and Lunt, *op. cit.* It is our feeling that the class system is found in all communities, and that an increase in association of ethnics with natives within the same class is equally important as a criterion of increasing assimilation as the other indices. By permission.

In the absence of comparative time data or of breakdowns by generations, one can only say that the large number of associations involving mixed native and ethnic membership indicates a very substantial degree of association assimilation on the part of the ethnics by 1933. Many of the mixed associations are related to other social structures such as churches, auxiliaries of hospitals, etc. Unfortunately for our purposes, data concerning the more purely "social" groups, which reflect better the acceptance of ethnics as equals are not available. Likewise, statistical data on mixed clique membership, a still more intimate relation, are not presented.

Variables affecting assimilation. Having focused attention on delineating the general process of native-immigrant interaction, we have not given extensive attention to the many variable factors which have hastened or retarded the assimilation of European nationality groups. Of the hypotheses which have been generally accepted in this connection, four will be listed. In each case the variable mentioned should be read as if preceded with the phrase, "other things being equal."

1. *The Recency Factor.* The more recently the ethnic group has come into the community, the slower the degree of assimilation.

2. *The Cultural Similarity Factor.* The more divergent the culture of the ethnic group from the normative culture of the dominant status group, the slower the degree of assimilation.

3. *The Concentration Factor.* The larger the numerical proportion of the ethnic group, in relation to the total population of the area, the slower the degree of assimilation.

4. *The Physiognomic Factor.* The "darker" the general physical appearance of the group, the slower the degree of assimilation.[45]

THE PRESENT POSITION OF IMMIGRANT GROUPS IN AMERICAN SOCIETY

The foregoing analysis of native-immigrant relations in the United States implies that the process leads, in the case of the European nationality groups, to eventual assimilation. To judge by the present concentration of attention in intergroup relations upon the minorities with racial or religious visibility, it would appear that students of the field, on the whole, consider the problems which arise from the presence of these nationality groups in American community life are from now on self-liquidating. The general acceptance of this viewpoint has prompted our abbreviation of the treatment of European

[45] Cf. with the list given by Warner and Srole, *op. cit.,* p. 102. On pp. 290-291, Table 7, "Ethnic and Racial Assimilation," these authors use the term "dark Caucasoids" in contrast to "light Caucasoids." The European types whom they list as qualifying in the former are Armenians, Sicilians, Portuguese, and a part of the Jewish population.

immigrant groups in contrast to earlier texts in our field. However, it is appropriate before leaving this subject to essay a general appraisal of the position occupied by the descendants of the later immigration at the midcentury. In the absence of any standard, combined index scale by which to measure comparative degrees of assimilation, anything approaching a definitive appraisal is not possible. Approximate conclusions may, however, be reached from many scattered sources.

An appraisal of the social position of the ethnic groups of the later immigration concerns itself with two main queries. How far do the people from these backgrounds remain identifiable as ethnic groups? And to what extent are they discriminated against? The earlier descriptions of Burlington, Yankee City, and Greenwich Village clearly indicated that at the time these studies were made, all in the early 1930's, ethnic differentiation was a marked feature of community life; that the ethnics were treated as minorities; and that the cleavages and animosities engendered by the relations of the ethnics to the dominant status peoples were a source of community conflict. To what extent are these same things true of community life in 1950?

The nationality groups are now American. To begin with, it is clear that the population of southern and eastern European lineage is now basically American and not foreign. The preliminary report of the 1950 census gives 6 per cent of the population as foreign born; more than twice this percentage is made up of native born of foreign parentage. The foreign born, moreover, are for the most part naturalized. The census figures of 1940 shows only 3.3 per cent of the total mainland population as aliens and a 1944 estimate reduces this figure to 2.2 per cent.[46] Still further, the foreign born speak English. Even 20 years ago (1930) only 6.6 per cent of the total foreign born population was unable to speak English; the number today must be negligible. Since the majority of the present foreign born population has now lived in this country more than 20 years, it is clear that they consider the United States their real home country.

The Americanization of the native born of Europe lineage is even more obvious, although systematic check as to its degree is lacking. The writer ventures the hypothesis that in a systematic study of the entire range of activities pursued day by day in the lives of families entirely composed of native born people of the later immigrant lineage, a wide preponderance of the activities listed would give no clue at all to their ethnic heritage. On the basis of their range of activities, as such, without reference to their name, their associates, or a few other matters, our identification of their ethnic origin, if cor-

[46] See William S. Bernard, ed., *American Immigration Policy* (New York: Harper and Brothers, 1950) p. 143.

rectly made at all, would be made by a small percentage of the total number of activity items.

Nationality groups still remain ethnically differentiated. In spite of their increasing acculturation, ethnic group differentiation, in communities where any substantial number of persons of later immigrant heritage reside, still remains a basic feature of community life. General observation shows that in communities where the later immigrants settled in numbers, identifiable ethnic groups are still to be found. For example, in the writer's industrial community, there developed before the turn of the century a large Hungarian subcommunity which is still a recognizable structure: a Hungarian area of the city, although it is not exclusively Hungarian; many churches whose membership is almost entirely Hungarian even though the main services now tend to be conducted in English; a local Hungarian newspaper; and a great number of fraternal, benevolent, and civic organizations whose members are largely Hungarian in lineage. In the sociological journals, there continue to appear articles describing particular aspects of the social organization of nationality groups in specific communities. For example, a study of the ways in which the formal organization among Greeks in Boston contributes to their Americanization appeared in 1949.[47]

Whenever reference is made to these ethnic groups it should be remembered that by no means all the persons in a community of, for example, Polish origin, are now identified with the local Polish community. Many have lost this identity. The process by which the native born particularly pass over into the dominant status community frequently involves upward social mobility, as illustrated in the Yankee City data. In a study of the Hungarian community of Detroit, it was found that the more successful Hungarians as they move upward in the social scale develop hostile attitudes toward lower class Hungarians and attempt to gain acceptance among native status groups.[48, 49]

Discrimination on ethnic grounds continues. Whether or not the persons still remaining ethnically identifiable are discriminated against for that reason, and if so, to what extent, are more difficult questions

[47] Mary B. Treudley, "Formal Organization and the Americanization Process, with Special Reference to the Greeks of Boston," *American Sociological Review*, Vol. 14, No. 1, Feb. 1949, pp. 44-53.
[48] Erdmann D. Beynon, "Social Mobility and Social Distance Among Hungarian Immigrants in Detroit," *American Journal of Sociology*, Vol. 41, No. 4 (Jan. 1936) pp. 423-434.
[49] Studies are needed to indicate the possibilities of loss of ethnic status without upward mobility which might show in varying degrees either the acquisition of a sort of general foreign status without reference to a particular nationality, or the acquisition of native status within the lower classes. Where a foreign status woman, for example, acquires a native status name through marriage, one would suppose the latter to occur.

to answer. In exploring this topic, we shall turn to specific studies, the first of which is a study by William F. Whyte of the life of a group of Italian young men as they lived in an Italian area located in a slum section of an American city in 1940.[50]

Cornerville. The activities which the young adults pursue are not so typically Italian as they are characteristic of American youth in general, when brought up in low economic areas of American cities. Their activities revolve around the club, operated with typical parliamentary procedures of American club life, through which they engage in group recreational activities, such as bowling and dog racing. In their civic activities, these young men are adjusted to the "racket-political structure"—a highly indigenous institution in American city life. They are identifiable as Italians because of their name, because they live in an Italian area, because they associate primarily with Italians, and because the rest of the community considers them Italians. Their identification with European Italian heritage is largely symbolic. In this sense, these young men are different from the rest of the community, and because of this difference, they are, in milder manifestations, discriminated against. For the more ambitious, there are two courses to be followed.

To get ahead, the Cornerville man must move either in the world of business and Republican politics or in the world of Democratic politics and the rackets. He cannot move in both worlds at once; they are so far apart that there is hardly any connection between them. If he advances in the first world, he is recognized by society at large as a successful man, but he is recognized in Cornerville only as an alien to the district. If he advances in the second world, he achieves recognition in Cornerville but becomes a social outcast to respectable people elsewhere. The entire course of the corner boy's training in the social life of his district prepares him for a career in the rackets or in Democratic politics. If he moves in the other direction, he must take pains to break away from most of the ties that hold him to Cornerville. In effect, the society at large puts a premium on disloyalty to Cornerville and penalizes those who are best adjusted to the life of the district. At the same time the society holds out attractive rewards in terms of money and material possessions to the "successful" man. For most Cornerville people these rewards are available only through advancement in the world of rackets and politics.[51]

Some of the difficulties in the way of these young Italian Americans becoming fully Americanized are indicated by Whyte.

Some ask, "Why can't those people stop being Italians and become Americans like the rest of us?" The answer is that they are blocked in two ways: by

[50] Whyte, *op. cit.*
[51] *Ibid.*, pp. 273-274. By permission.

their own organized society and by the outside world. Cornerville people want to be good American citizens. I have never heard such moving expressions of love for this country as I have heard in Cornerville. Nevertheless, an organized way of life cannot be changed overnight. As the study of the corner gang shows, people become dependent upon certain routines of action. If they broke away abruptly from these routines, they would feel themselves disloyal and would be left helpless, without support. And, if a man wants to forget that he is an Italian, the society around him does not let him forget it. He is marked as an inferior person—like all other Italians. To bolster his own self-respect he must tell himself and tell others that the Italians are a great people, that their culture is second to none, and that their great men are unsurpassed.[52]

Community S. A survey in the dynamics of intergroup relations in a suburban community in the East in 1950 confirms the presence of a distinctive Italian ethnic group and discrimination against Italians as such. This community, here called "S," is divided ethnically into four groups: Negroes, Jews, Italians, and people of native status. In the interviewing of a representative sample of this city, the respondents were asked to indicate whether or not they considered any groups in the community discriminated against, and if so, in which areas of life the discrimination occurred. Both the community as a whole and the Italians themselves agreed that in regard to hospital care and in service in shops, there is no discrimination. In public welfare services, a few Italians felt that some discrimination existed. A substantial number of the community believed that the Italians incurred some discrimination in education and in employment, and a larger proportion of the Italians testified to the same belief. It is in regard to the choice of a place to live and to social activities that the majority of the community recognized discrimination against Italians. In this the Italians themselves most emphatically concurred. In short, the community was aware of the presence of discrimination against Italians although not all elements were equally conscious of the ways in which it expressed itself. The Italians likewise felt themselves accorded differential treatment because of their Italian origin.[53, 54]

[52] *Ibid.,* p. 274. By permission.
[53] The data given indicate a minimal expression of the awareness and belief in discrimination toward Italians in "S," in the opinion of the research team. In the planning of the survey, it early became evident that both the native status element and the Italian element were inclined to minimize in verbal responses the extent of the discrimination which they really believed existed. The tendency was for the dominant status people not to want to admit how much their group discriminated; and the Italians were inclined to feel that open discussion of discrimination might result in worsening their situation in the community.
[54] The writer was given these data on Community S by John W. Riley, Jr., and Katherine F. Ruttiger of Rutgers University in advance of the publication of a study in process.

Summary statement of the position of ethnic groups. In summary, the position of the Americans of southern and eastern European nationality lineage in 1950 appears approximately as follows:

1. The people of this background are overwhelmingly American, not foreign, in their habits of life, activities, interests, and civic sentiments.

2. Distinctive ethnic groups still remain in communities where the numbers provide visibility and permit distinctive organization.

3. While by no means all the people of this lineage remain identifiable in their respective ethnic groups, nevertheless, loss of group identification lags behind acculturation.

4. Those who are part of the ethnic group are identifiable largely by name and by the fact that they associate primarily with others of the same ethnic background. Their attachment to the original foreign cultural heritage is mainly symbolic.

5. Those who do remain identifiable as ethnics are still, to some extent, discriminated against as such by the dominant status groups.

6. Since the native born, at least, and many of the foreign born, lack either sufficient foreign cultural traits or sufficient interest in the lands of their forebears to account for their remaining group identification, the persistence of these ethnic groups is in considerable measure a function of discrimination.

As a final comment, we call attention to the absence anywhere in the studies of ethnic groups of a situation where an ethnic group has retained its cultural identity and yet lost its minority status. Individual persons or families have become fully assimilated, which it will be recalled means, in our definition, accepted as equals as well as becoming acculturated, when they lost their ethnic group identity. But there is no account of a group differentiated in ethnic culture which is at the same time considered equal in status to the native status group. The implications of this general observation to the idea of a future United States composed of equal though different ethnic cultural groups, i.e., "cultural pluralism" on an ethnic basis, will engage our attention at subsequent points.

TOPICS FOR DISCUSSION AND PROJECTS

1. How would you account for the fact that there has been so little immigration to the United States from South America?

2. Recalling your high school education, what did you learn about the cultural heritages of the immigrant groups to be found in the American population?

3. Ask a number of people who migrated to this country from continental Europe to talk about their first year or two in this country. Try to direct

the conversations to the difficulties they experienced and particularly how they got along with the natives. Write an account of these conversations.

4. In what ways does the situation of the native born child of foreign parents encourage or discourage his interest in learning more about the culture of his parents' homeland?

5. Select some one immigrant group available to you for first-hand study. Make a list of five to ten of the basic customs or institutional practices of this group. Interview ten to twenty families in this group where the father and mother are native born. Find out the extent to which they continue to practice the traditional items on your list. Summarize and report your results.

6. Would you say that the formation of distinctive ethnic colonies is an inevitable development when a foreign group migrates to live among other people?

7. Suggest some ways in which the disorganization typically attending the marginal stage might be lessened.

SUGGESTED READING

Brunner, Edmund deS. *Immigrant Farmers and Their Children*. Garden City, N. Y.: Doubleday & Company, Inc., 1929.
> *The most complete single volume study on European immigrant minorities in rural areas.*

Park, R. E. and Miller, H. A. *Old World Traits Transplanted*. New York: Harper and Brothers, 1921.
> *One of the earliest sociological studies of the process of immigrant adjustment with much interesting case material.*

Schermerhorn, R. A. *These Our People: Minorities in American Culture*. Boston: D. C. Heath & Company, 1949. Chs. 11–15.
> *Contains good one-chapter treatment of each of five immigrant groups: Italians, Poles, Czechs and Slovaks, Hungarians (or Magyars), and Yugoslavs.*

Smith, William C. *Americans in the Making*. New York: Appleton-Century-Crofts, Inc., 1939.
> *A systematic treatment of the stages in the process of adjustment of immigrants with materials based largely on European immigration.*

Stonquist, E. V. *The Marginal Man*. New York: Charles Scribner's Sons, 1937.
> *Systematic treatment of the marginal stage in the process of assimilation.*

Thomas, W. I. and Znaniecke, Florian. *The Polish Peasant in Europe and America*. New York: Alfred A. Knopf, 2nd ed., 1927, two vols.
> *A monumental treatment of the process of disorganization accompanying the adjustment of the Polish peasants to American life. Makes extensive use of personal life history documents of Polish immigrants.*

Warner, W. Lloyd, and Srole, Leo. *The Social Systems of American Ethnic Groups*. New Haven: Yale University Press, 1945.
> *A study of the status of ethnic groups in a small New England city. The third in a series of studies of Newburyport, Mass., called the Yankee City Series.*

CHAPTER 5

The Effect of the Later Immigration upon the United States

At the turn of the 20th century, public opinion in the United States began to look upon European immigration as a serious problem. While there had been difficulties arising from the adjustment of the older immigrant groups and strong feeling against the Irish, somewhat localized, in the 19th century, it was not until after the frontier had closed and the newer immigrant groups became highly visible that native Americans began to be seriously disturbed about immigration. In the main, two broad questions were raised: (1) Should immigration be restricted? (2) What should be done to bring about a more satisfactory adjustment of immigrants to American life? The final answer to the first question was the adoption of a policy of drastic numerical restriction of European immigration on a nationality quota basis. With reference to the second question, various schools of thought arose ranging from the advocacy of programs of rapid assimilation to promotion of the idea of "cultural pluralism" in which the various nationality cultures would remain in high degree distinctive, and the ethnic groups involved would be considered equal to the native ethnic group. The development of American thought and action concerning these two questions will constitute the first portion of this chapter.

The adoption of restrictive immigration brought to an end a colorful and highly significant phase of American history. Since, as we have seen, by the third generation at least, the ethnic group tends to be assimilated, America would soon cease being a land of foreigners. Long before this, Asiatic immigration had become negligible. Thus only the other nations of the Americas were left as future sources of large-scale immigration. In fact, since 1924, Canada and Mexico have been the main sources of numerically extensive immigration. French Canadian immigration which had reached a peak ealier continued to keep alive the typical pattern of native-immigrant interaction. Mexican immigration commencing on a large scale after 1910 reached its peak in the later 1920's. This latter immigration became in a sense the new immigrant "problem," although highly localized in the Southwest. In fact, this reached such dimensions as to warrant separate treatment in Chapter 6.

While restriction became the national policy toward European immigration, there has continued an articulate public which considers this policy in some particulars unsatisfactory. In general, it was felt that the total quota was too small, and even more strongly opposed was the manner by which the allocation of quotas discriminated for or against the nationalities of the later immigration. Ever since the restrictive policy has been in practice, numerous native status groups have called for its revision in these respects. In order to furnish a background against which to weigh the arguments for and against revision of our present immigration policy, we shall consider in another section the effects of the later immigration upon the developing American civilization. Whatever may have been the merits or demerits of the restrictive policy at the time it was adopted, subsequent events abroad, perhaps more than those at home, have exerted pressure for some change. First arose the problem of the political refugees created by the rise of Naziism in central Europe prior to World War II; second came the problem of the persons displaced by the war; and third there developed the problem of the political refugees from the areas of communist expansion in eastern Europe. And beyond all these specific problems, lies the fact that with the establishment of United Nations, it became both appropriate and inevitable that immigration and emigration would be considered more from an international, rather than from an exclusively national reference. The present chapter, therefore, concludes with consideration of these current international aspects as they relate to the immigration policy of the United States.

THE RESTRICTION OF EUROPEAN IMMIGRATION

Until the year 1882, immigration into the United States was practically unrestricted. A few states had passed laws which established some selective, but not exclusive, standards, but the effect of

these was negligible. There was ample room for a growing population
and plenty of work for all to do, disregarding cyclical unemployment.
Under these conditions, it is not surprising that the first general Federal legislation, the Act of 1882 (not to be confused with the Chinese
Exclusion Act passed the same year), should do no more than to
bar obviously undesirable immigrants. This act prohibited the entry
of convicts (political offenders excepted), lunatics, idiots, and other
persons liable to become paupers. As has been previously indicated,
this law placed little restraint upon the total volume of immigration,
which continued to rise to new heights until 1914.

The movement to restrict immigration gained backing from three
public groupings. The first, and probably most influential, was organized labor.[1] Labor's position was based primarily on practical considerations that immigrant labor accepted low wages and was generally
more tractable, and therefore retarded union efforts to improve the
workers' economic position. A second public favoring restriction
was composed of those various individuals scattered throughout the
country who attributed many of national ills to the presence of "too
many ignorant foreigners." These were the "racist" minded people to
whom the racialist writers, referred to in Chapter 3, appealed. In
examining the newspapers and magazines from 1900–1930 Woofter
found that from 1907–1914 a marked change in public sentiment
toward immigration occurred. "The undesirability of certain racial elements" was coming to predominate over economic arguments against
restriction.[2] Finally, there was a growing feeling among the more
thoughtful and scientific circles, that the nation could not go on indefinitely trying to assimilate such large, continuous masses of people
of different cultures. This point of view is reflected in the report of the
United States Immigration Commission in 1911 which recommended
restriction on economic, moral, and social grounds. The first congressional act to give expression to these pressures for restriction was the
measure to bar as immigrants any aliens who were illiterate (a measure
passed in 1917 over President Wilson's veto).[3] This kind of test was
aimed at curtailing southern and eastern European immigration. Actually, however, it failed to reduce materially the volume of immigration, so Congress turned to a system of numerical limitation.

The quota system. First Congress passed the Immigration Act of 1921,
the most important aspect of which was that it restricted immigra-

---

[1] See Mary Beard, *A Short History of the American Labor Movement* (New York:
The Macmillan Company, 1927) p. 72.
[2] T. J. Woofter, Jr., *Races and Ethnic Groups in American Life* (New York: McGraw-
Hill Book Company, Inc., 1933) p. 31.
[3] Literary test bills were passed by Congress in 1896 and again in 1909, but were
vetoed by Presidents Cleveland and Taft, respectively.

tion on a basis primarily numerical—the first time this principle had been applied. The act provided that the number of aliens of any nationality admissible to the United States in any one year should be limited to 3 per cent of the number of foreign-born persons of such nationality who were residents of the United States in 1910. The Act did not apply to the Western Hemisphere or to the countries otherwise regulated, such as China and Japan. (See Ch. 7) The total yearly quota admissible under this Act was 357,803. The effect, although not the wording, of this law was discriminatory against southern and eastern European nationalities. The quotas set up permitted about 200,000 from the northern and western countries and 155,000 from the others. Since from 1910–1914 the average annual immigration from the northern European countries has been less than the quotas now allowed, in practice this law did not greatly limit emigration from these areas. But it did greatly restrict southern and eastern European immigration which had averaged 738,000 annually during the 1910–1914 period.

The Immigration Act of 1921 at its expiration was supplanted by the Immigration Act of 1924. Two different systems of quota apportionment were now set up, one temporary, in order to give the Immigration Commission time to work out proper quotas for the other, the permanent quota allotment. The temporary quota to operate for three years provided that "the annual quota of any nationality shall be 2 per cent of the number of foreign-born individuals of such nationality resident in continental United States as determined by the United States Census of 1890, but the minimum quota of any nationality shall be 100." The effect of this Act was to reduce the number of yearly immigrants still further to 164,667 and to discriminate even more strongly against the "newer" immigrant countries. Northern and western Europe now was allotted 80 per cent, whereas the southern and eastern nationalities had only 20 per cent of the quota. The permanent provisions of the Act of 1924 to take effect in 1927 reduced the annual quota now based on "national origins" plan to 153,774.[4] The law called for the apportionment of the total quota among the countries to which the Act applied according to their relative contribution to the American population as enumerated in 1920. For the quotas to be correctly apportioned was a difficult task involving retracing the entire immigration figures almost since the beginning of the nation, for which many of the essential statistics were lacking. No records of immigration by nationality were kept before 1820; and the recording of the country of origin of persons born here

[4] The revised quota system under the Act of 1924 actually did not go into effect until July 1, 1929.

of foreign-born parents was not started until 1890. The extent to which this final quota allotment favored the northern and western nations of Europe at the expense of the southern and eastern is seen in Table 10, where specific quotas for most of the nations involved are indicated.

TABLE 10

Quotas Allotted under the Immigration Act of 1924[5]

Southern and Eastern Europe		Northern and Western Europe	
NATIONALITY OR COUNTRY OF BIRTH	ANNUAL QUOTA	NATIONALITY OR COUNTRY OF BIRTH	ANNUAL QUOTA
Poland	6,524	Great Britain and	
Italy	5,802	Northern Ireland	65,721
Czechoslovakia	2,874	Germany	25,957
Russia	2,712	Eire	17,853
Austria	1,413	Sweden	3,314
Hungary	869	Netherlands	3,153
Yugoslavia	845	France	3,086
Finland	569	Norway	2,377
Portugal	440	Switzerland	1,707
Lithuania	386	Belgium	1,304
Rumania	377	Denmark	1,181
Greece	307	Other Countries	200
Spain	252		
Latvia	236	Total	125,853
Turkey	226		
Estonia	116		
Other Countries	700		
		Other Quota Regions	3,428
Total	24,648	All Countries	153,929

Immigration from Europe: 1924–1949. The adoption of the policy of restriction of immigration by the quota method had the effect of drastically curtailing the flow of immigrants to the United States. Table 11 presents the immigration flow from Europe by five-year intervals following the passage of the Act of 1924. An examination of the table reveals marked fluctuations in the volume of immigration for the period.

Immigration Adjusts to the Quota Limits: 1925–1930. During this period practically all European nations utilized their quotas to the full. The fact that the total immigration exceeded the quotas is ac-

[5] U. S. Immigration and Naturalization Service, *Annual Report* for year ending June 30, 1947, Table 7.

counted for by the admission of nonquota immigrants as permitted by the Act of 1924, the largest numerical group of which were the wives, husbands, or minor children of resident immigrants. The effect of favoring the "old" immigration over the "new is seen by the fact that between 1924 and 1929 slightly over 650,000 immigrants were admitted from the northern and western nations and slightly less than 100,000 from the southern and eastern countries.

TABLE 11

European Immigration to United States by Five-Year Intervals, 1925–1949[6]

1925–29	872,800
1930–34	309,163
1935–39	213,523
1940–44	132,355
1945–49	417,349
	1,945,190

Immigration Far Below the Permissible Limits: 1931–1935. The drastic decline in European immigration indicated in the table beginning with 1930 clearly reflects the effect of the economic depression of these years. This circumstance made coming to America less attractive to Europeans. In addition, the Federal Government instructed its consulates abroad to apply rigidly the clause in the immigration legislation denying entry to persons liable to become public charges.

Refugees Increase the Totals: 1936–1940. While the rise in European immigration beginning in 1936 may have reflected in part the improved economic conditions in the United States, it was substantially advanced by the arrival of thousands of Europeans who sought asylum in this country from persecution in the expanding Nazi Reich.

World War II Virtually Cuts off All Immigration: 1941–1945. Interestingly enough, due to the manpower shortage during the war, the United States imported on temporary visas from Mexico, Canada, and the West Indies some 350,000 laborers.[7]

Displaced Persons Increase Immigration: 1946–1951. Further discussion of the immigration of both the refugees and the displaced persons will be pursued below.

[6] *Annual Report of the Immigration and Naturalization Service,* U. S. Department of Justice, Philadelphia, for the year ending June 30, 1949.
[7] Maurice R. Davie, *What Shall We Do About Immigration?* Public Affairs Committee, Inc., Pamphlet, No. 115, 1946, p. 16.

THEORIES OF ASSIMILATION

From public discussion of the problems involved in the adjustment of the immigrants already living in the country emerged three main points of view concerning assimilation: (1) the "Americanization" theory; (2) the "melting pot" theory; and (3) the "cultural pluralism" theory. The "Americanization" school saw the problem as one of making over the immigrants, if possible, and their children in any case, into Anglo-Americans. This school was characterized by a marked ethnocentrism highly confident in the superiority of everything in the normative native culture. Those who shared this view had little understanding of the difficulties involved in reacculturation of adults to a new way of life; and they had not learned that their very attitude and the methods of Americanization they supported would engender strong resistance.

The "melting pot" adherents saw emerging out of the interaction of all these various groups a broadly uniform, but more highly variegated and richer, American culture. These were more cosmopolitan in outlook and appreciative of the many values in the foreign cultures. As an ideal, this approach was highly congenial to liberal democracy and was prevalent among the intellectual, democratically minded segment of the dominant status population.

The "cultural pluralism" school advanced the theory that the ethnic groups should be encouraged to retain as much of their traditional heritages as was consistent with their new civic responsibilities and sentiments of loyalty to their adopted country. Spiritually akin to the "melting pot" school, the cultural pluralists nevertheless considered the retaining of ethnic differences a value in itself in the great democratic society.

Each of these philosophies of assimilation found expression in the formal programs of agencies and institutions concerned with the adjustment of ethnic groups, and in the behavior toward them of the professional persons who came in direct contact with them, school administrators and teachers, welfare executives and social workers, probation officers and policemen. When World War I broke out, at the peak of mass immigration, it was not surprising that the nation at large should be anxious concerning the loyalty of the recent comers. During and following this war, programs of rapid assimilation were vigorously promoted, particularly in the public schools including evening class for adults. The trend in recent years in educational theory has been toward the cultural pluralism viewpoint, interestingly enough at a time when the Americans of European lineage have already become so acculturated that their interest in and attachment to their old world heritage is quite minimal.

None of the theories here under review gave adequate recognition to the dynamic character of the social process. On the one hand, the native, Protestant, Anglo-Saxon culture itself was undergoing constant change. On the other hand, the cultures of the nations whence the immigrants came have undergone change since the majority of the foreign born in the United States today left Europe. Thus whatever process of acculturation the members of ethnic groups followed they were bound to develop into a different sort of American than a mature American of 1900. In view of this dynamic situation, it will never be possible to determine to what extent the immigrants became like "Americans" or "Americans" became like immigrants. Nevertheless, the broad outlines of social change in the United States during the period of the later immigration are discernible and the way in which the later immigration either facilitated or retarded these changes can be approximately indicated.

THE EFFECTS OF THE LATER IMMIGRATION UPON THE DEVELOPMENT OF THE UNITED STATES

Among the main social trends present in the United States in 1880, the following appear most significant to note as a background against which to evaluate the effect of the later immigration: (1) The population was growing at a rapid rate, although signs of a decreasing rate of natural growth were already discernible. (2) The economy of the nation was rapidly shifting from a primarily agricultural basis to an industrial basis under the stimulus of the private enterprise system which it was generally believed should have minimum regulation by government. (3) Correspondingly, community life was shifting from a primarily rural to a primarily urban basis. (4) The preoccupation with pecuniary values was retarding interest in the arts, efficient government, and social welfare problems. (5) The secular approach to problems of life, derivative from Protestant tradition, was stimulating scientific discovery and invention and its application to social problems. It was into a society undergoing these processes of change that the southern and eastern Europeans came. While the ethnic groups varied, nevertheless for the purposes at hand the people of the later immigration may be characterized broadly in the following terms: they were rural, peasant folks used to working on the land, and possessing in other instances skills in the hand crafts; were accustomed to a simple social life based on kin relations, the church—for the most part

Greek or Roman Catholic—and communal festivals; were strongly familistic, that is, patriarchal with high family integration and stability; and finally, were essentially supernaturalistic rather than scientific in approach to the problems of life.

Effect on population growth. Reuter has calculated the relative contributions of net immigration as against natural growth for the United States since 1820. For each of the decades ending 1880 to 1920, he has shown that growth by immigration accounted for between 25 and 35 per cent of the total growth.[8] Reuter included not only net immigration but also the natural increase of immigrants arriving during the period, and their rate of natural increase was assumed to be the same as that of the total population. Such a procedure underestimates the contribution of immigrants to population growth because the immigrants were for the most part young adults at the most reproductive ages. Furthermore they were derived from peasant, Catholic cultures whose mores encouraged large families. While most studies show that the longer these immigrants were here and the more they rose in social status, the smaller their families became, nevertheless it seems reasonable to suppose that during the lag attendant upon their assimilation to the small family mores of America, they contributed a more than proportionate share to the birth rate.

Controversy arose concerning whether the gain in population coming from the latter immigration was a real net addition to the population. Walker, noting the decline of the native birth rate contended that this was due to the unwillingness of the native status population to compete with the lower economic standards of the immigrants. In essence he argued that the population would have grown as fast, or even faster, without immigration because then the original stock would have had larger families.[9] Such an argument overlooks the many other factors which influenced the declining birth rate, more marked among the native Protestant groups, such as urbanization, the desire for a constantly higher standard of living, and the changing status of women. Indirectly it is possible that the differential family size of the old stock and the new, may have been affected by the greater upward social mobility made possible for the native stock by the constant replenishing of the lower class levels by newcomers. The relatively low birth rates, however, of Australia, Canada, and other pioneer nations of Anglo-Saxon stock, suggests that the fertility of this stock in the United States would have declined if there

[8] E. B. Reuter, *Population Problems* (Philadelphia: J. B. Lippincott Company, 1937) pp. 59-60.
[9] Francis A. Walker, *Discussion in Economics and Statistics,* ed. by Davis R. Dewey (New York: Henry Holt & Company, Inc., 1899) pp. 417-454.

had been no further immigration. The idea has been advanced that immigration indirectly hastened the approach to a stationary population by accelerating the process of urbanization and industrialization. Whether or not in the long run, the population of the United States would have been any different in size with or without immigration, there is no doubt that during the period in which it took place immigration contributed to the rapidity of national growth by providing a larger base upon which natural reproduction operated. Without immigration, the emergence of the United States to the size of a leading world power would not have occurred so soon.

The differential rate of population growth between the northern European stocks and the southern and eastern has resulted in an increasingly larger proportion of the total population being derived from the latter rather than the former. In line with the discussion of the relation of race to nationality and culture pursued in Chapter 3, no biological significance is attached to this change.[10]

Economic effects. Mass immigration greatly stimulated the rapid industrial growth of the United States both by furnishing the needed supply of labor and, through population growth, an ever increasing domestic market for goods. The role which immigration played in furnishing the brawn is indicated by a number of characteristics in the situation.[11] (1) Immigration was a fluid method of matching labor demand and supply through its tendency to increase or decrease in relation to the business cycle. (2) Immigrants came at an age when they were ready to work. (3) Immigrants tended to flow to those places and industries where the demand was greatest. (4) Because they needed work right away and lacked skills suitable for employment at other levels, they were willing to do the most menial and unskilled jobs which the native workers tended to shun. Thus immigration was in a sense almost "made to order" as a device for meeting the needs of expanding industrial growth under the private enterprise system. On the other hand, it is argued by some writers, that the very cheapness and availability of immigrant labor may have retarded the technological advances in labor saving devices, which were later to characterize so markedly the American industrial system.[12]

The argument formerly advanced that immigration aggravated unemployment is scarcely ever voiced today. Unemployment is now understood to be related to a wide set of factors connected with the

[10] Cf. Maurice R. Davie, *World Immigration* (New York: The Macmillan Company, 1947) pp. 285-289.
[11] See *The Immigrant Problem in the United States*, Research Report, No. 58, National Industrial Conference Board, New York, 1923, pp. 29-36.
[12] *Ibid.*, p. 32.

cyclical nature of the free enterprise system and to many conditions involved in world trade upon which neither immigration nor emigration have any marked influence. Furthermore, as indicated in the previous paragraph, immigration has a tendency to decrease in periods of depression, irrespective of legal regulations governing it. The complaint that immigration had the effect of lowering the wage scale and therefore the standard of living of the nation has merit only in a short run sense. Immigrants did work more cheaply than native labor at first. But as they became more adjusted to life in America, and as they became unionized, they pressed for higher wages and adopted higher standards of living. In the meantime their labor contribution had helped to create the greater general national wealth essential to a higher standard for all classes.

In a somewhat similar manner, the short run effect of mass immigration may be said to have retarded the growth of unions, and through this to have increased the relative power of private enterprise over the expanding economy. On the one hand, industrialists took advantage of the weak bargaining position of the immigrants. "That employers make capital out of racial rivalries, playing off 'Wop' against 'Hunkie,' for example, and so preventing a united labor front, is well enough established." [13] On the other side, the unions made it difficult for the new immigrant to obtain membership. "Foreign born craftsmen have been driven to unskilled labor, for the conditions imposed on them . . . were utterly beyond their reach." [14] Eventually, the later immigrant groups became a substantial portion of union membership. But the barriers to their admittance imposed by the unions themselves retarded the development of a united labor movement, and in the interval the employer group strengthened its bargaining and controlling position.

Effects upon political life. Discussion of the influence of the later immigration upon American political life revolves largely around two topics: their influence upon "radicalism," and their connection with the development of the "Tammany Hall" type of urban machine politics.

The role of the later immigration in the development of the unsavory, and frequently corrupt, pattern of machine politics characteristic of American city life is succinctly summarized by Donald Young: "The immigrant has been a tool of corruption because of his ignorance and political tractability, but a tool in the hands of native politicians, in the unsavory meaning of the term, who lost their con-

---

[13] Robert F. Foerster, *The Italian Emigration of Our Times* (Cambridge: Harvard University Press, 1919) p. 402.
[14] Peter Roberts, *The New Immigration* (New York: The Macmillan Company, 1912) p. 73.

trol over him in proportion to his assimilation." [15] Admitting that rival factions existed and that local ethnic groups were scarcely ever a solid block for any party or faction, it is generally true that these typical urban political machines were supported by the mass of later immigrant groups. As was indicated in the preceding chapter, this political behavior of the later immigrant groups is due to the personalized character of the machine politics and to the minority status accorded the immigrants by the natives. That these machines provided something less than "good" government one could hardly have expected immigrants to understand. What they could understand was that the ward boss could and did do them many personal favors and, above all, did not treat them in a patronizing manner.

Nativist elements and organizations based upon opposition to foreigners and foreign ideas in their propaganda have attributed radicalism in the United States to immigrants. While it is true that some leaders of politicoeconomic movements, now commonly described as "leftist", have recent immigrant lineage, there is much to support a quite opposite thesis. The hypothesis that mass immigration retarded unionism, set forth above, should be recalled in this connection. Various "progressive" movements had their greatest strength in the Midwest where, insofar as the ethnic element may have been an influence, it was the northern European rather than the southern and eastern European cultural influences which predominated. In particular, the cooperative movement had its greatest strength in this area. The various socialist movements and parties have arisen in the industrial-metropolitan areas where the heaviest concentrations of recent immigration are to be found. But both the small size of the organizations and the insignificant vote which they have generally received for candidates for the political office indicate that only a small numerical minority of the population of recent immigrant lineage has been attracted to their causes. As Hansen has put it, "Probably more immigrant Socialists were lost to the cause in the United States than were won from the ranks of the newcomers. Those who did not join the Republican party as the protector of the industries that employed them, found a home in the more liberal atmosphere of the Democratic party. Neither group, of course, questioned the fundamentals of capitalism." [16]

Impact on volume of personal disorganization. Writers about immigrant problems have struggled with the question, "To what extent did immigration affect the volume of various sorts of personal mal-

[15] Donald Young, *American Minority Peoples* (New York: Harper and Brothers, 1932) p. 224.
[16] Reprinted by permission of the publishers from Marcus Lee Hanson, *The Immigrant in American History*, 1940 (Cambridge, Mass.: Harvard University Press, 1940).

adjustment in the United States?" with frequently inconclusive results. Comparisons of the rates of criminality, delinquency, mental disease, and pauperism of three groups, the foreign born, the native born of foreign parentage, and the native population, are difficult to interpret particularly because of wide differences in age compositions and in socioeconomic levels of the three groups being compared. For example, Davie cites these figures on mental disease for 1923. "The rate per 100,000 . . . was 159.8 for native whites of native parentage, 207.0 for native whites of foreign parentage, and 513.9 for foreign born whites." [17] But the foreign born population contains relatively few children, and mental disease appears more frequently in adult groups. Furthermore, the foreign born population especially in this country is highly concentrated in urban areas, and the rate of admission to mental hospitals upon which the statistical comparisons are based is twice as great in urban as in rural areas. Finally, the foreign born is predominantly male and the rate of admissions of males exceeds that of females by about 4 to 3. This is an object lesson concerning the difficulties involved in answering the question posed at the opening of this paragraph. The reader might well practice it by trying to interpret the real meaning of some facts about juvenile delinquency, to wit: A 1910 census report on juvenile delinquency indicated that the ratio per 100,000 population was 99.8 for native born whites of native parentage and 153.3 for native born whites of foreign parentage. A number of factors other than those related to minority status per se are needed to explain these comparative figures. In spite of the difficulties involved in the statistical approach, substantially every writer who has described the life of ethnic groups in American cities places emphasis upon such factors as cultural conflict and marginal status in accounting for personal disorganization in such groups.[18] Thus it is difficult to avoid the conclusion that in the over-all sense, mass immigration did add to the total volume of personal disorganization, not because of the nature of the immigrants or of their cultures per se, but because of the problem of adjustment to a new situation.

Effects upon American "culture". We use culture here in the delimited sense, as concerned with arts, sciences, religion, and recreation, in contrast with government and economics, and other instrumental phases of civilization.[19] The Anglo-American culture placed little value on

[17] Davie, *World Immigration*, p. 279.
[18] See for example, Mabel A. Elliot and Francis E. Merrill, *Social Disorganization*, 3rd ed. (New York: Harper, 1950) Ch. 28.
[19] See R. M. MacIver and Charles H. Page, *Society* (New York: Rinehart & Co., 1949) for this distinction, especially pp. 486-487.

the arts and its people were markedly inconspicuous in aesthetic expression. In contrast the folk cultures of the continental nations, and those of the later immigration in particular, were far more elaborated in music, the dance, colorful folk festivals, and the arts in general.[20] Thus the later immigration enriched the aesthetic quality of American life not only through the contributions of their great artists but also by diffusing a greater sensitivity and heightened evaluation of the arts. The Puritan influence which inhibited the development of the arts among the Anglo-Americans carried over into their whole concept of enjoying life. The pursuit of pleasure for its own sake was in a sense a "sin." This stands in marked contrast to the continental cultures which placed high value upon spontaneous gaiety, less inhibited expressions of passion, and enjoying life each day as it came. Again the later immigration contributed to the decline of the Puritan outlook on pleasure and its replacement by a more hedonistic view.

The Anglo-American culture became increasingly secular in its approach to human problems, not only in the sphere of economics but also in such fields as health and welfare. In contrast, the folk cultures of the later immigrant nationalities were more supernaturalistically oriented. In the earlier periods of the adjustment of these newcomers to their new environment, many difficulties were encountered in such matters as enforcing regulations pertaining to sanitation and public health and in rationalizing the approaches to problems of human conduct, particularly in the area of family relations. The later immigration had the effect of retarding the trend toward the application of a secular as, distinct from supernaturalistic, approach to the problem of human relations.

Finally, the later immigration, since it was predominantly Catholic by religion, greatly altered the religious composition of the nation. Since their Catholicism is the one differentiating aspect of the later ethnic groups which has been most completely retained, this change may be considered one of the most profoundly important permanent effects of the later immigration. Indeed, we consider it so significant that we shall devote Chapter 14 to its implications.

Immigrant contributions limited by minority status. No brief discussion can, of course, exhaust the list of contributions of the later immigrants to the development of American culture. Among the many millions of immigrants were many highly creative minds whose artistic creations and scientific discoveries added enormously not only to

[20] Cf. William C. Smith, *Americans in the Making* (New York: Appleton-Century-Crofts, Inc., 1939) pp. 423-431. The continental Europeans of the earlier immigration had a creative influence on the development of the arts in the United States.

American but to world civilization.[21] Innumerable scattered items, such as food dishes, words, and clothing styles, have been incorporated into the general mode of American life. Nevertheless, as we recall the processes by which immigrant adjustment took place and as we look at the cultural product now prevailing, the potential contribution of the immigrant groups can be seen to have been limited by their minority status. Native Americans who considered these foreigners as inferior people were not disposed to borrow elements from these Old World cultures. Even more important was the impact of minority status upon the native born of the later immigration. Since rise in status and acceptance by the dominant group was contingent upon the loss of ethnic visibility, those of immigrant lineage themselves looked down upon their own heritage and failed to perpetuate even those elements consistent with modern American living.

Thus the European ethnic groups became Americanized, if not quite into the Protestant, Anglo-Saxon mould. The melting pot boiled, but the emergent product was indigenously American rather than a mere amalgam of variegated European cultures. The result was more a creation of the reciprocal responses of many groups to the rapidly changing circumstances of the 20th century in an environment fortuitiously rich in natural resources, than a static reintegration of elements of times gone by. The product is now American rather than foreign and the possibility of cultural pluralism along ethnic lines, as far as European heritages are concerned, is now passed. For what remaining time European ethnic groups continue to be differentiated, they will be so because those of native status still refuse to accept them as Americans.

Summary of the effects of the later mass immigration upon American society. The foregoing discussion suggests the following propositions as a summary statement of the effects of the later mass immigration upon American society:

1. It accelerated the population growth of the United States during the period in which it took place and thus further advanced the position of the United States among the world powers.

2. It expedited industrial expansion and urbanization.

3. It temporarily retarded the growth of unionism and trends toward industrial democracy; and thus indirectly increased the relative power of private enterprise in the control of American economic life.

4. Immigration facilitated the perpetuation of "Tammany Hall" type of urban politics and conversely retarded the development of "good government" movements.

[21] See Francis J. Brown and Joseph S. Roucek, *One America* (New York: Prentice-Hall, Inc., 1945) Part II for the most exhaustive listing in one volume of the significant contributions to American life of each of the 39 different ethnic groupings described.

5. In its total impact, it increased the volume of personal maladjustment with particular reference to ethnic persons in marginal status positions.

6. It elaborated the artistic and esthetic elements of the general culture, and facilitated the trend away from Puritan outlook on pleasure and personal morality toward a more hedonistic value system.

7. It retarded the trend from a supernaturalistic toward a secular approach to problems of human welfare, particularly the application of newer social science approaches to the problems of human relations.

8. While innumerable specific items in the various ethnic cultures became incorporated into the general national or regional cultures, the minority status of ethnics limited the extent of this influence.

FUTURE IMMIGRATION POLICY OF THE UNITED STATES

Whether or not the present immigration policy of the United States should be revised, and in what ways, is related to questions of population, economics, international relations, and harmonious community life, which interrelate in so many ways that it is difficult to discuss each separately. Whatever may have been the motivation behind the adoption of the Immigration Act of 1924, it seems indisputable that some limitation of immigration is a necessity for the United States as well as for any other modern state. The problem thus centers upon how many should be admitted and what qualifications should be required.

Population considerations. Prior to 1950 students of population were in substantial agreement that the population of the United States would increase at a decreasing rate and reach a stationary point, at least by the end of the century, of less than 200,000,000. The greater increase in population from 1941–1950 in comparison with the previous decade has probably not altered the long time trend, however much it may change the predictions as to the time and size of the anticipated stationary mark. Whether or not this prospect is desirable in terms of general national interest, we do not argue. If, however, a more substantial growth than that in prospect is considered desirable, an increase in the number of immigrants to be admitted is a ready method to accomplish the purpose. Immigration, especially at the youthful adult ages, the ages at which it most frequently occurs, constitutes a way of adding immediately to the working and reproducing portion of the population.

Economic considerations. The United States is not overpopulated in the sense that a substantial increase in its present population would lower its standard of living. For a nation so situated it seems reasonably clear from past experience that growth in population aids economic expansion and the long range raising of the standard of living. Immigration, therefore, is a possible means of insuring a more substantial growth than natural growth at present affords. Immigration, can aggravate the short run problems arising from the business cycle. However past experience indicates that immigration tends to regulate itself, according to the ebbs and flows of employment opportunity. In an expanding and changing economy, development is frequently retarded by shortages in the size of the labor force at the moment in particular occupations. Immigration constitutes a flexible means of correcting these situations. For example, a recent writer predicts a sharp drop in the labor force during the first half of the 1950's, then a rise in the late 50's, when the bumper crop of postwar babies will enter the labor market.[22] Such considerations suggest the desirability of elasticity in the numerical quotas adjusted to fluctuations in employment indices. Likewise, selection may be made in relation to shortages in particular skills.

International considerations. Justification of the differential quotas favoring the nations of the older immigration as against those of the newer, is, however, a more difficult matter. Neither our past experience with immigrants nor our present social science furnishes objective bases for assuming that ethnic lineage as such affects the relative capacity of any foreigner to adjust successfully to American life. The case is therefore strong for the adjustment of national quotas so that all nations are considered equal. As a temporary procedure in this direction, Bernard recommends that quotas unused under the present system, should be placed in a general pool which in the immediate subsequent period could be used by countries whose quotas have been exhausted, or be made available for special groups in distress.[23]

Finally, the question of political affiliation must be considered. When a nation is engaged in a sharply poised struggle against another nation, it is inevitable that it will want to bar as immigrants people whose loyalty is on the other side, as is the case with many European Communists today. A real danger to democracy in the application of political tests for admission to the United States is the danger of confusing beliefs, as for example, communism with other beliefs in social change.

[22] Ewan Clague, "America's Future Manpower Needs," *The Annals of the American Academy of Political and Social Science,* Vol. 262, March 1949, p. 105.
[23] William S. Bernard, ed., *American Immigration Policy* (New York: Harper and Brothers, 1950) p. 275.

Summary considerations. Bearing all the above considerations in mind, it may be suggested in summary that the present immigration policy of the United States calls for revision in the following directions:

1. It is obvious that some numerical limitation should be imposed. The present figure of 150,000 a year is easily within the capacity of the nation to absorb without economic or social disturbance, and should not be lowered. Whether it should be raised or not depends on the position taken on the controversial question, "Is it desirable to stimulate the present rate of population growth in the nation?"

2. Two considerations suggest flexibility concerning the number to be admitted in any given year: (a) the fluctuations in the business cycle; and (b) the varying need to provide refuge for groups in distress.

3. While nationality quotas are essential to give opportunity for all foreigners to compete for admission, their allocation on a somewhat more equitable basis than now prevails seems called for. At the minimum, a provision that the unused quotas of nations might be pooled for the use by other nations would seem to balance in part the present disparity.

4. Since the migration of the peoples of the world will come increasingly under the purview and administration of United Nations, the United States should stand ready to supplement or revise its basic policy in relation to any future international programs.

The significance of this last consideration has been illustrated already in two situations arising since the present policy was adopted, that of the refugees from Naziism and that of the displaced persons of World War II.

THE REFUGEES

Throughout our entire history, American society has been added to periodically by immigrants who left their native lands primarily to escape persecution for their political or religious opinions. The term "refugees" was applied to individuals who fled from the Nazi persecution beginning in Germany in 1933 and carried on further in the Nazi-occupied areas after 1938. To quote Davie and Koenig:

The recent refugee movement has also been marked by (1) the extremely cruel treatment of the victims of political, religious, and "racial" persecution; (2) by the difficulty which these victims encountered in escaping and in finding a secure refuge as Naziism spread to ever larger areas; (3) by the reluctance of the countries not immediately affected to admit them because of the deep economic depression then existing; and (4) by the breaking up of families on a scale previously unknown. Such has been the refugee movement which began with the rise of Hitler to power in 1933.[24]

Davie and Koenig estimate the total number of immigrants in the United States who can be called "refugees" at 243,862. The period 1938–41 marked the peak of this particular immigrant movement. America was not, as many natives put it, "swamped" with refugees since the total amount of all immigration to our shores from Europe from 1933 to 1944 totaled only 365,955, only 16.8 per cent of the total permissible from Europe under the quota laws. In terms of nationalities represented, over half came from Germany or Austria, with Poles, Czechoslovakians, Russians, French, Italians, and Hungarians following in this order. Of the entire group, about two-thirds were Jewish, a fact explained by the Nazi persecution of Jews which was most systematic and categorical. These refugees eventually were distributed throughout the country, although they settled largely in cities. New York City absorbed a larger number than any other community.

This particular group differed from the earlier mass immigration in having a far larger proportion of highly educated, professionally trained, and commercially experienced persons than the earlier immigration. For example, 5000 were physicians; 25,000 merchants; 1800 manufacturers; and 3500 college and school teachers. The proportion of skilled and unskilled laborers was far below that of the earlier immigration. This unusual distribution of occupational backgrounds was in part due to the difficulties of escaping and the need of some wealth to get away. Relatively more of the refugees were wealthy, although many of the well-to-do who did not come early were unable to bring their wealth with them.

Davie and Koenig sum up their answer to the question, "What do Americans think of the refugees?" as follows:

The general reaction of Americans toward the refugees may be summed up as one of compassion for the victims of persecution seeking a haven here. The refugees report that, on the whole, Americans have shown an attitude of friendliness and helpfulness. As the number of refugees increased, however, a certain amount of antagonism developed. Refugees began to be looked upon as serious competitors, especially by certain professional and wage-earning groups and in certain communities. These fears were allayed with the increased demand for labor brought about by the war.

Nevertheless, a certain degree of resentment has persisted in certain quarters and against certain groups of refugees.[25]

These people were not, of course, a new minority group since they lacked specific visibility different from other immigrant descendants

---

[24] Maurice R. Davie and Samuel Koenig, *The Refugees Are Now Americans,* Public Affairs Pamphlet, No. 111, 1945, p. 4. By permission.
[25] *Ibid.,* p. 28. By permission.

from the same backgrounds. Nevertheless, they incurred antagonism particularly from the occupational segments in which they were potential competitors. Physicians, for example, complained about them, especially for filling places left by American physicians in service; this, in spite of the inadequate number of physicians in the country and of the fact that altogether the refugees comprised only 3 per cent of the total of all doctors. Complaints were heard of refugees amassing wealth in stock dealings and other large scale enterprises. The number of refugees engaging in large scale operations was few. That small percentage of refugees who composed "café society" were criticized for their arrogance toward Americans. It is probable that these well-to-do refugees were acting as they had been accustomed in Europe.

Within a short time, these refugees became well adapted, if not assimilated, to American life. On the one hand, their relatively few numbers offered little serious competition to Americans, except in an occasional locality; on the other hand, they had a beneficial influence out of proportion to their numbers. Some started new business enterprises and introduced new manufacturing processes; others were highly skilled workers in trades where a dearth of native trained workers existed. If in any sense the presence of the refugees constituted a "problem," it has long since ceased to be one.

DISPLACED PERSONS AND THE UNITED STATES

In the years since World War II, the United States has been receiving a new category of immigrants who have become technically designated displaced persons, a term which is frequently shortened to read DPs. It refers to those Europeans who were rendered homeless through the destruction of the last war, or for various reasons could not with safety resume residence in their prewar community. By the end of 1950, the heart-rending task of resettling these people has been substantially accomplished. It would therefore perhaps be adequate for us to confine our discussion of the topic to indicating how many came to this country, who they were, and how they fared among us. But the role which the United States played in this cooperative world problem is a good barometer for evaluating the present climate of American sentiment toward certain minorities, and a good test of the attitude of the American people toward international cooperation. We shall therefore treat the topic of the displaced persons in these terms.

The circumstances creating displacement. During the period of the German conquest up to 1943, millions of persons were evacuated by the German army or fled before it. At the same time prisoners of war and slave labor from non-German nationals were taken to Germany.

Again over two million Poles, French-speaking Alsace-Lorrainers, and Slovenes were expelled from border areas incorporated into the Reich in order to make room for foreign nationals of German stock who were thus repatriated nearer the homeland. As the tide of the war reversed, a series of other population movements took place. Inhabitants of German cities, perhaps as many as six million, were evacuated to other places within the Reich. As Russian victories occurred, Reich Germans from eastern and southeastern Europe together with some non-Germans who feared the Communists fled back to the fatherland. At the conclusion of the war, the Allied armies liberated from the notorious Nazi concentration camps the surviving Jews and non-Jewish political opponents of the Nazi regime. More recently, as the Iron Curtain began to surround their countries, thousands fled from their homes to seek asylum in the lands controlled by the Allied governments.

The characteristics of the displaced persons. It must be borne in mind that due to the changing aspects of the displaced persons movement any statistical statement of the characteristics of displaced persons as a group must be taken as estimates of the particular times when surveys were made. In a survey made late in 1947 it was estimated that there were 55 per cent males and 45 per cent females. In age distribution, those from 18 to 44 comprised 62 per cent of the total, 24 per cent being under 18 and 14 per cent 45 or over. This highly atypical age distribution accounts for the very high birth rate of 35.5 per thousand and the very low death rate of 4.9 per thousand, in spite of residents of DP camps receiving a bare subsistence diet.[26] In terms of religion, one estimate indicates that seven out of ten were Roman Catholics and that 20 per cent were Jewish.[27] The percentage of skilled laborers is high due in part to the fact that many were selected for slave labor because of the skills they possessed and that others were given training in the camps after the war as an aid to their resettlement.

Distribution by nationality is given in Table 12.

Adequate data to show the distribution of the displaced persons according to the causes for their displacement are not available. Kulischer, however, gives this general picture: "Among the original millions of displaced persons the largest group was probably composed of slave laborers, and the second largest, of prisoners of war.

---

[26] Eugene M. Kulischer, "Displaced Persons in the Modern World," *The Annals of the American Academy of Political and Social Science*, Vol. 262, March, 1949, pp. 172-173.
[27] William S. Bernard, "Homeless, Tempest-Tossed," *Survey Graphic*, Vol. 37, April 1948, p. 189.

TABLE 12

Distribution of Displaced Persons by Nationality, July 31, 1948[28]

	RECEIVING IRO CARE AND MAINTENANCE	OTHERS IN GERMANY AND AUSTRIA
Poles	142,352	⎫
Ukranians	89,208	⎬ 56,000
Balts	132,379	21,000
Yugoslavs	27,762	41,000
Jews	136,848	34,000
Others, including stateless	59,529	85,000
Total	588,078	237,000 [29]

Smaller groups consisted of those who fled with the retreating German armies, Jews who escaped extermination, political deportees and hostages, and others." [30]

The process of resettlement. From all of these millions of uprooted people, many returned to their former homes, and many others were resettled in the nations to which they belonged. Repatriation was carried on in the first years of the postwar period by Soviet authorities, by Allied military authorities, and by the United Nations Relief and Rehabilitation Administration. But before this period closed it was clear that for many of the displaced persons there was no place to go. UNRRA began the process of trying to locate these remaining people in foreign lands but had up to the time it disbanded, July 1947, resettled only some 90,000.[31]

The second phase of the resettlement process dates from July 1947 when the above mentioned agencies turned over the problem to the International Refugee Organization, a United Nations agency established for this purpose. While a precise count of the total number of persons still in need of resettlement could not be made, the number placed in IRO's charge exceeded 700,000. To add to the problem, the new refugees began to arrive in greater number from the expanding areas of Communist control.[32] The IRO sent out pleas to the member

[28] Sources: IRO *Statistical Reports;* Reports of the Military Governments in Germany; communication of the American Jewish Joint Distribution Committee.
[29] Not including an estimated 50,000 in Italy.
[30] Kulischer, *op. cit.,* p. 173.
[31] *Ibid.,* p. 175.
[32] The number who applied to the IRO for assistance from April 1, 1948, to May 31, 1950, was over half a million, almost all of whom fled from Iron Curtain countries. International Refugee Organization, *Statistical Report,* Geneva, Table 27, p. 35, May, 1950.

nations to arrange for the resettlement among them of these homeless people. By March, 1951, most of them had been resettled in the places indicated in Table 13 (p. 126).

The role of the United States in the displaced persons problem. During the UNRRA administration, a very small number, some 20,000, of displaced persons entered the United States, each one of whom was sponsored by a particular citizen who guaranteed that the immigrant would not become a public charge. During the first year of administration by the IRO, slightly over 200,000 displaced persons were resettled in the many nations. In relation to its size and world position, the 16,836 admitted by the United States during that year was relatively small. One reason for this was that most of the displaced persons were ineligible for admission under our quota system. The Administration urged Congress immediately upon IRO's call to pass special legislation to make it possible for a substantial number of displaced persons to be admitted on a nonquota basis. Congress did not act until the closing hours of its 1948 session, on June 2. The bill then passed had the following main provisions.

1. Permitted the admission of 205,000 DPs over a two-year period.
2. Charged the displaced persons entering up to 50 per cent against future annual quotas of the countries of birth.
3. Restricted eligibility to those entering Germany, Austria, and Italy prior to December 22, 1945.
4. Required that at least 40 per cent of the total admitted must be persons coming from areas annexed by foreign powers.

With the passage of this bill, the United States finally assumed a share of its responsibility more commensurate with its size and position. Considering, however, that our normal annual quota of immigrants was 150,000 and that the 1948 Act required that half of the entrants were to be charged against present or future national quotas, this measure does not appear unduly generous. But it is even more in the qualifying restrictions embodied in the Act that the limitations of the Act to meet the need are clearly indicated. The restrictions made it difficult to find 205,000 DP's who could qualify. The cutoff date excluded the large number of Jews who fled from eastern Europe after December 1945. The areas which had been annexed by foreign powers, from which 40 per cent must be drawn, included the Baltic States whose population contained substantial numbers of Protestants. Since, as indicated above, 90 per cent of the DP's were either Roman Catholic or Jewish, it is not surprising that the bill was considered by many as highly discriminatory against peoples of non-Protestant faith. Sharing this sentiment President Truman in his message following the signing of the bill put it in these words:

"In its present form, the bill is flagrantly discriminatory . . . It is a close question whether this bill is better than no bill at all . . . [It] discriminates in callous fashion against displaced persons of the Jewish faith . . . [It] also excludes many persons of the Catholic faith who deserve admission."

As the admissions began to lag, the Administration pressed for the revision of the 1948 Act, and on June 16, 1950, a new bill was signed by the President containing the following provisions:

1. The Act permits the entry of 228,514 more displaced persons and others from special groups, in addition to the 172,230 admissions already granted up to May 30, 1950, under the 1948 act.

2. The qualifications as to occupation and nationality of the previous bill were removed. The cutoff date was extended to make eligible any who entered the camps prior to January 1, 1949, thus including as eligibles, Poles, Rumanians, and Catholics in general who had fled in 1946 and 1947 from Communist controlled countries.

3. Among the special groups made eligible for admission were: "Volksdeutsche" from eastern Europe; the Polish army in England; Greeks displaced by guerilla warfare. Some 15,000 people in the United States, most of whom were students, who for political reasons could not go home, were granted permanent visas.[33]

Significance of American reaction to the displaced persons problem. The response of the American Government and public to the problem presented by displaced persons is indicative of the postwar national attitudes toward minorities. The account just presented reflects the characteristic ambivalence illustrated by its previous treatment of immigration and immigrants. As before, certain employer interests have been eager to get laborers who presumably would be willing to perform tasks which native labor is reluctant to perform, particularly in this instance, in agricultural labor. As before, liberal elements have favored a generous policy in accordance with democratic principles. Opposed to these publics, as previously, have been those "nativist" elements of the population, to whom "foreigners" are *ipso facto* undesirable. Overlapping the general nativist public in opposition to further immigration of displaced persons is the anti-Semitic public. Different from before has been the shift in the position of organized labor, which officially at least has supported the entrance of displaced persons. The fact that the United States has finally provided for the admission of enough displaced persons to terminate the problem, with no qualifications which could be interpreted as discriminations, indicates that in the balance of forces at present the

[33] *The New York Times,* July 17, 1950, p. 1.

liberal viewpoint is in the ascendancy. The same conclusion emerges from apparent response of the people among whom the displaced persons have settled in America. No comprehensive analysis of the adjustment has been made and it is perhaps too soon for such a study to be made. While some criticism has been voiced of the treatment of displaced persons as agricultural laborers in some areas, in general it appears that these new immigrants have been welcomed and have made rapid adjustment. A significant new element in this latest immigration situation has been the more systematic social planning attending the process all the way through. This new feature may well be adopted as a permanent procedure in all subsequent immigration policy.

The destinations of the displaced persons resettled up to February 28, 1951, are given in Table 13. On May 31, 1950, 261,033 persons still remain to be resettled but the United States Displaced Persons Act of 1950 will go far to liquidate the original problem. As has already been indicated, the problem of the refugees from behind the Iron Curtain continues.

TABLE 13
Places of Resettlement of Displaced Persons up to Feb. 28, 1951 [34]

United States	253,706
Australia	174,001
Israel	121,025
Canada	97,441
United Kingdom	85,513
France	38,139
Argentina	31,336
Brazil	24,911
Belgium	22,380
Venezuela	16,207
Other Countries	39,225
Total	903,884

TOPICS FOR DISCUSSION AND PROJECTS

1. Which of the three viewpoints presented in this chapter concerning the manner in which immigrants should be assimilated to American life appears to you as most consistent with the democratic ideal? Why?
2. Consult a number of general histories of the United States covering the period since the Civil War and compile the views expressed therein concerning the effects of the later immigration upon the development of

[34] Source: International Refugee Organization, *Advanced Statistical Report for April 4, 1951.*

American social life. To what extent do the views expressed agree or disagree with the hypotheses advanced in this connection in the summary on pages 116-117?

3. Do you think the present international situation is more likely or less likely to bring about a revision of our present immigration laws? Why or why not?

4. Analyze in detail all the possible effects which mass immigration had upon the composition and size of the population of the United States.

5. Discuss in detail the effects of immigration upon the economy of the receiving nation. Do these effects vary at different stages in a nation's development?

6. Consult the files of periodicals dealing with current affairs for the first half of 1948 for material concerning the Congressional debate on the first Displaced Persons Act. Summarize the leading views expressed.

SUGGESTED READING

Bernard, William S. ed. *American Immigration Policy: A Reappraisal*. New York: Harper and Brothers, 1950.
> *Brief comprehensive account of the effects of immigration and an appraisal of national policy from a liberal viewpoint.*

Bowers, David, ed. *Foreign Influences in American Life*. Princeton: Princeton University Press, 1944.
> *Contains essays on the influence of European immigrants upon politics, economic ideas, and cultural life of the United States.*

Davie, Maurice R. *Refugees in America*. New York: Harper and Brothers, 1947.
> *The most comprehensive account of the pre-World War II refugee immigration.*

———*World Immigration*. New York: The Macmillan Company, 1936.
> *Chapter 6. "Characteristics of Immigrants and Their Effects upon American Society."*

Gross, Feliks. "Political Emigration from Iron Curtain Countries", *The Annals of the American Academy of Political and Social Science*, September, 1950, pp. 175-184.
> *Discusses the political emigration from eastern Europe since World War II and analyzes its implication in relation to Western democracy.*

Hansen, Marcus L. *The Immigrant in American History*. Cambridge: Harvard University Press, 1940.
> *A historical treatment of the role of European immigration in American history, especially during the 19th century.*

"Reappraising Our Immigration Policy", *The Annals of the American Academy of Political and Social Science*, Vol. 26, March, 1949.
> *The number is devoted to the background of the immigration policy of the United States and the reappraisal is based upon world conditions following World War II.*

Thompson, Warren S. *Population Problems*, 3rd ed. New York: McGraw-Hill Book Company, 1942.
> *A specialist in population considers the effects of migration upon both the receiving and the sending countries.*

CHAPTER 6

Mexican Immigrants and Other Spanish Americans

In the decade of 1920–1930, *Readers' Guide* lists 51 articles on "the Mexican Problem" by comparison with 19 articles on the same subject for the previous decade.[1] With the slowing down of immigration and its final drastic limitation, Mexican immigration began to be discussed as the new immigrant problem. In many respects, this new immigrant situation bore resemblance to the one involving the southern and eastern European immigration, and in other respects the situation was different. Mexicans immigrated in large numbers and concentrated largely in one region which made them conspicuously visible. The region was, however, the Southwest where the circumstances were greatly different from the Northeast. Again like European immigrants, these Mexicans possessed a rural, peasant background which handicapped their adjustment to American life and insured their starting off on the lowest rungs of the economic ladder. Because of their cultural difference and their low economic status, and the reaction of the Anglo-Americans to them, Mexican immigrants tended to live together in colonies which were characterized by a slumlike appearance, low indices of health and welfare, and lack of integration with the native community around them similar to the immigrant colonies of the Northeast in their accommodation stage. Finally, as in the case of European immigrants, the native Americans, to whom we shall refer as Anglos, reacted to Mexican immigrants with the preju-

[1] Carey McWilliams, *North from Mexico* (Philadelphia: J. B. Lippincott Company, 1949) p. 206.

128

dice and discrimination which clearly marks the Mexicans as a minority, as we shall presently detail. However, the intensity of the discrimination against Mexicans exceeded that directed at European immigrants.

Much of the difference in the immigrant pattern as it unfolded in the Southwest as contrasted with the Northeastern situation grew out of the different social setting in which it occurred, a setting in which historically the Spanish cultural influence which the Mexican immigrant shared had far deeper roots than that of the ascendant Anglos.

The background of the relations between Anglos and the Spanish peoples of the Southwest. Spanish speaking people have been in the Southwest for 350 years. Some of the villages north of Santa Fe, New Mexico, were founded in 1598. A century later Spanish settlements were made in Texas, and almost two centuries later, in California. In each of these three areas, separated in time of establishment and by wide spaces, distinctive cultures developed within the broad Spanish base. These varying Spanish-Mexican cultures were likewise influenced by the relations of the Spanish to the many different Indian groups with which they came in contact.[2] "Until about the middle of the 19th century, the *californios,* the *nuevo mexicanos,* and the *texanos* went their separate cultural ways, held together only lightly by at first the slender threads of Spain, and later, for a brief incident, by the uncertain and flimsy bonds of independent Mexico." [3]

In consequence of this historical background as well as the cultural development affected by Spanish Mexican and Indian elements, the Southwest today bears the indelible marks of these influences. In the technological field, many of the methods and processes of sheep raising, cattle raising, mining, and irrigation farming were borrowed from the Mexican-Indian culture of the area. Now blended with new techniques which developed after annexation, these contributions are not adequately accredited to the people who should receive the credit. Likewise, some Mexican influence is reflected in state laws governing land use and property rights between husband and wife. More visibly recognized as "Spanish influence" are architectural forms, clothing, and language. American vocabulary in the region includes many Spanish words, the whole nomenclature of the rancho and vaquero (cowboy) culture complexes being largely Spanish.[4]

From the turn of the 18th century to the Mexican-American war, intergroup relations formed a complex pattern of individual friend-

[2] The writer is indebted to Prof. George I. Sanchez of the University of Texas for supplying "Spanish-speaking People in the Southwest—A Brief Historical Review" (mimeographed), which has been drawn upon in this section.
[3] *Ibid.,* p. 2.
[4] See McWilliams, *North From Mexico,* Ch. 8.

ships, competition, antagonism, and, in many instances, violent conflict based upon ethnic and racial distinctions. The Mexican society was sharply divided between upper class property owners and the peons. The invader-immigrant Anglos as individuals on the one hand competed, and sometimes came in conflict with the upper class Mexicans for economic gain; on the other hand, many Anglos cooperated with the ruling Mexican elements and through intermarriage became part of Mexican society. Both upper class Mexicans and Americans considered the peons as an inferior, servile class. With the increasing infiltration of Americans, however, relations between the two groups became more antagonistic. In Texas, where Americans by 1836 far outnumbered Mexicans, this antagonism expressed itself in a successful revolution resulting in the Republic of Texas. By the treaty of Guadalupe Hildago, terminating the Mexican-American War, all the Mexican territory north of the Rio Grande became a part of the United States. From this point on, American influence became dominant over Spanish-Mexican; upper class Mexicans attempted to join American society; and the poorer and illiterate Mexicans became a distinct ethnic minority, notwithstanding the fact that they were now citizens of the United States. The antagonistic character of Anglo-Mexican relations is reflected in the terms "gringo" and "greaser" which each group came to apply to the members of the other, with contemptuous implications. In popular usage prior to the conquest, "gringo" referred to any foreigner who spoke Spanish with an accent. The term "greaser" referred to a native Mexican or a native Spanish-American, originally applied disdainfully by the Americans of the southwestern United States to Mexicans. Given this intergroup situation against the setting of the "trigger-fingered" frontier, it was not surprising that violence should frequently arise. Paul S. Taylor in his study of a border community testified to many instances of violence from both groups. Illustrative of the situation in the late 19th century was a comment of a local official: "Undoubtedly robberies and murders by Mexicans have continually been perpetrated in Texas, but in retaliation Americans have committed terrible outrages upon citizens of Mexican origin." [5] McWilliams assembled a series of instances of violence visited upon Mexicans by Anglos. Examples of such instances are: "the first person to be lynched in California was a Mexican," and "Leonardo Cordoba, Clement Lopez, and Jesus Saguaripa were lynched in Tucson . . . (1873), with a coroner's jury defending the lynching." [6]

[5] Paul S. Taylor, *An American-Mexican Frontier* (Chapel Hill: University of North Carolina Press, 1934) p. 65.
[6] McWilliams, *op. cit.,* pp. 127-128.

The size and composition of the Spanish-speaking population. More confusion exists concerning the size of the Spanish-Mexican element in the population of the United States than of any other ethnic element with the possible exception of the Indians. Concerning the efforts made by the United States Bureau of the Census to count this population and the results obtained, Lyle Saunders writes:

Much of the lack of adequate demographic information about the group is due to the difficulty of finding any single criterion by which they can be distinguished. The Bureau of the Census in 1930 attempted to enumerate them under the heading "Mexican," defining them in their instructions to enumerators as "all persons born in Mexico or having parents born in Mexico, who were not definitely white, Negro, Indian, Chinese, or Japanese." The principal difficulty with this definition, aside from the confusion of racial and cultural concepts it contained, was that it excluded persons whose grandparents, great-grandparents, or even more remote ancestors had come to the Southwest by way of Mexico. In New Mexico, for example, where the Spanish-speaking people have lived for more than three centuries, only 61,960 "Mexicans" were enumerated although it was a matter of common knowledge that the Spanish-speaking group made up about half the population of the state, or something over 200,000 persons.

In 1940 the Bureau of the Census dropped the classification "Mexican," except for foreign-born persons actually natives of Mexico, and attempted to determine the size of the Spanish-speaking and other foreign language groups by asking of a five per cent sample of those enumerated the question: what was the principal language, other than English, spoken in your home during your childhood? From the answers to this question an estimate was made of the number of Spanish-speaking people in states and large cities, but the sample was not large enough to permit estimates for counties, small cities, or rural areas.[7]

The extent to which the census enumerations have underestimated the total population of Spanish-Mexican lineage is indicated by Saunders' own careful study of the population in Texas. For this state alone, he found in 1949 "between 1,100,000 and 1,300,000, plus an undetermined number of illegal aliens which may include as many as several hundred thousand persons." His Texas findings led Saunders to estimate that throughout the country, the total Spanish-speaking population would be 3,000,000 to 3,500,000.[8] This estimate, much larger than that obtained by the 1940 census enumeration, is further confirmed by the findings of the National Resources Planning Board which put the figure at about 3,000,000 in 1938.[9] Spanish-speaking

[7] Lyle Saunders, "The Spanish-Speaking Population of Texas," *Inter-American Education Occasional Papers V* (Austin: University of Texas Press, 1949) p. 8. By permission.
[8] *Ibid.*, pp. 7, 14.
[9] Cited by Carey McWilliams, *Brothers Under the Skin*, p. 116, from *The Problems of a Changing Population*, 1938, p. 224.

Americans thus constitute one of the largest ethnic elements in the United States who remain in considerable degree differentiated from the Anglo population. The indications are that this Spanish-Mexican ethnic element is growing somewhat faster than the general population. For Texas, Saunders concluded, "The Spanish-speaking group is increasing more rapidly than the population as a whole and may be expected to make up an increasing proportion of the total population." [10]

In view of the inadequacy of the official statistical counts as a whole to demarcate the population with which we are here concerned, we shall not present the official figures to indicate the distribution by regions. Students of this group agree on the following points: (1) that a large majority of the Spanish-Mexican group lives in the Southwest; (2) that the Hispano element is concentrated in northern New Mexico and southern Colorado; (3) that the Mexican immigrant element (including the native born who now outnumber the foreign about two to one) is concentrated in Texas, California, and Arizona, numerically in the order given; (4) and that something less than 20 per cent of the Mexican immigrant group now lives outside the Southwest in scattered groups, many of which are in or near urban centers in Illinois, Michigan, Minnesota, and Ohio. Mexican migratory workers are a more or less permanent feature of the agricultural life of many other states. Many of the migrants, however, consider the Southwest their permanent home.

Race consciousness in Anglo-Mexican relations. In Anglo-Mexican relations, the element of "race consciousness" on the part of the Anglos has been more pronounced than where European immigrants were involved. From an objective basis, the Mexican immigrant group does possess greater racial variance. The racial composition of the population of Mexico was returned in 1921 as 9.8 per cent white; 59.3 per cent mestizo; and 29.2 per cent Indian.[11] Since the immigrants to the United States have been drawn largely from the latter two elements, especially the mestizo, it is not surprising that the results of the United States Census of 1930, enumerating the Mexican stock by racial designation as "white" and "colored" for the first and the only time, showed less than 5 per cent as "white," 65,968 out of 1,422,533 total Mexican stock listed.[12] This considerable admixture of Indian traits would not from the scientific viewpoint carry with it

---

[10] Saunders, *op. cit.*, p. 14.
[11] Maurice R. Davie, *World Immigration* (New York, Macmillan, 1936) p. 215. Data taken from Department de la Estadistica Nacional, *Resumen del censo general de habitates de 30 de Noviembre de 1921*, Mexico, 1928, p. 62.
[12] U. S. Census, 1930, Population, Vol. 2, pp. 27, 34.

any significance. The mestizo cultures are more Latin-American than Indian. There is no evidence that Indians are inferior in innate capacity to Caucasians.[13] The Indian strain does, however, give the Mexican-American group a "darker" appearance in general. This racial visibility further strengthens Anglo attitudes of dominance over people of "color." Writing concerning the significance of this race consciousness in 1930, Manuel Gamio stated:

The darkest-skinned Mexican experiences almost the same restrictions as the Negro, while a person of medium-dark skin can enter a second-class lunchroom frequented also by Americans of the poorer class, but will not be admitted to a high-class restaurant. A Mexican of light-brown skin as a rule will not be admitted to a high-class hotel, while a white cultured Mexican will be freely admitted to the same hotel, especially if he speaks English fluently.[14]

In the contemporary scene can be found four categories of American people of Spanish-Mexican lineage whose situation requires separate treatment; (1) The Mexican immigrant population living in the Southwest, including their native born descendants; (2) The Mexican immigrant population, similarly defined, living in groups scattered outside the Southwest; (3) Middle class Americans of Mexican lineage, who are frequently distinguished from the immigrant Mexicans by the term "Spanish American"; and (4) Hispanos, as the relatively isolated, rural groups descended from the Spanish colonial settlers are called.

THE MEXICAN IMMIGRANT GROUP IN THE SOUTHWEST

From one viewpoint, the Mexican immigrant should be defined as any foreign born person living in the United States who was born in Mexico. From the point of view of the sociology of minorities, it includes not only the immigrants but all of their native born descendants who are still identified both in their own view and that of the Anglos as of the immigrant group. Viewed in this sense, the Mexican immigrant group today is preponderantly native born. Mexican immigration virtually ceased with the establishment of the Border Patrol in 1929, except for the "wetbacks," the Mexicans who cross the border illegally, often by swimming a river, who do not get caught and deported. An indication of the degrees of native lineage is found in the distribution reported in the special enumeration by the Bureau of the Census in 1940 of all Spanish-speaking people according to Spanish mother tongue. The percentages given were as follows: about 24 per

[13] *Infra.,* pp. 318-319.
[14] Manuel Gamio. *Mexican Immigration to the United States.* (Chicago: University of Chicago Press, 1930) p. 53. By permission.

cent foreign born; about 38 per cent native born of foreign or mixed parentage; and about 38 per cent native born of native parentage.[15]

While, as we have seen, Anglo-Mexican relations have a long history prior to the large-scale immigration, it was not until after 1920 that these relations began to assume the magnitude of a pressing problem. In order to describe the nature of these relations we shall draw upon two of the most extensive of the several studies made, namely, the series of monographs on Mexican labor in the United States by Paul S. Taylor[16] in the late 1920's and a penetrating study undertaken by Ruth Tuck of a Southwestern community in the early 1940's.[17]

In the Southwest, 1927. Taylor studied Anglo-Mexican relations in four different areas in the Southwest. While the carefully drawn picture which is delineated in each of the four areas differs in detail, it is the general picture emerging which we shall outline.

Mexican immigrants in the Southwest found employment in unskilled occupations, chiefly as agricultural laborers. Their wages in common with agricultural labor generally were low and usually lower than that paid any Anglos employed in the same kind of work. Employers often maintained that this differential was justified because Anglo laborers were more productive than Mexican. These Mexican laborers were slow to become unionized and the earlier efforts at organization were opposed strongly by the agricultural employers and were generally unsuccessful. While, by the late 20's an increasing number of the Mexicans were buying or building homes of their own, they did not however buy farm land for themselves and, in the areas where the economy was appropriate, showed little interest in share cropping. Few opportunities existed for Mexicans in higher ranking occupations both because they were not equipped to fill them and because of the discrimination against their employment in occupations involving Anglo fellow workers or serving Anglo trade. Some Mexican clerks were employed in low priced stores for the purpose of encouraging Mexican trade.

The housing of the more settled Mexicans was of the lowest standard; and that of Mexicans employed at the field, of a nondescript

[15] *Mother Tongue of the White Population for States and Large Cities,* Sixteenth Census of the United States, 1940. Population, Series P-15, No. 10.
[16] Paul S. Taylor, *Mexican Labor in the United States* (Berkeley: University of California Press, Publication in Economics, Vol. 6, 1928). In this volume are included three monographs: No. 1 on Imperial Valley, California; No. 2 on Valley of South Platte, Colorado; and No. 5 on Dimmit County, South Texas. Taylor also wrote *An American-Mexican Frontier* (Chapel Hill: University of North Carolina Press, 1934). While Taylor as an economist was primarily interested in the labor situations of the Mexicans, his field of inquiry embraced the general pattern of social relations between the Anglos and Mexicans.
[17] Ruth D. Tuck, *Not With The Fist* (New York: Harcourt, Brace & Company, Inc., 1946).

variety, sometimes hay mows or improvised shelters in the woods. In spite of these low economic conditions, Mexicans were not found often on relief rolls, partly due to their strong habit of mutual aid. Neither did Taylor find evidence that their record of criminal arrests was more than proportionate to their numbers in the population.

The pattern of group relations established distinctly separated the Mexican from the Anglo group in each community. The Mexicans lived apart. Although their low economic status and their desire to be with fellow compatriots in part account for this, the studies clearly indicate that in the case of those few more successful Mexicans who aspired to rent or buy in Anglo areas, where restrictive covenants were not specific, social pressure in the Anglo group kept them out. Keenly sensitive to their not being wanted as neighbors, few Mexicans made the effort to live outside their colony. The social line drawn between the two groups was as sharp as that in housing. An interesting comment cited by Taylor is that of a soda clerk in the Texas border area. "We serve Mexicans at the fountain but not at the tables. We have got to make some distinction between them and the white [sic] people. The Negroes we serve only cones." [18]

The attitude of the Anglo community toward the Mexicans is well illustrated in the sphere of education, about which Taylor found two points of view. The viewpoint represented by the farm employing group is well summarized in the following statement: "The historical tradition of the American farmers and their assumed interest in maintaining an uneducated labor class leads them to an attitude of indifference and even opposition to the education of the persons whom they do not class as whites." [19] An attitude held by other Anglos was that since the Mexicans were in Texas to stay, they would have to be given some education after all. Although some of the Mexicans were qualified for better than menial tasks as a result of the education they had received, Taylor found that better education had not appreciably improved their occupational status.

In short, the picture Taylor draws is that Mexican labor was welcome in the Southwest because it filled a labor need which was not likely to be met by workers of Anglo status at the wages and under the working conditions which the farmers of the Southwest were prepared to provide. The warmth of their welcome was in proportion to their willingness to continue to fill this need without becoming ambitious for something different, and to their willingness to keep their place in matters social. To what extent the situation had

[18] Taylor, *An American-Mexican Frontier, op. cit.,* p. 250.
[19] *Ibid.,* p. 113.

changed in the next 15 years can be seen by turning to Dr. Tuck's study of "Descanso," a Southwestern community in the early 40's.

Descanso: the colonia. Descanso is a small Southwestern city set in fertile valley, half cupped by mountains. It is a railroad junction, surrounded by large-scale farm operations. "Railroads and ranching . . . set the tempo" of its economy. While it lacks the clear-cut ecological pattern of Eastern cities, the tendency is for the east and north sections toward the mountains to be the preferred native residential section. The south section is the delapidated area of shacks and cheap bungalows now inhabited in about equal parts by Mexican-Americans, poor native Americans, and Negroes. It is in the western section, the Monticello district, where the Mexican colony lives. To quote Dr. Tuck:

On both sides of Monticello Avenue, a small Mexican business district has grown up—cafés, grocery stores, *cantinas,* a barber shop, a bakery, a drugstore, and a couple of *tortillerias.* The hiring and provisioning agency for the Santa Fe is also here. Much of the life of the Mexican-American colony centers on this street, and the colony itself is larger, more homogeneous, and more progressive than the smaller group in Spring Valley. The district has one or two Italian families, a few Filipinos, and recently the area has experienced a considerable invasion of Negro families from its east end, close to the railroad tracks. Practically no Anglo-Americans live in the heart of the district, although, toward the north, Mexican-Americans of higher economic status are beginning to occupy houses on streets with Anglo-Americans.[20]

The social life of the colonia is rooted primarily in the family system, secondarily in the church. The family system follows the usual Latin patriarchal form, resembling the Italian pattern previously described; subordination of women, although much reverence for mothers; subordination of children with a differential training of the sexes in line with patriarchal ideals; permanency in family relations; strict parental protection of girls together with a double standard of sex morality. While most Mexicans in Descanso were and are today Catholics, Dr. Tuck feels that the local church does not constitute as important a focus of the life of the Mexican-Americans as it does in Mexico. In practice, the males scarcely ever go to church. "The most admired and influential man in the colony is non-Catholic. . . . . Another outstanding and respected man is a frank, effective critic of the Church." [21] The Church made no effort to adapt itself to the changed situation. It made few attempts to offer recreational facilities to youth or cultural stimulation for the adults.

[20] Tuck, *op. cit.,* p. 5. By permission of the publishers, Harcourt, Brace & Company, Inc.
[21] *Ibid.,* p. 153.

"Most of the social life of the *colonia* is essentially informal in nature." [22] The proliferation of societies, clubs, and associations which distinguishes American life has not yet intruded on the *colonia*. The friends of the Mexicans are their relatives but the number of kin of each family is extensive enough to provide a wide circle of friends. There is one large men's organization, the Confederation of Mexican Societies, a council of four mutual insurance groups, coordinating their efforts. Its chief activity is to celebrate two Mexican national holidays. It rather vaguely acts for the "economic, moral, and cultural improvement of the Mexican people." [23] Its constitution specifically restricts any civic activity which is political in nature. From time to time, other organizations arose more definitely political in nature. However, "most of them have had brief, fitful lives."

Descanso's *colonia* falls into a two-class division: the "big people" and their satellites; and the commoner folk. "The top group contains some persons whose origins in Mexico were 'folk,' many quasi immigrants whose parents had such origins, and an increasing number of second generation persons who have risen within the structure of the *colonia*." [24] The criteria of class mobility are much the same as with other people with one exception. Higher education, higher status occupations, money, service to the group, raise one's status. The exception seems to be pride in being a Mexican. To quote Dr. Tuck:

This self-respecting pride in one's background and origins strikes a rather new note in American immigrant histories. The man who changed his name, denied his background, and was ashamed of the old folks with the accented English and foreign ways is a commonplace type among other immigrant groups. He is a distinct rarity among Mexican-Americans, except for some badly confused adolescents; and his actions, rather than being admired as a hallmark of success are described as "his misfortune," as though he had a strange affliction. "Assimilation! I am tired of that word," said one of the *colonia's* leaders. "Fusion is what we want—the best of both ways." A young American of Mexican descent, speaking at a club luncheon, was told by a gentleman of Swedish ancestry: "We Scandinavians get ahead because we dropped our old-country ways." "Perhaps that was your misfortune," was the reply.[25]

How does the native community react toward these Mexicans? Broadly speaking, they exhibit all the characteristic dominant group attitudes and discriminations, applied "not with the fist" but in all other possible ways. Examples quoted are:

[22] *Ibid.*, p. 157.
[23] *Ibid.*, p. 160.
[24] *Ibid.*, p. 133.
[25] *Ibid.*, p. 134. By permission of the publishers, Harcourt, Brace & Company, Inc.

"I'm for giving everybody a fair chance, but will you tell me what good it does to educate the average Mexican? They just don't take to it." (A native businessman)

"Of course, I pride myself on my tolerance, but I simply won't have my daughters attending a youth center where there are Mexicans." (A club-woman)

"Sure, I'm hiring skilled Mexicans now. I've got a war contract and I have to . . . But I'm not going to have them after the war. A Mexican's a darned good worker, but you don't want to have too many of them around in top positions." (An employer)

"This town will never stand for Mexicans in the same pool with white kids. Okies? But Okies are white." (A public official.) [26]

While there are Mexican-Americans who can honestly say that they have never encountered any of the cruder forms of discrimination and others who experience them only infrequently, still, "it is safe to say that the entire population . . . is aware of barriers against it." [27]

A young college graduate said—"Discrimination? Of course, all of my life, since I was a little boy. I make my way, I enjoy myself, I have good Anglo-American friends, in spite of it, but I never forget."

An extremely successful man [Mexican] by colony standards, said: "I don't know why it is, but I've had to fight ever since I first crossed the threshold of a public school. Even now, I seldom sit down in a restaurant without expecting the waiter to come up and say, 'Sorry, we can't serve you.' I'm careful to go where I know such things won't happen, but I still half expect them." [28]

What does native Descanso think of its own treatment of Mexicans? To quote Dr. Tuck:

There is nothing Descanso will deny more stoutly than any intention of keeping its Mexican-Americans disadvantaged in order to derive an economic gain from their position. That is why it resents the words caste or semicaste being applied to its practices. Descanso argues, rather, that the bulk of its Mexican-Americans are so low in type that they could not profit by advantage. It seems rather odd to prove this point by making sure that they have continued inferior advantage, but Descanso sees no hint of a vicious circle in this procedure. The "low type" of Mexican, says Descanso, is getting about what he deserves. If he encounters segregated schooling, segregation in use of public facilities, unequal employment opportunities, unequal pay for equal work, or prejudiced law enforcement and justice—what of it? Descanso does not see that, in making these and a thousand other decisions, it is casting a vote that amends, not only the rights and liberties of a certain group, but

[26] *Ibid.*, p. 53. By permission of the publishers, Harcourt, Brace & Company, Inc.
[27] *Ibid.*, p. 52.
[28] *Ibid.*, pp. 52-53. By permission of the publishers, Harcourt, Brace & Company, Inc.

the very nature of its democratic procedure. Descanso would not think of revising a certain historic document so that it guaranteed life, liberty, and the pursuit of happiness somewhat more to "high types" than to "low types." No, says Descanso, we are just making a few social distinctions, several million of which cannot possibly affect a democracy. You have to recognize, argues Descanso, that some people are just born inferior, generation after generation. As the leader of a church study group put it, "there are always hewers of wood and drawers of water." [29]

The status of Mexican-native relations in Descanso just prior to World War II approximated semicaste. While there were no legal restrictions against them, in subtle ways Mexicans were kept in their place. They were never given supervisory positions, or employed as clerks in native stores, or schoolteachers in any but Mexican schools. While no restrictive covenants applied to them, they could seldom buy a house outside the western district. Until a fight was made against it, they were kept out of the public swimming pool. They were never called to serve on juries. Most significant was the school situation. While not officially segregated, sufficient schools were built in the western section to substantially segregate them in elementary grades. As late as 1936, Descanso built a new junior high school in the Monticello area in order to continue Mexican pupils in their segregation. Most Mexican children mixed with middle class natives only in the last three years of school. Under the economic and social handicaps they face, it is small wonder that most of them drop out at sixteen. Thus one of the avenues of assimilation open to most immigrants is less open to Descanso's Mexican-Americans.

Some bridges across the semicaste chasm were, however, apparent. They seem to have arisen during World War II. Employment opportunity rose during the war largely in terms of higher wages and more varied occupation, rather than in upgrading. Unionization of the steel mills started a new way of economic thinking among Descanso's Mexican-Americans. Some conciliatory moves were made by the native community. The display of signs reading "white trade only" was made illegal; some Mexicans were drawn on juries. On the whole, however, the fight to improve their civic position was not too successful since the Mexican-Americans were sadly lacking in experience in political activity. While 78 per cent of the individuals in the *colonia* were citizens, most of them were so by birth. On the whole Descanso's Mexican-Americans have not succumbed to typical machine political manipulation. According to Dr. Tuck, they are incredibly "lily white" but on the whole too naive. They fail to realize their own potential political power.

[29] *Ibid.,* pp. 53-54. By permission of the publishers, Harcourt, Brace & Company, Inc.

If the strides made during the war are to be capitalized on, it will probably result from the leadership of GI's of Mexican extraction back from service. On this Dr. Tuck writes:

There is scarcely a home in the *colonia* which did not have a son in service; many had three or more. The big families the social workers used to frown on have their uses in time of war. By and large, the experiences of the *colonia's* youth in the services have been satisfying ones. Unlike Negro youth, they have not found, in uniform, a denial of the democracy for which they are asked to fight. Few are commissioned officers, but many have had the satisfaction of working up to the top of noncommissioned ranks. They have made close friends among Anglo-Americans. They have, in some cases, married into Anglo-American families from other parts of the country and have found that the social prejudices of Descanso did not exist. They have found that they can do things well, that they can command and take responsibility. Even the misfits and comparative failures feel that they have been judged, not as "Mexicans," but as individual men, by the same standards as other men. The successful have had the heady experience of accomplishment free of the tag "pretty good for a Mexican." They are, as they say, "all steamed up." [30]

Discrimination against Mexicans in the Southwest. The story of Descanso clearly attests the minority status of Mexicans at the present time. That Descanso is typical of the Southwest, except for New Mexico, is further evidenced by considering differential treatment accorded Mexicans in other localities in the areas of employment and education, in the securing of justice and civil liberties, and in social life generally.

Employment. Data from a Texas survey in 1945 confirm the persistence of discrimination in regard to employment.

In the spring of 1945, the President's committee on Fair Employment Practices ordered the Shell Oil Company to upgrade three Latin Americans on the basis of seniority, in its Deer Park Refinery. The contract between the Shell and the union relegated Latin Americans to certain types of jobs, and their opportunities for advancement under the contract were greatly inferior to those of Anglo American employees. The FEPC not only ordered the upgrading of the three Latin Americans, but also directed the union and the company to revise their contract so as to comply with the Fair Employment Practices Act . . . the company advanced the three men, whereupon the union . . . went on a wildcat strike in protest. The strike was in violation of the established policy of the oil workers' union, and the CIO International opposed it.

In March, 1946, it was reported that twenty Latin American veterans of World War II had been employed by a Gulf Coast refinery, but at a wage of fifteen cents per hour less than that paid Anglo Americans in the same job classification: Latins, 91 cents per hour; Anglos, $1.06.

[30] *Ibid.,* pp. 220-221. By permission.

. . . the United States Employment Service office in Austin, one day in November, 1945, received a telephone call from a woman department-head at the University of Texas. She expressed the desire to employ a trained secretary-assistant and was told that, fortunately, the application of a young lady who possessed all the required qualifications had just been received and that she held a degree from the University of Texas. The prospective employer was delighted, and inquired as to the girl's name. When informed that it was "Martinez," she exclaimed: "Why, I wouldn't have a Mexican in my office! I want a white girl!" [31]

Education. Typically, Mexican children have been segregated in their schooling, although the line has never been drawn as consistently as for Negroes in the Deep South. According to a Texas study, although there was no official state policy for segregating Mexican school children, in fact it was found that "nine school districts provided separate housing facilities for the first two grades, 16 provided them throughout the third grade, 23 through the fourth, 13 through the fifth, 27 through the sixth, 13 through the seventh, 17 through the eighth, one through the ninth, one through the tenth, and two through the twelfth." [32] While the superintendents tried to justify this quasi-segregation on the familiar grounds that the Mexican children do not know enough English to keep up with the others and that "they feel more at ease" among their own kind, many of them frankly told Dr. Little that the main reason was the prejudice of the Anglo-Americans. How these prejudices often express themselves is indicated in the following interesting example:

In June, 1944, in a south Texas High School, a Latin-American boy and an Anglo-American girl were running a close race for the honor of being valedictorian . . . The competition was keen, and it appeared certain the boy would win, whereupon the principal . . . was warned that if he allowed a "Mexican" to become valedictorian, he would be discharged. During the final week of school the girl brought up her grades sufficiently to win the honor, but the principal resigned his position immediately after the close of the session.[33]

Civil Rights. Mexicans who are citizens are, in general, not denied the right to vote but the poll tax, their low economic status, and their own cultural inadequacy for political participation all conspire to make them singularly ineffective in Texas and California politics. The

[31] Pauline R. Kibbe, *Latin Americans in Texas* (Albuquerque: University of New Mexico Press, 1946). By permission. The excerpts quoted above are selected among the many others cited on pages 161-164. Much of the data in this volume resulted from a survey made in 1943 and 1944 under the auspices of the Good Neighbor Commission of Texas. The author of the volume cited was executive secretary to the Commission.
[32] *Ibid.*, p. 96. Kibbe has taken these data from Wilson Little, *Spanish-Speaking Children in Texas* (Austin: University of Texas Press, 1944). By permission.
[33] Kibbe, *op. cit.*, p. 92. By permission.

Anglos often try to make their political growth as difficult as possible. "For example, in four Texas counties qualified voters of Mexican extraction are not allowed to participate in the Democratic primaries, by virtue of a so-called "White Man's Union," which prohibits both Negroes and Latin Americans from entering the polls." [34]

The treatment encountered by Mexicans when they run afoul of the law illustrates the general proposition, which we shall see starkly revealed in the case of Negroes, that a people possessing minority status frequently receive differential and unequal justice even though the letter of the law gives this no sanction. Mexicans in court face almost invariably an all-Anglo jury. In an estimated fifty Texas counties with large Mexican populations, persons of Mexican descent have never been known to be called for jury service.[35] Kibbe cites one county (30 per cent Mexican) where a Latin American was indicted for killing an Anglo by an all-Anglo grand jury. After the first trial jury called failed to show one Mexican, the defense attorney moved to quash the indictment on the grounds that never in the history of the county had a citizen of Mexican descent been called to jury service. "Rather than establish the precedent of allowing a Latin American to serve on either a grand jury or a trial jury, the authorities released the accused. . . . . [36] Hart Stilwell writing about a case in which an Anglo is acquitted of murdering a Texas-Mexican felt certain that if the roles had been reversed or if both men had been Latin Americans, the verdict would have been different. He goes on further to write:

> What happened in this case is typical of what has been happening in Texas courts for a hundred years or more—twenty-five years to my personal knowledge. I have been a newspaper man in Texas for twenty-five years and I have carefully watched criminal cases in which members of the two races were involved. And if an Anglo-American has served one day in the penitentiary for the killing of a Latin-American during that period of time, I have not heard of it . . .[37]

While there are no city ordinances to this effect, restrictive covenants are included in real estate contracts which "ordinarily prohibit the transfer of property to, or occupation thereof, 'by Negroes, Mexicans, or Chinese.' " [38] Miss Tuck quotes a Descanso Mexican college student:

> One of the first things I remember is the time we tried to rent a house just north of here. We'd been there two weeks when the agent came around to

[34] *Ibid.,* p. 227.
[35] *Ibid.,* p. 229.
[36] *Ibid.,* p. 229.
[37] *The Texas Spectator,* October 11, 1946, cited by McWilliams, *North from Mexico,* p. 273. Also see Kibbe, *op. cit.,* pp. 226-232. By permission.
[38] *Ibid.,* p. 229.

say that we'd have to move at the end of the month—the neighbors had protested to the owner.[39]

These invisible housing bars are not airtight. In Descanso, 50 families of Mexican extraction live outside the *colonia*. Some are "Spanish" Mexicans who have always lived outside the *colonia*. A few are, however, of immigrant status. Once a single Mexican family settles in an Anglo neighborhood, they are frequently given friendly treatment; but if they are followed by other Mexican families, friction begins to arise.

Again conforming to the pattern of dominant discrimination, Mexicans are frequently denied equal access to public places and facilities, though not so frequently and systematically as in the case of Negroes in the South. Kibbe sums up the point thus:

> The one-syllable answer to the question "Are Latin Americans refused service in public places of business and amusement in Texas?" would have to be "yes." But in order to be truthful, . . . that reply must be modified by the addition of the phrases "some Latin Americans" are refused service in "some places of business" in "some Texas towns." At the same time it is admitted that in some rural and semirural communities, Anglo-American operators of cafes, beer parlors, barber shops, and theaters are adamant in refusing service to any and all Latin Americans.[40]

The welfare of Mexican-Americans. In the measurable indices of welfare, Mexicans in the United States rank close to the lowest in comparison with other minority groups. This lowly position is greatly affected by the large number of Mexicans employed as migratory, agricultural workers. Although there have been improvements, this form of work is still recognized as one of the problem areas of the American economy. How low the income and the standard of living in this occupation were in the period prior to World War II can be illustrated by a special study in south Texas. The average income of 300 Crystal City families primarily engaged in harvesting spinach, cotton, sugar beets, and onions was $506.00 in 1938. Making allowances for a small average additional income in cash and kind, the report concludes, "Since the families averaged 5.5 persons, the average yearly income among the Mexican migrants was approximately $100.00 per person in 1938." [41]

As one might expect, the low family income and the unsatisfactory working conditions of the Mexican workers are further reflected in their housing, health, and in their educational opportunities.

[39] Tuck, *op. cit.*, p. 201.
[40] Kibbe, *op. cit.*, p. 208. By permission.
[41] Kibbe, *op. cit.*, p. 198. Data taken from Selden C. Menefee, *Mexican Migratory Workers in South Texas* (Washington: Federal Works Agency, Works Progress Administration, U. S. Government Printing Office, 1941), p. 37.

Turning first to housing, several studies reveal the typical *colonia* homes to be well below minimum standards.

North Town [southern California] . . . is a fairly typical *colonia*. Located on the site of an abandoned subdivision . . . Today some 1,500 Mexicans live in the six square blocks of North Town. . . .

With as many as three shacks to a lot, the structures are unpainted, weather-beaten, and dilapidated. The average house consists of two or three rooms and was built of scrap lumber, boxes, and discarded odds-and-ends of material. Ten, twenty, and thirty years old, the houses are extremely clean and neat on the inside and much effort has obviously gone into an effort to give them an attractive appearance. Virtually all the homes lack inside toilets and baths and a large number are without electricity.[42]

A Works Progress Administration study in 1938 provides the following glimpse of living conditions for Latin Americans in a Texas rural area.

The Mexican sections of Crystal City form a large semirural slum. More than half of the Mexicans own their houses or shacks, but most of the dwellings in the Mexican quarter are crudely built and in very bad repair. Few have electricity or plumbing. The houses are badly overcrowded; there was an average of 2.6 persons per room at the time of the survey.[43]

In regard to health, the low welfare index of Mexicans is attested in such data as follows:

. . . The 1944 statistics of the Texas State Department of Health . . . indicate a tuberculosis death rate among Anglo-Americans of 31 per 100,000 population; among Negroes, of 95 per 100,000; and among Latin Americans, of 209 per 100,000.[44]

According to statistics furnished by Dr. Lewis C. Robbins of the San Antonio Health Department, the number of live births among Latin and Anglo-Americans during the five-year period 1940–1944 were about equally divided, despite the fact that the city's residents of Mexican descent comprise only 33 1/3 per cent to 40 per cent of the population. But the number of infant deaths were far from being equally divided. The number of infant deaths for Anglos, 781; and for Latins, 2,295. Again for San Antonio, 1942–1944 inclusive, the number of maternal deaths for Anglos, 14; for Mexicans, 77.[45]

In a booklet, entitled *The Latin-American Health Problem in Texas,* published by the Texas State Health Department, 1940, reference was made to death rate from diarrhea. Texas counties with a Latin-American population of more than 20 per cent showed a death rate from diarrhea in children under two years of age of 85.1 per 100,000 population, or more than eight times the death rate from

[42] McWilliams, *North From Mexico,* p. 218. By permission.
[43] Kibbe, *op. cit.,* p. 125, from Menefee, *op. cit.,* p. 15.
[44] *Ibid.,* p. 126. By permission.
[45] *Ibid.,* p. 131. By permission.

that cause in the remainder of the state; the rate in counties with from 50 to 60 per cent Latin-American population was 129.4.[46]

Inadequate schooling for Mexican Americans is indicated by the tabulated reports of school superintendents in Texas for the fiscal year 1942–43 which revealed that only 53 per cent of the Latin-American children were enrolled in the public schools. Of the remainder only about 10 per cent were accounted for through parochial schools.[47]

Mexican immigrants outside the Southwest. Today clusters from the Mexican immigrant group are found scattered throughout Midwestern industrial centers, Chicago, Detroit, and Saint Paul notably. The 75,000 of these people now found in Lorain, Ohio, represent a great growth from the original 1500 imported from Texas by a tube company and like most Northern immigrant groups the subsequent generations are being assimilated.[48] Migratory Mexicans are frequently drawn to the cities, and remain there rather than return to their former Southwestern homes.

In general in the industrial areas of the North, Mexicans appear to be treated much as any other immigrant group has been. While as the latest entering group possessing few industrial skills, they occupy low economic status, they do not seem to encounter any "special Mexican" discrimination such as that met with in the Southwest. Since their numbers are usually not proportionately great in any one community, they tend to mix more with other working class groups, and thus their acculturation is accelerated. McWilliams writes, "Archbishop Mooney in Detroit has strongly discouraged the development of group-consciousness among his Mexican parishioners." [49] A Minnesota survey states that "Facts and figures indicate . . . that the movement toward integration of the Mexican into Minnesota life, while it may be slow, is a steady one." Again, the same report after noting that "Many Minnesota Mexicans are of pure, or nearly pure, Indian descent, and very dark in color," goes on to conclude, "the Mexican does not seem to encounter . . . extensive discrimination based upon skin color." [50]

TRENDS AND PROSPECTS IN MEXICAN-ANGLO RELATIONS

In the past 20 years, the amount of new immigration from Mexico has been negligible compared with that which occurred from 1910 to

[46] *Ibid.*, p. 130.
[47] *Ibid.*, p. 86.
[48] McWilliams, *North From Mexico*, p. 222.
[49] *Ibid.*, p. 222.
[50] *The Mexican in Minnesota*, Report by the Governor's Interracial Commission, (St. Paul: August 15, 1948), pp. 60-61.

1930. The majority of Latins in the United States are now native born, and the proportion of foreign born is decreasing each year. It has been shown that with other immigrant groups assimilation generally occurs by the grandchild generation. Yet in the case of Mexicans, the process is already retarded and there are no clear-cut signs that their assimilation will ever be complete. If we attempt to summarize the factors which lie in the background of their retarded status, two factors perhaps distinguish them only in imperceptible degree from at least other Latin immigrants from Europe: (1) their peasant, nonliterate cultural background; and (2) their conspicuous lack of political adaptability, thus preventing them from exercising the potential political power, which their numbers warrant, to improve their conditions. In addition, a number of other factors and circumstances differentiate them from other minorities in the United States: (3) the recency of their immigration in large numbers; (4) their entrance into the Southwest with its long history of Anglo-assumed superiority over the Mexican and of Anglo violence and exploitation in dealing with Mexicans; (5) their high admixture of Indian blood; and (6) their original occupational concentration as agricultural laborers, very frequently migratory.

The broad picture of Anglo-Mexican relations in the decade 1940–50 was one of Mexicans accommodated to American life as a minority with no certain prospects of losing this status. This is a somewhat disconcerting picture in view of two of the basic theses of this book which will be tested as we move from one minority to another. One thesis is that no dominant-minority relations can be frozen at any level in 20th century United States; another, that the over-all trend of change is toward the removal of minority status from all. Looking again at the present scene one observes signs that Anglo-Mexican relations are changing and in the direction of greater equality.

Marginality and disorganization: symptom of change. From the analysis of the process of assimilation as presented in Chapter 4, we have learned that movement from accommodation to marginality characteristically involves an increasing degree of disorganization. During this stage the problems for the community are heightened, and, provided the barriers to assimilation are not insurmountable, they are temporary. In broader perspective, this type of disorganization is an indication that the pattern of relations is not frozen, that change in the direction of assimilation is taking place.

There are some indications that the amount of delinquency and adult crime among the Mexican-Americans began to increase around 1940, although to no alarming degree. In Descanso "the number of arrests of juveniles of Mexican extraction is large, compared to the proportion of the population their group represents." [51] The "zoot suit" riots in Los Angeles in 1942, much overpublicized and exaggerated, are likewise manifestations of the growing pains accruing to marginal status. Bogardus in his analysis of gangs of Mexican youth in Los Angeles puts their significance in proper perspective by indicating that perhaps 1,000 out of about 35,000 Mexican youth in the city ages 6 to 17 were members of juvenile gangs, and a small portion of these were members of Pachuco gangs, as the older groups and those more inclined to delinquency were called.[52] The causes for the formation of these gangs and their behavior follows the exact pattern found in every American urban slum. There is nothing peculiarly Mexican about it. The factors underlying it are the physical sordidness of the environment of the areas of residence, the growing inability of parents to control their children; lack of interest in school because of the handicaps which put them behind; the special handicaps they face in getting work; and the lack of adequate wholesome recreational outlets.

The differences in the problems of young Mexican gangs as well as all the youth of the group arise out of their relatively higher visibility and therefore the more definite character of their minority status. The evidence is clear that in some of the most serious clashes between "zoot suit" Mexican youth and Anglos, it was the Anglos who precipitated the riots by attacking the Mexicans. Because of the minority status of the Mexicans, however, the reaction of the community at large was to presume the Mexicans guilty; to exaggerate the prevalence of delinquent behavior among all Mexican youth; and to apply abnormally drastic penalties to the Mexican participants, and light or no punishment to Anglos involved.

The effect of World War II. World War II opened up for the Mexican minority new avenues of employment and increasing unionization leading toward higher status. Higher wages and more regular employment also improved their welfare. The continued education of Mexican children even though frequently unequal and segregated, nevertheless moved them toward assimilation. The experiences of Mexican-American veterans of World War II broadened their horizons and left them less willing to accept supinely minority status in civilian life. Of Miss Tuck's many illustrations of the effect of GI experience, the following is illustrative:

A discharged private in the infantry said: "I'm glad I'm going to have one of those little buttons to wear in my coat. And a flock of foliage to put on my

[51] Tuck, *op. cit.*, p. 213.
[52] Emory S. Bogardus, "Gangs of Mexican Youth," *Sociology and Social Research,* Vol. 28, Sept. 1945, pp. 55-56.

uniform for Armistice Day parades. I'm going into politics. There's seven or eight of us, all from Southern California, who've talked it over. Things are going to happen in these colonies, and we're going to see that they do." [53]

Changes in Anglo attitudes. Even more significant sign of change in Anglo-Mexican relations is the increasing recognition by Anglos that the traditional situation cannot be permanently frozen. Increasingly throughout the Southwest, local communities are forming intercultural committees to improve relations. In Texas, a Good Neighbor Commission has been established, one of the fruits of which is the survey frequently quoted in this chapter. The Commission's report closed with elaborate recommendations for action. The formation of the Southern California Council on Inter-American Affairs and the holding of numerous conferences to deal with these intergroup relations at various places in the Southwest portend an increasing sentiment toward assimilating Mexicans. It is significant to note that this sudden blossoming of Anglo interest in improving the status of their Mexican people occurred during World War II and received much stimulation from the Office of the Coordinator of Inter-American Affairs, a Federal agency.

Federal Court decisions end school segregation. Two recent decisions rendered by Federal Courts in the Southwest have definitely established the illegality of the practice of segregating children of Mexican extraction in public schools and have specifically forced its abandonment in California and Texas.

The Mendez Case. In 1945, Gonzalo Mendez, a moderately prosperous asparagus grower of Mexican immigrant extraction in Westminister, Orange County, California, joined with Mexican-Americans in filing suit against the school officials of the county for maintaining a segregated school which all children of Spanish-speaking background were required to attend. While there was no specific statute regarding this matter, the practice of segregation was widespread throughout the region. The judgment of the court supported the petitioners. The Court said:

By enforcing the segregation of school children of Mexican descent against their will and contrary to the laws of California, respondents [school officials] have violated the Federal law as provided in the Fourteenth Amendment to the Federal Constitution by depriving them of liberty and property without the due process of law and by denying to them the equal protection of the laws.[54]

[53] Tuck, *op. cit.,* p. 221.
[54] From a reprint of the *Mendez Case,* Ninth U. S. Circuit Court of Appeals, Judge Stephen's Opinion and Judge Denman's Concurrence, No. 11,310, April 14, 1947.

The Delgado Case. A similar action led by Minerva Delgado, who was joined by other parents of Mexican immigrant extraction, was filed against the officials of the school district of Bastrop County, Texas, and others in 1948. The District Court of the United States in the Western District of Texas rendered a decision likewise invoking the Fourteenth Amendment, and ordered: "The defendants . . . are hereby permanently restrained and enjoined from segregating pupils of Mexican or other Latin American descent in separate schools or classes . . ."[55] The Court made one exception. It permitted the maintaining of separate classes for the first grade only for students who have been in school less than one year and who clearly demonstrate that they do not understand enough English to perform first grade work. This exception is constructively helpful for the child who knows little English in adjusting to the American school system. The Texas State Board of Education on May 8, 1950 specifically directed compliance with this Federal ruling throughout the state.

Contract labor and "wetbacks." Recent developments reveal the persistent connection between the problem of migrant farm work and the problem of Mexican immigration. While few visas are granted now for permanent entry into the United States from Mexico, the recruitment of Mexican nationals to pick the crops of a particular season has since 1942 been permitted under contract, the terms of which are agreed on yearly by the government of the United States and that of Mexico. The agreements which have been made since that date have specified minimum wages, minimum living and working conditions, and other benefits which are more advantageous to the workers than those of previous years. The purposes of such agreements are to furnish needed labor when the domestic supply is inadequate, to protect the Mexican nationals from exploitation, and to protect the standard of living of the domestic migrant labor force. A spokesman for the National Farm Labor Union has recently protested that while such agreements have been advantageous to the Mexican nationals, relative to conditions in Mexico, it has nevertheless failed to protect domestic farm labor. For example, the intergovernmental agreement reached in 1949 called for a minimum wage scale of 60 cents an hour which the union maintains was from 20 to 30 cents an hour lower than the rate prevailing in California at the time. Again, while the agreements specifically prohibit the displacement of domestic workers by such contract labor, the union's position is that "Displacement, nevertheless, has been, and is taking place on a large scale where, as

[55] From the Final Judgment, No. 388 Civil District Court of the United States, Western District of Texas. *Minerva Delgado et al v. Bastrop Independent School District of Bastrop County, et al.*

in California, nationals and legalized 'wetbacks' are given jobs at lower wages when domestic labor refuses to work for these wages." [56]

Further related to the same problem has been the increase in the number of illegal entries of Mexican "wetbacks" since the close of World War II. The report of the Border Patrol for 1949 states that since 1944 "each year the number of Mexican farm laborers entering the United States is alarmingly larger than the previous year." [57] That this source of labor supply is agreeable to many farm owners is further indicated by the following passage from the same report: "Some of the farmers frankly state they prefer the illegal entrant to the American citizen laborer. They can pay him practically any wage they may desire, have to furnish the very least of living facilities, and can, in the majority of cases, control the movement of such aliens by threatening them with action by the immigrant service." [58]

Finally, it is pertinent to point out that the interrelation of the migrant labor problem and the problem of minorities goes beyond Anglo-Mexican relations, since Filipinos, Puerto Ricans, and Negroes are likewise major sources of seasonal farm laborers.

In summary, it may be seen that the present position of the group of Spanish-speaking people whom we have called the Mexican immigrant group is in flux. The relatively static pattern of accommodation on a dominant-minority basis was unsettled by the conditions of World War II. In the postwar period the direction of change has been toward increasing acculturation and decreasing discrimination, although the process is slow.

HISPANOS

Included in the population of the Southwest are those Spanish-speaking people who are descended from Spanish-Mexican lineage indigenous to the area at the time of annexation, some of whose ancestry goes back to the 16th century. In view of the general statistical confusion concerning Americans of Latin ancestry, their numbers and proportion are difficult to establish. It is, however, clear that in New Mexico and southern Colorado a large proportion of the Spanish-speaking people derive from this Hispano lineage as distinct from im-

[56] Report of the Address of Ernesto Galarzo, "Mexican–United States Labor Relations and Problems" at the Fourth Regional Conference of the Southwest Council on Education of Spanish-Speaking People, Albuquerque, January 23–25, 1950.
[57] U. S. Immigration and Naturalization Service, *Annual Report*, 1949, "The Border Patrol," pp. 30-38.
[58] *Ibid.*, p. 32. The persistent nature of the problem of illegal ("wetback") immigration of Mexican nationals into the agricultural labor force of the Southwest is attested by Gladwyn Hill, in a series of articles in *The New York Times*, March 26–29 inclusive, 1951.

migrant Mexican lineage, whereas in Texas and Southern California the situation is roughly reversed.

In New Mexico. Hispanos in New Mexico number approximately 200,000 and comprise about half the population of the state. There are seven counties where they number more than 80 per cent of the population. Both Spanish and English are official languages in the state. Compared with the obvious minority status of immigrant Mexicans in other southwestern states, Hispanos do not appear at first to be a minority at all. They are all citizens and no efforts are made by Anglos to deny them civic privileges. All over New Mexico there are Hispanos who participate actively in politics and in counties where they predominate heavily they frequently run the government. Free and equal access to all public places is accorded all ethnic and racial elements—the Indians, the relatively few immigrant Mexicans, as well as the Hispanos. In the entire southwest region, New Mexico exhibits the least "racial" intolerance. The reason for New Mexico's distinctiveness in this connection appears to lie in the fact that through a long part of the state's history as United States territory, Anglos were a distinct numerical minority, and that, therefore, a pattern of racial tolerance was developed at the outset of Anglo-Hispano contact which has over the years been strengthened by tradition. Anglo-Hispano relations in New Mexico show interesting similarity to haole (white) relations with the "colored" races in Hawaii (see Ch. 13). But beneath the surface of this substantial intergroup harmony lie subtle discriminations against the Spanish speaking of middle-class status; and the pitifully low welfare status of the lower class, largely rural, Hispanos.

Rural Hispanos: "forgotten people." In rural New Mexico live an Hispano folk whom Sanchez calls "forgotten people." [59] Relatively isolated for generations, these rural Hispano folk developed a "folk" community life based upon a subsistence, noncommercial agricultural economy organized on semicommunal lines. Over the years since annexation, the encroachment of Anglo "big business" agriculture has whittled down the size of their domain so that their economic resources coupled with their outmoded techniques have brought them to a pitifully low economic level. Their culture has not changed so much in its traditional character; rather, it has deteriorated as a result of their unequal struggle to survive in a modern civilization. Their low welfare status is reflected in New Mexico's statistics on health and literacy. The

[59] George I. Sanchez, *Forgotten People* (Albuquerque: University of New Mexico Press, 1940).

state has a death rate of 13.8, almost 3 more deaths per 1000 population than the nation at large. Its percentage of illiteracy in 1930 was 13.3, placing it third from the lowest when compared with other states.[60]

The native, rural Hispano New Mexicans are not so much discriminated against, in the usual dominant-minority sense, as they are neglected. They have been exploited in the impersonal ways characteristic of the free enterprise system where groups are unequally able to compete. But the Anglos have not assailed their culture. In this particular instance, Anglo toleration of their indigenous culture by ignoring its people, while consistent with democratic principles means, in fact, increasing disaster for the Hispanos themselves, and generally retards progress for New Mexico as a state. The situation of these rural New Mexicans presents interesting comparison with that of the Indians. The new Indian policy adopted in 1934 aimed to integrate the Indians of the United States into American society by encouraging them to retain as much of their tribal culture intact as is consistent with the development of modern economic practices necessary to self-reliant survival; and to provide the necessary special assistance through the Indian Service until such time as they can stand alone without help. The rural Hispanos need special assistance as much as the Indians. The culture of the Hispanos while not as "primitive" as most Indian cultures is scarcely more suited, at least in its economic aspects, for survival without aid. Social policy in the case of these people calls for special assistance, and since their plight is a matter of regional and national concern, calls for joint federal-state planning in terms of their specific needs, economic planning, increased educational opportunity, and improved health facilities. In a plea for such a social policy Sanchez writes:

. . . the generally inferior status held by the native New Mexican today is, in large measure, a result of the failure of the United States to recognize the special character of the social responsibility it assumed when it brought these people forcibly into the American society. Granting them technical citizenship did not discharge that responsibility. The legal right to "life, liberty and the pursuit of happiness" is an empty privilege when the bare essentials of Americanism and of social welfare are wanting.[61]

. . . the ultimate goal . . . is the proper incorporation of the New Mexican into the American fold. That incorporation requires that the New Mexican be fitted to make his contributions to American civilization. His ability to contribute . . . is suggested by the tenacity with which he has maintained himself . . . on this forbidding frontier for more than three centuries. That contribution might well embody . . . [his] language, music, folklore, architecture, food, crafts, and customs. [His] filial respect, his love of home and of

[60] *Ibid.*, pp. 29-33. Also see McWilliams, *Brothers Under the Skin*, pp. 131-132.
[61] Sanchez, *Forgotten People*, p. 40. By permission.

country, and his fortitude in the face of adversity are potential resources to Americanism. The democracy inherent in New Mexican culture bespeaks these peoples' preparedness to enhance American life.

Girded with good health, economic security, social self-sufficiency, education, and the ability to compete for a living wherever he may be, the New Mexican . . . need no longer be a problem child, a culturally unassimilated subject, but a respected and self-respecting American . . .[62]

Spanish-Americans. In the midst of the southwestern tradition of Anglo superiority over Latins and Indians, reinforced by the wave of Mexican immigration, the Spanish-speaking people who possess or aspire to middle or upper occupational and economic class status, tried to maintain, with some degree of success, the distinction of being "Spanish," not Mexican. Actually they have considerable basis for claiming to be different from, though not necessarily superior to, immigrant Mexicans. Some of them have descended from the upper class Spanish-Mexican of preannexation days, others have risen from more humble origins to higher educational and economic status and are not sociologically identifiable with the present Mexican or Hispano group structures. Certainly in New Mexico they do not incur the usual disabilities of a clearly defined minority. Nevertheless, they do face subtle discriminations by Anglos in the area of "social" life. Of this McWilliams says: "Most of the service clubs in New Mexico . . . systematically exclude Spanish-Americans . . . The fraternities and sororities at the University of New Mexico draw a sharp line against Hispano students . . . Spanish-speaking students do not, as a rule, attend school dances. . . ." [63]

Outside of New Mexico, where these higher status people live in communities with large immigrant Mexican populations, the relations of the Spanish-Americans with the latter are ambivalent. On the one hand, their attempt to be "Spanish," and therefore superior to Mexicans, creates hostility between the two Latin elements; on the other hand, Anglo discrimination against both groups creates a bond of common interest. Thus, the middle class, Spanish-speaking person appears to occupy a status of marginality in some degree comparable to that of middle-class Jews in Northern cities.

TOPICS FOR DISCUSSION AND PROJECTS

1. Do you think the story of the adjustment of Mexican immigrants to the United States would have been any different if the immigrants had migrated to the great industrial regions of the Midwest and Northeast during the twenties? Develop your answer.

[62] *Ibid.*, pp. 97, 98. By permission.
[63] McWilliams, *North from Mexico*, p. 79.

2. Often Spanish-speaking Americans prefer to live in communities where there is no Mexican immigrant group. What reasons would you advance for this preference?

3. Do you think the Southwest as a region would be more prosperous or less prosperous if there had been no Mexican immigration during this century?

4. What reasons would you suggest for the fact that some employers prefer "wetbacks" to Mexican-Americans better adjusted to life in the States?

5. Discuss the significance of the relations of Anglos to persons of Mexican origin in the United States to the achievement of Pan-American solidarity in international affairs.

SUGGESTED READING

Gamio, Manuel. *The Mexican Immigrant: His Life Story.* Chicago: University of Chicago Press, 1931.
> *Analysis of the adjustment of Mexican immigrants to the United States in the decade 1920–1930 through the medium of personal life stories.*

Humphrey, Norman D. "The Housing and Household Practices of Detroit Mexicans", *Social Forces,* Vol. 21, No. 4, 1946, pp. 433–437.
> *Describes the acculteration of Mexican families to Northern industrial urban life.*

Leonard, Olen, and Loomis, C. P. "Culture of a Contemporary Rural Community, El Cerrito, New Mexico", Rural Life Series, No. 1. Washington, D.C.: United States Department of Agriculture, Bureau of Agricultural Economics, 1941.
> *A single community study of the Hispanos of New Mexico showing the persistence of group solidarity in the face of economic decline.*

McWilliams, Carey. *North From Mexico.* Philadelphia: J. B. Lippincott Company, 1949, Peoples of America Series.
> *Covers the entire history of the relations between Anglos and people of Mexican descent living in the United States, in a short popularly written book.*

Sanchez, George I. "Pachucos in the Making", *Common Ground,* Vol. 4, No. 1, 1943–1944, autumn 1943, pp. 13–20.
> *The writer finds "Pachucos" are the product of Anglo discrimination and documents extensively the practice of discrimination against Spanish-speaking Americans.*

Taylor, Paul S. *An American-Mexican Frontier.* Chapel Hill: University of North Carolina Press, 1932.
> *A study of Anglo-Mexican relations in a Texas border county. The most sociological of Taylor's specific community studies.*

PART THREE

White-Colored Relations

Similar in many ways to the previous pattern and process of dominant-minority interaction has been the relation of those immigrant peoples who came from the Orient to the native white Americans. In their case, however, the most important difference affecting their assimilation has been their Mongoloid features, vaguely summed up in the white mental complex as yellow or brown. Since this racial visibility is hereditary and since there has been no extensive amount of intermarriage with the native population, the retaining of this physical visibility has retarded their assimilation, even though their acculturation has advanced to the point where the native born of these groups are now far more American than Oriental. Viewing their situation up to the time of World War II one could not have been too confident that their full assimilation would ever take place. As we shall see, the events of the 1940–1950 decade have altered the prospect. The Chinese and Japanese people in the United States are treated in Chapter 7.

In the case of Americans of Negroid appearance, we face discrimination based upon color visibility in its purest form unmixed with either "foreign" or "pagan" traits. Whatever the American Negro is, he is an all-American product. The aboriginal cultural traits which differentiated the slaves from their masters have long since been attenuated, substantially to the vanishing point, by the impact of their American experience. Because Negro-white relations are so vastly more important than all other minority situations we treat them at greater length in Chapters 8 through 11.

CHAPTER 7

Orientals in the United States

Included in the population of continental United States in 1950 were some 300,000 persons whose lineage can be traced to Asiatic nationalities. A special census study in 1947 estimated the numbers of such groups as indicated in Table 14. Altogether these people constitute only

TABLE 14

Asiatics Living in America, 1947[1]

Japanese	131,000
Chinese	87,000
Other races	60,000
	278,000

0.20 per cent of the total continental population, or one out of every 500 people. However, their relations with the dominant population over the hundred years since they first began to come has been a phenomenon of sociological significance far beyond their numbers. Their treatment by white Americans has had serious repercussions upon international relations between the United States and the Chinese and Japanese governments. The dramatic and tragic story of the evacuation of Japanese from the West Coast in the period following the Japanese attack on Pearl Harbor singularly manifested America's sociological immaturity.

[1] U. S. Bureau of Census, *Estimates of Nonwhite Population of Continental United States, by Race: 1940–1947*, Series P 25, No. 23. In April, 1940, the category "Other Races" comprised the following groups: Filipinos, 45,563; Asiatic Indians, 2405; Koreans, 1711; Polynesians, 657; and other Asiatics, 131.

In broad outline, the interaction of these Oriental immigrants with the native population parallels in the earlier stages that of all native-immigrant interaction. The intensity of the discrimination displayed against them was, however, stronger. While, as has been seen, the subsequent generations of European nationality lineage became assimilated, the Oriental immigrants, up to the time of World War II at least, still remained accommodated only to American society. The basic characteristic which accounts for their inability to assimilate was their continued racial visibility and the reaction of white Americans to it. It is true that in their cultural characteristics the immigrant generations of Orientals differed more markedly from the native American culture than did the European immigrants. But the facility with which the native born generations became acculturated, insofar as the barriers of discrimination permitted, indicates that the basic reason for the continued discrimination was "physiognomic" visibility.

All of these peoples are non-Caucasian—"colored" as American whites refer to them. Except for the Hindus and Polynesians, numerically negligible, they fall under the classification Mongoloid. A description of Mongoloid racial traits was given in Chapter 3. Since, as we have seen, these racial traits bear no necessary relation to cultural attributes or psychological capacities, there is little point in the further elaboration of those traits. To the average American the fact that a person is an Oriental is indicated by yellowish complexion (shading toward brown in the case of Filipinos), the "oblique" eye, and the straight hair.

In this chapter, the story of the relations, first of the Chinese, and second of the Japanese, to the native whites of the mainland will be related and interpreted. The Hawaiian situation in which Orientals figure so prominently will be treated separately in Chapter 13 as a phase of the minority relations accompanying the overseas expansion of the United States. Likewise, treatment of the Filipinos will be held for consideration in the same connection.

THE CHINESE IN THE UNITED STATES

The picture held in the mind of the average American of the Chinese living in this country is probably more compounded of myth and legend than in the case of any other minority. The word "Chinatown" is associated with things exotic, mysterious, curious, and strangely alien to American life. The popular stereotype is derived more from such sources as that typified by the cinematic doings of Fu Manchu than from actual contact with the Chinese in America themselves. For example, the prevalent notion that the Chinese are more criminally inclined is belied by the statistics which show them to be among the most law abiding group in our society. This superlative lack of real knowledge of the Chinese arises in part out of their small numbers, and their concentration in a few large cities. But it also arises out of the fact that even in the communities where they do live, they are the most socially isolated of all minorities, a point which takes on added significance when it is recalled that the Chinese immigration antedated the period of great European immigration.

The Chinese population in the United States. In 1947, the Bureau of the Census estimated that there were 87,000 Chinese people in the United States, by which is meant people, native as well as foreign born, with racial characteristics derived from Chinese Mongoloid ancestry. Chinese immigration to the United States, as Table 15 shows, beginning in large numbers in the 1850's, rose to a peak in the 1871–1880 decade, declined sharply after the first Exclusion Act (1882), rose only moderately from the new low trend established then, and has been negligible since 1930. How are we to account for the fact that while over 380,000 Chinese have migrated to the United States there are only some 90,000 in the country today? First, the Chinese Ex-

TABLE 15

Chinese Immigration to the United States[2]

1820–30	3	1891–00	14,799
1831–40	8	1901–10	20,605
1841–50	35	1911–20	21,278
1851–60	41,397	1921–30	29,907
1861–70	64,301	1931–40	4,928
1871–80	123,201	1941–47	4,811
1881–90	61,711		
		Total	386,984

clusion Act drastically curtailed, although did not completely eliminate, further immigration after 1882. Second, the number of Chinese returning to China during several decades exceeded the number of arrivals. "From 1908, when records of departures began, to 1930, while 48,482 Chinese immigrant aliens were admitted, 72,796 departed, thus showing a net loss." [3] In the third place, normal natural increase was prevented by the disproportion of the sexes. In 1910 there were 1430.1 males to every 100 Chinese females; in 1920, 695.5; and in

[2] *Annual Report of the Immigration and Naturalization Service,* U. S. Department of *Justice,* Philadelphia, 1947, Table 4: "Immigration by Country for Decades 1820 to 1847."
[3] Maurice R. Davie, *World Immigration* (New York: The Macmillan Company, 1936). By permission. pp. 315-316.

1940, 258.3. Finally, due to exclusion, there had been an undue proportion of elderly Chinese in the population which provides a relatively high death rate for the group. Thus, it is not surprising to find that the Chinese population declined from a peak of 107,488 in 1890 to a low of 61,639 in 1920. From 1921 to 1930 the Chinese population began to rise, showing an increase from 61,639 in 1920 to 74,954 in 1930. This first increase for several decades may have been due to the greater proportion of women, and possibly also to the smuggling of Chinese immigrants into the country, following the passage of the Exclusion Act.[4] During the decade 1931 to 1940 the number of Chinese in America increased but slightly to a 77,504 total in 1940, probably reflecting the smaller national increase. For the seven year period, 1941 to 1947, however, the Chinese mainland population was estimated to have increased by 9000 to an estimated total of 87,000 which the final 1950 census figures will probably carry over the 90,000 mark. It therefore seems probable, now that the Chinese population is more normalized in its age and sex structure, that it will grow proportionately to the national population in general. Some further increase was made possible through the change in immigration law during World War II establishing an annual quota of 105 for China. But from so small a base the Chinese will remain a numerically insignificant element in the population.

The Chinese population is now highly urbanized, and concentrated particularly in cities of over 100,000. Whereas in 1880, 97.8 per cent of the total Chinese population (then 105,465) was living in places of 25,000 or less, in 1940 71 per cent (of the then 77,504 Chinese) were living in cities of over 100,000 in population. Indication of the degree of their concentration is seen in the fact that in only 28 cities of the United States were there established Chinatowns in 1940.[5] While the West Coast cities still harbor a greater proportion of the Chinese— San Francisco and Oakland alone about 21,000—the rest are located in large cities across the northern portion of the nation. Interestingly, they have avoided the South.

Stages in Chinese-white relations. The story of the Chinese in the United States and their relations with the dominant population can be appropriately related in three historical phases: (1) from the beginning of Chinese immigration in substantial numbers in 1850 to the passage of the first Chinese Exclusion Act in 1882; (2) the settled accommodation period from 1882 to the Second World War; and (3) the contemporary period.

[4] *Ibid.*, p. 316.
[5] Rose Hum Lee, "The Decline of Chinatowns in the United States," *American Journal of Sociology*, Vol. 54, No. 5 (March 1949), p. 423.

The early period. The discovery of gold in California was the magnet which first attracted mass immigration of Chinese to California. Perhaps much of the peculiarly violent and rough treatment accorded these first Chinese immigrants can be understood when it is remembered that Chinese–native white interaction first took place in the especially lawless setting of the frontier. In their first occupation, gold mining, opposition to the Chinese arose because they were industrious and persevering, often taking on mining locations which whites considered worthless and making them pay. Thus began the cry that the Chinese depressed the wages and the living standard of the whites, an allegation which was to dog the Chinese as they subsequently became laborers in all the menial occupations available—in railroad construction, on the farms, and in domestic service. Antagonism toward the Chinese expressed itself in the form of lawless violence; in discriminatory city ordinances and state legislation; and finally in successfully persuading the Federal Government to exclude further Chinese immigrants.

Acts discriminating against the Chinese, imposing special taxes on them, and prohibiting them from entering the state were passed by the California legislature in the 1850's and 1880's. Opposition to the Chinese was manifested also in city ordinances which attempted to reach the Chinese indirectly. For example, "San Francisco had a laundry ordinance imposing a license fee as follows: on laundries using a one-horse vehicle, $2 per quarter; two horses, $4 per quarter; no vehicle, $15 per quarter. The Chinese laundries commonly used no vehicle. It was made a misdemeanor for any person on the sidewalks to carry baskets suspended on a pole across the shoulders—a typical Chinese practice." And because the loss of a queue was a disgrace to some Chinamen, the so-called "queue ordinance" was especially perturbing to them. It "provided that every person convicted of a criminal offense should have his hair cut to a length of one inch from his head." [6]

Frequently the Chinese were exposed to illegal violence, especially in periods of hard times. As a result of the panic of 1873, riots occurred during which the Chinese were robbed, beaten, and murdered by hoodlums who made the Chinese the scapegoats for the ills of the times. Eye witness accounts report that "it was a common sight in San Francisco and other cities to see Chinese pelted with stones or mud, beaten or kicked, having vegetables or laundry stolen from their baskets, and even having their queues cut." It was also reported that their washhouses were set afire and when they tried to escape

[6] The quotations are taken from Davie, *World Immigration*, pp. 310-311. By permission.

from burning houses, they were beaten and sometimes compelled to die in the flames. The police afforded little protection against these outrageous attacks and the victims did not retaliate. The Chinese Government, however, demanded an indemnity which was paid by the United States.[7]

All of the California city ordinances and state laws specifically discriminating against Chinese were eventually declared unconstitutional by either the state Supreme Court or the United States Supreme Court.[8] Furthermore, the violence exercised against Chinese persons was protested by the Chinese Government, prompting the Federal Government to investigate the situation. The ultimate result was that Congress passed the first Chinese Exclusion Act in 1882, suspending all Chinese immigration for ten years. This was repeated for another ten years in 1892; and in 1902, suspension of Chinese immigration was extended indefinitely and was to remain thus until 1943 when under the spur of the war situation, China was added to the quota immigrant nations and allotted a quota of 105 annual entries. Included in each of these measures were various other humilating provisions including the denial of the privilege of becoming citizens to the foreign born Chinese.

The exclusion of the Chinese by Federal legislation is a clear illustration of Congress yielding to the specific will of one of its individual states in the absence of any general national demand. McWilliams has noted the following factors in the situation which help to explain it: (1) All but one of some eight anti-Chinese measures passed by Congress were passed on the eve of national elections and for avowed political purposes; (2) the interrelationship of the Southern attitude toward the Negro and the California attitude toward the Oriental, prompting Southern representatives to side with California on a *quid pro quo* basis; (3) the absence of any real knowledge on the part of white Americans throughout the nation of the Chinese and their failure to recognize the issue as related to national interest.[9]

The period of Chinese accommodation. In time sequence, the above discussion of the legislation limiting Chinese immigration has trespassed briefly upon the second phase of native-Chinese relations in the United States. Numerically few, and destined by the exclusion acts

[7] *Ibid.*, pp. 311-312.
[8] Below we refer to the Alien Land Holding Laws passed in the three Pacific Coast States for the purpose of barring foreign-born Japanese from owning land. They constituted a legal discrimination against the Chinese as well. Since the Chinese were less inclined toward land ownership, this discrimination had less practical importance in their case than in that of the Japanese.
[9] See Carey McWilliams, *Brothers Under the Skin* (Boston: Little, Brown & Company, 1943), pp. 87-96, for an extensive account and interpretation of the legislation against the Chinese.

to remain so, and culturally conditioned from their Chinese heritage to be meek and pacific rather than aggressive and militant, the Chinese reacted to this vehement Caucasian opposition in the most inoffensively accommodative ways. They dispersed to a few of the largest cities in the nation, thus removing the concentration factor. In these large cities, they segregated themselves in very compact areas, and confined their lives within them. They have entered occupations least competitive, particularly domestic and personal service. The small professional and clerical group is limited to serving their own people. Since "Chinatowns" are a point of interest to tourists, some make their livelihood through curio shops and restaurants serving the tourist trade. They developed two distinctive types of business— entirely unrelated to their own cultural background—the Chinese laundry and the Chinese restaurants, both designed to provide low price service not conspicuously competitive with white businesses in the same field. Finally, as noted above, many reacted by going back to China.

Like other immigrant minorities in the accommodation stage, the Chinese developed a segregated community within the large city. But because of the racial barrier to their gradual assimilation, Chinatowns have become more compact and more permanent. No other ethnic folk remains so completely isolated from the rest of the community. No other group has continued its traditional customs with less change.

The Chinese in Philadelphia. A recent study of the Chinese in Philadelphia affords an intimate view of the Chinese urban colony. While the Philadelphia colony is quite small, it is nevertheless reasonably typical of American "Chinatowns." [10]

In 1940, there were 922 Chinese people living in Philadelphia itself, although the Chinese community which focused around Race and 10th Streets included other Chinese living in cities around the Philadelphia area. Chinatown proper occupied about one square block located in a so-called blighted area, bounded by cheap hotels, the loafing places of idlers and "bums," and at another point by poor residences occupied by Negroes. The Chinese population in 1940 had a sex ratio of 393 males to 100 females, as compared with 285 for the Chinese population throughout the country. By nativity, the foreign born comprised 53 per cent compared with 48 per cent for all the Chinese in the United States. The age structure was heavily weighted by people over 40 with youthful adult age groups being smaller than that of the age groups under 15 years.

[10] David Te-Chao Cheng, *Acculturation of the Chinese in the United States: A Philadelphia Study* (Foochow China: The Fukien Christian University Press, 1948). The account given is the writer's adaptation of portions of this study.

The occupational distribution of the Chinese is reflected in the estimate that of the 547 employed Chinese in 1945, 400 were engaged as laundry operatives. Next in number were about 100 restaurant workers, and 18 grocery store workers. The majority of Chinese laundries, widely scattered about the city were one-man shops and the remainder either were partnerships or family projects. The restaurants were more selectively scattered and divided into three classes, according to the main source of their patronage: Negro, white American (in which Jewish patronage was pronounced) and those places which Cheng describes as "set up to entertain Chinese friends, feed gamblers (who frequently have their meals sent out), and so on." [11] The organizational basis of these restaurants was similar to that of the laundries except that the larger emporia required a larger operating personnel. The few Chinese stores served a Chinese clientele and performed a far wider set of functions than supplying the Chinese with material goods. They served as a post office, bank, and a general community center. Making a living at these tasks required long hours of work with no vacations as the rule. In Philadelphia the very few Chinese employed in higher status occupations included two art goods dealers operating the curio shops patronized by non-Chinese trade, and interestingly enough 12 engineers. The latter represented the most acculturated group who according the Cheng, took lessons in Chinese from him in order to be better prepared to go back to China after World War II to practice their profession.[12]

The social organization of the Chinese community in Philadelphia as elsewhere centered about the family, organized upon the highly familistic basis which has been widely described in sociological literature; featuring a strong sense of responsibility to all one's kin; patriarchal dominance with the oldest male retaining power over his adult children; the formal subordination of women and children; and emphasis upon the filial piety among the latter. Cheng delineated four types of Chinese families on the basis of his Philadelphia study: (1) the *mutilated* family which was really the husband living here alone with an immediate family back in China whom he visited when he could; (2) the *grafted* family, so-called because it involved the marriage of a foreign-born Chinese to an American-born Chinese or white American woman; (3) the *divided* family, by which is meant the natural family formed in the United States but separated from the family in China; and (4) the *emancipated* family, formed through the marriage of two American-born Chinese persons or where one

[11] *Ibid.,* p. 93.
[12] *Ibid.,* p. 111.

partner is not Chinese. This latter type, as the label suggests live very much according to normative modes of American family life.[13]

Aside from the family, structure of the Chinese community in the United States, as exemplified in Philadelphia, included other organizations which may be classified as traditional and adaptive. Among the former were tribal organizations or "common room" groups composed of some 10 to 20 Chinese male immigrants with the same common surnames who owned or rented a common room. This type of group was informal and performed the functions of a recreational center, a place to go when out of work or sick; and a place in which to entertain visitors from out of town. Again of longer standing were the "regional organizations," larger groups whose membership was based upon regional origin in China. Their functions were to provide mutual aid, mutual protection, and, when necessary, a respectable funeral for members. Cheng also mentioned "economic associations," essentially occupational guilds. None of these has ever existed in Philadelphia although restaurant waiters were organized earlier in other cities, and likewise laundrymen in New York in 1943.

The more traditional organizations noted above have been added to, and in considerable part supplanted by, adaptive institutions. In Philadelphia, as the Chinese community grew, the Chinese Public Association was established. This was the over-all organization "formed to handle all the big affairs which concern all Chinese." [14] Over the past 40 or 50 years, this association has exercized a wide variety of functions including maintaining order, protesting violation of Chinese civil rights, aiding the destitute, and raising funds for China relief. As time went on both the significance and the activity of the Public Association waned as the famous tongs increased in importance and usurped many of the functions of the other organizations. Tongs are in Cheng's words "Chinese secret societies grown wild." [15] The circumstances connected with the development of these widely publicized Chinese associations and the nature of the functions they perform has been a subject of much dispute. They appeared in essence as well integrated factional groups performing functions of mutual assistance and protection which often meant fighting against a rival faction. In Philadelphia, Cheng found that the two tongs, Hip Sing and On Leong, maintain a "nice balance of power." "While the Hip Sing exceeds the On Leong in manpower, the latter exceeds the

[13] *Ibid.* Cheng pointed out, as have many other observers, that, of course, the traditional Chinese family has undergone much westernization in China itself during the past half century.
[14] *Ibid.*, p. 124.
[15] *Ibid.*, p. 125.

former in wealth and social reputation. In Race Street Chinatown, a definite geographical sphere of influence is clearly drawn in the middle of the block, using the 'Security' garage as the dividing line." [16] The tongs, in recent years at least, were closely connected with the organized vices of Chinatown, of which gambling was the most prevalent manifestation.

The welfare of the Chinese. The Chinese in the United States have made their own unique economic adaptation to American life, which together with their strong feeling of mutual responsibility for one another has resulted in their taking care of themselves. The relatively low standard of living derives from their places of residence in the deteriorated areas of cities. They dwell in such areas largely because of the discrimination which bars free choice of a dwelling place. The limited material presented in the Philadelphia study indicated that almost all the dwelling units of the Chinese were built prior to 1900, that the majority of them had no private bath, and that there was extreme overcrowding. Cheng's data showed that the death rate of the Chinese population was higher than the population at large, although this may be due to the large number of elderly people. The incidence of tuberculosis was much higher than that of the general population. The conditions under which the Chinese of San Francisco lived were seen in the following excerpts from a report of the San Francisco Housing Authority in 1941.

Expansion in Chinatown is limited. Fifteen thousand Chinese live in an area five blocks by four blocks which is dedicated not primarily to residence but to shops, restaurants and institutions. . . . Of the 3830 dwelling units in Chinatown approximately 3000 are totally without heating equipment. In all Chinatown there are only 447 homes acceptable by the Survey standards, and all of these are in a high rental bracket.

They [the Chinese] live crowded together above the shops and below the sidewalks. Their windows, if they have any, look out on streets that are noisy until the early hours of the morning. The children lack adequate homes; they play in the streets at night or sit with their mothers and fathers at the workshops until midnight. As a consequence of these living conditions, the Chinatown tuberculosis rate is three times that of the rest of the city . . .

Three of every five Chinese families are living in one or two rooms, rooms usually so small as to deserve the appellation "cubicles." [17]

The native born generation. In the case of Euopean ethnic groups, it was seen that education of the native born opened the door toward upward social mobility and outward toward assimilation into the larger society. This is not the case with the Chinese born in this

---

[16] *Ibid.*, p. 127.
[17] McWilliams, *Brothers Under the Skin* (1943), p. 101. By permission.

country, and is not characteristically the case with the other minorities who retain clear-cut racial visibility no matter how much their
American acculturation, as will be shown in the discussion of other
racially visible peoples. Generally speaking, Chinese children are not
segregated in their schooling and during their school life they intermingle with white children on an equal basis. But as they leave
school, they revert to minority status. Up to World War II almost all
avenues of employment above the menial level or outside the Chinese
community itself were barred to the Chinese through the unwillingness of whites to employ them. Thus highly educated Chinese are frequently found as waiters in restaurants or in similar capacities.

Again, the characteristic disorganization, the second generation conflict between the foreign and native born members of the ethnic
group attendant upon the marginal position of the native born and
noted among European immigrant groups, has not been as marked
among the Chinese. While this is partly accountable from the strongly
familistic nature of Chinese culture, it is also related to the adamant
barriers of aloof indifference erected by the white community against
the Chinese. Until at least quite recently, it appears correct to say that
even the third and fourth generations of Chinese in this country
have not approached the marginal social position. Two exceptions
may be noted. First, here and there an individual Chinese person or
family may live separated from his fellows and achieve a moderate
degree of acceptance into the white society. Second, there have been
a few upper class Chinese, associated with importing firms, officials of
Chinese governments, and the like, who are accorded a different
status by white society, albeit even these are not readily accepted by
whites of comparable educational status.[18]

Despite the persistent separation of Chinese from the larger society
around them, each successive generation of the native born has become increasingly acculturated to the normative American way of
life. In his Philadelphia study Cheng measured the degree of acculturation of the contemporary community by examining various aspects
of culture with reference to the extent the Chinese manifested Old
World traits, adopted traits, and mixed or changed traits. Bearing in
mind that the summary results are for the whole Chinese community,
native and foreign born, Cheng found as follows:

We find that (1) under material traits, with the exception of "food," the
adopted traits are very strong indeed. (2) Under nonmaterial traits, the Old
World traits in business, social organization, and religion are still very dominant, while in education and customs, they are greatly weakened by the

[18] See Pearl S. Buck's recent novel, *Kinfolk* (New York: The John Day Company,
Inc., 1948) for a story involving upper class Chinese in New York.

adopted traits. And, (3) both in family and customs we find that there are many traits which have been mixed and changed. (4) In language and recreation, both the old and the adopted traits are about the same. (5) All in all, it is quite clear that so far as the Philadelphia Chinese are concerned, the culture traits which they have adopted from the American culture are definitely more than the culture traits which they have transplanted from the Old World and retained.[19]

With this increasing acculturation appear signs of cultural conflict between the "Americanized" and the Old World oriented Chinese, of which the following incident is illustrative:

My mother frequently drinks from my cup. I told her several times that it is unsanitary. My mother finally answered, "You think it is unsanitary to drink from the same cup, but why do you let your boy friends kiss you? I think it is far more unsanitary than to drink from the same cup." [20]

The rift in the generations within the family and between the more and the less acculturated elements within the Chinese group is further heightened by a language cleavage. The second generation speak English perfectly but know little Chinese. For the Chinese users, English is a mark of superiority, higher class status, and to them, at least, a sign that they are not foreigners.[21]

The current period. Surveying the over-all position of the Chinese minority in the United States in 1940, 90 years after their first mass migration, one would have been tempted to conclude that their status as a segregated minority, tolerated but disregarded by the Caucasian majority, was permanently frozen. The events of the past ten years, however, may temper that conclusion. World War II has introduced new factors. The shortage in manpower during the war period opened up to Chinese occupational opportunities hitherto barred to them—as clerical workers, in war industries, and even in some professional positions. Little, if any, material is available to indicate how far these occupational gains have been maintained; how far the contacts with the white world thus experienced has undermined the exceptional communal solidarity of the Chinese; or how far the whites associated with Chinese in these new situations have changed in their attitudes and behavior toward the Chinese. A number of circumstances or factors in the current situation may well be discussed in relation to the possibility that the Chinese may yet be accepted as real Americans.

[19] Cheng, *op. cit.*, p. 238. By permission of the author.
[20] *Ibid.*, p. 243. Quoted from Homer C. Loh, *Americans of Chinese Ancestry in Philadelphia,* unpublished doctoral dissertation at the University of Pennsylvania.
[21] Cf. William C. Smith, *Americans in Process* (Ann Arbor: J. W. Edwards, 1937), pp. 182-183.

1. *The General Trend Toward Reducing Minority Status.* As will be elaborated in more detail in the discussion of the larger minorities, the general trend of the decade has been toward the lessening of discrimination toward minorities. While this should operate in favor of greater equality for the Chinese, it is pertinent to observe with Rose and Rose that "organized efforts to improve the position of minorities seldom include the Chinese in their specific programs." [22]

2. *The Present Demographic Situation.* As discussed above, the normal growth of so small a population as the Chinese Americans comprise offers no biological threat to the white population.[23] The possibilities of Chinese assimilation, amalgamation, and possible disappearance as a distinct ethnic element in American society is conjecturally envisioned by Miss Lee in these terms:

It is probable that, as the Chinese reside longer in this country and the Chinese-Americans increase in population, another redistribution of their numbers may occur, with settlements in cities under metropolitan status. Where only a few Chinese reside in a community, they are socially well accepted. Acculturation and assimilation are more rapid for 'marooned families' and isolated individuals than for concentrated populations. Examples are found in Erie, Pennsylvania, where the one Chinese family residing in a middle-class neighborhood is highly regarded by its neighbors; in Milwaukee, Wisconsin, where a restaurateur has been accepted into the Masonic order and where a drugless physician maintains an office in a leading medical center and treats only American patients; and, in Arizona, where a Chinese has been elected a member of the state legislature. . . .

. . . It appears that the number of Chinatowns in this country will decrease almost to the vanishing point. Only those of historical or commercial importance, as in San Francisco and New York, will remain. Both these cities are important seaport and commercial centers linking the Orient and the United States. The Chinese population engaged in work needed by firms dealing in goods and services for international trade will be situated there. The smaller Chinatowns where sojourners predominate will lose their Chinese-American population to the larger ones.

As Chinese-Americans become acculturated and strive for higher status through education and enter professions or become employed by American industries, their dispersion will be similar to that of any other small minority group already an integral part of the American society. With acculturation and settlement among the members of the larger society, amalgamation will increase, and in time assimilation will be attained.[24]

3. *Communist China.* Until the past decade, dominant Americans in their behavior toward ethnic minorities in this country have been

[22] Arnold and Caroline Rose, *America Divided* (New York: Alfred A. Knopf, Inc., 1948), p. 317.
[23] See p. 160.
[24] Rose Hum Lee, *loc. cit.*, p. 432. By permission.

little affected by the attitudes of the home governments of these nationalities concerning it. As the nation reaches a point where more
people are aware that our treatment of minorities does affect America's position in world affairs, this awareness itself becomes a factor
favoring equality for the minorities. While protests by Chinese governments against treatment of Chinese in this country were occasionally made, the relations between the two governments have on the
whole been friendly. In contrast, the relations between the Japanese
Government and the United States, have been acrimonious.

Ironically, the postwar events in the international areas practically
reverse the situation. At the mid-century, it appears that Japan will enjoy more cordial relations with the United States, and a Communist-
dominated China, the opposite. Chinatowns in the United States could
serve as convenient anonymous bases of operations for Chinese Communist espionage. Bearing in mind the characteristic attitude of white
Americans toward "colored" peoples, one may well consider with some
foreboding the reaction of white America toward its citizens of Chinese
descent should the Chinese communities in this country inad-
vertently shelter "red" Chinese. In the conflict between the United
Nation forces and those of Communist China in Korea, the loyalty
of the Chinese in the United States to their adopted country apparently has not been publicly questioned up to the summer of 1951.
However, an attack upon Chinese-Americans by white Americans
was reported in the *Chinese Journal* in December, 1950.

In Woodland, California, a family lost their son recently in the battlefield in
Korea. When the Defense Department notified them, parents, wife, and
brother were deeply grieved. Filled with a desire for revenge, they gathered
their friends and relatives and headed toward a Chinese restaurant in that
town. They broke into the establishment and destroyed everything within.
Dishes, glasses, furniture, etc., were all ruined. The damages were estimated to
be very great.[25]

The dilemma facing certain classes of Chinese in the United States
by the rise to power of a Communist controlled government in China
is analyzed by Rose Hum Lee.[26] The "sojourner" group, composed of
Chinese males whose main objective has been to retire to China to enjoy a higher economic status with their savings in this country, does
not know whether or not to return. The policy of confiscation of
private wealth may place them where they were before. The "foreign

[25] The excerpt is from an editorial in the *Chinese Journal*, New York, December 1,
1950. The editorial as a whole warns the Chinese in America that they face close
scrutiny from the FBI under the present circumstances, particularly those who would
be classified as enemy aliens in the case of a formal declaration of war. The author
is indebted to Victor Chin of Rutgers University for the translation.
[26] Rose Hum Lee, "Chinese Dilemma," *Phylon*, Vol. 10, No. 2 (1949), pp. 137-40.

born intellectual" group, those Chinese students in this country pre-
paring to return to professional and managerial positions, are likewise uncertain of their status under the new regime. Their prior political and class affiliations make their fate uncertain should they return. Many would like to remain here but since they have only
transient visas, will find difficulty in obtaining permission to stay. If
they do remain here, they will, in all probability, fail to find positions
commensurate with their training. For the American born of Chinese descent, the new political situation in China will raise fewer
problems. Even though these are treated as a minority, they are nevertheless more firmly rooted in American life.

Finally, the extent of anti-American attitudes in China today has
been influenced by the patronizing, superior manner often adopted by
Americans sojourning in China. While many of the American missionaries and educators have been valiant exceptions, perhaps the more
characteristic attitude of Americans is expressed by the comment of an
American sociologist, who was stationed in China during World War I,
who wrote the present writer as follows: "Americans in China, including troops during the war, often have treated Chinese with ill-concealed
contempt."

THE JAPANESE IN THE UNITED STATES

The story of the Japanese in the United States presents a number of
interesting parallels and contrasts with that of the Chinese. Like the
Chinese, the Japanese settled on the West Coast, but in a more
stable period in that region's history. While perhaps it may be said
that eventually they incurred more antagonism from the natives
than the Chinese, they were spared the physically violent maltreat-
ment visited upon the latter in the lawless frontier days. While a
majority of the Chinese remained on the West Coast, a substantial
minority scattered in cities throughout the northern tier of the country, whereas, up to the time of relocation, the Japanese remained
highly concentrated in the Pacific coast states. Japanese culture was
Asiatic like the Chinese, but their technological level was higher.
Their literacy was greater and their agricultural skills better suited
to rapid economic adjustment. It is perhaps because of this superiority
from the viewpoint of making a living that their subsequent relations
with the natives followed a different course than that of the Chinese.
While the Chinese reacted to native opposition with extreme pas-
sivity, as has been shown, the Japanese were less tractable. They held
their ground—almost literally since they were farmers—and refused
to disperse like the Chinese, and made ingenious adaptations to the
various economic discriminations inflicted upon them. Consequently,

while the native population came to think of the Chinese in terms of stereotype A, the inferior, humble, ignorant who could be condescendingly tolerated, the Japanese came to be treated in terms of stereotype B, the aggressive, cunning, and conspiritorial requiring more active dominant effort to keep them in their place.

The Japanese, like the Chinese, retained a greater interest in their homeland than the European nationality peoples, as manifested in the large number constantly returning to Japan. Yet the Japanese population in the United States shows an almost steady rise, while that of the Chinese until recently showed considerable decline. Finally both groups suffered from the humiliation of severe legislative discrimination, culminating in drastic Federal action. The manner, however, of handling the Federal restriction of immigration was noticeably more diplomatic in the case of the Japanese, a contrast attributable to the greater power possessed by the Japanese Government, a government able to protest more effectively against the discriminatory treatment of their nationals in this country.

The sociological formulation of the story of the Japanese in America will be presented in stages or periods similar to that employed in the Chinese story with one notable exception. The evacuation of the Japanese from the West Coast following Pearl Harbor, their relocation in temporary centers, and subsequent resettlement constitute a unique episode in America's minority history requiring special attention. Before turning to describe these stages, a brief survey of pertinent demographic facts about the Japanese in the United States will be presented.

Japanese population trends. For over 200 years, 1638 to 1868, Japanese citizens were forbidden to go abroad, and foreigners, with minor exceptions, were forbidden to enter Japan. The first to go out from the land of the Rising Sun were students, sent to gain knowledge throughout the world. Subsequently, a limited number of laborers were permitted to leave. But it was the agreement signed by the Japanese Government and certain Hawaiian sugar plantation owners in 1885 by which Japanese contract laborers were permitted to go to Hawaii, which set emigration into substantial momentum. From then until 1924, substantial Japanese migration took place to Asiatic Russia (302,946), Hawaii (238,758), the United States (196,543), and to China (105,258); and in more limited numbers, Japanese emigrated through this same period to Canada, Brazil, the Philippines, Peru, Korea, and Australia. Considering the enormous rate of population growth in Japan during these decades and the subsequent population pressure, the relatively modest amount of emigration is surprising. The failure to emigrate in larger numbers to the areas of the world settled by Europeans is in part due to the unfriendly manner with which they were received and to the legal restrictions imposed. But this does not adequately explain their failure to migrate to other Asiatic areas in more substantial proportions. Considering its limited size, Hawaii may be considered the most popular magnet of Japanese emigration. As will be pointed out in Chapter 14, the present Hawaiian population is about one-third Japanese.

With overlapping in the 1881–1890 decade, Japanese immigration to the continental United States takes on where Chinese immigration falls off. Tables 16 and 17 respectively show the number of Japanese immigrants admitted from 1861–1947, and the total Japanese population, which of course includes the native born, at the decennial years.

TABLE 16

Japanese Immigration to the United States[27]

1861–70	186
1871–80	149
1881–90	2,270
1891–00	25,942
1901–10	129,797
1911–20	83,837
1921–30	33,462
1931–40	1,948
1941–47	503

TABLE 17

Japanese Population in the United States[28]

CENSUS YEAR	NUMBER	DECADE	PERCENTAGE RATE OF INCREASE
1860	0	1870–80	169.1
1870	55	1880–90	1,277.7
1880	148	1890–00	1,093.0
1890	2,039	1900–10	196.6
1900	24,326	1910–20	53.8
1910	72,157	1920–30	25.1
1920	111,010	1930–40	−13.1
1930	138,834	1940–47 (est.)	4.0
1940	126,947		
1947 (est.)	131,000		

[27] *Annual Report of the Immigration and Naturalization Service*, 1947, Table 4.
[28] U. S. Census, 1940, Vol. II, Table 4, p. 19; also *Estimate of Nonwhite Population of Continental United States, by Race, 1940 to 1947*, Series P 25, No. 23.

The increase in the Japanese population from 1880–1910 was largely due to immigration itself since the great preponderance of the newcomers was male. Due to the clamor of the West Coast for restricting Japanese immigration, President Theodore Roosevelt negotiated directly with the Japanese Government—the so-called Gentlemen's Agreement—in 1907. This provided that Japan would not issue passports for the continental United States to laborers unless they were coming to resume a formerly acquired domicile, to join a parent, husband, or child or to assume control of a farming enterprise which had been possessed before. Since this agreement did not completely close the door to further Japanese immigration, the continued growth of the population was partly due to the continued, though greatly diminished, immigration. But the growth in this period was due more to the fact that much of the post 1907 immigration consisted of women, many of whom were "picture brides." By 1930 the sex ratio among the Japanese in this country had declined to 143.3 males for every 100 females—much more normal than that of either the Chinese or the Filipinos living here. The only decennial decline in Japanese population occurred in the decade 1930–40, during which the number of returning homeland emigrants exceeded 8000, while slightly less than 2000 new immigrants came in. This trend of decline apparently continued up to the time of Pearl Harbor since the estimated population in 1942 was 122,000. Since then the Japanese population has increased again, reaching in 1947 an estimated total of 131,000, of which a 3000 increase was estimated for the year ending April 1, 1947. This suggests that in the postwar period, the population of Japanese-Americans on the mainland is resuming a more normal rate of increase, roughly comparable to that of the national population.

The Japanese population, unlike the Chinese, remained heavily concentrated on the West Coast, particularly in California, up to the time of the attack on Pearl Harbor. In 1940, of the 127,000 Japanese, both foreign-born and native-born citizens, 111,000, or about 88 per cent, resided on the West Coast. Eighty-three per cent were in California alone, and most of these in Los Angeles County. Outside of the West, the only two cities having enough Japanese to form a distinctive colony were Chicago and New York. Chicago, in fact, had a larger Japanese population than any other city except Los Angeles, estimated at 15,000 to 20,000.[29] In New York a Japanese colony has existed since the late 19th century, reaching at one point nearly

[29] *People in Motion: The Postwar Adjustment of the Evacuated Japanese,* United States Department of Interior Publication (Washington: Government Printing Office), p. 168.

5000, but at the outbreak of the war numbering about 2000.[30] The distribution of the Japanese resulting from their evacuation from the West Coast and their resettlement has considerably changed the pattern of distribution, as will be discussed below.

Cultural backgrounds of the Japanese immigrants. The culture in which the Japanese immigrants had been reared differed more markedly from that of America than the culture of the European immigrants; yet in some aspects it had prepared the Japanese for more successful adjustment to their life in this country. Prior to the period of Japanese immigration, Japan had begun the process of transforming itself from a semifeudal to a modern industrial nation. Thus its culture was a mixture of the traditional and the new. Basic in its traditional culture was the intricate set of mores which defined the strong obligation of the individual to the group, to the family, to those of superior class, and to the state. Japanese social organization was authoritarian and perhaps in no other 19th century nation was there a greater integration of the individual and his groups. Predominant in Japanese personality were the traits of obedience, self-control, and self-effacement. The strong sense of the subordination of the individual to the welfare of the group was reflected in marked solidarity of Japanese groups in this country. Deriving from long tradition was the intricate pattern of etiquette and ritual which prescribed the proper way of behaving in every situation. To conform punctiliously to these elaborate social rituals was a major drive in Japanese personality, accounting for the reputation for courtesy and good manners which the 19th century Japanese acquired.

The ferment of rapid change had already begun in earnest since the beginning of the Meiji Era (1868–1912). To transform Japan into an industrial nation with western technological methods under a centralized government was the conscious policy of the ruling elements. To the already great skill in the practice of intensive farming, acquired under the stern necessity created by population pressure upon a small tillable acreage, new practices of scientific agriculture were added. Public education was in the process of development to a high level. Likewise the development of scientific medicine and programs of public health were in process. While it is difficult to know how far all these new influences had affected the mass of the Japanese people from whom the immigrants to America derived, nevertheless in the willingness to learn and to experiment in matters technological and economic, the Japanese surpassed not only all other Asians but many European immigrant groups.

[30] Bradford Smith, *Americans from Japan* (Philadelphia: J. B. Lippincott Company, 1948), p. 336.

First phase: rural accommodation. The very first Japanese in the United States were employed in domestic service. As their numbers increased, some became engaged in a wide variety of menial jobs and others began to operate small shops. Because at first their numbers were small and the jobs they took did not affect the employment opportunities of white American workers, little opposition to the Japanese occurred. Beginning about 1890, antagonism began to be displayed by members of labor unions. In that year Japanese cobblers were attacked by members of the shoemakers' union. In 1892, a Japanese restaurant in San Francisco was attacked by members of the local cooks' and waiters' union.[31] From then on anti-Japanese activity became a permanent phenomenon in California rising to a climax in the famous School Board Affair in 1906, when the San Francisco Board of Education passed a resolution requiring the segregation of all Oriental children in one school. At the time there were exactly 93 Japanese attending the public schools of San Francisco and these were distributed in 23 schools. This action brought protest from the Japanese Government and developed a crisis between the Imperial Government and that of the United States, which led to the signing of the Gentlemen's Agreement in 1907. By the terms of the agreement, the Japanese Government agreed to limit passports to Japanese nationals to non-laborers, laborers returning from a visit in Japan, and immediate members of families of Japanese already here.

The rising antagonism toward the Japanese in the cities led the Japanese in increasing numbers to turn to agriculture.[32] They started out as farm laborers and began to outnumber the Chinese in this capacity in the late 1890's. By 1909 they constituted a large part of the farm labor force in the Western States. It was natural for the Japanese to turn to agriculture because they brought with them knowledge of intensive cultivation of the soil superior to that of many American native farmers. It was likewise natural that more and more Japanese should aspire to operate farms themselves. By 1909, 6000 Japanese were operating farms, the greater number by far as tenants.[33] They experimented with small-scale farming, finally concentrating in fruits and vegetables. Adaptable, thrifty, and industrious, the Japanese operated farms increased up to 1920.[34]

The success of the Japanese in moving from laborer to entrepreneur, even though on a small scale and usually involving the payment of rent to white owners, led to opposition from white farmers, culmi-

[31] Yamato Ichihashi, *Japanese in the United States* (Stanford: Stanford University Press, 1932), pp. 229-230.
[32] *Ibid.*, see Chs. 11, 12, 13, for progress of the Japanese in American agriculture.
[33] *Ibid.*, p. 178.
[34] *Ibid.*, p. 193.

nating in the passage in California of the first alien land holding act in 1913. According to this act, aliens ineligible for citizenship were prohibited from owning agricultural land. Aliens could lease land for periods not to exceed three years. Following the passage of this act, it appeared that Japanese were buying stock in land-owning corporations and buying land in the name of their native born children. In consequence, further pressure resulted in a new act which in substance prohibited the leasing of land by any method by Japanese foreign born. Similar laws were passed by other western states, and in a test case in 1923 their constitutionality was upheld by the United States Supreme Court. From then on the role of the Japanese in agriculture declined and return to the cities increased.

Second phase: urban accommodation. As with all urban dwelling minorities, the Japanese established a separate community within the larger community. On the West Coast, the main "Little Tokyos" were in San Francisco, Los Angeles, and Seattle. For a close-up view of the life within a Japanese American urban colony we turn to Seattle around 1935.

The Seattle Japanese community, 1935.[35] Japanese began to come to Seattle in numbers around 1900 and the colony they established had a transient character reflecting the "frontier" nature of Seattle itself at the time. Since in a growing community there was plenty of work to do, the few Japanese were welcome. The Japanese were largely males eager to make money and return to Japan. As however many stayed and as, after the Gentlemen's Agreement, more Japanese wives came to the community, a more settled community life developed. While discrimination against the Japanese now became pronounced, the opportunity to earn a living continued to be present, furthered by labor demand during World War I. The Immigration Act of 1924, which prohibited further Japanese immigration, marked the beginning of what Miyamoto called the "second generation" period. "From a community geared to expect a constant flow of immigration," it became a community geared to the greater opportunity which the American born could claim as their birthright. By 1930, 47 per cent of Seattle's 8448 Japanese were native born.

The Japanese colony was located directly to the southeast of Seattle's central business district. Between 1920 and 1935, the distribution of Japanese residences showed a marked trend away from solidly Japanese areas to a scattering about the central areas. The

[35] Shotaro Frank Miyamoto, *Social Solidarity Among the Japanese in Seattle,* University of Washington Publications in the Social Sciences, Vol. 11, No. 2 (Dec. 1939), pp. 57-130.

more successful Japanese families were diffused throughout practically every section of Seattle.

While the entire range of occupations of the Japanese was notably wide, concentration of 31 per cent of those employed in 1935 in domestic and personal service and of 45 per cent in the trades indicates a decided identity of occupational interests.[36] In general, however, the range of family incomes was not great, which meant that the absence of class difference was added to the forces uniting the members of the Japanese colony. The large number of Japanese operating small mercantile enterprises of their own reflected a considerable individual initiative and adherence to the private enterprise system. On the other hand, bcause so few could accumulate enough capital for these ventures, most of them required the aid of friends and relatives for the start. In fact, mutual aid in this connection was institutionalized in the form of pools formed by small groups from which various members in turn could draw in initiating new enterprises.

The social life of the Japanese colony in Seattle revealed a mixture of Old World, accommodative, and acculturative institutions. The traditional heritage was most clearly seen in the continuance of the patriarchal Japanese family with its extreme emphasis upon male authority and filial obligations. In recreation likewise, Miyamoto writes: "their play life tends to revolve about activities that are essentially Japanese in character." [37] The two Japanese daily newspapers in Seattle in 1935 were heavily oriented to activites of the homeland and few of the foreign born Japanese read American papers.

Among the accommodative institutions there were, in the economic area, the *tanomoshi*, or "pools" described above, and a Japanese chamber of commerce, patterned after the similar American form. In addition there were the *Ken-jin* and the Seattle branch of the Japanese Association of North America. The former were organizations of Japanese who came from a particular region, or *ken*, of Japan, whose functions were primarily sociable, and occasionally, charitable. The Japanese Association embracing the entire colony was the non-official equivalent of community government. It acted as the agency of social control throughout the Japanese community and represented the community in its relations with the larger white community.

In addition to the acculturation to American economic institutions noted above, the Japanese were highly acculturated to the American belief and practice concerning education. While most of the immigrants themselves lacked higher education, in all possible ways they

[36] *Ibid.*, p. 71.
[37] *Ibid.*, p. 122.

encouraged their children not only to continue in their attendance in the public schools but also to succeed in their studies. Between 1930 and 1937 in the nine Seattle high schools 15 Japanese students were either valedictorians or salutatorians of their respective classes. The strong discipline of the Japanese parents over their children was employed to reinforce the authority of the school. Turning to the sphere of religious affiliations, it is somewhat striking to note that 1200 Seattle Japanese belonged to Christian churches in 1936,[38] more than belonged to all the Japanese religious groups combined. Miyamoto suggests that the many practical services rendered by the Protestant mission churches encouraged Japanese membership.

The general picture emerging from examining the situation of Japanese in Seattle, which was representative of their situation throughout the West Coast, showed the Japanese successfully adapted to American life but still living as a group apart. Much of their continued ethnic identity can be accounted for by forces within the group itself, which have been described above. Nevertheless without question their continued solidarity and distinctiveness were manifestations of their rejection by white Americans as full-fledged participants in the larger community life. Following the more strongly voiced opposition to the Japanese noted earlier, the Japanese accommodated themselves to limited opportunity on a separate and discriminatory basis, so that the pattern of native American–Japanese American relations were frozen approximately upon this level up to the time of Pearl Harbor. Increasingly however the succeeding generations of Japanese born in this country were becoming acculturated. We turn to consider the native born as a group and the effect of their increasing acculturation upon the position of Japanese in American society.

The American-born Japanese. The increasing acculturation of the Nisei, as the Japanese born in America of foreign parentage are called, developed cleavages in the closely integrated and self-sufficient Japanese communal life. Cultural conflict similar to that noted in the European groups produced similar strains in family life. The younger Japanese considered their parents "too Japanesy" and began to defy the attempts of the parents to discipline them according to the traditional family pattern. The children became interested in American sports, desired freedom in their out-of-school life, and wanted to dress in the prevailing fashion of their white schoolmates. For the parents this Americanization of their children brought much sorrow. They could not understand that this desire on

[38] *Ibid.*, p. 99.

the part of their children to act like Americans was dictated by the wish to be accepted as Americans.

The typical generation conflict among immigrant groups was made more intense among the Japanese by the unusual age distribution of their population. The great disparity in the sex ratio of the earlier immigrant group created a great preponderance of males in the older generation. The middle-age classes were proportionally small, and not until the third generation were large numbers of both sexes present. "As late as 1940, only 27,000 of the 80,000 Nisei were over twenty-one." [39] As a way of meeting this problem some Japanese parents sent their children back home to be brought up in the fatherland culture. In 1942, it was estimated that at least 25,000 United States citizens of Japanese ancestry had been educated in schools in Japan. Among these Kibei, as they were designated, were the Japanese considered most probably disloyal in sentiment at the time of Pearl Harbor.

As with the Chinese, the stage of the conflict of the generations, typical in immigrant patterns, had a different sequel than that of the European nationalities. As anxious as the Nisei were to become Americans and forget Japan, they found that in spite of their acculturation, the native community looked upon them as "Japs" because they had racial visibility. They continued to be discriminated against in three areas—employment, in public places, and in social contacts.

In employment the educated Nisei had three choices.[40] He could accept prejudice for what it was—and assume the inferior tasks of houseboy, dishwasher, migratory laborer, cannery hand—just what the dominant group expected him as an inferior to do. He could go to Japan and forsake America. Or if he tried hard, perhaps he could get a job at a higher level but far below his actual qualifications.

Many barbershops, restaurants, and hotels refused to serve Orientals. Several large coastal cities had restrictive covenants which kept Japanese out of any of the attractive neighborhoods. Further illustrative of discrimination in the social sphere is the following:

The fear of rebuffs, the constant horror of being humiliated in public, made the Nisei draw together in a tight circle, even at college. They formed their own clubs even though some felt that such organizations only perpetuated their difficulties. They formed noticeable groups on campus. "There's a barrier between Nisei and the other students," said one. "You can feel it. They never feel easy with each other."

Hostility in the social sphere did not as a rule become noticeable until adolescence. The fear of "miscegenation," the old superstitions about racial

[39] Bradford Smith, op. cit., p. 245.
[40] The remainder of this section is adapted from Bradford Smith, Ch. 19.

"hybrids," the fear that friendship might be construed as having a sexual intent introduced, at courting age, a stiffening of attitudes. Yet the Nisei were quite as set against intermarriage as the Caucasians, their own fears and superstitions as deeply rooted.[41]

These discriminations had different effects upon the Nisei, depending upon their varying personalities. The strongest were stirred to even greater competitive spirit, as will also be seen in the case of similarly placed Jews. Some of them developed an exaggerated sense of humor. Others got relief by talking out their feelings of inferiority with fellow Nisei. Because of the keenly developed competitive spirit thus engendered, the Nisei had less solidarity than their elders and often took it out on one another.

To all this were added love frustrations.

Chief trouble was the difficulty young Nisei men had in getting jobs. Another was the expense of the usual Japanese wedding. Then too there was resistance to the old method of mating and not much experience with the new. A young man fortunate enough to have a job that would support a wife might want to marry American style. But Japanese parents were old-fashioned, so there was no chance for the American kind of courtship—dates, parties, a ripening acquaintance. Yet he resisted an arranged marriage, and so things drifted along.[42]

A final difficulty facing the Nisei in his assimilation was his lack of political maturity. Since the foreign born were barred from citizenship, the Nisei were slow to realize that they were in a position to use political pressure to improve their position. Because of their background and position as minorities they tended to start off as conservatives. Eventually a Japanese American Citizen's League was formed holding its first national convention in 1935. More and more Young Democrat and Young Republican clubs began to be organized, "still as racial units, but at least applying themselves to national problems . . . providing an outlet for all the aggressions their narrow economic communities had pent up." [48] Thus the Nisei were becoming of age but very impatient to enter into the fullness of American life. But unfortunately for their rising hopes, Pearl Harbor was to prove more disastrous to them than to any other single ethnic group in America.

Third phase: evacuation and relocation. The processes of second generation conflict and partial assimilation was rudely shattered by Pearl Harbor. On February 19, 1942, the Army was given authority to establish military zones from which any persons, citizen or alien, might be evacuated and excluded. All Japanese people were ordered to leave the

---

[41] *Ibid.*, p. 250. By permission.
[42] *Ibid.*, p. 255. By permission.
[48] *Ibid.*, pp. 258-259.

West Coast. This action was the most unprecedented single national action in our history against a large group of people. Analysis of its causes provides penetrating insight into the dynamics of dominant-minority relations in the United States. We return to this after carrying forward an account of what happened to the Japanese after February 19.

At first the Japanese were to be given time to remove themselves. A few did leave, but it was soon discovered that they were not wanted elsewhere. A quote from the Los Angeles *Times,* March 24, 1942, reads: "Japanese evacuees moving inland from California in a great mass migration will be put in concentration camps if they enter Nevada, Governor E. P. Carville warned tonight." [44] Therefore on March 27, the Japanese were ordered to stay where they were pending their mass evacuation under military supervision. A new Federal agency, The War Relocation Authority, was established to plan for the supervision of the Japanese under detention. Between then and August 8, all West Coast Japanese numbering over 110,000 were transferred to 10 hastily built centers located in the Rocky Mountain States and in Arkansas.

Aside from the shocklike psychological effect upon the Japanese and the bitterness which evacuation engendered, the Japanese faced enormous economic loss. While the Government took steps to protect the material property owned by the Japanese, the guarantees appeared so uncertain that many sold their effects, and under the circumstances, of course at a loss. A business enterprise and a crop in the field could not be frozen. They had to be disposed of for whatever they would bring at hurried sale or lease, or abandoned.

Life in the Settlement Centers. The War Relocation Authority faced a unique problem in American history. How the personnel met these problems and how life in the centers affected the Japanese has been thoroughly studied by highly qualified social scientists.[45] The policy of WRA was to organize the center community life with the maximum possible self-control by the Japanese. All the evidence indicates that the personnel was highly sympathetic to the Japanese for which it was criticized by the same elements of the white population which clamored for evacuation in the first place. As was almost inevitable under such circumstances, a number of rebellious activities arose among factions of the evacuees. Of these the most serious was a strike by some evacuees at Poston Center arising out of a feeling that two alleged attackers of a white official had been unfairly punished. In con-

[44] Alexander H. Leighton, *The Governing of Men* (Princeton: Princeton University Press), 1945, p. 36.
[45] *Ibid.;* see also Dorothy Swaine Thomas and Richard S. Nishimoto, *The Spoilage* (Berkeley: University of California Press, 1946).

sequence of incidents of this nature, Tule Lake Center became the segregation camp where active malcontents from all other centers were placed and controlled under strict discipline.

Resettlement. The other wing, so to speak, of WRA's operation was engaged through regional offices throughout the nation in trying to find employment opportunity for Japanese outside the centers. This phase of operations has not been given the systematic study which it deserves as a reflection of dominant attitudes. Its activities beginning in the spring of 1943 included the resettlement of the Japanese on a "retail" basis particularly in the Midwest and the Mountain States. Lack of extensive resettlement in the East was due to Army opposition. Those most frequently leaving the camps were young adult Nisei who, when and if they became successfully resettled, often sent for relatives to join them. WRA also assumed responsibility for helping the resettler to adjust to his new community as well as to his job. One of the hardest tasks in this connection was to find a place for him to reside. From informal although highly reliable first-hand sources, some interesting sidelights on this resettlement program may be gleaned. In the large metropolitan centers it was fairly easy to place Japanese in a wide range of menial and semitechnical jobs. It was difficult to place them in industries with war contracts or in positions calling for contact with the public. Frequent opposition from unions to their employment arose. Among the reasons often given for not hiring the Japanese were distrust of their loyalty; that other employers would resent; that customers would resent; and "my son is in the Pacific." While many of the resettlers left their jobs for the same reasons many other people did, the Japanese differed mainly in leaving because of their interest in work where they could acquire new skills in preparation for getting ahead.[46]

Prior to January 1, 1945, the date after which evacuees were permitted to return to the West Coast, WRA had resettled 31,625 Japanese in other parts of the country. Interestingly enough, when the opportunity came, the vast majority of the evacuees returned to their former community. Since the date for terminating WRA had been set, their choice at this point had to be quick and WRA was no longer able to give them individual assistance. It is probable also that many of the Japanese who had been resettled in other areas subsequently returned to the West Coast.

Japanese evacuation: a case history in white American dominant behavior. The evacuation of all persons of Japanese ancestry from the West Coast followed by their internment was a governmental action

[46] The writer is indebted to Gordon Berryman, a former employee of WRA for procuring these qualitative insights into the resettlement process.

without precedent in American history, involving constitutional issues of grave significance. The Supreme Court of the United States did in fact uphold the constitutionality of evacuation in wartime,[47] although strong dissents were written by a minority of the justices. However, in retrospect, the whole incident appears as a serious error in judgment. For this reason some analysis of the circumstances which led to such action is highly pertinent to the student of dominant-minority relations. The central question engaging our attention is: To what extent was the decision for evacuation and internment of the Japanese arrived at as a logical necessity for national security; or to what extent was the decision made in response to regional pressures unrelated to security? Since the Western Defense Command of the United States Army was responsible for the decision, it is appropriate to consider first the case which it presented in justification.[48]

Military Authority. The Final Report refers to as fact some illegal signaling from shore to sea on the West Coast, although it presents no specific proof that Japanese were involved in this. It cites the result of one spot raid made by the Federal Bureau of Investigation upon Japanese homes in which "more than 60,000 rounds of ammunition, and many rifles, shotguns, and maps of all kinds" were found. Such articles as well as some others had been declared contraband for enemy aliens. To what extent such articles were possessed by enemy aliens or by American citizens of Japanese ancestry and to what extent the articles found were evidence of conspiracy is not stated. The report indicates that in three instances where Japanese submarines shelled West Coast areas, the particular spots chosen were the very ones most out of range of American coastal batteries at the time. The assumption is that the Japanese Navy must have had inside information although no evidence is presented to connect West Coast Japanese with this knowledge. The above is in substance the entire case made which implies acts of sabotage or espionage.

Much more of the case presented by the Western Defense Command concerning the security menace of the Japanese is based upon the fact that the Japanese were in a position to do much damage and upon assumptions that many of them should logically be expected to take such opportunities. The military authorities were much impressed by the actual residence distribution of Japanese which seemed too singularly adjacent to strategic points to be fully coincidental. Surprisingly enough for a military document, the report rests much of its case upon sociological phenomena. Reference is made to "ties of

[47] Koramatzu vs. United States, 323 U.S. 214.
[48] *Final Report, Japanese Evacuation from the West Coast,* 1942. Washington, United States Government Printing Office, 1943, Ch. 2, "Need for Military Control and for Evacuation," pp. 7-19.

race" as well as strong bonds of common traditional culture which make the Japanese a tightly knit group. Major emphasis is placed upon the considerable number of Japanese associations on the West Coast whose purposes and activities reflected great interest in the ancestral homeland, and in some instances involving contributions in behalf of the war of Japan with China. Finally the report stresses and statistically verifies the fact that a considerable number of the American born Japanese had been educated in Japan and subsequently returned to live in the States. The military authorities conceded that many Japanese living in the country were loyal but felt that the task of screening the loyal from the disloyal presented too much of a problem and that therefore the only safe course was to evacuate everybody of Japanese ancestry.

The sociological observations just noted comprised facts about the Japanese in the United States well known to many people on the West Coast. In fact, the Japanese had been the subject of much detailed study by Pacific Coast social scientists for years prior to Pearl Harbor. Such students could have greatly assisted the military in making more valid interpretations of Japanese society on the West Coast. In this connection Grodzins writes, "as later research has shown military officers did not in a single instance rely on the large mass of scientific materials that had been gathered about American Japanese by such men as Steiner, Park, Strong, Bogardus, and Bailey." [49] Espionage and sabotage are inevitable concomitants of war. It is reasonable to suppose that some of the enemy aliens should be engaged in the task, although it is also logical to suppose that among the enemy agents will be some who would not be, for example, in this case Japanese at all. Even in the absence of much specific proof of disloyal behavior on the part of Japanese Americans, the general logic of the situation clearly called for especial vigilance over this group by the agents of the Justice Department and prompt action against any particular individuals even perhaps on reasonable suspicion. With such a policy, already in actuality in practice before evacuation orders, few Americans, and perhaps even few Americans of Japanese ancestry, would have quarrelled. This was the policy advocated by the Justice Department. As late as January 12, 1942, Attorney General Biddle said: "Wholesale internment, without hearing and irrespective of the merits of individual cases, is the long and costly way around, as the British discovered by painful experience; for by that method not only are guiltless aliens themselves demoralized, but the nation is deprived of a valuable source of labor supply at a time when every available man must be at

[49] Morton Grodzins, *Americans Betrayed: Politics and the Japanese Evacuation* (Chicago: The University of Chicago Press), 1949, p. 305.

work." [50] But the case submitted is highly unimpressive as a justification for such drastic action as mass evacuation. For this reason the hypothesis emerges that in adopting this extreme policy, the Western Defense Command was unduly swayed in its judgment of the situation by these elements of West Coast opinion who were either exaggeratedly hysterical or imbued with strong antagonism toward the Japanese.

West Coast Pressure Groups. The presence of pressure groups and their activities in the situation have been systematically studied by Grodzins. "The most active proponents of mass evacuation were certain agricultural and business groups, chambers of commerce, the American Legion, the California Joint Immigration Committee, and the Native Sons and Daughters of the Golden West." [51] The organizations advocating evacuation fall into two main classes. One class was composed of economic groups with a history of general opposition to Japanese on grounds of self-interest. While for public propaganda purposes, these groups stressed the danger of the Japanese to national security, Grodzins assembles evidence that in private conversation and in written communications to various key people, special economic interest was indicated. For example, "If all the Japs were removed tomorrow, we'd never miss them in two weeks, because the white farmers can take over and produce everything the Jap grows, and we don't want them back when the war ends, either." [52] Another class of groups pressing for evacuation was composed of those who were characteristically antiforeign, or nativistic in sentiment and behavior. Illustrative of the attitude of groups in this category is the following excerpt from a resolution adopted by an Oregon American Legion Post.

    . . . this is no time for namby-pamby pussyfooting . . . that it is not the time for consideration of minute constitutional rights of those enemies but that it is time for vigorous, whole-hearted, and concerted action . . . toward the removal of all enemy aliens and citizens of enemy alien extraction from all areas along the coast and that only those be permitted to return that are able to secure special permit for that purpose . . .[53]

In sequence this pressure was next reflected in Congressmen from the area and in state officials. To these pressures the Federal Government finally capitulated. Some counter pressure against evacuation was voiced by individuals and groups friendly to the Japanese on the West Coast, especially religious organizations and leaders but because they "lacked precise information on the conduct of the Japanese at Hawaii"

[50] Leighton, *op. cit.,* p. 17. By permission.
[51] Grodzins, *op. cit.,* p. 21.
[52] *Ibid.,* p. 28.
[53] *Ibid.,* p. 42. By permission.

and "were beset by fears of the then victorious Japanese enemy" they were completely ineffective in their opposition.[54]

Summary: The Hawaiian Contrast. Comparison of the handling of the problem of the Japanese in Hawaii at the onset of World War II with the procedure adopted on the West Coast further supports the conclusion that the mainland policy was a serious mistake. In order to draw the contrast in the two areas, we shall first summarize the above discussion of the West Coast situation, and then turn to the Hawaiian scene.

The evacuation of the Japanese from the West Coast was the resultant of a series of interacting factors and forces in which the following appear as most significant: (1) Inevitably there was much fear among citizens of the Pacific Coast concerning the possible actions of some Japanese, a fear heightened by Japan's early military success. (2) Suspicion of the possible disloyalty of some Japanese was not wholly illogical in view of the substantial number of Kibei who had been schooled in Japan during the period of Japan's militant expansionism. (3) Adequate information on the part of the West Coast whites, even those friendly and sympathetic to the Japanese, by which to evaluate the specific rumors of sabotage was lacking. (4) A general pattern of dominant-minority relations, long nurtured throughout the history of native American–Japanese American relations on the West Coast, prevailed with consciousness of racial differences a basic factor. (5) The situation was ripe to evoke in active form the ever-present nativist elements. (6) The opportunity was favorable for specific white economic interests to remove the Japanese from competition. (7) The Federal Government was under the necessity of making a quick decision at a time when it was beset with many critical and new problems.

At the outbreak of war with Japan, persons of Japanese ancestry comprised about a third of Hawaii's population. Following Pearl Harbor, rumors arose of alleged espionage activities on the part of some island Japanese. Both the military and the insular authorities, failing to find specific evidence to support these rumors, placed their official weight on the side of allaying these rumors and indicating their confidence in the loyalty of the Hawaiian Japanese as a group. Limited restrictions were imposed on the alien Japanese similiar to those imposed on the West Coast, and similarly a few Japanese whose active records prior to war rendered them suspicious were interned. There were elements of the general insular population who were fearful of the possible dangers from the Japanese and other groups who called for firmer action. As Lind indicates there was an increase in public

[54] *Ibid.,* p. 361.

demonstrations of antagonism against Japanese persons, apparently more from the Filipinos in Hawaii than from the white or other ethnic elements.[55] However the authorities held firmly to their policy of active vigilance over the Japanese and arrest of only those who acted in a suspect manner. General suspicion and fear of the Japanese as a group subsided and the relations of the Japanese to the rest of the archipelago's population resumed, in the main, its prewar character. The correctness of the official judgment that the Japanese in general constituted no serious security threat to Hawaii was borne out by future events. Subsequent hearings on the charges of subversive activity by local Japanese brought forth emphatic denials from the War Department, the Federal Bureau of Investigation, and from various insular authorities.[56] On the positive side, the Japanese were cooperative in accepting the mild restrictions, continued their economic role in Hawaiian production, and ultimately made contributions to the armed services. In this connection Lind states: "The final count of Hawaiian war casualties revealed that 80% of those killed and 88% of those wounded throughout the war were of Japanese ancestry." [57]

How are we to account for the strikingly different policy adopted toward the Japanese in Hawaii in contrast to that of the West Coast? Contrary to what one might at first think, the much greater proportional Japanese population in the islands operated against a policy of internment. To have tried to police one-third of the population would have been a costly process. More important, however, the removal of the Japanese from the general labor force would have drastically reduced the productive capacity of Hawaii at a time when the maximum possible increase in production was essential to the war effort.

Moreover, underlying the more favorable treatment of the Japanese were certain facets of the general pattern of intergroup relations in Hawaii which are discussed in more detail below in Chapter 13. At this point we shall briefly call attention to two factors which stand in sharp contrast to the West Coast situation. First, in Hawaii prevailed a more friendly and less discriminatory pattern of intergroup relations. Tradition in Hawaii frowned upon any public or explicit discrimination based upon the consciousness of color. In the second place, the economic position of the Japanese in Hawaii had developed few antagonisms based upon occupational competition. While by 1940, the Japanese had as a group moved far out of their earlier role as plantation workers toward various city occupations, this transition had

[55] Andrew Lind, *Hawaii's Japanese* (Princeton: Princeton University Press, 1946), pp. 56-61.
[56] See Lind, *op. cit.*, pp. 38-47.
[57] Lind, *op. cit.*, p. 126.

not up to this time brought them into much direct competition for jobs with the socially dominant white population.

The effects of evacuation. The short-range effects of the evacuation and temporary resettlement upon the national welfare were costly indeed. Particular segments of the West Coast population, as we have seen, made substantial gains out of removal of the Japanese from competition. For these gains, the nation paid a heavy price. The removal of the Japanese retarded the war effort. While eventually many of them did find useful work to do during the war, they would have contributed more if they had remained where they were. In fact, many more Mexicans and Negroes migrated to California attracted by the high paying opportunities the wartime manpower shortage created. The whole process of evacuation, the operation of the centers, and the heartbreaking effort of WRA to relocate them cost time, money, and energy which could have been used to more constructive purpose.

The effect of the evacuation upon the prestige of the United States in world opinion is difficult to appraise. Because of their imperialist activities in Asia, Japanese abroad were thoroughly hated by many Asiatic peoples. Nevertheless, the way in which the Japanese in this country were dealt with in contrast to our treatment of Germans and Italians reflected our color bias, and cannot have raised our moral stock with nonwhite people in general.

Fourth phase: postevacuation adjustment. The short-run effects of relocation upon the Japanese have been noted in our discussion of their life under the jurisdiction of the WRA. The long-range effects will be seen as we now turn to consider the fourth phase of the life of Japanese in the United States, their readjustment after evacuation.

Economic Readjustment. Bloom and Riemer have estimated that the evacuated Japanese sustained an economic loss of $367,500,000 if income losses were added to all other losses incurred from forced sale of their assets, loss of business good will, and other losses attendant on their rapid removal.[58] Making a sample survey of 206 Japanese American families, these authors found the median loss per family to be $9870, counting household and personal loss, total property loss, fees and expenses, and loss of income figures at the 1941 values of the dollar.[59]

Expressed in individual terms, economic loss is illustrated in the words of a Santa Clara County Issei.

"Before war I had 20 acres in Berryessa. Good land, two good houses, one big. 1943 in camp everybody say sell, sell, sell. Maybe lose all. Lawyer write, he

[58] Leonard Bloom and Ruth Riemer, *Removal and Return* (Berkeley: University of California Press), 1949, pp. 202-204.
[59] *Ibid.,* p. 144.

say sell. I sell $650 acre. Now the same land $1500 acre. I lose. I cannot help. All gone. Now I live in hostel. Work like when first come to this country. Pick cherries, pick pears, pick apricots, pick tomatoes. Just like when first come. Pretty soon, maybe one year, maybe two years, find place. Pretty hard now. Now spend $15,000 just for land. No good material for house. No get farm equipment." [60]

Some fraction of their great loss will ultimately be compensated under a bill passed by Congress in July 1948 by which the Attorney General was empowered to reimburse any one person not to exceed $2500 for "damage to or loss of real or personal property . . . that is a reasonable and natural consequence of the evacuation. . . ." [61] Under the terms of the bill claims must be filed within 18 months of the date of enactment, and any claims for loss of anticipated profits or earnings must be excluded. Under this bill 24,409 claims were filed by Japanese Americans. By January, 1951, 231 cases had been adjudicated, and of these 156 persons had been paid.[62] One of the problems in settling these claims is the difficulty in proving the losses. At the time of evacuation few Japanese had considered obtaining documentary proof of sales on any disposition of properties in anticipation of such indemnity.

Further in economic terms, evacuation undermined the occupational position which the Japanese occupied prior to evacuation, and forced readjustment upon return at lower socioeconomic levels. Few farmers could reestablish themselves again, and produce dealers were fewer than before the war. Many of these went into contract gardening which provided a measure of the independence they formerly enjoyed. The great shortage of housing available for the Japanese increased the number of boarding and rooming houses where Japanese who did have homes added to their income by charging high prices to fellow Japanese. The housing shortage likewise increased the number of returnees who went into domestic service because it often provided housing. In general the pattern of employment upon return involved a shift from being either independently employed or working for other Japanese to working for non-Japanese employers. Bloom and Riemer estimate that prior to the war, not more than 20 per cent of the Japanese labor force in Los Angeles County worked for non-Japanese, but place the figure in 1948 at 70 per cent.[63] In partial

[60] People in Motion, The Postwar Adjustment of the Evacuated Japanese, United States Department of the Interior Publication, p. 53.
[61] Public Law 886, HR. 2999, cited and discussed by Bloom and Riemer, op. cit., pp. 198-200.
[62] Data obtained from the Japanese American Citizens League, Eastern Office, New York City.
[63] Ibid., pp. 67-68.

compensation for their generally lower occupational position, the wages in their present occupations are relatively higher than before.

While the welfare of the Japanese as a whole was lowered by the losses incurred through evacuation, several circumstances in the postwar situation have been accelerating the process of assimilation.

In Chapter 4, the hypothesis that dispersion of an ethnic group accelerates both acculturation and social acceptance was advanced as a principle of dominant-minority relations. The indications are that the Japanese in the United States in 1952 are more dispersed throughout the nation than they were prior to evacuation. By the end of 1946 —one year after the wartime centers were closed—the Interior Department estimated that only 55 per cent of the Japanese were living on the West Coast as against 86 per cent residing in the same region in 1940. Since then some of the Japanese relocated by the WRA outside the West Coast have remained where they were, and in some cases have been joined by their families; others, after a temporary sojourn elsewhere, have returned subsequently to the West Coast. Definitive statement concerning the effect of evacuation upon dispersion awaits publication of the findings of the 1950 Census on the distribution of the Japanese population.

Japanese Solidarity Weakened. We have seen above how the occupational shifts necessitated after evacuation have weakened the in-group economic solidarity of the Japanese. Other developments weakened both the communal and familistic control. While reaction to evacuation first brought families even closer together, the experience in relocation gave the Nisei more independence. They often earned more by working in the vicinity of the centers than their elders. They more often left the centers for places farther east. In marriages the tendency was for the Nisei to choose their own mates. "Of fundamental importance to the Japanese social system, the institution of arranged marriages is very nearly out of the picture as far as Nisei are concerned." [64] Again, "none of the community managed Japanese language schools have been reopened" since return from exile.[65] Finally, the number of Japanese language daily papers—all of which suspended publication during the war—is far fewer today (1946), and none of those now published has attained its prewar circulation or strength in the community.[66]

Favorable Change in Caucasian Attitudes. The attitude of the white population in the United States has changed in the direction of greater tolerance toward the Japanese. Outside the West Coast, the change be-

[64] *People in Motion,* p. 201.
[65] *Ibid.,* p. 201.
[66] *Ibid.,* p. 203.

gan during the war itself, in considerable measure due to the planned activities of the WRA in resettling many Japanese. As we have seen, in eastern cities particularly relocation met with considerable success. Smith writes, for example, "Acceptance was good in St. Louis from the very first, thanks to good planning. . . . . Social acceptance went as far as the Nisei were willing to carry it." [67] While acceptance in rural areas of the East was generally not good, Seabrook Farms at Bridgeton, New Jersey, is illustrative of a number of exceptions. When C. F. Seabrook, operator of the extensive farms where vegetables are grown for canning and freezing, announced in 1944 that he was going to employ Nisei, the community anticipated their arrival with considerable foreboding of trouble. Rather quickly however the natives adjusted themselves to the idea of having Japanese in their community.

Their fears died out as they got to know the people. "These people are clean and they're polite," one storekeeper said. "We didn't know what we might be up against when they came. Tell the truth, I'd rather wait on them now than a good many of my white customers."

At Bridgeton High School the Nisei students have the reputation of being well behaved. Caucasian parents were apprehensive when Nisei kids practically took over the grammar school near the farms, but their cleanliness and intelligence put any legitimate fears to rest.[68]

On the West Coast, knowledge that the Japanese were coming back evoked reaction from "racist minded" groups who had been instrumental in causing their evacuation in the first place. The American Legion, Veterans of the Foreign Wars, Native Sons of the Golden West, the California Farm Bureau all protested. New "Ban the Jap" committees sprang up. Certain newspapers ran scare headlines which made many Californians uneasy. "Hood River had jumped the gun by erasing the names of its sixteen Nisei soldiers from the honor roll" [subsequently restored].[69] In the first half of 1945 more than 30 serious incidents occurred throughout California, though most of these were concentrated in particular areas.

This time, however, there was a second set of reactions which had been lacking before. Many individuals and groups arose to demand that the Japanese be given fair play and became active in insisting that they get it. The Fresno Fair Play Committee organized to file eviction suits for Japanese unable to return to their homes. In Hood River, a Christian pastor organized the League for Liberty and Justice which "made a frontal attack on the shameful practice of refusing to sell

[67] Bradford Smith, *op. cit.,* p. 335.
[68] *Ibid.,* pp. 342-343. By permission.
[69] *Ibid.,* p. 346.

groceries and other necessities to Nisei." [70] When machinists of the San Francisco Municipal Railway threatened to strike in protest against the employment of a Nisei, Mayor Roger Lapham averted the strike by going to the shop in person explaining to the men why the Nisei was entitled to the job. Churches up and down the Coast were focal points of support for the Nisei. This second reaction finally won out.

The pressure of public opinion all over the country put California on the defensive. It came to a point where the civic pride of the several communities was challenged and race baiting lost favor. At the beginning of 1945 the West Coast papers had been four to one against the Japanese. A year later they were four to one in favor of fair and equal treatment.[71]

The Nisei Move Toward Marginality. Under these more favorable circumstances of the postwar period, the Japanese are moving more actively forward toward assimilation. One indication is more positive civic activity. Because the Issei could not become citizens and had for so long dominated the life of the segregated Japanese community the American born Japanese acquired far less experience in American civic and political life than the comparable generations of European nationalities. While there were some Japanese organizations established prior to 1930 to protect their group interests, in that year there was founded the Japanese American Citizens League (JACL) which was to emerge in the postevacuation period as the most influential organization. In its earlier years, JACL had failed to win the united support of their people, but by the end of 1947, this association had reached a membership of 7000 with local chapters in 50 cities. Its activities involved not only efforts at reducing discrimination but also the formulation of a streamlined American welfare program, dealing with juvenile delinquency, recreation, health. Although concerning itself with problems peculiar to Japanese, JACL invites membership from other than Japanese.

In the process of Americanization, the Japanese are reacting to other minorities in typical American fashion, as the following conclusions reached in the Report of the United States Department of Interior indicate:

Attitudes of Japanese Americans toward Negroes, Mexicans, and other minority peoples vary as greatly and in about the same proportion as may be found in the general population.

One result of the evacuation was to place a large number of Negroes in the former Little Tokyos. As we have seen, adjustments have been made so far with no appreciable trouble. The fact that the Japanese businessmen have

---

[70] *Ibid.*, p. 348.
[71] *Ibid.*, p. 349. By permission.

a considerable amount of trade with Negroes, which they did not have before the war, has already resulted in some shifts in attitude. In general, Negro attitudes towards Japanese Americans have been friendly . . . There is, however, some resentment of the favorable attention and the community assistance given Japanese Americans.

Among Japanese American leadership there is some division of opinion whether their group should become involved in problems relating to discrimination against Negroes. In a number of cases the JACL has appeared as a "friend of the court" in legal actions resulting from restrictive covenants on residential property where Negroes were involved . . .

Conversely, the degree of economic and social discrimination affecting Japanese Americans is so far below that placed upon Negroes, Mexicans, and most other minority groups, that there is very great hesitation among many in associating themselves with problems which do not immediately concern them. Japanese Americans living in cities which maintain a segregated social pattern may attend white schools, use white playgrounds, and be admitted to all hospitals. The fear on the part of Japanese Americans that identification with efforts to open these institutions to Negroes might result in added disabilities to themselves has undoubtedly had a deterrent effect on closer association between the two groups.[72]

Psychological Barriers. The psychological state of many Japanese at present illustrates clearly the principle of dominant-minority relations that long conditioning to minority status becomes a strong barrier within the minority itself toward assimilation. Nisei themselves have put it in these words:

Most of the Nisei are not prepared psychologically and by experience to lose themselves in the larger community. Most of the Nisei I've talked to have told me themselves that they preferred to stick to their own group, largely because they feel much more at ease in their own group. . . . The Nisei must first replace the fear he possesses with confidence. One way this can be accomplished is by being active in his own group which provides him with opportunities for developing leadership and in general gives him a sense of security.[73]

The self-consciousness of the Nisei is further seen in this pithy sentence taken from an article in the *Pacific Citizen* captioned "I'm tired of being a guinea pig."

I've been probed and dissected and discussed and directed till I am but a shell of flesh surrounding a well-nurtured inferiority complex.[74]

Court Decisions Undermining Discrimination Against Japanese. A number of court decisions invalidating laws and practices which discriminated against both Japanese and Chinese in America were handed

[72] *People in Motion*, pp. 224, 226.
[73] *Ibid.*, p. 245.
[74] *Ibid.*, p. 248.

down in the years 1948 through 1950. In June, 1948, the United States Supreme Court (*Takahashi* vs. *Game Commission of California*) declared unconstitutional a California law prohibiting the issuance of fishing licenses to persons ineligible for citizenship. In October, 1948, the Supreme Court of California ruled that this state's law barring interracial marriages was unconstitutional.

Three significant court decisions bearing upon West Coast laws prohibiting Oriental aliens from owning agricultural land were handed down in the same period. The United States Supreme Court in January, 1948, ruled in the case of *Oyama* vs. *California* that that section of the California alien land law raising presumption of fraudulent ownership and occupation of agricultural land by persons ineligible for citizenship was unconstitutional. In March, 1949, the Oregon Supreme Court held unconstitutional the state's 1923 Alien Land Law which prohibited the renting and leasing of land to Japanese aliens. The District Court of Appeals sitting at Los Angeles in April, 1950, held that California's law barring aliens ineligible for citizenship from owning land was contrary to the Constitution of the United States. In this case the Court made a further point of great significance when it also stated that the law involved was contrary to the Charter of the United Nations. The invoking of this international sanction in relation to a domestic issue has profoundly significant implications for the future of dominant-minority relations in the United States.

TOPICS FOR DISCUSSION AND PROJECTS

1. What reasons would you suggest for the fact that the Chinese who moved away from the West Coast have settled in or near large cities in the Midwest and Northeast rather than in other types of communities and other regions?
2. Suggest as many reasons as you can for the fact that the number of Chinese immigrants who settled permanently in this country is so much less than the number who ever came here.
3. Some writers on minorities have drawn parallels between Jewish-gentile relations and West Coast white–Japanese American relations. What parallels occur to you?
4. In view of the greater antagonism toward Orientals on the West Coast, how do you account for the fact that the great majority of the evacuated Japanese returned to this region to live after release from internment?
5. Discuss the significance of white-Oriental relations in the United States in connection with the present international situation.

SUGGESTED READING

Bloom, Leonard, and Riemer, Ruth. *Removal and Return*. Berkeley: University of California Press, 1949.
> *A careful study of the readjustment of the Japanese to the West Coast since World War II, with particular reference to economic adjustment.*

Embree, John E. *The Japanese Nation: A Social Survey*. New York: Rinehart & Co., Inc., 1945.
> *Provides a short but comprehensive description of the culture and social organization of modern Japan.*

Haynor, Norman S., and Reynolds, Charles N. "Chinese Family Life in America," *American Sociological Review*, Vol. 2, October, 1937, pp. 630-637.
> *Describes the changes occurring in Chinese-American families in the 20th Century.*

Leighton, Alexander. *The Governing of Men*. Princeton: Princeton University Press, 1934.
> *A study of the administration of the Japanese evacuation centers concerned with the contribution of the experience to social science theory.*

McKenzie, R. D. *Oriental Exclusion*. Institute of Pacific Relations Study. Chicago: University of Chicago Press, 1927.
> *An authoritative account of effects and implications of the acts attempting to exclude further Oriental immigration.*

Mears, Eliot G. *Resident Orientals on the Pacific Coast*. Institute of Pacific Relations Study. Chicago: University of Chicago Press, 1928.
> *A general study of both the Chinese and Japanese on the West Coast.*

Strong, Jr., E. K. *Japanese in California*. Stanford University Publications, University Series, Education-Psychology, Vol. 1, No. 2. Stanford: Stanford University Press, 1933.
—— *The Second Generation Japanese Problem*. Stanford: Stanford University Press, 1934.
> *These two volumes give a comprehensive picture of the situation of the Japanese in California up to 1930.*

Thomas, Dorothy S. "Some Social Aspects of Japanese-American Demography," *Proceedings of the American Philosophical Society*, Vol. 94, No. 5, October, 1950.
> *An authoritative, brief summary of Japanese immigration, population growth, the evacuation phenomenon, and the social consequences of these demographic trends.*

—— and Nishimoto, Richard S. *The Spoilage, Japanese-American Evacuation and Resettlement*. Berkeley and Los Angeles: University of California Press, 1946.
> *An intensive study of those Japanese who either were or became bitter enough about evacuation to renounce their citizenship or went back to Japan following World War II.*

CHAPTER   8

Negro-White Relations:
Biology and Background

Whenever and wherever the subject of minorities or of race relations in the United States is raised, the relation of Negroes to the rest of the population predominates. Among the manifold dominant-minority situations occurring under the American flag, Negro-white relations occupy first place as a social problem. This fact alone would require a more extensive treatment of the topic in a general text on minorities in the United States. Moreover, while the pattern and the process of Negro-white relations resemble in some measure the generalized dominant-minority type, there are elements of uniqueness which make it necessary to treat them as a distinctive type. In terms of numbers, Negroes constitute about one-tenth of the total continental United States population, 14,894,000 or 9.9 per cent in 1950. In terms of time, the Negro minority is by far the oldest.[1] Slaves were brought to Jamestown in 1619. On the eve of the American Revolution, Negroes comprised about one-fifth of the population. In terms of status, Negroes are accorded the lowest rank among all the minorities. In terms of welfare, a large portion of the Negro population stands well at the bottom, although, as we shall see, at the present time the welfare of Negroes is highly variable. In terms of culture difference, one of the significant barriers to immediate social acceptance on the part of immigrant groups, American Negroes are Ameri-

---

[1] Indian-white relations did not become dominant-minority relations in the true sense until the Indians became wards in 1870.

can, their original primitive cultures having been largely eliminated through long sojourn in America under slave and caste conditions.

Two factors which explain why Negroes have remained so long a minority in the United States are (1) that they are Negroid in their visible racial characteristics or in their known lineage; and (2) that their ancestors were slaves. Therefore it seems appropriate in the first of these four chapters devoted to Negro-white relations to focus attention upon the racial characteristics and population trends of the Negro; and to deal briefly with the period of slavery and its immediate aftermath.

THE CHARACTERISTICS OF THE AMERICAN NEGRO POPULATION

The past and present minority status of Negroes in the United States has rested in large measure on the beliefs developed and sustained in the minds of the dominant white population that American Negroes are Negroid in their biological traits and that being Negroid means that they are innately inferior. Accumulated scientific evidence establishes beyond question important qualifications to any truth that these beliefs possess. In the first part of this section, attention will be directed toward the first of the beliefs, that the American Negro is Negroid; and the second part to the belief that being Negroid means being innately inferior.

Racial ancestry of the Negro population. The "visibility" of the Negro minority derives from the fact that all the members have some genetic lineage from Negro ancestry. In the United States, a person is considered a Negro if he has any known Negro lineage whether he can be identified as of such lineage by his appearance or not. No precise data exist to indicate what distribution of the basic Negroid traits are now present in the population known as Negro. The United States Census count in 1920—the last year a distinction between mulatto and black was made—gave the figure of 15.9 per cent for mulattoes, which all students of the problem consider a gross undercount. Obviously census takers are not physical anthropologists. Herskovits made a study of 1551 Negroes by combined genealogical and anthropometric methods.[2] In Table 18 is to be found the distribution of his sample by racial ancestry according to the statements of the subjects themselves. The subjects were likewise measured for four traits: nostril width; height when seated; lip thickness; and skin color. A high correspondence was found between the measurements and the genealogical data. While Herskovits' sample contained a disproportionate number of more ed-

[2] Melville Herskovits, *The American Negro: A Study in Racial Crossing* (New York: Alfred A. Knopf, Inc., 1930).

ucated Negroes, known to have a greater proportion of white ancestry, the probability that many Negroes in his sample did not know of possible white ancestry from several generations back may have served to counterbalance the selective bias.

TABLE 18

Classification of 1551 American Negroes According to Racial Genealogy[3]

CLASS	NUMBER OF INDIVIDUALS	PER CENT OF TOTAL
Unmixed Negro	342	22.0
Negro, mixed with Indian	97	6.3
More Negro than white	384	24.8
More Negro than white, with Indian	106	6.9
About the same amount of Negro and white	260	16.7
The same class, with Indian mixture	133	8.5
More white than Negro	154	9.3
More white than Negro, with Indian	75	5.5
Total	1551	100.0

About all that can accurately be said is that the majority of Negroes in the United States show one or more of the basic Negroid traits—dark skin, thick lips, "wavy" hair, and prognathism; in a minor proportion, the evidences of these traits are so faint that one cannot be sure of identifying them; and in a relatively small percentage there is absolutely no somatic evidence of their Negro lineage, but either they themselves, or others who know them vouch for some Negro ancestry. In any event, the American Negro population of today is, biologically speaking, quite different from that of colonial days. The processes by which this change has come about will now be described. Since the matter of sexual relations is a subject particularly tabooed for scientific investigation, even more so when, as in the case at hand, they have been so frequently illicit, we shall find the evidence none too exact.

Selective mating processes influencing the genetic composition of the American Negro

Intertribal Mating. Knowledge of the ancestry of American Negroes is not very precise. However, it is now considered that most of the present Negro population traces the Negro part of its ancestry back to slaves who originally came from the West Coast of Africa, from

[3] *Ibid.*, p. 9. By permission of the publishers, Alfred A. Knopf, Inc.

Gambia down to Angola.[4] Although there is little accurate knowledge concerning their genetic traits, there can be little question that persons from as wide a tribal range as is indicated presented considerable variation. Since under slavery in the United States, their mating was not tribally endogamous, the first process was to intermix these original tribal variations. This would have had the result of producing a new, but African, Negro type if it had not been for the crossing of slaves very early with both Indians and white people.

Negro-Indian Crossing. In the United States prior to the 19th century, extensive intermingling between Indians and Negroes took place. Some of the admixtures disappeared into the Indian population. A few Indian tribes appear to have been lost almost completely by this process. In the sample study of Negro racial traits by Herskowits, 27 per cent of the subjects were found to have some Indian lineage.[5] Further Indian genetic strains resulted from the increasing importation, in the later periods, of slaves from the West Indies where comingling with the natives had occurred.

Negro-White Crossing. The population from which the African slaves were recruited already had some admixture of Caucasian genes, as a result of miscegenation with the Portuguese who settled on the Guinea Coast for slave trading purposes; and through contact in Europe whence some slaves were brought to the West Indies.

In the colonies themselves, the indications are that the first extensive Negro-white crossing took place between indentured white servants and Negro slaves involving either sex of one with either of the other. As the indentured servant disappeared and the Negro slave system developed, miscegenation between white and colored people continued through the access to Negro slave women which the slave system gave the white male owners of slaves, and to white men in general. Mulatto women were favorites in this connection.

A third stage came with the Civil War and its aftermath. "The Northern army left an unknown amount of Yankee genes in the Southern Negro people."[6] Under the caste system supplanting slavery, interracial crossing resumed more or less the same pattern of white male exploitation of Negro women, although the latter had more freedom of person than under slavery. While admitting that evidence is difficult on the matter, most writers on the Negro agree that the amount of miscegenation, that is to say, reproductively effective mating, has declined in the 20th century. Among the factors fre-

---

[4] E. Franklin Frazier, *The Negro in the United States* (New York: The Macmillan Company, 1949), pp. 4-6.
[5] See Table 18, p. 199.
[6] Gunnar Myrdal, *An American Dilemma* (New York: Harper and Brothers, 1944), p. 127.

quently cited to account for this tentative conclusion are, from the white side, a decline in demand for sexual congress with Negro women due to an increasing casualness in white female sexual behavior. From the Negro side, in the 20th century increasing numbers of Negro people have adopted white middle class attitudes toward sexual conventionality and have developed a maturing sense of racial pride. The increasing practice of contraceptive measures has also affected the selective process, since such sex relations as do occur between the two races are for the most part casual. In urban areas, both North and South, Negro prostitution involving white patrons developed as a special aspect of commercial vice. Prostitution has always been, however, a highly sterile sexual process.

"Light" Selection in the Negro Population. It is generally acknowledged even by Negro students of race relations that mate selection within the Negro population itself has been in favor of those Negroes who possessed the greater visible indices of Caucasian traits. The higher status ranking of mulattoes has been due not only to their "lightness" but also to the fact that the dominant white population has been somewhat more favorably inclined to them. Thus in general mulattoes had more economic and educational opportunity. This selective mating bias among Negroes has had the effect of increasing the distribution of white genetic factors in the Negro population. This effect is partially offset by the further consideration that "lighter" Negroes, tending to be more middle class in their standards, incline to have fewer children. The trend toward the development of Negro race pride, stimulated by certain elements of Negro leadership, may well reverse the effect of the process here being considered. To the extent that the present trend toward the devaluation of lightness increases, the Negro population will veer toward a mulatto norm and toward greater homogeneity about that norm. The extensive use at present of the term "brown" Americans in place of "black" in the literature concerning Negroes symbolizes the effect of this most recent process.[7]

Passing. By "passing" is meant the successful and permanent assumption of "white" status by a person who knows he has Negro ancestry. We shall have occasion to refer to this interesting phenomenon in other connections. Here we are concerned with its effects upon the two population groups involved. The number of persons involved in this process, according to Davie, are estimated to range from 2000 to 30,000 a year.[8] Drake and Cayton believe the number is 25,000 and

---

[7] For further discussion of this subject, see Otto Klineberg, ed., *Characteristics of the American Negro* (New York: Harper and Brothers, 1944), Pt. V, Ch. 9, "The Future of the Hybrid," by Louis Wirth and Herbert Goldhamer.

[8] M. R. Davie, *Negroes in American Society*, McGraw-Hill Book Company, Inc., 1949, p. 406.

probably more.[9] The effect of such passing as does take place is to remove from the Negro population strains which would increase the Caucasian admixture in the Negro population. The process adds some Negroid admixture to the white population but very little since the Negroes who pass have very few Negroid genes to add. The Negroid influence is further diluted by the tendency of "passers," if they marry, to select either white mates or equally white Negro mixtures. In this connection, it is pertinent to call attention to the fear which many white people and many "passable" Negroes have concerning the possible Negroid characteristics of children resulting from marriages of two white-appearing Negroes or of one of them to a white person. The probabilities of progeny from such unions are now known with high precision. As representative of the accepted view are these summary statements by Julian Lewis, Negro biologist:

Two very fair-complexioned Negroes will produce children 18 per cent of whom are pure white, 65 per cent the same color as the parents, and 17 per cent a shade darker than both parents.

When a white person mates with a very fair Negro who is sometimes able to pass for white but not of the 'pure white' type, 40 per cent of the resulting children are of the same color as the white parent, less than 60 per cent are the color of the Negro parent, and less than 1 per cent is darker than the Negro parent. The possibility of this one exception frequently causes untold worry and concern in such unions.

Some of the children of matings involving fair Negroes are pure white according to accepted standards of whiteness. Such types are known to geneticists as "extracted whites." When an extracted white mates with a full white or another extracted white, none of the children will ever be darker than the parents.[10]

Summary and future possibilities. Through the operation of these many selective processes, and differential birth rates, to which we next turn, the Negro population of contemporary America varies widely in its biological traits. The range is fairly well known, but the frequencies at various intervals of the range are not all well known. Therefore, in the strict scientific sense of the term, it is not clear that the term "race" should be applied to the American Negro population. Future trends in the biological characteristics of American Negroes depend in large measure upon social and cultural influences, many of which have already been discussed above. In general, there appear two alternative possibilities. First, the Negro population may tend toward

[9] St. Clair Drake and Horace R. Cayton, *Black Metropolis* (New York: Harcourt, Brace & Company, Inc., 1945), p. 160.
[10] Julian Lewis, "What Color Will Your Baby Be?" *Negro Digest*, Vol. V, Nov., 1945, pp. 6-7. For fuller treatment see Julian Lewis, *The Biology of the Negro* (Chicago: University of Chicago Press, 1942). By permission.

a more homogeneous type which for short may be symbolized by the term "brown Americans." This development would be favored by the continued decline in miscegenation, illicit or legal, by passing, and by the continued increase in the development of Negro race consciousness and pride. The second possibility to be considered is the gradual disappearance of the Negro population through absorption into the white population.[11] Only a steady increase in the amount of miscegenation between Negroes and whites, contrary to the present trend, could bring this about and it would take, like all similar biological processes, centuries in any case. Therefore, as a possible "solution" of America's 20th century Negro problem, amalgamation into the white population may for all practical purposes be counted out. As yet, no mention has been made of the possibility of the Negro population in the United States absorbing the white. In order to deal with this theoretical alternative, the facts concerning the present trends in the growth of the Negro population are necessary.

THE GROWTH OF THE NEGRO POPULATION

Numerical increase but proportional decrease. Table 19 shows that the number of Negroes in the United States has grown each decade since 1790, the time of the first census count. It also shows, with some temporary decennial rises, that the proportion of the Negroes to the total population has declined down to 1930. Between 1930 and 1950 the proportion increased slightly. Although influenced by net reproduction rates, the proportional decline is primarily due to the proportionally great increase in the white population brought about by immigration from Europe. Since an analysis of the population growth in the past would serve little purpose in understanding the current scene, attention will focus upon the recent rise. The net reproduction rates[12] for the white and Negro population in 1930 were substantially the same—110 and 111 respectively. From 1940, the comparable rates for whites were 94 and for Negroes, 107. The tentative conclusions reached by Myrdal in his analysis of this recent proportional rise are

[11] Ralph Linton has stated this thesis in an article, "The Vanishing American Negro," *The American Mercury*, Vol. 64, No. 278, pp. 133-139, Feb., 1947, and further suggests that the Negro will thus "vanish" in about two hundred years. An effective criticism of Linton's position is to be found in the *American Sociological Review*, Vol. 13, No. 4 (Aug., 1948), "Is the American Negro Becoming Lighter? An Analysis of the Sociological and Biological Trends," pp. 437-443, by William M. Kephart.

[12] The net reproduction rate (NRR) is a measure of the average number of daughters that will be produced by women throughout their lifetime if subject to prevailing birth and death rates, or life-table rates on which such calculations may be based. Many nations (and the United Nations) express the NRR in terms of one woman (U. S. NRR 1946, 1.359) while the United States Bureau of the Census expresses the NRR in terms of 100 women (U. S. NRR 1946, 135.9).

T A B L E 19

Growth of the Negro Population Since 1790[13]

Census Year	Number of Negroes	Percentage of Total Population	Percentage Increase of Negroes During Decade	Percentage Increase of Whites During Decade
1950	14,894,000	9.9	15.8	14.4
1940	12,865,518	9.8	8.2	7.2
1930	11,891,143	9.7	13.6	15.7
1920	10,463,131	9.9	6.5	15.7
1910	9,827,763	10.7	11.2	21.8
1900	8,333,940	11.6	18.0	21.2
1890	7,488,676	11.9	13.8	26.7
1880	6,580,793	13.1	34.9	29.2
1870	4,880,009	12.7	9.9	24.8
1860	4,441,830	14.1	22.1	37.7
1850	3,638,808	15.7	26.6	37.7
1840	2,873,648	16.8	23.4	34.7
1830	2,328,642	18.1	31.4	33.9
1820	1,771,656	18.4	28.6	34.2
1810	1,377,808	19.0	37.5	36.1
1800	1,002,037	18.9	32.3	35.8
1790	757,208	19.3		

presented as the most carefully drawn, despite, as he says, many errors in the data. They are:

1. That Negroes, like whites, are not reproducing themselves so rapidly as they used to.

2. That probably their rate is now higher than that of the whites.

3. That this differential is a new phenomenon, at least insofar as it is significant. If such a differential continues into the future and if it is not fully compensated for by immigration of whites, the proportion of Negroes in the American population may be expected to rise, though slowly.

4. Even within regions and rural-urban areas taken separately, Negroes are no longer reproducing themselves at a lower rate than whites. In fact, the figures suggest that they are reproducing themselves more—thus reversing the position they held in 1930 and earlier.[14]

Summary prediction. The significant probabilities emerging from this analysis of the qualitative and quantitative changes in the Negro population are these: (1) that beyond this century the United States will

[13] Source: U. S. Bureau of the Census, *Negroes in the United States, 1920–1932*, pp. 1-2; *Sixteenth Census of the United States, 1940, Population*, Vol. II, *Characteristics of the Population*, p. 19. 1950 figures from U. S. Census, 1950, preliminary report, Series PC-7, No. 1.

[14] Myrdal, *op. cit.*, p. 160-161. By permission of the publishers, Harper and Brothers.

have a Negro element sufficiently visible in somatic characteristics to be distinguished from the rest of the population; and (2) that this Negro element will remain for the country as a whole a definite numerical minority. Thus this Negro population will possess two attributes useful to the dominant white group in keeping Negroes in minority status, if the dominants so wish to utilize them. Whatever social policy is adopted concerning Negro-white relations must reckon with these biological probabilities. Only a policy of annihilation or one of emigration of Negroes can afford to disregard them.

Distribution of the Negro population. The Negro population in the United States has been highly concentrated in the South throughout the entire period of their sojourn in the area. In 1790 only a scattering of Negroes lived outside the South;[15] in 1940, 77 per cent of all American Negroes still lived in that region. Since 1860 the two most important regional migrations have been the so called "Great Migration" to the North commencing in 1915; and the small, but hitherto unprecedented, westward movement beginning about 1940.

Under slavery, Negro migration was of course governed by the owners and traders of slaves. The southern and southwestern expansion of the plantation economy from the upper South was paralleled by a corresponding expansion of the growing Negro population in these areas. In spite of the technical freedom for Negroes to move where they desired after the Civil War, very few Negroes migrated to the North, and almost none to the West. In the post-bellum period, there has been considerable shifting about of the Negro population in the South itself, the net result of which was to increase the proportion of the Negro population living in Southern cities. Between 1910 and 1940 the proportion of the Southern Negro population living in cities increased from 22 per cent to 37.3 per cent. Aside from this urban drift, the other most important demographic change in the South has been the decreased concentration of the Negro population in the "Black Belt," composed of counties in eastern Virginia and North Carolina, all of South Carolina, central Georgia and Alabama, and a detached tier of counties in the lower Mississippi River Valley. From 1900 to 1940, the Negro population in this area declined from 4,057,619 to 2,642,808. While in 1880 over half (57 per cent) of the total Negro population of the country was located in the Black Belt, only about one fourth (26.15 per cent) was residing in this area in 1940.[16]

[15] Throughout this book the term *South* will mean, unless otherwise stated, the following states: Alabama, Arkansas, Delaware, Florida, Georgia, Kentucky, Louisiana, Maryland, Mississippi, North Carolina, Oklahoma, South Carolina, Tennessee, Texas, Virginia, and West Virginia, and the District of Columbia.
[16] Frazier, *op. cit.*, pp. 187-190.

The Great Migration of Negroes to the North began in 1915 in response to the great demand for labor created by World War I. Between 1910 and 1940, this migration netted about 1,750,000 additional Negroes to the Northern population. Almost all the migrants moved to Northern cities, concentrating particularly in the largest urban centers. By 1940, 16.19 per cent of the Northern Negro population was in New York City, and large Negro populations were located in Chicago, Philadelphia, Detroit, Cleveland, and Pittsburgh.[17] Because of the total numbers involved the concentration of Negroes in the metropolitan North is especially noted, yet the distribution of Negroes in many smaller cities of the North reached such a proportion even before 1940 that race relations had become a significant community problem. For example, there were 15 cities in New Jersey in which in 1940 Negroes comprised 10 per cent or more of the population and 12 more in which the Negro population ranged from 5 to 9 per cent.[18]

The most recent trend in the movement of Negro population has been migration to the West, more specifically to the larger cities of the West Coast. Up to 1940, few Negroes lived in the West. In 1940 Negroes comprised 1.2 per cent of the total population of the West, and these constituted 1.3 per cent of the total Negro population.[19] Just as World War I precipitated the northward migration, the labor demands created by World War II stimulated this westward trek.

Preliminary reports of the 1950 census show that the northward and westward trends in Negro migration have continued in the decade 1941–1950. The proportion of the total Negro population living in the South dropped from 77 per cent in 1940 to 69 per cent in 1950. Whereas the population of the white South increased 16.5 per cent over 1940, the Negro South increased only 3.1 per cent. The percentage increase over the same period in the Negro population in the Northeast was 44.2 per cent and in the North Central Region 50.2 per cent, obviously reflecting substantial migration. In the West the Negro population increased during the decade 237.4 per cent against a 40.9 per cent increase in the white population. Because, however, so few Negroes lived in the West before, the percentage of the region's total population which was Negro in 1950 was only 2.5 per cent, and in actual numbers, approximately 576,000.

The significance of Negro population movements. We shall have occasion to consider later the bearing which the size of the Negro population in any community, state, or region has upon the character of race relations in a given locality. For example, in those local areas of

[17] Myrdal, *op. cit.*, p. 183.
[18] U. S. Census, 1940, *Population*, Vol. II, New Jersey, Tables 32, 34.
[19] See 1940 Census.

the South where Negroes exceed whites in number, it is understandable that the thought of a breakdown in the caste system should create a fear in the minds of most whites that approaches the intensity of an obsession. In contrast, in some Northern cities where a few Negroes live in the community, from the white side at least, there was scarcely a conscious awareness of race relations as a problem. Up to now the shifts in Negro population have been primarily affected by the pull of fortuitous economic opportunity; and secondarily by the desire to move into a community where there are a sufficient number of other Negroes to permit sociability among them. Since the reaction of the white community to Negroes is affected by their proportional numbers among them, the suggestion that efforts be made to induce Negroes to distribute themselves in numbers favorable to harmonious adjustment has been advanced as one solution of the problem of Negro-white relations.[20]

CHARACTERISTICS OF AMERICAN NEGRO PEOPLE

The stereotype of the American Negro current in popular white thought characterizes him in about this way: The Negro is lazy, won't work unless he has to, and doesn't know what to do with money when he gets it. He is dirty, smelly, careless in appearance, yet given to flashy dressing. He is much more "sexy" than the white man, and exercises no restraint in its expression. He has low mental ability incapable of anything but menial labor. He is naturally religious, but his religion is mostly emotion and superstition. On the other hand in his simple way, the Negro is a likable fellow, clever in a childlike way, and has natural abilities as a singer, dancer, and actor which surpass those of most white folks.

Guy Johnson made an extensive study of the opinions concerning the personality and cultural traits of the American Negro as found in the literary characterizations of an assorted collection of writers, both Negro and white, ranging from plain journalism to varying degrees of "scientific" authority. He then essayed to combine the various opinions and judgments into a composite picture which represents in his words "a 'boiling down' of popular notions, common sense observations, and semiscientific pronouncements." Before reading this list as presented below it is imperative that the reader understand that it is "simply a descriptive list, based on a fair degree of consensus, of the interests, habits, and tendencies which might serve to characterize the 'typical' Negro." Insofar as it has any validity, it tells us nothing concerning

[20] Joseph H. Dougas and Albert N. Whiting, "An Approach to Negro-White Relations," *Phylon*, Vol. 10, No. 2, 1949, pp. 146-152.

how the "typical" Negro got this way. Furthermore the "typical" Negro represents the Negro masses, not the minority of "highly sophisticated" Negroes.

Negro personality and culture traits [21]

Mental. Relatively low intellectual interests; good memory; facile association of ideas.

Temperamental. Gregariousness or high interest in social contacts; philosophical or get-the-most-out-of-life type of adjustment; high aesthetic interests; love of subtlety and indirection; adaptability.

Emotional. Warmer emotional tone in every sphere of life; less inhibition of the expression of emotion.

Aesthetic. Love of music and dance; oratory and power of self-expression; high interest in and appreciation of the artistic.

Economic. Relatively low interest in material things, such as care of money, property, tools, etc.; line of least resistance in habits of work; relative lack of self-reliance.

Personal Morals. Double standard of morals and ethics, i.e., one for his behavior toward Negroes and another for his behavior toward whites; personal honesty, e.g., not up to standard in behavior toward whites; in sexual conduct, higher interest in sex, high sexual indulgence, and larger sphere of permissive sex relations.

Family and Home Life. Relatively low solidarity; high frequency of common-law matings and separations; role of mother strong; warmth of affection toward children; high rate of illegitimacy.

Religion and the Supernatural. Rather high emotional tone; personalization of God and saints; high interest in "superstition"—i.e., belief in various supernatural forces and ways of controlling them.

Law Observance. Relatively high incidence of social disorder; drunkenness, fighting, gambling, petty stealing, etc.; resentment against the white man's law.

Public Manners. Tendency toward extroversion in public contacts; easy sociability, loud talk; relative carelessness in speech and dress.

Race Pride. Not yet highly developed; inferiority feelings common; acceptance of white standards of physical beauty to a large extent.

Race Consciousness and Leadership. Lack of cohesion; high intragroup conflict and cleavage; distrust of leaders; lack of strong race-wide leadership.

This characterization by literary consensus tends in some degree to confirm the unreflective stereotype of the general white American public, even though the wording is more discriminating and objectively phrased, as for example, "relatively low intellectual interests" rather than "naturally mentally inferior." Furthermore, in locating traits more flattering to the Negro this list is more discerning than the popu-

---

[21] Guy B. Johnson, "The Stereotype of the American Negro," in Klineberg, *op. cit.,* pp. 18-19. By permission of the publisher, Harper and Brothers.

lar stereotype. The Negro is "adaptable," has a "good" memory, "high interest in and appreciation of the artistic"; and possesses "warmth of affection" toward children.[22]

As one reads this somewhat detailed characterization, the question arises, even if these traits do broadly characterize the Negro, how far do they really distinguish him from other ethnic types? Would not "high interest in the artistic" apply to the Italian? or "love of subtlety" perchance to the Chinese? or "gregariousness" to any number of other ethnic types? Again while some traits are so stated as to show comparative reference to white norms, for example, in the high rate of illegitimacy, who knows in the case of other alleged traits, for example, "drunkenness," whether they are more marked among Negroes than among many other American groups?

Another source of information concerning the characteristics of American Negroes lies in the results of psychological tests of various sorts designed to determine comparative differences between Negro and non-Negro groups. Since we reviewed the results of tests of general intelligence in Chapter 3, we need here only recall the broad conclusions. The results showed that the performance of Negroes in general is less satisfactory than that of general white samples. Studies of differences in other personality traits are not extensive and, according to Klineberg, have yielded few definite conclusions. The testing of small samples has indicated that Negroes are more extravertive than whites; that they are more suggestible; and that Negro children are more sociable in their play habits than white children. Other studies of particular traits have failed to show significant differences, for example, in color preferences, handwriting, and in the perception of emotional expression.[23]

Determinants of American Negro personality and culture. In the absence of more precise studies of Negro characteristics, the profile outlined by Johnson may serve as a rough description, provided we remember that the type to which it applies is the Negro population brought up under the conditions which generally surround Negroes in American life. Each year the number of Negroes to whom the stereotype applies, however, grows fewer. We turn attention next to inquire what the determinants of these type characteristics have been. For this purpose exploration of three main areas of determinants is pertinent: genetic racial determinants; aboriginal African cultural determinants; and the impact of the experience of Negroes in the United States. In this section we shall consider the first two of these sets of influences.

[22] Cf. the "lady of the races" description of Negro personality by Robert E. Park in R. E. Park and Ernest W. Burgess, *Introduction to the Science of Sociology* (Chicago: University of Chicago Press, 1931), pp. 138-140.
[23] Klineberg, *op. cit.*, Part III, "Experimental Studies of Negro Personality," pp. 99-138.

The third will be treated in the subsequent three chapters, 9, 10, and 11.

"Race" and Negro characteristics. The point of view of contemporary social science concerning the role of racial heredity in determining the behavior and culture of human groups was set forth in Chapter 3. The application of these current views on racial factors to the topic at hand can therefore be treated briefly. In restatement, social science has shown that none of the evidence purporting to establish connections between the racial genetic factors and either the general range of intellectual capacity or of predispositions toward any particular personality traits or cultural expressions is adequate. As far as general intelligence is concerned, the study of Negro-white groups was used in Chapter 3 to demonstrate this general point. Concerning other psychological differences between Negro and white in the United States, we refer to Myrdal's conclusions. High significance may be attached to the fact that in his monumental treatise on the Negro in America, Myrdal devotes only 20 pages to the topic of racial characteristics, and that in large part those are devoted to criticizing any racial interpretation of the findings of the studies which have been made. Myrdal indicates, with reference to studies comparing Negro and white psychological traits, that while the first of such studies shows significant average differences between the two groups, the later studies throw presumptive doubt on a racial interpretation.

The large amount of overlapping brought out the fact that both Negroes and whites belonged to the same human species and had more similarities than differences. The averages themselves tended to come nearer each other when the measurements were refined to exclude more and more the influence of differences in environment, such as education, cultural background and experience, socioeconomic class; and the social factors in the test situation itself, such as motivation and rapport with the tester.

The intensive studies of these last influences proved, in addition, that no psychological tests yet invented come even close to measuring innate psychic traits, absolutely undistorted by these influences. *They rather rendered it probable that average differences would practically disappear if all environmental factors could be controlled.*[24]

Much of the error involved in racial genetic interpretations of group differences has grown out of inadequate comprehension of the complexity of environment. Social science has penetrated the depths of "environment" at a rapid rate in recent years. Environment is more than geography and more than the immediate material setting, such as a slum or a suburban residential area. Included as well is the entire

[24] Myrdal, *op. cit.*, p. 147. Italics ours. By permission of the publishers, Harpers and Brothers.

configuration of social relationships in which the individual interacts, for example, the social situation of the only child, or the child brought up in the home of an alcoholic mother.

One aspect of the environment of the Negro in the United States, which makes it distinctive, in degree perhaps from that of all other people, and in kind, shared only with other minorities is minority status itself. As long as the stigmatism of minority status exists, it renders the environment of the minority and the dominant different. To take a hypothetical research problem in this connection, let us set ourselves the task of measuring the relative quantum of ambition to be found in a white and a Negro group. Since we recognize that the economic and living conditions of the two groups as a whole are quite disparate, we first seek to equalize the factors in our selection of a sample for measurement. We seek whites as well as Negroes who are poor, who have less schooling, who live in overcrowded homes. Let us assume that our results still show a significant lesser quantum of ambition in the Negro sample. Before attributing this remaining difference to racial heredity, we would do well to investigate what the effect of minority status, a factor which is still different in our samples, may contribute to the difference.

The influence of African culture. In the case of all the minority groups thus far considered, cultural differences derived from their nationality and ethnic origins have played a major part in influencing their adjustment and final acculturation to American life. The situation of Negroes in this respect is considerably different. The sharp impact of slavery went far to destroy the many and varied tribal cultures which the Negroes brought with them. Scholarly controversy prevails among the students of Negro history in the New World concerning the extent to which African culture traits have survived, or to what extent Negro cultural adaptations in the New World were influenced by their aboriginal culture.[25] A considerable number of scattered, specific cultural traits have been found in specific Negro groups which can be directly traced to African origin. It is, however, significant that more of these have been found among Negro groups in the West Indies, and that among those found in the United States the groups involved were especially isolated. Concerning other more prevalent aspects of American Negro culture and behavior which present a vague, general similarity to African cultural forms, the continuity of the African heritage is highly debatable. We may cite these examples to illustrate the point

[25] A brief introduction to this historical problem is found in Frazier, *op. cit.*, Ch. I, "Significance of the African Background." For fuller discussion of the topic, see Melville J. Herskovits, *The Myth of the Negro Past* (New York: Harper and Brothers, 1942).

at issue. Is the frequency of common-law marriage in Negro rural life derivative from African customs, or is it interpretable in terms of the highly destructive impact of slavery upon stability of Negro family life? Or again is the predilection of American Negroes toward the Baptist denomination which features total immersion, due to the surviving influence of West African "river cults" upon their choice, as Herskovits speculates, or is it more simply attributable, as Frazier suggests, to the vigorous proselytizing activities of the Baptist denomination.[26] In any case, there are few facets of Negro personality type or cultural expressions for which a logical explanation cannot be derived in terms of Negro adaptation to the conditions of slavery and minority status.

In view of the rapidly accelerating rate at which the Negro people in the United States are becoming acculturated to the normative white culture, the question of African survivals has little significance for the future, except in one respect. The advancement of American Negroes to full-fledged acceptance has been, and still is, retarded by their own feeling that Negroes have never amounted to much in human history.[27] Viewing history in broad perspective, at the primitive level and in the historic periods prior to the white man's domination, African civilizations showed high levels of development. Because of the servile position occupied by Negroes under white dominance, their historic position has not been adequately publicized. A more adequate and accurate treatment of Negro history, both African and American, would have two effects. It would increase the feeling of racial self-respect among Negroes and decrease the feeling of racial superiority among white people.

Stages in Negro-white relations. The history of Negro-white relations in the United States may be divided into four broad stages: (1) the period of slavery, 1619 to 1863; (2) the period of reconstruction, 1864 to 1880; (3) the period of biracial accommodation, 1881 to 1940; and (4) the period of emergent assimilation, 1941 to the present. The first and second of these stages engage attention in the remainder of this chapter.

THE PERIOD OF SLAVERY

The colonial period. Since there was no precedent in English law dealing with slaves when the first 20 slaves were bought by Virginia settlers from a Dutch ship in 1619, it seems to have been assumed that their status was similar to that of the white indentured servant, with stipulated ways of being manumitted. However, early in colonial history,

---

[26] Frazier, *op. cit.*, pp. 10-18.
[27] Interrelated with this inferiority reaction is the feeling of "self-hatred," which some writers attribute to the personality of minority people. See pp. 418-419.

differential treatment of Negroes from other bonded persons began. For example, three bound servants, two white and one Negro, had been brought back to Virginia from Maryland after attempting to escape from servitude. While the court ordered thirty lashes for all three, it further ordered that the white servants should serve three years extra time in bondage, but that the Negro should serve his master for the rest of his life.[28] By court actions such as these, the differential status of Negroes evolved into a clear pattern of slavery which eventually became established by more explicit law. In Virginia, the slave status was fixed by a law making all non-Christians who came into the colony as servants from across the seas slaves for the rest of their lives. In 1682, this law was repealed and in its place another substituted "making slaves of all persons of non-Christian nationalities thereafter coming into the colony, whether they came by sea or land and whether or not they had been converted to Christianity after capture." [29]

Although early developing into a fixed institution, Negro slavery grew indispensable only as the plantation system of agriculture became important and more widespread. This system involving the large-scale production of a staple crop for commercial exchange required cheap labor. White men at a time when land was either free or cheap, wanted to work as independent farmers, not as wage earners. Thus Negro slaves filled the manpower need and the demand for more of them increased. The colony of Georgia, founded in 1735, first prohibited the importation of Negro slaves. But by 1750, as the plantation system began to spread into the new colony, this act was repealed. As a result the number of Negroes in Georgia increased from a reported 349 in 1750 to 15,000 by 1773.[30] The nexus between the plantation economy and slavery is further illustrated by the differences between the two Carolinas. The plantation economy failed to develop on a large scale in North Carolina and so did slavery; in South Carolina where the plantation system developed on a large scale, "the number of Negroes had become so numerous that it was felt necessary to encourage the importation of white servants to secure the safety of the colony." [31] Finally, as is well known, in the North where there was no plantation economy no large-scale slavery developed. By 1790 when the first Federal census was taken, the proportion of free Negroes to those in slavery ranged from the all-free Negro population (5,462) in Massachusetts to other states where from a third to a half of the few resident Negroes were still slaves.[32]

[28] Frazier, *op. cit.*, p. 24.
[29] *Ibid.*, p. 26.
[30] *Ibid.*, p. 32-33.
[31] *Ibid.*, p. 32.
[32] *Ibid.*, p. 34.

The introduction of slavery into the colonies came as an extension of the slavery institution already established in the West Indies. The slave trade to the colonies was largely carried on by the British although subsequently colonists themselves took a hand in it, especially New England port merchants.[33] This trade was a highly hazardous and adventurous occupation. It was not easy to procure slaves in the first place and not easy to deliver them in the second place, since, aside from the problem of holding them by force, great mortality occurred from the usually overcrowded conditions prevailing in the "Middle Passage" journeys. However, when the risk succeeded, as it obviously so often did, the profits were high. Franklin writes, "It was not unusual for a ship carrying 250 slaves to net as much as £7,000 on one voyage. Profits of 100 per cent were not uncommon for Liverpool merchants." [34] The number of slaves imported to the colonies, and later to the states is not known, the estimates ranging from 500,000 to 700,000. In spite of the fact that the importation of slaves was officially prohibited after 1808, the evidence is incontrovertible that a substantial contraband trade continued after that date. Collins estimates that about 270,000 slaves were imported into the United States between 1808 and 1860.[35]

The total number of slaves imported from Africa to all the New World from the 15th century to the 19th century from all accounts must be reckoned in the millions. Williams writes "The importation into Jamaica from 1700 to 1786 was 610,000, and it has been estimated that the total import of slaves into all the British colonies between 1680 and 1786 was over two million." [36] Bearing in mind the number who died resisting capture and the heavy mortality on shipboard, it can be seen that the slave trade constituted a terrific drain on the manhood of Africa, particularly in the West Coast area, and especially since the traders tried to procure the youngest and healthiest men.

From the Revolutionary War to the War Between the States. In spite of the fixed position of slavery in colonial economy during and for a short period following the Revolutionary War, signs developed that the slavery system might be abolished. Slavery came under increasing attack from a moral viewpoint, not only from Northerners but from enlightened slave holders such as Washington and Jefferson. The first President desired "to see a plan adopted for the abolition of it

[33] Davie, *op. cit.*, p. 18.
[34] John Hope Franklin, *From Slavery to Freedom* (New York: Alfred A. Knopf, Inc., 1947), p. 57.
[35] Winfield H. Collins, *The Domestic Slave Trade of the Southern States* (New York: Broadway Publishing Company, 1904), p. 20.
[36] Eric Williams, *Capitalism & Slavery* (Chapel Hill: University of North Carolina Press, 1944), p. 33.

[slavery];" [37] Jefferson wrote in his autobiography, "Nothing is more certainly written in the book of fate than that these people are to be free." [38] The division of the public attitudes was affected by economic interests as well as moral idealism. Frazier indicates that opposition to slavery was expressed in Delaware, Maryland, and Virginia where a diversified agriculture was supplanting the production of tobacco, whereas in the lower South, where the production of tobacco, rice, and indigo was still important, there was strong opposition either to suspending the slave trade or the emancipation of the Negro.[39] In the midst of these conflicting public attitudes toward slavery, the Constitution of the new republic compromised on the issue by setting 1808 as the date after which the importation of slaves was to be abolished. The abolition of slavery in many state constitutions in the North and its declining economic significance led many people to share with Jefferson the belief that slavery was on its way out.

The hopes of those opposed to slavery were destined to be dashed by the invention of the cotton gin. With this invention Southern cotton planters were able to solve the technical problem necessary to meet the rapidly growing demand of the English market. The expansion of cotton economy increased by leaps and bounds, especially from 1815 on. This development was accompanied by the growth of the slave system and the slave population. (See Table 20.)

TABLE 20

Growth of the Slave Population in the United States, 1790–1860 [40]

CENSUS YEAR	SLAVE POPULATION	DECENNIAL INCREASE
1790	697,624	
1800	893,602	28.1
1810	1,191,362	33.3
1820	1,538,022	29.1
1830	2,009,043	30.6
1840	3,204,355	23.8
1850	3,204,313	28.8
1860	3,953,760	23.4

From 1790 to 1808, the natural increase of the slave population was supplemented by foreign importation in excess of 100,000. While, as Table 20 shows, the percentage of increase after 1810 declined, a substantial number of slaves were smuggled in to augment the natural

[37] Myrdal, *op. cit.*, p. 85.
[38] *Ibid.*
[39] Frazier, *op. cit.*, p. 35.
[40] Source: U. S. Bureau of the Census, *A Century of Population Growth*, p. 133.

increase. Moreover the increasing demand for slaves in the face of legal prohibition of new imports resulted in the development of a great domestic slave trade. As the plantation system spread south and west away from Maryland, Virginia, and Kentucky, many slaves were sold by owners in the latter to those in the former.

Having then built not only its economy but a total society upon the foundation of slavery, the South needed rationalizations which would justify it. Thus there began to emerge in the pre-Civil War period learned treatises solemnly concluding that "the Negro" was naturally meant to be a slave, that he was obviously inferior to the white. Many of these treatises invoked Biblical sanction and two of the most scholarly were written by Presbyterian ministers.[41] The growing intellectual support for the established system reached its climax in the words of Chief Justice Taney who in the course of his famous decision in the Dred Scott case declared, "A Negro has no rights which a white man need respect." [42]

Thus, far from declining, it appeared clear that the slave system during the early 19th century in the South grew constantly stronger. This is important to keep in mind as we turn to the reconstruction days. It does much to explain why the Emancipation Proclamation which freed slaves in the legal sense did not free them from the caste barriers which were erected to supplant those of slavery.

The American slave system: comparison with Latin America. The general character of a slave system and the nature of master-slave relations is implicit in the words themselves. Among the many instances of such systems, however, there is considerable variation. The degree of authority accorded to the master is affected by many factors of which the economic role of the slaves and the character of the other institutions in the society are important. The actual exercise of the permitted authority is always colored by the common human qualities of affection, on the one hand, and of aggressiveness, on the other, qualities which are in part structured by the general culture but always to some extent vary with individual personalities. Likewise the responses of

[41] Frazier, *op. cit.*, p. 42.
[42] Part of the decision rendered in the Dred Scott Case (Mar. 6, 1857) as quoted in *The Columbia Encyclopedia* (New York: Columbia University Press, 1940), p. 1728. Dred Scott, a Negro slave, was taken by his master from the slave state of Missouri into free territory. Upon return, Scott sued for his freedom on the ground that residence in Illinois, a free state, and in Minnesota, a free territory, made him a free citizen. The case came up in the Missouri courts, but after Scott was purchased by a citizen of New York, suit was filed in the Federal courts. Financed by Abolitionists, the case reached the Supreme Court, where Chief Justice Roger B. Taney rendered the opinion taken as that of the majority. (1) It upheld the Missouri courts in declaring that Scott, still a slave, was not a citizen. (2) It declared the Missouri Compromise unconstitutional. The Negro was branded inferior, "altogether unfit to associate with the white race."

slaves to their condition vary with their cultural level and their personality variables. In order to gain perspective upon the particular nature of the prebellum slave system in the United States, it may be compared with that of Latin America.[43]

In Latin America, law, religion, and the mores of the society made the status of slaves vastly different, and on the whole superior, to that of slaves in the British-settled area of South America and in the southern United States. In the first place, in Latin America slaves, as slaves, had rights protecting them against many specific abuses from their masters. The power to inflict certain physical punishments upon slaves was limited by law and slaves could obtain legal redress if the master overstepped these bounds. Married slaves could not be separated from each other against their will. "The children followed the status of their mother, and the child of a free mother remained free even if she later became a slave.[44] By contrast, in the American system, the slave had practically no protection at all by law from the arbitrary exercise of authority by the master.[45] He had no property rights. Married partners could be separated from each other, and children from their parents. That they were is attested by Tannenbaum in a number of advertisements of which the following is typical.

> NEGROES FOR SALE. A negro woman, 24 years of age, and her two children, one eight and the other three years old. Said negroes will be sold SEPA-RATELY, or together, *as desired*. The woman is a good seamstress. She will be sold low for cash, or EXCHANGED FOR GROCERIES.
>
> For terms, apply to Matthew Bliss and Co., 1 Front Levee.[46]

A second contrast lies in the facts that the Latin system favored manumission and that under it there was a more-or-less steady change from slavery to freedom going on all the time. "A hundred social devices . . . encouraged the master to release his slave, and the bondsman to achieve freedom on his own account." For example, in Cuba "a slave worth six hundred dollars could buy himself out in twenty-four installments of twenty-five dollars each, and with each payment he acquired one twenty-fourth of his own freedom." [47] The American system operated to prevent manumission. While some slaves were

---

[43] Much of the material for this comparison is derived from Frank Tannenbaum, *Slave and Citizen* (New York: Alfred A. Knopf, Inc., 1947).
[44] *Ibid.*, p. 49.
[45] Myrdal, *op. cit.*, pp. 530-531.
[46] *New Orleans Bee*, quoted in Tannenbaum, *op. cit.*, p. 77. By permission of the publishers, Alfred A. Knopf, Inc.
[47] *Ibid.*, pp. 53-54.

freed, as the system grew in strength during the early 19th century the pressures against freeing slaves became greater.

A third contrast arises in the difference in status of former slaves in the two systems once they became free. In Latin America, the freed person whatever his racial lineage assumed a place equal to that of all others in the civic community. While authorities differ as to whether or not Negro ancestry might have been a handicap in the class status system of Latin America, there seems little doubt many Negroes came to occupy high public position and that white-colored intermarriage had never been looked upon with the abhorrence that it is looked upon in the United States. Although the position of those American Negroes freed prior to general abolition was in some respects higher than that of those still enslaved, the fact that he was still a Negro meant that he was an inferior person.

Among the various social forces which Tannenbaum offers in explanation for the contrasts in these two slave systems was the presence in the Latin American legal system of Spanish law with its already established precedents of specific definition of slave status, and the absence of any corresponding precedents in British law. Again, the influence of Catholic doctrine in contrast to the position of Protestantism on slavery should be noted. Although the Church did not interfere with the institution when the domestic law accepted it, it had early condemned the slave trade and prohibited Catholics from participating in it. Still further, the Church doctrine considered that slave and master were equal in the sight of God, gave slaves the right to baptism, and insisted that masters bring their slaves to church. This stands in sharp contrast to the total neglect of Negroes by the Episcopal Church in British West Indies, and in strong contrast to the position of the Protestant sects in the South of the United States. After 1700, there was no systematic opposition to teaching the Christian doctrine to the Negro slave. But the churches in the South generally made no attack on the institution of slavery itself.

Slavery as a social system. Slavery as a system of human relations cannot be maintained without the use of force. While most slave states passed statutes designed to protect the slave from unnecessary sufferings, Myrdal writes, "In general, the Negro slave had no 'rights' which his owner was bound to respect." [48] Thus the disciplining of Negroes was left largely to the volition of the master, or his white overseer, and in exercise of this function, the overseer was restrained only by his own conscience and such group pressure as the white mores of the community in this regard brought to bear on him. When it was necessary, the

---

[48] Myrdal, *op. cit.*, p. 530.

masters did inflict corporal punishment and even death upon the slaves.

Nevertheless, the relations between the two racial groups came to be ordered by a system of etiquette and ritual which more or less explicitly defined the proper reciprocal behavior whenever members of the two races were together. The actual relations between groups never perfectly coincides with the formal status. Thus it is clear enough that white-Negro relations under slavery were often overlaid with a sense of mutual responsibility and reciprocal affection. This was particularly true in the case of house servants who identified themselves with the family, and who were often biologically related to it.

Slavery has two effects on the personality of slaves. In some cases it conditioned them to accept the definition of themselves which the system implied. By this we mean that the slave came to believe in the propriety of the status itself and to acquire a sense of security in this acceptance. Certainly many slaves born into the system in the South felt about it in this way. In other cases, being enslaved incited bitter resentment which may or may not have been expressed in open rebellion depending upon the external circumstances and the personality of the slave. We have of course no way of knowing the relative prevalence of these two types of personality reaction among the slaves of the American South. That there was far more of the rebellious reaction than the apologists for the slave system liked to admit is, however, now well known. Aptheker has documented about 250 slave insurrections and rebellions in the United States throughout the entire period of slavery.[49] All of these cases are on record and involve 10 or more people. Yet it is only a partial list of planned or attempted group rebellions, not to mention the many instances of open resistance offered by individuals.

THE RECONSTRUCTION PERIOD

The emancipation of slaves had been forced upon the South against its will and the implication of freedom could be carried through only by a large-scale program of the Federal Government at a huge cost, and the application of considerable compulsion upon the South. The problem posed was twofold: how to implement and guarantee the new political status of Negroes as free men; and how to reconstruct the economy of the South in such a manner that Negroes would have a secure economic position.

The war had wrought enormous material property losses on Southern whites as well as the loss of the slaves. Many of the freed slaves both

[49] Herbert Aptheker, *American Negro Slave Revolts* (New York: Columbia University Press, 1943), p. 162.

during the war and immediately after it flocked to the cities or to the vicinity of Northern army camps and had no means of livelihood. In recognition of the need to cope with the chaotic situation from the economic side, the Bureau of Refugees, Freedman, and Abandoned Lands was established in 1865 to aid, among other things, in the economic rehabilitation of the freedmen, as well as the propertyless whites, and to promote an educational program for the Negroes. The general plan was to furnish land and tools with which the freedman and landless whites might become self-sustaining farmers. During the seven years of its existence (1865–1872) the Bureau was unable to accomplish the economic objective for a number of reasons. It had woefully inadequate funds for the size of the job. The amnesty granted former Confederates restored to them the land which had already been leased to Negroes who consequently became landless again. When efforts were made to resettle both white and Negro tenants on public lands in the Gulf areas, inability to raise enough capital and general discouragement at the whole program led few to take advantage of this opportunity. Underneath all these circumstances militating against the success of the Freedmen's Bureau was the desire of the more influential portion of the white South to retain the traditional system of agricultural production and to keep the Negro in his servile place. Likewise, the half-hearted support of Northerners contributed to the failure of the Government to carry through the program. The lukewarm support of Northern opinion was in part due to the usual reluctance to appropriate the rather large funds needed for the task. Northerners, although believing in theoretical freedom for Negroes, were far from advocating that they be accorded full equal status. The combination of proprietary interest in the South and the traditional white attitudes toward the proper status of Negroes, shared by many Northerners as well as nearly all the white South, conspired to defeat what appears in retrospect to have been a validly conceived plan for the economic rehabilitation of the South.

The same combination of interests and attitudes appeared in opposition to the fulfillment of the other objective in the Northern plan for reconstruction of the South, namely the civic and social integration of Negroes and rehabilitation of Negroes as first-class citizens. Soon after the close of the war eight Southern states instituted the so-called Black Codes. By various statutes affecting apprenticeship, labor contracts, debts, and vagrancy these codes went far to reestablish the servile position of Negroes. Of the examples of these codes which Frazier cites, the following is significantly illustrative. "The Florida code states that if any person of color failed to fulfill the stipulations of a contract into which he entered with a plantation owner or was impudent to the owner, he should be declared a vagrant and be subject to punishment for vagrancy." [50]

When the Republican government of the North realized that the South was in fact nullifying the emancipation, it set about to exert pressure to force acceptance. Through the Fourteenth Amendment to the Constitution, declared effective in 1866, abridgement of the full civic equality of all citizens was declared unlawful, and the supplementary Fifteenth Amendment, effective in 1870, specifically denied the right to abridgement of the voting privilege on "account of race, color, or previous condition of servitude." Still further, Congress passed in 1867 a series of reconstruction acts. These called for the temporary governing of the South by military rule until such time as genuinely democratic elections could be held and governments so elected should get under way. In the governments which followed, many Negroes were elected to state assemblies, and 20 were sent to Congress. Some of these Negro officials demonstrated unusual ability. In these turbulent years the majority of Southerners naturally resented the attempt of the "carpetbaggers" to reconstruct their society, aided by their own "scalawags," as the Southerners who cooperated with the Yankee officials were called. They made much of the point that complete civic equality for Negroes would give the colored population control over the South. Actually in no state were Negroes ever the dominating factor in the government though in several states they constituted about half of the population. It matters little for our purposes what judgment historians pass upon the motivations of the outsiders or the efficiency of the efforts made to force reconstruction. The basic point is that the Southern attitude toward the Negro was not reconstructed, as the testimony of Carl Schurz on the basis of his personal investigation indicates:

Wherever I go . . . I hear the people talk in such a way as to indicate that they are yet unable to conceive of the Negro as possessing any rights at all. . . . The people boast that when they get freedmen's affairs in their own hands . . . "the niggers will catch hell."

The reason of all this is simple and manifest. The whites esteem the blacks their property by natural right, and however much they admit that the individual relations of masters and slaves have been destroyed by the war and by the President's emancipation proclamation, they still have an ingrained feeling that the blacks at large belong to the whites at large.[51]

The third phase of the reconstruction drama opened as the Republican Congress began to weaken. In 1872, the disabilities imposed

---

[50] Frazier, *op. cit.*, p. 127. Italics ours.
[51] Report of Carl Schurz, Senate Executive Document, No. 2, 39th Congress. 1st Session, cited by W. E. B. DuBois, *Black Reconstruction in America* (New York: Harcourt, Brace & Company, Inc., 1936).

upon the former Confederate leaders, which prevented their participation in political affairs, were removed. The Freedmen's Bureau was abolished, depriving many Negro laborers and tenants of much-needed economic support and moral aid. The climax came when the Civil Rights bill of 1875 was declared unconstitutional. This bill, as Myrdal puts it, "represented the culmination of the Federal reconstruction legislation, was explicit in declaring that all persons . . . should be entitled to the full and equal enjoyment of the accommodations, advantages, facilities, and privileges of inns, public conveyances on land and water, theaters, and other places of public amusement . . . applicable alike to citizens of every race and color, regardless of previous condition of servitude." [52] When this bill was declared unconstitutional at least as far as the "social" equality phases were concerned, the North seems to have given up.

From 1875 on, the door was open for the unreconstructed white Southerners to carry on their own process of reconstruction which resulted in the establishment of the biracial pattern of race relations in which the dominance of white over colored was assured. This social system has remained broadly intact down to the present and will be the subject of detailed examination in the next chapter. Reconstruction on this basis involved the use of both legal and illegal procedures. Since in the white Southern view, Negroes had already advanced too far, it was first necessary to apply illegal force and terror to compel a return to their original status. This phase of the reconstruction was spear-headed by a number of secret societies, of which the Ku-Klux Klan is the most widely known. These extralegal activities were supplemented by further Black Code legislation which segregated Negroes and otherwise accorded them unequal privileges. While it took some years to accomplish the task, the white South succeeded in establishing a color-caste system.

Reconstruction: an object lesson. What happened in the reconstruction period is an excellent object lesson in social science. It illustrates the consequences of attempting swift and radical social change without adequate social planning. In hindsight, it is clear that the Federal Government attempted to accomplish too sweeping objectives in too short a time, against too strong a set of opposing forces, and with too little public support from the North itself. For example, how could it have been expected that white Southerners, long steeped in the tradition of slavery, could change their complex attitudes and habits concerning Negroes overnight? Again, how could it have been expected that slaves, held to such a low level of literacy and moulded into a ser-

[52] Myrdal, *op. cit.*, p. 579. By permission.

vile, dependent, personality pattern, could immediately become self-reliant and civically active? Furthermore, how could it have been expected that such a program could be carried on without a greater consensus of Northern opinion to support it? To raise such questions in hindsight and to leave the matter there is obviously unfair to the many intelligent and socially conscious white people both North and South who set the objectives and tried to carry them out. It is not reasonable to have expected them to possess the foresight which hindsight now reveals. Neither the theoretical knowledge of human nature and social processes nor the accumulated practice of social engineering had advanced to a point in 1865 to have made this foresight possible. We cite the lesson for its value at the present time. The United States in 1951 is again in a period of rapid flux and uncertainty in Negro-white relations, highly provocative of serious conflict unless new adjustments are carefully engineered. We face the current situation, however, with a greatly expanded body of knowledge of social theory, techniques, and practice in intergroup relations, not available in 1865, which can be put to use if the consensus of public opinion both permits and demands its use. The nature and scope of this accumulated knowledge will be presented in Chapter 17.

TOPICS FOR DISCUSSION AND PROJECTS

1. Discuss the relative importance of (*a*) sociological factors and of (*b*) biological factors in determining whether an American is or is not a Negro.
2. The "Negro" population of the United States could decline even with higher birth rates and lower death rates among people of Negro ancestry. Explain how this could happen.
3. Discuss the various effects upon Negro-white relations which you would see following from the increasing development of race pride among American Negroes.
4. Trace carefully the role which economic and technological factors played in the development of the slavery system in the South.
5. Consult appropriate historical sources with the view of determining the extent to which Negroes in the South following the War Between the States were or were not prepared for citizenship.

SUGGESTED READING

Aptheker, Herbert. *American Negro Slave Revolts*. New York: Columbia University Press, 1943.
   The most complete history of the subject.
Coulter, E. Merton. *The South During Reconstruction, 1865–1877*. Baton Rouge: Louisiana State University Press, 1947.
   A Southern view of the Reconstruction Period.

DuBois, W. E. B. *Black Reconstruction*. New York: Harcourt, Brace & Co., Inc., 1935.

A Negro leader presents his view of the role of Negroes in Reconstruction.

Holmes, S. J. "The Trends of the Racial Balance of Births and Deaths," in *Race Relations and the Race Problem*, Edgar T. Thompson, ed. Durham: Duke University Press, 1939.

The analysis anticipates increasing proportional gain of Negro population in relation to the growth of the white population.

Lewis, Julian H. *The Biology of the Negro*. Chicago: University of Chicago Press, 1942.

Most complete summary and analysis of the subject.

Myrdal, Gunnar, et al. *An American Dilemma: the Negro Problem and Modern Democracy*. New York: Harper and Brothers, 1944.

The most comprehensive assemblage of facts about Negroes in relation to whites in American society. The Swedish writer has presented his own interpretation of the data and researches provided by scores of American scholars. Chapter 7, "Population"; Ch. 8, "Migration"; and Ch. 10, "The Tradition of Slavery" bear upon this chapter.

Phillips, Ulrich B. *Life and Labor in the Old South*. Boston: Little, Brown & Company, 1939.

An interesting social history of the region before the War Between the States. Chapters 9 and 11 especially describe the slavery system.

CHAPTER 9

Negro-White Relations:
The Southern Pattern

·In the previous chapter, the period of Negro-white relations in the United States from 1880 to 1940 was given the designation, "the period of biracial accommodation." This phrasing was selected as the most suitable to subsume the two markedly different patterns of these relations prevailing in the South and outside of it. Negroes clearly occupied a minority status position throughout the United States but the difference in their position in the two regions was so great as to require separate treatment. Considering in this chapter the Southern pattern first, we shall in common with many other, although not all, students of minorities designate it as a caste system. In its ideology and in the institutions which govern race relations, the categorical segregation of the two races in a large number of social relations is clear. Intermarriage is flatly prohibited. While specific identification with a particular occupation, as was characteristic of the traditional Hindu caste system, is not so marked, nevertheless the Southern pattern has generally not permitted the performance together of the same tasks by members of the two races. Furthermore the rising middle class of Negroes in the South was in the main segregated from the white middle class. The absence of explicit religious sanctions for its biracial system most clearly distinguishes the Southern pattern from other caste systems.

This chapter delineates the system of race relations in the South as a whole. The area considered as South comprises the District of Columbia and the 16 states designated as Southern in the discussion

225

of the distribution of the Negro population (see p. 205). We are here concerned with the general characteristics of this regional pattern. Some of the main variations will be considered under a separate heading at the end of the chapter.

In our treatment the Southern system will be viewed as a more or less fixed structure rather than in developmental terms. The caste system reached its perfection around the turn of the 20th century. While from 1900 to 1940 the pattern had not been completely frozen, it was sufficiently so to permit its delineation as an essentially unchanging pattern of intergroup relations. Such changes as have taken place in the more recent years of this period have been in the direction of the elimination of discrimination. In fact since 1940, this democratic trend has been so greatly accelerated that we devote Chapter 11 to describing the changes in detail. Because the main characteristics, however, of the Southern pattern still prevailed in 1951, the present tense may be properly employed for describing race relations in the 20th century South.

This caste system operates first, by segregating Negroes and whites physically to the maximum extent possible for two groups living in the same community, and in that segregation by clearly defining the Negroes as inferior. Second, since Negroes earn their living primarily by working for whites and therefore must unavoidably mingle spatially with whites, caste superordination and subordination is maintained by an elaborate set of caste rules of etiquette which symbolize the superior-inferior racial position.

CASTE SYSTEM [1]

Caste segregation. Residentially, in rural areas, Negroes are scattered but do not live close to whites, except on plantations where the mansion is separated conspicuously, often not far from Negro shacks. In small towns, there is a definite clustering of Negro homes on edges of the community. In Southern cities there are varieties of Negro residential patterns: the back-alley residence plan as seen in Charleston; the isolated community as in Tulsa; the one large Negro area with smaller scattered clusters found in many cities. Interestingly enough, Southern whites do not appear to object to having Negro families live near them as do Northern whites. However, where in the South homes of Negro families are spatially proximate to those of white families, there is usually some outward manifestation of the superior-inferior status, for example, whites facing the streets, Negroes the alley, or the comparatively more run-down appearance of the Negro homes. Neighborliness

[1] See Charles S. Johnson, *Patterns of Negro Segregation* (New York: Harper and Brothers, 1943), for the fullest single-volume discussion of all phases of segregation.

may prevail but always in conformance to the etiquette of race relations.

In education, 17 states have entirely separate school systems. No contact at all takes place between the teachers or pupils of the two systems except the unavoidable contact of the superintendent who is white. This separation in schooling at these early years goes far to root firmly in the attitudes and habits of children of both races the practice of race segregation. Negroes are not admitted generally into public libraries in the South, and a Negro has no access to library facilities unless he can get a white friend to take out a book for him. However, in a few large cities Negro branch libraries have been established.

Public recreational facilities are generally scarce in the South outside the large cities, and Negroes in the nonurban areas do not share those that exist with the whites. Negroes are generally excluded from public parks in Southern cities, and only in a few cities do they have parks of their own. Except in a few instances where a special section of a public playground is set aside for Negroes, the colored people are not permitted to utilize public playgrounds.

In hotels and restaurants, the segregation is absolutely complete. This works extreme hardship upon traveling Negro people. Outside the larger cities, where some Negro hotels and restaurants exist, it is literally impossible for Negroes traveling to get a meal or lodging except as some Negro family gives them hospitality. In public buildings, such as post offices, tax offices, etc., Negroes usually wait in line until every white person appearing has been served. Separate toilets for each race are the general rule in public places where both races are admitted. "Jim Crow" transportation is the best-known device of the segregation system. In local transportation where the vehicles are often not physically partitioned, Negroes go to the rear and whites to the front, the dividing line being set on each trip by the proportion of each race aboard. Of this Johnson writes: "The operator is empowered to regulate the space occupied by each race in accordance with the respective number of passengers. This system is subject to abuse since it permits the attitude of the operator to become a factor in segregation." [2]

One of the most serious examples of segregation is in hospitalization. In some places there are isolated wards for Negroes. But more often the hospitals will not admit them, and there are few Negro hospitals. Instances have occurred of deaths of Negroes in need of emergency operations because the nearest hospitals would not admit them.

Segregation in economic life has two main aspects; in employment and in the role of the Negro as a customer. In regard to employment,

[2] *Ibid.*, p. 49.

the basic principle is that Negroes must not work alongside whites on equal functional terms. For instance, one restaurant may have all Negro waitresses; another across the street may have all white waitresses; but no restaurant will mix the two. The first will probably have a white cashier; the second will probably have Negro dishwashers; but but here the functional differentiation is clear. This principle operates to limit Negro employment to those occupations which whites do not care to enter. The one important exception to this is tenant farming in which both races engage, but in which they do not work together. As a result, occupations which are the most menial and the poorest paid tend to be left for Negroes. When technological improvements came along to make any particular occupation more rewarding, the whites tried to keep the Negroes out, as they did following the introduction of farm tractors and the mechanical cotton picker. (In these particular instances white farm labor has not been wholly successful in keeping a race monopoly.)

Prior to 1935 labor unions in the South excluded Negroes from membership, or at the most permitted them to organize in separate auxiliary locals. Since in the earlier days of the caste period, Negroes were a majority in certain semiskilled or skilled trades, the development of unions had the effect of driving them from these occupations. The elimination of Negroes as engineers on railroad locomotives, and the gradual decline in the number of Negro firemen and brakemen correlated with the rise of the railway workers' unions.

The color line is less rigidly drawn against the Negro as a customer in commercial establishments. Two generalizations hold largely true. The cheaper the price level of the goods to be sold, the more welcome is the Negro trade. Thus the "five and ten" stores and the chain food stores generally welcome Negro trade and provide reasonably courteous service, while the more exclusive stores either refuse or discourage Negro patronage through discourtesy. The other general rule is that the more intimate the personal relationship involved in a commercial transaction, the more likely the Negro is to be excluded. In beauty parlor and mortuary services the races are strictly separated. Where however the services to be rendered, though involving considerable interpersonal relationships, are such that the position of the vendor is clearly superior to that of the buyer, as in the case of medical or legal counsel, white professional people as a rule will take Negro clients.

The code of race etiquette. Since Negroes are an important part of the economic life of the South, they cannot be totally segregated. They must have some interpersonal relations with whites. To give expression to the lower caste position of Negroes in such situations there has developed an elaborate pattern of racial etiquette.[3] The essence of this etiquette governing these interpersonal relations is to make clear the superordinate and subordinate caste positions. For example, a white man does not shake hands with a Negro when introduced to him. An exception would be when a white man visits a Negro college or, sometimes, a Negro home. The white person does not address the Negro person as Mr. or Mrs., but rather by his first name, or if it is not known, his last; in turn the Negro always addresses the white person as Mister, Marse, or Misses, or better still by some such title as Colonel which, in fact, the white man may not possess. Interestingly enough, professionally trained Negroes may be addressed as Professor, Doctor, or Reverend. Consequently most Negro male school or college teachers are "Professors," however limited their education may be. Negro women are never referred to as "ladies," but either just women, or, irrespective of age, as "girls." Negro men are expected to doff their hats when they speak to white men, but the latter are not expected to reciprocate. Whenever Negroes have occasion to call at or enter into white men's homes, they do so at the rear door; reciprocally, of course, the white man who has occasion to call at or enter a Negro home, always appears at the front door. Whenever circumstances bring Negroes and white people together at mealtime or on recreational occasions, the races are not expected to sit together at the same table or play together. For example, when a white person visits a colored home, if the Negro hostess wishes to provide food for her guest, etiquette prescribes that they do not eat together. With the exception of quite young children, Negroes and whites do not ordinarily play together. A significant exception is the case where there is opportunity for the Negro to serve his white companion in a servile role as in hunting or fishing with a white friend. On the other hand, where interracial associations, aimed at improving Negro-white relations, meet together there may be no barriers regarding eating at the same table.

Endogamy is the primary principle of caste. Marriage across caste lines cannot be recognized and is forbidden by law in Southern states. Therefore, most adamant of all is the taboo against any sort of casual interpersonal relations between a white woman and a Negro man. No one thing is more dangerous to a Negro male than to be in any situation that can be even remotely construed as indicating personal interest in a white female. That Negro men understand this and act accordingly is seen in the following instance. A white woman, the wife of a white man in charge of a migrant labor camp for Southern Negroes in the North, in walking about the camp attempted to engage Negro men in friendly conversation and was nonplussed at their passive at-

[3] See Bertram W. Doyle, *The Etiquette of Race Relations in the South* (Chicago: University of Chicago Press, 1937), for a fuller description of the subject.

tempts to avoid the situation. Brought up to know that the rope or faggot awaits the Negro accused—falsely or otherwise—of "sexual" interest in a white woman, Negro men in the South, as a general rule, avoid white women.

The interrelation of class with caste. In the South, the class system is linked with the caste system in significant ways. In most Southern communities, particularly in cities, class differentiation has developed within the Negro caste as well as in the white caste. Negroes performing higher ranking functions, for example, ministers, teachers, doctors, farm agents, and others have achieved a higher-class status within their racial group. The class position of such Negroes is generally recognized by the white people, and the Negroes so recognized are accorded differential treatment from that accorded the lower-class Negroes. For example, upper-class whites often come to the defense of upper-class Negroes who get into trouble with lower-class whites. Warner and Davis cite the case of a colored professional man who accidentally ran down and killed with his car a drunken lower-class white man. Local bankers offered money for the Negro's defense, and upper-class white women called at his place of business to indicate that they supported him in his difficulty.[4] The class bond cutting across caste lines prompts upper-class whites upon occasion to attend special functions conducted by upper-class Negroes and at such occasions special courtesies not generally accorded Negroes by caste etiquette may be extended by the whites, such as addressing the Negro women as "Mrs."

This class differentiated aspect of the caste system operates more to strengthen caste than to undermine it. While it accords upper-class Negroes some differential privileges, these are limited and always fall clearly short of implying equality. To receive these class privileges, upper-class Negroes must accept caste, at least outwardly. This special relation also serves practical purposes in the maintenance of the biracial system. While caste relations are fundamentally antagonistic, they cannot exist without some degree of cooperation. In spite of the vastly superior power position of the whites, an orderly community under caste requires cooperation from the Negro group. In their function of leaders, the middle and upper-class Negroes are expected to exert their influence to control the Negro masses in the interest of preserving caste.[5]

[4] W. Lloyd Warner and Allison Davis, "A Comparative Study of American Caste," in Edgar T. Thompson, ed., *Race Relations and the Race Problem* (Durham: Duke University Press, 1939), p. 243.
[5] These class-linked relations should not be confused with intergroup relations which are in substance nonconformity to caste. There have been, of course, throughout the whole period considered, a few white people here and there, more particularly in cities, who did not believe in caste, and who, with due deference to the personal costs of nonconformity, have participated in informal mixed gatherings on a plane of social equality.

METHODS OF ENFORCING CASTE

The methods employed for sustaining this caste pattern of race relations in the South may be conveniently treated under the headings: legal methods; illegal force and intimidation; and custom. Bearing in mind that at many points these three categories of methods of social control reinforce each other, we shall discuss each separately.

Legal methods. Specific local and state laws require segregation of the two races in many of the categories noted above. Southern state supreme courts have upheld these laws. Until recently the Supreme Court of the United States has upheld Southern segregation laws in the cases reaching it. One important exception concerns housing segregation by state or municipal law. In 1915, a Louisville, Kentucky, city ordinance forbidding Negroes to reside in certain areas was declared unconstitutional by the United States Supreme Court.[6] In its rulings this highest tribunal has insisted that the segregated public facilities and services provided Negroes should be equal to those provided for whites. As we shall presently detail, every description of the facilities for Negroes in the South documents the fact that Negroes have not, and still do not, receive equal public facilities in spite of this interpretation of the Constitution. Segregation is still, in part, upheld by law.

Illegal violence and intimidation. The whole pattern of segregation and race etiquette, however, is not upheld by law. That part of it not so covered is reinforced by intimidation and extralegal violence. The Negro who violates the customary etiquette finds himself brought to order by whites by abusive language and warnings. If he persists in violation, or if the breach is considered particularly heinous from the dominant caste viewpoint, he may be physically maltreated or lynched. If the violations appear to be in any sense en masse, a whole Negro street or area may be destroyed by white groups as a way of "teaching the nigger to keep his place." In *Deep South,* Davis and others write:

In fact, it is considered entirely correct for the white person to resort directly to physical attack upon the Negro. Thus, if a Negro curses a white, the white may knock the Negro down; and failure to do so may even be considered as a failure in duty as a white.

It is a common belief of many whites that Negroes will respond only to violent methods. In accordance with the theory of the "animallike" nature of the Negro, they believe that the formal punishments of fines and imprisonment fail to act as deterrents to crime.

The same authors quote a planter who puts the traditional Southern white viewpoint in these words:

[6] See Johnson, *op. cit.,* p. 175.

The best thing is not to take these young bucks into the courthouse for some small crime but to give them a paddling. That does them more good than a jail sentence. If I catch a Negro stealing a hog or some chickens, what is the use of taking him into court? He would get a fine or a jail sentence and unless I pay him out he will lie up in jail, and when he gets out he will keep on stealing.[7]

As a result of this traditional support of intimidation and violence when needed to keep Negroes in their caste status, law itself is caste patterned. It applies very unequally to the two races. When any altercation occurs involving a white and a Negro person, the Negro is most likely presumed to be wrong. The word of a white person is ordinarily taken against that of a Negro—even when privately many whites know the white person is lying. Again, the law fails to protect the Negro against extralegal violence on the part of whites. It is generally impossible to get anybody to testify that he has any knowledge at all about illegal acts of violence perpetrated against Negroes. As a result lynching after lynching has occurred in the South. Even those reported in the national press, where the fact of lynching is incontrovertible, seldom result in indictments and trials. Negroes have been kept off juries in the South. However, recent Federal Supreme Court reversals of Negro convictions where the defense argued successfully that Negroes in the communities involved were purposely not called to jury duty has broken this caste practice to a degree.[8] Some measure of justice for Negroes is obtained by having a white protector who will intercede for them. Frequently a landlord or other employer will say a good word for his Negro employee and get the case dismissed or the sentence lightened.

Custom. The casual traveler in the South would not notice this intimidation. He sees on the whole an orderly pattern of segregation and race etiquette. On the surface he sees no resentment. Even though indications of intimidation are not present each day, no Negro brought up in the South is unaware of the threat of violence. Because of this, Negro children are brought up by their parents and conditioned by their earliest experience with white people to conform to the established pattern. Negro parents have to punish the rebellious inclinations of their children who naively approach white persons as equal human beings. Reciprocally, white children in the South are, of course, conditioned to assume all the appropriate attitudes and behavior patterns of the dominant caste. The common human tendency to really like Negro children must be sternly disciplined to make sure that they are

[7] Allison Davis, Burleigh Gardner, and Mary R. Gardner, *Deep South* (Chicago: University of Chicago Press, 1941), pp. 45-46. By permission.
[8] Myrdal, *American Dilemma,* p. 549.

not treated as equals. Thus the Southern caste pattern is supported by the conditioning and habituation of Southerners of the two races to assume the reciprocal social roles required to keep it intact—the white to be arrogant, exploitative, superior; the Negro to be submissive, exploited, and inferior. Most of the time this combination of implicit intimidation and habituation works quite successfully. The Negro who occasionally throws caution to the wind and rebels against the pattern is dealt with summarily. The white person whose conscience occasionally pricks him submerges his charitable inclination under the pressure of public sentiment.

Caste control illustrated: keeping Negroes from voting. The mixture of law, intimidation, and custom in sustaining caste is well illustrated in the devices by which Negroes in the South have been prevented from exercising the ballot. As noted in the discussion of reconstruction, Negroes after emancipation had voted and been elected to office. Between 1890 and 1910, 11 Southern states adopted special requirements for voting designed to deny Negroes the franchise. One such device was the poll tax. In order to vote the citizen was required to pay a special tax of a dollar or two for the privilege. While this is not a large sum, by various other devices it was made to serve its purpose. Sometimes the tax was retroactive, that is to say, in order to vote in any one year, poll tax receipts back over a number of years must be shown if asked for by the election official. An arrearage of $10 to $20 is effective in keeping a Negro from voting. Likewise the poll tax encouraged corruption by affording politicians the opportunity to pay up the tax of poor whites to get their vote and not offering the same to Negroes.

Negroes were barred from voting in the Democratic primary on the theory that any political party may restrict its membership. Prior to 1941 the United States Supreme Court in decisions concerning these white primary regulations had failed to overrule the specific laws in this connection. Other qualifications for voting left opportunity for discrimination through their administration. For example, educational tests were sometimes stipulated. By asking Negro applicants for registration difficult questions concerning government, and finding the answer incorrect, Negroes could be kept off the list. Or again, such devices as giving the Negroes only a day for registration when perhaps the white officials were not available have been further employed.

In addition to these state statues of questionable constitutionality and to administrative discrimination, white Southerners have at times resorted to intimidation and violence for the purpose of preventing Negroes from voting. Davie furnishes the following example:

There are numerous instances of Negroes who attempted to register or vote being driven away, beaten up, or killed. More generally the opposition takes the form of intimidation. For example, a Negro went to the registration booth in his county and asked if he could register. The white official replied: "Oh, yes, you can register, but I want to tell you something. Some God-damn niggers are going to get killed about this voting business yet." Intended to terrorize Negro citizens who might seek to vote in the primaries in Dennison, Texas, in the fall of 1932, handbills were scattered throughout the town, reading as follows:

NIGGER!

The white people do not want you to vote Saturday.
Do not make the Ku Klux Klan take a hand.
Do you remember what happened two years ago, May 9th?
George Hughes was burned to death, the county courthouse
destroyed . . . "For good reason."

Riots on election day in which both whites and Negroes have been killed have occurred in various sections of the South.[9]

EFFECTS OF CASTE SYSTEM

The effects of the race caste system as it operates in the South will be discussed in terms of its effect upon personality and behavior; upon the welfare of the Negro; upon social organization in Southern communities; and upon the political and economic development of the region.

Negro personality and behavior. Students of social life know that personality is determined through the interaction of the individual with the total system of social relationships which circumscribe his life. As was shown in Chapter 3, the factor of biological racial heredity has little to do with it. The personalities of the many individuals who are brought up in the same cultural society tend to possess a certain degree of similarity. In heterogeneous societies such as ours, group personalities or social types can be noted, such as Babbitt or the "club woman," the "worker" or the "bohemian." The experience of being a dominant or a minority person likewise tends to structure a certain kind of personality. What this kind of status experience does to the personalities of Negro and white in the Southern scene is analyzed with penetration by John Dollard as a result of an intimate study of class and caste relations in a Southern cotton community.[10]

Dollard has analyzed the "gains" which accrue to white people under the caste system which are in turn "losses" to the Negroes. First,

[9] By permission from *Negroes in American Society*, by M. R. Davie. Copyright 1949. McGraw-Hill Book Company, Inc., p. 266.
[10] John Dollard, *Caste and Class in a Southern Town* (New Haven: Yale University Press, 1937).

there is the economic gain. The system enables the white people to exploit Negroes as workers and consumers. The year cycle of the Negro tenant farmer runs as follows. After the cotton has been sold and the Negro has paid his debts, he is broke. The landlord advances him "furnish" to carry him through the next harvest. The charges for this "furnish" are not regulated and, due to lack of Negro education, the accounting is often largely in the landlord's hand. This offers opportunity for exploitation. Dollard does not maintain that this exploitative advantage is always completely utilized to the maximum, but it is difficult for the Negro to get justice if his accounting differs from that of the landlord.

Second, Dollard mentions the "sexual gain." By this is meant that the caste system operates to give white men exploitative advantage in sexual satisfaction among Negro women, as well as among whites, while any sexual advances of Negro men toward white women are absolutely tabooed and infractions punishable by death. The caste system does not require Negro women to accept the sexual overtures of white men, but the economic and social disadvantages which Negro women suffer through the caste system often make acceptance of these advances desirable. While by no means all white men take advantage of this opportunity, it is a general part of the rationalization of the white caste ideology that Negro women are sexually promiscuous and therefore such behavior on their part is hardly to be taken seriously in an ethical sense. The third gain Dollard sees accruing to the white caste is "ego" gratification. The daily expressions of superiority toward all Negroes which the whites can indulge and the reciprocal responses of submissiveness by the Negroes bolster the self-esteem of the whites, especially among the less privileged ranks of whites.

In the face of these "gains" to the whites, what can Negroes do? Obviously these advantages to the whites generate an enormous amount of additional frustration among Negroes. Dollard has suggested five ways in which Negroes may react.[11] (1) They may become overtly aggressive against the white caste. This some Negroes have done though infrequently and unsuccessfully in the past. (2) They may suppress their aggression and supplant it with accommodative attitudes. This was the slavery solution and it still exists under the caste system. Negroes sometimes get what they want from whites by exaggerated flattery and thus exploit the "ego inflation" of whites to their own advantage. The cleverer Negro may act "dumb" in order to get around the white person. Frequently Negroes lie to white people because they fear to refuse to agree to anything whites ask them. (3) Negroes may turn their aggression from the white caste to individuals within their own group.

[11] *Ibid.*, Ch. XII.

While the stereotype of Negroes carrying razors is highly exaggerated, a very considerable amount of physical violence toward one another does take place. The homicide rate among Negroes is high. (4) Negroes may give up competition for white values and accept other forms of gratification than those secured by whites. This is the solution characterizing lower class Negroes. Since in tenant farming they are dependent upon the planter, they can enjoy the privilege of being lazy— assume a "let's enjoy today," attitude, "since tomorrow will be no better." Again, sex gratifications may be indulged more fully since no "social climbing ambitions" will be jeopardized. "Flashy" dress is a direct satisfaction which no "keeping up with Jones" interferes with. Broadly speaking this caste system encourages Negroes to give direct, emotional expression to their basic desires because restraint in the interest of "getting ahead" has no meaning. (5) Dollard suggests that some Negroes may compete for the values of white society by attempting to raise their class position within the Negro caste. This involves managing "aggression partly by expressing dominance within their own group and partly by sheer suppression of their impulse as individuals. This is the solution characteristic of the Negro middle class." [12]

The oppression psychosis. From such an analysis of the impact of caste upon Negro personality, it can be seen that the presence of "minority consciousness" is a phase of Negro personality which serves to differentiate it clearly from whites, even lower class whites whose material conditions of life may not be any better than that of many Negroes. In general this minority consciousness reveals itself in two forms. The majority of Negroes, at least up to the past decade, have accepted their inferior status with resignation and have organized their lives as well as they could in an apparently unalterable situation. A smaller number think of themselves more or less constantly as oppressed people, and devote a great deal of energy in whatever ways possible to change the situation. The personalities of the latter more clearly reveal what Herbert A. Miller, among the first, called "the oppression psychosis." Sutherland and Woodward have succinctly delineated this psychological characteristic.

Common among minority groups subject to domination, the "oppression psychosis" involves attitudes of fear, hatred, resentment, jealousy, suspicion, and revenge. When in this state of mind, a group interprets any action of the oppressor as another injustice. Although the Negroes do not have this complex to the extent to which it is found among some of the oppressed minorities of Europe, there are evidences of its presence.

[12] *Ibid.,* p. 253.

A perusal of the news columns and editorials in the Negro weekly *The Chicago Defender* will show story after story praising achievement of Negroes and condemning acts of discrimination of the white man. This group reaction has its counterpart in the personalities of some individuals; certain Negroes (as would be true with any oppressed group) became highly sensitive to comments which cast reflection upon them as individuals or upon their race as a group. A quick, impulsive flash of anger, a sharp retort, or even physical resistance may be expected from such a person. To him are attributed radical acts and impertinences, much resented by a similar element in the white group. Out of such antagonisms race riots and lynching parties develop.[13]

The fact that Negroes seldom manifest hatred for white people as a class openly should not be interpreted to indicate that they do not cherish such a feeling inwardly. Warner and Davis write: "Anyone who believes that the hostile statements uttered by Southern whites toward Negroes are extreme should be allowed to hear those uttered by Negroes, even Negro children and adolescents toward whites."[14]

White personality. Reciprocally, the caste system has its effects on the dominant caste personality, a subject which has received little scientific attention. However, in the description of the effect of caste upon Negro personality and behavior, the white reciprocals are revealed, as in Dollard's study. It can be seen that the common human tendency to exploit and to "bully" are intensified by the dominant position of whites in the caste situation. Also there arises a disdain for certain forms of physical labor which have been traditionally associated with the minority caste. Obviously the cultivation of a genuinely democratic personality is made difficult by the kind of upbringing which white children get in a caste stratified community.[15]

Effects on social organization: the Negro community. Under the caste system the organization of Southern communities is a dual structure in which the white community and Negro community are distinct. In the latter are found parallel associations and institutions, Negro churches, lodges, schools, recreational places. As the description of segregation above indicated, there is not a completely parallel set of economic institutions. For many of their goods and services, Negroes patronize white stores and salesmen. However, in regard to economic services of a personal sort such as eating places, beauty parlors, undertaking services, etc., separate Negro enterprises exist.

---

[13] Robert L. Sutherland and Julian L. Woodward, *Introductory Sociology* (Philadelphia: J. B. Lippincott Company, 1948), pp. 394-395. By permission.
[14] Warner and Davis, *loc. cit.*, p. 237.
[15] It is also true that class differentiation has some similar effects but this is beyond the scope of this book.

Myrdal characterizes the Negro community as a "pathological" form of the average American community.[16] It is like the white community except that it is more deteriorated in its physical structures; its associational structure tends to exaggerate parallel aspects of the white community, for example, in the number of lodges; and many of its institutions express an earlier stage of the parallel white institutions, for example, in the case of the church. The social organizations within the Negro community are not the product of a distinctive cultural heritage. Few traces of African cultural heritages are to be found. They are American, developed by people American in their culture. The pathological manifestations grow out of the discriminations attached to the lower caste position. These general characteristics of Negro community life are revealed by looking at the basic institutions.

Negro family life is characterized by a greater maternal dominance and weaker institutional stability than white family life.[17] Both of these characteristics arise in part from the heritage of slavery and from the difficult conditions under which Negro families live, especially in cities. The frequent enforced separation of father from mother and children under slavery; the greater frequency of monogamic unions without legal sanction; and the low economic status stimulating married Negro women to work outside the home all contributed to increasing the independence of Negro women in the family and to making the mother-child relationship the more enduring bond. The high frequency of common-law marriage and the high rates of illegitimacy are indices of greater institutional instability. An official table for 1936 shows Negroes having eight times as much illegitimacy as native whites and 16 times as much as foreign born whites for the United States as a whole.[18]

The actual "social disorganization" of the Negro family is somewhat less than it appears as measured by white standards. In the rural South particularly, adaptive mores have developed which greatly mitigate the disorganizing tendencies in the situation. Illegitimacy does not have attached to it the stigma found in the white community and therefore does not produce the same psychological effects. A high value is placed on children and the larger kin groups of the rural family tend to provide group security to all children however irregular their status. According to Myrdal this type of family is "conducive to social health, even though the practices are outside the American tradition. When

---

[16] Myrdal, op. cit., p. 927.

[17] See E. Franklin Frazier, The Negro Family in the United States (New York: The Dryden Press, Inc., 1948), for the most complete description and interpretation of the subject.

[18] U. S. Bureau of the Census, Births, Stillbirths and Infant Mortality Statistics, 1936, pp. 9-13.

these practices are brought into closer contact with white norms, as occurs when Negroes go to the cities, they tend to break down partially and to cause the demoralization of some individuals." [19]

The church, particularly in the South, is a most fundamental institution in Negro life. In form it resembles that of lower-class white Protestant churches: small in congregation size; fundamentalist in belief; its services characterized by great emotionalism; puritanical in its views of morals, but unable to do much to stop "sin" except preach against it. Generally speaking, its chief function is to furnish an opportunity for release of frustrations attached to caste status and to bind the members of the community together. Because of this orientation, the lower-class churches are not as important as agencies for intellectual growth or as centers for promoting constructive activity to improve the Negroes' status as are some middle-class Negro churches in Northern cities. The limited range of other avenues of cultural expression open to Negroes appears in part to explain the high rate of church membership among Negroes; the frustrations of the caste status account for its "escapist" character.

In the tendency to form an unusual proliferation of social clubs, lodges, and sundry other kinds of "voluntary" associations, Negroes are truly American. They appear in a sense to outdo the whites. "In Natchez, Mississippi, where the total Negro population was about 7500, there were more than 200 Negro associations discovered in one week in 1935." [20] In form, these multifarious Negro associations reflect the white pattern of a generation ago; secret lodges; formal ritual; exact parliamentary procedures; much talk and little accomplishment beyond the pleasure of meeting together.

The welfare of Negroes in the South. In all indices of human welfare, the Negro population of the United States as a whole, as well as in the South considered separately, ranks conspicuously lower in comparison to the white population in general. The facts attesting this differential condition are among the most amply demonstrated phenomena in the literature concerning minority groups.

We shall present some of the salient facts in this connection with reference to the material standard of living, health, the level of education, and the extent of crime and delinquency. The striking difference between the two groups has been a continuous phenomenon through the entire history of the Southern racial system. The welfare of the Negro has improved in some aspects with the general advance of the South, and the relative gains made by the Negroes have in some respects been greater than the relative gains of the whites; that is to say, the gap

[19] Myrdal, *op. cit.*, p. 935.
[20] *Ibid.*, p. 952.

between the two racial groups has somewhat narrowed. Here we are concerned with the constant influences which produced the racial differential. The continuous factors have been the concentration of the Negro population in the South in the lower occupational and income brackets, the continuous influence of certain distinctive cultural traits developed among Negroes in their adaptation to American life, and the effect of the discriminations imposed upon Negroes by the Southern racial system. These three factors are, of course, constantly interacting upon one another.

Occupation and Income in the United States. The comparative occupational distribution of Negroes and whites gainfully employed in 1940 is given in Table 21. In this table sharecroppers were placed in

TABLE 21

Employed Workers in the United States Classified into Social-Economic Groups, by Color, 1940[21]

SOCIAL-ECONOMIC GROUPING	PER CENT DISTRIBUTION BY COLOR	
	NEGRO	WHITE
Professional persons	2.6	7.5
Proprietors, managers, and officials	16.1	20.2
Clerks and kindred workers	2.2	19.5
Skilled workers and foremen	2.9	12.4
Semiskilled workers	12.3	21.4
Unskilled workers	63.9	19.0
Total	100.0	100.0

the proprietor, managerial class. Since these obviously belong in the same status as the unskilled, the proportion of all Negroes in the lowest socioeconomic class exceeds the two-thirds figure indicated in Table 21. In terms of income, a 1935–36 study compared incomes of families not on relief, finding a median of $1100 for whites and $480 for Negroes. In Southern cities of 2500 or more the median income for white families was $1570 against $525 for Negroes.[22] Comparison of total family income obscure the fact that in Negro families, more members are gainfully employed, that is wives and older children more frequently seek work. The number of Negroes in the higher ranking levels in the South has been too few to have had much effect upon average family income. Since Negro private enterprisers and professional people large-

[21] U. S. Bureau of the Census, *Comparative Occupation Statistics for the United States,* 1870–1940, p. 189.
[22] U. S. National Resources Committee, *Consumer Income in the United States,* p. 28.

ly do business with Negroes, their average incomes fall below those of white people in similar categories.

The low income of the Negroes in the South is in part a result of the relatively poorer level of Southern economy in comparison with the rest of the country. But the continued concentration of Negroes in the lower paid occupations is directly affected by the caste system which limits Negro employment in higher occupational ranks and operates to prevent their training for these occupations. Because of the general race division of labor, it is not easy to determine in mass statistics whether or not Negroes get less pay for the same work. Studies of special local rural areas show that white tenant farmers have an average higher family income than Negro tenant families.[23] One of the reasons given for this is that more Negro tenant farmers operate on credit while more white farmers operate on cash. The evidence from all studies of the tenant farm system clearly show that white land owners vastly prefer their Negro tenants to operate on credit since it ties them to one place and affords opportuntiy for profitable credit terms.

Housing. Housing conditions in the South are inferior to those of the nation in general and Negro housing is of poorer quality than that of white. Illustrative data are these: 3 per cent of all Negro farm homes had screens in good condition in contrast to 24 per cent of the white homes; 10 per cent of Negro homes were without toilet or privy of any kind as against 2 per cent of white homes lacking a similar facility. In Southern villages, two-thirds of the large Negro families were living in homes with 1.5 persons per room, as against 28 per cent of the white families of similar size in the same area.[24] The comparison in Southern cities runs along similar lines.

Education. Comparing the educational level of the Negro population in the South in 1940 with its level at the time of emancipation indicates tremendous strides. In 1870, 81.4 per cent of Negroes were illiterate; in 1930 this figure had been reduced to 16.3 per cent.[25] Comparing the educational facilities for Negroes with those of white persons in the South at any given time, however, gross disparities are consistently seen. During the year 1939–40, the Southern States spent $58.69 per white child in average daily attendance in schools as against $18.82

[23] See Myrdal, *op. cit.*, p. 1284. Source of data: U. S. Department of Agriculture, Bureau of Home Economics, *Consumer Purchases Study, Farm Series, Family Income and Expenditures, Southeast Region,* Miscellaneous Publication No. 462, Part 1, *Family Income* (1941) pp. 5 and 77-80.
[24] Myrdal, *op. cit.*, pp. 376-377 and 1291. Data based on U. S. Department of Agriculture, Bureau of Home Economics, *Consumer Purchases Study, Urban, Village, and Farm Series, Family Housing and Facilities, Five Regions,* Miscellaneous Publication No. 399 (1940) Table 36.
[25] Davie, *Negroes in American Society,* p. 139.

for each Negro child.[26] Regarding the value of the equipment used in the two racial school systems in 11 Southern states in 1940, a study showed that $162 was spent for every white pupil in contrast to $34 per Negro pupil.[27] In 1940, 29 per cent of the Negro school teachers had completed four or more years of college against 53 per cent of the white teachers.[28] Almost three-fourths of the Negro elementary schools in 18 states in 1935–36 were one and two room schools.[29] In the higher educational levels, the differential opportunity of Negroes is even more striking. In 1933–34, only 19 per cent of the Negro children of high school ages were in high schools as compared with 55 per cent of the white children of the same ages. In many counties of the South with substantial Negro populations, there were, prior to 1940, no high schools available for Negroes.[30]

Education of Negroes at the college level in the South prior to 1890 was exceptionally limited and the schools available had been largely supported by private contributions, largely from Northern religious denominational sources. In 1890 an amendment to the original Morrill Act, adopted in 1862, required that Federal funds be divided fairly between the white and the Negro institutions in states having the dual system. Subsequently, 17 land-grant agricultural and mechanical colleges for Negroes were established, receiving some of their support from Federal funds under this Act. Wide disparities have continued to exist both in the quantity and quality of Negro higher educational institutions in the South.

Part of the immediate cause for the difference in the levels of educational achievement of the two races in the South lies in the lower motivation for education in the Negro group. A similar situation is characteristic of all low economic status groups. In the case of Negroes, however, it is further accentuated by the limited vocational opportunities which discrimination imposes. Since such Negro schools as there are, however, have been community by community markedly inferior to the white schools, primary causation may be attributed to the discrimination of the Southern racial system.

Health. Most studies of comparative Negro-white health conditions show widely disparate conditions unfavorable to the Negro. On a nationwide basis, some of the significant figures run as follows: The expectation of life of Negroes at birth was ten years less than that of whites in 1939; the infant mortality rates per 1000 live births in 1945

[26] See Frazier, *op. cit.,* p. 437.
[27] Davie, *op. cit.,* p. 150.
[28] *Ibid.,* p. 153.
[29] Frazier, *op. cit.,* p. 435.
[30] *Ibid.,* p. 436.

was 56.2 for Negroes and 35.6 for whites; the maternal mortality rates in 1940 show that of Negro mothers to be about two and a half times that of white mothers. The National Health Survey of 1935–36 found that the amount of disability per person due to illness which incapacitated for a week or longer was 43 per cent higher for Negroes than for whites.[31]

Studies are lacking which compare the health of Negro with white groups of comparable economic situation to which we might turn to locate factors related to Negro health other than their low income. However, other considerations point to the influence of discrimination. Good health conditions are highly dependent upon the provision of adequate facilities, and these in turn are dependent upon community cooperation and financing, both governmental and voluntary. We noted above the policy of hospital segregation of the races. In Mississippi for example in 1938 there were 0.7 hospital beds per 1000 Negroes against 2.4 beds per 1000 whites.[32] Discrimination in this instance directly contributes to Negro ill health.

It is in the field of health perhaps more than other aspects of welfare that the influence of Negro folk custom can be seen. The tuberculosis rates among Negroes are three to four times as great as among the white population, and the disparity in the incidence of the venereal diseases is still greater. Since the incidence of these diseases, particularly tuberculosis, is correlated with socioeconomic status, the low status of Negroes as a group would of itself be expected to produce high rates of these diseases. However, in this instance the survival and prevalence of folk superstitions concerning disease and its treatment make a further contribution to high rates of these diseases and to Negro ill health in general.

Crime and Delinquency. The rates of crime and delinquency for the Negro population as a whole compared with the white population as a whole generally show the Negro rate to be significantly higher. In 1933 among the prisoners in the county and city jails the rate per 100,000 population 15 years and older was 236.8 for Negro males as compared with 71.9 for white males, and 24.4 for Negro females as compared with 3.4 for white females.[33] Negroes accounted for 22.8 per cent of the arrests reported to the Federal Bureau of Investigation in 1940, whereas they comprised about one-tenth of the population. In other words, in the same year, there were 1078.4 Negroes arrested for every

[31] Davie, *op. cit.*, pp. 234-238.
[32] Frazier, *op. cit.*, p. 586.
[33] U. S. Bureau of the Census, *County and City Jails, Prisoners in Jails and Other Penal Institutions under County or Municipal Jurisdiction, 1933* (Washington: Government Printing Office).

100,000 of the Negro population, against 391.6 white arrests for every 100,000 of white population.[34]

Students of criminology constantly caution against the use of such statistical data as that submitted above without qualification. The reporting of crime data is far from uniform and therefore we rarely have a full count. Again there are many factors which influence the categories of criminals who are arrested and who are placed in penal institutions. We have seen above that the administration of justice is caste patterned, particularly in the South. This in itself affects the statistical figures. Where the offenses of Negroes are against the white race, or disturb the white community, Negroes are more frequently arrested and more often found guilty. On the other hand, crime within the Negro community is often left unpunished or treated lightly. Bearing in mind such considerations as these, an exact comparison of the actual amounts of criminal behavior in the two groups cannot be made. What is perhaps of practical concern is the high prevalence among Negroes as compared with whites of arrests for murder, assault, and petty larcenies.

Applying the three types of causes hitherto employed to interpret race differentials to crime and delinquency, we again begin with the concentration of the Negro population in the lower socioeconomic levels. In general, the positive association of crime rates and low economic position is well established irrespective of the social characteristics of the groups involved. Further, there are certain persistent influences carrying over from the traditional servile position of Negroes which operate in the situation. Petty thievery, for example, such as the stealing of food or a piece of cast-off clothing, has been generally condoned by whites much as one treats a similar act among little children. The traditional pattern of sexual exploitation of Negro females by white males persists to aggravate the volume of prostitution among Negro women. Again, from Dollard's analysis of Southern town race relations it is clear that the frustrations engendered by discrimination provoke a larger volume of aggression which in the case of Negroes to whom other aggressive outlets are limited, results in much criminal aggression against their own people and against whites.

Violent conflict: lynching. The caste system generates periodic violence directed against Negroes by whites. The two characteristic modes of expression of this violence are lynchings and riots. Lynching may be defined as the murder of a person by a group of people infused by the crowd spirit. In American history lynching of native status people and of minority persons other than Negroes has taken place. Statistics of lynchings have been provided by Tuskegee Institute for the years since

[34] See Frazier, *op. cit.*, p. 648.

GRAPH 2

Number of Negroes Lynched in the United States Yearly, 1882–1949 [35]

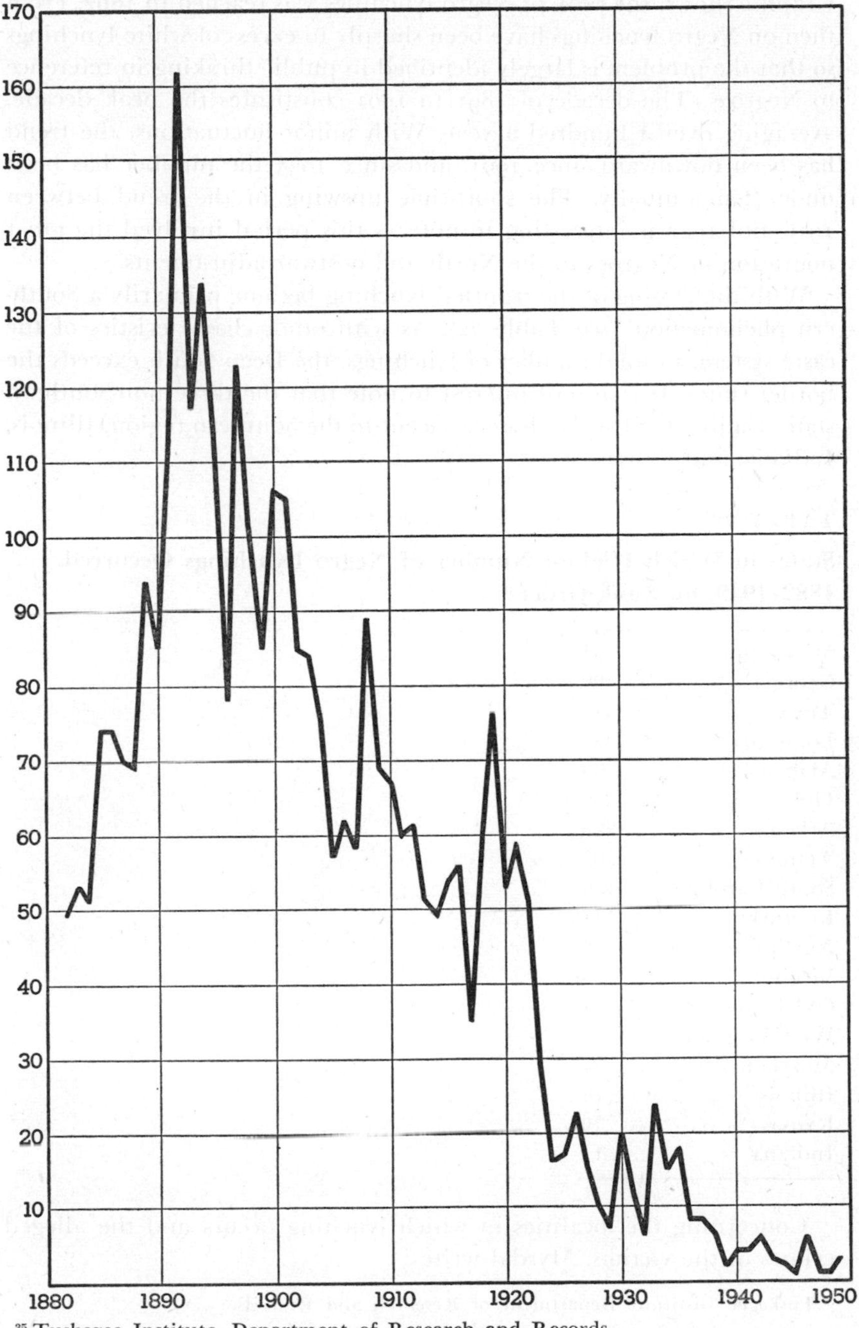

[35] Tuskegee Institute, Department of Research and Records.

1882. In 1884, lynchings of white people still exceeded the lynchings of Negroes by a substantial margin—whites, 100; Negroes, 51. As Graph 2 shows, the peak of Negro lynchings was reached in 1892. From then on Negro lynchings have been sharply in excess of white lynchings so that the problem is largely identified in public thinking in reference to Negroes. The decade of 1891 to 1901 constitutes the peak decade, averaging over a hundred a year. With minor fluctuations, the trend has been downward since 1901, and since 1935 the number has been under ten annually. The short-time upswing in the trend between 1916 and 1922 is interesting to note as this period involved the great migration of Negroes to the North and postwar adjustments.

With the closing of the frontier, lynching became primarily a Southern phenomenon (see Table 22). As with other characteristics of the caste system, in total number of lynchings, the Deep South exceeds the border states. It is also of interest to note that the three non-Southern states leading the list are those adjacent to the Southern region, Illinois, Indiana, and Kansas.

TABLE 22

States in Which Highest Number of Negro Lynchings Occurred, 1882–1949, by Rank Order[36]

Mississippi	534
Georgia	490
Texas	346
Louisiana	335
Alabama	299
Florida	256
Arkansas	226
Tennessee	203
South Carolina	156
Kentucky	141
North Carolina	84
Virginia	83
Oklahoma	41
West Virginia	28
Maryland	27
Illinois	19
Kansas	19
Indiana	14

Concerning the localities in which lynching occurs and the alleged crimes of the victims, Myrdal writes:

[36] Tuskegee Institute, Department of Research and Records.

Lynching is a rural and small town custom and occurs most commonly in poor districts. There are some indications that lynchings go in waves and tend to recur in the same districts. The accusations against persons lynched during the period for which there are records were: in 38 per cent of the cases for homicide, 6 per cent for felonious assault, 16 per cent for rape, 7 per cent for attempted rape, 7 per cent for theft, 2 per cent for insult to white persons, and 24 per cent for miscellaneous offenses or no offense at all. In the last category are all sorts of irritations: testifying at court against a white man or bringing suit against him, refusal to pay a note, seeking employment out of place, offensive language or boastful remarks. Regarding the accusations for crime, Raper testifies: "Case studies of nearly one hundred lynchings since 1929 convince the writer that around a third of the victims were falsely accused." The meaning of these facts is that, in principle, a lynching is not merely a punishment against an individual but a disciplinary device against the Negro group.[37]

As was indicated above (in the discussion of methods of maintaining caste) lynching and the ever-present threat of it constitute a powerful social control mechanism for maintaining caste. Lynchers are seldom held accountable for their acts. They are seldom indicted; even more seldom convicted; and if convicted, are usually pardoned. "While state police can be used to prevent lynching, the local police often support the lynching." [38] Raper estimates that "at least one-half [of 100 studied] of the lynchings are carried out with police officers participating, and that in nine-tenths of the others the officers either condone or wink at the mob action." [39]

The composition of lynching mobs is indicated by Myrdal as follows:

The actual participants in the lynching mobs usually belong to the frustrated lower strata of Southern whites. Occasionally, however, the people of the middle and upper class take part, and generally they condone the deed, and nearly always they find it advisable to let the incident pass without assisting in bringing the guilty before the court. Women and children are not absent from lynching mobs; indeed, women sometimes incite the mobs into action.[40]

Among the various background conditions which have been suggested as related to lynching are: poverty and economic fear; social fear that the Negro is "getting out of place"; the dullness and general

---

[37] Myrdal, op. cit., by permission of the publishers, Harper and Brothers, p. 560. See Arthur Raper, The Tragedy of Lynching (Chapel Hill: University of North Carolina Press, 1933) for an extensive analysis of the lynching problem.
[38] Myrdal, op. cit., p. 562.
[39] Arthur Raper, "Race and Class Pressures," unpublished manuscript prepared for Myrdal study, 1940, p. 275.
[40] Myrdal, op. cit., p. 562. By permission of publishers, Harper and Brothers.

boredom of everyday life in the rural areas and small towns of the South.

Lynching has a "psychological importance out of all proportion to its small frequency." [41] Analyzing its effects, the Myrdal study has this to say:

The effects of lynchings are far reaching. In the locality where it has happened and in a wide region surrounding it, the relations between the two groups deteriorate. The Negroes are terror stricken and sullen. The whites are anxious and are likely to show the assertiveness and suspicion of persons with bad, but hardened, consciences. Some whites are afraid of Negro retaliation or emigration. Every visitor to such a community must notice the antagonism and mutual lack of confidence between the two groups.[42]

Lynchings in the United States affect adversely world opinion of this country. Accounts of them are widely publicized in other countries. In Davie's opinion, "lynching is without question our best advertised disgrace." [43]

Lynching falls in the category of social behavior whose control and eventual elimination must be accomplished by a change of opinion and mores within the communities where it has long been approved, or at least condoned. It is, therefore, pertinent to observe that organized efforts dedicated to this purpose have arisen in the South itself. Influential among such regional activities was the organization of the Association of Southern Women for the Prevention of Lynching, founded in Atlanta in 1930. In the basic statement of the association's purpose, lynching is declared "an indefensible crime destructive of all principles of government, hateful and hostile to every ideal of religion and humanity, debasing and degrading to every person involved." [44] This association has succeeded in securing the signatures of 50,000 white women of the South to its pledge which reads in part: "We solemnly pledge ourselves to create a new public opinion in the South which will not condone for any reason whatever acts of mobs or lynchers." [45]

Race riots are more characteristic of the Northern scene and will be discussed in that connection. In the South, they tend more to be white mob action directed at defenseless Negro areas.[46]

Political effects. The South as a region has had a political development which differs from the rest of the country. (1) The proportion of peo-

[41] *Ibid.*, p. 564.
[42] *Ibid.*, p. 564. By permission of the publishers, Harper and Brothers.
[43] Davie, *op. cit.*, p. 357.
[44] *Ibid.*, p. 354.
[45] *Ibid.*, p. 355.
[46] For dramatic accounts of violence in the Southern scene, see Walter White, *A Man Called White* (New York: Viking Press, Inc., 1948).

ple who participate in politics is markedly smaller than in the rest of the nation. We have already referred to the virtual disfranchisement of Negroes. As an example of the effectiveness of means adopted to keep the Negroes from voting, Bunche estimated that in 8 Southern states, the so-called Deep South, never more than 80,000 to 90,000 Negro votes had been cast in general elections up to 1940, and only a handful in the primaries—the elections which really count.[47] Again in the South, the proportion of the white electorate which participates in politics is decidedly less than in the rest of the nation. In 1940 only 28 per cent of the adult population of 12 Southern states went to the polls in contrast to 53 per cent for the rest of the country. (2) The South for all practical purposes has had a one-party system, the Democratic party. The primary contests in this party constitute in essence the final decision. (3) From this it followed that political opposition has been more confined than elsewhere to rivalries between factions and personalities in which the basic issues contested in the nation as a whole have not been debated. Since the Democratic party in the South has represented traditional and conservative interests, the South itself had remained conservative, and exercised a conservative influence in the National Congress. The same kind of liberal political pressures which have arisen elsewhere in the nation, representing broadly liberal and human welfare interests as opposed to conservative and propertied interests, have not manifested themselves in any marked degree in the South. Since wide exercise of the franchise, a two (or more) party system, and the vigorous debate of new ways to further the democratic ideal are signs of a healthy democracy, the democratic political process may properly be regarded as retarded.

To what extent are these distinctive developments in Southern politics attributable to the effect of its system of race relations? Since we adhere to the general principle that the causal factors in such complex social phenomena are always multiple and are interactive upon one another, we shall not suggest that the system of race relations is all-determinative. Nevertheless, the interrelationship between the phenomena of race relations and these political developments is highly impressive. The elaborate devices to limit the electorate arose primarily as a way of preventing Negroes from exercising active citizenship. Likewise the one-party system with its "white" primary developed for the same reason. Once established, these political phenomena have furthered the politicoeconomic interests of the middle and upper classes of the white South in opposition to those of the lower class whites. The failure of the latter group to generate more effective political expres-

---

[47] Ralph J. Bunche, "The Negro in the Political Life of the United States," *Journal of Negro Education*, Vol. 10, July, 1941, pp. 567-84.

sion of its interests is in considerable measure related to its preoccupation with keeping the Negro in his place.

Effect on the economy of the South. Rupert Vance, an outstanding student of the Southern region, has defined the South's position in the economy of the nation in these terms: "The statistical indices of wealth, education, cultural achievement, health, law and order reduced to a per capita basis combine in every instance to give the Southern states the lowest rankings in the Union." [48] After a careful appraisal of the natural resources of the region, Vance concludes that it is not lack of adequate natural resources which accounts for the South's relative poverty. He finds the chief explanation in the manner in which the Southern economy has been organized.

Southern reconstruction on the economic side called for carrying on the plantation agricultural economy, with chief emphasis upon cotton production, with such modifications as the emancipation of the slaves required. Since this economy required cheap labor, the caste system developed in part as a means of guaranteeing the continued employment of Negroes in their accustomed occupational role at subsistence wages. Furthermore, in order to hold its place competitively in a national economy generally more efficient than its own, the Southern cotton economy was forced to exploit the soil to the point of diminishing returns. In this way, a cycle of reciprocal forces was established which operated to retard the economic development of the region. The relatively inefficient economy could produce only subsistence wages for the laborers involved. Their marginal income in turn retarded the regional demand for goods which would have favored the development of industrial enterprise. Furthermore, the marginal economy was unable to produce enough to furnish the capital needed for industrial development. This capital had, therefore, to be furnished from outside the region, which meant that part of the gains were drained from the region itself. In order to get this capital, the South offered the inducement primarily of cheap labor costs, which still further aggravated the low standard of living, extending it in this instance to a wider segment of its white population. While the expanding industrial economy offered some opportunity to transfer Negroes from farm work to city work, the caste system prevented their employment in other than the lowest paying capacities.

Clearly many factors are involved in interpreting the cycle just described. Nevertheless the influence of the caste system is apparent at every turn. As Vance has written: "The South holds the Negro back; the Negro holds the South back; and both point in recrimination." [49]

---

[48] Rupert B. Vance, *Human Geography of the South* (Chapel Hill: University of North Carolina Press, 1932), p. 442. By permission.
[49] *Ibid.*, p. 43.

VARIATION IN THE SOUTHERN PATTERN

The foregoing description has disregarded the variations in order to indicate the generalized Southern pattern. Variations exist from state to state in minor details but not in essential form. Some significant rural-urban contrasts are to be noted. The city environment permits more relief to Negroes from the omnipresent impact of caste through the opportunity it affords to build a separate community structure in which they may live a fuller life. At least within this area, Negroes can live their own lives.[50] Compared with the smaller places, there is less actual personal interaction between the members of the two races in the city. Traditionally, the caste system carries with it much direct personal dependence of individual Negroes upon particular white people, through which conformance to the mandates of caste can be closely scrutinized. The greater drawing apart of the two races in the Southern cities places the control of caste upon a more impersonal basis.

The border states. A major variation in the Southern pattern of race relation is seen by considering certain border states, including Oklahoma, Kentucky, West Virginia, Missouri, Maryland, Delaware, and the District of Columbia. In none of these states is to be found the "white primary"; among them, only Oklahoma has "Jim Crow" streetcars. Likewise, in these states, the code of etiquette is frequently less explicit and less binding. On the other hand, in all these states intermarriage between Negroes and whites is prohibited by law and the segregation of Negroes in schools has remained, at least to 1940, the general practice.[51]

Washington, D. C. The pattern of race relations in Washington, D. C. is of particular significance because it is the Capital of the nation, visited by foreign officials of all nations. On the one hand, Washington is in tradition part of the Southern area and therefore reflects in many ways the Southern attitude and behavior in Negro-white relations. On the other hand, the influence of the Federal Government has imposed certain exceptions to the traditional Southern pattern. To illustrate the latter first, Negroes are not "Jim Crowed" in District transportation; they have equal access to all institutions and services directly operated as Federal Government property, for example, Federal cafeterias, and playgrounds operated for Government employees. Prior to the past war, the National Government as an employer offered to a limited number of Negroes employment in higher ranking occupations, qualified by the

[50] The writer was told by a professional Negro in a Louisiana city that the members of his family went "down town" as seldom as possible because they so profoundly disliked the caste requirements.
[51] See Myrdal, *op. cit.*, p. 1072, Table 1, "Various definitions of the South," for a check list of the various features of the caste system for the Southern states.

tendency to place them in special assignments dealing with Negro problems. Aside from these exceptions, Washington in the period prior to World War II presented substantially the same picture as other border cities. For example, school segregation still prevailed and Negroes were, and still are, denied the use of general restaurant and amusement facilities in the city. From the Negro viewpoint, housing segregation in the Capital City presents a most critical problem but in this respect the situation is substantially like that of Northern cities in general.[52]

CHANGES IN THE SOUTHERN PATTERN

Between 1880 and 1940, race relations in the South reveal changes which went rather rapidly in one direction, and rather slowly in another. As we have seen in the short period when Northerners directed the reconstruction program, Negroes achieved certain gains in status, especially in politics. When the white South regained control, its efforts were to put the Negro back into his inferior status through the establishment of the caste system. In the decade of 1900–1910 this adjustment had been perfected, and remained broadly unchanged to World War II. The change in the opposite direction is revealed in the improvement in the welfare of Negroes as a group, even though at all times with wide discrepancies, in comparison with the welfare of the whites as a group. Among the forces operating to effect this improvement was the opportunity presented by World War I for Negroes to find employment in the North, which had some effect upon improving their bargaining position in the South. Again, the tendency of the Federal Government to insist on the more equitable use of Federal funds for Negroes, especially during the 1930's, improved Negro welfare. Furthermore, the beginnings of a crack in the color line hitherto drawn in the unions began to show in the mid-1930's.

White liberals. The earnest efforts of a small band of Southern white liberals in behalf of Negroes deserve recognition among the forces operating to keep the Southern pattern unfrozen. The group comprised a few writers, journalists, educators, and some club women whom Myrdal has described as "mostly a fraternity of individuals with independent minds, usually living in, and adjusting to, an uncongenial social surrounding." [53] Because for the most part they possessed high social prestige either through their lineage from Southern aristocracy or through the national preeminence they had acquired in professional fields, their espousal of the Negro's cause was tolerated. Their first ef-

---

[52] See *Segregation in Washington*, A Report of the National Committee on Segregation in the Nation's Capital (Chicago: 1948) for a summary of the Negro-white relations in Washington, including the situation after World War II.
[53] Myrdal, *op. cit.*, p. 467.

forts were directed at striving for equal justice, particularly against lynching, and gaining for the Negro a fairer share of public monies spent for education, health, and other aspects of welfare. They were unable to challenge the system of segregation itself. The Southern liberals have not been able to influence political life to any marked extent and their influence has been largely confined to higher social and educational levels of Southern society. The main organization through which Southern liberalism found expression was the Commission on Interracial Cooperation, founded in 1919. In Myrdal's judgment its most far-reaching effect is *"to have rendered interracial work socially respectable in the conservative South."* [54]

As relatively ineffectual as the efforts of the Southern liberal group have been in the past, its presence in the South is of enormous importance in the present situation when the nation as a whole is pressing the South for significant readjustment in the position of Negroes. Insofar as this outside pressure can be channeled through the Southern liberals, the conservative position can make less use of the argument of outside interference.

Negro leadership. Finally, we consider the role of Negro leadership and organization upon the course of Southern race relations, during the caste period. Under slavery, the organized activities of Negroes in their own behalf, as we have seen, consisted largely of abortive slave revolts. Prominent in the abolition movement, however, was Frederick Douglass, the outstanding leader among Negroes in the 19th century. Following emancipation, which he urged upon Lincoln, he worked to secure for the Negroes full equality, but saw the fight lost during the Southern reconstruction. Organized movements among Negroes subsequently have divided into main types usually referred to as of the "protest" variety or of the "accommodative" variety. The former, of which Douglass was an example, aimed to secure full equality for Negroes; the latter, aimed to secure the betterment of the conditions of Negroes without challenging the institution of caste itself. During the 20th century, the protest type of activity was almost exclusively confined among Negroes in the North, which we shall consider in Chapter 10. In the South, the unquestioned spokesman for the Negro was Booker T. Washington who is generally considered a leader of the accommodative type, although some of his biographers think that the extent of his compromising has been overstressed, particularly in view of the circumstances which he faced. Rose summarizes the role which Washington played and the philosophy behind it in these words:

[54] *Ibid.,* p. 847.

It is wrong to characterize Washington as an all-out accommodating leader. He never relinquished the right to full equality in all respects as the ultimate goal. But for the time being he was prepared to give up social and political equality, even to soft-pedal the protest against inequalities in justice. He was also willing to flatter the Southern whites and be harsh toward the Negroes—*if* the Negroes were allowed to work undisturbed with their white friends for education and business. But neither in education nor in business did he assault inequalities. In both fields he accepted the white doctrine of the Negroes "place." In education he pleaded mainly for vocational training. Through thrift, skill, and industry the Negroes were gradually to improve so much that later the discussion could again be taken up concerning their rights. This was Washington's philosophy.[55]

However one views the relative merits of the protest as against the accommodative program of action, beyond question Washington had the greatest influence of any single Negro upon the development of Negro welfare during his time. His influence was most concretely evidenced in the development of Tuskegee Institute over which he presided for many years.

TOPICS FOR DISCUSSION AND PROJECTS

1. Interview two or more Northern bred whites who have traveled in the South and two or more Southern bred whites who have traveled in the North. Ask each to talk about their first experiences with the different etiquette in race relations and their reactions to it. Present the findings of your interviews.
2. Debate the topic: Biracial segregation in principle is consistent with equality of opportunity for both groups.
3. How would you account for the fact that some Negro women in the South accede voluntarily to the sexual overtures of some white men?
4. Discuss the topic: The effects of the Southern caste system upon the personalities of Southern white people.
5. How do you account for the apparently greater volume of overt antagonism manifested by lower class Southern whites in contrast to that shown by middle and upper class whites?

SUGGESTED READING

Cayton, Horace R. "The Psychology of the Negro Under Discrimination," in *Race Prejudice and Discrimination*, Arnold M. Rose, ed. (New York: Alfred A. Knopf, Inc., 1951) pp. 276-290.
> *A brief but incisive analysis of the effects of discrimination upon Negro personality.*

Davis, Allison. *Children of Bondage*. Washington, D. C.: American Council on Education, 1940.

---

[55] Arnold Rose, *The Negro in America* (New York: Harper and Brothers, 1948), p. 240. By permission.

An intensive study of eight Negro adolescents in the Deep South, indicating the effects of the Southern pattern upon Negro personality.

———, Gardner, Burleigh B., and Gardner, Mary R. *Deep South: A Social Anthropological Study of Caste and Class.* Chicago: University of Chicago Press, 1941.

A community study of race relations around Natchez, Mississippi, distinguishing class relations from the interracial caste relations.

Johnson, Charles S. *Growing Up in the Black Belt.* Washington, D. C.: American Council on Education, 1941.

Study of the impact of Southern system upon the personality development of Southern rural Negro youth through intensive case studies.

Johnson, Guy B. "Patterns of Race Conflict," in *Race Relations and the Race Problem,* Edgar Thompson, ed. Durham: Duke University, 1939.

Traces history of race conflict showing that the patterns had not changed much in spite of changing conditions.

Raper, Arthur F. *Preface to Peasantry.* Chapel Hill: University of North Carolina Press, 1936.

First-hand study of two black belt counties in Georgia, emphasizing the role of tenant farming system upon the poverty of the farmers of both races.

———, *The Tragedy of Lynching.* Chapel Hill: University of North Carolina Press, 1933.

A detailed analysis of the lynchings occurring in 1930. The study was sponsored by the Southern Commission on the Study of Lynching.

Vance, Rupert P. "Racial Competition for the Land," *Race Relations and the Race Problem,* Edgar Thompson, ed. Durham: Duke University Press, 1939.

Shows how racial competition for land in the rural cotton South has contributed to depressed conditions for both races and stimulated migration to the cities.

CHAPTER 10

Negro-White Relations: The Northern Pattern

Introduction. While the status of Negroes outside the South is in some ways similar to that found within that region, the differences to be found in the North are sufficiently striking to make a separate discussion essential. In the North, Negroes are discriminated against substantially everywhere but not in as many aspects of life nor so intensely as in the South. The welfare of the Negro in the North is relatively the lowest of all large minorities but the relatively higher general standard of living in the North is reflected in the higher standards of Northern Negroes as compared with Southern Negroes.

A basic difference between the Northern and Southern situation lies in the absence in the North of any such precise institutionalization of the minority position of Negroes as the Southern caste pattern involves. In the South caste relations are well defined in law and in the regional mores; and control mechanisms for maintaining the caste pattern have become standardized through years of experience in their operation. In contrast, in the North the discrimination and segregation which does exist lacks explicit sanction in the mores; and there are lacking well established control devices for holding the Negro within minority status. For Southern white people in general the attitudes and values of the caste system are an integral part of their personalities; and for Southern Negroes brought up under this system the reciprocal attitudes and behavior patterns are deeply structured in their personalities. Caste is an intrinsic part of the Southern social structure and daily

256

touches the lives of the people of both races. In the North, the segregated position of Negroes is only a fragmentary aspect of Northern community life and many white people, even in communities with sizable Negro populations, are scarcely aware of its presence.

Many contrasting circumstances in the two regional situations account for this basic difference, some of which can only be stated briefly in this introductory overview. The North does not have the tradition of slavery in relation to Negroes, having abolished slavery prior to emancipation. In no community of the North has the number of Negroes approached a majority. While Negroes have been highly useful in the development of the economy of the North, their labor has never been considered specifically essential to Northern economic life, especially as long as European immigration furnished cheap labor. The concentration of Negroes in the larger cities of the North where their residential segregation resembles that of other ethnic and racial minorities makes their position appear less sharply in contrast to the dominant white community than in the South where Negroes are essentially the only minority.

The significance of this difference can be seen from the contrasting reactions of the North and South to the present disequilibrium in Negro-white relations precipitated by World War II. Faced with the situation of increasing pressures to accord Negroes more and more equality, the white North reacts with less unanimity, with less intensity, and most significant of all with less concern. Let us disregard for the moment the Northerners who are ready to accord Negroes full equality in status and those actively working to bring it about. The rest of the North may grumble at Negroes, or get irritated with them at times, try to prevent new Negro advances, and try to keep Negroes out of their neighborhoods, often successfully. But on the whole even these people, once a new advance has been made, tend to accept it. While their acceptance is partly due to the fact that they cannot help it, it is even more important that these Negro advances are not a matter of paramount concern to Northerners. Without wishing to overdraw the unanimity of Southern response to pressures to improve the status of Negroes, it seems fair to say that in contrast to the North, the South is gravely concerned and perplexed about the probability of a change in Negro-white relations.

THE PATTERN OF DISCRIMINATION

A close-up view of the general pattern of Negro-white relations in the North may be obtained from the comprehensive study of the Chicago scene made by Drake and Cayton. While confined to this one city, in essence *Black Metropolis* typifies the Northern situation. Much of the material was gathered for this volume in the 1930's, although some of it refers to the impact of World War II. While the decade of 1940–1950 has seen some changes in Chicago and elsewhere, the Black Metropolis scene still prevails in the main.[1]

Residential segregation: the black ghetto. Negroes in Chicago were highly concentrated in residence; 337,000—90 per cent of all—lived in the Black Belt.[2] The difference between this and other ethnic colonies found in cities is that while the latter tended to break up in time, the Negro area became increasingly concentrated. The particular area was on the lower South Side, long considered by Chicago planning boards a "blighted area," the most dilapidated area of the city. The degree of congestion is indicated by the fact that Negroes were living 90,000 to the square mile as compared to 20,000 in adjacent white apartment house areas.[3] This high degree of spatial segregation "is primarily the result of white people's attitudes toward having Negroes as neighbors. Because some white Chicagoans do not wish colored neighbors, formal and informal controls are used to isolate the latter within congested all-Negro neighborhoods." [4]

The real force of the measures to contain the Negro area began when the mass invasions took place. "It was only after 1915, when 65,000 migrants came into the city within five years, that resistance became organized." [5] Property owners associations began to take active measures to forestall sale and rent of property to Negroes outside the Black Belt. "A wave of violence flared up, and between July 1917 and March 1921 fifty-eight homes were bombed. . . . The victims of the bombings were Negro families that had moved into white neighborhoods, as well as Negro and white real-estate men who sold or rented property to them." [6] Since 1925, the major device for controlling the Negro community has been the restrictive covenant—an agreement between property owners within a certain district not to rent or sell to Negroes.[7]

Occupational discrimination: the job ceiling. Discrimination in jobs against Negroes was seen first of all in the tendency to deny them jobs when white people were out of work. In 1940 according to Drake and Cayton sources. *"While Negroes made up only 8 per cent of the availa-*

---

[1] St. Clair Drake and Horace R. Cayton, *Black Metropolis* (New York: Harcourt, Brace & Company, Inc., 1945).
[2] *Ibid.*, p. 174.
[3] *Ibid.*, p. 204.
[4] *Ibid.*, p. 174.
[5] *Ibid.*, p. 177.
[6] *Ibid.*, p. 178.
[7] The effectiveness of this device has been greatly weakened although not completely destroyed by a 1948 Supreme Court decision denying the support of courts in enforcing restrictive covenants.

ble workers, they constituted 22 per cent of the unemployed. All along the line, Negroes had been displaced in a ratio of roughly three to one. Almost half of the Negro domestic servants, a third of the semi-skilled workers, and a fourth of the unskilled were unemployed in 1935." [8] Job discrimination was seen in the fact there were numerous pursuits from which Negroes were substantially barred. "The job ceiling for Negroes tends to be drawn just above the level of semiskilled jobs, with the skilled, clerical, managerial, and supervisory positions reserved for white workers." [9] The third index of job discrimination was seen in the fact that the Negroes had not consistently held their competitive position in certain occupational fields. For example, during the depression, Negroes lost out to whites in restaurants and hotel jobs. In the occupational areas where Negroes and whites competed for jobs, it should be remembered that prior to World War II, whites in general were able to refuse to work with Negroes in the same level job. Thus if a restaurant desired to employ white waitresses, there could not be any Negroes in a similar capacity.

As compensation for these inequities in competition for such occupations as they were fitted for, Negroes had a substantial monopoly in the two occupations of Pullman porters and "redcaps." In both these occupations "the earnings and the prospects of advancement are dependent upon cheerful and, if necessary, ingratiating service. . . . Even very well-educated Negroes did not scorn such jobs." [10]

The low economic position of Negroes is in part explainable by their relative lack of skills and training for the higher ranking jobs. It is further accounted for by the tendency of Southern Negroes to flock to the North in numbers in excess of the job opportunities available to them, in search of the real but exaggerated "freedom" of the North. But in considerable measure, it is due to racial discrimination: to the tendency of white workers to refuse to work alongside Negroes and of employers to assume this is true even more than it is; to the tendency of white customers to resent being waited on by Negroes, except in the most servile services, and of employers to assume the universality of this reaction by white clients; and to the tendency to consider the Negro as somehow different, not quite one of us, and of course inferior.

Limited equality in public. In contrast to the South, Negroes in Chicago were not segregated in their utilization of many public facilities. Public parks, public transportation facilities, stores, and public toilets were open to them. However, the more intimate the situation the more doubtful the acceptance of Negroes in equal terms. In theaters, restau-

[8] Drake and Cayton, *op. cit.,* p. 217. By permission.
[9] *Ibid.,* p. 262.
[10] *Ibid.,* p. 237.

rants, and particularly in swimming places, Negroes were discouraged by every possible means from associating with whites. In the Midwest metropolis, bathing beaches and swimming pools were among the primary tension points. The Negro press reports:

POLICE OBJECT TO MIXING OF RACES ON BEACH; ARREST 18. SAY THEY ARE TRYING TO PREVENT RACE RIOT.[11]

While the color line was seldom drawn in theaters or at large public gatherings, in recreational situations that emphasized active participation as distinct from merely looking on, Negroes were barred; and in all situations where men and women participated together, there was a rigid line.

"Equality" in education, political life, and before the law. In marked contrast to the South was the "equality" accorded Northern Negroes in these areas indicated by the headings. However, the term "equality" is here placed in quotes because what Negroes had in Chicago and elsewhere in the North was the substance of equality so far as it can be institutionalized within the framework of dominant group attitudes toward minority groups. It is hard to prove a teacher "looks down" on Negroes, or that a juror will not believe Negro testimony when it contradicts that of a white person. But it is equally difficult to study the events which occur in such connections without being convinced the equality is qualified by prejudice.

Law. To take up these equalities in reverse order, Drake and Cayton wrote: "To Negro migrants, fresh from the South, Midwest Metropolis presents a novel experience—a substantial measure of equality before the law. Here, they can expect a reasonably fair trial in the courts, with a choice of colored or white counsel. There are no lynchings." [12]

Politics. In Chicago, as elsewhere in the North, Negroes had full political rights. Even though thought of as a minority group, their right to vote and participate in political organization has not been denied. In fact since they were then able to influence the outcome of elections, the politicians, being realists, worked with them and assisted them in adjusting to Northern city life. Being of low economic status and not experienced in politics, the Negro vote tended to swing to the political machines as distinct from the reformers. Machine politicians who had experience in organizing various foreign groups made it a point to learn how to appeal to and influence this new mass of voters. To most Southern Negroes this opportunity to be a citizen was a new experience.

[11] *Ibid.,* p. 105.
[12] *Ibid.,* pp. 108-109.

Politics became an important, perhaps the most important, method by which the Negro sought to change his status. It was often the only avenue open for struggle against caste tendencies. This struggle invested his political behavior, even when corrupt, with an importance and a dignity that similar behavior could not command in any other portion of the population. To paraphrase Lincoln Steffens, the Negro favored *representative* government, even if it was not always *clean* government.[13]

As a result of their political activities, Negroes have made substantial gains in Chicago.

Within a decade after the Great Migration, Black Metropolis had elected two Negro aldermen, one State Senator, four State Representatives, a city judge, and a Congressman. This political activity led Gosnell to comment in 1935 that "the Negroes in Chicago have achieved relatively more in politics . . . than have the Negroes in other cities of the United States." Wielding such political power, Negro politicians have been in a position to demand appointive positions for a few hundred individuals and equitable treatment in the courts for the masses (as well as dubious "benefits" from the great Chicago enterprise of "fixing" and "rigging" everything from traffic tickets to gambling dens). They have also been able to expose and check discrimination in the administration of the civil service laws and in the enforcement of the Civil Rights Law. They have created, among influential white politicians of all parties, an awareness of the Negro's desire for equal opportunity. The appointment of the Mayor's Committee on Race Relations, to which we have frequently referred, was as much an evidence of the political power of the Black Metropolis as it was an expression of spontaneous civic foresight and virtue.[14]

The minority status of Negroes was, however, reflected in politics as in all other phases of their lives. Of this Drake and Cayton write:

The color line in politics is also reflected in the types of political plums that go to Negro politicians and their henchmen. The big contracts and the heavy graft are reserved for whites. Negroes get the petty "cuts" from gambling and vice protection. In fact, a tradition has developed that Negroes will not demand big political rewards. Also, in matters of street cleaning, garbage disposal, and general city services, Negro areas are neglected. During the period of the Depression, however, when vast Federal funds were at the disposal of the machine in power, the Black Belt was able to secure some expansion of social services. Political leaders in Midwest Metropolis, balancing the pressures of ethnic, economic, and religious blocs, are forced to grant some of the demands of Negroes, and Negro politicians shrewdly demand all that they think the traffic will bear.[15]

[13] *Ibid.*, p. 343. By permission.
[14] *Ibid.*, pp. 109-110. By permission.
[15] *Ibid.*, p. 111. By permission.

Education. Curiously in view of the exhaustive coverage of Negro life in Chicago, Drake and Cayton write very little about education. For the North in general, Myrdal, however, notes:

There is little school segregation required by law in the Northern and Western states: Arizona requires it in elementary schools and makes it permissive in secondary schools; Kansas, Wyoming, Indiana, and New Mexico make school segregation permissive in the elementary grades and sometimes also in the secondary grades. Some communities in the southern parts of New Jersey, Indiana, Pennsylvania, Ohio and Illinois use organized pressure contrary to law to segregate Negroes in at least the elementary grades. In practically all other areas of the North there is partial segregation on a voluntary basis, caused by residential segregation aided by the gerrymandering of school districts and the system of "permits." This segregation is fairly complete for elementary schools, except where Negroes form only a small proportion of the population, but there is much less segregation in secondary schools. In few cases—if any—is this segregation accompanied by discrimination, however, except that form of discrimination which inevitably arises out of isolation. In fact there is probably more discrimination in the mixed schools than in the segregated ones in the North: frequently Negroes in mixed schools are kept out of swimming, dancing, and other athletics, and out of social clubs. There are, however, some Negro teachers in mixed schools in many Northern cities, and Negroes sit on the boards of education in a few big Northern cities.[16]

The opportunity for Negroes to procure higher education in the North has been less equal than for secondary schools. Northern state universities have not prohibited Negro enrollments, although the vast majority of the private institutions either categorically did not accept Negroes, or accepted a "token" Negro or two. Myrdal concluded that there was no serious restriction upon higher education of Negroes in the North, supporting his view by pointing out that only four Negro colleges, all of these established before the Civil War, have been located in the North. However, it is pertinent to note that prior to 1940, a large number of Northern Negroes had gone South to attend Negro colleges, 3000, for example, in 1938–39.[17] They may have done this because these colleges are less expensive or because they received scholarships. However it is also possible that in some case they did so because of the feeling that, though admitted to a Northern college they would still face a number of unpleasant discriminations. Caliver writes that Negro students "seldom lived on campus and in general, they seemed not to belong in the same way that white students felt themselves a

[16] Myrdal, *An American Dilemma,* p. 633. By permission of the publishers Harper and Brothers.
[17] Ambrose Caliver, United States Office of Education, *National Survey of Higher Education of Negroes* (Washington: Government Printing Office, 1942–43), Vol. IV, p. 13.

part of the university." [18] Discrimination in higher education is likewise seen in the fact that prior to World War II, not more than five
white colleges had had a Negro member on their faculty.

Social segregation: no social equality. The color line holds most adamantly in the North in the field of social life, even though here it cannot be said to be absolute. Negroes seldom mix with whites in voluntary associations, except for civic purposes; in church congregations,
the Catholic parishes more frequently excepted; in cliques; and of
course in family life. To the typical dominant white American, the
specter of social equality with the Negroes is the most feared. The
meaning of "social equality" is variously interpreted. In our usage, it
means the association of colored and white on equal terms in the more
intimate areas of interpersonal relations such as those indicated above.
Whatever may be their ultimate hope, Negroes themselves lay less
stress on the desirability of achieving equality in this more intimate
sphere than upon the other equalities. This difference in the relative
importance attached to social equality by the two races is favorable to
facilitating adjustment in Negro-white relations in the North in the
immediate future. The reaction of Negroes to social inequality is more
marked in the borderline situations where occupational or civic associations of which Negroes are members with whites have "social" affairs. Drake and Cayton write of this:

> Whenever Negroes in such a situation are ignored, barred, or subjected to
> "special arrangements" they usually resent it. Nobody likes to feel "left out"
> or to be regarded as a "problem." Sometimes Negroes will put up a fight for
> inclusion in such activities. More often they will withdraw and mask the
> snub by feigning a total lack of interest in the proceedings or by professing a
> preference for the company of Negroes. Those who elect to fight usually make
> it clear that they consider the issue one of "civil" or "economic" rights
> rather than one of *social* equality. Those who decide to withdraw accept the
> definition of the situation as *social* and disavow a desire to participate.[19]

METHODS OF ENFORCING
THE NORTHERN PATTERN

Generally speaking, segregation outside the South is not supported
by law. A few non-Southern states ban intermarriage; certain local
communities have officially segregated Negroes in schools, but such
laws have usually been overridden by court decisions.

Attempts are made in some communities by police to keep Negroes
out of certain public areas, such as beaches, but such actions are nowhere actually legally supported. Subterfuges, such as making the

[18] *Ibid.*
[19] Drake and Cayton, *op. cit.*, p. 123. By permission.

commercial recreational place a "club" are sometimes successful. In a left-handed way law enforcing agencies frequently support segregation by refusing to arrest whites who molest Negroes exercising their legal privileges. Broadly speaking, however, when Negroes press cases of discrimination involving civil rights outside the South, they win these cases. However, since legal vindication is a costly process, such cases are not numerous.

The use of restrictive covenants to prevent Negroes from occupying homes in many white areas has been the most prevalent device of a legal discriminatory nature employed by Northern whites against Negroes. This device is a compact, frequently included in deeds of sales, by which real estate operators and property owners agree for a definite period of time not to sell or lease property to certain prescribed categories of people, usually Negroes.[20] The two most usual arguments advanced to justify such agreements are (1) that Negroes have lower standards than whites and will not keep up the property to the standard prevailing in the area, thus affecting property values; and (2) that white people do not like Negroes as neighbors and that therefore the value of properties in the section deteriorate with the admission of any Negroes. When Negroes come in, white people try to get away and thus sell more cheaply, it is argued. On the first point concerning Negro care of their homes, the Washington study gives much evidence that, compared with white tenants of a similar socioeconomic level, Negroes are, if anything, better tenants than whites.[21] The second point that whites do not like Negroes as neighbors must of course have much truth or there would be no point in convenants of this kind. However, it should be observed that restrictive covenants are always highly profitable to certain local real estate interests. On the one hand, properties which are so restricted can command a higher price for this reason. On the other hand, since Negroes are restricted in their choice, the rental and sale value of the limited supply of housing which is open to them is higher than it would be otherwise. According to Weaver, recent studies have shown that "the nonwhite family receives less housing value for the same price than does the white group which has access to an open housing market."[22] Since these specific local realty interests stand to make a two-way gain, so to speak, at the minimum they can hardly be expected to make any efforts to change the situation. Weaver puts the point more strongly by stating that it is cer-

[20] Cf. Robert C. Weaver, *The Negro Ghetto* (New York: Harcourt, Brace & Company, Inc., 1948). Ch. 13. "The Villain—Racial Covenants."
[21] *Segregation in Washington,* A Report of the National Committee on Segregation in the Nation's Capital, Nov. 1948, Chicago, NCSNC, p. 31.
[22] Weaver, *op. cit.,* p. 261.

tain that racial housing covenants are carefully promoted by property owners' associations, developers of subdivisions, financial institutions, and in some instances by the Federal Housing Authority.[23] Attempts legally to upset these agreements were for a long time unsuccessful. In 1917 the Supreme Court (245 U.S. 60) ruled that a municipal zoning ordinance which segregated Negroes and whites deprived the real estate owner of property without due process of law. Thus government, at least, could not segregate Negroes. But private contracts involving restrictive covenants were upheld by United States Supreme Court decision in 1926 (Corrigan v. Buckly, 271, U.S. 323). Not until 1948 did the United States Supreme Court declare that these covenants could not be upheld by law.

Except then as theoretical equality before the law is qualified in the ways just indicated, the pattern of discrimination against Negroes outside the South is maintained by the nonlegal means which a dominant group has at its disposal. Employers refuse to hire Negroes in many kinds of jobs (in the absence of specific laws prohibiting this, of which more later); white workers often indicate they will not accept Negroes as co-workers. Some theaters refuse to sell any but balcony seats to Negroes; many restaurants make it clear that they do not welcome colored patronage by being curt, delaying service, overcharging, and making meals unpalatable. Segregation in the North is upheld by common practice—practices by whites to keep Negroes within the bounds of minority status and the reciprocal practices of Negroes to accept this status. While Negroes bitterly resent this, to have some peace of mind, they put up with discrimination most of the time. The fact, however, that these practices are of doubtful legality means that Negroes can and do challenge civic discrimination on occasion, and by this means keep the pattern of relationship unfrozen. Thus, sporadic gains here and there are made.

As in the South, the Northern pattern is supported by the prevalence of the "racial ideology" which looks upon Negroes in the mass as inferior. There is, however, a wider variation in racial attitudes and beliefs in the North. What in comparison appears clearest is that Northern attitudes are not crystallized into any uniform public opinion. As Drake and Cayton write: "In the South, every white man feels impelled to protect *every* white family, clique, and church from 'Negro contamination.' In Midwest Metropolis, each person is concerned only with his own." [24] Toleration of the deviations from the usual relations is due in part to the fact that the average person is not aware of how

[23] *Ibid.*, p. 249.
[24] *Ibid.*, p. 119.

much intermingling goes on. So long as it does not affect him personally, Negro-white relations do not greatly excite the typical Northerner.

VARIATIONS IN NORTHERN PATTERN

Negroes in New Haven. Of all regions of the nation, New England
had a traditional reputation for having accorded the relatively few
Negroes who dwelt in its communities a substantial measure of public
and civic equality. When, however, the Great Migration brought large
numbers of Southern Negroes into many New England cities, the position of Negroes in this area deteriorated, so that their situation in
general has come to resemble the pattern of the North in general,
which we have just depicted through the Chicago example. We draw
upon an intensive study of Negro-white relations in New Haven, Connecticut, to attest further the generality of the Northern pattern.[25]

Concerning the ecological position of New Haven Negroes Warner
writes, "The physical Negro town within the city of New Haven is not
distinct and clear-cut, as is the Negro social structure . . . yet there is
a town of color with a main street, churches, halls, hotels, and movie
theater." [26] The operation of the color bar in employment is attested
at many points. In the employment of Negro men as operatives, the line
is only less sharp and less general than in the employment of Negro
women. However, there are in New Haven industries certain jobs
designated for Negroes, ". . . usually unpleasant by reason of heat,
dust, dirt, or moisture. . . . In some few factories, they work side by
side with white men on the same jobs." [27] The older craft unions in
New Haven had never been favorable to Negro membership, and the
greater development of unions in general worked to the disadvantage
of Negroes up to World War II. Again in some unions which admitted
Negroes to membership, discriminative practices within the unions
tended to make their membership of little value.[28] White collar employment was categorically barred to Negroes with the one exception
of government service.

The general similarity of the reaction of New Haven Negroes and
those of Chicago to their minority position is seen in the greater
amount of crime, violence, and immorality in the Negro areas in general. In the older resident, middle class, Negro families, however, the
highest codes of behavior are maintained. Among these likewise
"white standards of beauty are secretly, but generally, held; yet race

[25] Robert A. Warner, *New Haven Negroes* (New Haven: Yale University Press,
1940).
[26] *Ibid.*, p. 195.
[27] *Ibid.*, p. 239.
[28] *Ibid.*, pp. 241-242.

pride (which means respect for Negro characteristics) has to be maintained." [29]

According to Warner "most colored New Haveners also hope, like other Americans, to gain their ends by means of government influence and assistance." [30] Although Negroes share equal political privileges with whites, they have not been given jobs proportional to their political activity. Nevertheless, they show little inclination to espouse radical politicoeconomic movements.

Recency of migration. The status of Negroes in Northern cities varies with reference to the extent which a given city shared in the Great Migration. Generally the status of Negroes in the North as a whole declined in the years attending this migration. Furthermore, the occurrence of the depression of the 1930's, during which so large a proportion of Negroes were on relief, retarded improvement. Even in New England, which did not greatly share in the Great Migration, the traditional tolerance toward Negroes declined. Frazier writes, "The increase in the Negro population [of Boston] during and following World War I accentuated race consciousness among Negroes as well as whites." [31] Illustrative of the point Frazier further cites a study of Milton, Pennsylvania.

The [Negro] population of this town had continued inconsequential until Negro laborers were brought in during World War I. Before that time the few Negroes had found employment in personal and domestic service among the well-to-do white families. Negroes had been accepted to the extent that white and colored children went to school together and they mingled socially to some extent. The importation of Negro laborers from the South created race consciousness among both Negroes and whites. Since the Negro laborers have left, race relations have tended to assume their former character.[32]

Interesting confirmation of the principle that animosity to a minority rises with the sudden influx of a new group into a particular area comes from a study of the situation in the Northwestern communities to which Negroes migrated during World War II.[33] Prior to 1940 Negroes comprised less than 0.5 per cent of the population covered in this study, whereas by 1945 the Negro population had increased 300 per cent. The very small and inconspicuous group of Negroes living in the area prior to this recent migration "had learned gradually to adjust themselves to white patterns, and whites had in

[29] *Ibid.,* 187.
[30] *Ibid.,* pp. 288-289.
[31] E. Franklin Frazier, *The Negro in the United States* (New York: The Macmillan Company, 1949), p. 254.
[32] *Ibid.,* p. 253. By permission of The Macmillan Company.
[33] T. H. Kennedy, "Racial Tensions Among Negroes in the Intermountain Northwest," *Phylon,* Vol. 7, 1946, pp. 358-364.

turn more or less come to accept this small Negro minority as a natural part of the population." However, "with the appearance of new faces, unfamiliar with the community's mores, tensions began to be apparent." Contributing to the tension was the fact that the white "newcomers" to these localities came from areas with more discriminatory patterns, and translated their usual attitudes into behavior in the new situation. Furthermore, the change in white attitudes was resented by the oldtime Negro families whose status deteriorated in the face of the general rise of antagonism toward Negroes, producing friction within the local Negro group. Insofar as social policy can be brought to bear upon future adjustment of Negro-white relations, these Northern and Western experiences point toward discouraging a large influx of Negroes over a short period of time into any one community.

The smaller city versus the metropolis. Since the major portion of the Northern migration went to the large cities prior to 1940 little attention has been given to Negroes in the smaller cities. In Muncie, Indiana, the Lynds found in 1929 that "the sense of racial separateness appears in widely diverse groups." Negroes were not permitted in the Y.M.C.A., for example. "News of the Negroes is given separately in the papers under the title 'In Colored Circles.'" [34] In 1935 in their postdepression study of the same city, the authors found Negroes had better leadership and organization but that they "occupy a more exposed position . . . than before the depression." [35] In the Yankee City study, the position of Negroes is summarized thus: "Negroes have been present in Yankee City from the days of the New England slave trade . . . [By 1933] the Negro group had dwindled to eighty individuals, only 0.48 per cent of the population. The caste barrier, or color line, rigid and unrelenting, has cut off this small group from the general life of the community." [36] The writer's own knowledge of New Brunswick, N. J., with about 6 per cent Negro population, confirms the conclusions of these studies, which indicate that Negroes are no better integrated in these smaller cities than in the great metropolis. In addition they suffer the further handicap that their numbers are not adequate to furnish for themselves as complete a separate community life.

The influence of the Southern pattern upon the North. From what we have considered in this chapter so far, it is clear enough that white Americans living in the North are not prepared to accept Negroes

---

[34] Robert S. and Helen M. Lynd, *Middletown* (New York: Harcourt, Brace & Company, Inc., 1929), p. 479, footnote 1.
[35] Robert S. and Helen M. Lynd, *Middletown in Transition* (New York: Harcourt, Brace & Company, Inc., 1937), p. 465.
[36] William Lloyd Warner and P. S. Lunt, *The Social Life of a Modern Community* (New Haven: Yale University Press, 1941), p. 217.

into full equality. In concluding the discussion of variables in the Northern scene, it is pertinent to note two influences of the Southern pattern upon the North and West. First, we call attention to the migration of Southern workers to the North which, where it is recent and in substantial numbers, tends to disturb the pattern of toleration of Negroes in many Northern communities. This was notable as a factor in the tense Detroit situation of World War II. Again, in those Northern states bordering upon a state with a Southern pattern, variation in race relations from south to north has been noticeable. In the state of New Jersey, prior to recent state government policies inaugurated in the 1940's, school segregation was more pronounced in the southern than in the northern portion of the state. The part of Illinois, which dips down into the South shows more Southern caste influence than the northern section of the same state.

THE IMPACT OF THE NORTHERN PATTERN UPON NORTHERN COMMUNITIES

The kind of pattern of Negro-white relations which we have described in this chapter thus far affects the life of those Northern communities with any substantial Negro population in many ways. We shall consider in turn the four following effects: (1) Negro minority status creates, and more or less perpetuates, a "black ghetto," which as a physically deteriorated area yields the high rates of crime, delinquency, ill health, and other social pathologies characteristic of slums everywhere. (2) The discriminations imposed upon Negroes directly engender frustrations in the personality structure of Negroes, further provocative of antisocial behavior. (3) The dominant-minority character of race relations creates a continuous intergroup tension in community life which sporadically breaks out into violent intergroup conflict. (4) The more dynamic, less rigid character of race relations in the North, on the one hand, leads to confusion, handicapping adjustment, but on the other hand affords greater opportunity than in the South for Negroes themselves to advance the race.

The black ghetto: a blighted area. The assignment of Negroes to minority status in Northern cities has resulted in the establishment in each city of another separate subcommunal structure within the larger community. While in many cities, there are a few scattered Negroes living among whites, most Northern Negroes live together either in one large area or in several intermittent, but nevertheless compact, Negro areas. Irrespective of the degree of compactness of Negro residential segregation, there is the distinctive sociological community composed of separate churches, clubs, recreational organizations, and civic groups. Off the job, Negroes associate almost exclusively with Negroes whether in informal or formal relations. The development of separate Negro communities fitted easily into the ecological pattern of Northern city life where various ethnic colonies were no new phenomena. But as time has gone on, while the ethnic colonies tend to disappear through assimilation of subsequent generations, the Negro separate colony tends to persist and grow. Growth of the Negro population in the city almost always poses a problem of serious dimension. Resistance to permitting Negroes into new areas results first in fantastic overcrowding. In Detroit "Rates for overcrowding are . . . twice as high as for the white population." [37] When finally the walls of the black ghetto must burst, infiltration of Negroes into other dilapidated areas begins. If some Negroes do get a foothold, whites begin to move out, and more Negroes move in until the new block, or section, comes to be generally Negro. This process is attended by a considerable degree of reciprocal animosity between both racial groups, provocative of race rioting. Through it all Negroes have had substandard housing for which they have paid abnormally high rents.

It has been demonstrated that all slum areas, regardless of who lives in them, although highly profitable to particular special interests, are an economic drain on the community at large, and unvaryingly yield a disproportionate share of the various social pathologies—delinquency, crime, high disease rates. That the presence of a Negro ghetto in a Northern community is no exception has been amply demonstrated by many studies of such areas.

Pertinent illustrations are these:

. . . in Chicago the percentage of Negro boys among juvenile delinquents increased from 4.7 in 1900 to 21.7 in 1930. . . . During this same period, the proportion of Negro juvenile delinquents in Indianapolis, Gary, and Dayton was three to four times as large as their relative numbers in the population.[38]
. . . it is practically certain that Negroes have more mental disease in the North than do whites.[39]
Tuberculosis rates in five Northern cities for 1939–41 run from three to five times as high for all Negroes as for all whites.[40]

Thus, the persistence of Negro ghettos constitutes a major social problem in the Northern communities where they exist.

The effect of discrimination on Negro personality. Kardiner and Ovesey studied 25 urban Negroes by psychoanalytic methods and concluded that the neurotic personality manifestations found in these cases were

[37] Weaver, *op. cit.*, p. 115.
[38] Frazier, *op. cit.*, p. 649. By permission of The Macmillan Company.
[39] Myrdal, *op. cit.*, p. 980.
[40] Dorothy J. Liveright, *Tuberculosis Mortality Among Residents of 92 Cities of 100,000 or More Population: United States, 1939–41*, U. S. Public Health Reports, July 21, 1944, pp. 942-55.

in considerable measure the result of discrimination.[41] A penetrating exploration of this aspect of social psychology was undertaken by Lewin, largely focused on the position of Jews as a minority. He cites, however, the following example of a young Negro woman:

> A young Negress in one of the Northern industrial centers who is engaged in housework is encouraged by her white teacher to take the civil service examination. She passes at the top of the list and is assigned to a public swimming pool. Negro patronage of this swimming pool has been prohibited; nor does the director wish to employ Negroes. His objections are overruled by the civil service authorities. He employs the Negro girl in a lower capacity than she merits—in cleaning work. The girl works without complaint. After a few weeks she thinks of swimming in the pool herself. Immediately a group of white boys approach her, treat her none too gently, make her stop swimming. The shock is so great that she not only quits her job but refuses to try for any other job to which she is eligible in the civil service. The white teacher from whom I got these facts told me that she came upon the Negress some time later as an elevator girl in a department store. The teacher tried to encourage her to apply once more for a civil service position, but the girl seemed to have lost all faith and all interest in anything better than a subservient place.
>
> Such a degree of breakdown made me suspect that as a child this Negress had had particularly friendly relations with white children on an equal footing. An inquiry showed that she had indeed grown up in a group of children without discrimination between whites and Negroes.[42]

While in the above case, discrimination led to withdrawal and passive reaction, in the following case of Arthur Brown, the ultimate result was aggression.

Arthur Brown applies for a job.[43] "Hey, you lazy 4-F," growled the cop, "why don't you get yourself a job and stop hanging out on street corners?" His nightstick swung menacingly.

Arthur Brown choked back the anger and resentment that rose in his throat. His fist itched to take the measure of that cop, but he knew too well that in Harlem that just didn't go. Hit a cop and the whole force gangs up on you.

"Mind your business," he said sharply. "I can take care of myself."

Actually Arthur had tried during the day to get employment as an International Business Machines operator or supervisor in which he was well qualified. While there were such positions open in the community at the time, Arthur was turned down for reasons indicated. In

[41] Abraham Kardiner and Lionel Ovesey, *The Mark of Oppression, A Psychosocial Study of the American Negro* (New York: W. W. Norton and Company, 1951).
[42] Kurt Lewin, *Resolving Social Conflicts* (New York: Harper and Brothers, 1948), pp. 172-173. By permission.
[43] Edward H. Lawson, "Arthur Brown Applies for a Job," *The Journal of Social Issues*, Vol. 1, No. 1 (Feb. 1945), pp. 11-14. By permission.

irst personal interview, he faced a woman employment officer in a
ness Survey Systems Office. In turning down Arthur for the job, the
white woman said in part as follows:

"But you realize we've never had a colored supervisor. Now so far as I'm
concerned, personally, I'd take you on in a minute. I haven't any prejudice
at all. I have a great many Negro friends. But these girls we have here—
they're young, impressionable—and some of them are very prejudiced. I just
couldn't put you over any of them. They'd walk out on me—right smack out
of the place."

Arthur tried his second reference, this time in the office of a ship-
yard building naval vessels. His conversation with the assistant general manager ran as follows:

"So they sent you down to get that I.B.M. job, huh?" he asked. "Well, son,
I can't give you that."
"Nope. But I'm afraid you wouldn't fit into our office. We have five men on
those machines. As it happens, they're all white."
"I'll get along with them."
"Well—" The general manager chewed speculatively on a big cigar. "Maybe
you would and maybe you wouldn't. My experience says you wouldn't."
"How about letting me try?"
"Nope, couldn't do it. And I'll tell you why. About five or six years ago I
took a colored fellow outa' the yard and put him on an office machine. He was
no good—just couldn't do the work. The other fellers said he balled up the
whole department, and I had to take him out. I learned a lesson from that—
colored boys are all right for the heavy yard jobs, but they don't work out
in an office."
"But he wasn't competent," Arthur Brown argued. "I've had experience.
Besides, you can't judge a whole race just by one guy—"
"Son—" The general manager's tone was patronizing. "When you've been
in business as long as I have you learn what works and what don't work. We're
too busy now with war orders to try out experiments. I'll give you a job, this
minute, as a shipfitter's helper. It's a good trade for you to learn. But I'm
not going to buck human nature and put you on an office job, and that's that."

Later the same evening, while walking up Lenox Avenue, Arthur
spied a couple approaching in his direction.

Suddenly he ducked into the sheltering darkness of an unlighted storefront.
A tall, good-looking brownskin girl brushed by without a second look at him.
A merchant seaman held her arm, and they laughed together as at some great
joke. Lucy!
Lucy was Arthur Brown's girl—or was she, any more? Since he'd lost his
last job, since he'd no longer been able to take her out, buy her drinks, show
her a good time—

Lucy was a fine girl. But after all, what more could he expect?

Arthur Brown walked along the avenue, shoulders hunched against the gathering twilight chill.

He paused before a theater, fingering the fifteen cents remaining in his pocket. He'd need the fifteen cents for breakfast in the morning.

He reached an intersection and stood there on the corner, watching traffic. He didn't see the cop until he tapped him on the shoulder.

"Hey," growled the cop, "didn't I tell you to stop hanging out around here? Why don't you get yourself a job—do some work to help the war effort?"

It was then he hit the cop. Why he did it he could never quite explain. He knew in Harlem that just didn't go. But somehow he didn't care.

The above two cases suggest that minority status imposed upon Northern Negroes has similar effects upon the personality structure and behavior as does the caste system in the South. The passive reaction of the young woman in Lewin's case in contrast to the aggressive reaction of Arthur Brown may reflect the variables in the psychological constitution of the two as individuals; but the intensity of the reactions noted can be considered as arising from discrimination.

Constant tension generates sporadic violence. The presence of Negroes in minority status is a constant source of tension and a sporadic source of race rioting in Northern communities. While there had been race riots in the North prior to the Great Migration, such as one in Springfield, Illinois, in 1908, most of the serious riots occurred during and following the two great wars of this century. During World War I, aside from a notorious riot in Houston, Texas, involving service men of both races, the most important riot occurred in East St. Louis, Illinois, during which at least 39 Negroes and 8 whites were killed. In the first year following this war, 1919, riots occurred in at least 26 American cities. After this flurry of disturbances, race riots were relatively few until the beginning of World War II.

In Detroit in 1942 occurred one of the worst race riots in recent history. Myrdal writes of it:

. . . in trying to move into a government defense housing project built for them in Detroit, Negroes were set upon by white civilians and police. The project was built at the border between Negro and white neighborhoods but had been planned for Negroes. Encouraged by the vacillation of the federal government and the friendliness of the Detroit police (many of whom are Southern born) and stimulated by the backing of a United States congressman and such organizations as the Ku Klux Klan, white residents of the neighborhood and other parts of the city staged protest demonstrations against the Negro housing project, which led to the riot.[44]

[44] Myrdal, *op. cit.*, p. 568. By permission of the publishers, Harper and Brothers.

In the same city there occurred one year later a still more serious race riot. The specific spark which started mass rioting between Negroes and whites at Belle Isle Bridge, near a recreation park in Detroit on Sunday evening, June 20, 1943, has never been fully established.[45] But within a short time, the conflict spread over wide areas of the city, especially into the Negro ghetto. The rioting continued over two days before it spent itself, partly curbed by the imposition by the city authorities of temporary curfew regulations and a special contingent of the Army. The story of the police efforts during the period provides much evidence of discriminatory treatment of Negro participants, alleged or actual, as contrasted with the handling of white participants, and of the tendency of the authorities to place the blame solely upon Negroes.[46]

The conditions which favor riots are the infiltration of unusual numbers of Negroes into the community; Negro "invasion" of new residential areas; additions to the community of large numbers of Southern white workers; and circumstances which promote the entrance of Negroes into new occupational fields in competition with whites. In general, any unusual or rapid change in the prevalent Negro-white situation in a community is provocative of rioting. Precipitating factors are altercations developing between individuals or small groups of the two races, which then spread to other people in both races. In the process rumors spread, distorting and enlarging the facts about the original incident. Underlying all the particular conditions and precipitating incidents is the general pattern of dominant-minority relations which calls for the subordination of Negroes to whites and resents the assumption of equal privileges by Negroes.

The present situation in the black ghettos of the North is provocative of a somewhat different pattern of race riot, illustrated by the Harlem Riot of 1935. This was an outbreak of sporadic violence in the Negro area itself, an outgrowth of the inevitable high degree of social disorganization to be found in physically blighted, "burstingly" overcrowded, and socially depressed areas such as the black ghettos of the North comprise. Ottley describes this riot in these words:

The morning of March 20, 1935, the nation awoke to learn to its dismay that the home of happy feet, Harlem, had exploded into violence. Whipped to a frenzy by radical street speakers, upwards of ten thousand had tumbled from taverns and tenements, barber shops and basement dives, and surged through the streets grappling in hand-to-hand struggles with the police. They

---

[45] See Alfred M. Lee, and Norman D. Humphrey, *Race Riot* (New York: The Dryden Press, Inc., 1943), for a full account of the Belle Island race riot, and analysis of its implications for the general problem.
[46] *Ibid.*, p. 69.

smashed store windows, hurled bricks and assaulted white merchants. Bands plundered and looted stores with amazing discrimination—choosing only those owned by whites. When the police finally restored order in the early morning, three Negroes had been killed, thirty-odd hospitalized for bullet wounds, and two hundred white and Negro persons treated for injuries. Two hundred shops were smashed and gutted, and two million dollars in property was destroyed. One hundred Negroes were in the lockup for inciting to violence, unlawful assembly, and looting.

The police hunted the answer in poolroms, basements, and gambling joints, places where the criminal elements gathered. But actually the outburst was a manifestation of deep social unrest and unhappiness.[47]

Ambiguity of the Northern pattern and Negro adjustment. It is a well demonstrated sociological principle that the adjustment of adult migrants to a new social environment is characterized by a certain amount of disorganization. A large proportion of the Negroes living in the North, certainly prior to 1940, have been brought up in the South; and of the remainder many are children born in the North to Southern bred parents. In a number of instances, the Negro migration involved movement from a rural or small town Southern setting to a Northern urban milieu. These shifts in environment would of themselves account for some of the problems arising from the adjustment of Negroes to Northern life. Adjustment, however, is further complicated by the fact that this migration likewise involves a shift from a clearly defined and firmly established pattern of caste relations to a less rigid and more ambiguous dominant minority pattern.

The particular kind of conditioning which Negroes have had, however, makes the Northern scene peculiarly upsetting. The Southern Negro generally had adjusted himself, with whatever inner psychic costs, to a lifetime of minority status. In the North, this pattern of adjustment is considerably upset. He is in many ways freer to do things he could not do in the South but is frequently at a loss to know just how much freer. He can go to this restaurant, but that one refuses him service. He can play on the school team, but he cannot go to the dances. The lack of definiteness in the expected behavior in relation to white people in the Northern city increases the difficulty of his adjustment.

Again while treating him as a minority person, Northern practice holds the Negro more accountable to behave according to the general norms of the community. Petty thievery is expected of Negroes by the white Southerner, and is dealt with more as one ordinarily deals with it in the case of children. The Northerner puts him in jail for it. "Illegitimacy" in the South (often occurring within stable monogamic

[47] Roi Ottley, *Black Odyssey* (New York: Charles Scribner's Sons, 1948), p. 258. By permission.

unions) is laughed off by Southern whites as "natural for darkies," but in the North it frequently brings investigation by a white welfare worker.

Finally, while the South holds out no prospect to the Negro of ever rising above the confines of caste (allowing for some upward class mobility within caste), the Northern situation, as ill defined and perplexing as it is, is sufficiently fluid to portend possible complete integration. But since Northern white attitudes are by no means ready for the full step, the Negroes' hopes are frequently raised too high only to be dashed. The relatively better education offered the Negro in the North encourages him to prepare himself for occupations, employment in which he will subsequently be denied. His desire for better housing, and often the means to pay for it, are raised only to be frustrated by restrictive covenants. He is on the one hand encouraged to develop higher cultural interests and on the other often refused a seat in a theater.

Thus the lack of clear definitions of expected Negro behavior, and the uncertainties and the fluidity characterizing their relations with whites place considerable strain upon Negro personality.

Impact of Northern "freedom" upon Negroes. In spite of the disorganizing affect of the none too well defined situation of the Negro and of the very considerable discrimination against him, compared with the South, the North affords far more real freedom and opportunity. Two advantages in the North are (1) the opportunity for individual Negroes to reach higher levels of success, and (2) greater opportunity to work effectively to advance the race.

Rise of individual Negroes. Although Negro society in the South has some class differentiation, in the North the class structure is more elaborated reaching, as with the white class structure, its greatest complexity in the metropolis. The social class structure of "Black Metropolis" is described as follows:

The process of differentiation among Negroes in Bronzeville has given rise to a loose system of social classes which allows for mobility upward and downward. This class structure operates as a system of social controls by which the higher-status groups "protect" their way of life, but admit "strainers" and "strivers" who can make the grade. Individuals and organizations on the higher-status levels become models for imitation and also serve as an incentive toward social mobility. . . . At the top are the uppers, oriented predominantly around "Society" and Race Leadership, and with a small group of Gentlemen Racketeers who have gained some status as Race Leaders but who are not accepted socially. Below them is the middle class with four "centers of orientation"—church, social club, "racial advancement" (including *individual* advancement), and "policy." At the bottom is the lower class with a large "disorganized segment," but also with a "church-centered" group and a small group of "secular respectables" interested in "getting ahead." Underlying the whole structure is the "underworld" of the Black Ghetto.[48]

Prior to 1940, a few individual Negroes in the North had gained fame and fortune in areas competitive with white people. Joe Louis and, even earlier, Jack Johnson in prizefighting; Roland Hayes and Paul Robeson in concert singing; Paul Lawrence Dunbar, Countee Cullen, James Weldon Johnson in the field of literature are a few examples. It is to be noted also that the theme upon which these artists played was often related to Negro life and problems.

For the larger part of the Negroes who achieved higher social and economic status, it was the very separation of the Negro community from the rest that provided much of their opportunity.[49] Negroes have been conspicuously underrepresented in business, even compared with some other racial minorities, such as Chinese and Japanese. Rose writes, "In 1939, there were not quite 30,000 Negro retail stores, giving employment to a total of 43,000 persons. The total sales in 1939 were less than $\frac{2}{10}$ of 1 per cent of the national total.[50] Nevertheless the pattern of segregation itself creates a monopoly for Negroes in certain kinds of businesses—those involving intimate contact with the person of the Negro, such as hairdressers, restaurant and hotel service, and undertaking.

In professional service, however, where the relationship to the client is less personal and also not servile, aspiring Negroes, when they managed to hurdle the difficulty of acquiring professional training, are in competition with white professionals for the trade of the Negro population while being generally barred from competition for the white trade. In 1940 there were about 3500 Negro physicians in the whole country, which means about 45 times as many white doctors as Negro. Negro physicians are handicapped by the lack of hospitals for their patients, and are frequently not permitted to treat their patients in mixed hospitals. In 1940 there were 1063 Negro lawyers in the United States. In spite of the fact that this is less than 1 per cent of all lawyers in the country, the North provides an opportunity here which is substantially closed in the South. Thus two-thirds of this small number of Negro lawyers are to be found outside the South, where less than one-fourth of the Negro population lives.

[48] Drake and Cayton, op. cit., pp. 710-712. By permission.
[49] This is not to imply that many of these same people would not have achieved comparable status in competition with whites in a social structure in which racial distinctions did not prevail.
[50] Arnold Rose, The Negro in America (New York: Harper and Brothers, 1948), p. 108.

The occupation of the ministry in Negro churches is, of course, a monopolistic avenue for aspiring Negroes all over the country. Clergymen are the second largest group among Negro professionals. School teaching exceeds the ministry largely because in the South only Negro teachers are allowed to teach Negro children. While the influence of ministers as leaders of the church-going Negro people is strong, in the North their leadership is shared and sometimes overshadowed by other educated Negroes.

Interestingly, one of the largest of all Negro businesses is in the insurance field. Frazier writes, "For the year 1945, the 44 member companies of the National Negro Insurance Association reported nearly 4,000,000 policies in force, of which 3,860,890 were health and accident and nearly 80,000 unspecified." [51] The opportunity here arose because of the reluctance of general insurance companies to underwrite Negro policies on the same actuarial basis as employed for whites due to the known wide differentials in risks in health and mortality prevailing between the two races. That the reluctance to underwrite Negroes is by no means absolute, however, is indicated by Frazier's statement that "one large white insurance company has insurance in force on Negro lives amounting to more than twice the insurance in force in all the Negro insurance companies.[52]

The very fact of the semisegregation of Negroes in the North together with the necessity of integrating them somehow into the civic life of the community has provided opportunity for some Negroes to become the liaison agents, or specialists, representing Negroes in community-wide civic activity. Much more in the North than in the South, although the tendency is increasing there, such liaison activity is assigned to Negroes. The very real participation of Negroes in Northern politics, as described below in Chicago, affords opportunity for leadership in party politics, with occasional appointment to public positions either as reward or through civil service.

It is of course inevitable that among a people so situated there should arise an "underworld," often abetted and patronized by whites affording opportunity for some Negroes to achieve financial, if not social class, reward.

Thus the Northern scene affords qualified opportunity for getting ahead as Negroes and accounts for the growing upper and middle classes to be found in the Northern Negro communities. The values and modes of life to be found among the middle class Negroes are similar to those in the white middle class. Drake and Cayton put it thus:

---

[51] Frazier, *op. cit.*, p. 401.
[52] *Ibid.*, p. 401.

The whole atmosphere of middle-class life is one of tension, particularly at upper-middle-class level, or among people on the way up, but not yet secure in their position. The drive to get ahead, to "lay a little something by," to prepare for the education of children, and at the same time keep up "front" by wearing the right kind of clothes, having a "nice home," and belonging to the proper organizations—the pursuit of these goals brings into being definite social types which Bronzeville calls "strivers," and "strainers." With limited incomes, the problem of striking a balance between the conspicuous consumption necessary to maintain status, and long-range goals like buying property and educating children, becomes a difficult one. During the depression years particularly, Bronzeville's middle-class families faced a continuous crisis.[53]

Opportunity to advance the race: Negro leadership and organization. We have seen that throughout the long sojourn of Negroes in the New World there have always been some members of the group who have actively protested against their minority status. Under slavery, Negroes organized rebellions which in the United States were never successful; under caste, Negro leadership took the accommodative road of trying to improve the welfare of the group and to obtain better treatment without challenging the basic principle of segregation. In the North through this half century, Negro leadership and organization to advance the race have embraced a wider range of activities and programs.[54]

Among the many Negro movements brief attention may be pertinently directed to those which partake of an escapist character directed by charismatic leadership. Of these in time sequence, the "Back to Africa" movement led by Marcus Garvey comes first. Garvey, a West Indian full blooded Negro, rejected the idea that Negroes in the United States could ever become fully assimilated into the general white society, and developed an organization, The Universal Negro Improvement Association, whose broad aim was the establishment of an African Republic to be led by Negroes. Garvey was ultimately imprisoned in 1925 on the charge of using the mails to defraud in connection with his financial manipulations and the movement collapsed. During the brief period of its existence, the Garvey movement elicited great outpouring of response from the Negro people. Myrdal contends that this movement was the first organized Negro activity of the protest variety which really gripped the imagination and enthusiasm of the Negro masses in this country.[55]

[53] Drake and Cayton, *op. cit.*, pp. 667-668. By permission.
[54] See Ira DeA. Reid, "Negro Movements and Messiahs," *Phylon*, Vol. 10, No. 4, 1949, pp. 362-368, for a brief treatment of the leading Negro movements of this century.
[55] Cf. Myrdal, *op. cit.*, pp. 746-749.

Likewise of an escapist variety, although in many other ways completely opposite to Garvey's movement, is the much publicized movement headed by George Baker, now generally known as Father Divine. Preaching a doctrine of love among all peoples, Father Divine established a cult. Those who joined one of his "heavens" turned over their possessions and lived under his protection and security. This in many ways remarkable leader has been shrewd in managing the affairs of the movement and has, on the whole, taken care of the followers who have placed their trust in him. While the large majority of his followers are Negroes, some white people have entered his "heaven." Although rumors have arisen in connection with this cult, as is usually the case with movements of this sort, as far as the outside community is concerned, the followers are exemplary in their conduct.

The role of "glamour" personalities as leaders among Negroes calls for mention not so much for their actual activities in that capacity as for the reason why they are thought of as leaders. By glamour personalities is meant that small—but increasing—number of Negroes who have achieved national popular fame and considerable fortune through their phenomenal success in their occupations, such as Duke Ellington, Jackie Robinson, Marion Anderson. White people in comparable positions do not necessarily play a leadership role in community affairs. In the case of Negroes in this position, however, a sort of "race" leadership is thrust upon them by the very unusualness of their success as members of a minority group, whether they have either the capacity or inclination to assume the role.

We turn now to consider those movements and organizations which have had a more enduring and a more far-reaching effect upon improving the position of Negroes in American society.

The development of protest activity. The first effort, following Southern reconstruction, to organize a movement among Negroes to protest actively against their minority status was launched in 1905 when 29 Negro intellectuals met at Niagara Falls. From this conference emerged the plan for the formation of a national organization to challenge all forms of segregation and discrimination. Such a bold program was opposed by Booker T. Washington and thus in part the Niagara movement was a challenge to his accommodative leadership. Although the organization itself ceased to be effective after 1910, it had prepared the way for the formation of the National Association for the Advancement of Colored People (N.A.A.C.P.) presently to be considered, through which in part the spirit of the Niagara movement lived on.

Following the Great Migration and World War I, some younger Negro leaders in the 1920's of whom A. Philip Randolph, late president of the Brotherhood of Sleeping Car Porters was to become the most influential, saw the Negro's greatest hope in alignment with the postwar radical movements of Socialist vintage. It is clear from the relative failure of urban radical movements as far as election results were concerned that the majority of Negroes aligned themselves politically with the major parties. Generally, it appears that this element merged with the New Deal element of the Democratic Party in the F. D. Roosevelt era, except for an occasional convert to Communism. As we shall see in our account of the 1940–1950 decade, the protest line of activity continued to gain ascendancy over the accommodative approach.

The Negro intelligentsia. The 1920's saw the emergence of a group of Negro intellectuals whose purpose was to enhance the self-respect of Negroes by glorifying the great accomplishments of Negroes past and present. Prominent among the leaders of this movement were W. E. B. DuBois, editor of *The Crisis*; Charles S. Johnson, editor of *Opportunity*; Alain Locke, editor of the volume, *The New Negro*; and Carter G. Woodson, who had in 1915 organized The Association for the Study of Negro Life and History, and began the publication of *The Journal of Negro History*. This movement had much moral support and financial aid from liberal minded white people.

The high position occupied by Negro college and university professors in the leadership of American Negroes is worthy of note. To take the field of sociology alone, one may cite Dr. Charles S. Johnson, president of Fisk University; Dr. E. Franklin Frazier, professor of sociology at Howard University, and formerly president of the American Sociological Society; Dr. Ira DeA. Reid, chairman of the sociology department of Haverford College, among a constantly increasing number. The influence of Negro academic men upon Negro society in the United States is far greater than the influence of comparably placed white academicians upon white American society.

The leading Negro organizations. The two organizations which since their formation have continued to be the most influential in working for the improvement of Negro welfare and status have been the National Association for the Advancement of Colored People and the Urban League. Strictly speaking these two organizations are not exclusively Negro but interracial with substantial white membership. Again, while they operate in the South, their origin in the North and the greater support accorded them in this region make it appropriate to discuss them in this chapter.

The N.A.A.C.P. was formed in 1909 following a severe race riot in Springfield, Illinois, the previous year. It was started on white people's initiative but its active workers are usually Negroes. The long-run objective of the association has always been to win full equality for the Negro as an American citizen. Its specific activities have been in the field of civil liberties, constantly fighting legal cases of discrimination, such as antilynching legislation, the abolition of poll taxes, etc. The strategy of its approach has been practical and opportunistic. The association has not conducted an omnibus legal campaign against the Southern caste pattern but has selected strategically important cases in specific fields of discrimination. It has saved many Negroes from unequal court treatment; prevented the extradition of Negroes from North to South for trial; helped to establish the precedents by which the exclusion of Negroes from jury service constitutes a denial of equal protection of laws as guaranteed by the Fourteenth Amendment —to select only a few of its many legal successes.

The Urban League was founded in 1910, also as an interracial movement on white initiative. It arose primarily to help the recent Negro migrants adjust to Northern city life. It has become a general social welfare agency performing all sorts of welfare services varying in time and local circumstance—health work, recreational work, delinquency prevention, and acting as an informal employment agency for Negroes. Local branches are established in about 50 cities, of which 12 are in the South.

Myrdal considered that one great weakness of both these organizations was their lack of support from the Negro masses.[56] This has been due in part to the generally low educational and economic status of the Negro masses, and the widespread prevalence among Negroes of a resigned and hopeless attitude as far as cracking the color line is concerned. The lack of mass support is also due to the fact that, as in all class structures, the interests of the Negro middle class and the Negro lower class are not identical in all respects. In the 1940–1950 decade, however, these two organizations made substantial gains in mass support.

Race relations: a regional issue. Before turning to consider the 1940–1950 decade where great changes in Negro-white relations occurred, it is pertinent to emphasize that the very existence of regional attitudes and practices as disparate as those portrayed in the past two chapters have been a perennial source of regional conflict affecting in many ways the political and civic unity of the nation. The earlier manifestations of this conflict have been treated in Chapters 8 and 9. The slavery issue threatened national unity until the close of the War Between the States. From 1880 to the First World War, the North in general tended to leave the Negro problem, as far as it was thought of as

[56] *Ibid.*, pp. 835-836.

such, to the South. The Great Migration created a new Northern Negro problem. The discriminatory pattern of adjustment in the North appeared at first to suggest a moving of the region closer to the view of the South. However, throughout the entire period a segment of Northern opinion has continued to propagandize against discrimination toward Negroes. Finally, there began to emerge a new definition of the problem as one of national significance. More Northern people began to believe that the prevailing patterns of dominant-minority relations between the two races could not permanently endure in a political democracy. This emerging new definition of the race problem received great impetus from the New Deal. In the operation of large-scale relief and in other government planned projects, the tendency was toward providing Negroes a fairer share. Here and there Negroes were being placed in new situations alongside whites. The number of Northern organized groups, especially religious groups, who became interested in democratizing race relations, grew. Among the minorities themselves, a trend toward integration of their protest activities in behalf of all began, in which Jewish associations took a prominent lead.

Since the North is the predominant center of national opinion making and likewise exerts a more potent influence in forming national policy, this emerging new conception of the Negro problem as a problem for all Americans inevitably disturbed a South not prepared to accept this new definition. Prior to World War II, the South reacted to Northern pressure with aggressive defense of its traditional race relations. Thus the approach of World War II found a long standing regional issue becoming again more sharply poised.

TOPICS FOR DISCUSSION AND PROJECTS

1. If you have lived in or are well acquainted with any community, outside the South, which has any Negro population, compare the extent of their segregation in this community with that of Chicago as depicted in this chapter. If your comparison shows the community to reveal any marked difference from that of Chicago, suggest any circumstances which seem to you to explain why your community so deviates.
2. It is frequently said that Negroes prefer to associate with their own kind. Do you think this is the case or not?
3. Since the indications are that Negroes do have a considerably larger measure of opportunity in the North, how do you account for the fact that far more of them have not left the South?
4. Consider carefully all the reasons which occur to you to explain why it is that Negro youth, although accorded equal right in the North to complete their high school education do in fact drop out of school in larger proportions than white children.

5. Find out from the best available sources whether or not the delinquency rate is higher for Negroes than it is for non-Negroes in some delimited local area. Having established the comparative rates, study the situation and account for them.

SUGGESTED READING

Cantril, Hadley. *Psychology of Social Movements*. New York: John Wiley & Sons, Inc., 1941.

> *Chapter 5, "The Kingdom of Father Divine," interprets this movement as a search for satisfaction which the "real" society denies.*

Kardiner, Abraham, and Ovesey, Lionel. *The Mark of Oppression: A Psychological Study of the American Negro*. New York: W. W. Norton and Company, 1951.

> *Twenty-five urban Negroes were studied by psychoanalytic techniques and the results indicate how the neurotic symptoms present had been effected by the impact of discrimination.*

Lee, Alfred M., and Humphrey, Norman D. *Race Riot*. New York: The Dryden Press, 1943.

> *Provides excellent analysis of the Detroit Belle Island race riot and suggests a program for prevention which has general application.*

Locke, Alain. *The New Negro*. New York: Albert and Charles Boni, Inc., 1925.

> *One of the first books surveying the literary and artistic contributions of the Negroes to American culture.*

"Race Relations on the Pacific Coast," *Journal of Educational Sociology*, November 1945, Vol. 19.

> *Issue contains a number of special accounts of race relations in Pacific Coast cities in 1945.*

Reid, Ira DeA. *The Negro Immigrant*. New York: Columbia University Press, 1939.

> *Most definitive account of the subject, treating especially the West Indian migrant.*

Warner, W. Lloyd, Junker, Buford H., and Adams, Walter A. *Color and Human Nature*. Washington: American Youth Commission, 1941.

> *Studies the impact of the Chicago milieu upon the personality of Negro youth. A companion volume to those mentioned in bibliography of Chapter 9 conducted under the same auspices.*

Weaver, Robert C. *The Negro Ghetto*. New York: Harcourt, Brace & Company, Inc., 1948.

> *A long-time student of the effect of housing segregation upon Negroes provides a comprehensive treatment of the subject in this volume.*

CHAPTER 11

Trends and Prospects
in Negro-White Relations

In this chapter, attention is focused upon the current trends and immediate prospects in Negro-white relations, with special emphasis on the effects resulting from World War II. The urgency of the war situation breached the wall of caste at many points. In the postwar period thus far these breaches have been widened and many new ones developed; and the process shows no signs of halting. At the midcentury, Negro-white relations are more unstable than at any time since reconstruction days. Whether the present trend toward greater equality for Negroes will continue steadily forward to its logical conclusion, the complete assimilation of Negroes into American society, or whether these relations will crystallize on a new level of accommodation will be determined by the balance of many social forces, some of the more significant of which we shall consider at the conclusion of this chapter.

In the analysis and interpretation of these current changes, the distinction between change in welfare and change in status which we drew briefly in Chapter 2 should be kept in mind. Improvement in the welfare of the group does not necessarily signify improvement in status, in dominant-minority terms. An event occurring in the writer's community a few years ago will serve as a preliminary example. In order to improve the housing situation of Negroes, the city government cooperated with the Federal Government in financing a new housing project for Negroes only. As a result, 60 of the some 500 Negro families in the community were provided with greatly improved hous-

285

ing. In the many other new housing developments in the area, both publicly and privately financed, there has been no mixing of the white and Negro groups. If we were making a systematic measure of change in status as distinct from welfare in this particular city, on the housing index, we should score no change.

THE EFFECT OF WORLD WAR II ON NEGRO-WHITE RELATIONS

World War II marked a significant point in Negro-white relations primarily because a nation engaged in a great war must of necessity utilize its manpower to the utmost. It is also probable that, as in all war periods when the nationality sentiment rises to its highest intensity, the dominant people acted more democratically toward Negroes, as well as other minorities, except those of "enemy" background. Moreover, the appeal to democracy was utilized to persuade, cajole, or force white people—as in the instance of the Fair Employment Practices Committee—to alter their traditional attitudes enough to permit a more effective utilization of Negro manpower. For whatever reasons, the facts are clear enough that the welfare of Negroes improved greatly throughout the war years, and that some changes in status occurred.

In economic life. The greatest gain accruing to Negroes in the World War II period was to have constant employment, at considerably higher real wages, in a wider range of occupations. Weaver cites these gains:

In 1940 . . . only 4.4 per cent of all male Negro workers were in skilled industrial jobs; in 1944, the figure was 7.3 per cent. In 1940, about 13 per cent of the same group was in semiskilled and industrial work; by 1944, the figure was 22.4 per cent . . . really significant gains occurred in single-skilled and semiskilled occupations. In 1940, for example, Negro males were 5.9 per cent of all male operatives; four years later, they were 10.1 per cent. Negro women constituted 4.7 per cent of all female operatives in 1940; in 1944, they were 8.3 per cent of the total.[1]

Further Weaver shows that Negroes gained greatly in Federal jobs in Washington. Even more significant is the fact that in 1938, 90 per cent of Negro Federal employees were engaged in subclerical capacities; whereas in 1942 almost half of the colored employees were in clerical and professional capacities.

This improved occupational situation led to advancement in Negro standards of living as Weaver points out in a still later volume.[2] After

[1] Robert C. Weaver, *Negro Labor, A National Problem* (New York: Harcourt, Brace & Company, Inc., 1946), pp. 79-81. By permission.
[2] Robert C. Weaver, *The Negro Ghetto* (New York: Harcourt, Brace & Company, Inc., 1948), pp. 125-138.

citing statistics from Government documents showing increased averages in family incomes, he concludes:

> Thus, . . . colored, as all defense workers, bought more and better food, clothing, and, when available, household equipment. The crowded waiting rooms in the offices of Negro professional men and women and the high earnings they enjoyed during the war . . . attested to the fact that the residents in the Black Belt were demanding more and better medical and dental attention, spending more time and money on personal appearance, and seeking legal advice when such was needed. All of this meant that colored people, who had always accepted the American standards of living, rapidly took steps to achieve them once they had more money.[3]

The improved occupational situation of Negroes during the war period meant not only an improvement in welfare but also improvement in status. In many of the new sorts of war jobs Negroes worked alongside whites under equal terms so far as wages and work privileges were concerned. In Chicago, for example, Drake and Cayton write, "Colored girls . . . became salespeople in a few Loop stores, and colored Western Union messengers appeared on the streets of Midwest Metropolis for the first time." [4] Again, Embree noted during the war: "Over two thousand Negroes were employed in fifteen cities as streetcar conductors, motormen, and bus drivers. Certain railroads have upgraded waiters to stewards and are employing Negro firemen for the first time in a generation." [5]

What was to prove in the long run most significant in improving the status of Negroes was their increasing acceptance into labor unions. Johnson cites several estimates ranging from a total Negro union membership in 1943 of 400,000 to claims of the unions themselves which would put the figure at over a million at the close of the war.[6] The successful unionization of Negroes was not accomplished easily. Acceptance of Negroes into unions was by no means wholehearted on the part of white workers. The national trade unions often had to discipline local groups for their refusal to accept Negroes, sometimes striking over the matter. Nevertheless, Embree wrote in 1945:

> The greatest asset in employment is the new attitude of the unions. The Congress of Industrial Organizations is the strongest force against discrimination that has arisen in these fervid years. The older unions are not so aggressive but they are feeling the new movement for a united front of all laborers. The

[3] *Ibid.*, p. 136.
[4] St. Clair Drake and Horace R. Cayton, *Black Metropolis* (New York: Harcourt, Brace & Company, Inc., 1945), p. 296. By permission of the publishers.
[5] Edwin R. Embree, "Balance Sheet in Race Relations," *Atlantic Monthly,* Vol. 175, No. 5 (May 1945), p. 89.
[6] Charles S. Johnson, *Into the Main Stream* (Chapel Hill: University of North Carolina Press), 1947, pp. 114-115.

Farmer's Union, not yet firmly established against the big landowners organization, is also committed to fair play for the Negro farmers and farm workers.[7]

While, as would be expected in the South, in many instances separate Negro unions were formed, significant was the trend toward more mixed unions, and as time went on the discarding of the rules of caste etiquette in the association of both races in the same unions. Memphis reported not only mixed unions but the development of the practice of electing a white president and a Negro vice-president. Similar developments were noted in Georgia and in New Orleans. Of Alabama, Northrup writes:

> The results of this policy of gradualism are already discernible. According to a number of informants of both races, "Negro members of grievance committees, who a few years ago would have risked physical violence had they raised their voices in joint union-management meetings, now argue their cases quite as freely as their fellow white members." Local meetings are no longer featured by such "formal" relationships between the races as . . . was the case in 1934–35. White members no longer hesitate to call a Negro unionist "brother," or to shake hands with Negro delegates without displaying embarrassment.[8]

The Fair Employment Practices Committee. As a further influence upon wider employment opportunity for Negroes, as well as other minorities, the Fair Employment Practices Committee came into being, when on June 25, 1941, President Roosevelt issued his now famous executive order No. 8822. The order provided:

1. That all government agencies concerned with training programs should take measures designed to prevent discrimination.
2. That all government contracting agencies should include in defense contracts a provision obligating the contractor not to discriminate against any worker because of race, color, or country of national origin.
3. That there should be established a Committee on Fair Employment Practices to investigate complaints of discrimination and to take appropriate steps to redress valid grievances.

This action was taken in part as a result of a movement to organize a Negro march on Washington, led by A. Philip Randolph, head of the Brotherhood of Sleeping Car Porters, and had the immediate result of forestalling this march.[9] The Committee was strongly opposed in many communities, and violently opposed throughout the South. It had neither legislative sanction nor any real powers of enforcement. In spite of these handicaps, in the first 80 weeks of its existence "Ne-

---

[7] Embree, *loc. cit.*, p. 89. By permission of *Atlantic Monthly.*
[8] Herbert R. Northrup, *Organized Labor and the Negro* (New York: Harper and Brothers, 1944) p. 167. By permission of the publishers.
[9] For fuller details of this movement see Myrdal, *An American Dilemma*, pp. 851–852.

gro employment increased in commercial shipyards from 6952 to 12,-820; in navy shipyards from 6000 to 14,000; and in aircraft from 0 to 5000." [10] Thus FEPC as a new device against discrimination appears to have proven its worth, enough so that while it was abolished on the Federal level in 1945 it has been subsequently resumed on the state level in New York, New Jersey, and elsewhere. In its final report, the Committee stated, "FEPC during its five years satisfactorily settled cases by peaceful negotiation, including forty strikes caused by racial differences." [11]

Except, however, in the area of greater job opportunity and in increasing mixed unionism, the caste line between white and Negro remained substantially the same. The situation in regard to housing is admittedly difficult to appraise in a period of widespread national housing crisis. However, the exhaustive account which Weaver presents leaves little doubt that the traditional discrimination against Negroes in this respect generally held fast.[12] A few examples may be given. "An estimated 85 per cent of Detroit's area is shut off from colored homeowners or renters by restrictive covenants. And Negro housing projects are not to be built in neighborhoods predominantly white." [13] In Cleveland "There were no houses for sale to Negroes (in 1945) and the proportion for rent to them was only one-third the low figure of 0.9 per cent for whites." [14] In Los Angeles, while the nonwhite population increased about a third between 1940 and 1947, it still had to crowd into the same number of dwelling units.[15]

In the postwar study of segregation in Washington, it was found that the limitation of Negro residence to the previous Negro areas continued virtually unbroken. Even the National Capital Housing Authority bowed to the prevailing community pattern in race relations in its building low rent housing units. The 2700 housing units built by this Federal agency for Negro occupancy were all located in the existing Negro areas, thus reducing the space available for all Negroes. On the other hand, some units constructed for whites were built in the Negro areas, still further restricting available Negro residence.[16]

In the still more intimate area of social relations, substantially no change took place during the war. Nowhere was this more dramatically and conspicuously illustrated for the benefit of the many foreign

[10] Carey McWilliams, *Brothers Under the Skin* (Boston: Little, Brown & Company, 1946), p. 314.
[11] Fair Employment Practice Committee, *Final Report*, June 28, 1946, Washington, 1947, pp. viii-ix.
[12] Weaver, *The Negro Ghetto*, Ch. 7.
[13] *Ibid.*, p. 116.
[14] *Ibid.*, p. 120.
[15] *Ibid.*, pp. 121-123.
[16] *Segregation in Washington*, A Report of the National Committee on Segregation in The Nation's Capital (Chicago: Nov. 1948), p. 43.

emissaries than in the capital of Washington. To the numerous other materials about Washington's race situation the present writer here adds his own personal observations.

In common with many other governmental agencies during the war, the X division of the armed services numbered about one-third Negroes in its more than a thousand employees. While the occupational range of the Negroes employed was skewed in the lower direction, several Negroes held occupational ranks higher than many whites. One cafeteria served the entire personnel. Negro employees had equal access to the cafeteria and kept their position in line when ahead of whites. Casual, but nevertheless regular observation indicated that unvaryingly individual tables observed the color line. To the best of my knowledge there was no official pressure to prevent mingling at lunch, but it did not take place. Again there were two recreation libraries and rest rooms. In one of these a white worker was in charge; over another, a Negro worker presided. In the latter, all Negroes were to be found; in the former, whites were present except for an occasional Negro or two of higher rank. I suspect the latter were there more on principle than preference. A river excursion was planned for the employees. Two boats were chartered. The problem of the possible mixing of the two races was met by assigning tickets to the appropriate racial boats. The recreational staff was embarrassed by the attempt of some Negro workers to insist on tickets for the white boat.

In the armed services. The armed services, with a few exceptions noted below, practiced a policy of segregation. In the Army, Negroes were assigned to colored units and the great majority of these units were in supply services where the actual tasks performed were largely menial labor. A few thousand Negro officers were trained and placed over Negro troops frequently under the command of a white captain. In army posts, separate recreational rooms were maintained, and nearly all communities which any considerable number of Negro soldiers frequented—North as well as South—restricted colored troops to the Negro areas, and set up separate USO's. For the most part Negro units were kept out of combat. According to Rose, "In Europe there were some efforts made to keep Negroes from fraternizing with the civilian population, when no such bar was set up against the white troops." [17]

The policy of segregation of Negro troops reflected the wishes of the white troops. A survey of the attitudes of servicemen on the matter of race segregation made in March 1943 found that about 80 per cent of the white troops preferred to have the two groups separated in PXs, in service clubs, and nonmilitary units.[18] While, as would be expected,

[17] Rose, *Negro in America*, p. 138.
[18] Samuel A. Stouffer et al. *The American Soldier*, Vol. I (Princeton: Princeton University Press, 1949), pp. 566-580. Chapter 10 of this volume, "Negro Soldiers," contains probably the most definitive research material ever gathered on how the young adult males of both races look at one another and think about the "race" problem.

the study showed that over 90 per cent of the Southern white respondents on each of the three counts listed above approved segregation, it is significant that over 70 per cent of the Northern white troops likewise indicated approval.[19] Again, as would be expected, the Negro respondents showed far more opposition to being segregated, but the detailed findings in this respect were highly significant as an indication of how Negroes viewed their situation generally. Of the Negro sample 37 per cent disapproved separation in military units; 36 per cent approved; 17 per cent thought it made no difference; and 10 per cent were undecided.[20] Comments made on the questionnaire by some of the anti-segregation Negro soldiers emphasized primarily the democratic principle involved. Illustrative of these comments was this, "Separate outfits shows that the Army continues segregation and discrimination. Is this the Democracy we are told we are fighting for?" [21] On the other hand the 36 per cent of Negro soldiers who approved of segregation did so on the basis of expediency, based upon their realistic appraisal of white prejudice. Among the reasons given for taking the pro-segregation viewpoint were: a fear of interracial friction, illustrated by the comment, "A white soldier would call a colored soldier 'nigger' and it would be a fight"; a desire to withdraw from the situation of not being wanted, or, as one soldier put it, "so long as there are so many prejudiced white people, it would be too unpleasant"; a desire to prove that Negro groups can match the achievements of white groups; and finally, a desire to associate with those who understand each other, illustrated by the remark, "I had rather be with my own color. Then I know where I stand." [22]

Ultimately some cracks appeared in the race segregation pattern of the services of which Dollard and Young write:

The first was a decision to abandon segregation in all officers' candidate schools except those for Air Force flying personnel. At the peak, there were about a score of such integrated camps, each producing specialists for some one branch of the service—artillery, tank corps, infantry, and so on. White and Negro slept, ate, and trained together with a minimum of friction and with no "incidents" worthy of record.

The second crack in the pattern resulted from a single experiment. On December 26, 1944, Lieutenant General John C. H. Lee issued an order permitting Negro enlisted men in service units within his command to volunteer for duty as infantryman, with the understanding that after the necessary training, they would be committed to front line service with white companies. In spite of the fact that all volunteers had to sacrifice any ratings they held,

[19] *Ibid.*, pp. 568-570.
[20] *Ibid.*, p. 568.
[21] *Ibid.*, p. 575.
[22] *Ibid.*, p. 574.

about twenty-five hundred took advantage of the opportunity and eventually saw combat duty. For the first time in the recent history of the army, Negroes and whites operated as members of a single company.[23]

In spite of segregation policy and practice, the total impact of experiences in the armed services had effects disturbing to the traditional pattern of caste relations. More objectively measurable was the introduction of colored servicemen to new standards of welfare—in diet, health, and sanitation; and the increased training in many new skills, some of which could be useful in peacetime. One measure of the Negro soldiers' own feeling about the vocational value of their army experience is provided by a study made by the office of Army Education and Information. Asked to indicate whether or not they felt that their army training would help them to get a better job after the war than they had ever had before, 61 per cent of the Negro respondents replied in the affirmative as contrasted with only 39 per cent among the whites.[24] Less tangible but perhaps in the long run more significant was the impact of service experience on the attitudes of GI's of both races. Northern born Negro servicemen trained in the South came face to face with the stricter Southern caste system. Southern Negro GI's came north to experience some measure of unaccustomed freedom. In Europe, many Negro GI's found white people wishing to accept them as any other American soldier. All this was unsettling to these troops.

Equally disturbing to traditional attitudes and habits was the impact of war service upon many white Southerners. This is most dramatically illustrated by Margaret Halsey's account of her experiences operating a servicemen's center in a large Northern city where the policy of accepting all men in U. S. uniform on the same terms was successfully maintained. Some Southern bred young women were among the hostesses who found it possible to dance with Negro servicemen; many Southern white servicemen, though first somewhat shocked to see white women dancing with colored servicemen, both in conversation and in correspondence with Miss Halsey, indicated that they were doing some inner struggling with their attitudes. One series of correspondence involved a lieutenant from the Deep South who wrote Miss Halsey that he wants his colored friends to have the vote, real justice in court, college education, decent living conditions, etc. and that he will work hard to see that they get them. But he goes on, "I do not want him to be my house guest, . . . to live next door to me . . . [or] dance with my daughter. How can I reconcile these conflicting desires?"

[23] Charles Dollard and Donald Young, "In the Armed Forces," *Survey Graphic,* Vol. 36, No. 1 (Jan., 1947), p. 68. By permission.
[24] Stouffer, *et al., op. cit.,* p. 537.

To Miss Halsey's well thought out reply, the lieutenant finally wrote:

Perhaps without knowing it, you have supplied me the answer to my dilemma. That answer I find in two points made by you. The first is that we are not born with racial prejudices. We are educated to them, perhaps not formally, but certainly effectively. So it is with me. Your second and all-important point is that everything I do in the interest of the Negro brings him closer to dancing with my daughter. You point out that my efforts in their small way will lead to equality, not in my lifetime, but in hers. After about the tenth reading, light broke like a flare in the darkness.

The answer to my problem is in two words: SO WHAT? What right have I to say with whom my daughters shall dance? Certainly I have no right to dictate the likes and dislikes of my *granddaughter!* If the next generation should by a miracle of education grow up to believe in true democracy and accept all men as equals, what is it to me? That is my daughter's business. All I can or should do is to see that she has an open mind and picks up from her lovely mother or myself enough sense to discern between dead right and dead wrong. With this attitude, I can write what I please and fight racial prejudice with an eye to ultimate victory.[25]

The situation at V-J Day. To take stock of the position of Negro-white relations at the close of the war as a base from which to analyze the trends since 1945, Myrdal's summary observations, though written prior to the war's end, will be employed.

Of the North, Myrdal observes:

The social paradox in the North is exactly this, that almost everybody is against discrimination in general but, at the same time, almost everybody practices discrimination in his own personal affairs.

It is the cumulation of all these personal discriminations which creates the color bar in the North and for the Negro causes unusually severe unemployment, crowded housing conditions, crime, and vice. About this social process the ordinary white Northerner keeps sublimely ignorant and unconcerned. This aloofness is, of course, partly opportunistic but it can be fought by education. When now, in the war emergency, the Negro is increasingly given sympathetic publicity by newspapers, periodicals, and the radio, and by administrators and public personalities of all kinds, one result is that the white Northerner is gradually waking up and seeing what he is doing to the Negro and is seeing also the consequences of his democratic creed for his relations with Negroes. We have become convinced in the course of this inquiry that the North is getting prepared for a fundamental redefinition of the Negro's status in America. The North will accept it if the change is pushed by courageous leadership. And the North has much more power than the South. The white South is itself a minority and a national problem.

[25] Margaret Halsey, *Color Blind.* Copyright, 1946, by Margaret Halsey. Reprinted by permission of Simon and Schuster, Publishers, pp. 125, 127-128.

In contrast, Myrdal writes of the South:

The situation in the South is different. Unlike the white Northerner, who is most inclined to give the Negro equality in public relations and least inclined to do so in private relations, the white Southerner does not differentiate between public and private relations—the former as well as the latter have significance for prestige and social equality. Moreover, he is traditionally and consistently opposed to Negro equality for its own sake, which the Northerner is not. He may be privately indulgent much more than the white Northerner, but he is not as willing to give the Negro equal treatment by public authority.[26]

Myrdal further observes that "At this juncture, the white North is moving in a direction contrary to the South." [27] The present writer feels that it is more accurate to state that at the close of World War II, the South had not moved in any marked degree from its prewar position while the North had moved considerably toward equality. Such a restatement would not negate Myrdal's further prediction of a growing tension between the two regions over the race issue in the postwar period. Since the white South lacks the power to resist a Northern solution if determinedly pushed, which Myrdal predicted would be the case, he feels the South must eventually capitulate. He took hope, however, in the further observations that "the white South is not united against a redefinition of the Negro's status"; that "Southern liberalism has been coming to be a force"; and that "in the long run . . . the conservative white Southerner himself can be won over. . . ." [28]

Myrdal's entire study is based upon the value premises of democracy. He maintains that since America is first of all democratic and since race discrimination is obviously undemocratic, the only conceivable ultimate solution of the race problem is the elimination of all discrimination and the complete acceptance of all minorities as equals. In terms of this value premise, the final tone of his monumental treatise is optimistic concerning the destiny of Negro-white relations in the United States. He is more optimistic than many American students of the problem. The trend of events in the postwar period, to which attention is now directed, provide much justification for Myrdal's optimism.

THE POSTWAR PERIOD

The gains made by Negroes in the war period were wrought more from urgency than from any sweeping change in the hearts and minds of the white people of the country. Nevertheless, the cumulative effect

[26] Myrdal, *op. cit.*, pp. 1010-1011. By permission of the publishers, Harper and Brothers.
[27] *Ibid.*, p. 1014.
[28] *Ibid.*, p. 1015.

of these changes in addition to the new situation faced by the nation in the emerging international society developed a vastly greater national self-consciousness about the American race dilemma. More than ever before, or certainly since reconstruction days in the South, race relations became defined in wider public segments as a social problem of the first magnitude. For the past few years, almost every issue of the metropolitan press has had items of news or comment on race incidents or issues. Most of the magazines have had several articles a year concerned with racial topics. Committees and organizations concerned with racial interaction have grown apace. Social science has begun to turn more serious attention to the field of race relations and to make it the object of more systematic study.[29] It is, then, this new national self-consciousness about race relations and its increasing definition by wide segments of the public as a "problem" which most of all characterizes the current postwar period.

Again the tone of this new national discussion of Negro-white relations, as well as of all dominant-minority relations, is, with some discordant notes, pitched within the framework of the democratic value system which Myrdal insisted Americans must accept as a basis of social policy. Outside the South, and here and there within it, the publicly acknowledged *ultimate* goal appears to be the elimination of ethnic, religious, and racial minority status from American society. Public debate turns more on the questions: How can we proceed to reach this goal? and How rapidly can we move?

While this is the direction of change, it must not be forgotten that the base from which the present trend was somewhat rapidly projected, beginning with war mobilization, was one of systematic discrimination. Negroes are still more discriminated against than not. Furthermore, this rapid acceleration toward increasing equality for Negroes in the North has been sustained by the propitious circumstance of a high national level of employment. Any substantial recession will test the permanency of these gains. Finally, in regard to any social issue involving a clash of interests which becomes a major focus of public attention, as has race relations, strong pressure in one direction engenders determined efforts in the opposite direction. Witness the Thurmond candidacy for the presidency as a counter movement against President Truman's civil rights program. With these general reflections in mind, attention now turns to the record of events transpiring since V-J Day.

[29] Some penetrating hypotheses, by no means flattering to sociologists, concerning why sociology did not find race relations a respectable field of sociological investigation earlier may be found in the presidential address of Professor E. Franklin Frazier, published in the *American Sociological Review*, Vol. 14, No. 1 (Feb. 1949), pp. 1-11.

Increased integration into civic life. While the most conspicuous advances of Negroes in the war period were in employment and income, it is their increasing integration into civic life which stands out in the postwar period. In many Northern communities it has become a fixed practice in the unofficial community organization activity such as chest drives, health programs, and other civic welfare enterprises, to give representation to Negroes on the committees and boards. Heretofore they have been chosen largely to function as representatives of the "Negro element"; in time, Negroes may be chosen as persons in their own rights.

In governmental agencies, likewise, Negroes have been getting increased representation. Again, the first step has been to have Negro officeholders limited to authority over their own people, such as, a Negro probation officer to deal with Negro probationers. But in other instances, of which Negro police officers are illustrative, Negro officials function in authority over white people.

Court decisions in recent years have greatly strengthened the right of Negroes to first-class citizenship. Convictions of Negroes for criminal offenses have been overruled by higher courts when there was evidence of systematic exclusion of Negroes from jury duty in the area of original jurisdiction.

A number of recent decisions by the United States Supreme Court have made it now illegal to refuse qualified Negro applicants admission to state supported graduate schools anywhere in the country. In 1947 in a case involving the refusal of the University of Oklahoma to admit a qualified Negro woman applicant to its law school, the highest tribunal ordered provision for the applicant of legal education equal to that given any other Oklahoma resident. In another Oklahoma case, where a Negro teacher had been admitted to the graduate school of education but segregated in anterooms for his classes, the court ruled by unanimous decision on June 6, 1950, that all segregation rules in the institution must be abolished. On the same day, the court rendered another unanimous decision ordering the State University of Texas to admit a Negro applicant to its all-white law school. This case is of great interest because Texas had provided for the Negro applicant in this case a special law "school" for this one Negro applicant. In deciding that this did not provide "equal" training, the court said in part, "the law school, the proving ground for legal learning and practice cannot be effective in isolation from the individuals and institutions with which the law interacts." [30]

The report of the Civil Rights Commission appointed by President Truman contained a large number of recommendations pertaining to

[30] *New York Herald Tribune,* June 7, 1950, p. 34.

the civil rights of minorities. While the recommendations have been vigorously urged upon Congress, to date none of them has been passed. The provisions of the report most directly pertinent to Negro-white relations are:

Action by the States or Congress to end poll taxes as a voting prerequisite.

The enactment by Congress of a statute protecting the right to qualify for, or participate in, federal or state primaries or elections against discriminatory action by state officers based on race or color, or depending on any other unreasonable classification of persons for voting purposes.

The enactment by Congress of legislation, followed by appropriate administrative action, to end immediately all discrimination and segregation based on race, color, creed, or national origin, in the organization and activities of all branches of the Armed Services.

The enactment by Congress of legislation providing that no member of the armed forces shall be subject to discrimination of any kind by any public authority or place of public accommodation, recreation, transportation, or other service or business.

The conditioning by Congress of all federal grants-in-aid and other forms of federal assistance to public or private agencies for any purpose on the absence of discrimination and segregation based on race, color, creed, or national origin.

The enactment of a Fair Employment Practice Act prohibiting all forms of discrimination in private employment, based on race, color, creed, or national origin.[31]

While these are as yet only recommendations, they point toward the still greater integration of Negroes into full citizenship.

In the armed services. The postwar period has seen a decided trend toward the elimination of segregation in the Armed Services and the equalization of opportunities for Negro servicemen with those for whites. On July 26, 1948, President Truman ordered "equality of treatment of all persons in the Armed Services without regard to race, color, religion, or national origin." [32] The following April, the Secretary of Defense directed the elimination of discrimination in all branches of the service. Substantial progress in this direction has occurred in the Navy and Air Forces. Segregated units have been eliminated and the equalization of opportunities for Negroes to train for officers has taken place. In the Army, change in the same direction has

---

[31] *To Secure These Rights*, The report of the President's Committee on Civil Rights (New York: Simon & Schuster, Inc., 1947), pp. 160-163, 166-167.
[32] See *Civil Rights in the United States* (New York: National Association for the Advancement of Colored People and American Jewish Congress, 1948).

proceeded more slowly. The national press reported in July, 1951, while the cease-fire negotiations were going on at Kaesong, that the Army had abandoned all segregation in units fighting in Korea. However, segregation of Negro ground troops stationed in the United States still continued.

Expansion of Negro job horizons. The gains made by Negroes in employment opportunity during the war period on the whole have been sustained, making allowance for the necessary adjustments in employment which affected many categories of workers. Among the factors which underlie this sustained Negro employment status are the continued high general level of employment and the increased extent to which Negro workers are union members with whites, thus affording them the protection of all union workers. However, even where employment opportunity has declined, discrimination against Negroes, is less noticeable than formerly. In New Jersey, for example, the first noticeable postwar decline in employment began in early 1949, yet there was no evidence that any racial or ethnic minorities were experiencing discrimination in the process of being laid off.[33]

The Bureau of Labor Statistics reported that "the proportion of Negroes employed in industrial jobs (craftsmen and operatives) was about the same in 1947 as during the war." [34] However, "employment of Negroes as skilled craftsmen and foremen appears to have declined somewhat since the war's end, in contrast to the significant increase in craftsmen and foremen among whites." [35] The postwar trends to date seem to confirm Weaver's hypothesis that "the whole industrial history of minority groups in the nation indicates that once a discriminated group gets its members in better and new types of jobs, *some of them remain in those occupations,* becoming the beachhead from which subsequent participation of additional members of the group is projected in the next period of boom." [36]

In addition to holding broadly fast to the war employment gains, in the North, at least, the postwar period has seen sporadic Negro advances into still wider occupational areas, especially into positions involving higher remuneration and connoting middle-class status. In addition to the widely publicized "firsts" such as Jackie Robinson becoming a Dodger, and Dr. Ralph Bunche becoming the Palestine Mediator and in 1950 being awarded the Nobel Peace Prize, here and there Negro young women have become telephone operators, salesgirls, teachers of mixed classes. Government service has provided

[33] See the *Annual Report, 1948–49,* Division Against Discrimination, Department of Education, State of New Jersey, pp. 3-4.
[34] *Monthly Labor Review,* Vol. 15, No. 6, December 1947, p. 665.
[35] *Ibid.*
[36] Weaver, *The Negro Ghetto,* p. 135.

greater opportunity for Negroes than private establishments, eloquent testimony to the importance of political power, which Negroes in the North possess, as a pressure for lifting discrimination.

State antidiscrimination law and administration. The consolidation and further expansion of the wartime gains of Negroes in employment have been strengthened in several Northern states by the passage of special antidiscrimination legislation and the setting up of agencies by state governments modeled upon the Federal Committee on Fair Employment Practices.[37] Among these little "FEPCs," those of the states of New Jersey and New York have had several years of operation. An appraisal of the effects of such agencies has great theoretical significance in evaluating the possibilities and limitations of legal measures as a means of adjusting friction in dominant-minority relations. We shall have occasion to refer to the work of these agencies in the concluding chapter on social policies. At this point, we shall describe their activities in relation to Negro employment opportunity. In both states, these divisions of government entertain complaints of refusal to hire, or of dismissal allegedly due to discrimination on account of race, color, religion, or nationality origin. If upon investigation, the agency finds the complaint justified, it first attempts to secure for the complainant willing compliance from the guilty employer or union by informal conference. This may mean hiring the aggrieved person, or if this is no longer feasible, an agreement to alter employment practices. While these agencies have the power to institute formal legal proceedings against the guilty party, in practice thus far in these two states, the agencies have managed to close the cases satisfactorily by the informal procedure. While the scope of their functions covers all minorities, in practice the overwhelming majority of their cases involved discrimination on the basis of color, substantially all being Negroes. Up to 1948, in New York State 69 per cent of all investigations involved discrimination on the basis of color; in New Jersey up to July 1, 1949, about 90 per cent of the complaints were on the same ground.

How these agencies have operated and the kinds of adjustments they affect may be seen in the following cases cited from the New York State experience.

A woman was fired because of her color. She filed a complaint; the Commission investigated and sustained her charges. Her foreman, who was prejudiced and made discriminatory remarks about her color, had filed a report saying that her work was not efficient. When the employer was shown the results of the Commission's investigation, he fired the foreman. . . .

[37] At the beginning of 1950, New York, New Jersey, Massachusetts, Connecticut, New Mexico, Washington, Oregon, and Rhode Island had enacted laws against discrimination in employment and set up special agencies to administer such laws.

Meanwhile the woman had obtained another job at a higher salary. The original employer said that he would give her her job back and offered to meet her present wage.

A Negro man was refused membership in a union because of his color—yet the union had sent him out on jobs for five years when it could not supply enough men from its membership. The complainant was told that his membership was refused not because of his color but because he could not meet the requirements of other locals (some of which were located in the South). After conferences between the Commission and the union, the Negro was given membership in the union and also a temporary work permit while his regular papers were being made out.

Clearly the successful operation of an agency of this sort depends on its ability and willingness to insist that adequate proof of discrimination is forthcoming from the complainant. Typical of a complaint which was dismissed is the following case:

. . . man claimed that he was fired because of his race. The Commission's investigation showed that the man was inefficient and spoiled a good deal of material. The employer offered to let the man give a demonstration before any group of workmen inside or outside the plant who know the work, but the complainant refused. The case was closed without proving discrimination.[38]

It is not possible to appraise the exact contribution of this legislation and administration among the many other factors which have influenced the highly favorable opportunities for broader and higher level employment for Negroes in these two states. For example, relative to the entire nation, the attitudinal climate among white people in these two states, except for the less populous southerly section of New Jersey, was more favorably disposed toward Negroes even before this new social machinery was instituted. This in part explains why New York and New Jersey were among the first to adopt such measures. It is also true that employment opportunities in general have been favorable during the period of their operation. On the other hand, the cases cited indicate actual change in specific employment situations which was wrought by the activity of the antidiscrimination divisions. Finally, high significance may be attached to the fact that these agencies devote much effort to an educational program designed to influence public attitudes in these two states in support not only of the law itself but of the broader aims in intergroup relations toward which it is directed.

[38] The three cases cited are from Felix Rackow, *Combating Discrimination in Employment in New York State*, New York State School of Industrial and Labor Relations, Research Bulletin No. 5 (Ithaca: Cornell University, No. 1949), pp. 28-29. By permission of the school.

Segregation declines in public accommodations. The trend toward equal access by Negroes to public acommodations and places in the North has continued forward since World War II. Both New Jersey and Connecticut have empowered the state antidiscrimination agencies operating in the employment field to enforce nondiscrimination in public places. While in some Northern cities, incidents of violence have been reported over the increasing pressure by Negroes to be accommodated in places hitherto denied them, on the whole, this process has occurred with relatively little of the anticipated friction.

The color line in interpersonal relations. The extent to which the color line in informal interpersonal relations has held fast, or has been breached, in the Northern postwar scene is difficult to measure. Prior to the 1940–50 decade, the actual amount of intimate association on the basis of equality between whites and Negroes did not appear to be substantially greater than in the South. Clearly, it is still not the usual practice for Northerners to mingle with Negroes as social equals. Nevertheless, the trend is toward increasing social equality. Increasingly "forced" by the new legal pressures to accept Negroes in jobs and in public places as nominal equals, whites are getting more accustomed to associate with Negroes more freely in general.

Acceptance of minority persons into voluntary associations provides a more measurable device than informal relations for determining change in interpersonal relations. The greatest gains accruing to Negroes in the North have been scored in professional associations, in churches, and in various educational associations. Significant illustrations are these: the election of the first Negro member to the Albany, N. Y., Junior Chamber of Commerce; the election of a Negro student to the Amherst Chapter of Phi Kappa Psi, and the subsequent reorganization of the chapter as an independent local when it was suspended by the national organization for its action; the naming of a Negro to the policy making body of the American Medical Association; and the admission in 1950 of a Negro woman applicant to the national women's tennis championship competition.

The Negro ghetto continues. Living side by side connotes in American cities a general equality in social status and a presumption that neighborliness could properly take place. It is therefore not surprising that, next to and pertinently related to interpersonal segregation, housing segregation in the North remains substantially unbroken and that the Negro ghetto described in Chapter 10 remains substantially intact. Weaver shows that in the postwar period in cities with low indices of restrictive covenants, the tendency has been for the proportion of the total supply of housing available to nonwhites to vary with the proportion of nonwhites in the population. In the cities where racial restrictive covenants are more general, nonwhites failed to get their proportionate share of housing.[39] Recalling that Negro housing areas have been dangerously overcrowded in the North for years, housing discrimination remains the most tragic disability which minority status imposes upon Negroes. It cuts more deeply now than before the war since an increasing number of Negroes can in fact pay for better housing and their improved education has raised their standards of desirable living conditions.

Two new developments indicating some change away from segregated Negro housing have occurred in the postwar years. One is the Supreme Court decision in 1948 which ruled that racial restrictive covenants could not be enforced by law.[40] While this does not make covenants illegal, it makes them more risky, and therefore should promote their less frequent use. The other new development has been in new housing entirely or partly subsidized by the government. By far the greater majority of public housing projects has been racially segregated, although some all-Negro projects have been constructed. On the whole, whenever such Negro projects could not be located in the existing Negro areas, opposition to their location anywhere else near white people unvaryingly arose. However, more experiments in mixed housing projects are being undertaken and the results seem to mark a continuing trend in this direction.

Chicago, already in the process of abandoning a segregated program, found the basis and occasion for completing the process in its wartime and veterans' housing experience. The Housing Authority of the City of Los Angeles substituted a nonsegregated policy for one of racial quotas during the war; and San Francisco, pressured during the war to change its policy, announced a nonsegregated one in 1946. In Cleveland, too, the war experience spurred the local Housing Authority to accelerate a movement toward unsegregated living in the projects it managed. New Haven indicated that it was at least pleased that nonsegregation worked in a war housing project. Buffalo, under pressure from the State Commission Against Discrimination, adopted a nonsegregation policy in 1947. With the exception of Detroit and possibly Philadelphia, all the metropolitan cities in the North with large Negro populations either had, or were on the way to achieving, a policy of nonsegregation in public housing. Progress in many of the smaller cities, and in a few larger ones, however, was less apparent.[41]

In spite of gains in this direction, pressure against the color line in housing still remains a most explosive force. Up to 1950, little progress

[39] See Weaver, *The Negro Ghetto,* Ch. 7, especially pp. 120-124.
[40] Shelley vs. Kraemer, 334 U.S. 1; Hurd vs. Hodges, 334 U.S. 24.
[41] Weaver, *The Negro Ghetto,* p. 208.

had been made in mixed housing projects under private enterprise. In 1949 numerous reports were received of assaults and, in Chicago, of two major riots occasioned by the purchase, or rumors of purchase, of homes in white residential areas by Negroes.

The Cicero incident of July 1951 illustrates both the increasing pressure of Negroes against the housing bars and the persistence of white opposition to Negroes as neighbors. In this Illinois urban community, a college educated Negro man working as a truck driver rented an apartment in a new housing project in a community which had no Negroes. A mob of local white residents, predominantly of European immigrant background, rioted and damaged the property of the project in protest against the admittance of a Negro family. Because of the failure of local law enforcement agencies to restrain the rioters, state militia had to be brought to the scene to restore order. Further events following this incident, however, reflect the changing climate of public attitudes toward race relations: the mob action received widespread condemnation from many groups; legal agencies proceeded to act against rioters and criminals; and plans to make Cicero the subject of intensive study by intergroup agencies were announced.

Movement toward equality in the North. Up to the present time, the Northern trend toward increased equality and opportunity for Negroes since the war has occurred without any significant counter trends. From the viewpoint of those interested in seeing the Negro get ahead, failures have been failures to move forward in many communities, or defeats in particular efforts of forward movement, not in actual reverses. The instances of violence reported growing out of new Negro gains have been sporadic and have not as yet contained the general forward movement. In the absence of detailed knowledge for the entire nation, one would assume that in some communities where large groups of Negroes have entered for the first time, the status of Negroes has declined. Here and there certain fanatical "racist" elements have reasserted themselves momentarily but seem on the whole to have aroused more ridicule than anything else.

The South is stirring. The direction of change in the South since World War II is similar to that of the North although the inclination of the trend is small and the base from which it should be plotted starts at a much lower point. Differing from the North, the Southern reactions to the postwar period are affected by the influences from without as well as those from within the region itself. Over the years the South has developed a keen sensitivity to criticism and "interference" from the rest of the nation, especially concerning the race question. But as we have noted, the North particularly in regard to civic rights for Negroes, is putting more, not less, pressure on the South. The North also is making the discrepancy between its own treatment of Negroes and that of the South still more conspicuous. The South can less cogently fall back on an earlier claim, which had much truth in it, that when Northerners were actually brought face to face with the presence of large numbers of Negroes it would act the way the South traditionally has.

In any event, the evidence is clear that the South today is less uniformly committed to retain the traditional pattern of race relations than at any time since Thomas Jefferson's day. There are at least three varieties of publics to be found in the white South today. One group holds the traditional view which was described in Chapter 9. A second embraces those Southerners who are attempting to make the idea of equal welfare within a biracial pattern more a reality through the improvement of Negro schools, hospital facilities, etc. The third is that small group of Southerners who realize that segregation must eventually go. Except for the opinion that the latter group is small, it would be hazardous to assay the relative numbers holding the first and second views.[42]

Recent Southern events

In Politics. Increase in Negro voting in the South is attested in the following summary concerning the 1948 presidential election:

The Negro vote in 1948 has been estimated at 700,000 as against 250,000 in 1940. Yet even the former figure represents only 14 per cent of the Southern Negro population of voting age. Despite the victories won in court and elsewhere, new devices are being found every year to keep Negro voting at a minimum and the outright use of violence against those Negroes who dare to exercise their newly won right remains a potent threat. [43]

Further Negro voting is restricted by the continuance of the poll tax, which in 1950 still limited the franchise in seven Southern states. Negroes have been running for public office in increasing numbers. In Richmond, Virginia, in 1948, a Negro was elected to the City Council, an election in which it is estimated that the Negro councilman received about 20 per cent of his vote from white people.

Legal Protection. Negroes are serving on juries with increasing frequency, in part because of the disposition of the Federal courts to

---

[42] We do, however, hazard the guess that any public opinion polling on the subject would err on the side of finding more people appearing to hold the traditional view than is actually the case. It has long been known that many Southerners in private conversations talk more liberally about race relations than they dare express in public. To the contrary, in the North public opinion polling would likely err in finding more liberal ballots than actually exist in the minds and behavior of the respondents. Public pressure operates in opposite ways in the two regions.
[43] Civil Rights in the United States in 1948, *loc. cit.,* pp. 9-10.

throw out convictions where the absence of Negro jury service is attested. White people who commit crimes of violence against Negroes are being more frequently arrested and brought to trial. Although the number of convictions of white people in such cases is few, the fact that some white criminals in these cases have been fined and even imprisoned is a significant change in the Southern scene. The trend toward employing Negro police officers to cover Negro areas greatly reduces a provocative source of friction. By the end of 1948, 68 Southern cities in 12 states were employing a total of 361 Negro police officers.

Education. The improvement of the facilities and the quality of the segregated Negro public school education in the South has continued. More significant, however, has been the breaching of the color line in education at the higher levels, particularly in the graduate schools. It was estimated that more than 200 Negroes were enrolled in hitherto exclusively white graduate schools in the academic year, 1950–1951.

Counter trends in the South. As would be expected, all these pressures both from without and within against the accustomed pattern of Southern race relations generated stronger counter activity than in the North. The civil rights program of the Truman Administration engendered the States Rights Party in the 1948 Presidential election carrying the electoral vote of four states. Although the effect of this bolt from the Democratic party was diminished by Mr. Truman's election in spite of it, nevertheless the Administration had up to 1951 lost all rounds in the battle to advance its program in the 81st Congress. Thus far, those Southerners liberal on the race question have not had much influence on the political machines which control Southern politics.

From the mounting tension observed in the wartime South, an increase in violence would be anticipated. The data available do not indicate any precipitate rise, or consistent trend in the amount of violence against Negroes in the postwar period. The continued persistence of the traditional pattern of violence in race relations is, however attested. Reported lynchings of Negroes are as follows: 1945, one; 1946, six; 1947, one; 1948, one; 1949, three. "Official brutality to Negroes has continued to be a serious problem." [44] In 1949, 34 Negroes were killed and another 33 injured while in police custody.

The counter reaction toward the pressure of current trends in race relations in the South is also seen in the activities of organized racist minded groups, here and there with renewed vigor. A typical example is the following:

Early in March (1948), some three hundred Ku Klux Klansmen paraded through the town of Wrightsville, Georgia, after hearing Grand Dragon

[44] *Ibid.*, p. 9.

Samuel Green of Atlanta promise that "blood will flow in the streets of the South" if the Negro takes a place at the side of white men; "the Klan will not permit the people of this country to become a mongrel race." The demonstration, staged strategically on the eve of the Johnson County primary elections, effectively discouraged some four hundred registered Negroes from voting the following day. Governor M. E. Thompson and State Attorney General Eugene Cook were petitioned to halt the Klan parades, but indicated they were without authority to do so as long as demonstrations were conducted in an orderly manner.[45]

Again it should be noted that public sentiment in opposition to Klan activities is more articulate than before, as is evidenced, for example, by the outlawing of masked gatherings in some Southern cities.

The rising militancy of the Negro protest. White Americans have persistently underrated the resentment by Negroes of the discrimination imposed on them in the United States. We have noted in the previous chapter the trend toward the "protest" as distinguished from the "accommodative" attitudes and programs of Negro leaders and organizations. With the appearance of a volume, *What the Negro Wants,* in 1944, any doubt concerning what the educated Negroes want now disappears.[46] In this volume, 14 Negro leaders of widely varying political persuasions indicate the same goal even though they vary in their views concerning how to reach it. In essence they all want first-class citizenship for Negroes without any reservations.

But what about the Negro masses? On the surface they appear to many white people to have resigned themselves to minority status and to have worked out a reasonably contented way of life on this basis. That underneath this surface the real attitudes and feelings among Negroes about their position in this country differs from this superficial white impression is well documented in a survey conducted by the Army in 1943 among the soldiers. A representative sample of all Army troops was asked the question, "If you could talk to the President of the United States, what are the three most important questions you would ask him about the war and your part in it?" Upon analyzing the replies of the Negro troops in this study, Stouffer and his associates have this to say:

Four out of five Negroes came forward with at least one question, the same proportion as in a cross section of white soldiers queried at the same time . . . half of the Negroes who responded with questions to the President wrote explicit questions or protests about racial discrimination. Of the remaining comments, an unknown proportion were stated in terms which at least implied a racial emphasis but could not clearly be placed in this category on

[45] *Race Relations,* April–May, 1948, p. 166. By permission of Fisk University.
[46] Rayford W. Logan, ed., *What the Negro Wants* (Chapel Hill: University of North Carolina Press, 1944).

the basis of explicit statement. For this reason, the proportion of men reported as making racial comments is a minimum estimate of the racial response to the question. It will be noted that the question was so worded as to encourage focusing attention on the war and contained no manifest reference to race. While the results must be interpreted in the light of evidence . . . that the better educated and more critical were more likely to offer free answers, the fact that four-fifths of the Negroes volunteered at least one response means that a correction for nonrespondents would not alter the picture much. The high incidence of "racial" comments, therefore, is evidence of the Negro soldiers' concern with racial questions.[47]

Further indications of the preoccupation of Negro young adult males in general with their minority group status and of the specific aspects of discrimination which they resent can be seen in the kinds of questions which were raised in the Army survey, which are classified under seven headings substantially as follows:

1. Will there be less discrimination after the war?
2. Why doesn't he (the President) make people stop discriminating against us?
3. Why is there discrimination in the Army?
4. What does the Negro have to fight for?
5. If we have the duty to fight, why shouldn't we be given equal rights now and in the future?
6. What is the Negroes' part in the war?
7. Why can't Negro troops be moved out of the South?[48]

This survey, more definitively than any other materials, strongly indicates that the Negro masses as well as the more articulate leadership of the group are profoundly discontented at being treated as a minority. The wide discrepancy between the way in which the white population thinks the Negro views the situation and the way the Negro actually views it may be accounted for in part by the social isolation between the two groups which so minimizes personal contact that whites learn little about the Negro's real feeling. This is further aggravated by the tendency of Negroes even when in conversation with white people to conceal their real feelings. Still further, however, the prevalent white interpretation of the Negro's position as one in which he is on the whole contented is in considerable measure a matter of wishful thinking. Many whites believe in this connection what they want to believe, which helps to justify their part in maintaining the situation.

Relation of Negroes to other minorities. Since all minorities share the common experience of discrimination it would be logical to suppose

---

[47] Stouffer, *et al, op. cit.,* pp. 503-504. By permission of publishers, Princeton University Press. Among the white troops asked the same question, there were **no** questions listed pertaining to racial discrimination.
[48] *Ibid.,* pp. 504-506.

that they would be sympathetic toward one another and make common cause. There is not much material in the literature of minorities to help us test this logical hypothesis. The most recent general discussion of this topic, with particular reference to Negroes in relation to other minorities, has been provided by Rose.[49] The Negro press has championed the cause of the colored peoples in their 20th century conflicts with their white "imperial" rulers, e.g., the Ethiopians against the Italians, the Indonesians against the Dutch. In World War II, a tendency for Negroes to sympathize secretly with the Japanese because they were, in the initial stage, beating the white people was overbalanced by a sympathy for the Chinese and their basic loyalty to the United States. Because of their concentration in the South, prior to the Great Migration, Negroes at home had not come in much contact with the other minorities. We have seen that World War II brought Negroes in numbers to the West Coast for the first time, often to fill positions and to occupy homes made available by the evacuation of the Japanese. The return of the Japanese thus afforded a situation ripe for antagonism between the two groups. However, Rose writes, "Reports indicate that Negroes and Japanese are now living amicably side by side in West Coast cities." [50]

Of the other minorities, Negroes have come in contact most often with Jews. Lacking a strong "color" consciousness, Jews have more often sought to do business with Negroes and by their more cordial attitude have been more successful than other white groups. By that very fact, however, Jews have laid themselves open to the criticism that by opening enterprises in Negro areas they have retarded the efforts of Negroes to become enterprisers themselves; and to the feeling that their main interest in Negroes is in making money out of them. According to Sheppard's study of Negro businessmen in Chicago, struggling Negro merchants find anti-Semitism a useful weapon in their competition for customers.[51] Among the Jewish liberal and intellectual circles, particularly in the period following World War II, a tendency to recognize the common interest of all minorities is to be noted, and is reflected in the programs and research projects undertaken by organizations whose major interest is the reduction of anti-Semitism.

Of the various European nationality groups in the Northeast, it is the Italians with whom Negroes have been in closest contact. In the absence of systematic study of the relations between these two groups, the (present) writer offers the following comments. Following

[49] Arnold Rose, *The Negro's Morale* (Minneapolis: University of Minnesota Press, 1949).
[50] *Ibid.*, p. 128. See also *supra*, p. 291.
[51] Harold L. Sheppard, "The Negro Merchant: A Study of Negro Anti-Semitism," *American Journal of Sociology*, LIII (Sept. 1947) pp. 96-99.

the Great Migration, the relations between these two groups who so often resided near one another, were on the whole friendly. As time went on, the social atmosphere changed bordering at present in some communities upon antagonism. While the repercussions of the Ethiopian-Italian conflict abroad upon the sentiments of Negroes and Italians in the United States precipitated some antagonism, the change in relations is more basically related to the difference in the operation of the assimilative process respecting the two groups. Italians were not considered categorically unassimilable; Negroes have been so considered. Part of the process of assimilation is the adoption of the normative white American standards. These include the conception of Negroes as permanently an inferior and separate group. Thus Italians, as well as other white ethnic groups, in the process of becoming Americanized tend to adopt the normative attitudes toward Negroes.

Our analysis suggests that the relations between Negroes and the other minorities are ambivalent. On the one hand, the common bond of minority status tends to prompt some members of another non-Negro minority to identify their interests with the case of Negroes; on the other hand, since the door is open for the full assimilation of the noncolored minorities, disassociating their interests from those of the nonassimilable Negroes hastens their entrance into dominant status.

The present situation in summary. The present situation in Negro-white relations in the United States presents two outstanding aspects: These relations are in an extraordinary state of flux; and the direction of change is inclined sharply toward elimination of discrimination. In concluding the discussion of Negro-white relations, we summarize the factors and forces present in the current social scene which operate to produce this situation; and follow with a summary of the counter forces operating to retard this trend.

Outstanding among forces upsetting the prewar equilibrium of Negro-white relations and pressing for readjustment upon a more equalitarian level are: (1) the dynamics of democracy; (2) the continued prosperous condition of the American economy; (3) the position of the United States in the United Nations; and (4) the cumulative effects of Negro advance upon Negroes themselves.

1. The democratic process inevitably presses toward its own greater fulfilment. Thus the agencies of democratic government tend toward increasing consistency between stated principles and actual behavior. This has been strikingly demonstrated in the past few years by Supreme Court decisions which one by one undermine the specific basis of discrimination.

2. The continued high level of employment, the sustained purchasing power, and the increasing trend toward greater individual economic security have kept to a minimum the motivation to discriminate generated by the feeling of insecurity. This is reflected in the tendency toward acceptance of Negroes into white unions.

3. In the United Nations, the representatives of the United States are more closely allied with those nations who, on the whole, are working toward the expansion of freedom and equality for the colored peoples of the world. This role in international affairs inevitably constrains the Federal Government toward a similar policy in regard to its own domestic minorities. It further constrains wide segments of the American people to view our minorities problem in a newly evaluated light.

4. Each new Negro advance has a cumulative effect upon the behavior of Negroes, which further accelerates the trend. Each advance encourages Negroes to press for more. Each advance helps to destroy the illusion of the white stereotype of the Negro. The categorical inferiority of Negroes is undermined by each individual demonstration of equality in performance. The successful integration of Negroes into a mixed union undermines such familiar clichés as "whites won't work with Negroes."

Among the forces and factors in the current situation which operate to retard the present trend toward increasing equality for Negroes are: (1) the cumulative effect of tradition; (2) the economic motivations for discrimination in specific groups; and (3) the effect upon Negroes of their long possessed minority status.

1. Traditional attitudes and patterns of conduct tend to carry on of their own momentum. Tradition in the United States defines the Negro as inferior and sanctions discrimination along the lines of caste in the South and in terms of dominant-minority relations in the rest of the country. Traditions change but they do not change easily or rapidly.

2. We shall discuss in more detail in Chapter 16 the influence of economic motivations upon discrimination toward minorities in general. Our analysis there leads us to conclude that the private enterprise system does not consistently operate toward such discrimination. It is however clear that in the present situation there are specific groups who have a strong, direct pecuniary interest in maintaining discrimination, for example, owners of cotton-growing land, and real estate interests in particular communities. Such economic groups tend to resist the trend toward equality. Still further, there are special groups and particular individuals within the Negro group itself who have strong personal economic and status interests in retaining segregation. To

maintain their influence upon other Negroes, these individuals must openly espouse the aspiration for ultimate equality for Negroes. But it is asking much of human nature to expect that they should want to see all segregation disappear tomorrow.

3. The impact of minority status upon Negroes continues to develop in the personality structure of the Negro people attitudes and behavior patterns which retard their own advancement. As we have noted before, this is a circular process. Being born and reared under adverse welfare conditions and restricted in freedom of activity by the system of dominant discrimination, Negroes tend to develop behavior patterns which in various ways keeps them a minority. The widely prevalent apathy precludes their active cooperation with those social action groups who would advance their cause. The greater prevalence among them of behavior defined by the white groups as disorderly further confirms the white stereotype of the Negro.

Other significant trends in American society deserve consideration for their possible effects upon the future course of Negro-white relations. For example, we call attention to the hypothesis noted in recent sociological literature that class lines in the United States are growing less flexible.[52] It is possible that this trend, if it be validated, will retard the rising advance of Negroes. We shall consider the implications of this trend in our general interpretation in Chapter 16. The fact is that Negroes have advanced rapidly in the 1940–1950 decade while this tightening of class lines has been continuing.

Also deserving attention is the possible effect of the sharply poised struggle against Communism upon the trend of Negro-white relations. Based on past experience the increasing employment resulting from an accelerated armament production, and the heightening of the sense of national unity which the presence of a foreign threat always engenders, would be expected to sustain or accelerate the democratic trend. Against this is the experience that preoccupation with an external threat tends to divert attention from domestic reform. Since the further extension of equality to Negroes is often identified as "radical," the fear of being considered "red" may prompt a slackening of the efforts of American liberals in both racial groups to advance further the present trend.

TOPICS FOR DISCUSSION AND PROJECTS

1. Ask a number of white people in your community what changes, if any, they expect to see in Negro-white relations in their area in the next decade,

---

[52] See, for example, the discussion of trends in American social classes in W. F. Ogburn and M. F. Nimkoff, *Sociology* (Boston: Houghton Mifflin Company, 1950), pp. 156-158.

and why. Report your answers. In each case, identify the sex, age, occupation, and religion of the respondent.

2. Do you think the rapid trend toward greater opportunity for Negroes occurring in the North since World War II will continue at the same pace in the next decade? Develop whichever position you take on the question.

3. Consult appropriate sources for material concerning the integration of Negroes into the armed services since World War II and report on your findings.

4. Consult appropriate sources for material on housing projects where both white and Negro tenants have been accepted. Report on the planning and results so far of such projects.

5. Consult Supreme Court decisions since 1935 in cases involving alleged discrimination against Negroes. Develop fully the implications of these decisions upon the future of Negro-white relations in the United States.

SUGGESTED READING

Davie, Maurice. *Negroes in American Society*. New York: McGraw-Hill Book Company, Inc., 1949.
> *In Chapters 21 and 22, "The Future of the Negro," the author predicts a slow but steady advancement of the position of Negroes in the democratic direction.*

Frazier, Franklin E. *The Negro in the United States*. New York: The Macmillan Company, 1949.
> *Chapter 28, Prospects for Integration of the Negro into American Society," stresses the interrelation of the Negro's prospects with the developments of America's position in world affairs.*

Logan, Rayford W. ed. *What the Negro Wants*. Chapel Hill: University of North Carolina Press, 1944.
> *Fourteen Negro leaders indicate the Negro wants first-class citizenship.*

Moon, Henry L. *The Balance of Power: The Negro Vote*. New York: Doubleday & Company, Inc., 1948.
> *Summarizing the position of Negroes in American politics, this book reveals the extent to which Negroes are able to manipulate their vote for the purpose of improving their group's position.*

Myrdal, Gunnar, et. al. *An American Dilemma*. New York: Harper and Brothers, 1944.
> *Chapter 43, "America at the Crossroads," shows how the prospects in Negro-white relations looked to the distinguished Swedish scholar in 1944.*

Rose, Arnold. *The Negro in America*. New York: Harper and Brothers, 1948.
> *Chapter 19, "America at the Crossroads," is an abbreviated presentation paralleling the last chapter of the Myrdal volume with, however, later developments.*

"Segregation," *Survey Graphic*, Vol. 36, No. 1, January 1947.
> *Entire issue devoted to describing Negro-white relations in the United States.*

PART FOUR

Ward-Wardship Relations

In the next two chapters, minority situations are described which may be distinguished from those yet considered by the fact that the dominant group assumes and acknowledges certain specific obligations toward the minority. While de facto patterns of paternalism, on the one hand, and dependence, on the other, have emerged in other minority situations, as for example, in the case of the tenant farmer and his landlord in the South, the obligations of the dominant in such cases are not explicit. The designation ward-wardship pattern seems the best term to describe this type of situation, of which the clearest example is the relation between the Indians of the United States and the Federal Government. Likewise the status of the peoples of the territories acquired by the United States in its 20th century expansion which have not been given statehood, Hawaii and Puerto Rico, and formerly the Philippines, approaches in some respects this ward-wardship type. The Indian situation will be analyzed in Chapter 12 and the situation of the territorial peoples in Chapter 13.

Indians in the United States

Anglo-Latin contrasts. A broad review of the relations between the Indians of the Americas and the white Europeans who invaded their domain reveals significant contrasts in the areas dominated by the conquerors from the Latin nations and those dominated by the English. The Spaniards employed various devices to force the Indians to work for them. While their labor exploitation greatly decimated the Indian population, the population of the Spanish American areas are composed today in substantial measure either of Indians or of mestizos. In the Latin American nations which Gillen has described as Mestizo America, are to be found today many Indian groups who remain distinctively Indian in their culture. But the large mestizo populations of these nations indicate that, to a far greater extent than north of the Rio Grande, the descendants of the Indians of colonial times have been integrated into the general national societies, largely into the peon class. The general cultures of Mestizo America have therefore pronounced Indian influences.

In contrast, the English settlers in North America pushed the Indians off the land to work it themselves, subsequently with the aid in the South of Negro slaves. As in Latin America, the Indian population in the United States was greatly decimated but more as a result of unsuccessful warfare with the whites and the expropriation of their land and resources rather than through harsh conditions of slavery or peonage. Again as in Latin America, many Indian societies survived and retained their tribal cultures. But they survived largely on the fringes of the new North American society, apart from it rather than as a part of it.

As a consequence of this broadly contrasting pattern of Indian-white relations in the two areas, the problems arising likewise differ. In Mestizo America, the groups remaining Indian in their ways of life constitute substantial portions of the population; and the welfare of such groups effects in high degree the welfare of the nations involved.[1] The problems of the large mestizo group are not peculiarly Indian but are interrelated with the broad problems of class difference and the development of democratic institutions. In the United States and Canada, on the other hand, the Indian problem is more particularistic in its nature and minor in its dimension. The special character of the Indian problem in the United States is attested by the establishment of the Indian Service as a branch of the Federal Government with no counterpart in all the other minority situations. Its minor place is seen in that the Service concerns itself with less than 0.5 per cent of the total national population.

Racial characteristics. The aborigines of the American continents are generally classified in racial terms as a variety of the Mongolian stock. Their distinguishing physiognomic features, according to Kroeber, are: straight hair, slight facial and body hair, variable in head form, medium in nasal index, medium in prognathism, brown skin color, tall to medium in height, and generally broad faced. Having migrated to the Americas beginning perhaps 18 thousand years ago and having subsequently been hemispherically endogamous down to 1492, the Indians developed a type distinguishable from the original Asiatic strains. It is interesting that Kroeber considers the Indians along with present day Malaysian types earlier developments of the Mongoloid family than the so-called Mongoloid proper, typified by modern Chinese. The oblique or "Mongoloid" eye, typical of the latter, which the Indians generally lack, is considered by Kroeber as a later development.[2]

Population trends. Estimates of the number of aborigines in the Western Hemisphere at the time of the white man's coming vary widely. Lorimer cites estimates ranging from 8 to 13 million.[3] Means, how-

[1] John Gillen, "Mestizo America," in Ralph Linton, ed., *Most of the World* (New York: Columbia University Press, 1949) pp. 156-174. Mestizo America includes all the nations south of the Rio Grande, except Argentina and Uruguay, which are practically all Caucasian in composition, and Brazil, which has a proportionally smaller Indian population, and where Indians have not been as integrated into the total national life as in Spanish America.
[2] A. L. Kroeber, *Anthropology* (New York: Harcourt, Brace & Company, Inc., 1948), pp. 136-137.
[3] Frank Lorimer, "Observations on the trends of Indian population in the United States," in Oliver La Farge, ed., *The Changing Indian* (Norman: University of Oklahoma Press, 1942), p. 11.

ever, estimates the number of Indians of the Inca Consolidation alone to have been 16 million.[4]

Any estimate of the present Indian population of the Americas is exceedingly unreliable not only because of inadequate statistical counts but also because persons of varying degrees of Indian ancestry have been so largely incorporated into the common national populations that the lines of racial division have become highly obscured. Lorimer summarizes the situation as follows: "The number of pureblood Indians in the Western Hemisphere may be greater today than at the time of Columbus; with the number of persons usually considered as Indian it is almost certainly greater; and the total Indian stock, including its fractional elements in the whole population, is far greater."[5] The same author further observes: "Mestizos, or Ladinos, who draw their genetic heritage in part from Amerindian and in part from other stocks now outnumber pureblood Indians both in Latin America and in the United States."[6]

Estimates of the number of Indians in the area now the United States, in 1492, range from 700,000 to 1,000,000. By the time Indians became official wards in 1871 their population had become decimated to below the half million point. It is generally agreed that under the impact of the earlier reservation regime, the population declined still further, reaching its lowest point around 1900 when it began to rise again. In the official census count, these trends are reflected in the following figures:

TABLE 23

Indian Population[7]

1890	248,253
1920	244,437
1940	333,369
1947 *est.*	402,000

Most students of Indian affairs consider the census count an underestimate. For example, as against the 1940 census figure given above, the Department of Indian Affairs reported 401,384 on their rolls in 1943, and estimate the entire Indian population at above 430,000.

[4] Philip A. Means, *Ancient Civilizations of the Andes* (New York: Charles Scribner's Sons, 1931).
[5] Lorimer, *loc cit.*, p. 11. By permission.
[6] *Ibid.*, p. 12.
[7] U. S. Census, 1940, Vol. II, p. 19; and *Estimates of Non-White Population of Continental United States, by Race, 1940–1947*, Series P-25, No. 23.

The difficulties in determining the actual number of Indians stem from the problem of definition, particularly in regard to the classification of mixed bloods. Census enumerators are instructed "to return as Indians, not only those of full Indian blood, but also those of mixed white and Indian blood, except where the percentage of Indian blood is very small or where the individual is regarded as a white person in the community where he lives." [8] On the other hand, persons of whatever admixture of Caucasian genetic strains, or in many instances, of Indian-Negro mixture, who have remained in the tribes and therefore on the Indian Service rolls are considered Indian because they live as Indians. Clearly this problem of definition complicates the problem of predicting the future Indian population, a matter of important concern in the light of present Indian policy. Adapting estimates made for the National Resources Committee, Lorimer finds that they would call for a legal Indian population in 1980 of about 700,000.[9] While the death rates of the Indians, as well as their birth rates, are above the average for the national population, the rate of growth of the Indian population is greater than that of the total population.[10] The future size of the Indian population depends not only on national growth but also upon the extent to which mixed bloods choose to remain "Indian" or to pass into the white world. In any event, the number of mixed bloods in the present legal Indian population is increasing, a fact which prompts Shapiro to write, "Already many of the Indian wards of the state are more white or more Negro than Indian, and this anomaly is likely to become more and more frequent." [11]

The intelligence of Indians. A number of earlier studies in which the intelligence of Indians as measured by intelligence tests in comparison with either white norms or actual white groups showed results broadly below the white norms, and the greater the extent of white admixture the higher the scores.[12] The interpretation of the results of the Indian-white comparisons with those of the Negro-white presents similar problems. Like the Negroes, Indians have a depressed economic environment and lack motivation to perform their best on the tests. The linguistic difficulties are even greater in connection with Indians than in the case of Negroes, and in general, the Indian cultural background is more divergent than that of any other minorities. For example, in one "logical selection" test an item read: Crowd (closeness,

[8] H. L. Shapiro, "The Mixed-Blood Indian," in LaFarge, *op. cit.*, p. 20.
[9] Lorimer, *loc. cit.*, p. 14.
[10] See Laura Thompson, "Personality and Government," *America Indigena,* Vol. 10, No. 2, Nos. 3 and 4 (1950) for further details on Indian vital statistics.
[11] Shapiro, *loc. cit.*, p. 26.
[12] See Otto Klineberg, *Characteristics of the American Negro* (New York: Harper and Brothers, 1944), pp. 70-71 and also pp. 86-88 for a brief summary of comparative Indian-white mental test studies.

danger, dust, excitement, number), the correct answer is *closeness* and *number*. Many Indian children chose *danger* and *dust*. From the experiential background of Plains Indian life, these Indian answers are just as logical as the officially correct ones. While these considerations militate against a racial interpretation of the "inferiority" of Indians as indicated from the earlier tests, more recent findings coming from a comprehensive testing program of Indians made by Shailer Peterson clearly dispute the notion of their inferiority. Samples of these findings are as follows:

One group of Hopi children had an average IQ of 112 and a second had 111, both on the Arthur Scale. These two groups measured 111 and 117 on the Goodenough test. White children scored an average IQ of 103 on the Arthur test and 101 on the Goodenough.

Pine Ridge Sioux children had a range of from 101 on the Arthur to 114 on the Goodenough.

Every Indian group had a higher average on the Goodenough test than the white children.[13]

The summary findings reported by Laura Thompson[14] show some Indian groups with lower ranges and averages than those just quoted above. But the over-all results of mental testing of Indians provide no basis for making, in their case, any exception to the general conclusion elsewhere stated concerning the relative intelligence of racial groups. For all practical purposes, it may be assumed that taken as a group, Indians are innately as capable as any other racial group.

Present distribution of the Indian population. While there are people classified by the census as Indian in every state in the Union, our interest focuses upon those who live as Indians in groups. Some Indian landholdings are to be found in 32 of the 48 states. The areas of their distribution can be summarized as follows:

1. *The Southwest.* Primarily Arizona and western New Mexico. Major groups are the Navaho, Hopi, Papago, Pueblo, and Apache.
2. *California and the Northwest.* An intermittent scattering of Indian tribes through California, Nevada, and Utah, including many Shoshone and Paiute. A further intermittent but less wide scattering of reservations in Washington, Oregon, Idaho, Montana, and Wyoming.
3. *The North Central.* The area of greatest concentration here is in South Dakota with its large Sioux population, followed by substantial reservations

[13] Cited in the *Annual Report of the Secretary of the Interior* for the Fiscal Year ending June 30, 1948 (Washington, U. S. Government Printing Office, p. 383) from Dr. Shailer Peterson's findings.
[14] Thompson, *loc. cit.*

in North Dakota and Minnesota and scattered small bands in Nebraska and Iowa on the south and in Wisconsin and Michigan on the east.

4. *Oklahoma*. It is not surprising that this former Indian territory has more Indians than any other one state, only exceeded by the Southwest region. Linked with this area may be considered the small bands in northern Kansas.

5. *North Carolina*. While some small Indian groups are located in widely scattered places in Texas, Louisiana, Mississippi, Alabama, Florida, South Carolina, and Virginia, the Cherokee tribes of North Carolina far outdistance in total population all other Indian groups combined in the South.

6. *New York*. Of the relatively few Indians to be found in the Northeast, most of them are located in the rural areas of New York State, including the Seneca, the Onondaga, and the Tonawanda. Very small bands may be found in Rhode Island and in Maine.[15]

INDIAN SOCIETIES AND CULTURES

From the viewpoint of current minority problems, it is more important for the Americans of dominant status to understand the culture and personality of Indians than similar characteristics of immigrant groups. The latter, as we have seen, early desire to become American and are now, for the most part, nearly assimilated. In considerable measure, Indians do not want to become assimilated. The future of Indian culture and welfare depends very largely upon the policy adopted by the white population. No policy will be successful which is not based upon a reasonable understanding of Indian culture. To acquire such an understanding is immeasurably complicated by the fact that Indian culture is not one but a variety of cultures developed over thousands of years before the white man's coming and greatly changed by the presence of the white man in their continental domain. Space permits here only a brief tracing of the post-Columbian development of Indian societies and a general statement of their characteristics.

At the time of discovery by the European invader, there existed north of the Rio Grande in the area to become the United States, more than 600 distinct tribal societies. Contrary to the trend in Mexico and South America toward consolidation, the North American natives had remained in small units. Further, the process of subjugation of the North American Indians tended to keep them distinct from each other and to retard their acculturation to colonial societies. In spite of this, nevertheless, the general principle that cultural diffusion always takes place when different peoples meet, was operative between the Indian and white societies. Illustrative of the influence of white culture upon the Indians are Radin's comments:

[15] G. E. E. Lindquist, *The Indian in American Life* (New York: Friendship Press, 1944). This volume contains a map showing Indian tribes and reservations in the U. S.

The use of iron, the adoption of the horse, and the impact of Christianity and of European culture in general, often produced new expansions of native culture that were rarely felt by the Indians themselves to be anything but legitimate extensions and growths of their own civilizations. . . .

In the United States proper the three outstanding examples of such new developments and recreations are the Iroquois, the Southwestern Pueblos, and the Navajos. The three major traits we ordinarily associate with the last tribe—sheep-herding, silverwork and blankets—all represent borrowings from the Spaniards. Practically all the great rituals, so distinctive of their life today, come from other Indian tribes with whom they have come into contact indirectly through the intermediation of their white conquerors. And yet no Navajo would understand what an anthropologist or an historian meant if he pointed out that most of what he possessed today had come to him from non-Navajo sources.[16]

Among the many elements of white culture which the North American Indians borrowed to which Wissler calls special attention are the horse, the gun, and alcohol drinking.[17] Of these, the horse was clearly the most useful. For example, on the Great Plains where the hunting of buffalo constituted a main economic activity the greater speed and safety which the horse provided was highly advantageous. The role of the gun was more ambivalent. Its value for hunting and for warfare with other tribes was in part offset by its very efficiency. It promoted too great a decimation of Indian populations and likewise of the game. The drinking of alcohol which Indian tribes first learned from the white man was altogether a disorganizing influence, the more so because with no previous experience with this beverage, the Indian cultures lacked mores to control its use within reasonable limits.

The contributions of the Indian to the normative American culture and indeed to world culture have been more considerable than the average American probably realizes. We draw upon Wissler for a summary account.[18] In the material realm first may be noted the many food plants introduced to the white man by the Indian—maize, potato, kidney bean, tomato, peanut, tobacco, chocolate, and many others. The Indians are credited with the original use of such medicinal plants as cascara, cocaine, and quinine. Among the inventions used by the colonists, many of which are still used today, were hammocks, birchbark canoes, maple sugar, snowshoes, moccasins, and toboggans. The American English language has been enriched by the adoption of

[16] From *The Story of the American Indian* by Paul Radin. Published by Liveright Publishing Corporation, New York City. Price $2.98. Copyright, 1934 and 1944, by the Liveright Publishing Corporation, pp. 374-375.
[17] Clark Wissler, *Indians of the United States* (Garden City, L. I.: Doubleday & Company, Inc., 1946), Ch. 20.
[18] Clark Wissler, "Contributions of the American Indians," in Francis J. Brown and Joseph S. Roucek, eds., *One America* (New York: Prentice-Hall, Inc., 1946), Ch. 32.

many words either from the original Indian or in adaptation, to mention a few, powwow, council fire, ambush, wigwam, and whole phrases as, run the gauntlet, bury the hatchet, smoke the pipe of peace. Further in the nonmaterial realm is the contribution of Indian art directly and indirectly. "In the use of geometric patterns and flat even tones the Indian was a genius, and so characteristic is the decorative style of his pottery, basketry, and textiles that they are easily recognizable on sight." Finally, the Indians have stimulated the intellectual development of the new North American society. For example, the development of anthropology stemmed largely from studies of American Indian tribes and the numerous problems presented by their languages, their origins, and the distribution of their culture traits.

General characteristics of Indian societies. Notwithstanding the difficulties of generalizing about such widely varying cultures, certain broad characteristics of Indian societies may be noted with especial reference to their contrast with the cultures of the white invaders. In delineating these characteristic features, we shall ignore changes effected during the whole wardship period.

1. The Indian cultures were all preliterate. Thus knowledge and mores were inculcated through the spoken word and the teaching of youth by the elders.

2. While all preliterate societies appear small scale in contrast to modern societies, Indian societies north of the Rio Grande tended to be small even by primitive standards. Tribal relationships were almost entirely personal and the Indians lacked experience with those secondary, impersonal, formalized relationships characteristic of larger scale civilization.

3. The Indian economies were primarily hunting and gathering economies, with fishing in certain appropriate areas. Hoe agriculture was practiced among the eastern tribes and in the Southwest where the maize growing complex was more prevalent. Even where hoe agriculture was practiced, it was usual for the women to perform the gardening tasks,[19] a point to keep in mind when, later, efforts were made to transform Indian men into farmers. The attitudes taken by the nonagricultural Indians toward the land is revealed in the words of Wowoka, a Nevadan Indian who founded a new religion among the western Indians in the 19th century.

"You ask me to plow the ground," he said, "Shall I take a knife and tear my mother's bosom? Then when I die she will not take me to her bosom to rest.

[19] Robert H. Lowie, *Primitive Society* (New York: Liveright Publishing Corporation, 1947), p. 75.

"You ask me to cut grass and make hay and sell it, and be rich like white men but how dare I cut my mother's hair?" [20]

4. In the organization of economic life, the Indian societies were generally communal rather than individualistic. While individuals frequently owned items of personal adornment and also many forms of incorporeal property such as the right to sing certain songs and to certain crests, the land itself and the flora and fauna which furnished their living were thought of as belonging to the groups as a whole. Whatever individualism in economy existed was clearly qualified in terms of tribal interest. It was inconceivable that any individual member of the tribe should lack the necessities of life as long as they were available to anyone else.

5. Although Indian societies were often elaborately differentiated along kinship lines, there was lacking marked distinction in those forms of status which connote inferiority and superiority. Even in those few instances, illustrated by the Northwest Coast Indians (in Canada), where marked class distinctions were present, the actual standard of living, measured in terms of necessities of life, did not vary greatly from commoner to noble. Likewise among the Indians of the United States, individual power was greatly limited. Comparing the position among four widely contrasting North American tribes, Goldenweiser writes, "in no case is he [the chief] permitted to exercise actual control over the actions of his people—barring such drastic situations as war or other temporary exploits—and that in his daily life he is scarcely distinguishable from any of his subjects." [21] Thus the Indians of the United States were equalitarian, more generally so than preliterate cultures in other areas.

6. Life presented to the Indian many fearful experiences and in the absence of scientific explanations, tragedy and disaster or good fortune were thought of as being caused by spirits. Therefore, elaborate ceremonies developed whose purpose was to ward off the evil spirits and to propitiate the good. The behavior of the individual was rigidly controlled in the interest of the group. The in-group ethics of each tribe were comparable to these of in-group folk ethics of historic peoples but likewise did not apply when dealing with outsiders.

RELATIONS OF INDIANS TO WHITE AMERICANS

Among all the minorities in American society, the Indians hold a unique status, acquired in 1871, as official wards of the Federal Gov-

[20] Radin, *op. cit.*, p. 368. By permission of the Liveright Publishing Corporation.
[21] Alexander Goldenweiser, *Early Civilization* (New York: Alfred A. Knopf, Inc., 1922), p. 120.

ernment. Therefore, a description of white-Indian relations falls into
two parts: (1) the relation of Indians to the Government and (2) the
informal, noninstitutionalized relations of white people and Indians,
especially in the areas where the two groups live close together and
come into more direct interpersonal relations.

Indians and the white government. The ancestors of the Indians of
present day United States came in contact with four groups of white
people, the Spaniards, the French, the English, and the Dutch. The
Spaniards, as has been indicated, although quite ruthless when necessary to their interests, aimed at integrating the Indians into the new
Spanish American civilization. Since the French came primarily to
trade rather than to settle, they aimed on the whole to keep on friendly
terms with the Indians. The French interfered little with the Indians,
and those who remained borrowed much of the Indian culture. They
frequently made permanent marriages with Indian women. In the
struggle between the French and the English for control of the eastern portion of North America, various Indian tribes became involved
on opposite sides thus sometimes pitting Indian against Indian in a
conflict in which they were to become the losers whichever European
power prevailed. Since the English finally prevailed, further discussion
will be limited to their relations with the Indians.[22]

The period of community diplomacy: 1607–1778. During the colonial
period, each local English or Dutch settlement dealt with the Indians
by whatever means seemed best to it. In Virginia, the first settlement
which began in 1607 lay within the territory of the Powhatan Con-
federacy. Its chieftain, Waukunsenecaw, left the small white group in
peace. When, however, a new wave of settlers appeared, the succeeding
chief, Opechancanough, fought to drive them out. But in 1644 he was
decisively beaten.[23] In Massachusetts, peace prevailed between the
Indians and the white men for more than 10 years, in part because of
an illness which heavily depopulated the tribes nearest the shores.
Again, however, as the white settlers became more numerous and began
to press westward, many tribes grew hostile. While in some cases Indian
resistance was temporarily successful, the ultimate outcome was always
white victory.

In 1754, the British Crown formulated a policy for dealing with the
Indians which took jurisdiction away from the individual colonies or

---

[22] The Dutch established the policy of buying the land from the Indians, as in the
case of the world famous purchase of Manhattan Island for a purported $24. The
Quakers in Pennsylvania developed a friendly policy with the Indians and tended,
in the early days at least, to fulfill with scrupulous honesty the bargains they made.
[23] From *Indians of the Americas* by John Collier, copyright, 1947, by John Collier
(New York: Mentor Books, The New American Library of World Literature, Inc.,
1947) p. 114.

border groups. Under this policy, "the tribes were independent nations, under the protection of the Crown; Indian lands were inalienable except through voluntary surrender to the Crown; and any attempt by an individual or group, subject to the Crown, or by a foreign state, to buy or seize lands from Indians, was illegal." [24] The attempt of the British Government to carry out this policy amidst innumerable local violations increased the antagonism of the colonists, especially those in the border areas, toward the Crown. Thus the Indians indirectly contributed to the final issue of the American Revolution.

Period of control by treaties, 1778–1871. This policy of the British Crown was in essence taken over by the new American Government. For the first hundred years of the national period, the relation of the Indian tribes to the Federal Government was characterized by treaties, nominally negotiated by the Government with so-called sovereign Indian nations. Whenever the Indians failed to agree with what the Government wanted, they were met with military force. Frequently special local groups moved against the Indians irrespective of the National Government as when the Georgia Legislature passed an act confiscating all Cherokee land and declaring their tribal laws invalid within the state. Persistently when the white people rode roughshod over their own treaties, the Indians fought back, and a number of Indian wars of considerable dimension took place east of the Mississippi. The Seminole War in Florida and the Black Hawk War in Illinois Territory were among the more famous. The final outcome east of the Mississippi was that most of the Indian tribes were forced into the newly established Indian Territory, now the state of Oklahoma. The exceptions were a few small, relatively harmless bands in Maine, New York, Virginia, Florida, and a considerable number of Cherokees in North Carolina who put up so much resistence that they were left alone in the wilds of the Smoky Mountain Region.

West of the Mississippi, much of the story of Indian-white relations centers around, first, the situation in California following the Gold Rush and second, about the subjugation of the Plains Indians throughout the vast Midwest. In California, the white men in search of gold drove the Indians out of any area they wanted by force. From 1851 on the Federal Government negotiated treaties with many local tribes by which the Indians agreed to surrender more than half of California. These treaties, due to frontier political pressure, were never ratified by the Senate and the Government subsequently sold to white people much of the land pledged to the Indians. The subjugation of the Plains Indians is described by Collier in these terms:

[24] *Ibid.,* pp. 116-117.

Contact between the government and most of the Plains tribes dated from the close of the American Civil War. Beginning about 1870, a leading aim of the United States was to destroy the Plains Indians' societies through destroying their religions; and it may be that the world has never witnessed a religious persecution so implacable and so variously implemented. The successive and evolving reactions of the Indians to the irresistible proscription supplied a moving chapter to the religious history of mankind.

The assault against the tribal and intertribal religions was part of an all-out offensive against Indian land and society. The offensive, including its religious part, reached far beyond the Plains region, but nowhere else was it so intense. The main features of what may be called the secular part of the onset can be briefly indicated.

First there was military assault, on slight pretexts or no pretexts at all, and the government exploited tribal rivalries in order that Indians should kill Indians. The limited and disciplinary war customs of the Plains turned into total warfare, aimed at annihilation, with the United States Army as the driving power. The tribes were finally beaten, however, not through overwhelming numbers or superior armament (though these existed) but through starvation after the whites had destroyed the buffalo. . . . That revelry of slaughter, which had no sportsmanship in it, was recognized as a war measure against the Indians and was deliberately encouraged.[25]

Reservation period: phase one; forced assimilation. In 1871, Congress decreed that no Indian tribe "shall be acknowledged or recognized as an independent nation, tribe or power, with whom the United States may contract by treaty." [26] This marks the beginning of a definitely new phase in Indian-white relations. The Indians were now wards of the United States. The policy and practices of the Indian Office from now on were aimed at weakening the tribal organization of the Indians, destroying their culture, and forcing the assimilation of Indians as individuals into the normative American way of life. After several years of public and congressional debate, a new land policy was adopted with the passage of the famous Dawes Act in 1887. This legislation empowered the President to divide the lands of any tribe by giving allotted individual portions to family heads or other individuals. These plots so allotted were, however, to be held in trust for 25 years after which they were to become the unrestricted property of each owner. In the meantime they could not be sold. Allegedly the object of this program was to force each Indian breadwinner to become a self-supporting individual by working his own land. In the meantime the Indians were to be supported directly by the Government.

[25] *Ibid.*, p. 133. By permission of the author, John Collier.
[26] Ray Allen Billington, *Westward Expansion* (New York: The Macmillan Company, 1949), p. 668. Chapter 32, "The Indian Barrier," pp. 651-670, describes the history of Indian-white relations from 1860 to 1887.

The effect of the land allotment policy was extremely disastrous to the Indians. The Indians did not possess the technical knowledge to make their holdings pay. They lacked the credit with which to acquire materials needed to operate the land. Further difficulties were created concerning the division of land through inheritance. Finally the policy called for selling any "surplus" left over after allotments to white people. While some Indians made an attempt to make a living on their allotments, many chose the easier course of leasing their land to white people. For example, white graziers would rent a large number of contiguous allotments and then operate a range. Over the entire period in which this allotment policy was operative (1887–1914), the lands held by the Indians shrank from about 138,000,000 to 47,000,000 acres.[27]

Another phase of the policy of forced assimilation concerns the educational program. Indian children at school age were taken out of their tribal homes and placed in boarding schools. Here the use of Indian languages and the practice of Indian ways, such as dress and hair styles, were forbidden. The curricula of the schools were largely that of the white schools of the times without any adaptation to the particular needs of the Indians. In Macgregor's opinion, whatever practical training the Indian children obtained either for making a living or making better homes was gained from the labor they performed to help support the school.[28] Thus a not too-efficient school system tried to prepare Indian children to live like white people, although in fact most of them left the schools to return home to live as Indians.

In retrospect this first phase of the Indian reservation policy can be viewed as a failure. When it was replaced by the New Deal policy in 1934, it is a fair question whether the over-all Indian problem was any nearer solution than it was in 1887. From the economic point of view the Indians were a pauperized people. The education which the younger Indians had received had made them marginal individuals not yet ready to take their place in the white American world but also unsettled for Indian life. The health of the Indians was subnormal although it improved somewhat toward the later part of this period. This policy failed in part because it attempted the rapid, forced acculturation of one cultural group to another, a procedure which social science now knows cannot be done. It is least surprising that such a policy should have failed when applied to the Indians, whose cultures were more markedly divergent from white American culture than in the case of any other minority. For example, many well meaning

[27] Ward Shepard, "Land Problems of an Expanding Indian Population," in LaFarge, *op. cit.*, p. 76.
[28] Gordon Macgregor, "Indian Education in Relation to the Social and Economic Background of the Reservation," in LaFarge, *op. cit.*, pp. 116-127.

white people could not understand why it should be so difficult to teach Indian men to be hardworking, competitive, economic individualists—to the white American the proper way of economic life—in contrast to the traditionally established Indian way of working together for the interests of the group. That Indians should desert their jobs when working for white people in order to participate in their tribal ceremonies on the accustomed date was construed by many whites to be an example of the Indian's incorrigible laziness.

The first reservation policy further fell short of its object because of inefficient administration. The Indian Service, particularly in the earlier years of this period, was not conspicuous for the high standards of its personnel. Nor was a particular interest in Indians and their welfare a prerequisite for employment in the Service. Furthermore, the appropriations granted it were inadequate to the task. Even when well-intentioned officials attempted to carry out a badly conceived policy, they were beset with powerful pressures from special interests to twist the policy to the latter's advantage. Finally, underlying all these factors accounting for the failure was the characteristic race consciousness of dominant status Americans which saw Indians as "colored" peoples and therefore, like all nonwhite people, as inferior. Even among the more acculturated Indians, the color prejudice militated against their adjustment to white society.

During the 1920's, constant pressures were brought to bear by certain vested white interests to procure legislation which would have expropriated further the rights of Indians to their resources. These efforts were defeated and as one result of the publicity attending the hearings in this connection, a comprehensive study of the problems of the administration of Indian affairs was undertaken in 1927 by a private agency, the Institute for Government Research, at the request of Secretary of the Interior, Hubert Work. The findings of this study, usually known as the Merriam Survey, went far to create a more favorable attitude toward the Indians.[29] In the Hoover administration, Government policy was orientied toward a more genuine concern in protecting Indian interest. This changing attitude was most specifically expressed in the revamping of the educational program for Indian children.

Reservation period: phase two; the "New Deal." The phrase "New Deal" coined to characterize the earlier years of Franklin D. Roosevelt's administration was peculiarly apt with reference to Indian affairs. While the time was ripe in 1933 for reorganization of Indian policy, the sweeping character of the changes undertaken at this time was in considerable measure due to a long standing sympathetic interest in

[29] *The Problem of Indian Administration,* Institute for Government Research (Baltimore: John Hopkins Press, 1928).

Indians of the new Secretary of the Interior, Harold I. Ickes, and to the appointment of John Collier as Commissioner of the Bureau of Indian Affairs.

The Philosophy. Back of the efforts which culminated in the passage of the Indian Reorganization Act, sponsored by Senator Burton Wheeler of Montana, was the new philosophy concerning Indians held by the new Commissioner and strongly supported by the new Federal Administration. In essence, this philosophy aimed at integrating Indians into the national life as Indians, to make Indian groups as such self-sustaining and yet retain as much of their tribal culture and group identification as was consistent with life in a modern civilized nation. Collier not only admired the Indians as persons but held the conviction that much of their culture should be preserved, that there was a place for Indians as Indians in a multigroup democratic society. Collier's philosophy as expressed in his own words follows:

The new Indian policy . . . seeks to reinstate the Indians as normally functioning units, individual and group, into the life of the world. It makes them equal in the management of their own affairs and the direction of their own lives.

On the purely cultural side, only sheer fanaticism would decide the further destruction of Indian languages, crafts, poetry, music, ritual, philosophy, and religion. These possessions have a significance and a beauty which grew patiently through endless generations of a people immersed in the life of nature, filled with imaginative and ethical insight into the core of being. . . .[30]

The Provisions of the Indian Reorganization Act. The point of view of the new commissioner was reflected in the Indian Reorganization Act passed by Congress in 1934, the chief provisions of which are as follows:

1. With certain qualifications, Indian societies were to be empowered to undertake political, economic, and administrative self-government.

2. Land allotment was to be stopped, and under certain conditions, additional lands could be added to their present holdings.

3. A system of agricultural and industrial credit was to be established, and the needed funds authorized.

4. An Indian Civil Service was to be established and provisions for the training of Indians themselves in administration and the professions were called for.

The Reorganization Bill called for the acceptance of its provisions by each tribe individually, determined on the basis of a referendum using secret ballot. Those who voted to accept could organize under it

[30] From Report of House of Representatives Subcommittee on Appropriations for the Interior Department, 1934.

for self-government and also organize themselves as a Federal corporation to conduct economic enterprise.[31]

Results from the new policies. The results which this reoriented and reinvigorated Indian policy produced are attested in recent official reports.

> *Economic Rehabilitation.* In the years since 1930, Indians have increased the acreage of crop lands farmed by themselves by 400,000 acres. In addition, they have taken over the operation of more than 7,000,000 acres of grazing land.
>
> . . . since the beginning of agricultural extension work on Indian reservations, more than 12,000 families have been completely or partially rehabilitated and are now wholly or nearly self-supporting.
>
> On loans from the United States under the revolving credit program, 96.7 per cent had been repaid at the end of last fiscal year. . . .
>
> During the calendar year, 44 million acres of Indian range lands were grazed. Of this area, 34,500,000 acres were used by Indians.
>
> Crafts furnish a significant supplemental income to thousands of Indians. Although machine-made products are increasingly competing with Indian handicrafts, there is still a flourishing demand by buyers who want handmade articles of Indian form and design.[32]

Two of the major problems faced in the efforts to rehabilitate the Indians economically have been the problem of preventing soil deterioration and the problem of depletion of the Indian land resources through the desire of many Indians to sell their land to non-Indians. In regard to the latter point while it is clear that the new policy went far to stop alienation of Indian land resources, a recent marked increase in requests by Indians to be permitted to sell their holdings is noted in the reports of the Commissioner of Indian Affairs for 1948 and 1949. After a belated start due to inadequate authority and funds, the Indian Service began a program to prevent further erosion and subsequently to improve the land, and to encourage stipulation in contracts to prevent deterioration of the lands leased by Indians to whites.

Education. The 1948 report indicates improvement in the school system for Indians in the following ways: great reduction in the "overage" number of Indian pupils, a natural problem in an uneducated group; greater facilities at the top grade levels; strengthening of teacher training requirements; and increase in teachers' salaries. The report does not indicate to what extent Indian teachers are replacing white teachers, nor to what extent Indian children are being educated in mixed schools off the reservation, data which would be pertinent measures of assimilation.

[31] Collier, *op. cit.*, pp. 157-158. By permission.
[32] Taken from *Annual Report of the Secretary of the Interior*, 1948, pp. 369-392.

Political Self-control. Under the provision that the tribes themselves should vote to accept or reject the terms of the Indian Reorganization Act, "258 tribal elections were held, in which 181 tribes adopted the law and 77 tribes rejected it. Subsequently, 93 tribes adopted written constitutions and 73 of these . . . [received] a charter of incorporation." [33] The terms of these charters usually provide that after a term of years, the supervisory rights of the Secretary of the Interior may be terminated and the tribes take over fuller independent responsibility for conducting their own business.

How the development of self-government among Indians has proceeded can be illustrated from the observations found in recent monographs studying in detail the life of three different Indian tribes: The Dakota Sioux on the Pine Ridge Reservation in southern South Dakota;[34] the Papago living on their reservation in southern Arizona;[35] and the Navaho, living in northern Arizona, the most populous of all Indian tribes whose growth at present presents a serious welfare problem.[36] The first two of these tribes organized under the Indian Reorganization Act and now operate on tribal constitutions. The Navaho rejected the terms of the act, which adds to the difficulty of helping them to become self-governing. All three of these studies indicate that the Indians are becoming more self-governing. In each case there is a Tribal Council which suggests measures of administration and approves or rejects proposals of the Agency staff; has considerable control of the tribal finances; and appoints a Tribal Court of Indian judges who try all cases of criminal law except in regard to the ten most serious offenses where the Federal court still retains jurisdiction. On the other hand, the great gap between tribal legal and political practices and those of the white democracy cannot be closed at once. For example, it was the practice of both the Navaho and the Papago to decide important matters by face-to-face meetings of all concerned in which the issues were discussed until full unanimity was reached. Under American democracy, issues are decided by majority vote. It is clear that the process of self-government for the Indians must be approached by degrees.

With reference to the voting status of Indians, the 1948 annual report of the Indian Service states, "Although all Indians . . . were made citizens by the act of June 2, 1924, seven states, as recently as

---

[33] *Ibid.,* p. 388.
[34] Gordon Macgregor, *Warriors Without Weapons* (Chicago: University of Chicago Press, 1946).
[35] Alice Joseph, Rosamond B. Spicer, and Jane Chesky, *The Desert People* (Chicago: University of Chicago Press, 1949).
[36] Clyde Kluckhohn and Dorothea Leighton, *The Navaho* (Cambridge: Harvard University Press, 1947).

1940, barred Indians from voting either by discriminatory state laws or by interpretations of state law resulting in discrimination. Five of these states had allowed their restrictive provisions to go unenforced and the Indian citizens of those states were permitted to vote." However, in 1948, "favorable court decisions in Arizona and New Mexico opened the door to full voting privileges for the approximately 100,000 Indians in those two states." Thus "it seems unlikely that any of the states in which discriminatory laws remain on the books will attempt in the future to enforce them against their Indian citizens." [37]

Indian welfare still below normal. Despite the rapid gains made by the Indians in the past two decades, their welfare is still well below the general national norms. As late as 1947, 30 per cent of the Indians were still illiterate. In nearly all the indices of health, the Indian rates show unfavorable contrasts with white population in general. For example, the Indian death rate from tuberculosis remains more than 10 times as high as that of whites. While some Indian persons and some groups became wealthy through the discovery of oil on their allotted land, most Indians are poor, economically in the bottom tenth of the population.

INTERPERSONAL RELATIONS BETWEEN INDIANS AND WHITES

The attitudes of white people toward Indians in the United States have varied widely, perhaps more so than in regard to any other minority. In the past the attitudes ranged from conceiving of the Indian as a "noble savage" to picturing him as a "savage beast." The one extreme has been expressed in literature of the Hiawatha type and in many children's books; in the Indian lore incorporated in such conventional groups as the Boy Scouts; in the contemporary "Tonto" of Lone Ranger fame. The opposite extreme is expressed in the stereotype which looks upon all Indians as cruel warriors who enjoyed scalping white people. As the Indians became "tamed" and pauperized, the range of white attitudes tended to swing from benovolent pity and sympathy at one extreme, to disdain and contempt at the other. In the absence of adequate systematic data on the point, we venture the hypothesis that in this century there has been a rough correlation between the attitudes of white people and their proximity to the Indians. By this we suggest that the concept of the Indian as a noble, mistreated person is more frequently found among those white people whose picture of the Indians has been derived from secondary sources; whereas, the notion picturing the Indian as an inferior, lazy fellow is

[37] *Annual Report of the Secretary of the Interior*, June 30, 1948, p. 391.

more widely prevalent among whites living in areas close to reservations. The studies which will presently be cited offer considerable
support to this thesis.

Race consciousness plays a part in determining white American responses to Indians, but there are some indications that negative
white reactions to the Indian's "color" is less intense than in the case of
other racial minorities. The census definition of the Indian given
above suggests that mixed-bloods with Indian genetic lineage may
"pass" as whites much more easily than Negroes. Bogardus' study of
the reactions of a sample of white Americans to 40 different ethnic and
racial groups supports the above statements. To take admission of a
member of another group to close kinship by marriage as one criterion
of acceptance, his data show that only 8 per cent of his respondents expressed a willingness to admit Indians to this degree of intimacy, a
lower percentage than applied to most nationality immigrant groups.
This supports the reality of color consciousness. On the other hand the
position of Indians in comparison with other "colored" groups is
significant. Only 2.3 per cent of the sample expressed willingness to
accept Japanese into their families, and the percentage for the other
visibly colored groups was still smaller.[38]

From these general observations, we turn now to view interpersonal
relations between Indians and their white neighbors as revealed in recent monographs on particular Indian tribes. Reservation Indians
come in contact with four categories of dominant status white people:
members of the Indian Service personnel assigned to their reservation;
traders; missionaries; white employers for whom some of the Indians
work and white neighbors among whom they sometimes dwell for
periods of time.

The Indian Service personnel. The relations of the Agency staff members to their Indian wards vary with their own personalities and attitudes toward their task. While in many instances warm friendships
develop between staff members and particular Indians, the general
impression drawn from these accounts suggests that the relations are
more official and impersonal than neighborly. Spicer finds that teachers
do not usually become intimately integrated with the Indian life in
their school community, and the effectiveness of Agency medical
workers to get Indian acceptance of modern health methods depends
upon their attitude toward Indian beliefs. Furthermore, "nominally,
every staff member . . . is accessible to any Indian who desires to talk
with him, but relatively few Indians seek such contacts." [39] Kluckhohn

[38] Emory S. Bogardus, *Immigration and Race Attitudes* (Boston: D. C. Heath &
Company, 1928), p. 25.
[39] Joseph, Spicer, and Chesky, *op. cit.*, p. 103.

and Leighton find that while some of the employees of the Indian Service are motivated by a genuine desire to help the Indians, nevertheless, a large number are thus employed largely because it is the best job they can get even though they have no real interest in Indians. "Many are highly conventional, prejudiced, and of limited imagination and flexibility." [40]

The traders. Because the traders on the reservations are the white people with whom the Indians are best acquainted, they symbolize the white world to the Indians. The character of the traders, and therefore the reaction of the Navahos to them, varied widely. Some traders are very fond of the Navahos and perform a wide variety of friendly services; others "have mercilessly and shamefully exploited the Indians' ignorance of markets and of simple arithmetic." [41] While the role of traders is declining as the Indians get to town more often, nevertheless they "are still significant in helping the Navahos market their goods, in encouraging native handicrafts, and in otherwise promoting the economic development of the tribe." [42] To the Papago, "the trader is still a main channel of white culture." [43]

The missionaries. Franciscan Fathers and a number of Protestant groups carry on missionary work among the Navahos. Of these missionaries, about 300 in number, about one-fifth are Navaho themselves. In addition to their religious activities the missionaries operate schools and hospitals and offer other social services. In their zeal to teach the Indian children English, the mission schools in some instances have forbidden their pupils to speak their native tongue anywhere about the school. Kluckhohn and Leighton find that the missionaries have made few practicing converts to Christianity. This they attribute in large measure to "their efforts to suppress native custom or to urge strenuously the substitution of white customs, oftentimes in spheres which seem to the Navahos outside the province of the missionaries." [44] The resistance and, sometimes, ridicule which the missionaries encounter in trying to make the Navahos give up their traditional ways are illustrated in the following comment of a young mission school graduate:

That missionary came here today and tried to make my husband buy a marriage license, but my husband said he didn't have a dollar. He has been trying to get my brother to buy a license for a year. The other missionary tried for two years and got tired of it. His wife said, "We're married all right.

[40] Kluckhohn and Leighton, *op. cit.*, p. 107.
[41] *Ibid.*, p. 79.
[42] *Ibid.*, p. 80.
[43] Joseph, Spicer, and Chesky, *op. cit.*, p. 96.
[44] Kluckhohn and Leighton, *op. cit.*, pp. 81-82.

We don't need any paper. You tell him you don't know, you'll have to ask your wife—then he won't talk so long to you." [45]

Among the Papago likewise, missionaries have not yet had any great influence. On the other hand, the Dakotas have by now become almost completely Christianized, in part as Macgregor suggests, because their own religion was more akin to that of Christianity than in the case of many other Indian groups, and in part because, in its principles at least, Christianity was the one aspect of the white man's culture which defined Indians as equal to whites.[46]

White employers and neighbors. In the Papago area, "the general public looks upon these Indians as a lower-class group with a tendency toward drunkenness, and, though they are not subjected to as marked social discrimination as are Negroes, they must endure a certain amount of racial prejudice." [47] In the vicinity of the Pine Ridge Reservation the neighbors of the Dakotas react to Indians in accord with class position.

To sum up, attitudes vary generally with the social status of the white man. The tradespeople, well-to-do farmers, and Government employees, who form the middle class of South Dakota and Nebraska, look upon most Indians as socially and economically inferior. The Indians who are acceptable to this white group are those whose education, employment, and social behavior are like their own.

There is, however, another group of whites in the area to whom the Indians, especially the mixed-bloods, are more acceptable and with whom there is some intermarriage. This group is largely composed of the poorer farmers and townspeople, often those who live on the "wrong side of the track." Because of the greater freedom of social relationships with these white people, the Indians are adopting their pattern of living and their social attitudes and values. In other words, the Indians are merging to a greater degree with the lower than with the middle class of South Dakota whites.[48]

Kluckhohn and Leighton call attention to the relations of special interests among the white groups toward the Navahos.

There is tremendous organized political pressure or threat of pressure, from white residents of the surrounding country who want to get Indian lands, or to keep Indian standards of living low in order to secure cheap labor or make large profits on sales to Navahos. There are many others who want to cut down appropriations for government services to all Indians. Some lawyers in

[45] Reprinted by permission of the publishers from Clyde Kluckhohn and Dorothea Leighton, *The Navaho*, 1947 (Cambridge, Mass.: Harvard University Press, 1947), p. 82.
[46] See Macgregor, *op. cit.*, Ch. VII, "Power, Ceremony, and Church," pp. 85-104.
[47] Joseph, Spicer, and Chesky, *op. cit.*, p. 110.
[48] Macgregor, *op. cit.*, p. 84. By permission of the publishers, University of Chicago Press.

nearby towns foment Navaho resistance to the government in order to profit by litigation.[49]

In each of the areas here under review, an increasing number of the Indians are working outside the reservation for white employees in menial occupations, such as harvesting crops, ranching, and in the case of the Papago, in a mine nearby. In these capacities the Indians are generally considered good workers, although slow. Their unwillingness to work steadily is a frequent complaint made by white employers. "Navahos are good workers but not steady. . . . They disappear for days at a time to attend a sing or to help their families out." [50] Such a comment by white employers indicates the inability of the white people to realize that going out into the white man's world of work presents a considerable problem of adjustment for Indians. As Spicer put it, "Working on a definite schedule in the white fashion is not a normal life for the Papago, but he seems to be able to adjust, perhaps because he likes the wages, which give him a higher cash income than most people can earn on the reservation." [51] It is interesting that Spicer reports that some of the employers of the Papago are adjusting their work to enable the Indians to return home periodically, and are providing better working and living conditions in order to make the Indians more contented and steady in their work.[52]

Tribal interrelationships. Since each Indian tribe has a separate society with its own particular culture, each has looked upon the other with the characteristic "in-group" attitude of ethnic groups toward one another. Navahos considered Pueblos to be effete town dwellers, and the Pueblos in their turn regard the country dwelling Navahos as ignorant and barbaric. The Papago look upon the Apaches as mean and cruel, although they admire the latter's prowess as warriors. Thus, because of their tribal insularity and ethnocentrism, the sense of the common solidarity of all Indians as opposed to whites has been comparatively weak. However, just as changing conditions have brought each Indian tribe more in contact with white people, likewise they have increased social contacts between the tribes. Among the Navahos can be found more or less systematic exchange of goods with many other tribes. For example, "the Navahos trade rugs and silver to the Utes for the baskets used in the Navaho ceremonies like that of marriage." [53] Furthermore there is considerable interest shown by neighboring tribes in

[49] Reprinted by permission of the publishers from Clyde Kluckhohn and Dorothea Leighton, *The Navaho*, 1947 (Cambridge, Mass.: Harvard University Press, 1947), pp. 107-108.
[50] *Ibid.*, p. 111.
[51] Joseph, Spicer, and Chesky, *op. cit.*, p. 110.
[52] *Ibid.*, pp. 109-110.
[53] Kuckhohn and Leighton, *op. cit.*, p. 76.

each other's ceremonies. The Papago, for example, "never tire of watching the Yaqui *pascola* dancers perform." [54] In the off-reservation boarding schools, Indian children of different tribes are often brought together, further facilitating inter-Indian acculturation. Boarding school romances often lead to intertribal marriages, which their elders, of course, do not favor but to which they are apparently becoming reconciled.

Indians and other minorities. Concerning the Papago and the Mexican Americans, Spicer observes:

Mexicans are known to the Papago as "Smarties" (*chuchkam*), and relations between the two groups vary. At present Mexicans living in the United States and the American Papago usually meet on friendly terms. Several factors tend to draw them together: in the towns both groups do the same kind of low-paid work; they are equally discriminated against by the white Americans, who frequently cannot tell them apart; and they often have a common religion in Catholicism. A Papago will trade at a Mexican store in preference to an American. When he is working in a town, he will live either with his tribesmen in "Papago Town" or with Mexicans (and perhaps lower-class white Americans). Papago in Tucson live in the "Barrio Libre" along with Mexicans and Yaqui.[55]

The fact that Indians are forbidden to buy liquor legally and that Mexicans, of course, are not, provides a special basis for trade and social relations between the two groups. Mexicans are willing to resell liquor to Indians at a profit. While the Papago "are aware that the 'Smarties' bear watching" and fights occur sometimes from this illicit trade, the Papagos "accept exploitation docilely in order to insure their liquor supply." Aside from the liquor trade, "there are few friendships between individuals and little real social intercourse." Further, "mixed marriages are frowned upon, and Indians known to have or suspected of having Mexican blood are looked down upon by full-blood Papago." [56]

The Navaho study reveals in general a similar pattern of relations between these Indians and their Mexican-American neighbors. Mexicans often protect Indians from Anglo law in such minor offenses as drunkenness. While it is rare for Mexicans in towns to invite Indians to their homes, in rural areas intimate, neighborly relations between the two groups are more frequent. On the other hand, gangs of Mexican youth often beat up and rob Indians and bloody fights occur between small bands of these two groups. It is of considerable interest that Kluckhohn and Leighton note that violence of this sort hardly

[54] Joseph, Spicer, and Chesky, *op. cit.*, p. 95.
[55] *Ibid.*, p. 95. By permission of the publishers, University of Chicago Press.
[56] *Ibid.*, p. 96.

ever occurs between either of these minorities and the Anglos.[57] In our discussion of the Negroes we saw the tendency of minorities to deflect their frustration through aggression toward other members of their own group. In this instance we see a more acculturated minority taking it out on a lesser minority in a situation where aggression directed toward the dominant would be far more dangerous to the aggressor.

THE IMPACT OF MINORITY STATUS UPON INDIANS

In the case of other minorities, we have noted how the pressures to acculturate to normative American life and the frustrations engendered by discrimination have imposed strain upon the personality organization of members of minority groups, and in the development of the personality of children of the groups. The same phenomenon is to be found among Indians, although there are some differences in their situation. Reservation Indians have the security of their identification with their own tribe. They likewise have the advantage of the special guidance and protection of the Indian Service. Nevertheless the gap between their cultures and that of the world around is so much wider than in the case of most other minorities, that even with this special assistance the strain of adjustment is great. In the case of those Indians who go off the reservation into the white world either temporarily or permanently, the problem of adjustment is still greater. Illustrative of ways in which Indians react under these difficult circumstances are the following comments of Kluckhohn and Leighton concerning the Navahos:

Different sets of Navahos (depending partly upon age, schooling, location of residence with respect to intensity of non-Navaho contacts, and other factors) have shown different major responses to the insecurities, deprivations, and frustrations of the immediate past and especially to the "between two worlds" problem. . . . Some focus their energies upon trying to be as like whites as possible. Some find relief in becoming followers of vocal leaders. Others dissipate much hostility in factional quarrels or scatter their aggression in family fights, in phantasies about witchcraft or in attacking "witches," in verbal and other indirect hostilities toward whites, or they turn their aggression inward with resultant fits of depression. The culturally patterned releases in humor and in "joking relationships" with certain relatives continue to play some part. The central response of certain individuals is in flight—either in actual physical withdrawal or in the escape of narcotics, alcohol, and sex. Still others turn to intensified participation in rites of the native religion and to new cults (e.g., peyote). Partial solutions are achieved

[57] Kluckhohn and Leighton, *op. cit.*, pp. 77-78.

by a few individuals by rigid compartmentalization of their lives and by various rationalizations.

Those who have set themselves to follow the white man's trail find themselves—as have representatives of other minority groups—in a (rationally) odd dilemma. While as youngsters they are rewarded by school teachers and others for behaving like whites, as adults they are punished for having acquired skills that make them competitors of their white contemporaries. The more intelligent ones had, by early maturity, realized that their education would bring them into conflict with or isolation from their own un-schooled relatives. But the experience of being turned on by their white mentors comes as a painful surprise. They find they are seldom received on terms of social equality, even by those whose standards of living, dress, and manners they have succeeded in copying almost perfectly. They learn that they must always (save within the Indian Service) expect to work for a salary at least one grade lower than that which a white person of comparable train-ing and experience receives. They overhear remarks by those same groups of whites who had goaded them to give up "those ignorant Indian ways." "You can never trust these school boys." "Give me a 'long hair' every time. They may be dumb but they are honest and they work hard." "Educated Indians are neither fish nor fowl. They give me the creeps." Rejected by the white world they have made so many emotional sacrifices to enter, some attempt a bitter retreat to the Navaho world. Others, in sour disillusionment, abandon all moral codes. Still others achieve a working (but flat and empty) adjustment.

Navahos are well aware of the difficulty of their situation. Surrounded by powerful pressures to change, they know that indifference and withdrawal can no longer serve as effective responses. They are conscious of the need to develop some compromise with white civilization. But doubt as to the best form of compromise makes them angry and anxious. Thus suspicion and hostility are becoming a major emotional tone of their relationships with whites.[58]

THE INDIAN PROBLEM

From the value frame of reference of democracy, the essential prob-lem of the Indians is their minority status. While the submarginal conditions of welfare which prevail among Indians constitutes a serious situation, the critical problem is how to effect the integration of In-dians into American society as equal and self-reliant citizens. In terms of this broad objective, the major issue revolves around the concepts of cultural pluralism versus total assimilation. Should Indians be en-couraged to integrate into American society as Indians—as groups re-taining their group identities and as much of distinctive cultures as can be successfully adapted to a self-reliant group life? Or should Indians

[58] Reprinted by permission of the publishers from Clyde Kluckhohn and Dorothea Leighton, *The Navaho*, 1947 (Cambridge, Mass.: Harvard University Press, 1947), pp. 113-115.

be encouraged to acculturate as rapidly as possible to the typical American way of life leading to complete assimilation, amalgamation, and the disappearance of Indian society and culture? The student of minorities will appreciate that in issues of this sort, adherence to either of these views is often motivated by self-interest rather than concern for the Indians. For example, some Indian Service personnel may favor the nonassimilation viewpoint because it will more likely require the Indian Service as a special agency for a longer period. On the other hand, it is clear that some of the protagonists of assimilation as rapidly as possible have designs on Indian properties and resources. However, among specialists on Indian affairs with long records of sympathetic interest in the welfare of Indians, difference of opinion on the issue likewise prevails.[59] Those who favor integration through cultural pluralism believe that there is much in Indian culture which should be preserved or modernized and that the Indian societies should be retained for this purpose. Since former Commissioner Collier, as we have seen, holds this view, during his administration the policy of the Indian Service was directed to this end. On the other hand, the Indian specialists who incline to the policy of the integration of Indians through their complete assimilation argue that Indians will not be in fact autonomous members of our society until they cease their Indian ways. The policy of the Indian Service since Collier's retirement appears to have veered toward this latter view.

On the basis of our study of minorities, we bring to bear upon this issue two considerations. The present situation of Jews in the United States, and of certain minor religious sects, suggests that it should be theoretically possible for Indian communities with modernized Indian cultures to become self-reliant in the economic and political sense in due time. In democratic society, if this is what Indians themselves continue to want, democratic principle logically calls for protecting their right to such a solution. On the other hand, whether by this course they could shed completely their minority status is debatable. We have advanced the hypothesis (in Chapter 4) that cultural pluralism based on ethnic differentiation, due to the special circumstances in the development of dominant-minority relations in this country, carries with it, inevitably, a degree of discrimination. If Indians remain physiognomically visible, culturally distinguishable, associate primarily with Indians, and remain numerically a small proportion of the national population, it does not seem probable that they will cease to be a social minority.

[59] See John F. Embree, "The Indian Bureau and Self-Government," *Human Organization*, Vol. 8, No. 2, Spring, 1949; and John C. Collier, "The Indian Bureau and Self-government: A Reply," Vol. 8, No. 2, Summer, 1949.

TRENDS AND PROSPECTS
IN THE INDIAN SITUATION

The situation of the Indians in the United States at the present time may be summarized in the following terms:

1. The Indians are minorities in two respects. They are wards of the Government in a manner distinctive from all other American groups. The Indians are also minority people in the manner of other minorities. That is, they are categorically discriminated against by white Americans wherever they live in numbers in the proximity of whites.

2. The Indian population is growing at a rate greater than that of the national population, and probably at a rate too great to be adequately supported on the areas now assigned to them. The Indian Service reports: "On a number of reservations, most notably the Navajo, Hopi and Papago, even if maximum development of resources were possible many thousands of Indians would still be left without any means of livelihood." [60]

3. Thus, while Indian welfare is improving, their progress in this respect is retarded by the inadequacy of their present material resources for their growing population and by the lag in the modernization of their material culture.

4. The Indian groups are becoming increasingly self-governing.

5. The Indian population, in general, still shows a marked tendency to remain Indian in the cultural and social sense. No large scale tendency to "pass" over into the non-Indian society and to lose their tribal identification is yet discernible.

6. The strain imposed upon Indian groups by the pressure to acculturate on the one hand, and the desire to remain Indians on the other, manifests itself in the behavioral difficulties of many Indian persons. In the case of those Indians either working off the reservations or residing in white communities, discrimination against them as Indians aggravates still further personality maladjustment.

7. As with other minorities, the progress of Indians toward full equality is retarded by the pressures of vested interests among the dominant group. This factor, however, operates with peculiar force in the case of Indians due to their ward status, and to their ownership of valuable lands and mineral resources.

TOPICS FOR DISCUSSION AND PROJECTS

1. Point out as many ways as possible in which the situation of Indians in the United States differs from that of the other minorities with physiognomic visibility.

[60] *Annual Report of the Secretary of the Interior,* June 30, 1948, p. 389.

2. Discuss the significance of the "forced" assimilation policy practiced by the Indian Service from 1878 to 1928 in relation to its contribution to the science of human relations.

3. Discuss (a) color, or race consciousness, on the part of white people in relation to the Indians, and (b) the direct economic interest of certain white groups as factors affecting the status and welfare of Indians in this country.

4. Study any pertinent material you can locate with the view of verifying or disproving the following hypothesis: The prevalence of unfavorable and discriminatory attitudes on the part of whites toward Indians varies directly with the nearness of white communities to Indian reservations. Report your findings.

5. Do you think it is possible for Indian groups to become ultimately self-reliant and still retain any of their distinctive ways of life? Develop whichever position you take.

SUGGESTED READING

Aginsky, Burt W. "The Interaction of Ethnic Groups: A Case Study of Indians and whites. *American Sociological Review,* Vol. 14, No. 2, April, 1949, pp. 288-293.
> *Finds the only workable solution "functionally integrated participation" of Pomo Indians into surrounding white society.*

Collier, John. *The Indians of the Americas.* New York: Mentor Books, The New American Library of World Literature, Inc., 1947.
> *The story of Indian-white relations in the Western World, as told by the inaugurator of the "new deal for the Indians," as former Commissioner of Indian Affairs.*

Haas, T. H. "The American Indian in Recent Perspective". *Race Relations* Vol. 5, 1948, p. 58. Reprinted by the United States Government Printing Office: 1948-0-780-468.
> *The prospect for the Indians as indicated by the situation following World War II.*

Leighton, Dorothea, and Kluckhohn, Clyde. *Children of the People.* Cambridge: Harvard University Press, 1948.
> *A systematic study of the personality development of the Navaho child.*

Linton, Ralph. *Acculteration in Seven American Indian Tribes.* New York: Appleton-Century-Crofts, Inc., 1940.
> *From a detailed study of seven tribes, the author derives generalizations on cultural change.*

Loram, C. T., and McIllwraith, T. F., eds. *The North American Indian Today.* Toronto: University of Toronto Press, 1943.
> *A symposium of Indian life in Canada and the United States.*

Thompson, Laura. *Culture in Crisis.* New York: Harper and Brothers, 1950.
> *An exceptionally complete study of the Hopi Indians. Good example of coordinated research in social science.*

CHAPTER 13

Minority Wards of
Twentieth Century Expansion

At the turn of the 20th century, the United States embarked upon a modest career of overseas expansion. As a result of the Spanish-American War, the Philippine Islands and Puerto Rico were added to the nation's domain. In consequence of prior economic penetration of Hawaii by various white groups in which Americans came to predominate, revolution took place and Hawaii was annexed under territorial status. One result of these·overseas ventures was the creation of minority situations, which had a twofold aspect. Eventually, emigration from the new territories to the mainland began to take place. In broad outline, the pattern of interrelationships between these island immigrants and the mainlanders resembled that of all other immigrant situations. Because these new immigrants came from backgrounds of greater divergence from American cultural norms than those of European immigrants and because in varying degrees their racial genetic heritages were colored, white American discrimination was more intense than with the Europeans. The fact, however, that these peoples were under American jurisdiction meant that, in contrast with other immigrants, they were in a sense a special responsibility.

The other aspect created by this territorial expansion has to do with the relation of the white mainland Americans who lived in these territories to the natives. These Americans comprised largely officials of the Federal Government, emissaries of mainland economic interests, or individual enterprisers who developed businesses in these areas. Here,

343

in general, it may be said that Americans, along with the northern Europeans present possessed a higher status ranking than the native populations, and that thus their relations with the natives resembled the dominant-minority pattern. In this chapter, both the mainland phase and the territorial phase of the situations involving Filipinos, Puerto Ricans, and Hawaiians will be considered.

The manner in which the United States as a government and in which the Americans as a people act in respect to these wards gains heightened significance when considered in relation to the current, unstable, international scene. The Pacific area and Asia are now of much more vital political significance to the United States than ever before. The attitudes of Asiatics and Pacific Islanders toward Americans have been and will continue to be affected by the developments in our territorial affairs. In this connection, passing attention may be called to the fact that the United States has political control over Guam, a part of Samoa, and scattered islands designated in administrative terms as Trust Territory of the Pacific Islands. Whatever may be the legal political status of the various islands in this area, it is probable that their destiny is in a sense under American control. Thus Furnas writes:

. . . This or that island may fly the tricolor, the Southern Cross, or the Union Jack, but the destiny of this stretch of salt water is determined by the world force implied in the words Pearl Harbor, Guadalcanal, Tokio Bay.

So the South Seas are Uncle Sam's baby. Power over an area implies responsibility for it and responsibility makes understanding highly advisable.[1]

It now seems more probable that the United Nations rather than the United States will assume the responsibility of which Furnas writes. But the discharge of these responsibilities will bring American military and civilian personnel in wider contact with non-Caucasoid peoples. Under the territorial jurisdiction of the United States there are also to be found other ethnic groups with considerable racial visibility: Eskimos, Indians, and Asiatics in Alaska, and the preponderantly Negro population of the Virgin Islands. All these peoples are colored races in the eyes of most Americans.

FILIPINOS

The Filipino people, since the granting of independence to this island nation in 1946, have ceased to be wards of the United States. In view, however, of present international power relations, this new republic is likely to remain for some time to come within the protective sphere of influence of its former ruler.

[1] J. C. Furnas, *Anatomy of Paradise* (New York: William Sloane Associates, Inc., 1948), pp. 3-4. By permission.

Americans in the Philippines. The subject of Americans in the Philippines divides into the relations of the Government and its officials to the Islands and the Islanders, and the interpersonal relations of Americans to the Filipinos. Regarding the former, it may be said in general that the policy and practice of the United States Government, initiated by the first civil governor, William Howard Taft, was one of the least exploitative of occidental colonial policies. At the outset, the United States had declared publicly its intention of ultimately granting independence to the Philippines, and stated that its efforts would be directed to bringing the Islands to the point where independence would be feasible. Specifically, this meant education of the islanders, stimulation of the capacity for self-government, and development of the economy of the Islands to a self-sustaining point. Most writers on American rule in the Philippines agree that in the main this policy was followed. Increasing capacity for self-government was developed among the Filipinos through the encouragement given to wider native participation by American officials. This development followed an irregular course in which American liberal governments granted new degrees of participation followed by conservative governments which froze the situation. While Philippine government had its many shortcomings, nevertheless according to Hayden, "it has been worked by genuinely representative Filipinos who have made it in a real sense a Filipino government, as it has touched the masses of the people." [2] The modern school system introduced by Americans advanced greatly during the American control. By 1939, however, only 45 per cent of the estimated number of Filipino children 7 to 17 years of age were enrolled in schools, although nearly 90 per cent of the children of primary school age, 7–10 years, were enrolled in the first four grades.[3]

While the economy of the Philippines was greatly developed during American administration, the trade advantages accruing from the fact that their agricultural products were admitted into the United States duty free, resulted in the expansion of agriculture to the neglect of industry. This geared Philippine economy to American economy with the result that when the time for freedom came, its economy had difficulty standing on its own feet. While much of the capital invested in the development of Philippine economy came from the mainland, actual control of economic life was in Filipino hands. The vast proportion of the acreage of the Islands belonged to Filipinos. As late as 1938, tax declarations showed a greater number of Filipino-owned corporate declarers than American, who were, however, second. Of in-

[2] Joseph R. Hayden, *The Philippines: A Study in National Development* (New York: The Macmillan Company, 1942), pp. 288-289.
[3] *Ibid.*, pp. 469-471.

dividual owners of taxable property Filipino owners far outshadowed all the rest, with the Chinese second.[4] The latter had acquired a virtual monopoly upon retail trade. Interestingly, it was the success of Chinese immigrants in this field which led to Filipino manifestations of antagonism toward the Chinese, very similar to the attitudes and behavior of the West Coast Americans toward the Japanese.

The over-all record of American administration in the Philippines resulted in the Islands' readiness for the independence they finally received in 1946. In Hayden's opinion, the Philippines were well qualified for nationhood, in population, in area, in economic resources, and in cultural and racial homogeneity.[5] "Upon the basis of its agricultural, pastoral, forest, and fishery resources alone the Philippines should be able eventually to readjust its economy to separation from the United States and to support a steadily growing population at a standard of living which the masses of its people would accept."[6] A large majority of the people of the Philippines belong to one great racial group, the Malays. A great unifying influence of the Spanish period was the Christianizing of the population, so that by 1939, more than nine-tenths of the people were Christians. The greatest deficiency still retarding nationality consciousness was the lack of a common language among the masses, although the upper classes everywhere spoke Spanish or English or both languages.

Filipino-American interpersonal relations in the Philippines. The number of Americans who have taken up permanent residence in the Philippines is small. Therefore, it is not surprising that little research material is available concerning the interpersonal relations of Americans in the islands with the Filipinos. Forbes writes that "the policy inaugurated by Governor Taft and followed by other officials in the Islands has been to treat the Filipinos as social equals."[7] He further recounts an official ball in which the Governor and Mrs. Taft danced with the socially ranking Filipinos present as partners. Forbes makes passing reference to the fact that the Americans in Manila formed a group apart, although in the provinces he indicates that being very few in numbers they tend to mix socially with the native population. Florence Horn makes this observation on the subject: "Americans in Manila are like Americans in Mexico City and Americans in Maracaibo and Hong Kong and Rio de Janeiro. They build for themselves a barricaded American life wherever they are. They in-

[4] *Ibid.,* p. 702.
[5] *Ibid.,* Ch. 1, pp. 3-31.
[6] *Ibid.,* p. 7. By permission of The Macmillan Company.
[7] W. Cameron Forbes, *The Philippine Islands* (Cambridge: Harvard University Press, 1945), p. 301.

sulate themselves as thoroughly as possible against the life of the country they are in." [8]

Filipinos in the mainland United States. Filipinos in the mainland of the United States comprise a very small minority, according to the Census of 1940, only 45,563. They came here chiefly during the 1920–30 decade. They will remain a small minority, because from the time the territory became a Commonwealth in 1935, their immigrant quota was only 50 per year, which was advanced to 100 when they gained their independence in 1947. Two closely related facts contribute to their probable disappearance as a separate group in this country. The present ratio of men to women is about 14 to 1 which, while it indicates on the one hand that a large number are unmarried, also means that more than other Oriental groups, they marry across ethnic lines. The Filipinos are concentrated heavily in the West Coast region, although small clusters are found in some of the larger cities of the nation. In occupations they are employed as unskilled farm laborers in the country and in housework and hotel work in the cities.

In the main, the story of the relation of Filipinos to Americans follows the pattern revealed in the case of other Oriental immigrants. The Americans reacted to them in much the same way, although the adjustment of the Filipinos themselves varies from that of other immigrants largely in relation to their small numbers.

American reaction to Filipinos. Prior to the economic depression of 1929 most of the Filipinos who came here managed to find employment largely as field workers in agriculture and in service capacities. While the evidence that migration here was encouraged by the transportation interests or by American entrepreneurs is not convincing (the Hawaiian story is different), nevertheless Americans were glad to employ them in the capacities noted partly because they were good workers and partly because they could be employed at lower wages. Mounting antagonism toward the Filipinos rose in localized small towns and cities in the West as their numbers increased sufficiently to bring them into direct competition with other argicultural and service employees. A series of "race riot" incidents occurred beginning in 1929. Illustrations of these are to be found in Lasker's study of Filipino Immigration.

[Early in 1930, in Watsonville, California, a riot occurred.] Here resident youths rather than migrant workers were implicated, and economic rivalry merely formed a background for a conflict which arose from the attention of

[8] Florence Horn, *Orphans of the Pacific* (New York: Reynal & Hitchcock, 1941), p. 90.

Filipinos to white girls and the introduction of other white girls into the community for their entertainment.

In May 1930, anti-Filipino agitation again appeared in Washington—this time in the White River Valley, south of Seattle, where forty or fifty white farm laborers, displaced by Filipino workers in their jobs of packing peas and lettuce, raided camps where some two hundred Filipinos were housed, kidnapped some of them and forced others to flee, without their belongings, to the nearby hills. The complaint here was that the Filipinos, for some time employed at harvesting the vegetables for white and Japanese growers, were being employed to pack vegetables for shipment, an occupation previously given to white workers, cutting the wage from 60 to 25 cents an hour. Though these wage rates lack confirmation, the motive obviously was one of resented competition, and the incident is in line with those experienced earlier in the lettuce regions of California.[9]

Illustrating antagonism from another source and for another reason, the following incident is cited:

In August 1934, about 3000 Filipinos went on strike in the lettuce fields near Salinas, California. An army of special deputies descended on the Filipino picket line and herded a group of 700 Filipinos together, and drove them from the community. As a part of this campaign, a Filipino labor camp was raided and burned to the ground. Many Filipinos were corralled and held incommunicado; and, of course, the strike was broken.[10]

Economic discrimination is further illustrated in the following account by a Filipino immigrant himself:

Yet Filipinos, six of us, worked eleven hours a day there, with no day off. Sozimo Belmonte worked eleven hours a day, no day off, and got $8.00 a week. Remigio Santiago was head bus boy, and was paid $12 a week. I worked eleven hours a day and was paid $16 a week. The Filipino chef worked twelve hours a day and got $23 a week.

But was it because business was rotten that we had to work so many hours and be paid such low wages? Honestly, no! If the business didn't make a good profit, how was it that it was able to expand its plant during this time? No, it was just that the employer knew we Filipinos couldn't squawk. We would rather work at these wages than not work at all. We aren't allowed to join unions, or to have the weapons that organized labor uses. So it was "take it or leave it," and we took it.[11]

[9] Bruno Lasker, *Filipino Immigration*, published for the American Council Institute of Pacific Relations by the University of Chicago Press, Chicago, Ill., 1931, pp. 14, 17. By permission.
[10] Carey McWilliams, *Factories in the Field* (Boston: Little, Brown & Company, 1939), p. 133. By permission of author.
[11] Manuel Buaken, *I Have Lived with the American People* (Caldwell, Idaho: The Caxton Printers, Ltd., 1948), pp. 85-86. By permission.

Treated as "colored people" by native Americans, Filipinos encountered discrimination in housing, in recreational places, and when they sought companionship of non-Oriental women.

The demand for exclusion. As in the case of all other Oriental immigrant groups, the demand for the exclusion of Filipinos arose first in California, and first by that group most affected by their competition, organized labor. At the hearings in Washington, the demand for exclusion was supported by professional nativist organizations. Since, however, the Philippines were a part of the United States, no exclusion act was passed. Actually the conditions in the early 1930's were such that in any event few Filipinos would have immigrated. At this point, however, the famous Repatriation Act (July 10, 1935) was passed. It provided that the United States would pay the transportation of Filipinos back home but further provided that those accepting such benefits should not return to the States again. In spite of the fact that economic conditions were not favorable here for the Filipinos, relatively few of them actually accepted this offer.

Reaction of Filipinos to American discrimination. The adjustment of Filipinos to American life was complicated by the many discriminations imposed upon them and by the peculiarities of the composition of their group, namely, the smallness in number and the preponderance of males. In the latter connection, they were too few to form separate colonies and the absence of Filipino women hindered normal family life. Rejected almost completely from association with stable American community influences, they were perforce limited to association with the least stable elements of community life. In view of this it seems almost incredible that the Filipinos did not have a high delinquency record. The migratory and otherwise irregular nature of the occupations in which they could find employment further contributed to an unstable existence. Yet there are no indications that the Filipinos caused any serious problems for the communities in which they lived other than those created by American attitudes toward their, on the whole, harmless presence.

While all minorities resent discrimination and suffer from it, the Filipinos' resentment was affected by certain circumstances which in their own way of thinking at least distinguished them from other Oriental immigrants. They considered themselves in a sense Americans, and such education as they have had was patterned after American models, including indoctrination into the American democratic ideals. They were Catholic Christians. Because of their closer cultural affinity to Americans they did not think of themselves as Oriental or "colored"

and were thus not prepared for the intransigeance of color consciousness among mainland white Americans.

Trends and Prospects. World War II had the effect of lessening the
discriminations against Filipinos in the Mainland.

The war has promoted a new justice in treatment of the Filipinos in both
the negative and positive happenings.

In the negative happenings—there is a complete stoppage of publicity that
sneers at and ridicules us. No more merchants of hate parade their stuff in big
weeklies. No more learned sociological studies purporting to show the great
superiority of other racial groups, such as the Japanese over the Filipinos as
components of American life, as candidates for citizenship. In fact I can't cite
you an example of race-hatred inciting publicity directed against the Filipinos
since Pearl Harbor, where there used to be floods of such to plague and tor-
ment and destroy us, and to destroy American democracy.

In the positive happenings, there is something intangible in the air that
says that America has learned to respect us. No longer on the streetcar do I
feel myself in the presence of my enemies. We Filipinos are the same—it is
Americans that have changed in their recognition of us. . . .

. . . The radio has been open to us—various programs have featured
Filipino speakers—something they never did before. Women's clubs and civic
organizations have invited Filipinos to be their guest speakers. . . . Maria
Dayoan, a young Filipino missionary worker from the Philippines and a
refugee from the Japs in northern Luzon has a weekly speaking engagement
in the various churches in the west coast. . . .

Agitation for citizenship of Filipinos is being carried on now by Americans,
whose sense of justice has finally come on to play this subject.

The employment of Filipinos in offices of the Federal Government is a
decided change from our former status of being excluded from all such skilled
work by being excluded from citizenship.[12]

This change in attitude toward Filipinos is in part an aspect of the
general change in attitude toward all minorities. It is further accentuated in the case of the Filipinos by their clear demonstration of
loyalty to the United States in its war against the Japanese during
which the Philippine Islands suffered enemy occupation.

PUERTO RICANS

The present situation with respect to Puerto Ricans is in considerable contrast to that of the Filipinos. The United States has solved the
problem of its relation to the Philippines as a territory by granting the
islands their independence, whereas the status of Puerto Rico is still
inadequately defined. The problem created by Filipino immigration
has been roughly solved by refusing to admit any more, whereas the re-

[12] Buaken, *op. cit.*, pp. 322-324. By permission of the publisher, The Caxton Printers,
Ltd.

cent influx of Puerto Ricans mostly to New York City constitutes the newest minority situation. The "Puerto Rican problem" is twofold. The island constitutes a political and economic problem and the migrants to the mainland create a minority situation. The two are related. The depressed conditions of the island stimulate more immigration to the mainland; which in turn aggravates the minority problem there. Thus any planned approach to the mainland minority situation problem should properly be integrated with plans for the island itself.

Puerto Rico is one of the most densely populated areas in the world, 628 persons per square mile. Its approximately two million inhabitants occupy 3425 square miles of territory, and three-fourths of this acreage is mountainous.[13] Its economy has been based upon agriculture, raising part of its food stuffs and specializing in the production of sugar for export purposes. The pressure of population in an economic area which cannot adequately support so large a population on a primarily agricultural economy has kept the island poor. High rates of ill health, malnutrition, poor rural living conditions, and urban slums accompany its poverty.

As a sociocultural group, Puerto Rico had at the time of annexation to the United States, a homogeneous civilization of the Latin American variety, with its own peculiar distinctiveness. The main status differentiation was that of social class in which a small upper class, chiefly of landed proprietors, was distinguished from the peasant mass of workers. Into the composition of the population had gone Indian, Negro, and white genetic strains. Today the Indian strains are a minor factor, but the Negro and white strains are blended in all degrees of variability. Officially the racial composition of the population is considered about one-fourth Negro and three-fourths white, but since the definition of the Negro on the island means a definite preponderance of visibly Negroid traits in contrast to the mainland definition, comparable data for mainland and island cannot be used. We shall presently consider in what ways this physiognomic variation affects social relations on the island, but in general we shall see that it does so far less than on the mainland.

Americans in Puerto Rico. Since there are only about two thousand mainland descended Americans permanently living in Puerto Rico, relations between Americans and Puerto Ricans on the island are largely of an impersonal nature, confined to the formal relations involved in economic and governmental activity.

[13] *The Puerto Ricans of New York City,* a publication of The Office of Puerto Rico, Washington, D. C., p. 1. This monograph was written by the Columbia University Bureau of Applied Research on the basis of their findings. The advance report of the 1950 Census estimates Puerto Rico's population at 2,210,273. The rate of increase during the decade was 18.3 per cent.

The Federal Government and Puerto Rico. Much of the difficulty which has beset the Puerto Rican situation stems from the general apathy of mainlanders concerning the territory, and the consequent lack of any definite long range aim in government activity. Acquired by the United States as an incidental consequence of the Spanish American War, Puerto Rico has been governed by shifting administrations with shifting policies. Whether like the Philippines, Puerto Rico was to be prepared for independence, or on the other hand to be made ready for eventual statehood has never been clearly defined in mainland thinking. By somewhat faltering steps, democratic political institutions have been established, with increasing degrees of self-government permitted. On November 2, 1948, Puerto Rico elected its own governor for the first time. Except for the Presidential appointment of the auditor and supreme court justices, and for the power of the United States Congress to annul any law passed by the Insular Legislature (something which has not yet been done), Puerto Rico has attained complete self-government. By the Jones Act of 1917 Puerto Ricans were made citizens of the United States, yet they do not have voting representation in Congress nor can they vote in Presidential elections.

Under American control, a free public educational system has been established, although in the 50 years in which this system has been developing, it has not yet reached normative mainland standards. A basic problem has been the matter of educational policy concerning the use and teaching of languages in the schools. At first when the schools were more dominated by mainland teachers and officials, English was required and emphasized, although Spanish was taught. As the system has become more controlled by Puerto Ricans, Spanish has come to the fore as the basic language with English encouraged as a second language.

Prior to 1932 the Federal Government assumed a laissez-faire attitude toward the island's economy. In consequence, American investment in the island's economy came from mainland private economic concerns. The extent of mainland interest in Puerto Rican economy was summarized as of 1930 by Diffie and Diffie as follows:

. . . Sugar is 60 per cent absentee-controlled; fruit is 31 per cent, or more; tobacco is 85 per cent; banks are 60 per cent; railroads, 60 per cent, or more; public utilities, 50 per cent; and steamship lines, approximately 100 per cent. There is no important source of wealth that is not partially in the hands of outsiders, and in some instances, such as steamships, outsiders control the entire business. Any estimate of Porto Rico dependence on absentees which places the total at less than 60 per cent of the island's wealth is certainly too low. Not all of the industries belong to absentees, but those which do not are so indebted to continental banks as to be virtually in their possession. Not all of the good land is in the hands of outsiders, but a large portion of it is, and much of the remainder is heavily mortgaged. And finally, there is that type of dependence on absentees which Porto Rico suffers, because of her long dependence on a monopolizing mother country, the necessity of importing vast quantities of food, clothing, machinery, chemicals, and drugs. The control of the absentee is all but complete and with the aid of the Coastwise Shipping Act and the American Tariff bids fair to absorb all of the profitable enterprise.[14]

Under the earlier Roosevelt Administrations, governmental efforts at reorienting Puerto Rican economy in terms of the welfare of the islanders themselves was undertaken. The Puerto Rico Relief Administration was supplanted by the Puerto Rico Reconstruction Administration which undertook projects for irrigation systems, the building of new highways, new schools, new houses, and many other projects. According to Pattee, "there is little doubt that the present [Roosevelt] administration . . . postponed, at least, a collapse in Puerto Rican economy." [15] However, the same writer further observed, "The Puerto Rico Reconstruction Administration . . . made definite progress but did not achieve that complete reform that was so desperately needed." [16] An indigenous reform program developed from the emergence of a new political party in the island, the Partido Popular Democrato. The most important reform accomplished by this new administration has been its efforts to redistribute land and to restrict the holding of the landed sugar interests. While it is possible that the Puerto Ricans, with increasing political maturity, will go far to solve the island's economic problems by themselves, the continued pressure of population will make this difficult.

Finally, the definition of Puerto Rico's status as a part of the United States remains ambiguous.[17] There have been times in the past when it seemed possible that as far as mainland sentiment was concerned, Puerto Rico might have had independence if she wanted it. Today, because of the increasing significance of its strategic location from a military defense viewpoint, it is doubtful if the United States would grant complete independence. From the Puerto Rican viewpoint, it is doubtful whether the islanders in general desire complete independence. Under the Organic Act of 1917 when citizenship was conferred upon the Puerto Rican, the right to enroll themselves as citizens of any other country was provided. Only 288 citizens of Puerto Rico did

---

[14] W. Bailey Diffie and Justine Whitfield Diffie, *Porto Rico: A Broken Pledge* (New York: The Vanguard Press, 1931), pp. 135-136. By permission.
[15] Richard Pattee, "The Puerto Ricans," *Annals of the American Academy of Political and Social Science*, Vol. 223, Sept. 1942, p. 52.
[16] *Ibid.*, p. 52.
[17] *The Puerto Ricans of New York City*, p. 13.

so.[18] While from the practical point of view of distinguishing islanders from mainlanders, Puerto Ricans refer to themselves as such, and refer to mainlanders as Americans, they nevertheless go on to indicate that they consider themselves American citizens too.[19]

"Race" relations in Puerto Rico. Puerto Rico has acquired a reputation for the absence among its people of prejudice and discrimination based on the factor of color visibility. More recent students of the island scene seriously challenge the validity of this reputation. The present confusion concerning the actual situation may well arise from the fact that mainland observers, accustomed to the patent and easily validated pattern of discrimination between Negroes and whites in the states, have failed to observe the more subtle aspects of color discrimination on the island.

Since the abolition of slavery, there has been no civic and public discrimination against a Puerto Rican related to physiognomic features. None of the forms of interracial violence, such as lynchings and race riots, characteristic of other interracial populations has occurred. Back of this formal absence of race prejudice lies the Latin tradition which we have noted elsewhere. There is also to be taken into consideration the fact that the population of Puerto Rico presents so wide a range of combinations of Negroid-Caucasoid-Indian physiognomic features that a formal pattern of dominant-minority relations on the basis of physiognomic features would be difficult to maintain, except perhaps to distinguish a small upper class of supposedly "pure" Spanish lineage from the rest of the population.

Against this traditional view, recent students of the Puerto Rican scene indicate that in its more subtle and less explicit aspects prejudice and discrimination based on color visibility are widespread. Maxine Gordon writes, "we maintain, however, that no Puerto Rican is unaware of his position in the Puerto Rican society as determined by the color of his skin." [20] In support of this position, the writer cites the elaborate classificatory terminology by which the varying degrees of Negroid appearing people are labeled in informal conversation; folklore which makes much of whether one has a Negro ancestor or not; firsthand knowledge of social discrimination based on color in the university; and evidence that while intermarriage is outwardly tolerated, social

[18] Trumbull White, *Puerto Rico and Its People* (New York: Frederick A. Stokes Company, 1938), p. 181.
[19] *Ibid.*, p. 181.
[20] Maxine W. Gordon, "Cultural Aspects of Puerto Rico's Race Problem," *American Sociological Review*, Vol. 15, No. 3 (June 1950), p. 382. Also by the same writer, "Race Patterns and Prejudice in Puerto Rico," *American Sociological Review*, Vol. 14, No. 2 (April 1949), pp. 294-301.

discrimination nevertheless follows for certain kinds of mixed marriages. Armstrong expresses a somewhat similar view although disclaiming systematic study of the subject.[21] President Truman's Civil Rights Committee reported discrimination in the employment of Negroes on the island.

The milder form of color prejudice and discrimination on the island has been influenced by three factors. (1) It is in part a reflection of class prejudice, since Negroes in general occupy lower economic positions. (2) It is in part derivative from the Spanish colonial influence and slavery. (3) Race consciousness as a determiner of status has increased as a result of the affiliation of Puerto Rico with the United States. Mainland white tourists tend to project their mainland attitudes toward Negroes upon Puerto Ricans. During World War II, Army camps on the island segregated Puerto Rican troops and the Navy would not take them.[22] Knowledge of the mainland reaction toward migrants to the United States also affects the island viewpoint. Although the mainland influence increasing race consciousness is resented by the islanders, it produces ambivalent reactions. It promotes, on the one hand, a tendency for those Puerto Ricans whose physiognomic variable may make it possible for them to succeed in being considered white to draw apart from those who cannot. On the other hand, those who cannot establish white status or feel insecure about it resent the increasing emphasis upon color. When, as is often the case, members of the same family vary sufficiently to place some in the white category and others in the Negro category, even family harmony is disturbed.

Puerto Ricans on the mainland. The ambiguous status of Puerto Ricans as Americans is likewise demonstrated in the situation of those islanders who migrate to the mainland. On the one hand, since they are American citizens, they have formal civic equality. They are free to migrate to any part of the nation they desire; and upon establishing residence in a state are entitled to voting privileges and all other civic rights. On the other hand, in the places where Puerto Ricans have congregated in numbers, they are generally treated by the mainland whites as an alien minority.

The number of Puerto Ricans living in the States is considered to be about 250,000, over 90 per cent of whom are located in New York City alone. A 1947–48 survey estimated that the number living in the two areas of Harlem and the lower East Bronx ranged between 160,000 and

[21] Robert G. Armstrong: "Intergroup Relations in Puerto Rico," *Phylon*, Vol. 10 (1949), No. 3, pp. 220-224.
[22] Gordon, *op. cit.*, p. 387.

200,000.[23] During World War II and since then, the situation of these New York Puerto Ricans was the subject of considerable public interest as reflected in journalistic feature stories about them in the metropolitan press.

Puerto Rican migrants in New York City.[24] The problem of adjustment which the Puerto Rican migrant to New York City faces is broadly similar to that of other immigrants to the United States, differing in nuances related to his particular cultural background. (1) While 70 per cent of Puerto Ricans on the island live in rural areas, about 79 per cent of the migrating population is urban. To them, as well as to their rural cousins, New York City, as the apogee of urbanism, presents a bewildering contrast to Puerto Rican cities. (2) The climate of Puerto Rico is milder and less extreme at both ends than that of New York City. These differences in climate require readjustment of the migrant's clothing habits. Further his lack of experience with refrigeration had built attitudes of waste of food which the Puerto Rican finds costly with his low wages. (3) In New York City, and the mainland in general, the migrant faces a consciousness of color distinction in which people are either Negro or white, and nothing in between. Since in his homeland, people with widely varying ranges of physiognomic features combining Caucasoid and Negroid traits have lived together with less consciousness of "race," the Puerto Rican migrant faces a perplexing psychological problem. While he considers himself white, he may be treated as a Negro by white New Yorkers. Often he tries to escape this dilemma by isolating himself as much as possible within the secure confines of Spanish Harlem, thus retarding his acculturation. (4) The Puerto Rican migrant has been brought up in a society where people do not often rise out of the class status in which they are born. In New York he faces a fluid class situation in which success is determined by competition. While he enters at the bottom of the status scale, he finds he is supposed to try to better his position which places great strain on his personality. "The Puerto Rican migrant suffers . . . under the handicap of knowing little English, of coming from a culture which stresses enjoying life through poetry, music, and dancing rather than the accumulation by money by hard work, conscientiousness, promptness, dependability, and toadying to the foreman." [25] (5) The community life to which the migrant is accustomed was controlled by rigid mores defining the proper conduct of individuals to one another. He

---

[23] Bureau of Applied Social Research, Columbia University, summary of findings of a study of New York City's Puerto Ricans conducted for the government of Puerto Rico, June 15, 1948, p. 3.
[24] *The Puerto Ricans of New York City*, Ch. 2, "Metropolis—the Panorama of Contrasts," p. 32-39.
[25] *Ibid.*, p. 36.

finds in New York a bewildering variety of customs and practices, and further finds that his own mores are looked down upon by higher status New Yorkers. For example, he finds that women are not as subordinate to men as in his island family culture, and that as his Puerto Rican migrant woman begins to utilize her greater opportunities, conflict in family life increases.

Welfare of the Puerto Ricans. In terms of welfare, Puerto Ricans as a group occupy a position about as low as any minority group in New York City. On the whole, the migrants in the past decade have not had much difficulty finding employment in menial tasks, although it is somewhat easier for the migrant women to find employment than the men. Likwise, the migrants consistently have been able to get jobs paying better wages than those they had received on the island. Nevertheless these wages are at the lowest scale paid in New York City. Most of the Puerto Ricans live in "slum" areas with the usual run-down appearance and lack of repair. Overcrowding is high, a little under one person per room (in 1940), although not as absurdly so as some journalistic accounts have intimated. While precise data for comparing the health standards of Puerto Ricans with other ethnic groups are lacking, expert opinion considers the incidence of illness to be at about the same high rate characteristic of all slum dwelling groups. Tuberculosis rates, for example, are high.

Acculturation. Acculturation to the great metropolis by Puerto Ricans is occurring but on the whole slowly. Organizations of Puerto Ricans for their own mutual self-aid and improvement are few and weak. The migrants are generally slow and reluctant to seek out city agencies which help them with many of their needs. Protestant Puerto Ricans have formed churches within their own group rather than joining those already established. Although membership of Puerto Ricans in labor unions is reported increasing, except where the union itself makes a special effort to deal with them through Spanish language, their participation in union affairs is not active. The transitional nature of their situation is reflected in high rates of delinquency and crime, although these are about the same as of groups with similar ecological location. Still further, the marginal position of an increasing number is reflected in reports of Puerto Rican women rebelling against male dominance and in the inability of parents to control their children.

If we think in terms of a temporary hierarchy among the minorities in New York City in 1950, Puerto Ricans as a group are close to, if not on the bottom level. That they are now so situated is in considerable measure due to their divergent cultural background, in which lack of facility in English and their traditional attitudes toward illness and diet play a prominent part; their concentration in the lowest paid occupations, in part due to their lack of training for better jobs; and the relative recency of their entrance upon the New York City scene. Because all these factors are still preeminently operative, it is difficult to appraise adequately the influence of dominant discrimination against them as a factor in their present situation. As increasing acculturation occurs, we shall be better able to judge whether the Puerto Ricans are destined to follow the course of nationality minority groups, or the course followed by racially visible groups, or in other words, how far other New Yorkers and other mainlanders are going to react with color consciousness to the variable physiognomic visibility of Puerto Ricans. We have noted previously the tendency of many New Yorkers to look upon many Puerto Ricans as Negroes, perhaps at times being unable to tell the difference. The Columbia Survey indicates considerable prejudice and gang violence against the Puerto Ricans by other groups, themselves minorities (notably Italians), whose social worlds overlap with that of these island newcomers. Little friction was found between Negroes and Puerto Ricans except that developing out of the sex rivalry[26] arising from the association of Puerto Rican men with Negro women.

Trends and prospects concerning Puerto Ricans. From the foregoing discussion of Puerto Ricans, it can be seen that the United States faces two different problems which are closely interrelated. The island itself possesses a level of welfare far below the normative American standards. Until such time as the extreme pressure of population growth upon its resources and economic organization achieve a decidedly more optimal balance, the island will continue to be a special problem area. During the lag attendant upon the achievement of this optimal balance, the better opportunity for employment at higher wages on the mainland will continue to stimulate migration from the island to the mainland. The difficulties faced by the migrants in adjusting to mainland life create another problem, and in the absence of constructive measures designed to reduce the difficulties in the migrants' adjustment, we may anticipate that this problem will increase in the foreseeable future.

This summary statement of the Puerto Rican situation suggests several lines of social action which are in limited scope already being tried. (1) The situation calls for long-range planning for the economic development of the island together with encouragement of a lower

[26] *Ibid.*, pp. 61-62. The writer has heard reports of the opposite, that is, of strong antagonism by Puerto Ricans to Negro men dating Puerto Rican girls. Since there is a substantial number of Negroes in Harlem who are economically better off than the typical Puerto Rican migrant, it is logical that some Puerto Rican girls should find them congenial companions and suitable marriage partners.

rate of human reproduction. Steps in this direction are noted above in our discussion of the island's development under United States tutelage.[27] Further treatment of such a program lies beyond the scope of this book. (2) Since increased migration from the island to the mainland is in prospect, projects carried on the island itself designed to prepare the prospective migrant more adequately for occupational adjustment on the mainland can serve a constructive purpose. Programs of this character have already been tried on a limited scale. For example, an occupational training program for female domestics was conducted on the island preparatory to their being placed in specific jobs in New York, involving cooperation by public educational and employment agencies on the island and in New York. (3) Measures aimed at encouraging the wider distribution of Puerto Rican migrants throughout the mainland are advocated by some students of the problem. In this connection the Columbia research associates write: ". . . diverting the flow [of Puerto Rican migrants] to other localities where jobs and living facilities could be found . . . would probably require an extensive educational campaign on the island and in New York City, as well as some arrangement to assure prospective migrants of the existence of opportunities. The Puerto Rican Department of Labor has recently worked out cooperative arrangements with federal and state employment services for work along these lines. Several groups have been recruited for work in the steel mills of the Akron-Youngstown area in Ohio." [28]

Related to the possibility of greater distribution of Puerto Rican migrants is the recent development of importing agricultural labor directly from the island to rural areas in the Midwest for temporary employment. This situation is comparable to that noted in the Southwest involving Mexican nationals and creates similar problems, except that the Puerto Ricans are American nationals. Since some of these temporary migrants will no doubt decide to remain in the United States, further geographical distribution of Puerto Ricans may result from this kind of migration.

THE PEOPLES OF HAWAII

Hawaii, from the viewpoint of the study of America's minorities, is an area of special interest because the pattern of its intergroup relations appears, on the surface at least, to be unique. The impression is generally held that this archipelago is a paradise of interracial harmony. The fact of its great ethnic and racial heterogeneity can be seen in Table 24 where the composition of Hawaii's population by ethnic

[27] *Ibid.*, see Appendix, pp. 84-102.
[28] *Ibid.*, p. 79.

origin at specified dates is given. Likwise the absence of public discrimination against any of these peoples is a clearly verifiable fact. On
the other hand, all writers seem to agree that the affairs of Hawaii for
the past 75 years have been run the way the white Americans wanted
them run, in fact very largely as the so-called "Big Five Corporations"
desired. Furthermore, there are indications that in the informal, less
readily observable areas of social relations, intergroup prejudice and
discrimination are present, particularly in the relations of the white
Americans with the "colored" groups. Unfortunately for our purposes,
systematic study of these informal relations is lacking. One clue as to
why more such study has not been undertaken may be obtained from
the testimony of one sociologist studying minority groups in Hawaii
when he reports, "Very few on the United States mainland know what
is going on in the Hawaiian Islands at present, because of a rigid cen-
sorship. The writer has endeavored to secure information, but has been
informed that the significant materials would probably not pass the
censor." [29] This was, however, during World War II.

With so many different peoples to consider, the problem of consistent
nomenclature arises in describing the Hawaiian situation. With one
exception, the peoples involved can be labeled by the terms used in
Table 24. By Hawaiians we mean the descendants of the native group
present in the islands when white contact was first established. All but
one of the other groups can be called by their nationality names. The
term "other Caucasians" as it appears in the official classification is,
however, hardly adequate to designate the one group which in fact
has the highest prestige and plays the most influential role in the territory's life. For these people the term *haole*—pronounced "howley"
—bestowed upon them by the native Hawaiians will be employed.
The original meaning of this term was "stranger." Having given this
label to the first strangers to appear in Hawaii, the Euro-American
whites, it has come to be restricted to this group and their descendants,
and not to all the other strangers who subsequently immigrated to the
islands. It identifies white people of American or northwestern European descent. The story of ethnic intergroup relations in Hawaii
will be related in terms of three periods: (1) the period of European
invasion and the decline of Hawaiian civilization, from 1778 to about
1850 when the immigration of Asiatic people began; (2) the period
of haole dominance over both the Hawaiians and the other subsequent
immigrant peoples from 1850 to the second World War; (3) the period of rise of the nonhaole population in status, which is just beginning to unfold in the postwar period.

[29] Wiliam C. Smith, "Minority Groups in Hawaii," *Annals of the American Academy
of Political and Social Science*, Vol. 223 (Sept. 1942), p. 43.

TABLE 24

Population of Hawaii by Ancestry at Specified Dates[30]

	1853	1878	1896	1910	1940	1950 [31]
Hawaiian	71,019	44,088	31,019	26,041	21,063	
Caucasian-Hawaiian [32] } Asiatic-Hawaiian }		3,420	8,485	{ 8,772 / 3,734 }	44,228	87,400
Portuguese	—	486	15,191	22,301	—	—
Puerto Rican	—	—	—	4,890	—	—
Spanish	—	—	—	1,990	—	—
Other Caucasian	1,262	3,262	7,247	14,867	115,836	114,000 [32]
Chinese	364	6,045	21,616	21,674	28,809	33,000
Japanese	—	—	24,407	79,675	156,849	183,600
Korean	—	—	—	4,533	6,761	—
Filipino	—	—	—	2,361	52,148	60,100
All others	493	684	1,055	1,071	960	21,700 [32]
Total	73,138	57,985	109,020	191,909	426,654	499,800

The decline of the Hawaiians. At the time of the first white contact with Hawaii in 1778, the archipelago was inhabited by a people of Polynesian origin and physiognomic features, brown skinned, black haired, and considered handsome by Caucasian people. Their society, although preliterate, was highly elaborated. Earlier estimates of the native population in 1798 placed the number around 300,000, although contemporary Hawaiian scholars believe the number to have been far less than this. The early explorers saw only the settlements near the coast and based their estimates of the total population on the assumption that the interior was equally densely populated. It is now known that the island of Hawaii, for example, where so much of the interior is covered by bare lava, was sparsely populated. The Hawaiians had developed a distinctive way of life quite suitable to themselves and had sufficient resources available to sustain them. Within a century after the coming of the white man, this civilization was virtually destroyed. The population had declined almost to the point of extinction, and the relatively small group of white newcomers had supplanted the natives

[30] *Ibid.*, Table 1, Population of Hawaii by Ancestry, 1853–1940, p. 38. By permission of the publishers of *The Annals of The American Academy of Political and Social Science.* Smith used territorial reports for 1940 which differ slightly from the 1940 census figures.

[31] U. S. Census, 1950, preliminary report. All persons with any Hawaiian lineage are combined into one group.

[32] The category "other Caucasian" is here changed to Caucasians, and includes Portuguese and Spanish. Puerto Ricans are however here included in the category "other races" which supplants "all others," and which further includes Koreans, Samoans, and the small number of Negro people in Hawaii.

as the controlling element in the further development of Hawaii as an insular community.

The few Euro-Americans who came to Hawaii prior to the middle of the 19th century came with specific individual economic interests in mind, except for the missionaries. First confining themselves to trading, the whites gradually became interested in cattle raising, rice growing—introduced first by the Chinese—and finally sugar growing, destined to become the economic foundation of the future Hawaii. Thus the whites became interested in securing permanent tenure of more and more of the valuable lands for these purposes.

The reactions of the Hawaiians to the haoles was compounded chiefly of awe and friendliness, both of which aided the haoles to gain their immediate ends. The technological superiority of the haole evoked admiration from the natives and thus began the development of haole prestige. As Burrows writes, "They [the natives] seem to have made the generalization that because the foreigners were superior to them in certain points of technology, they were superior in everything." [33] While some local tribes opposed the haoles as they encroached upon their land, in general, infiltration was accomplished peacefully. In 1845, an act was passed prohibiting aliens from acquiring fee simple title to the land.[34] As in the case of the Indians, however, when this act was repealed in 1850, native Hawaiians sold their land for ready cash.

During the period under review, and extending beyond it, the Hawaiian population declined at a staggering rate. From an estimated 300,000 in 1778, the 1940 count shows 21,063 pure Hawaiians, and 44,228 part Hawaiians. (See Table 24)

Adams has summarized the causes for this phenomenal population decline as follows: (1) the sanguinary wars which continued for 17 years after Captain Cook's first visit; (2) the introduction by foreigners of diseases new and highly fatal to the natives; (3) the hardship and exposure incident to their new relations with foreigners, such as the cutting and carrying of candlewood, service on whaling ships, and the contributions of foodstuffs required for trade; (4) the serious disorganization of production due to trade and to contacts with the foreigners; (5) the decadence of the old moral order; and (6) the inability of a primitive people to meet the requirements of the new situation promptly.[35] In short, it is clear that this rapid decimation of the Hawaiian population was influenced by haole infiltration, even

[33] Edwin G. Burrows, *Hawaiian Americans* (New Haven: Yale University Press, 1947), p. 17.
[34] *Ibid.*, p. 40.
[35] Romanzo Adams, *Interracial Marriage in Hawaii* (New York: The Macmillan Company, 1939), p. 7.

though haoles as a group or as individuals did not directly contribute to it or desire it.

In this early period began to emerge a pattern of interracial relations quite contrary to those established by north Euro-Americans in their imperialist expansion elsewhere. The number of white people in Hawaii was quite small. They came from various nations and no one nation had gained ascendancy. Hawaiian political autonomy, although influenced by white intrigue, was maintained. The power situation called for treating Hawaiians with due respect and with at least formal equality. Furthermore, the white population was predominantly male, and thus many of those who remained permanently often married Hawaiian women. Such intermarriage was further facilitated by the freedom with reference to marriage within the loosely organized native Hawaiian system.[36] Thus many conditions in the Hawaiian situation conspired against the drawing of the color line by the white people. Haole prestige, obvious even in the early days, was based more upon social class position than upon race consciousness. In terms of dominant-minority relations, this is the most significant development in the early period.

The establishment of American haole dominance. In the latter half of the 19th century, white people established a firm control over Hawaiian society. The issue of nationalistic rivalries between the whites from imperialist nations was resolved in favor of the Americans. Agitation in the islands for annexation to the United States arose, ultimately producing a revolution and the formation of a provisional government favorable to annexation. Official transfer of sovereignty from the Republic of Hawaii to the United States occurred on August 12, 1898.

Economic Dominance. Prior to annexation, control over the Hawaiian economy by American haoles had been substantially accomplished through the concentration of control over the elaborated plantation system and its auxiliary financial and shipping enterprises. This control was vested substantially in five corporations.

[The Big Five] act in the capacity of factors or agents for all but three of the sugar companies operating in Hawaii, and have substantial stock holdings in these companies. Together, the Big Five control about 96 per cent of island sugar production. Largest of these agencies is American Factors, Ltd., which was formed in 1918 to take over the business of the German firm of H. Hackfeld & Company, and which in 1945 represented nine plantations responsible for 30.8 per cent of the total sugar produced. The others are C. Brewer

[36] *Ibid.,* pp. 46-48.

& Company, Ltd., with 23.5 per cent; Alexander & Baldwin, with 20.8 per cent; Castle & Cook, Ltd., with 14.5 per cent; and Theo. H. Davies & Company, Ltd., with 6.9 per cent. The agency system is less used in the pineapple industry, although some of the Big Five have an interest in that industry. The Big Five have holdings in other important enterprises such as public utilities, docks, shipping companies, banks, hotels, department stores, and affiliated concerns. Power is held not only through direct stock ownership but through financing and supply contracts, through holding companies, through complicated land-leasing systems, through control over transportation agencies, through personal interfamily relationships, through trusteeships, and through a web of interlocking directorates.[37]

This great economic development in Hawaii under American corporate direction would not have been possible without an additional labor supply. Due to their population decline, there were not enough Hawaiians. Futhermore, the natives were not a success as plantation workers. Burrows writes, "The whole idea of steady work for wages was so foreign to their old culture that it had no value to appeal to them. . . . when an Hawaiian was hired to work on the plantations, he would work, as a rule, only until he had enough money to buy what he wanted at the moment, and to give his friends a good time."[38] The labor problem was solved by the importation, under contract in some cases and by active persuasion in others, of a succession of immigrants from various parts of Asia and elsewhere. The order of succession of these ethnic groups is seen in the population composition in Table 24, the Chinese, the Portugese, the Japanese, and, considerably later, the Puerto Ricans and Filipinos.

This process of immigration to Hawaii developed into a pattern. The need was for cheap and tractable labor. Each new ethnic group as it came in would at first serve the purpose as plantation workers. As its members became better adjusted to island life, some would grow discontented with their menial lot. Of these, some began to desert the fields for the city, and others returned back home. As a result the planters needed constant new replacements. As the numbers of any one ethnic group became more numerous, the characteristic antagonism seen in similar situations arose, first showing itself among other competing workers. It was strategic for the planters to try a new ethnic source in order to allay public antagonism against any one group. Another circumstance likewise suggested this course of action. The longer any group of workers stayed in Hawaii, the less tractable they became. While the growth of a strong labor movement in Hawaii is a quite recent development, there was some organization among workers with

[37] Ralph S. Kuykendall, and A. Grove Day, *Hawaii: A History* (New York: Prentice-Hall, Inc., 1948), pp. 271-272. By permission.
[38] Burrows, *op. cit.*, pp. 41-43. By permission of the publishers, Yale University Press.

attempted strikes in the early 19th century. An ethnically divided working group was less likely to develop strong labor solidarity.

The drawing of racial lines in labor activities has, indeed, been one of the chief causes of lack of labor solidarity. Early in the century, the policy of denying to Orientals membership in the skilled trades unions smashed all hopes for effective organization, for a "one-nationality" union arouses prejudice and may be crippled by competing workers from another national or racial group, who will work for lower wages or even act as strikebreakers. Discrimination has been charged; it was once a common saying in Hawaii that there are three kinds of payment for the same kind of work—what *haoles* pay *haoles,* what *haoles* pay Orientals, and what Orientals pay Orientals. Racial loyalties have conflicted with labor-group loyalties, although racial antagonism in Hawaii has never been acute. Language difficulties and differences in culture and outlook have further divided allegiances to working-class ideals.[39]

Although after annexation, contract labor became illegal, the planters still managed on the one hand to locate the further labor supply needed and on the other to control the inflow in terms of their requirements.

Political Dominance. Wherever the economic control of an area is highly concentrated in relatively few hands, the same economic interests in large measure control the politics and government. Hawaii has been no exception. While it is true that under American rule, all the formal democratic institutions of the American governmental system have been established in Hawaii, practically all writers on the Hawaiian scene conclude that the Big Five substantially control the political life of the territory. Illustrative are these remarks of Barber.

Moreover, they [the Big Five] are represented indirectly in the political affairs of the Territory, members of the legislature being linked with the Big Five, either through former association (or as in the case of the Speaker of the lower House, through being legal counsel for the sugar industry), or through the bonds of kinship.[40]

In spite of the fact that the nonhaole groups combined constituted a numerical majority, they did not until the past two decades seriously challenge haole political domination. Although the Japanese are by far the largest of the ethnic groups, "it was not until 1930 that a number of Japanese-American candidates appeared in the primaries." [41] It will be recalled that Federal law made foreign-born Orientals ineligible for citizenship.

[39] Kuykendall and Day, *op. cit.,* p. 275.
[40] From Hawaii, *Restless Rampart,* by Joseph Barber, Jr., copyright 1941, used by special permission of the publishers, The Bobbs-Merrill Company, Inc., p. 46.
[41] Bradford Smith, *Americans From Japan* (Philadelphia: J. B. Lippincott Company, 1948), p. 166.

An analysis of the class structure of Hawaii reveals the over-all social dominance of haoles, even though the picture is complicated by class division within the major nonhaole groups. The upper class is composed of haoles entirely. Almost all the other haoles are in the middle class. White people, prior to World War II, were not imported as laborers in the expanding economy. The small number of lower class haoles are, or are descended from, sailors or other occasional travelers who decided to stay there. Some of those belong in the "beachcomber" category; others are conventional workers' families. Since the other racial groups are largely of lower class status, haole social dominance is in considerable measure a function of their position in the over-all class structure. Within the other racial groups, class differences are distinct and important. Among the Hawaiians the families descended from chiefs are superior to the commoners; among the Chinese the Punti are superior to the Hakka; and the "regular" Japanese consider themselves above the Okinawans.[42] Nevertheless a "color line" in social status separates the higher class colored segments from both the middle and upper class haoles, and the line is drawn by the haoles.

Interpersonal relations: haole discrimination. The reality of the formal, institutionalized pattern of racial equality in Hawaii is attested by practically all writers on the Hawaiian scene. There are no Jim Crow rules in Hawaii; no segregation in schooling; no laws against intermarriage. On the other hand, practically all writers indicate that underneath the surface there are indications of prejudice and discrimination in which race consciousness is a predominant factor. Burrows writes:

. . . throughout their school years the Hawaiian born of Oriental stock have become more and more American. The process was favored by an atmosphere kindlier toward their race, and more tolerant of racial and cultural differences, than that of the American mainland. But when they got out of school, and set out to win their way toward prosperity, as good Americans are expected to do, they met with a rude shock. They found that the tolerance and friendliness among races, for which Hawaii has been justly celebrated, prevailed only within limits, and at a price. The price demanded by the dominant haoles— never in so many words, but nevertheless insistent—has been cheerful acceptance by other peoples of a subordinate place.[43]

Fortune found in 1940:

But with land control what it is, there just isn't room for the sons of the Japanese, the Portuguese, and the Filipinos to graduate from field work to small scale ownership of agricultural lands. Racial differences prevent their rise to important posts within the haole setup.[44]

[42] The writer is indebted to Edwin Burrows who by correspondence has provided information on the Hawaiian class structure.
[43] Burrows, *op. cit.*, p. 85. By permission of the publishers, Yale University Press.
[44] *Fortune*, August 1940, "Hawaii: Sugar-Coated Fort," p. 81. By permission.

Referring to haole relations with the Japanese, Bradford Smith cites instances of occupational and social discrimination.

Discrimination appears in social life as well as in business. . . . The principal of a Honolulu school told me that in sixteen years as a teacher . . . he had come to know only three or four haoles well enough to enter their homes, and all of them were from the mainland. Even in the faculty lunch rooms racial lines hold in the table groups.

Social considerations also affect advancement in jobs. A plantation manager wanted to appoint a Nisei chief electrician. If he did, the Nisei and his family would move into a house in the supervisor's area and his wife would have to be invited to social affairs with the other supervisors' wives. The ladies refused to do this. So the man was not appointed.[45]

Beaglehole finds that the haoles look at the Hawaiians in the typical stereotype A, as an inferior, lazy, happy-go-lucky people. Those haoles who have little contact with the natives react toward them with a paternalistic, sentimental attitude, partly out of envy that as good Americans they themselves must work hard to get ahead. Other haoles who come in closer contact with the Hawaiians find these same traits annoying.[46] Indications of racial prejudice are also seen in the attitudes of nonhaole groups toward others. Attitudes of youth are indicated in a study of a group of Hawaiian and part-Hawaiian pupils, ranging in age from 12 to 20, in the Kamehameha Schools. These children were asked to check the cultural groups toward whom they felt friendly, moderately friendly, tolerant, or only unfriendly. Beaglehole found that "in general . . . Hawaiian youth feels most friendly to members of those cultural groups who are friendly to them, who are good neighbors, workmen, servants, playmates, or with whom it mingles closely for any purpose whatever. . . . irrespective of the racial antecedents of the individual making the judgment." "The pupils felt most friendly to the Hawaiians, and then in order follow haoles (whites), Chinese, Japanese, Portuguese, Koreans, and Filipinos. . . ."[47]

The same writer cites a study by Masuoka on Japanese attitudes toward others.

When each racial group in the territory is rated according to socioeconomic status, it appears that the Japanese have a prejudice against the Puerto Ricans, Filipinos, and probably the Portugese. They are positively attracted to the whites and the Chinese. Intermediate between these two groups are the white-Hawaiians, Hawaiians, and Asiatic-Hawaiians in this order.[48]

[45] Bradford Smith, *op. cit.*, pp. 160-161. By permission of the pubishers, J. B. Lippincott Company.
[46] Ernest Beaglehole, *Some Modern Hawaiians,* University of Hawaii Research Publications, No. 19 (1937), pp. 119-120.
[47] *Ibid.*, pp. 128, 131.
[48] *Ibid.*, pp. 121-122.

Nonhaole reaction to haole dominance. How have nonhaoles as individuals and as groups reacted to haole dominance? Since Burrows studied the Hawaiian scene from this point of reference, his findings will be drawn upon. Burrows adopts Leighton's scheme of analysis and applies it to the Hawaiian scene. According to this procedure there are three main ways in which minorities react to the stress and frustration engendered by minority status: by aggressiveness, by withdrawal, and by cooperation.

Aggression. This has not been characteristic of any of the groups except the Hawaiians at the two periods of their maximum stress: around 1830, when the haoles were rapidly assuming dominance; and in the period of the 1880's when haoles assumed control of the government. Also for a brief period, suicide seems to have been more frequent among the Chinese. The only form of aggression which has been at all common among the minorities has been the mildest one of grumbling.

Withdrawal. The extreme forms of withdrawal seem to have been more frequent among the Hawaiians than among the Orientals. They are manifested in happy-go-lucky apathy, such as drinking extensively and in reverting to the extreme exaggeration of taking life easy—going fishing, strumming the ukulele, and other ways. Extreme withdrawal is further manifested by religious reversion, sometimes by revival of traditional Hawaiian rites and practices and other times by embracing new cults.

According to Burrows, "recreative reversion" is gaining ground during the last generation in pronounced forms.[49] This mildest form of withdrawal is illustrated by the revival of interests in the traditional culture of their native lands. Among the Hawaiians the revival of ancient pageantry, the hula-hula dance, and folklore; among the Chinese, the revival of Chinese drama and music; among the Japanese likewise, revival in Japanese arts, in which dancing is conspicuous, are all manifestations of recreative reversions. While withdrawal has been more frequent than aggression, it is still confined to a minority of the persons in the groups involved.

Cooperation. Cooperation has been the main form of reaction to haole dominance. For the most part, this has been in the form of passive conformity to the demands placed upon them by the haoles. In fewer instances it takes the form of ascetism where the individual meticulously avoids all that is forbidden and drives himself to do his full duty. During the war, this expressed itself often among Japanese-American soldiers who drove themselves to heroic martyrdom in acts "above and beyond the call of duty."

[49] Burrows, *op. cit.*, pp. 167-198.

The rise of the nonhaoles. World War II marks a turning point in Hawaiian intergroup relations. The circumstances of war introduced new tensions which were of a temporary nature. However, the war further accelerated certain trends which had commenced in the period of haole dominance.

Wartime Tensions. The exigencies of war brought to the islands an influx of mainland civilian workers and military personnel, not accustomed to Hawaii's pattern of race relations.

As early as 1940 the mounting tide of defense workers, which was to more than double the size of the civilian population of Caucasian ancestry in Hawaii within six years, had begun to make its impact upon the sensitive balance of race relations within the territory. Despite the fairly frequent instances of "shacking up" with local girls, the defense workers generally were highly critical of the free and easy association of the various racial groups in the Islands. Most of them came with fixed ideas, derived from experience with the Negro in the South or with the Oriental and the Filipino on the West Coast. Although living in Hawaii, the psychological barriers they brought with them, along with the limitations imposed by their occupations and their segregated residence, prevented most of them from really becoming "at home" in Hawaii.[50]

The onset of World War II placed the Japanese in Hawaii in a peculiarly difficult situation. As the largest of the archipelago's ethnic groups, the Japanese had always been suspect to many of the haole population. It was almost inevitable that in consequence of the attack on Pearl Harbor, suspicion of their possible disloyalty should arise. Andrew Lind, sociologist at the University of Hawaii, made an intensive study of the situation of the Japanese in Hawaii following Pearl Harbor.[51] As Lind indicates, numerous stories of alleged sabotage by Hawaiian Japanese aiding in the success of the Pearl Harbor attack and of other sabotage activities were widely circulated through the islands and on the mainland United States. On the whole, however, he finds that the stories were given more credence on the mainland than in Hawaii itself. As we pointed out in Chapter 7, Hawaiian authorities imposed limited restrictions upon those Japanese who were enemy aliens but not upon the whole group. As to facts concerning Japanese, Lind cites from a number of official sources, to the effect that there was no evidence of sabotage on the part of Hawaii's Japanese.[52] The generally cooperative behavior of the Japanese, including the service of

[50] Andrew W. Lind, "Recent Trends in Hawaiian Race Relations," *Race Relations,* Vol. V, Numbers 3 & 4 (Dec. 1947, Jan. 1948), p. 60. By permission of the publisher, Fisk University.
[51] Andrew W. Lind, *Hawaii's Japanese* (Princeton: Princeton University Press, 1946).
[52] *Ibid.,* pp. 43-46. Among the authorities quoted are Henry L. Stimson, Secretary of War, the Federal Bureau of Investigation, the Army Intelligence in Hawaii, and the Police Chief of Honolulu.

many Hawaiian Japanese young men and women in the armed services, demonstrated their loyalty to the United States. "The net effect of
the war upon the Japanese," writes Lind, "has been clearly to hasten
and assist their participation in the broader life of the Hawaiian community." [53]

The Acculturation of the Nonhaole Peoples. A more lasting consequence of World War II was the impetus given toward the assimilation of Hawaii's minorities which increasingly challenge haole dominance. The children of immigrant Orientals were being acculturated
rapidly to the haole way of life. All the native born were educated in
public schools of a modern American type. "By 1940, approximately
65 per cent of the American citizens of Japanese ancestry over the age
of twenty-five had completed eight or more years of American schooling
as compared with only 30 per cent in the entire population of the
Territory." [54] The public school system has encouraged all its pupils
to conceive of themselves as full-fledged members of a free and democratic society. As the native born come of age, which did not occur in
Hawaii in any considerable number except for the Chinese and Hawaiians prior to 1920, they began to participate more actively in political
life. Illustrative of the American orientation of the native born Japanese in comparison with their foreign born parents, is Bradford
Smith's comment concerning Nisei reaction to Issei attitudes toward
Japan's informal war against China after 1931. "The Nisei resented
the partisanship of their parents. They resented anything which set
them apart from other young Americans. They resented the contributions to Japanese militarism. Family arguments grew bitter, family relations more strained." [55]

Following in the footsteps of the earlier Chinese, the more enter-
prising of the Japanese moved from agricultural work into the cities,
and there have shown upward occupational mobility. "By 1930 the
Japanese were operating 49 per cent of the retail stores in Hawaii and
provided 43 per cent of the salesmen." Again, "Fifteen per cent of
the Japanese gainfully employed in 1940 were in preferred professional, proprietary, and managerial occupations as compared with
13.7 per cent of the total population." [56]

The war gave great impetus to this process of acculturation through
the opportunity it offered to participate in the common community
war activities and through the improved economic welfare it afforded.

[53] *Ibid.,* p. 258.
[54] *Ibid.,* p. 18. By permission of publishers, Princeton University Press.
[55] Bradford Smith, *op. cit.,* p. 147.
[56] Lind, *Hawaiia's Japanese,* pp. 17-18. By permission of the pubishers, Princeton
University Press.

Toward economic democracy. We have noted above the absence of any substantial unionization of nonhaole labor in Hawaii. As late as 1935 the membership of all unions was only 500. Between then and the Pearl Harbor attack, the numbers grew to 10,000. While the active list dropped to 4000 during the war largely because Federal Government regulation virtually dictated wages and working conditions at high levels, its postwar growth has been very rapid. "In 1947, two years after V-J Day, there were 47 organizations in the territory affiliated with the American Federation of Labor, 18 with the CIO (including five I.L.W.U. locals), 4 independent unions, and 5 government employees' organizations. Total membership claimed by the unions, exclusive of governmental employees, was 55,000 to 60,000." [57]

The significance of this postwar development of unionism to race relations in Hawaii has been summarized by Lind.

The sudden spread of the labor movement in Hawaii since the close of the war has widened somewhat the breach between the haole elite and the combined nonhaole laboring groups. The plantation character of Island economy has long given rise to the myth that the haoles had a monopoly of the preferred positions, while the nonwhite groups performed only the menial tasks and occupied the inferior positions. The rapidly expanding labor unions, particularly those on the plantations, have drawn their membership as well as their lay leadership chiefly from the nonhaole groups, and the subsequent conflicts between the unions and the employers have reenforced the sense of a schism on racial lines. Actually, of course, the professional leadership in the unions is largely Caucasian, and an increasing proportion of the recently acquired wealth in Hawaii is held by nonhaoles. As time goes on, it will become progressively more difficult to maintain even the fiction of a racial hierarchy in Hawaii.[58]

Lind in 1948 gave his summary of the present trends in race relations.

It is difficult to assess with any great precision the present state of race relations in Hawaii. There is a greater willingness than ever before to discuss the situation freely and openly, but this is by no means a necessary evidence of greater tension. The less privileged groups are more disposed than ever to speak out for their rights under the Hawaiian code of race relations, and there is an increasing recognition throughout the community that the various immigrant groups "have come of age" and that the individual must be judged on his own merit rather than on the basis of his racial ancestry. Whatever limitations the Islands may present in the way of hidden prejudice and of racial exclusiveness, these barriers appear far less restrictive and ominous

[57] Kuykendall and Day, *op. cit.*, p. 283.
[58] Lind, "Recent Trends in Hawaiian Race Relations." *Race Relations*, Vol. 5, Nos. 3–4 (Dec. 1947–Jan. 1948), p. 62. By permission of the publishers, Fisk University.

in Hawaii than in most other parts of the world. There are difficulties and conflicts, but the prospects of building a genuinely interracial community are considered bright.[59]

Prospects of statehood. The only special problem presented by Hawaii for the United States relates to its future political status, the question whether or not it should be admitted to statehood. Our interest in this problem lies in the implications of the problem with respect to dominant-minority relations. Viewed by rational criteria of readiness for statehood, Hawaii ranks high in nearly every item. It is a prosperous area with a specialized economy whose products are essential to mainland economy. It is not overpopulated as is Puerto Rico. Fifty years of free education have produced a highly literate population. Both education and practice in political democratic processes qualify an increasing part of its population for participation in full American citizenship. The younger members of the nonhaole group are substantially American in their culture. Their loyalty has been well tested and was not found wanting.

The obstacles to statehood in the past have been Big Five opposition, mainland apathy, and mainland racialism. Big Five opposition has changed to favor statehood. As a result of the declining isolationism attendant to the postwar era, mainland public interest in all the territories has increased.

The admission of Hawaii to statehood continues to be resisted by those elements of mainland opinion with racialist attitudes, those who still hold to the idea that colored races are unassimilable. Objectively their case is weak. Hawaiian haoles now consider the nonhaoles assimilable, and the latter are likely to stay in Hawaii since their economic outlook and their status prospect are brighter there than on the mainland. All the race conscious have to fear from Hawaiian statehood is the probability that eventually some of the Senators and Representatives from Hawaii will be of Asiatic ancestry. But since there are now Negro Congressmen, Hawaiian members would set no color precedent. Representatives from Hawaii of Oriental background would logically be expected to ally themselves in Congress with those actively working to remove all American minority disabilities.

SOME IMPLICATIONS OF THE HAWAIIAN SITUATION FOR THEORY OF DOMINANT-MINORITY RELATIONS

The power of the mores. The power of mores alone as a factor influencing the course of dominant-minority relations is strongly illustrated in

[59] *Ibid.*, p. 62. By permission of the publishers, Fisk University.

the Hawaiian situation. Due to a particular set of circumstances in the early haole-nonhaole relations, a formal pattern of racial equality developed and as through the years it became explicit and traditional, it has operated persistently against the many forces present in Hawaii pressing in the opposite direction. In contrast, in the mainland South other circumstances conspired to establish the mores of inequality and segregation. The mores once established become powerful factors to check the many influences in the Southern situation operating toward the undermining of caste.

The cumulative effect of democratic political institutions. The Hawaiian story likewise well illustrates the persistent effect of political democratic institutions in creating still more democracy. It is to be doubted that the haole group in Hawaii at the time of annexation foresaw that the introduction of free education and the democratic franchise in Hawaii would, in time, lead to the challenge of haole dominance by the colored peoples of Hawaii. Yet it now seems clear that the rise of nonhaoles to complete equality in status cannot be prevented without explicit reversals in democratic institutions.

TOPICS FOR DISCUSSION AND PROJECTS

1. Discuss the similarities and the differences in the situations of Filipinos and Puerto Ricans living in the mainland United States at present.
2. Discuss the significance of the record of the government of the United States in governing the Philippines as a territory in relation to the present international situation. In the same connection, consider the effects of the attitudes of white Americans in their interpersonal relations with Filipino people at home and abroad.
3. To what extent would migration from Puerto Rico on a scale three or four times that now taking place help to solve the economic problem of the island?
4. How do you think your community would react to the suggestion that it encourage the settlement of a sizable group of Puerto Ricans in its midst? What groups do you think would be more favorably disposed to such a project, and why? Which groups would oppose the move, and why?
5. Compare and contrast the development of dominant-minority relations in Hawaii with those which developed in the northeastern states as a result of the mass immigration from southern and eastern Europe. Explain any contrasts you find.
6. How do you account for the contrast in the manner with which the dominant group treated the Japanese in Hawaii and on the Pacific coast during World War II?
7. Discuss the question, "Why is Hawaii not admitted to statehood?" The *Congressional Record* and reports of committee hearings on the issue may give some clues.

SUGGESTED READING

Adams, Romanzo. *Interracial Marriage in Hawaii*. New York: The Macmillan Company, 1937.
> *While primarily concerned with intermarriage, the book contains much material on the intergroup relations in Hawaii in general.*

Bogardus, Emory. "Filipino Repatriation", *Sociology and Social Research*, Vol. 21, pp. 67-71.
> *An analysis of the reasons why few Filipinos went home under the terms of the Repatriation Act.*

Buaken, Manuel. *I Have Lived With the American People*. Caldwell, Idaho: The Caxton Printers, Ltd., 1948.
> *The story of the Filipinos in the United States as described by a Filipino American.*

Gordon, Maxine. "Race Patterns and Prejudice in Puerto Rico," *American Sociological Review*, Vol. 14, No. 2, pp. 294-301.
> *Finds much evidence of prejudice against color in the traditional sanctions, if not in the overt institutions of the island.*

Kirk, Grayson. "The Filipinos," *The Annals of the American Academy of Political and Social Science*, Vol. 223, September, 1942, pp. 45-48.
> *A brief discussion of the legal complications and the social problems arising from Filipino immigration to the mainland United States.*

Kuykendall, Ralph S. and Day, A. Grove. *Hawaii: A History*. New York: Prentice-Hall, Inc., 1948.
> *Best brief and up-to-date history of the islands, treating the subject in a way highly useful to the sociological student.*

Lasker, Bruno. *Filipino Immigration*. Chicago: University of Chicago Press, 1931.
> *The most comprehensive treatment of the subject up to 1931.*

Mills, C. Wright, et al., *Puerto Rican Journey*. New York: Harper and Brothers, 1950.
> *Final presentation of the Columbia University Bureau of Applied Social Research Studies of the Puerto Rican Migrants.*

Perloff, Harvey S. *Puerto Rico's Economic Future*. Chicago: The University of Chicago Press, 1950.
> *An excellent study of the economic development of Puerto Rico with emphasis on the trends since the New Deal program was inaugurated.*

Smith, Bradford. *Peoples from Japan*. Philadelphia: J. B. Lippincott Company, 1948. The Peoples of America Series.
> *Part 1 of this book gives a popularly written account of the Japanese people in Hawaii.*

Smith, W. C. "Minority Groups in Hawaii," *Annals of the American Academy of Political and Social Science*, Vol. 223, 1942.
> *An account of the minority situation in Hawaii during World War II.*

PART FIVE

Religious Difference
and Minority Status

Involved in the complex of cultural differences which have served to make certain minorities visible, has been the difference of religion. A large number of the members of European immigrant groups have been Catholics; and a preponderance of the Oriental immigrants have been non-Christian. In the process of acculturation, this religious difference from the normative Protestantism of the native Americans has been retained in larger measure than any of other cultural differences. How far this religious difference has affected dominant-minority relations engages attention in Chapter 14.

There still remains one large minority group to which we have not given specific attention—those Americans of Jewish ancestry—whose position not only in American but also in world history is unique. Involved in the complex of differences which serve to set Jews apart from the host groups among whom they dwell is their identification with the traditional heritage of the religion of Judaism. However as we attempt, in Chapter 15, to explore the enigmatic facade of Jewish-gentile relations in the United States, we shall discover reasons to doubt that it is their religious difference alone which explains their role as the perennial minority. Whatever other role Jews may play in human history, their relations with gentiles have furnished social science profound insights into the nature of the mentality of the dominant.

CHAPTER 14

Catholic-Protestant Relations
and the Minor Sects

The phenomenon of religious difference has been involved in a number of the minority situations already analyzed. Since the American population up to 1830 was predominantly Protestant, it is not surprising to note that among the cultural differences by which the Irish and, in the later immigration, many other nationality groups were identifiable by the dominant native population was their Catholicism. The majority of Oriental immigrants were likewise, of course, non-Protestant. The one large ethnic group which has not yet been considered, the Jews, are often classified as a religious, rather than a nationality, group. The relation between Jews and gentiles in the United States is so important a topic that it is dealt with in considerable detail in a subsequent chapter. In this chapter, attention is directed toward evaluating the role of religious difference per se as a determining factor of dominant or minority status. Such an inquiry is logically called for in any systematic analysis of America's minority situations. Changing aspects of the contemporary situation give to the topic, however, special significance. The assimilation process has narrowed the range of general cultural difference among American minorities, but the basic religious difference between Protestant, Catholic, and Jew remains. There are some indications that these religious differences have precipitated sharper conflict creating a potential basis for new developments in dominant-minority relations along religious lines.

Preliminary considerations. To approach the topic of religion in rela-ation to minorities, it is essential at the outset not to make certain as-sumptions. First, it should not be assumed that religious difference alone necessarily leads to conflict. While modern European history does contain abundant evidence of conflict between religious groups, a number of nations have by now reached a point in which widely vary-ing religious groups live together amicably in the same national com-munity. Secondly, it should not be assumed that all conflict which divides on a religious basis is of the nature of dominant-minority con-flict. For example, an American Protestant may oppose the policy of the Catholic Church in his community on civic issues on quite logical grounds not necessarily reflecting the dominant stereotype of Cath-olics. There are two forms of anti-Catholic behavior which it seems appropriate to designate by the terms *intergroup antagonism* and *in-terinstitutional antagonism*. In the former, the antagonism is di-rected toward the members of the religious group as persons who by their identification with the group are considered inferior. Where the power differentials permit, it results in discrimination against Cath-olics as such. In the latter, the antagonism is directed toward the reli-gion as an insitution whose policies and practices are considered by the Protestant to obstruct certain community enterprises or to jeopard-ize the freedom of Protestants. While it may be possible that the two forms reinforce each other, and that an individual Protestant may manifest both kinds of attitudes, it seems pertinent to advance this theoretical distinction as we turn to the general topic at hand.

A further preliminary consideration involves the definition of per-sons in religious terms. Who are to be considered Protestants and who Catholics? For a discussion of religious difference as a factor in inter-group relations, the religious designation applies in a broad sense. A person is a Protestant who comes from Protestant lineage, from a Prot-estant family which is identified with an ethnic background gener-ally considered Protestant. Whether an individual person from such a group is a member of a Protestant church or not, or whatever may be the degree of his religiosity is not of much moment in the counting of the size of the Protestant group. While there may be some relation be-tween active participation in church life and antagonism toward other religions, there appears to be no available research material to support any hypothesis in this connection. The definition of Catholics fol-lows the same broad line as in the case of Protestants. As compared with Protestants, far more of all the persons of Catholic background belong to a church, although again there is wide variability in the degree of participation in religious life. Again, however, in connec-tion with dominant-minority relations, it is the typical religious designation of the ethnic group which is involved. Thus both Irish and Italians are considered "Catholic" ethnic groups, even though there have been numerous enough conversions to Protestantism to note. Who are to be considered Jews in religious terms presents additional difficulties to be given attention in the following chapter.

The plan of inquiry. Among the contemporary writers on minority problems, Warner and Srole in their "Scale of Subordination and Assimilation" [1] have evaluated the factor of religious difference in the most definite terms. After first dividing all ethnic groups into five racial types, they secondarily divide within each racial hierarchical type on the basis of Protestant and non-Protestant. Still further they divide tertiarily on the basis of whether the group is English speaking or non-English speaking. The important point for the topic at hand is their insistence that Protestantism always takes prestige and precedence over non-Protestantism and that being Protestant (the racial types being equal) rates higher than speaking English. For example, among light Caucasoids the English speaking Protestants rank higher (highest of all) than all Catholics, but more important is their judgement that Protestants who do not speak English rank higher than Catholics who do speak English. While as will be indicated below, there is considerable doubt that this schema, if applied rigidly, is valid; nevertheless, we find that in adapted form it furnishes a plan for systematic pursuit of the inquiry.

PROTESTANTISM AND DOMINANT STATUS

English Protestants. Identification with an ethnic group which is Protestant is generally considered to be a mark of dominant status in American society. Historically this predominant status prestige of Protestantism derives from the fact that the earlier settlers were English Protestants and that up to 1820 they comprised an overwhelming majority of the population. Protestantism itself has been and still is highly differentiated, and this differentiation from time to time has precipitated oppositions and antagonisms which manifest some of the characteristics of a dominant-minority situation. Indeed religious intolerance is a marked feature of colonial history and persecution of those sects which branched off from those first established, or new sects which migrated directly from the Old World, were common occurrences. Illustrative is the following:

In 1656 there appeared in Boston two Quaker women, Mary Fisher and Anne Austin. By law Quakers had been adjudged as not "of the people," and

[1] William L. Warner and L. Srole, *The Social Systems of American Ethnic Groups* (New Haven: Yale University Press, 1945), p. 288. The table itself is reproduced on pp. 452-453 of the present volume.

so these two were immediately imprisoned. Their books were burned. They were examined for witch marks. For five weeks they were confined in a dark cell, denied a candle and all communication with the outside world was forbidden. Eight other Quakers who arrived later in the year were similarly treated; their imprisonment continued until a ship bore them away.[2]

In the Constitution of the United States the principle of the separation of church and state and the right of religious freedom were established. Thus, prior to the beginning of the earlier mass immigration, it may be said that all English-descended Protestant groups possessed equality in status, at least in civic terms. Subsequent however to 1820, new sects arose from within this ethnic population whose dissidence from the normative sects was so extreme as to incur persecution. Whether such groups ever occupied a minority status in terms of our concept of minority is debatable. In order to test this point, however, two of such minor dissident sects will be considered, namely, the Mormons and Jehovah's Witnesses.

Indigenous Protestant sects

Mormons. The story of the Mormons is generally well known to Americans who have studied American history. Its founders and its earlier adherents were native Americans of Protestant lineage. As a sect dissident from the major Protestant sects, the Mormons were persecuted and, moving about the country in search of a safe refuge, finally located their main center in what is now Salt Lake City, Utah. There they settled permanently, grew economically prosperous, and subsequently became a main political element in the new state. Utah was admitted to the Union in 1896 after the Mormons had foresworn the practice of polygamy hitherto permitted and encouraged, particularly for the leaders. At the present time it is clear that the Mormons are not a minority in the sense that the term is employed in this book. In fact, in Utah itself they occupy the highest prestige status. In recent years little indication may be found that the more scattered Mormons or their missionaries who travel about the country are discriminated against in minority fashion. It is even doubtful whether during the earlier years of their persecution their situation met our criteria of minority status. They had no physiognomic visibility; and furthermore their cultural visibility was limited largely to the religious aspect. With the one exception of permissive polygyny, which probably precipitated most of their persecution, their culture was not differentiated from native Protestant culture.

[2] Everett R. Clinchy, *All in the Name of God* (New York: The John Day Company, 1934), pp. 30-31. By permission.

Jehovah's Witnesses. This less known sect presents a generally similar parallel to the Mormons. Our brief discussion of this religion and its adherents is drawn from Stroup's study.[3] Jehovah's Witnesses, whose beliefs are dissident from the established Protestant sects, founded their order in Pittsburgh in 1872. Stroup calls it "one of the most complete examples in form and spirit of truly American religious society." The society has lacked the geographical identification which the Mormons achieved, and on the local community basis, the Witnesses do not form a distinctive colony. Their members, estimated at close to 100,000, are scattered in groups over much of the nation. Stroup presents little evidence that these people were or are discriminated against. Antagonism to them seems largely to have been confined to two issues: their unwillingness to "salute the flag," which has caused trouble in the school system, and their unwillingness to participate in America's wars. Stroup states that the latter is not due to categorical pacifism but to their conviction that the particular wars were unjust. This interesting little sect hardly qualifies as a minority since the reaction of the outside world is primarily indifferent. The Witnesses themselves, however, hold a dim view of the outside world. From Stroup's account it is clear that such vitality as the group possesses derives in large measure from its constant verbal attack upon everything in the general culture and society. Their earlier opposition to Catholicism was met by some local priests with counterattacks. From experience, Catholic leaders have discovered that to ignore the Witnesses altogether seems a better method of undermining their influence.

Protestant non-English speaking peoples. The leading Protestant Caucasoid non-English speaking ethnic groups in the United States are the Dutch and the three Scandinavian groups, the Swedes, the Norse, the Danes. The Germans might be included also since they are predominantly Protestant. That the minority status of these peoples in the United States has never been so pronounced as that of the non-English speaking Catholics, and that in any event their assimilation has been more rapid was indicated in Chapter 4. Because their general cultural kinship to the English is so much closer than that of the Catholic nationalities, it is impossible to evaluate precisely the relative importance of the factor of Protestantism among the many others. At the time of their great migration, their Protestant denominationalism was broadly distinguishable from the established English and Scotch denominations. Lutheranism was predominant. But appearing on the

[3] Herbert H. Stroup, *Jehovah's Witnesses* (New York: Columbia University Press, 1945).

scene well after the principle of religious tolerance among Protestants was well established, their sectarian divergence from the main English denominations seems to have been of little significance. Likewise, the fact that they came after the beginning of the first great Catholic ethnic migration, that of the Irish, seemed to identify them more closely with the other Protestants. It is interesting to note that Warner and Srole say of the Armenians in "Yankee City," a much more strikingly divergent cultural group, that their similarity in background "lies only in a religious affinity between the Armenian Apostolic Church and the Episcopal Church, which led to affiliation between the two and more rapid acculturation of the Armenian group." [4]

Immigrant sects. In contrast to the "home grown" minor Protestant sects discussed above, there have been a number of European dissenting sects who migrated to the United States during the 19th century and who came here primarily for the purpose of escaping persecution in their homelands. Most of these sects which were not English were of German or Swiss derivation. Among such may be mentioned the Dunkers, a dissident Baptist sect establishing their first colony in Germantown in 1719; and the Mennonites, the first group of whom also settled in Germantown, in 1683. Several Mennonite groups migrated from Russia to which their ancestors had moved from Germany under the promise of economic assistance and of religious toleration by Catherine the Great. Persecuted by later Tsars, they came to the United States, settling largely in rural areas. Among the Mennonites in the United States, schismatic tendencies were so pronounced that in the 20th century there were 17 distinctive religious organizations which had broken off from the original Mennonite church.[5] Among the small religious communistic sects, those not of English derivation were, again, primarily of German background. The Ephrata, Pennsylvania, colony was established by a German immigrant; and the Amana Society, established near Buffalo, was inspired by religious movements in Germany. A German immigrant from Wurtemburg founded in 1803 an experimental communistic sectarian community called Harmony, in Butler County, Pennyslvania. Later moving to New Harmony, Indiana, in 1814, this sect sold their property to Robert Owen in 1824. Moving then to Economy, Pennsylvania, the group survived to 1903.[6]

[4] Warner and Srole, *op. cit.*, p. 100. In view of the very small number of Armenians in "Yankee City," it would be unwise to assume that their status throughout the United States would be similar to that found in "Yankee City."
[5] Elmer T. Clark, *The Small Sects in America* (New York and Nashville: Abingdon-Cokesbury Press, rev. ed., 1949), p. 187.
[6] *Ibid.*, p. 139.

Our interest in these immigrant sects concerns whether or not they were discriminated against in the manner of minorities. The studies made of these groups provide little material pertinent for use in this connection. To explore the subject of immigrant sects further, however, we shall discuss in more detail the Amish, one of the most interesting of the many sects splintering off the main Mennonite stem.

The Amish. The Amish are a European bred religious sect whose dissidence from Protestantism traces back to the Mennonites, and ultimately to the Anabaptists. Of their religion Nimkoff writes:

[They] believed that religion was an individual matter, and that neither an elaborate ecclesiastical machinery of salvation nor a political organization could take the place of a living faith as a means of access to a loving Father. [They] rejected infant baptism and baptized only upon confession of faith. They believed in absolute religious toleration. They held the doctrine of nonresistance, believing that only love and good will could successfully combat such evils as spring from human passion and hatred. They had a strong sense of otherworldliness. They interpreted the Scriptures literally. They stressed the need of living a pure life.[7]

Although the Amish are commonly thought of in ethnic terms as Pennsylvania Dutch, they are in fact descended from Swiss, German, and Dutch lineage. Their first settlement was in Germantown, Pennsylvania, and they are still identified with Lancaster County in that state. They have, however, spread out in colonies intermittently located in the central United States and Canada and are now estimated to number between 25,000 and 40,000.

The central facts about the Amish most pertinent to our interest are that their religion and their whole culture are one and inseparable; and that being a dissident sect with long experience in being persecuted, they in fact desire only a limited acculturation and assimilation. For these purposes their choice of rural areas to establish their separate community life was felicitous. The studies of the Amish made by outsiders dwell more upon their culture than upon their relations with other groups; hence we lack materials to evaluate the dominant group relations with them. In the areas where they live, the Amish are highly visible by their garb and tonsorial customs. The men, for example, wear ankle length cuffless trousers and white muslin shirts at all times. Single and married men may be distinguished by the fact that the latter never shave. It is inevitable that the native population consider the Amish "queer" and poke fun at them. Yet it is questionable if they are actually discriminated against. In spite of religious

[7] Meyer F. Nimkoff, *Marriage and the Family* (Boston: Houghton Mifflin Company, 1947), pp. 242-243. By permission.

taboos which preclude the use of modern techniques in agriculture, they have been reasonably prosperous and for this they are respected. Their chief conflict with the larger community has been in connection with education and, in wartime, with military service. The Amish do not consider education beyond the eighth grade essential and they prefer to educate their children themselves. Nimkoff writes, "Recently a group bought an old discarded one-room schoolhouse, and are sending their children there to a private teacher rather than to the new consolidated PWA school with modern equipment." [8] Aside from these particular matters, the presence of the Amish creates no special community problems. They are largely left alone—which is what they desire. On the other hand, there are no indications that any of the Amish-descended people who wish to forsake their parental culture and to become assimilated into general community life would meet with barriers from the dominant status elements.

The Molokans. An immigrant sect more divergent in cultural background than those considered above are the Molokans. Between 1905 and 1907, about 5000 persons known as Molokans fled from Trans-Caucasia because of religious persecution and settled in the United States. The single largest colony, in Los Angeles, was made the subject of comprehensive study by Pauline V. Young.[9] The first group of Russian peasants to become Molokans dissented from the Russian Orthodox Church over 250 years ago. Like the other immigrant sects their entire culture is integrated with their religion, and their desire to maintain their distinctive religion developed a strong collective consciousness shutting them off from others. The Molokans, however, differed from the other immigrant sects in selecting an urban milieu, a fact which made it more difficult for them to hold their young people to the faith. In general, their experience in adjustment to American life was similar to that of other immigrant groups in urban areas, except that their strong desire to retain their religion retarded the process of assimilation.

The interrelation of these immigrant sects with the larger society appears to follow a general pattern. The sect typically isolates itself spatially as far as possible from the rest of the society, by choosing a rural locale and attempting to develop a self-contained economy. By limiting its contact with the outside world, the sect reduces to a minimum occasion for conflict. Such conflict as has arisen characteristically involved the failure of the members of the sect to perform certain civic duties required of all citizens, which were contrary to the tenets of

---

[8] *Ibid.,* p. 251.
[9] Pauline V. Young, *Pilgrims of Russian Town* (Chicago: University of Chicago Press, 1932).

the sect. Otherwise, there is little evidence that these sects were discriminated against in the typical manner of the minorities concerned with in this book. Neither is there any indication that persons from such sects who desire to leave and become part of the larger community find any barriers interposed to their assimilation. In this connection, it is to be noted that all the sects mentioned were composed of people of north European background and that despite their dissidence, they were, after all, Protestant Christians.

"Colored" Protestants. The one most conspicuous exception to the prestige status of Protestantism is afforded by the position of American Negroes. They are preponderantly Protestant,[10] and they occupy the lowest status of all the minorities. Perhaps no other fact in the whole minorities picture documents the vastly greater significance of race consciousness as a determiner of minority status than this. When race is involved, all other factors pale into insignificance. Below, in another context, attention is drawn to an increasing conversion of Negroes to Catholicism. Insofar as this is due to a greater willingness of Catholics to admit Negroes to mixed parishes, there arises the interesting possibility that Negroes raise their status by tranferring from the dominant prestige religion to the minority prestige faith.

Further light on the relevance of religious difference in affecting minority status when race is involved may be obtained by considering the religious affiliation of the Japanese. As was noted in Chapter 7, while 55 per cent of the Japanese in America were Buddhist in 1942, 29 per cent gave their religion as Protestant and 2 per cent as Catholic. Clearly the very considerable conversion of Japanese to Christianity is an aspect of their acculturation. Comparing the native and foreign born, one finds 33 per cent of the former are Protestant against 22 per cent of the latter.[11] The functional contribution of Protestant conversion in the adjustment to American culture is analyzed in Miyimato's Seattle study, in which he places the more passive resigned view of Buddhism in contrast to the more optimistic "reform the world" philosophy of contemporary Protestantism.[12] Research observation is lacking, however, to indicate whether the Japanese who became Christians are treated differently by white dominants because of their conversion. In Seattle in the late 1930's, the Japanese Protestants were organized in separate churches.[13] Concerning

[10] Jessie Bernard, *American Community Behavior* (New York: The Dryden Press, Inc., 1949). p. 252.
[11] *The Evacuated People*, United States Department of Interior, War Relocation Authority (Washington: Government Printing Office), p. 79.
[12] Shotaro F. Miyamoto, *Social Solidarity Among the Japanese in Seattle* (Seattle: University of Washington Publications, 1939), pp. 99-104.
[13] *Ibid.*, p. 99.

this situation, Smith writes, "So Christianity, which began by direct-ing its adherents to America, ended by keeping them in segregated churches and helping to calcify the shell which surrounded them." [14]

CATHOLICISM AND MINORITY STATUS

The religious differentiation of the American population between Catholics and Protestants became a phenomenon of social significance following the large Irish immigration. While in the colonial and early national population, there was a small number of Catholics, there appears to have been no marked interest in their relations with the native large majority of Protestant people. As was indicated in Chapter 4, the Irish as the first large non-English immigrant group were reacted to as a minority, especially by the native Protestants in the areas of greatest Irish concentration. The Irish were also the first great Catholic group to enter the United States, and thus there was interwoven in the constellation of dominant antagonistic atti-tudes toward the Irish a derogatory attitude toward their Catholicism. In the later immigration, the new ethnic groups arriving were also predominantly Catholic, notably Italians, Poles, and French-Ca-nadians. Because ethnic difference in general was associated with Catholicism, it is almost impossible to evaluate the relative impor-tance of their Catholicism alone as a symbol of minority status. Mac-Iver writes:

We do not dispute that difference of religion is sometimes a determinant of the type of discrimination we have in view. A Protestant employer, for ex-ample, may reject the most qualified applicant for a position solely because he is a Roman Catholic, and the Roman Catholic employer may similarly turn down the Protestant. But we do not find sufficient reason to regard religion *by itself* as of crucial importance in provoking the tensions and cleavages manifested in the everyday relationships of American society.[15]

While it is true that all Protestant north European peoples assim-ilated more rapidly, their cultural nearness to the English was more broadly similar. Better test cases for the problem at hand would be the Germans and Hungarians where, particularly among the latter, there were considerable numbers of both religious groups. Unfortu-nately, no studies seem to be available to indicate whether the status of Hungarian Protestants, for example, rose more rapidly than that of Hungarian Catholics. Further insight concerning the significance of Catholicism in relation to minority status may be gained from com-

[14] Bradford Smith, *Peoples from Japan* (Philadelphia: J. B. Lippincott Company, 1948), p. 228.
[15] R. M. MacIver, *The More Perfect Union* (New York: The Macmillan Company, 1948), p. 12. By permission.

paring the situation of two large Catholic immigrant groups, the Irish and the Italians, both of Caucasian stock.

The Irish as Catholics. In the general story of native-immigrant relations in Chapter 4, the earlier minority status of the Irish was indicated. Also noted in the community studies cited was the special role they came to play as the leaders of ethnic groups, especially those of Catholic persuasion. As the first great Catholic group, the Irish had approximately a generation of adjustment to life in the United States before subsequent Catholic ethnic peoples appeared on the scene. With this experience they became adept at politics especially on the local level. The common bond of Catholicism with the others, enabled the Irish to gain sufficient strength to wrest control of government in many northeastern cities from the dominant native group and eventually to play a leading role in state and national politics. Finally, within the Church itself the Irish acquired a dominating role both among the clergy and the laity.

Through these hundred years, Americans of Irish descent have become assimilated. The "Yankee City" Irish by 1933 had distributed themselves through all classes except the topmost level.[16] In formal association and in cliques, the Irish intermingle extensively with Protestant peoples. In the absence of specific studies on the point, it appears that persons of Irish Catholic lineage intermarry with Protestants especially in the middle and upper class levels more than do the other Catholic ethnic groups. It is also common knowledge that romances across these lines are often opposed by both sets of parents. From the Irish side, opposition arises out of intense loyalty to Catholicism. While, on the Protestant side, the opposition may contain residual elements of antipathy to "aliens," it is also frequently based more rationally upon the very real problems which Protestant-Catholic marriages precipitate. The assimilation of the Irish is further attested by the lack of in-group solidarity which their variable class statuses have accelerated. Concerning this the "Yankee City" study finds as follows:

Internally, the Irish group is now differentiated according to position in the city's class system. The growing identification with class level and the usual manifestations of extreme class distance have served to break up the Irish group's inner cohesion. The result is seen in the sharp antagonisms which exist between the Irish of the two lowest classes (lower-lower and upper-lower) and of the two higher classes (upper-middle and lower-upper). The former refer to the latter as "lace-curtain Irish," a term with reproachful connotations, and associate them with the Hill Street "codfish aristocracy."

[16] Warner and Srole, *op. cit.*, p. 93.

The higher-class Irish, when aroused, will apply to the Irish of the lower classes the familiar epithet, "shanty Irish." The lower-middle-class Irish seem to keep to the fence in this conflict between the two class factions in the group.[17]

Earlier studies of minorities refer to the Irish as the highest ranking minority. On the basis of the above discussion we advance the hypothesis that the Irish as such are no longer a minority at all. The two main elements which provide some common bond of union among the Irish in America are the still surviving anti-British attitude and their especial identification with Catholicism. The former was manifested in the spring of 1950 by the "snub" given to the Protestant Premier of North Ireland when he visited New York City, by the city administration. The latter was discussed previously. The prominence of the Irish in Roman Catholic leadership is in part a function of their relatively higher economic and political status. But above and beyond this, they continue to display evidences of being the most intensely loyal and devoted to the Church of all the Catholics in America. Because this is their only remaining basis of "visibility," it follows that to any extent to which the Irish are now, or may be in the future, a minority, it will be as Catholics and not as Irish. The above evaluation of the Irish as Catholics may be set in contrast to the status of Italians as Catholics.

The Italians as Catholics. Of the later immigrant groups, the Italians were numerically the largest. In Chapter 4, their minority status was attested. The Italians are generally considered as well an all-Catholic ethnic group. Yet in most of the literature concerning dominant reactions to the Italians, their Catholicism appears to be a less marked consideration. This may be due in part to their subordination, as with the French-Canadians in New England, to the Irish Catholics, a situation which has caused the Protestants to identify the Irish with Catholicism. In communities where the numbers of Italians have warranted the setting up of separate Italian Catholic parishes, the lower prestige rating of these parishes in relation to the Irish is apparent. Again the domination of the Irish in the Roman Catholic Church in America when placed against the traditions of Catholicism which the Italians brought with them, precipitated other conflicts. In southern Italy, local Catholicism had many adumbrations in the form of local superstitions which were less tolerated by the Irish priests than by the Italian clergy. In Italy, the communicants were not accustomed to large regular contributions to the Church; in the United States such contributions are expected. In Italy itself, the Italian men had not the

[17] *Ibid.*, p. 93. By permission of the publishers, Yale University Press.

habit of attending church as regularly as the Irish, or in other ways as actively identifying themselves with religious functions. In view of all these circumstances, it is not surprising to learn that Dr. Tolino, after considerable study of the matter, concludes that of the 6 million Italian-descended people in the United States, about one-third only are probably "good Catholics," that is, attend church regularly and go to confession.[18] Another contrast is seen in the difference concerning parochial schooling. "In school too, the two groups hardly met, for the Irish filled the parochial and the Italians the public school," writes Dr. Ware about Greenwich Village. Still further, "Most Italians, much less faithful in carrying out religious precepts, sent their children to parochial school only when the latter was more conveniently located." [19]

The above considerations suggest that what distinguishes Americans of Italian descent in the dominant stereotype is their "foreignness" and their Italianness rather than their Catholicism. However, they are becoming increasingly assimilated. Furthermore, however much less intense and active may be their manifestations of Catholicism, Italian Americans for the most part remain Catholics. There is little indication of their conversion to Protestantism. It may be therefore, that, as the Italians become more assimilated in general to the normative dominant culture, they, like the Irish, will retain visibility largely as Catholics. This possibility is further strengthened by the circumstances in the process of their assimilation leading to greater residential, occupational, formal associational, and romantic contacts first with other Catholic ethnics. While the Irish and the Italians have been used as test cases in this connection, it is probable that considering the other Caucasian Catholic ethnic groups would lead to a similar conclusion. The foregoing analysis suggests that however much the other forms of reciprocal visibility upon which dominant-minority relations rest may disappear, the distinction between Protestant and Catholic will remain a fixed difference in the foreseeable future. That this difference has been an aspect of minority situation in the past is clear. Whether it will be in the future depends in large measure upon the course of action pursued by the official institutions, the churches involved. For further consideration of this point attention in the concluding section of this chapter turns to anti-Catholicism, long an important factor in American social history, and to the bases of current opposition between the Catholic Church in America and organized Protestantism.

[18] The Rev. John V. Tolino, "The Future of the Italian American Problem," *Ecclesiastical Review*, 101:221-232, 1939.
[19] Caroline F. Ware, *Greenwich Village* (Boston: Houghton Mifflin Company, 1935), p. 132.

Anti-Catholicism. In the preceding section prejudice against Catholics has been seen to be interwoven with prejudice against foreigners, although in the case of Protestant attitudes against the now assimilated Irish, the religious prejudice appears more prominent. Anti-Catholicism, as such, has a long history in the United States. Since the great Irish invasion, it has been expressed in unorganized fashion. Such prejudice has frequently been manifested in the private conversation and humor in Protestant circles. Until recently notices of jobs have occasionally carried the stipulation that only Protestants need apply. Many social clubs and organizations refuse to admit Catholics to their membership.

Organized anti-Catholicism has been seen explicitly in organizations established since 1840. The oft-mentioned "Know-Nothing" party, officially known as the American Party, was one of its earliest expressions. It was both antislavery and anti-Catholic, and when the Compromise of 1850 temporarily allayed the antislavery agitation, the party directed its energies toward anti-Catholicism. A secret ritual of the party pledged its members to vote only for native-born Protestants. The American Protective Association, organized in 1887, was violently anti-Catholic. The new or revived Ku Klux Klan, developing after World War I, with considerable strength outside the South, was motivated by antagonism against Catholics as well as against Jews and Negroes.[20]

Present trends in Protestant-Catholic relations. With the increasing assimilation of Catholic ethnic groups and their wider social class distribution, Protestant antagonism toward Catholics had, in the opinion of Rose and Rose, by the 1930's "reached such a low point that it was questionable whether Catholics could any longer be called a minority group." [21] Since then, however, these authors indicate a marked increase of religious intolerance directed at both Catholics and Jews.

Certain actions of the Catholic Church, and the interpretation and extension of them made by certain Protestant leaders, have opened a new path toward hatred between the two dominant religious groups in the United States. Thus far the new Protestant attitudes have only occasionally been shifted from a hatred of the Catholic Church to a hatred of Catholic people, and these new attitudes have hardly been transmitted to the great masses of Protestants. Therefore it could not be said that there is today any great hatred between these religious groups. But the path has been opened, and it may be that the great bulk of the American people will move down it. The only significant

[20] For a more detailed account see C. F. Marden, "Secret Societies," in J. S. Roucek, *Social Control* (New York: D. Van Nostrand Company, Inc., 1949), Ch. 21.
[21] Arnold Rose and Caroline Rose, *America Divided* (New York: Alfred A. Knopf, Inc., 1948), p. 324.

factor preventing us from making a prediction that such hatred will flare out is the common opposition both of these groups have to Soviet Russia and Communism.[22]

The new chain of events which has led to the more sharply focused opposition between these two great religious groups appears to have been initiated by new activity from the Catholic side evoking more articulate reactions from the Protestant side. First in this connection, indications in the late 1930's appeared that the Catholic Church was engaging in a more active program to recruit new members, which in part involved conversion of persons of Protestant background or affiliation. "Great efforts were made to gain converts to the Catholic Church, and these had a notable success. Whereas the number of Catholics increased only from 18,600,000 to 19,900,000 between 1926 and 1936 (7 per cent), the number jumped to 25,000,000 by 1946 (an increase of 26 per cent)."[23] In the same connection, Bernard has written:

Perhaps the most important field of church competition is between Protestantism and Catholicism. Until recently the United States was a missionary field for the Catholic Church. That is, priests were sent from abroad to take care of Catholic parishes in American communities. . . . The Catholic Church was too busy keeping its members in line and establishing itself in their communities during the transition from Old World to New World to devote itself to converting others. Besides, proselytizing was scarcely possible with foreign-born priests.

Now that it is more secure, however, and has definitely established itself in American community life, the Catholic Church has become aggressively evangelistic. It seeks converts from other churches.[24]

Especially pertinent to the minorities field is the fact that in religious competition for new members, the Catholic Church has made a special effort to win over American Negroes, with noticeable success. The Catholic Church enters this competition with certain advantages, notwithstanding the fact that Negroes have been overwhelmingly Protestant, 70 per cent of them Baptist alone. The Roman Church has a long tradition of freedom from racism. Being primarily rooted outside the South, the Church has not been identified with Southern Protestant segregation. In practice in the North, Negroes have been admitted to white Catholic parishes far more widely than into white

[22] Ibid., p. 324. By permission of publishers, Alfred A. Knopf, Inc.
[23] Ibid., p. 55. By permission of the publishers, Alfred A. Knopf, Inc.
[24] C. C. Morrison, "Roman Catholicism and Protestantism," Christian Century 63; 747, 749 (May 12, 1946) as quoted in Bernard, op. cit., p. 248. By permission of the publishers, The Dryden Press, Inc. Readers interested in the general problem of Protestant-Catholic relations will find incisive discussion in this book in Chs. 12 and 18.

Protestant congregations. "In St. Louis, for example, while Washington University continued to exclude Negroes, St. Louis University, a Jesuit institution, opened its doors to them." [25] One of Dr. Bernard's astute observations is to suggest that the Catholic Church understands better than the Protestants that appeals in the modern world should be directed toward groups. "The Protestant group, with its evangelistic emphasis on the individual and on revivalism, still acts as though individual mentalities were the most important factor. The Catholic Church, with a more urban background, recognizes that a collectivist mentality now prevails." [26] Finally, it may be noted that in its efforts to integrate Negroes into white parishes, the centralized, authoritarian organization of the Catholic Church is highly advantageous. A student of the writer's reported eye-witness observation of the consternation and indignation arising in a predominantly Italian parish when with no warning at all at a particular mass, a strongly Negroid appearing priest presided. Of further interest is the fact that, although in the northeastern city concerned considerable tension existed between colored and white, nevertheless the parish quickly reconciled itself to the new situation.

As was to be expected, this somewhat aggressive Catholic behavior generated indignation among Protestants. However, effective counteraggression was hampered because of the lack of a centralized organization. Among the Protestant clergy may be found a considerable number who hold the most unequivocal views against discrimination and segregation. However, individual ministers are less able to change the practice of their church against the wishes of the congregation, because for American Protestantism there is no central authoritative body which determines policy for all.

More sharply defined Catholic-Protestant opposition has arisen over the contrasting stands taken in regard to specific civic issues, reflected sometimes at the national level, but more persistently in local communities where a substantial number of Catholic communicants reside. One major focus of such opposition is in the area of education. The Catholic Church urges parochial school education upon Catholic children where it is available. For this reason the official Catholic pressure may oppose additional taxes for public schools. In other instances pressure may be exercised to preclude the use of certain books or periodicals in the public schools, or to impede the introduction of certain curricula. A nationwide controversy was stirred up by the reply of Cardinal Spellman to some comments of Mrs. Eleanor Roosevelt in her newspaper column, which were construed as indicating the latter's approval of the

[25] Bernard, op. cit., p. 253.
[26] Ibid., p. 249. By permission of publishers, The Dryden Press, Inc.

Barden Bill, a measure which would have prohibited the use of Federal monies granted in aid of local education for the transportation of other than public school children to and from school.

Another common issue upon which the two religious groups divide is in the general area of family relations. Here the antagonism of non-Catholics is aroused not over the rights of Catholics to hold and practice their differing attitudes, but over what the Protestants conceive to be Catholic attempts to get the laws of the community written in such a way that they preclude Protestants from practicing their own differing concepts. Thus controversy arises over such matters as divorce laws, laws regulating the dissemination of contraceptive information, and education for family life.

Closely related to the above is the opposition arising over the matter of intermarriage. In general, it may be said that both religious institutions oppose marriage outside their own faith, although the pressure the Catholic Church is able to exert is clearly stronger. When an interfaith marriage occurs, the Catholic Church uses its influence to have the children reared in the Catholic faith and frequently to have them educated in parochial schools. In contrast, Protestant parents and clergymen claim to be more willing to approach such a situation in a spirit of compromise.

As has been suggested, this heightened religious conflict appears as yet to be in the nature of an interinstitutional conflict rather than an intergroup conflict in which reciprocal antagonistic attitudes are directed toward the persons of the opposing groups. Until such time as, if ever, it reaches the intergroup stage, dominant-minority aspects in the conflict will not be prominent. At such a time, the traditional force of anti-Catholicism, still latent in American society, would inevitably become more pronounced.

Religious difference, democracy and cultural pluralism. The foregoing treatment of Catholic-Protestant relations, past and present, has particular pertinence to the subject of cultural pluralism and democracy. A basic contrast between a large-scale democratic society and a totalitarian society is that in a democracy the right not only of individuals, but of groups as well, to differ from one another is assiduously protected. In essence, in democratic theory, groups thus differentiated have equality in status irrespective of their numerical size. The changing aspects of social differentiation in the United States have vastly altered the picture in relation to cultural pluralism. The acculturative process in due time will eliminate nationality cultural differences. Dominant Americans no longer need be taught to be tolerant of cultural differences of German or Swedish descended people in their society because the latter are no longer Germans or Swedes. While it would be enormously helpful in the further assimilation of the descendants of the later immigrant groups if the dominant status elements indicated more respect for and understanding of the cultural background from which these peoples originally came, the realistic fact of the matter is that Americans of Italian, Polish, or Hungarian descent are not going to be Italians, Poles, or Hungarians culturally, much longer, regardless of the reactions of dominant status people. The residual group differences will be racial and religious.[27] As far as race is concerned, the persons of different races, with the exception of some Indians, have no desire to remain different. Tolerance here is not tolerance of differences since the differences have no valid meaning. The religious differences on the other hand do have valid meaning and the adherents of each faith do desire to remain different to this extent. Tolerance and mutual respect for other religions is a matter of continuing practical importance if religious difference is not to become disruptive of American national unity.

TOPICS FOR DISCUSSION AND PROJECTS

1. Select some religious group in your community which is considered a sect as distinguished from a denomination. Study their situation with the purpose of determining whether or not they are a minority as the term is used in this book.
2. What issues have arisen in your community in the past ten years concerning which different religious groups have tended to oppose one another? Describe the situations and analyze them in terms of the distinction between intergroup antagonism and interinstitutional antagonism suggested in this chapter.
3. Arnold and Caroline Rose in *America Divided* consider Catholics in the United States to be a minority. Do you agree with their position? Develop whatever position you take on this question.
4. As a research project, interview a sample of middle class Catholics with a questionnaire designed to determine the extent to which they associate with non-Catholics. Why do you suppose we suggest selecting a middle class sample for this purpose? The project could be extended by selecting a sample of middle class Protestants and similarly measuring the extent of their association with Catholics.
5. As a term paper study the history of anti-Catholic movements in the United States with the purpose of delineating the social and psychological characteristics of the Protestant groups manifesting intense prejudice against Catholics, and of indicating the social conditions or circumstances under which anti-Catholicism rises or falls.

[27] This, of course, is not to preclude the possibility of new cultural group differences arising indigenously out of the processes of cultural creativity within American society.

SUGGESTED READING

Billington, R. A. *The Protestant Crusade, 1800–1860.* New York: The Macmillan Company, 1938.

> *A study of the origins of American nativism and its development to 1860.*

"Caste in the Church", *Survey Graphic,* Vol. 36, January 1947, pp. 59-66.

> *Liston Pope describes the Protestant experience with Negro-white relations and John La Farge S.J. describes the Catholic experience.*

Kollomorgen, Walter M. *The Old Order Amish of Lancaster County, Pennsylvania.* Rural Life Studies, No. 4, Bureau of Agricultural Economics, United States Department of Agriculture, September 1942.

> *An intensive study of Amish life and culture in the area with especial attention to their economic adjustment in relation to their religious principles.*

Myers, Gustavus. *History of Bigotry in the United States.* New York: Random House, 1943.

> *Extensive account of organized activities of a nativist, anti-Catholic, and anti-Semitic character in the United States.*

Silcox, Claris, and Fisher, Helen M. *Catholics, Protestants, and Jews.* New York: Harper and Brothers, 1934.

> *Extensive study of the relations between religious groups in the United States and Canada. The data for Canada are more complete than for the United States.*

Young, Donald. *American Minority Peoples.* New York: Harper and Brothers, 1932.

> *Chapter 15, "The Church and Race Relations", provides a good brief summary of the subject up to 1932.*

CHAPTER 15

Jewish-Gentile Relations

Introduction. No serious student of the American scene expresses any doubt that the position of Americans of Jewish ancestry is clearly that of a minority as we employ the term, notwithstanding their extraordinary adjustment and contribution to our national life. The fact that discrimination against Jews is not manifested in as many fields as with most other minorities, and that in the fields where discrimination does operate it is often subtle and indirect, tends to obscure the reality of their minority status, and to make the study of their position more difficult. Among all the minorities the situation of Jews is in many ways unique. In this introduction we wish to call attention to two of these unique features.

Unlike most of the other immigrants, the Jews who came to the United States have had long experience as a minority. Since the establishment of Christianity as the official religion of the Roman Empire in the 4th century, Jews, distributed among various European peoples, have been discriminated against almost everywhere. Intermittently, they have endured tragic persecution, particularly in middle and eastern Europe. Much of Jewish history is the story of the effort of Jews to retain their traditional religious heritage while living among Christians. It can therefore be explained as response to the ways gentiles have dealt with them. Driven from the land, Jews became city dwellers; discriminated against in many occupations, they concentrated on those which were open; placed on the defensive, Jews developed strong in-group solidarity; living in ghettos they developed a highly effective urban social organization; and being as individuals in marginal position, their innate capacities were stimulated to unusual development.

The course of Jewish-gentile relationships in the United States has differed from that of other European minorities. We saw in Chapter 4, that the course of native-immigrant relations in general followed a path which led by characteristic stages toward complete assimilation. In contrast Jewish-gentile relationships have followed a course fluctuating between periods of moderate discrimination and periods of intense anti-Semitism. With the composition of the Jewish population changing steadily from preponderantly foreign born to preponderantly native born, the acculturation of Jewish Americans has proceeded in a progressive fashion. Yet the degree of their full acceptance as Americans has followed no such linear trend. Jews remain in the United States a "perennial minority" [1] as they were for centuries in Europe. Much of the description and analysis of Jewish-gentile relations in this chapter will be directed toward finding out why this should be so. Preliminary to consideration of these relations, we turn attention to the growth and distribution of the Jewish population in the United States.

JEWISH IMMIGRATION AND POPULATION GROWTH

The growth of the Jewish population in the United States falls into three main periods, the first two of which involve substantial increments through immigration; and the third in which growth was dependent primarily upon the excess of births over deaths. The three periods are: (1) from colonial times to the great migration after 1880; (2) from the great migration to the passage of the restrictive quota act of 1924; and (3) from 1924 to the present.

Jewish immigration to 1880. The history of Jewish immigration to North America began with the arrival of 23 Sephardic Jews, men, women, and children, who settled in New Amsterdam in September 1654, interestingly enough according to Goldberg, "as fugitives from South American bigotry." [2] Individual Jews or families were to be found in nearly every colony prior to the American Revolution. "Jews organized religious communities in Georgia in 1733, in Philadelphia in 1745, in Charleston in 1750, and in Richmond in 1790." [3] The population is estimated to have increased from 6000 in 1826 to

---

[1] Term used by Richard A. Schermerhorn, *These Our People* (Boston: D. C. Heath & Company, 1949), Ch. 16.
[2] Nathan Goldberg, *Population Trends Among American Jews,* Jewish Affairs, New York, American Jewish Congress, April, 1948, Vol. II, No. 5. The data of this section are derived mainly from this study.
[3] *Ibid.,* p. 5.

230,000 in 1877. During these 50 years, natural growth was augmented by at least 50,000 immigrants who came from Germany, and some 25,000 from eastern Europe.

The great migration: 1880–1914. The great Jewish migration began in 1880 and increased to a flood which was damned up by World War I and the policy of restriction which followed it.[4] About half a million Jews came to the United States between 1881 and 1898; but about a million and a half entered between 1898 and 1914. Most of the Jewish immigrants in this period came from the Russian Empire which then included Poland and the Baltic states.

The Jewish immigrants came to stay. "Only 7.1 per cent of Jewish immigrants to the United States between 1908–1914 left the country compared with one-third of all other immigrants. Indeed, this proportion of departures fell to 1.7 per cent in the case of Jews between 1915–1943, while it rose to an average of 42.3 per cent for other immigrants."[5] Jews more frequently came as families, or the husband and father sent for his wife and relatives as quickly as possible. Thus the sex composition of the Jewish population had less excess of males than in the case of other immigrant groups. Likewise this pattern of total family immigration gave more immediately a youthful cast to the Jewish population. "One out of every four admitted in the years 1899–1914 was under fourteen."[6]

Growth since 1920. The large drop in the percentage of increase in the Jewish population between 1917 and 1937, as indicated in Table 25 indicates that increasingly the further growth was becoming dependent

TABLE 25

Jews in the United States, 1848–1937

(Estimated)[7]

YEAR	NUMBER OF JEWS	PER CENT INCREASE	PER CENT OF NATIONAL POPULATION
1848	50,000	——	0.2
1877	230,000	360.0	0.5
1897	938,000	307.8	1.3
1907	1,777,000	89.4	2.0
1917	3,389,000	90.7	3.3
1927	4,228,000	24.8	3.6
1937	4,771,000	12.8	3.7

[4] *Ibid.*, p. 6.
[5] *Ibid.*, p. 7.
[6] *Ibid.*, p. 8.
[7] *Ibid.*, p. 10. Also, see *The Jewish People, Past and Present* (New York: Jewish Encyclopedic Handbooks, Central Yiddish Culture Organization, 1948), Vol. 2, p. 25.

on the excess of births over deaths. The immigration part of this growth is estimated to have been 328,000 between 1921–29, most of which probably came prior to 1924, the date of the permanent quota system. Between 1930 and 1943, 188,101 are estimated to have come in. Many of these were the "refugee" element, fleeing from Hitler's control in the late 1930's.

After an extensive analysis of Jewish birth rates in comparison with the native white population, Goldberg finds "the conclusion is self-evident that the Jewish rate of natural increase in the United States lags behind the general population." [8] Among the interacting factors which he lists to explain this conclusion are: the high degree of urban concentration of the Jewish population; the desire for a higher economic status; and strong parental devotion, which leads in part to an average later age of marriage. While Goldberg is hesitant about future predictions, his material seem logically to point to the probability that the Jewish population will do well to maintain its present percentage of the total population, and may well lose proportionate ground. Only the possible admission of a considerable number of young Jewish immigrants will raise the birth rate.

Intermarriage. Over this century the rate of intermarriage between Jews and non-Jews has increased. In New Haven, the percentage of exogamous Jewish marriages rose from 1.1 per cent in 1900 to 6.3 per cent in 1940. One-tenth of the Jewish families in San Francisco, New London, and Jacksonville in recent years had one or more non-Jewish members. The rate of out-marriage for native-born Jews in Manhattan and the Bronx between 1908–1912 was seven times higher than for the foreign born.[9] Whether intermarriage reduces the size of the Jewish population or not depends upon the extent to which the gentile partners and the children either become converted to Judaism or become identified with the Jewish community. Jewish men out-marry more often than Jewish women, and Jews of both sexes marry Protestants more often than Catholics. In his Minneapolis study, Albert Gordon notes that intermarriage is taking place in increasing numbers. He further observes that while the Jewish community definitely disapproves of such marriages, nevertheless, "there is a growing tendency to accept such persons [gentiles] without prejudice in the synagogues and other Jewish organizations." [10]

Distribution of the Jewish population. The Jewish population is highly concentrated in large cities. As Table 26 shows, slightly more than

[8] *Ibid.*, p. 12.
[9] *Ibid.*, p. 16.
[10] Albert I. Gordon, *Jews in Transition* (Minneapolis: University of Minnesota Press, 1949), p. 206.

half of all Jewish Americans reside in New York City alone.[11] While Goldberg does not make the point, much of the remaining 22 per cent not accounted for in the 14 major centers indicated in Table 26 may well be found in the cities adjacent to the metropolis. For example, in the New York metropolitan area, Jersey City, Newark, and smaller satellite cities have substantial Jewish populations.

TABLE 26

Major Jewish Centers in the United States with Percentages of the Total Jewish Population[12]

CITY	1910	1940
Baltimore	1.6	1.7
Boston	3.4	2.6
Buffalo	0.4	0.3
Chicago	6.6	6.4
Cleveland	1.4	1.3
Detroit	0.6	2.1
Los Angeles	0.3	2.0
Milwaukee	0.5	0.4
New York	51.4	52.0
Philadelphia	7.2	6.7
Pittsburgh	1.2	1.0
St. Louis	1.1	0.6
San Francisco	0.3	0.2
Washington	0.2	0.6
Total	76.2	77.9

While the greater economic opportunity afforded Jews in the larger cities is one reason for their urban concentration, another reason is the preference for living with their coreligionists in a large enough sub-community structure to enjoy a more complete life. Jews in Europe had lived largely in cities and had developed an urban mode of life. In any event, this pattern of extraordinary urban concentration has remained substantially the same for 30 years, as Table 26 shows. A tabulation of the distribution of Jews on a state-wide basis for the twelve states in which 94 per cent of them lived in 1910 disclosed the fact that 94.5 per cent of the total Jewish population were found in the same states in 1940.

[11] Goldberg's estimate of the Jewish population of New York City is higher than that usually given. American Jewish Yearbooks for several years past have given 2,000,000 of the estimated total American Jewish population of 5,000,000 as resident in New York City. This is only 40 per cent of the estimated total American Jewish population.
[12] Goldberg, op. cit., p. 22.

Summary comment. The more significant aspects of this discussion of Jewish population trends are these: (1) Jews in the United States numbering about five million comprise less than 5 per cent of the total population. Furthermore, in every city where they live they constitute a definite numerical minority—and, aside from New York City, a small numerical minority. (2) Present population trends indicate the Jewish population is growing less rapidly than the general national growth. (3) No radical change has occurred in the urban concentration of Jews within the country.

JEWS IN THE AMERICAN GENTILE COMMUNITY

Wherever any considerable number of Jewish people reside in an American urban community, there has developed a separate Jewish substructure, usually called the Jewish community, which has a characteristic relation to the larger gentile community about it. We shall again draw upon a particular community study sufficiently typical to illustrate the generalized pattern, a study of the Jews in Buna by Leonard Bloom.[13]

Jews in Buna. Buna is a medium-sized metropolitan center of the American industrial Midwest. Bloom indicates the discussion is based on firsthand observation of several similar cities, although one is used as a kind of core and the characteristics regarded as minimum essentials occur in all.

The population of Buna is composed of 80 per cent native born, much of which is of Southern origin; 15 per cent foreign born; 8 per cent Negro. Included are 5000 Jews, somewhat more than 2 per cent of the total. To what extent do these people remain apart from and intermingle with the gentile population?

Their religious life is separate from gentiles, although Buna Jews reveal the same wide range of religious difference to be found in any sizable Jewish community. Bloom estimates 10 per cent orthodox; 40 per cent liberal; 30 per cent free thinking; and 20 per cent agnostic.[14] In fact an increasing number of Jews are breaking away from organized religious Jewish activity. But they are not embracing Christianity, and thus are not assimilated to the traditional American pattern in this respect. Closely reflecting their religious variation is the extent of out-marriage. Practically no out-marriage takes place in the orthodox and liberal groups; a small per cent of the "free thinkers"

[13] Leonard Bloom in *Jews in a Gentile World*, ed. by Isacque Graeber and Steuart Henderson Britt (New York: The Macmillan Company, 1942), Ch. 7, "The Jews of Buna," pp. 180-199.
[14] *Ibid.*, pp. 189-190. Bloom's religious division of the Jewish population does not conform to the classification usually employed, Orthodox, Conservative, and Reformed, to which, of course, should be added a category of Jews who profess no religious belief.

out-marry, and a considerable number of the agnostic groups marry gentiles.

With reference to residential distribution, Bloom finds:

> . . . the Jews of Buna are distributed through the north side of town. They are scattered in fanwise fashion through the areas adjoining the business district, where the poorest Jews are found, to the exclusive residential section of Long Hill. There are a few exclusively Jewish streets in the poorer and middle-class sections, but, for the most part, the Jewish population has sifted into this quarter of the Buna landscape. Only one section, Green Acres, is expressly and explicitly closed to Jews. The residence of Jews is mainly limited by the ability to pay and the ability to own property. The fact that there are some Jewish streets, but not a ghetto, must be emphasized.[15]

In occupation, Jews are found in disproportionate numbers in mercantile occupations—the most well-to-do Jews are department store owners—and in the professions of dentistry, law, and medicine. Bloom finds that numerous clerks and stenographers in Buna are Jews and observes that the fact that these are exceedingly "visible" occupations tends to make the non-Jews of Buna think there are more Jews than there really are. A fair number of Jews are found among manual workers, largely in the building trades. "The bulk of the poorer Jewish population are to be found working as small, independent merchants."[16] In general, one sees the tendency of Jews to gravitate to occupations of a relatively independent nature. This appears to suggest discrimination possibly in the larger industries. Concerning occupational discrimination, Bloom writes:

> One seldom finds in the *Buna Republican* advertisements specifying "no Jews need apply" or "Protestants only." On the other hand, Jews and non-Jews tacitly admit that the Jew is at a disadvantage in seeking employment. A minority of the larger concerns exclude Jews as a matter of policy either expressed or concealed. Following are some of the alleged reasons for not hiring Jews: "They are not strong enough for heavy work." "Jews don't have loyalty to the company." "Jews are too ambitious—they know too much for their own good. You can't trust them." "Other employees don't want to work with Jews." Here are the Jews' explanations for not being hired: "It's just a matter of prejudice." "A Jew has to be twice as good as a Gentile to get a job in this company." "All the Nazis aren't in Germany." "They're always afraid a Jew will get into competition and get their trade away." [17]

In political life, Bloom finds:

> The political affiliations of Buna's Jews largely depend on the economic group to which the individuals belong. There is nothing which could be

[15] *Ibid.*, p. 195. By permission of the publishers, The Macmillan Company.
[16] *Ibid.*, pp. 193-194.
[17] *Ibid.*, p. 193. By permission of the publishers, The Macmillan Company.

called a "Jewish vote" in Buna, although the disproportionate number of merchants tends to give a conservative cast to the Jewish electorate. However, the younger Jews and the working class are likely to favor the New Deal, as is true in the general population. The Old World "Socialist Bund" survivals do not figure appreciably, and it is not at all uncommon to find a member of one of the Bunds voting a straight Republican ticket.[18]

In organizational life, Jews are mixed with Gentiles in such organizations as the Masons, the Scouts, and the University Club. One might wish Bloom had presented more details on this point because membership in organized groups is a significant index of assimilation. His statement that "there is one exclusively Jewish organization for every fifty adult Jews in Buna," [19] however, markedly indicates the existence of a separate Jewish social structure.

Other community studies. Other community studies verify the generality of the Buna picture of Jews in American gentile communities, although revealing minor variations. Sophia Robison's summary of the findings from a survey of eight communities attests a typical residential and occupational distribution of Jews.[20] In all the eight cities, there was a concentration of Jewish residences in certain sections, but except in Minneapolis and Detroit, at least half of the Jewish families were distributed widely throughout the city. The marked occupational concentration of the gainfully employed Jews in retail trades and in the professions is likewise documented in these survey findings. Of all the Jews gainfully employed the percentage engaged in retail trades ranged from 43 per cent in Passaic to 60 per cent in Pittsburgh.[21] Again from these surveys, it was found that in each of the communities the proportion of Jewish people engaged in the professions was substantially higher than the proportion of Jews in the total population. Further reflecting occupational concentration is this conclusion: "In no city was the ratio of Jews in manufacturing, mechanical industries, public service, domestic service, in skilled and unskilled occupations anywhere near that of the ratio of Jews to the total population." [22] Because the total number of American Jews who live in small numbers in various scattered communities is so few, little study of their relations to gentile neighbors in such places has been made. The general impression is that Jews so located are more often assimilated into the gentile community. Pertinent in this connection is the finding in the Robison study that in the Norwich–New London community

[18] *Ibid.,* p. 194. By permission of the publishers, The Macmillan Company.
[19] *Ibid.,* p. 194.
[20] Sophia M. Robison, *Jewish Population Studies,* Jewish Social Studies Publications, No. 3, New York, Conference on Jewish Relations, 1943.
[21] *Ibid.,* p. 183.
[22] *Ibid.,* p. 184.

where the numbers of the Jewish population were the smallest, there was the least concentration of Jewish residences.

GENTILE DISCRIMINATION AGAINST JEWS

For purposes of analysis, it is essential in discussing gentile behavior toward Jews to make a distinction between those more ordinary and less intense sorts of discrimination which are widely manifested by gentiles among whom Jews live, and the phenomenon of anti-Semitism. Anti-Semitism as a term came into usage in Europe during the 1870's to denote social and political agitation, sentiments, and acts directed toward Jews.[23] Prior to that time, hostile attitudes and behavior against Jews have been thought of as anti-Judaism with the implication that its ostensible rationale was based upon the fact that Jews were not Christians. Beginning with the decade noted, a shift in the ideological content of antagonism toward Jews began, in which the religious difference played little part. Hostility against Jews, upon racial, social, economic, and political grounds in varying times and in various places replaced the rationale of religious difference. Organized movements against Jews became an important weapon in European political struggles. In Germany, for example, anti-Semitism became a part of the protest of insecure middle class elements against the excesses of capitalism, on the one hand, and against the rising socialist trend, on the other. In Russia in the late 19th century, Jews were discriminated against by law, and the Tsarist government made little effort to curb periodic pogroms. In the Hitler Reich, anti-Semitism as a political weapon reached its highest perfection, including a systematic program designed to annihilate the Jewish population.

Against this harsh background of European anti-Semitism the treatment accorded Jews in the United States, as we shall presently describe it, appears in so much more favorable a light that the milder discrimination encountered here has been regarded by many Jews themselves, as well as by many gentiles, of minor significance. Nevertheless, careful study of Jewish-gentile relations in this country reveals not only the persistent and prevalent minor discrimination but, since 1917 at least, the persistence of anti-Semitism in significant segments of the American population, latent at times but periodically becoming active. In this section, we shall first describe the major fields of discrimination against Jews; and secondly trace the fluctuating course which opposition to Jews by American gentiles has followed.

"Normal" discrimination. The fields in which gentile discrimination against Jews operates are those in which evidence in statistical form is

[23] Benjamin Ginsberg, "Anti-Semitism," *Encyclopedia of Social Sciences.* Vol. 1 (New York: The Macmillan Company, 1930), pp. 119-125.

the most difficult to document. No one doubts that many Jews incur social discrimination, occupational discrimination, discrimination in the opportunity for higher education, and in choice of residence. But the data are lacking to provide anything approaching a definitive measure of these phenomena. Further difficulty in this connection arises because the methods employed in such discrimination are frequently not in the open. Nevertheless, a typical pattern of discrimination against Jews is seen in all the American communities where Jews exist in any considerable number.

Social discrimination. Most characteristic of all is the prevalence of social discrimination against Jews. While gentiles are generally civil and friendly to Jews where the two mingle in civic and economic life, the former in various ways draw subtle lines against association in group life where sociability on a plane of equality is the main interest. Gordon cites the testimony of a Christian businessman in Minneapolis, which epitomizes the general pattern. "Most of my business associates are Jews . . . they invite me to play golf with them at their golf club. I have accepted their invitation on many occasions. But it has never occurred to me to invite them to join me in a game of golf at my golf club." [24] In many communities, Jews are not found as members of exclusive clubs one of whose functions is to denote the social prestige of its members.[25] On most college campuses where Jewish students are present in numbers, fraternity and sorority membership is divided on an exclusive gentile and Jewish basis. Social discrimination is further seen in the many hotels and vacation places which discourage Jewish clientele.

Whether these kinds of social discrimination, as irritating as they are to Jews, impose any serious handicap upon their equality of opportunity depends upon whether they affect indirectly more serious matters such as occupations and choice of residence. McWilliams has argued cogently that exclusion from social clubs where the contacts made are important adjuncts to business success is an indirect economic discrimination. This hypothesis is difficult to prove or to disprove.[26]

Occupational discrimination. While 78 per cent of all the complaints filed over a period of the operation of the wartime Federal Fair Employment Practices Commission were filed by Negroes, the next most numerous class involved Jews. The statistics of the New York Commission Against Discrimination were similar in this respect. Another ap-

[24] Gordon, *op. cit.*, p. 48.
[25] See Carey McWilliams, *A Mask for Privilege* (Boston: Little, Brown & Company, 1948), p. 123, for a documented instance.
[26] *Ibid.*, pp. 114-126.

proach to this matter is to look at the actual pattern of employment of Jews in the upper economic levels. The position of Jews in business was summarized in an article in *Fortune* in 1936, as follows:

> They [Jews] play little or no part in the great commercial houses . . . they have an inconspicuous place in heavy industry. . . . Something of the same situation exists in automobiles. . . . The coal industry is almost entirely non-Jewish. . . . Rubber [and] shipping and transportation are equally non-Jewish. . . . In brief, Jews are so far from controlling the characteristic of present day American activities that they are hardly represented in them at all.
>
> To find Jewish participation in industry it is necessary to turn to the light industries. And even there, it is necessary to turn from the manufacturing to the distributing end . . . the clothing business is the spectacular and outstanding exception to the statement that Jewish industrial interests are generally in the minority. . . . Jews are a definite retailing minority over the country. . . . At the most, half the opinion making and taste influencing paraphernalia (newspapers, radio, movies, theater) is in Jewish hands.[27]

In view of the acknowledged high level of education among Jews and the prevalence of acquired desires for economic success, one should expect a reasonably proportionate distribution of Jews in all fields of business life. The fact that they are seldom found in big corporations appears only to be explained on the basis of discrimination. The apparent overrepresentation of Jews in professional life suggests that Jews incline toward the higher-ranking occupations which are open to them and where, for example, they do not have to be hired by someone else. Eli Cohen maintains that professionally employed Jews occupy a marginal position in these occupations. For example, he cites the difficulties encountered by Jewish physicians to acquire certified ratings for medical specialties; and further, that few Jewish accountants and few Jewish lawyers are employed by large firms.[28]

Educational discrimination. There is no denial of education to Jews at the public school level anywhere in the nation. There are, however, strong indications of limited discrimination at the collegiate and graduate school level. In a survey of practices regarding admissions of 700 liberal arts colleges, Dodson found sufficient evidence to conclude that a quota system is in effect in nearly all of them even though the officials denied it in all but a few instances.[29] In medical schools, one study indicates that Jewish enrollees have been reduced approximately 50 per cent in the last 20 years, which obviously cannot be ac-

---

[27] "Jews in America," *Fortune,* Vol. 13, No. 2, Feb. 1936. The above material was adapted from pp. 133-136. By permission of the publishers of *Fortune.*
[28] Eli E. Cohen, "Occupational Status and Occupational Structure," *American Jewish Year Book,* Vol. 51 (1950), p. 65.
[29] Dan W. Dodson, "Religious Prejudice in Colleges," *American Mercury,* Vol. 63, No. 271 (July 1946), pp. 5-13.

counted for on the basis of a decline in qualified Jewish applicants.[30] Patently, discrimination in admission to professional schools places Jews at a disadvantage in the free competitive choice of an occupation.

Discrimination in other fields. Evidence of discrimination against Jews in regard to choice of residence are less convincing, although there is no other adequate explanation of their absence from certain middle and upper class sections than that of prejudice. While restrictive covenants have been mainly directed at Negroes and Orientals they have also been written to exclude Jews. More frequently, neighborly pressure is brought on exclusive gentile residents not to sell to Jews.

Outside the fields described above, Americans of Jewish ancestry do not appear to be discriminated against in specific ways. But the social distance maintained by gentiles generally in their contact with Jews colors all phases of interpersonal relations with at least a faint tint of the dominant-minority hue.

In this section, the continued existence of a general pattern of gentile discrimination against Jews in the United States has been noted. We shall presently show that anti-Semitism, the more intense form of prejudice, has also been displayed intermittently in the American scene. Historical experience suggests that sporadic outbursts of violent anti-Semitism occur in areas where patterns of general discrimination against Jews are a constant feature of Jewish-gentile relations. Perhaps the failure of many liberal gentiles and also of many Jews to recognize this point is what made the Nazi holocaust a tragic surprise to so many people of both groups. Jews were nowhere (where they existed in any numbers) more nearly assimilated to a gentile national life than in Germany. Yet there did exist in Germany the ordinary forms of discrimination out of which under appropriate economic and political conditions such as accompanied the rise of Hitlerism, anti-Semitism would find fertile ground. The possibilities of the recurrence of anti-Semitism are always implicit in any national society where Jews still possess minority status.

ANTI-SEMITISM IN THE UNITED STATES

We shall now consider the beginnings and subsequent course of anti-Semitism in the United States. As we shall see, the visible manifestations of this phenomenon show ebbs and flows in intensity which suggest that as a state of mind anti-Semitism has been constantly latent in particular segments of the gentile population beginning with the decade of 1870.

[30] Frank Kingdon, "Discrimination in Medical Colleges," *American Mercury,* Vol. 61, No. 262 (Oct. 1945), pp. 391-399.

Social anti-Semitism. Prior to 1870, there was little evidence of anti-Semitism in this country. In 1877 Joseph Seligman, the New York banker, was refused accommodation for his family at the Grand Union Hotel in Saratoga Springs. This is one of a number of incidents arising in this decade which provide the first overt manifestations of anti-Semitism. Since Seligman had lived in this country since 1837 and had been offered the post of Secretary of Treasury by President Grant, the refusal to accord him accommodations hitherto granted suggests the development of a new attitude toward Jews which was to continue from then up to the present time.

Economic anti-Semitism. The great immigration of Jews after 1880 did not provoke any strong anti-Semitic activity. This may in part be due to the fact that so many Jews in New York concentrated in the needle trades, removing themselves from general competition and insulating themselves in their self-developed ghettos. The real upsurge in feeling against Jews as economic competitors appears to have started after 1900 and had reached a high peak at the outbreak of the first World War. Drawing upon Severson's study of discriminatory want ads, one finds none prior to 1911. Beginning in that year, however, "ads requesting 'Christians only' or 'Gentiles only' appeared at the rate of 0.3 per 1000, rose to 4 per cent in 1921, to 8.8 in 1923, to 13.3 in 1926; averaged 11 per cent from 1927 to 1931; dropped to 4.8 per cent in 1931, and then rose to 9.4 per cent in 1937." Severson's thesis is that it was not immigration per se, nor cultural conflict, which developed this latent prejudice but "that the particular exigency of the occasion was the coming into the clerical labor market, particularly of girls into typing and stenography, of second-generation east European immigrants." [31]

Political anti-Semitism. About 1917, there began to arise anti-Semitism similar to that better known in Europe, political in its implications, more organized, and more vitriolic in its propaganda. In the few years following the close of World War I, large quantities of anti-Semitic literature identifying Jews with the rising European revolutionary ideology appeared; the new Ku Klux Klan arose in the North with its generally antiforeign orientation including anti-Semitism; the Fellowship Forum distributed widely copies of the forged Protocols of the Elders of Zion; and Henry Ford commenced his anti-Semitic campaign through the publication of the *Dearborn Independent.*[32] That these new anti-Semitic activities had repercussions upon Jews is

[31] Quotation taken from A. L. Severson, "Nationality and Religion in Newspaper Ads," *American Journal of Sociology*, V. XLIV, January, 1939, p. 545.
[32] Donald S. Strong, *Organized Anti-Semitism in America* (Washington: American Council on Public Affairs, 1941), p. 15.

indicated by an increase in various incidents of which the following are illustrative.

The board of directors of a Milwaukee golf club asked eight Jewish charter members to resign.

The secretary of the Chamber of Commerce in St. Petersburg, Florida, announced that the time had come to make St. Petersburg "a 100 per cent American gentile City."

Several large real estate concerns in New Jersey, New York, Georgia, and Florida were found to have restricted new subdivisions against Jewish occupancy.

Of more than passing interest, in this period, was President Lowell's graduation address at Harvard in June 1922, in which he advocated quotas against Jews. While the trustees of Harvard later rejected this suggestion, it was painfully apparent that the quota system was spreading.[33]

Abating somewhat during the late 1920's, anti-Semitism rose again in the early 1930's as the depression deepened. Strong has indicated that there were 121 organizations actively spreading anti-Semitic propaganda during 1933 and 1940.[34] In the late 1930's anti-Semitism began to be used for the first time openly in political campaigns. The manager of the nativist third party in the 1936 Presidential election is quoted by McWilliams as stating, "the trouble with this country now is due to the money powers and Jewish politicians." [35] While the sweeping victory of President Roosevelt in 1936 temporarily set back the agitation, it resumed with new intensity in the late 1930's and continued down to Pearl Harbor. Involved in this activity was the Christian Front, led by Father Charles Coughlin, and the Silver Shirts, directed by William Pelley. In a period of 19 months prior to July 31, 1938, Pelley mailed approximately three and a half tons of anti-Semitic propaganda from his headquarters. All of this organization and propaganda obviously cost considerable sums of money. Conducted by relatively unimportant people, it occasionally received support in high places. For example, McWilliams quotes Congressman John Rankin as stating to Congress that "Wall Street and a little group of our international Jewish brethren are still attempting to harass the President and Congress into plunging us into the European War." [36] It is interesting to note that this new crescendo in anti-Semitic propaganda was correlated with the increasing strength of the Nazi movement in Europe.

---

[33] McWilliams, *A Mask for Privilege,* pp. 38-39. By permission of the publisher Little, Brown & Company.
[34] Strong, *op. cit.,* pp. 146-147.
[35] McWilliams, *A Mask for Privilege,* p. 42.
[36] *Ibid.,* p. 46.

During World War II, overt manifestations of anti-Semitism disappeared. They were considered inimical to the war effort and were discouraged by the Government. Furthermore, the ideological inconsistency of anti-Semitism when we were fighting the arch Jew hater, Adolph Hitler, had some deterrent effect. In the few months following the end of World War II, the Fair Employment Practices Committee noted an increase in discrimination against Jews in employment. However, the *Fortune* Survey which had found the incidence of anti-Semitism in the adult population to be 9.3 per cent in 1943, found it to be 8.8 per cent in 1946.[37] Organized anti-Semitic activity failed to resume its prewar intensity although it was, nevertheless, far from dormant. The *American Jewish Year Book* for 1950 noted a tendency for individual agitators to combine operations and to favor the distribution of inflammatory literature in preference to the holding of meetings and demonstrations.[38] These trends indicate that the agitators were having a more difficult time.

Viewing this fluctuating course of anti-Semitic behavior suggests that it is more responsive to changes in socioeconomic conditions in the national community rather than to changes in the behavior of Jews. These conditions are manifold and it is rarely that we can single out one factor as being the sole determinant. At times it may appear that economic changes have a direct bearing. For example, in the first of the periods of marked discrimination, 1910–1914, the competition of increasingly Americanized Jews for employment in white collar occupational positions began to be felt by gentiles at these socioeconomic levels. At other times conflicts in ideologies loomed as the more significant factor. Thus the rise in anti-Semitism following the close of World War I seemed related to the spread of radical philosophy in this country, which raised anxiety in the middle classes. Or again, the sharper political orientation of the anti-Semitism of the 1930's occurred at a time when legislation was enacted which made the position of the working class more secure, and in consequence, increased the anxieties of the other economic levels. These observations will contribute to the explanation of anti-Semitic behavior which will be further considered below.

Interpretations of anti-Semitism. The reader will recall our contention in Chapter 1 that Jewish-gentile relations are the most enigmatic of all our dominant-minority situations. It is, then, not surprising to learn that many reasons have been advanced for the perennial minority status of Jews. In order to place these many explanations under manageable treatment within the space available for their consider-

[37] *Fortune,* "The Fortune Survey," Vol. 33, February, 1946, p. 237.
[38] *American Jewish Year Book,* Vol. 51, 1950, p. 110.

ation, we shall consider them under two general headings: nonassimilation theories; and "scapegoat" theories. The nonassimilation theories find the main reasons for gentile discrimination against Jews in the behavior and characteristics of Jews themselves. Here belong such ideas as that the Jew is different racially and/or culturally; that furthermore he desires to remain different, and that therefore gentiles should not be expected to consider him "one of them." The anti-Semite adds to this alleged unassimilability the idea that Jews possess certain undesirable traits which are inimical to the general welfare. It is therefore necessary for gentiles, they argue, to discriminate to some degree in order to protect the general welfare. What these undesirable traits, as seen in the gentile stereotype of the Jew, are thought to be, we shall presently consider.

Under the broad heading of "scapegoat" theories we subsume a variety of hypotheses about anti-Semitism which view it as an aberration of the gentile mind, meeting certain psychological needs. Often people who feel highly insecure and have feelings of frustration are not aware of the real sources of their difficulty. This psychological conditon generates aggression which seeks on outlet. Because aggression is often dangerous, unconsciously such people seek an object toward whom they can direct this hostility with relative impunity. "The Jew" constitutes a convenient target for this purpose.[39]

THE CHARACTERISTICS OF AMERICAN JEWS

The gentile stereotype of the Jew. As in all minority situations, Jewish-gentile relations are influenced by the gentile stereotype of the Jew. A 1942 study by Angus Campbell illustrates some of the ideas about these characteristics held by gentiles. The respondents were asked to make any specific criticisms they had concerning Jewish behavior. No criticisms at all were made by 55 per cent of the sample. The kinds of criticism made and how frequently each was made are summarized in Table 27. The high prevalence of the idea that Jews are aggressive and sharp in economic behavior stands out among the classified replies. Based on studies of this sort and other sources of evidence, the gentile stereotype of the Jew in the United States appears as follows. They are racially different. They have hooked noses, dark hair, and distinctive facial features which are allegedly unattractive by gentile aesthetic norms. They are culturally different. They have a different way of life, based on a religion, involving many strange rituals and family customs which vary from the Christian way of life. They are "smart" but unethical. They are so ambitious to get ahead that they incline toward

---

[39] See Talcott Parsons, "The Sociology of Modern Anti-Semitism," in Graeber and Britt, *op. cit.*, p. 114, for development of the frustration-aggression thesis.

TABLE 27

Specific Criticism Made of Jews[40]

	PER CENT OF ALL RESPONDENTS
In Relation to the War Effort	
"They're not doing their share."	
"They're draft dodgers."	11
In Relation to the Political Field	
"The Jews caused the war; they got us into it."	
"The Jews are running Washington."	
"They are trying to take over the government."	5
In Relation to the Economic Field	
"The Jews are too wealthy."	
"They don't treat you fairly when you buy from them."	
"They all grab as much money as they can."	
"They don't treat their workers right."	
"The Jews are running Wall Street."	
"They're taking over business, pushing the gentiles out."	30
In Relation to Personal Characteristics	
"They're dirty, pushy, greedy."	
"They stick together too much. You don't see them joining in our activities."	
"Their religion teaches them bad ways."	
"They think they are too superior."	30
No Criticism Made	55

aggressive and often underhanded business methods particularly when dealing with gentiles. They are lacking in Christian modesty in their approach to sex behavior; and are rather vulgar, ostentatious, and boisterous. Finally, they are conspiratorial in civic life, always scheming to get the gentile world into trouble from which the Jew always somehow benefits.

It will be seen that the stereotype differs in important ways from that held by white people concerning other minorities. To illustrate, comparison may be made with the white stereotype of the Negro. Whereas the Negro is considered lazy, the Jew is considered too ambitious; whereas the Negro is considered mentally inferior, the Jew is considered smart. On the other hand one notes some similarity in the

[40] Angus Campbell in Newcomb and Hartley *Readings in Social Psychology* (New York: Henry Holt & Company, Inc., 1947), pp. 518-527. By permission. The table totals to more than 100 per cent since some of the 45 per cent who made criticisms made more than one type of criticism.

stereotype of the Japanese and the Jews with respect, for example, to aggressiveness and the conspiratorial tendency.

Further consideration of the Jewish stereotype reveals that the gentile concept is not altogether consistent. The Jew is considered by many or at one time a ruthless capitalist; by others, or at other times, thought of as a Marxist radical. Or again, the Jew is criticized on the one hand for being too clannish; or on the other hand for wanting to move into gentile neighborhoods.

We shall now consider what the characteristics of Americans with Jewish ancestry are, as far as can be ascertained from available data.

Physiognomic or "racial" features. Anthropometric studies of samples of Jewish population in Europe and the United States lead Coon to conclude that certain physical traits of genetic determination tend to be characteristic within these populations. These traits are a "combination of a relatively wide head and narrow face, with a slanting axis to the ears; a narrow lower jaw; a narrow interocular distance; and a considerable nose length, with convexity of profile and tip depression." [41] By characteristic is meant, as indicated in Chapter 3, that one or more of these traits will be found far more frequently in a Jewish sample than in one composed of non-Jews. The traits Coon lists are all found, however, among non-Jews, and they are all Caucasian traits. "It is the blending of Nordic and Alpine with eastern Mediterranean elements which gives the Jews their characteristic physical features." [42] The above description particularly applies to the Jewish branch known as Ashkenazim, from whom the majority of American Jews are descended. [43] Thus the Jews who were originally Mediterranean in their subracial features have developed a new type in the Diaspora, in which a limited amount of out-marriage and more frequent in-marriage has been involved. The conclusion is that there is just enough physical distinctiveness, or somatic visibility among Jews as a whole population to permit identification in a fair proportion of individual cases. This identification of a person as a Jew from his appearance is further aided by other than hereditary traits. Of these other aids Coon writes:

. . . the Jew of caricature becomes particularly Jewish-looking when he is given a beard, a black cap, and other cultural objects of a traditionally Jewish character. But he needs more than that; he needs a Jewish facial expression before the caricature is complete.

[41] Carleton S. Coon, "Have the Jews a Racial Identity?", in Graeber and Britt, *op. cit.*, p. 33.
[42] *Ibid.*, p. 33.
[43] *Ibid.*, p. 31. The other main branch known as Sephardic were Jews who lived long in Spain and through in-marriage tended to develop a degree of physical distinctiveness from the other Jews.

The cast of countenance which is commonly labeled "Jewish" is produced in part, without doubt, by the possession of the combination of facial and cranial characters under discussion. Jewish racial continuity, however, is not strong enough nor is the Jewish racial type under discussion different enough from types found among other peoples to explain its apparently distinctive nature. This cast of countenance must be partly produced by a community of noninheritable traits, culturally acquired, and including characteristic postures, facial expressions, and vocal habits.

Many Jews have no distinctive "Jewish" appearance; this is especially true in England, where social barriers between Jews and gentiles have been notably low, and in America among the newer generation of Jews, who have been brought up under traditions and conditions different from those in which their ancestors were reared in Europe. In the absence of "Jewish" facial expressions and mannerisms some Jews will continue to be correctly identified on somatic grounds alone, while others will not.[44]

Jewish culture. Immigrant Jews, whatever their European nationality, brought with them a distinctive culture, rooted in the religion of Judaism with its special beliefs and practices. Interwoven with this religion were family customs and dietary practices which served to differentiate the life of Jews from those among whom they lived. The traditional origin and early nature of Judaism is known to Christians from their own Old Testament. Of this religion, Hertzler writes:

> The immutable, eternal, uniform, and sacred truths of Judaism are embodied in sacred writings; in folkways and folklore; in customs, ceremonies, observances, written (Torah) and oral (Talmud) law; and in a host of peculiar institutions. About 400 A.D. the scholars of Palestine put the totality of their legal tradition into the Palestinian Talmud. A century later the Jewish teachers of Babylonia edited the Babylonian Talmud. Thus before the Diaspora had well begun, Israel was equipped with crystallized statements of its traditional law. At the same time interpretations of scriptural passages, legends, historical notes, moral epigrams, theological discussions, and other nonlegal traditions were collected and edited as the Midrashim. This meant that the Jews of the world obeyed a sacred legislation which made them eat, pray, do business, marry, die, and be buried according to universal fixed rules, some six hundred and thirteen in number.[45]

A key point in Judaism which affects the relations of Jews to gentiles is the concept of "The Chosen People." Like Christians, and all other religions for that matter, Jews consider their religion the only "true one." But unlike Christianity and some other religions, Judaism is less open to others. While some gentiles have been converted to Judaism and accepted as Jews, nevertheless Judaism has remained essentially

---

[44] *Ibid.*, p. 34. By permission of the publishers, The Macmillan Company.
[45] J. O. Hertzler, "The Sociology of Anti-Semitism through History," in Graeber and Britt, *op. cit.*, pp. 66-67. By permission.

"a tribal religion," not a universal one. The zeal to retain their Judaism has led to voluntary social isolation from the rest of the community around them. The "ghetto" was in the first instance a voluntary community which later, in some places, became compulsory by dominant gentile decree.

In the United States, the Jewish immigrants of the great migration formed distinctive colonies, New World ghettos, and were for a period culturally distinctive in the same manner as all other of the later immigrant groups. The Chicago ghetto as of 1926, as described by Wirth, centered around the synagogue, which exercised minute control over the lives of the orthodox, and about the strongly knit family. To observe faithfully the forms of their religion, Jews often sacrificed employment opportunity that interfered with their religious pursuit. In the ghetto were to be found colorful Jewish types, such as "the Chassidic Jew" with flowing beard and long black coat; and the characteristic institutions, the Kosher shops, the sacramental wine shops, the Yiddish theater, and a plethora of second-hand book shops. In comment on the ghetto, Wirth writes:

> The ghetto is a closed community, perpetuating itself, and renewing itself with a minimum of infusion of influences from without, biologically as well as culturally. It is almost completely shut off from the world as if it were still surrounded by a wall and its inhabitants were still locked nightly behind ghetto gates.[46]

Acculturation of Jews. The process of acculturation of Jews bears resemblance to that of all other European immigrant groups, but also presents significant differences. Eventually the ghetto as a distinct physical area began to disappear as the number of Jews living within it dwindled. Likewise, the immigrants themselves, and more particularly the children and grandchildren, became Americanized in large measure. Gordon documents in considerable detail the decline in orthodox practices in Minneapolis: the decline in Sabbath observance; the increasing disregard of dietary practices; modifications of the traditional burial customs; the use of physicians rather than mohels to perform the rite of circumcision; the disappearance of Yiddish as the language of the home.[47] Corresponding with this decline in the old traditions has been the taking on of normative American ways.

The acculturation of Jews, however, presents some striking differences to that of the other immigrant groups. In many ways the Jewish group became more rapidly and successfully adjusted to life in America than the other immigrant groups. This has been true with

[46] Louis Wirth, *The Ghetto* (Chicago: University of Chicago Press, 1928), p. 226. By permission.
[47] See Gordon, *op. cit.*, part II.

reference to economic success, participation in civic life, and educational achievement. An important factor which accounts for this adjustment was the acculturation of Jews to an urban way of life in Europe, in contrast to the rural, peasant background of some other European immigrant groups who settled in cities. This remarkable adjustment in America is reflected in the low delinquency rates, low alcoholic rates, and low percentages of Jews on relief rolls.

Again differing from other immigrant groups, increasing acculturation has not led to complete assimilation, nor are there any indications in 1952 that it will ever do so. The Jewish community within the larger gentile community, modernized and adaptive as much of its cultural content is, still remains distinct. For example, the middle class family of native born Jewish Americans lives a life which in large degree is like that of comparably situated gentile families. But it is a Jewish family and it associates in intimate social life with other Jewish families. Or again, in much of its activity and organization, the Reform synagogue resembles a Protestant church. But it is composed of Jews. In short, Jews as a group still possess what we have called associational visibility, often called by the anti-Semite "clannishness." Frequently the question, "Is X a Jew?" can be answered only by finding out whether or not he associates mostly with Jews. It is this associational visibility, we believe, even more than objective cultural differences, which sets apart the highly Americanized Jew from the gentile.

Personality traits. To what extent do Jews possess the personality traits implied in the gentile stereotype of the Jew? In the first place, a careful study of the personality traits of Jews and a comparison with appropriate non-Jewish samples has not as yet been made. All the common logical errors by which the stereotype of a minority is built up in the dominant mind apply in the case of Jews as in other instances. We have as yet no sufficient data to answer the question above. In the second place, all the alleged traits are common human traits found in all large populations, so that if Jews have any distinctiveness here, it can be only in prevalence or intensity of such traits. In the third place, from the viewpoint of modern social science, any such comparative differences would not be explainable on the basis of genetic factors. And finally, understanding of the manner in which the "vicious circle" operates in dominant-minority structures would lead the impartial student to expect that some of the alleged traits in the stereotype would in fact be more prevalent in a group with highly developed capacities who are obviously discriminated against. This is such an important aspect of the scientific problem at hand that we shall pursue it in more detail.

Impact of minority status upon Jewish personality. We have seen before, particularly with reference to Negroes, that being treated as a
member of a minority in itself tends to accentuate in minority personalities the very traits for which the stereotype calls. That the treatment accorded Jews in western society has this kind of effect, MacIver
has pointed out:

Only a people possessed of great tenacity of character and remarkable skill in
adapting itself to adverse conditions could have survived and overcome so
signally the peculiar hazards of its [Jews] lot. In the process it shaped out a
system of defensive-aggressive responses that enabled it members to open up
for themselves occupations disregarded by other peoples, such as the business
of the trader, or subject to social or religious taboos, as was the lending of
money in the Middle Ages. Thus they tended to combine a radical speculative-
ness in economic matters with a highly conservative socioreligious system.
Their very success in this respect roused new assaults and stimulated new
prejudices. Moreover, it was very natural, very "human," that in these later
days a number of the intellectuals among this people should seek a way out
of the experience of social frustration by becoming advocates of social revolution, and this in turn has become another source of general suspicion and
animosity. The fruits of prejudice and discrimination are the seeds of fresh
prejudice and further discrimination. As we shall see, this "vicious circle" is a
phenomenon of high significance, and it finds no more striking illustrations
than those furnished by the history of the Jewish people. The victim of discrimination, by his responses to it and his struggles against it, can scarcely,
unless he has all the cunning of the serpent and all the innocence of the dove,
avoid behavior that ratifies in the minds of the discriminators the discriminations they practice.[48]

The impact of minority status upon the personality of Jews varies
with reference to the extent that the individual Jew feels himself
identified with the Jewish group. Lewin has provided incisive analysis
of this topic.[49] For purposes of analysis two types of Jews may be
identified: the Jew who accepts the fact that he is Jew; and the one
who rebels against his Jewishness, at least inwardly, who may be
called the "marginal Jew." The former organizes his life around the
fact that he is a Jew, feels pride in the fact, does not try to hide it.
While as an individual he accepts his identity with a people who are
discriminated against, he expresses his opposition to the injustice of discrimination by working through the group to improve the status of the
group as an entity. The marginal Jew, on the other hand, is the Jew
who does not wish to be considered a Jew, who desires to "pass"
by himself into the gentile world. He inclines studiously to avoid act-

---

[48] MacIver, *The More Perfect Union*, pp. 30-31. By permission.
[49] Kurt Lewin, *Resolving Social Conflicts* (New York: Harper and Brothers, 1948).

ing "like a Jew," in his conversation with gentiles to deprecate any behavior by other Jews which gives the slightest plausibility to the stereotype. While a few Jews have successfully "passed," for many of the others who have tried to do so with only partial success, serious problems of mental conflict often arise. Lewin gives this example:

Recently an eastern college co-ed, keen, beautiful, successful, and therefore on the whole in a particularly desirable position, expressed this feeling as follows:

You may have noticed that I am the middle speaker. It's a very appropriate place for me, I think, not because I strike a mean between them, but rather because I am on the fence. I haven't quite made up my mind as to what I think or why I think it. And in that, I am typical of the Jewish people.

Look at me. I'm neither here nor there. As a Jewess, I don't amount to much. I come to services when I have to; I've been told that mine is a precious heritage, but I haven't the slightest idea what it is. I can name quite a number of relatively unimportant English poets—but do I know who is the greatest Jewish poet? No. My education has been exclusively Christian. My virtues are the Christian virtues—at least my conceptions are. Occasionally, I discover something in me that is characteristically Jewish—and I am surprised, almost estranged from myself. I know I'm Jewish because I've been told so, because I have Jewish friends. Aside from that, it doesn't mean very much to me.

So you see, as a Jewess I don't amount to much. But I'm not much better as an American either. Here at school I move in a charmed circle of Jews. The other circle, the non-Jews are oblivious of me, and I of them. Occasionally, the circles touch, sometimes more, sometimes less. I become friendly with some one in the other circle. But self-consciously friendly. If it's a boy, I wonder just how he thinks of me; he wonders what his fraternity brothers are saying. If it's a girl, we both congratulate ourselves mentally on our over-stepping the bonds of racial prejudice. When I read the Phi Beta Kappa list, I'm careful to point out how many of the chosen people are Jewish. I'm always conscious that I am Jewish whether I hide it or try to impress it upon others.

So what am I? According to Jews, I'm American. According to Americans, I'm Jewish. And I'm wrong, utterly wrong, in being that way. And so it is only by pushing people like me off the fence—that Jews are ever going to be freed from anti-Semitism. We must remove the beam from our own eyes.[50]

Underlying the surface aspects of the personalities of many marginal Jews is the phenomenon of self-hatred. According to Lewin, "that self-hatred is present among Jews is a fact that the non-Jew would hardly believe, but which is well known among Jews themselves." [51] This explains the anti-Jewish behavior of many Jews. This phenomenon is also known among Negroes. The refusal of a light-skinned Negro

[50] *Ibid.*, pp. 178-179. By permission of the publishers, Harper and Brothers.
[51] *Ibid.*, p. 186.

woman to marry a dark-skinned Negro man on no other basis than his darkness is often a manifestation of this hatred of oneself because one was born a member of a racial minority. From this kind of analysis, Lewin concludes that the marginal Jew "will be more frustrated than those members of the minority who keep psychologically well inside the group." [52] For this reason, he advises that in bringing up the Jewish child, parents should encourage the development of his allegiance and sense of belonging to the group as a prophylactic against the mental conflicts implicit in "marginality." Experience has shown that, at least in all nations where Jews are present in numbers, no matter how much they try to assimilate completely, they are almost certain to experience some rebuff from the gentile world. Therefore, Lewin maintains that the Jewish child should be taught the "facts of life" rather than be shielded from them, the facts here being that Jews are a minority. The very fact that the opportunities for children born of Jewish lineage to pass over into the gentile community appear to be more favorable than they really are is the reason this lesson is more needed for Jewish parents than, for example, in the case of Negro parents in the United States, where the temptation to pass can only arise among a relatively small percentage of Negroes.

While Lewin's interpretation is not universally accepted, it is a highly provocative analysis of how minority status structures the personality of many minority people. The sequence of cause and effect appears as follows in this order: Gentile discrimination leads to the desire to escape from being a Jew (and self-hatred because one is); this psychological complex leads many Jews to try to become non-Jewish; the failure in many instances to succeed leaves such Jews in a marginal position, belonging to neither group; and this insecure position leads to many mental conflicts.

Jewish protest activity. The minority status of Jews, as with other minorities, has led to organized activity by Jews themselves, to protest and render more secure their position in American society. Due to their high cultural level and their long experience in defending themselves, Jewish organizations for this purpose are the most intelligently conducted of all minority group organizations with similar objectives. Four major Jewish organizations have been engaged in such efforts. Their activities have been summarized by Schermerhorn in these words:

1. The American Jewish Committee, first formed in 1906 and supported largely by influential and relatively wealthy citizens from Reform congrega-

[52] *Ibid.*, p. 193.

tions; this group has preferred to work quietly and by means of indirect influence rather than by much more aggressive methods.[53]

2. The Antidefamation League of B'nai B'rith, organized in 1913 to combat anti-Jewish attitudes especially through publications refuting libelous attacks against the Jews; this organization includes members of different strata in the Jewish community.

3. The American Jewish Congress, which came into existence in 1917, adjourned in 1920, and re-formed in 1922 for the purpose of defending the political rights of Jews in the United States and overseas. It really originated in rebellion against the leadership of the American Jewish Committee and draws its members from middle class groups of Conservative and Orthodox supporters who were Zionists and militant in espousing the Jewish cause. It has recently established a research unit called the Commission on Community Interrelations that sponsors studies on prejudice and discrimination with their effects.

4. The Jewish Labor Committee, which began in 1933 to organize the efforts of workingmen against the antilabor movements in European countries and has more recently turned its attention to problems within the United States. This is a group of trade unionists or radicals of the noncommunist variety, largely nonreligious.

These four groups have frequently worked quite independently or at cross-purposes with each other but in 1943–1944 they arranged for mutual consultation and division of labor in the National Community Relations Council.[54]

Summary of Jewish characteristics. In summary, it can be seen that Jews in the United States today do retain a measure of distinctiveness in physiognomy and culture, and also in what has been called "associational" visibility. It is further to be noted that their cultural distinctiveness is declining; and that their associational distinctiveness ("clannishness") is highly intensified by social discrimination. Indirectly, social discrimination aids in retaining physiognomic similarity since it further limits intermarriage of Jews with gentiles. The minority position of Jews is reflected in the personalities of its members by a keen perception at the conscious level of their minority status, leading to the tempering of competitive aggressiveness with circumspectness, and to organized efforts to protect the group. The behavior of Jews reflects the presence at the unconscious level of the feeling of insecurity and in some cases of self-hatred.

It now remains to discuss the question whether or not this present degree of distinctiveness on the part of Jews precludes their acceptance on the same basis of social status as all other Americans. Is this degree of group difference in any way inimical to the national welfare or

---

[53] Schermerhorn notes that the pattern has changed to a more aggressive one in recent years.
[54] Schermerhorn, *op. cit.*, p. 407.

should it be considered as a form of cultural pluralism well within the legitimate limits of a multigroup democratic society?

JEWS AND AMERICAN SOCIETY

No biological threat. From the modern scientific viewpoint no threat is involved in the shifts in the proportionate numbers of the various stocks of mankind, nor in the intermingling of stocks. Nevertheless dominants frequently react with fear to these possibilities. In the case of Jews, it has been shown that the particular stock itself is a combination of Caucasian genetic elements. Again, Jews constitute about 3 per cent of the total national population and show no trend to increase disproportionately. Surely the Jews can hardly be said to present any biological threat.

Religion, exclusive but not aggressive. In spite of the peculiarly exclusive nature of Judaism, it nowhere tries to convert others to it. In its practical effects upon the gentile community, the most Jews have ever asked is to be left alone to practice their religion. In all its present-day forms, the ethical precepts of Judaism harmonize with those of Christianity. There have been almost no legislative issues in which the Jewish religious influence has taken sides. In this respect, Protestants and Catholics more frequently clash. In a modern nation founded on the principle of separation of church and state and guaranteeing freedom of worship, it is difficult to see any way in which the presence of people devoted to Judaism can threaten the national welfare.

Jews in the national economy. Two favorite theses of the anti-Semite have been: (1) that the scheming Jewish financiers try to control the nation's economy and policy to their own advantage and against the national interest; and (2) that the Jewish radicals are scheming to bring about revolution. The two themes are in themselves contradictory but we shall examine them in turn. The *Fortune* study of Jews in business (see p. 406) found few of them in higher ranking positions in the large corporations which were most influential in the control of our economy. Furthermore, the wide range of economic interests and socioeconomic class levels make their economic interests far from identical. There are Jewish entrepreneurs and Jewish laborers.

Civic loyalty. Jews in the United States have participated in the armed services and have shown no hesitation to fight against Jews of the enemy forces. A sample study of 13 communities showed a higher percentage of Jews represented in the total number supplied to the American service than Jews represented in the total population of these communities. This study further showed that from 60 to 72 per cent of the Jewish veterans were in combat units.[55]

No adequate data are available to indicate whether Jews are more than proportionately represented in political parties or movements of the left. Two factors in the Jewish situation would logically point to expecting them to incline in that direction. Parties of the left have always attracted "intellectuals." Given the high educational level of Jews, one would expect many of the Jewish intelligentsia to be drawn to them. In the second place, movements of the left have stood strongly against discrimination on ethnic and racial lines. This has a special appeal for all minorities. However, the exceptionally small vote which radical parties have received indicates that Jews generally support the two major parties.

The foregoing discussion suggests that Jews do not constitute any threat to the welfare of the nation. This is however only "eliminating the negative" without giving recognition to the positive contributions which Jews have made. The contributions made to our national life by the many outstanding Americans of Jewish ancestry are well known. As a group, Jews have, in the process of acculturation, undergone less social disorganization than most other ethnic groups, and have thus provided communities with fewer problems in such matters as dependency, crime and delinquency, and alcoholism. Furthermore, they have cared for their own in large measure through their welfare organizations, generally operated with a high degree of efficiency according to modern social work standards. At the same time, they have participated actively in support of general community welfare services.

CHARACTERISTICS OF ANTI-SEMITES

To explore the "scapegoat" theories of Jewish-gentile relations, we need to ascertain what the characteristics of the anti-Semites are. Paul Massing provides a penetrating analysis of this subject during the Imperial period in Germany.

The analysis of German anti-Semitic literature, movements, and agitators discloses some rather unexpected and puzzling facts. The most implacable enemies of the Jews were urban rather than rural; indifferent, if not hostile, to the church rather than devout Christians; and members of the "educated" rather than the "ignorant" classes. The most virulent kind of anti-Semitism was spread throughout Germany by teachers, students, industrial and commercial employees, petty officials, professional people, and followers of cults of every variety: members of "life reform movements," whole-rye bread dietitians, opponents of vivisection, and "back to nature" builders of body and

[55] *American Jewish Year Book,* "Jewish War Records," Vol. 47, 1945–1946, pp. 163-169.

soul. From these groups, not from the peasants or the land-owning aristocracy or the reactionary clergy, narrow-minded though they might have been, came the fanatical haters of Jews.[56]

In general, those German gentiles whose status was least secure furnished the hard core of anti-Semitic expressions. These insecure people needed some object upon which to project their anxieties, some one to blame for their unsatisfactory situation. Sometimes they considered their plight due to the upper classes; at other times to the rising socialist ideology of the working classes. Aggression against either of these powerful groups was however dangerous; thus, their mental conflict was resolved by blaming it all on the Jews who could be subtly symbolized either as rapacious capitalists or as radical revolutionists, and who were in any event a safe target to attack. During the Imperial period, anti-Semitism expressed itself largely in ideational form. Jews were seldom actually overtly attacked nor was their established position of civic equality altered. This was in part due to the fact that the conservative ruling class, while at times cynically manipulating anti-Semitism as a counterrevolutionary measure, nevertheless kept it within symbolic bounds. As Massing points out, during the Nazi period, the anti-Semites themselves finally gained political power; the hitherto manipulated anti-Semites became the manipulators; and anti-Semitism broke out in unparalleled physical violence.

Socioeconomic status. Against this German background, we shall consider what are the distinguishing characteristics of anti-Semites in the United States. Strong found the members of the 11 anti-Semitic organizations which he studied to be middle class, with numerous professional people included; and that the leaders of these groups evinced antilabor sentiment. He also found the names on membership lists to be primarily Anglo-Saxon and German, up to the time Father Charles Coughlin developed his movement bringing in an Irish following.[57] A *Fortune* Survey in 1946 found that anti-Semitism increased with wealth; was strongest in the Northeastern and Midwestern regions; and more pronounced in the age group 35–49.[58]

Levinson and Sanford found in their sample that Republicans were more anti-Semitic than Democrats; that sorority members were more anti-Semitic than nonsorority members; and that anti-Semitic scores in general were positively correlated with the amount of the father's income.[59] Bettelheim and Janowitz in a study of a sample of veterans

[56] Paul Massing, *Rehearsal for Destruction* (New York: Harper and Brothers, 1949), p. 75. By permission.
[57] Strong, *op. cit.*, pp. 172-173.
[58] "The Fortune Survey," Feb., 1946, p. 257.
[59] Daniel J. Levinson and R. Nevitt Sanford, "A Scale for the Measurement of Anti-Semitism," *Journal of Psychology*, 1944, Vol. 17, pp. 339-370.

found that it was not so much the economic and social background of people, but whether or not their status was changing, which was most significantly related to intolerance. The veterans who were in the process of downward mobility showed the most marked prejudice against Jews. These authors also found a high amount of intolerance among the few individuals in their sample who had made substantial salary increases ($1500 or more) since the war.[60] The net result which emerges from the researches cited points to the concentration of anti-Semitic attitudes in certain segments of the middle classes, although in the United States, the upper range in the anti-Semitic profile may perhaps extend to higher socioeconomic levels than it did in Germany. This latter difference may be interpretable by the presence in the higher levels of American society of many *nouveaux riches* whose status is less permanently established than was that of the European upper classes; and by the probability that an unusual amount of aggressiveness characterizes such people.

Class status alone by no means automatically determines or delimits anti-Semitism. No estimate of the prevalence of anti-Semitism in the United States has placed it greater than 10 per cent of the population. Some anti-Semitism was found in all social classes. For further insight into the nature of anti-Semitism, we shall now focus attention upon the personality characteristics of the anti-Semite.

The anti-Semitic personality. The most intensive research yet undertaken to probe the personality structure of persons having pronounced prejudices against Jews in American society has been carried out under the auspices of the American Jewish Committee. The findings are now available in the publication, *The Authoritarian Personality*.[61] Questionnaires designed to measure degrees of anti-Semitism were distributed among over 2000 West Coast urban gentiles including a wide range of status and occupational groups. This was followed by intensive interviews of approximately 100 of the original sample, selected from those scoring in the highest and lowest quarters of the anti-Semitic or prejudiced rating scale.[62] We shall present the summary profile of the high scorers; that is, those with greater degree of prejudice, as contrasted with the low scorers, or those more markedly tolerant.

The prejudiced personality tries to repress from his consciousness unacceptable tendencies or impulses in himself, whereas the unprejudiced person shows more awareness of his faults and is more will-

[60] Bruno Bettelheim and Morris Janowitz, *Dynamics of Prejudice* (New York: Harper and Brothers, 1950), p. 61.
[61] T. W. Adorno, Else-Frenkel-Brunswik, Daniel J. Levinson, R. Nevitt Sanford, *The Authoritarian Personality* (New York: Harper and Brothers, 1950).
[62] *Ibid.*, pp. 19-27.

ing to face up to them. The prejudiced person particularly attempts to repress fear, weakness, sex impulses, and aggressive feelings toward those in authority, for example, his parents. He shows also a tendency to compensate for this overrepression by manifesting a drive for power and success along conventional lines. The prejudiced gain little pleasure from sensuality, companionship, art, or music, in contrast with the unprejudiced. Outward conformance to conventions is a marked characteristic of the prejudiced whereas the unprejudiced are genuinely concerned with discovering a valid ethical value system for themselves. The prejudiced are more interested in achieving power, whereas the less prejudiced seek love and affection as satisfactory ends in themselves. The high scorers are extremely rigid in their standards of behavior, intolerant of any deviation from the conventional codes of morals or manners: in contrast, the low scorers are more flexible in their own adjustments to the mores, more appreciative of the complexities of human behavior, and more sympathetic with those who err.

The genesis of these two contrasting personality types in terms of prejudice is found by these research workers in the contrasting patterns of family life to which the subjects were exposed in childhood. The prejudiced report rigid discipline with affection made conditional upon the child's approved behavior. In the families of the prejudiced there were clearly defined roles of dominance by parents and submission by children in contrast to families where equalitarian practices prevailed. As the authors put it: "Forced into a surface submission to parental authority, the child develops hostility and aggression which are poorly channelized. The displacement of a repressed antagonism toward authority may be one of the sources, and perhaps the principal source, of his antagonism toward out-groups." [63]

It is of further concern to determine whether linked in the personality of the anti-Semites is a more general ideology toward social issues. The *Fortune* Survey previously quoted found that in 1946 anti-Semitic attitudes ran parallel with hostility to Great Britain and to Russia; with disapproval of large-scale government projects to help prevent unemployment; and with opposition to labor unions.[64] The American Jewish Committee research team likewise found a significant positive correlation, approximately +.5, between anti-Semitism and the "right" in the right-left dimension of politicoeconomic ideology.[65] Since the correlation was, however, far from perfect, they sought in their case studies to delineate more precisely any syndrome

---

[63] *Ibid.*, p. 482.
[64] "The Fortune Survey," Feb., 1946, p. 257.
[65] Adorno, *et. al. op. cit.*, p. 207.

of the anti-Semitic form of "rightism." While such procedure revealed a number of patterns, the most significant was what they label the "pseudoconservative" type. What this politicoeconomic type of person really wants is a fascist revolution which he believes will bring him security without his having to struggle so hard. But he wants the totalitarian order which will follow to be operated by those people usually conservative with whom he feels securely identified. "The psychological structure that corresponds to pseudoconservatism is conventionality and authoritarian submissiveness on the ego level, with violence, anarchic impulses, and chaotic destructiveness in the unconscious sphere." [66]

Summary statement of Jewish-gentile relations in the United States. Jewish-gentile relations in the United States may be summarized in terms of the following statements.

1. Widely prevalent in the gentile population is an attitude which defines the Jew as peculiarly different from other Caucasian peoples, as a person not fully acceptable. From this attitude flows the general practice of social discrimination.

2. Far less prevalent is a specific anti-Semitic prejudice expressed in ideological, symbolic terms. In 1950 about 10 per cent of the population were said to be so inclined. Anti-Semitic prejudice is constantly present in a dormant form. Intermittently it becomes more active, often in organized form. Both its latent and active types stimulate occasional acts of physical violence against Jewish property or persons, but this has not been frequent on any organized scale in the American scene.

3. The gentiles who possess this anti-Semitic prejudice are found more frequently in the middle and upper classes, particularly among the segments of those classes who at any given time feel insecure in their status.

4. Anti-Semitic gentiles possess the type of personality structure which markedly tends to project inner conflicts upon some out-group. The authoritarian personality stands out among varying types of anti-Semites.[67]

5. Social conditions which favor increased discrimination against Jews and outbursts of active anti-Semitism are any changes which render more insecure the position of the middle and lower-upper classes.

6. One way in which Jews themselves contribute to the situation is by remaining visible, by remaining identifiable as a group with a sep-

---

[66] *Ibid.*, p. 675.
[67] If the interpretation of Adorno, *et. al.*, is correct, the "authoritarian personality" should be found likewise among those people who manifest intense prejudice against other group objects which might be considered as threatening their security, e.g., Catholics as well as Jews.

arate social substructure. Many, probably most, Jews want to retain a substantial measure of identity with the Jewish community, although they consider this difference to be merely a form of cultural pluralism which is the legitimate privilege of any aggregate of people in a democratic multigroup society. This difference is therefore, in their view, no proper basis for discrimination. There is no evidence to dispute their position in this respect. There is also no evidence that their pursuit of Jewish cultural activities or their attachment to the Jewish community conflicts with their civic loyalty to the local community or to the nation. On the other hand, there is much evidence of their positive contributions to the general welfare.

7. Whether there is in the Jewish group a wider prevalence of certain personality traits as alleged in the gentile stereotype of the Jew, and considered in an unfavorable light, has never been sufficiently studied to permit verification or disproof. That their minority position makes its imprint upon Jewish personality is manifest, as in the case of all minorities. In certain aspects, the discrimination undergone logically stimulates the development of the very traits considered undesirable by gentiles; for example, aggressiveness in business competition. On the other hand, Jews as a group with long minority experience and a high cultural level are consciously and keenly aware of the necessity for extraordinary circumspectness in their behavior in order to avoid deterioration in their relations with gentiles.

TRENDS AND PROSPECTS IN JEWISH-GENTILE RELATIONS

The prospects for Jews in American society appear different from those of any other minority. With the possible exception of Indians, Jewish Americans as a group are the only minority who have a strong desire to retain a distinctive measure of identity. As we have seen, Judaism has become modernized and many Jews are highly nominal in their allegiance to it. Nevertheless, there is no clear sign that Jews are willfully going to permit Judaism to die. In fact since the rise of Hitler the solidarity of the Jewish community has increased. While this is in some degree a defensive reaction to increasing gentile discrimination, the experience thus encountered carries over in spite of Hitler's inglorious demise. The most significant event in Jewish history since the end of World War II has been the establishment of the nation of Israel.

Israel and American Jewry. The establishment of the new state of Israel—the fulfillment of the Zionist movement participated in by many, though by no means all, American Jews—while generally celebrated by Jews everywhere, creates new problems with respect to the

Jews in the United States. It calls for clarification of the relation of Jews elsewhere to the new nation.[68] At present Jewish opinion is divided on this matter. The Zionists take this position:

Summed up, the Zionist answer to the problem of the relationship of Jews outside of Israel to their new state is that the Zionist will continue to look upon American Jews as Americans of "Jewish" nationality. . . . While in the main formally observing the legalities of every country in which Jews live, they will sustain and exploit the concept of a world-wide nationality of Jews, only some of whom as yet, live in the "Jewish" national home. . . . It will be designed to segregate and distinguish Jews as derivatives of that nationalism, no matter where they may live.[69]

The contrasting position is taken by the Council for Judaism in these terms:

We therefore emphatically declare that the State of Israel is not a state or homeland for the Jewish people. To Americans of Jewish faith it is a foreign state. Our single and exclusive national identity is to the United States. Our exclusive spokesman in all international affairs is the Government of the United States through its authorized representatives.

If Americans of Jewish faith actively, consistently, and publicly disavow Israel-nationalism and act in accordance with their disavowal, the process of integration which has already brought us so much security and freedom, can go on to achieve still greater victories.[70]

No matter which of these positions Americans of Jewish ancestry have taken, the very presence of Israel will strengthen the will for the perpetuation of Jewish identity. Thus what Jews in America will do is reasonably predictable. They will remain Jews in a gentile society, and as such contribute in large measure to the general national welfare. Further than this, the future of Jewish-gentile relations is contingent upon the behavior of gentiles. Gentile behavior, as we have seen, varies in relation to certain general conditions.

Economic conditions. Historical experience shows that periods of relatively good economic conditions tend to lessen minority discrimination and depressed economic conditions to increase them. Looking ahead from the mid-century, the prospects are that the higher employment levels in general will decrease the competitive motivation for discrimination against all minorities. In the case of Jews, however, it is particularly the way in which economic conditions affect the relative position of middle and upper classes in the socioeconomic structure which is of primary significance. Viewed in this light one significant

[68] This problem is discussed briefly in *Race Relations*, June–Dec., 1948, Vol. 5, Nos. 9-12, pp. 279-280 under the caption "Israel and American Jewry."
[69] *Ibid.*, p. 279. By permission of Fisk University.
[70] *Ibid.*, p. 279-280. By permission of Fisk University.

trend in the economy is unfavorable to the position of Jews now and in the immediate future. The increasing extent to which private enterprise is conducted on large scale, corporate basis as contrasted with small business, limits the economic upward mobility of Jews, even more than it does gentiles. Since the same trend likewise limits social mobility in the gentile middle classes, it is likely to generate a great volume of anti-Semitic sentiment in the middle class gentiles with strong status aspirations, and inclined to search for a scapegoat for the ills besetting their class.

Political conditions. The political condition most favorable to Jews is government in the hands of those determined to sustain and to further implement democratic political institutions. Administrations in such hands tend to promote programs designed to create a greater economic security for all. This indirectly reduces the feeling of insecurity which nourishes anti-Semitic feeling. Such administrations cannot do much to change the attitudes of the true and chronic anti-Semite. It can, however, restrain the active expression of such sentiment by firm administration of democratic law. As a recent example, may be cited the effect of specific antidiscrimination legislation and agencies in curbing occupational discrimination against Jews as well as other minorities in many states. Since the administration of government in general in the United States has been markedly inclined in the direction noted above for at least two decades, this trend may be expected to prevent deterioration in the position of Jews, and probably to improve their position. In our summary of the Negro situation we had occasion to refer to the possibly adverse effect upon the status of minorities of rising anticommunist sentiment as in its more hysterical manifestations this feeling is directed toward putative as well as real communists within the country itself. Based upon past historical experience in which the Jew stereotype has been linked symbolically with the revolutionary radical, we should expect such a trend to increase anti-Semitism. However, two other trends in the mid-century situation may well serve to counterbalance this prospect: the inclination of the new state of Israel away from the Soviet orbit; and the increase of anti-Semitism within the Soviet sphere.

TOPICS FOR DISCUSSION AND PROJECTS

1. A number of writers have suggested that the rise and decline in the intensity or prevalence of anti-Semitism is one of the best single indices of the vitality of democratic sentiments and institutions in any nation having a Jewish population. Do you agree? Support your position.
2. Procure a series of at least fifty photographs with a ten per cent sample of Americans of Jewish background mixed in with a generally gentile

collection. A senior year book which could be cut up, using the last senior class before any of your respondents came to college would serve the purpose. Ask twenty-five or more of your fellow students to identify the Jews in the whole series from the photographs alone. Present a statistical analysis of your results. In your report include the photographs of any Jews who were rather consistently missed; and the pictures of any gentiles who were rather consistently identified as Jews.

3. Taking the general description of the position of Jews in Buna as your guide, compare the position of the Jews in your community. If your study shows any marked differences from the Buna picture, suggest some possible reasons why your community deviates.

4. Do you think Jews in the United States will ever cease to be a minority as long as any considerable proportion of Americans of Jewish ancestry form separate religious congregations? Develop your position.

5. Discuss the possible effects of the establishment of the nation of Israel upon the position of Jews in the United States, in the USSR, and in the world in general.

SUGGESTED READING

Ackerman, Nathan W., and Jahoda, Marie. *Anti-Semitism and Emotional Disorder.* New York: Harper and Brothers, 1950.
> *A psychological interpretation of anti-Semitism based on case histories of individuals with demonstrated anti-Semitic atttudes who had undergone psychoanalysis.*

Gordon, Albert I. *Jews in Transition.* Minneapolis: University of Minnesota Press, 1949.
> *A study of the Jewish community in Minneapolis.*

Lowenthal, Leo, and Guterman, Nobert. *Prophets of Deceit.* New York: Harper and Brothers, 1949.
> *A study of the techniques of the American agitator as gathered from the writings and speeches of the well-known American specimens.*

McWilliams, Carey. *A Mask for Privilege.* Boston: Little, Brown & Company, 1948.
> *A description and interpretative analysis of the anti-Semitic behavior of American gentiles from 1870 to date.*

Orlansky, Harold. "The Jews of Yankee City," *Commentary,* Vol. 1, No. 3, January 1946, pp. 77-85.
> *Observations on the position of Jews in small numbers in a small city, based on the data of the Yankee City study.*

Pinson, Koppel S., ed. *Essays on Anti-Semitism.* Jewish Social Studies Publications, No. 2, Conference on Jewish Relations, New York, 1946.
> *A series of analytical, historical, and regional studies of the subject.*

Zuckerman, Nathan. *The Wine of Violence.* New York: Association Press, 1947.
> *An anthology on many phases of anti-Semitism.*

PART SIX

Conclusion

The preceding Chapters 4 through 15 have portrayed and analyzed substantially all of the specific minority situations in the United States. We turn now to consider dominant-minority relations as a whole. In Chapter 16, we seek first a general interpretation of dominant-minority structures as a characteristic feature of American society, developing out of the interplay of a number of social forces and circumstances present in American history. Second, we essay to set forth such general principles as appear to have governed the process of dominant-minority relations.

Chapter 17 is concerned with social action undertaken for the purpose of changing these relations toward a desired end. From the value frame of reference of the American Creed, the central problem is the status of minorities, not their welfare. From this it follows that the elimination of discrimination becomes the only valid *ultimate* goal. Since, however, social science makes it clear that structures and processes as deeply rooted as the ones with which we deal cannot be made to vanish quickly, the immediate goal of democratic social action becomes one of constant reduction of discrimination wherever possible. The purposive efforts of many social action groups dedicated to this objective have already yielded valuable experience. The final chapter presents some of the lessons already learned from such activities as guides for further constructive action.

CHAPTER 16

Interpretation of Dominant-Minority Relations in the United States

Having described and analyzed in some detail each of the specific dominant-minority situations in the United States, we seek now a general interpretation of them all. For this purpose, we shall focus attention upon two uniformities in all these manifold situations: (1) In all the specific situations where a different people have come in contact with Americans possessing unquestioned first-class status, a dominant-minority situation has developed with the latter as dominant; (2) the structure of the relationship in each case has never been completely stable, and the long-run trend of change has been toward the elimination of minority status from each people who possessed it. Even though the former of the above two great uniformities will engage more attention, the latter must ultimately be explained as well. Why is it that all these "strangers" have been accorded minority status, and that so many of their descendants still retain this status. Is this just fortuitous circumstance? Is it the natural order of things—the result of some universal principle operative in all situations where people meet? Or is it peculiar to Americans, the result of social forces peculiary unique in American history, or of Western culture? Or is it perchance a combination of some or all of these circumstances, factors, or forces? In our search for the answer we shall bring into review some of the many theories which others have advanced.

Initial considerations. Some initial considerations need to be borne in mind as we proceed to examine typical theories of dominant-minority relations. First, some of them do not essay to encompass all the intergroup relations which have been considered as dominant-minority relations. Some are theories of "race relations"; others are theories of ethnic group relations. Second, not all of the theories are mutually exclusive. Their differences lie in considerable degree in the level of phenomena, biological, psychological, or cultural, upon which their analysis operates. But in general each theory aims at establishing some one factor or process as essentially determinative from which all the rest inevitably follows. Students of general sociology are familiar with monistic, or one factor deterministic explanations of social life; i.e., geographical, or racial, or economic determinism. Having learned to view all such theories critically, such students will not be surprised that they have shortcomings when utilized to explain dominant-minority relations. Our aim will be to examine these theories against the generally accepted principles of contemporary social science and against the facts of dominant-minority relations as they have been revealed. Proceeding in such manner, it will be shown that some of these theories may be rejected altogether. In others will be found substantial elements of truth for which, however, the expounders have claimed too much. Since in the second section of this chapter, we shall attempt to combine the valid elements which each theory contains into an integrated general interpretation, at this point our concern will be directed at weeding out the elements of error or overemphasis.

Biological "racist" theories. To those who hold in varying degrees the tenets of racism, which were discussed in Chapter 3, explanations of all dominant-minority relations in which race consciousness is a factor are simple. If one believes that the white race is in terms of hereditary capacity superior to the colored, it is both natural and inevitable that where the two live together, a superordinate-subordinate pattern of intergroup relations should prevail. Thus in the traditional Southern ideology, Negroes automatically possess inferior status because they are considered to be innately, and therefore permanently, inferior. Likewise, colonial Europeans penetrating areas of the world inhabited by "uncivilized" peoples naturally dominate the "natives."

In view of the thorough demolition of such "racist" philosophies by modern social science, it is unnecessary to discuss them further. As beliefs still held by those who know no better, or who against all evidence still wish to believe them, these ideas are factors to reckon with in explaining how dominant-minority relations are sustained. But since they are demonstrable myths, this is their only significance.

Natural aversion to other peoples. Another simple explanation of dominant-minority relations rests them upon an alleged instinctive aversion of each distinctive people, usually differentiated in "racial" terms, from other peoples. As will be more fully developed later, there is an element of truth in the idea that where two different peoples meet, it is usual for some amount of antagonism between them to develop. But insofar as the antagonism is attributed to instinct, such theories are contrary to current psychological and social science. Consciousness of one's own kind, or in-group identification, arises out of the experience of living together, whatever the range of physiognomic difference within the communal group, and out of the common sentiments and cultural values which living together generates. That consciousness of race difference is by no means universal is demonstrated by history and by empirical research. In racially heterogeneous Brazil and Russia, both Tsarist and Soviet, race consciousness approaches a minimum of significance. A number of empirical researches, involving situations where white American and Negro American children are brought together under conditions free of adult definitions, indicate that reciprocal responses and choices of friends are uninfluenced by racial features.[1]

Psychological factors. Like all sociological phenomena, dominant-minority relations have their psychological correlates—the attitudes, interests, and motivations which underly the reciprocal behavior of each group to the other. We are concerned here with the psychology of the members of the dominant group. Dominant behavior may be explained in terms of four general kinds of motivations: (1) the motives generated by the imperatives of the society's culture; (2) the desire to conform to the group; (3) calculated self-interest; and (4) psychological imperatives deeply rooted in the unconscious level of his personality.

A basic postulate of social science is that the culture of any society, diffused through group experience, tends to structure the personality of all its members in the mould reflecting its basic values. Thus Zuni culture structures the personality of the individual Zuni to become self-effacing; Chinese culture, to make all Chinese concerned with "saving face"; Dobu culture, to develop suspiciousness in all Dobuans.[2] An integrated interpretation of dominant behavior must therefore take into account the basis of the culture of the society in question.

[1] See Arnold Rose and Caroline Rose, *America Divided* (New York: Alfred A. Knopf, Inc., 1949), p. 281.
[2] See Ruth Benedict, *Patterns of Culture* (Boston: Houghton Mifflin Company, 1934), for further discussion of the influence of culture upon personality.

Every human being desires to be considered a part of the group and to have a secure place in it; he is constrained to conform to the prevalent specific practices of his group. In many instances, his conformance to particular practices lacks any specific motivation other than the desire to conform. He may indeed conform for this reason even when he possesses strong interest in doing the contrary. Many people discriminate against a minority for no other reason than to stay in the good graces of their fellows or, stated in another way, to avoid group penalties for failure to conform. Ultimately this repetitive conformance becomes habitual and continues more or less unconsciously. This process is best illustrated by children who learn to discriminate against particular groups and simply continue to do so throughout their life.

The intensity of the prejudice against minorities and the degree of discrimination against them varies, however, among the members of a society or a group. Greater discrimination is sometimes due to calculated self-interest, on the whole a rational motive understood at the conscious level of personality. This kind of motivation is illustrated by the role of the slave trader in the colonial slave system, or the housewife who offers a minority applicant for domestic service a lower wage than she would offer a dominant status applicant. Or again, the exploitative sexual bargaining of dominant men with minority women falls in this category.

In other instances, we have seen an intensely hostile attitude toward a minority for which there is no adequate explanation in terms of rational self-interest. This is best illustrated in the personality of the true anti-Semite. Interpretation of the attitudes and behavior of such individuals calls for probing into the dynamics of personality at the unconscious level. Theories of such behavior interpret intense prejudice as one mechanism adopted, unconsciously of course, by some persons of dominant status possessing a deep-seated or chronic mental conflict or frustration, in order to resolve their neurotic or psychotic feeling. The most general and least complicated of such types of theories suggests that chronically frustrated people alleviate their frustration by aggression upon available minority people. Minorities are convenient objects of this aggression because it is more dangerous to be aggressive against other dominants and because the dominant society is characteristically tolerant of violation of the rights of minorities. In other formulations, it is suggested that the guilt feelings of the dominant may be resolved by projecting the responsibility for evil upon the minority. For example, the businessman neurotically disturbed as a result of attempting to reconcile his aggressive economic behavior with his Christian ethics, resolves the problem by projecting the blame for the general character of capitalist business practice upon Jews. In still another psychoanalytic theory, McLean[3] interprets Southern white behavior toward Negroes in terms of "the loss of a secure dependence on a fixed social system" brought about by the destruction of the slavery system. Assuming the general validity of the modern functional interpretation of neuroses and psychoses, there can be little doubt of its general applicability to the more pathological dominant behavior toward minorities, however much a particular detailed interpretation may lack verifiability.

Sociological theories. Further contributing to the interpretation of dominant-minority behavior are theories which maintain their analysis primarily on the sociological level. First it may be mentioned that ethnocentrism contributes to explaining why opposition occurs when two peoples meet. Since this phenomenon will be included in our combined interpretation to follow, the development of the point will be held for later consideration. There are, however, important types of interpretative analyses of dominant-minority relations of a sociological character to which we shall give preliminary consideration here: theories based on economic determinism, primarily on the Marxist interpretation of modern history; and Myrdal's theory of white-Negro relations in terms of conflict of values.

Marxist theories. The main thesis of Karl Marx was that the struggle between the bourgeoisie and the proletariat was the determinative force in modern capitalistic society and that all other social relations were derivative from this basic process. From this it follows inevitably that later expounders of Marxist theory should essay to interpret dominant-minority relations in terms of capitalist exploitation. Thus Cox has written, "Racial antagonism is part and parcel of this class struggle, because it developed within the capitalist system as one of its fundamental traits;" and again, "the interest behind racial antagonism is an exploitative interest—the peculiar type of economic exploitation characteristic of capitalist society." [4]

American social science, though greatly stimulated by Marx's writings to explore more closely the connection between economic relations and other social phenomena, rejects the thesis that economic relations determine everything else. Representative of this point of view are MacIver and Page.

We can agree so far with Marx that our dependence on the economic means determines largely our attitude toward the whole social order which yields them to us in scantier or more abundant measure. . . . We can agree that

[3] Helen V. McLean, "Psychodynamic Factors in Race Relations," *The Annals of the American Academy*, Vol. CCXLIV (March, 1946), pp. 159-66.
[4] Oliver C. Cox, *Caste, Class, and Race* (Garden City, L. I.: Doubleday & Company, Inc., 1948), pp. xxx-xxxi.

the mode in which the economic means are acquired influences the nature of satisfactions we seek through them; that, for example, the competitive spirit engendered in the economic struggle affects our manner of living, our recreations, our philosophies, our ideals. We can agree that the struggle for the means of living must color, according to its character, the whole outlook of men. But in so agreeing we are simply admitting that the economic element is one highly important factor in the whole nexus of interactive factors which determine social phenomena. Its relative importance and its relation to other influences, varying according to the conditions, have still to be investigated.[5]

In line with the above appraisal of the influence of economic factors upon social life in general, it would be expected *a priori* that some causal connections between economic organization and dominant-minority relations would necessarily be found. The record of the actual events as recorded in previous chapters provides abundant evidence that such connections do in fact prevail. Therefore we shall include in our interpretation an analysis of the ways in which the dynamics of our economic system, capitalism, have encouraged the establishment and perpetuation of dominant-minority relations.

Myrdal's conflict in values theory. Myrdal's monumental study, quoted extensively, Chapters 8 to 11, is confined to Negro-white relations, although his basic interpretative thesis has more general application. To him, the situation of Negroes in the United States constitutes a conflict in values, a moral dilemma. Myrdal believes that the basic value in the American value system is the American Creed.[6] Since the traditional pattern of segregation of and discrimination against Negroes is obviously at variance with this creed, in time the dynamics generated by acceptance of the creed will force the abolition of the minority phenomena. On the one hand, the system continues because of the operation of the vicious circle. The dominant discrimination tends to make minorities appear to fit the stereotype of inferior, and their continued inferiority justifies the dominant rationalizations for the necessity of keeping them so. On the other hand, the circle is by no means absolutely closed. The dynamics of the American Creed force some improvement in the Negro's condition, and each such improvement undermines to a degree the traditional pattern. The principle of cumulative causation under the American Creed inexorably pushes the Negro step by step nearer equality. A major criticism of Myrdal's analysis is that it minimizes and understresses the role of the economic interests of the dominants in keeping the Negro in his accustomed place, whereas the Marxists writers consider this the whole story. On the other hand, Myrdal illuminates what seems to us essen-

---

[5] MacIver and Page, *Society*, p. 564. By permission of Rinehart and Company, Inc.
[6] Myrdal, *An American Dilemma*, Ch. 1.

tial aspects of a total interpretation. Especially does his interpretation help to explain why it is that even under capitalism the long run trend of change has been the movement of Negroes toward equality.

A SYNTHESIZED INTERPRETATION

The foregoing considerations suggest that an adequate interpretation of dominant-minority relations in the United States must combine a number of different factors and forces. The most significant of such factors and forces appear to us to include: the universal phenomenon of ethnocentrism and the principle of in-group–out-group interaction, fortuitous historical circumstances, the dynamics of the capitalist system, the sustaining influence of tradition, and the dynamics of democracy.

Universal principles of group interaction and ethnocentrism. The initial stages of interaction between a dominant and a minority group may be expected to follow the well established universal sociological principles of ethnocentrism and in-group–out-group processes. In order for any society to survive, each member as he grows up in the group must acquire a strong sense of loyalty to and identification with his own people—the in-group. Through this process also each member acquires the conviction that the culture of his own group, its ways of doing things, its values and goals are the "proper," the right ways and values. It is therefore to a degree inevitable that when two such in-groups find themselves suddenly faced with the problem of living together in the same area, each should consider the other an out-group and that some antagonism should arise. The immediate harmonious assimilation of two visibly different groups is impossible. Still further, the in-group sentiment requires some degree of sacrifice of individual desires in order to conform to the demands of the society. In psychological terms, this involves some degree of repression of individual desires and the resulting frustrations seek a permissible outlet. An out-group, a different people, afford such an outlet. Thus, for example, the in-group member in wartime, chafing at rationing regulations, may blame the necessity for it on the alleged black market operations of the members of an out-group.

Relation to historical circumstances. Since it is then sociologically natural for opposition to arise between two peoples living in the same area, the great prevalence of ethnic and racial antagonism in the history of the United States is in no small measure related to the fact that no other nation in modern times has faced so many such situations, so often and so continuously. Parisian French, for example, have a reputation for their indifference to race, but France, as a modern nation, has had no great influx of different peoples to absorb. While, as was pointed out in Chapter 1, southern Europeans have never been as "race conscious" as northern Europeans, it should be remembered that over the historic period being covered, the nations of southern Europe have not faced, nor invited, the situation of assimilating vast numbers of cultural and racial aliens. As we pointed out in Chapter 2, in Europe, particularly in the central and eastern regions, hostile attitudes between ethnic and nationality groups create minorities problems of a different character than those which have arisen in American history. To an extent then, the prevalence of ethnic and racial antagonism in the United States is due to the unique historical circumstances creating so many potential dominant-minority situations. While universal principles explain why intergroup antagonisms arise, and why historical circumstance has presented the United States with unequalled opportunity for their expansion, they do not explain why the outcome has been so unvaryingly of the dominant-minority pattern, and why in each case "white Americans" have been the dominants.

Native status Americans possessed superior power. The unvarying dominance of those Americans possessing native status resulted from their possession of superior power. In all situations with two exceptions, the combination of power factors, superiority in numbers, economic resources, and technological skills is so obvious as to need no summary retelling. One exception is the situation of white colonists vis-a-vis Indian peoples in certain localized areas. In delimited areas, sometimes the Indians annihilated the whites. Again, in the island territory situations where the white Americans are numerically in the minority, their dominant status arises out of the managerial economic position and their ruling political function, a status supported by a homeland power nation. Thus the opportunity to resolve their antagonism with the other peoples by assigning them the status of minorities, if they so desired, lay with native white Americans.

Capitalist dynamics furnish strong motivations for dominant behavior. In intergroup relations, there is no universal principle to the effect that the group which is stronger will automatically dominate the weaker. When the stronger group does establish a dominating relationship, the motivations for its members' behavior must be sought in the dynamics of its culture. In the case of those Americans possessing dominant status, by far the greatest cultural force motivating discriminatory behavior has been capitalism. Before analyzing the ways in which capitalism has stimulated dominant behavior we wish to suggest in advance, in line with the criticism of the Marxist writers previously indicated, that we do not consider the nexus between capitalism and the existence of minorities an inevitable connection. Some class differentiation is an inevitable concomitant of capitalism—and probably of any other alternative system by which large scale societies can conceivably be operated. But capitalism can operate without minorities. Furthermore, the dynamics of capitalism do not operate uniformly or consistently in the one direction, that of establishing and maintaining minorities. At certain times and in certain total societal configurations, capitalism operates to remove minority status, as will be illustrated at the conclusion of this section. With this general orientation, attention now focuses upon the pervasive manner in which capitalism has contributed to the establishment of minorities and continues to sustain their position.

For the purpose of this analysis, capitalism is here considered strictly as an economic system, and the human beings influenced by it will be considered strictly in their roles of "economic men." Such a procedure necessarily ignores the total man, who has many other interests than the economic one, and the problem of reconciling the other interests with the economic. It is useful to proceed in this manner in order to reveal the relation of capitalism to our problem.

Capitalism is a set of economic institutions in which all individuals strive by competition and bargaining to gain the most for themselves individually. The belief is widely held in the United States that the indirect result of this pluralistic striving is to provide the greatest possible economic welfare for the society as a whole. For our purposes the validity of this belief is irrelevant. What concerns us is the way in which motivations established by this individualistic economic endeavor influence dominant behavior toward minorities. The person acting in his "economic man" role in capitalist society cannot give *primary* consideration to the *common* welfare. The one criterion by which the individual must decide his attitude and behavior toward minorities is the pecuniary one. Decision rests upon the best calculated answer to the question, "What course of action will yield me the greatest economic gain?" Viewed in this light, attention now turns to indicate the ways in which this pecuniary incentive leads persons in a position of dominant status to behave as a dominant toward minorities.

The entrepreneur. The employing, managerial segment of the American economic order has gained by the presence of minorities in two distinct ways. First, each individual employer desires to get labor at the cheapest possible cost. The indications are clear that minority status characteristically constitutes an additional handicap for any applicant not shared by the applicant with dominant status. Minorities are a source of cheaper labor. During the colonial period and after the United States became a nation, vast opportunities existed for highly profitable private enterprise. Full exploitation of these opportunities required far more labor than population growth provided. To start with, African natives were forced to provide that need. At later periods, employers have welcomed immigrant newcomers for this purpose. It will be recalled that it was organized labor, not employers, who pressed for restriction of immigration. The differential handicap in wages suffered by minority workers has been partly obscured by the tendency to employ only minority workers in particular occupational functions; for example, Negro cotton workers and house servants, Mexican "beet pickers," immigrants on railroad building gangs. Here the collective minority status of all the workers helped to keep the general wage low. In the second place, in his pursuit of the cheapest labor, the individual entrepeneur opposed unionization. If he could not prevent it altogether, he tried to keep union strength at the lowest possible point. Antagonisms between dominant status labor and minority status labor, or between minorities themselves, contributed to weakening the bargaining power of labor. As a closely related point, in a number of instances, minority laborers were utilized as "strikebreakers."

While the relations of economic men to one another in the free enterprise system are primarily essentially competitive and bargaining relations, secondarily, considerable cooperation with others is a necessary condition to success. Such cooperation takes many forms. The form of most concern to us is that which prompts competitors to maintain common rules of competition. The advantages accruing to entrepreneurs from the presence of minorities are contingent upon general cooperation. If one by one, for example, entrepreneurs break the customary "color line," the economic advantage of it would soon be lost. Class consciousness impels each individual entrepreneur toward conformity with the prevailing patterns of dominant-minority relations, even in instances where the particular employer has no direct or immediate economic advantage.

Labor. In the economic system, laborers are in competition with each other for jobs and for better jobs. Laborers possessing either dominant status or a higher minority status than other minorities have a differential advantage in this competition. While perhaps in the long run, the differential position of all labor would be strengthened by resolving dominant-minority distinctions and opening up union membership to all, the immediate short-run advantage lies in a policy of exclusion. Of further significance is the long experience of labor with the effects of depression periods in the business cycle which gives strong impetus to an individual laborer or his restricted union to maintain their own particular job status by any means possible. Discrimination against minorities is one such means. The facts in any case are that American labor has characteristically discriminated against minorities both economically and socially, although in the last decade their position has been changing in this respect.

The indirect effect of the capitalist dynamics. Private enterprise economics also indirectly provides further motivation for dominant behavior. The success of the system in part lies in the holding out of great pecuniary reward for those most successful in the system. From this it follows that wide disparity in wealth and income is an essential part of the system. Consequently, there must be a substantial working class whose pecuniary reward is nominal. For many of the wage earning and low salaried groups the resulting situation inevitably generates a sense of economic deprivation. It is psychologically more frustrating to be "poor" in a rich country than to be poor in a poor country. The frustrations thus generated seek alternative compensations in whatever ways are possible. Dominant status constitutes one such possible compensating satisfaction. For example, it provides the low income Southern white an ego statisfaction to feel that he is better than any "Nigger," or the low income Anglo-American that he is better than any "Polack."

The private enterprise system and the relatively open class system in the United States has provided great opportunity for those born into humble circumstances to achieve higher economic reward and social status, probably to a greater extent than in any other modern nation. For this reason the system has generated strong competitive drives, particularly in the business world. On the other hand, the system offers little certainty of security at any level. Therefore there develops among those who acquire this intensely competitive drive a large volume of frustration at not being able to reach the desired level or at retaining a level already reached. As we have seen in the interpretation of gentile behavior, this condition motivates hostility against Jews. Likewise, the antagonism of some West Coast whites toward Japanese carries a similar interpretation. That this sociopsychological process does not appear operative in other minority situations may be explained by the fact that, as yet, the other minorities have not reached a point of effective competition in the area of business life.

The connection between the frustrations generated by deprivation and status anxiety, and strong antagonism toward minorities is, of course, not automatic. There could be other outlets, such as antagonism toward a foreign nation, or an 'ism, or in rationally organized efforts to improve their economic position. But for persons who fear the consequences of opposing those in powerful position, an available minority is a safer outlet for their aggression. These indirect effects of the private enterprise system are not, of course, always consciously perceived by the property holding classes or always consciously exploited for the purpose implied. Nevertheless the assumption that a vague awareness of the utility of minorities in this regard helps to make more intelligible the toleration by the upper class dominants of the cruder excesses of discrimination displayed by lower class dominants.

Special economic interests. The analysis of economic factors influencing dominant behavior reveals that wide segments of the dominant group gain economic advantages from discrimination against minorities. However, there are a number of particular interests who profit most highly from the situation. Among these are employers of unskilled labor, of whom large scale agricultural enterpreneurs would perhaps rank highest. Cotton production in the South, prior to the introduction of the mechanical cotton picker, utilized Negroes; for large scale vegetable production, particularly in the Southwest, Mexicans are employed in large numbers; and historically, immigrants in general supplied the least skilled labor in the great industrial areas. Other special economic interests are the owners of residential real estate in housing areas more or less restricted to minorities, where the limitation of choice of residence enables the charging of exhorbitant rents.[7] Ironically enough, certain minority people themselves have a special economic interest in the maintenance of segregation. For example, Negro ministers, undertakers, beauticians, have a stake in maintaining segregation. While in the long run, the removal of all segregation would improve the occupational opportunities of the minority in general, in the short run the particular persons now earning a living in these ways stand to lose.

The counterdynamics of capitalism favoring improvement of minority status. In spite of the manifold ways in which people, acting in their roles as "economic men" under capitalism, are motivated to seize the advantages accruing from dominant status, the connection between the two phenomena is not inevitable. Again it is the individualistic and pluralistic character of the capitalist order which makes it generate forces in the opposite direction. There are circumstances and conditions in which it pays economically not to discriminate. A Southern city department store owner may find it pays to welcome Negro trade

---

[7] See the report on *Segregation in Washington* for details.

and to be reasonably civil to Negro customers to keep it. An employer desperately needing labor to fulfill a lucrative contract may be glad to place Negroes in jobs hitherto denied them. An employer may be able to get a better qualified Negro for a job at less money than he would have to pay a white. These entrepreneurs have only to calculate the possible other effects which may offset the advantage, and when the balance appears to favor taking on the minority person, their economic interests lead them to do so. In fact, as has been indicated at many points, in the past decade, the total situation has so changed that in an increasing number of instances entrepreneurs have been opening up more opportunities to minorities in employment, even in jobs where they work alongside of dominant status people. While there have been many political and civic pressures which account for this, when the times and the rules change, the practices of the competitive economic man change also.

Finally, it is well to state again that the above analysis has considered the impact of an economic order as though it were the whole societal system, which is, of course, far from the complete reality. The total society has also a political order, a religiomoral order, and they all interact upon one another. Likewise, we have been analyzing the fractional responses of the total human being—his economic responses—without reference to the totality of his personality. Man likewise is a civic being, and as an American holds in varying degrees a belief in the democratic way of life; he is a Christian who believes, however myopically at times, in the brotherhood of man; and he has the capacity to sympathize and to like other human beings irrespective of color and creed. It is this conflict in values within the American man which keeps the structure of dominant-minority relations in flux.

Tradition supports the persistence of dominant behavior. In addition to the continued influence of the dynamics of capitalism, the persistence of the dominant-minority pattern is in large measure the product of tradition. It is an elementary principle of social science that once a pattern of social relationships has been established, it tends to carry on unchanged, except as the dynamics of other social forces operate to undermine it. Because this elementary principle of social science is so vital to attacking the problem of minority groups, it is important to apply it to our theme. In addition to the people who in their "economic men" roles have special reasons for maintaining "minorities," there are people who hold mythical stereotyped beliefs about minorities, who manifest prejudiced attitudes, and who in various subtle ways—as mild as repeating a minorities' story—practice discrimination for no other reason than that they have been "conditioned" that way. A student in the writer's class refers to gentiles as "white" in contrast to Jews. At a high school concert where Negroes participate with whites on merit, one act is an imitation of Al Jolson by a white student "colored" with burnt cork who imitates the supposed stereotype of Negro behavior. Traditional attitudes and corresponding behavior patterns once conditioned are hard to change in adult people. Scientific fact and logic are often unable to dislodge them, especially among the legion who are not trained to think about social phenomena in a scientific manner.

The strength of tradition lies in part in its generality and its explicitness—the fact is clearly understood that it is the right way of behavior for all good members of the group. In the South where caste segregation of Negroes is established, the liberal Southerner who desires to have it changed faces the harsh sanctions which tradition can command—ostracism, ridicule, stigmatization as a radical. On the other hand, tradition is not inflexible. In contrast to dominant behavior enmeshed with economic motives or compelling psychic needs, one finds that dominant behavior of the purely traditional type is more amenable to change, more responsive to intellectual persuasion, more willing to weigh scientific evidence, more influenced by broader ethical insights.

The dynamics of political democracy press toward the elimination of minority status. Dominant-minority relations in the United States have always been in a state of flux. The trend of change for any particular group has not always been in the same direction. Attention will be given subsequently to certain short-time ebbs and flows either in status or in the intensity of discrimination practices. One influence in American culture has, however, persistently pressed toward the elimination of minority status and its attendant disabilities, namely, political democracy. Political democracy is in part a set of beliefs and sentiments which taken altogether constitute what Myrdal has called the American Creed. Among the elements of the creed are the idea that government derives its authority from the consent of the governed, and that each citizen is entitled to equal participation in government and to equal protection from it. Furthermore, political democracy is a set of institutions through which the democratic creed is given explicit expression. Among these many institutions, those most pertinent for our consideration are democratic citizenship, democratic government, and public education.

Democratic citizenship. Democratic citizenship involves both equal opportunity to participate in government and equal protection from it. Participation includes the right to vote, join a political party, run for office, and to be appointed to a governmental job. Protection includes the right to trial by jury, equal treatment by law-enforcing officers, and equal protection from physical harm or property damage.

European immigrants, including Jews, have been able to acquire all these rights through naturalization, and their descendants born here are automatically citizens. Mexican immigrants have the same privileges, although local legislation has segregated them in schools and barred them from certain public places. Chinese and Japanese foreign-born have been denied citizenship, and have been denied the privilege of owning land. Except for a brief postbellum period, Negroes have been denied many of the privileges of citizenship.

The caste patterning of the administration of government and the intimidation implicit in the caste system often have nullified civic privileges which are not officially denied by local law, for example, voting and jury service.

In spite of these obvious inconsistencies, the basic institutions of political democracy remain to point up the incongruity; and by their continuous existence, press continuously for the abolition of discrimination. Foreign born Chinese acquired the right to citizenship in 1943, and current movements press vigorously toward similar opportunity for the Japanese. Federal court decisions have set aside many Negro convictions because of various discriminatory procedures involved in their trials, for example, the failure to call Negro citizens for jury service. While for a long period the United States Supreme Court upheld the principle that segregation was not unconstitutional where the services were "equal," in recent decisions, notably concerned with professional education for Negroes, it now indicates change in this respect. The same Court ruled in 1948 that restrictive covenants could not be enforced by law. While the wartime Federal Fair Employment Practices Commission designed to protect minorities from job discrimination was abolished in 1945, pressure to reestablish it continues. In the meantime a number of Northern states have established their own similar commissions, and in some cases, as in New Jersey, are making it specifically illegal to bar minorities from any public places.

Democratic government. While effective democratic citizenship itself requires an alert and efficient democratic government to maintain it, emphasis here is on the tendency of democratic government to press further toward its own greater democratization. Politicians, for example, are responsive to all elements of the population in a position to influence elections. Thus in areas of minority group concentration, the exercise of civic rights permits election of their members to councils and legislatures and their appointment to various governmental positions. Strong in a study of the rise of Negro voting in Texas shows how once Negroes do manage to vote in numbers, white politicians begin to bid for their votes. He cites, for example, the veteran Congressman who reacted in 1944 to the court decision outlawing the white primary by stating publicly that Negroes would vote in his district "over my dead body." Yet, "two years later when encountering appreciable opposition in the primary of 1946, he was to be seen putting in an occasional appearance at Negro fish fries and church picnics." [8] Comparison of governmental associations with other associations suggests in the main that the former reveal, outside the South, less discrimination against minorities. In Washington, D. C., the agencies of the Federal Government are far less discriminatory than the rest of the community. In, short, our thesis is that the very existence of democratic government furnishes a persistent dynamic to further democracy.

Public education. A strongly established belief of the American Creed is the right of all children in the nation to free public education. The institutional embodiment of this belief is the public school system. In consequence, the children of minorities have been educated at public expense. With three main exceptions, Negroes in the South, Mexicans in some areas of the Southwest, and Indian children on reservations, minority children have not been segregated.

Public education has been profoundly instrumental in undermining minority status. It has been a principal factor in the complete assimilation of ethnic minorities. In the case of racial minorities, it continues to lead toward their complete acculturation and improves the group welfare, but as yet has not been sufficiently influential to remove the stigmatism of minority status. Even in segregated and unequal schools, the education of minority children has one enormously important effect upon dominant minority relations: it undermines the dominant stereotype of the minority. Education brings out the varying ranges of talents and abilities which exist in every minority group, and thus makes it increasingly absurd to invoke the stereotype to support the dominant position. Minority valedictorians deflate the myth of categorical minority inferiority.

In its impact upon dominant children in unsegregated schools, public education likewise operates to remove the distinctions between dominant and minority. Admittedly, the education received for citizenship in the formal curricula is not totally free from prejudiced nuances reflecting the varying attitudes of their teachers. But the proc-

[8] Donald S. Strong, "The Rise of Negro Voting in Texas," *American Political Science Review*, Vol. 42, June, 1948, pp. 510-522.

ess of civic education in a democratic society must outwardly conform to democratic principles. At the minimum, "lip service" must be given against discrimination. Public education works in the same direction also through the association together of dominant and minority children on a plane of at least formal equality. Again, we are not unmindful of the formation of cliques manifesting prejudices or the subtle ways in which minority students are frequently kept out of certain school clubs and activities. But by its very nature a public school system in a democratic society cannot officially approve such tendencies. An increasing number of schools are in fact designing purposive policies to counteract these influences.[9] Finally, the "carry over" into adult life of the democratic impact of public education is of course by no means complete. Many college students liberalized in the cloistered atmosphere of the campus reveal anti-Semitic attitudes after several years out in the "hard" world. But it can be scarcely doubted that there is considerable permanent influence.

Summary. The two outstanding generalizations about dominant-minority relations in the United States have been (1) the imposition of minority status upon all the "different peoples" coming under the jurisdiction of the nation; and (2) the instability of the dominant-minority patterns thus formed, with the net trend of change in the direction of removing the disabilities of minority status from each minority. An interpretation of the first of these generalizations can be made only by considering a number of circumstances and social forces operating in conjunction. Since ethnocentrism is a universal phenomenon it engenders some degree of opposition wherever two peoples meet. The historical circumstances which brought so many other peoples in contact with "established" Americans presented the maximum of opportunity for the development of dominant-minority structures. The success of dominant Americans in imposing minority status upon all the others is in part due to their superior power. The desire to establish and maintain dominance has been powerfully motivated by the dynamics of the free enterprise system, especially in its development to the first World War. From the viewpoint of entrepreneurs, the exploitation of the possibilities for economic profit in the New World encouraged welcoming new labor willing to perform unskilled tasks. Their subsequent minority status contributed to keeping their wages lower directly by discrimination and indirectly by retarding unionization. Dominant status laborers likewise in an unstable employment economy were motivated to practice discrimination to protect their tenuous economic status. Indirectly, the individual economic in-

[9] See Theodore Brameld, *Minority Problems in the Public Schools* (New York: Harper & Brothers, 1946).

security of many elements in the American economy coupled with the strong urge to rise in socioeconomic status created a large volume of frustration. Discrimination against minorities served to attentuate these frustrations both by providing the ego satisfaction of having someone else to look down on and by proving an outlet for the aggressive tendencies which frustration generates by projecting it upon minorities. This diversion of frustration of the dominant status worker through discrimination also served the economic interest of the entrepreneurial elements. The dynamics of private enterprise are not in all ways and at all times in the same direction. Changing conditions create situations in which "it pays" for both employer and worker to relax their discriminatory practices. In the final analysis, the relation between capitalism and minority discrimination is not inexorable.

Once established, dominant-minority patterns tend to continue in part simply because they are traditional, supported by the mores of the dominant community. This tendency to conform is strengthened by conditioning dominant status children to accept them as "habitual," and by applying the penalties of nonconformism upon the would-be nonconformists.

Dominant-minority relations have never been completely frozen. The net trend toward the breakdown of minority status derives primarily from the dynamics of political democracy, from the beliefs in the American Creed and their expression through appropriate institutions. The institutions of democratic citizenship press persistently toward the equal participation of all and the equal protection of all. The process of democratic government likewise presses continuously for its fuller development, and in so doing affords increasing opportunity for minorities to help themselves. Democratic education tends to break down the dominant stereotype of the minority, an essential rationale for the discriminatory process. Free education for minorities destroys the illusion of their categorical inferiority. Democratic education of the dominant elements further undermines the racist ideology, as does the experience of association with minority students on a relatively equal footing. The course which dominant-minority relations has followed in the United States may be in considerable measure viewed as a conflict between the dynamics of capitalism and those of democracy. The conflict is not, however, "one to the death." However, ascendancy of the political over the economic interest is essential if the move toward "a more perfect union" between minorities and the dominants is to continue. Either the dynamics of democracy must control the exploitative tendencies of the free enterprise system or they must create conditions in which discrimination "does not pay off" in economic terms. The current trends suggest that the democratic dynamics possess this ascendancy.

CHARACTERISTICS OF DOMINANT-MINORITY RELATIONS IN THE UNITED STATES

The interactions between dominant and minority groups in the United States has shown certain general uniformities; and tendencies to vary in certain more or less consistent ways. These constitute in a sense "principles" of dominant-minority relations. It is possible that some of them would hold true in every dominant-minority situation, but since as we have seen, the course of intergroup relations in the United States has been greatly affected by the particular configuration of historical circumstances in the nation's development, we shall not consider them as principles but as characteristic uniformities and variables within the particular society of the United States in its history thus far.

"Visibility" variables. The process of assimilation has been differentially affected by the kinds of identifiable features of the minority which have been called "visibility." Warner and Srole have arranged these features in hierarchial manner, in which race (color), religion (Protestant or non-Protestant), and language (English-speaking or non-English-speaking) determine each minority's rank. First, the broad levels are determined by race color which rank from top to bottom as Light Caucasoids, Dark Caucasoid, Caucasoid Mixtures, Mongoloids, and Negroids. Within each of these primary levels, are sublevels. The other two variables noted, further determine the status. A table constructed with the three variables would yield thirty possible status positions. In the United States there are actual ethnic or racial groups representing only 17 of these possibilities. These are presented in Chart 2. Perhaps the most important comment to make concerning this scheme is that no adequate scale exists by which to measure the status of the minorities. Therefore, there is no way to test the validity of their rank order. Yankee City itself had largely immigrant minorities. Recognizing the lack of research tools by which to appraise this schema, certain queries however may be raised. The status of many minorities varies by regions; for example, the Japanese in California and those in New York City. Mexican status may vary from Chicago to El Paso. Likewise other variables, such as the recency of the group's entrance into the country and the size of the group, may operate in such manner as to preclude any fixed schema of assimilability such as the Warner-Srole system suggests. Again it is doubtful if their system adequately places the Jewish minority. Finally, Chapter 14 pointed out

CHART 2

Scale of Subordination and Assimilation [10]

RACIAL TYPE	CULTURE OF TYPE
Racial Type I Light Caucasoids	*Cultural Type 1* English-speaking Protestants Tests: English, Scotch, North Irish, Australians, Canadians
	Cultural Type 2 Protestants who do not speak English Tests: Scandinavians, Germans, Dutch, French
	Cultural Type 3 English-speaking Catholics and other non-Protestants Test: South Irish
	Cultural Type 4 Catholics and other non-Protestants most of whom speak allied Indo-European languages Tests: (fair-skinned) French-Canadians, French, Germans, Belgians
	Cultural Type 5 English-speaking non-Christians Test: English Jews
	Cultural Type 6 Non-Christians who do not speak English Tests: (fair-skinned) European Jews, Mohammedans from Middle East
Racial Type II Dark Caucasoids	*Cultural Type 2* Tests: Protestant Armenians, other "dark-skinned" Protestants
	Cultural Type 4 Tests: "dark skins" of racial type I, cultural type 4; also Sicilians, Portuguese, Near Eastern Christians

[10] W. Lloyd Warner and Leo Srole, *The Social Systems of American Ethnic Groups,* pp. 288, 290-292. The above constitutes an adaptation of their shorter and longer scales. Full description of the cultural types are given for Racial Type 1; the reader should refer to those cultural types as repeated under other racial types. The logical cultural subtypes which are not represented in the United States are left out. By permission of publishers, Yale University Press.

RACIAL TYPE	CULTURE OF TYPE
	Cultural Type 6
	Tests: ("dark-skinned") Jews and Moham-medans of Europe and the Near East
Racial Type III	*Cultural Type 2*
Mongoloid and Caucasoid mixtures that appear Caucasoid	Tests: small groups of Spanish Americans in the Southwest
	Cultural Type 4
	Tests: most of the mixed bloods of Latin America
Racial Type IV	*Cultural Type 1*
Mongoloid and Caucasoid mixtures that appear Mongoloid	Tests: most American Chinese and Japanese
	Cultural Type 4
	Tests: Filipinos (Catholic)
	Cultural Type 6
	Tests: East Indians, Chinese, Japanese
Racial Type V	*Cultural Type 1*
Negroes and all Negroid mixtures	Test: most American Negroes
	Cultural Type 3
	Test: some American Negroes
	Cultural Type 1
	Test: Negroid Puerto Ricans
	Cultural Type 6
	Tests: Bantu Negroes and West African Negroes

the difficulty of determining whether Catholicism per se is as important and as consistent a factor as the Yankee City writers imply.

The evidence is, however, overwhelming that the possession by a minority of enough physiognomic visibility to permit the dominant group to view them as "racially" different is the strongest barrier to assimilation. Concerning the factor of visibility, we state our first two propositions:

1. Physiognomic visibility is the strongest factor retarding assimilation. Color is the most significant physiognomic feature. The "darker" the color the slower the rate of assimilation.

2. The greater the cultural difference of ethnic group from the host group, the slower the rate of assimilation. Among these cultural differences those of language and religion are significantly determinative.

The size and concentration of the minority. The following proposition is generally accepted by students of minorities:

3. The larger the size of the minority proportional to the population of the given area, the slower the rate of assimilation.[11]

The rigidity of the Southern caste system appears roughly correlated with varying proportions of the Negro population in the South. North Carolina has a much smaller proportion of Negroes than South Carolina and the former has a less rigid caste system. Viewed in its entire historical context, the fear in the minds of Southern whites of the sheer number of Negroes in their midst is at least understandable. Most polls have shown that the incidence of anti-Semitism was greatest in the Northeast and the Midwest, the areas of greatest Jewish concentration. Students of the Jewish problem are, however, inclined to be cautious about relating anti-Semitic feeling to any specific phenomena because of the highly symbolic nature of anti-Semitism. The concept of the Jew can be opposed even if Jewish people are not seen.

Closely related to point 3 is the following:

4. Rapid increases in the numbers of any new group increase antagonism toward the group. In consequence the position of an ethnic group may deteriorate for a time until some new equilibrium is established.

A leading Negro sociologist once illustrated this point by his own experience. As a graduate student in New York City, he with two other colleagues went to work in the Connecticut tobacco fields to earn money in the summer. These three Negro young men were well received by their white associates, played on their ball team. Two years later, the young sociologist repeated the experience and found that the whole attitude had changed. Now white people would not associate with him. In the short interval, there had occurred a conspicuous "invasion" of the area by Negro people to which he attributed the change in white attitudes.

Economic conditions. In a general way the position of minorities improves in economic good times and deteriorates in depressions. However, the relationship appears to be more precisely seen in the effect of general changes on particular segments of the population. For the next two propositions, we quote directly from Williams:

[11] Robin M. Williams, Jr., *The Reduction of Intergroup Tensions* (New York: Social Science Research Council, Bulletin 57, 1947), p. 58. Permission to quote the propositions from this monograph which are cited in this chapter and Chapter 17 has been granted by the Social Science Research Council.

5. Conflict is especially likely in periods of rapid change in levels of living. The probability of conflict is increased insofar as the changes have a differential impact on various groups.[12]
6. Among the members of any dominant group the greatest incidence of open conflict behavior toward a given minority will be found among those classes which are most vulnerable to competition from the minority.[13]

Political conditions. It is a basic postulate of social science that conflict with outside groups intensifies the solidarity of the in-group. When the antagonistic out-group is another nation, the in-group nation shows more unity. Applied to dominant-minority conflict this would yield the following proposition:

7. In periods when the nation is preoccupied with the threat of conflict with another nation, the intensity of dominant-minority conflict within the nation declines.

One of the most striking facts revealed in our discussion of the different minorities was the great impetus to advancing their position which resulted from World War II. The main exception to this proposition is that the position of minorities who may be identified with the enemy may deteriorate, as with the Japanese in World War II.

We have placed great emphasis upon the dynamics of political democracy as a constant factor persistently operating toward assimilation. The influence of this factor varies however in relation to the amount of interest which the particular persons operating the government at any one time have in extending the applications of democracy. To put this in formal statement:

8. The pressures exerted by the dynamics of democracy toward the removal of discrimination varies in intensity with the degree of democratic sentiments held by those in possession of governmental authority.

Minority behavior. The behavior of a minority is affected by forces generated from within the group itself and by the impact upon the group of the manner in which the dominant group treats it. Among the characteristic forms of behavior generated from intragroup life are the following:

9. The minority moves toward acculturation to the norms of the dominant society.
   a) The less culturally different the minority is from the dominant society, the more rapid is its acculturation.
   b) The less determined the minority is to retain any parts of its cultural heritage, the more complete its acculturation becomes.

[12] *Ibid.*, p. 58.
[13] *Ibid.*, p. 59.

In subproposition 9*b* above, we have in mind groups like the Amish, and to some extent the Jews, who have shown strong tenacity in preserving their traditional culture. As we have shown repeatedly, it is difficult to evaluate properly this force because the discrimination from without generates a defensive reaction.

The typical forms of minority behavior which are more clearly interpretable in terms of reaction to dominant treatment embrace the following propositions:

10. Minorities react with sensitivity and withdrawal to dominant discrimination, producing in the personalities of its members in varying degrees of intensity a persecution complex.
11. Dominant discrimination sets in motion a "vicious circle" which tends to increase the prevalence within the minority membership of the very traits considered undesirable by the dominant.
    a) The above effect varies however with the general cultural level of the minority group. The higher the general cultural level of the minority, the more apt it is to struggle against this very effect.

By 11*a* above, we have in mind the behavior of Japanese and Jews who have tempered their competitive behavior with a circumspection growing out of their awareness of the dominant conception of them.

We have noted at various points that as some minorities improve their position they tend to act toward minorities still below them in rank much as dominants have acted toward them. This is in part a function of the process of becoming "Americanized," taking on the normative patterns of behavior of the dominant. But it is also interpretable in terms of the insecure, marginal position which such groups occupy. We have found this kind of behavior often enough to consider it a general characteristic.

12. Minorities in intermediary or insecure status tend to act toward the minorities below them in status in the manner of a dominant.

Finally, the variability of "militant" behavior by minorities in their own behalf shows a characteristic mode. Our previous discussion of "protest activity" is one measure of militancy. Our material supports Williams' formulation of this point:

13. Militancy, except for sporadic and short-lived uprisings, is not characteristic of the most deprived and oppressed groups, but rather of those who have gained considerable rights so that they are able realistically to hope for more.
14. A militant reaction from a minority group is most likely when (*a*) the group's position is rapidly improving, or (*b*) when it is rapidly deteriorating, especially if this follows a period of improvement.[14]

[14] *Ibid.*, p. 61.

THE GENERAL PROSPECT FOR MINORITIES

We have at times stated or implied throughout this book that the ultimate prospect for all minorities was complete assimilation. In general, we believe the materials of this book warrant this conclusion, on the assumption of the continuation of the political democracy as our form of government. There are, however, three recurring points in our materials which bear adversely on this prospect: (1) the color consciousness of white Americans; (2) the question of cultural pluralism; and (3) the changing class situation.

It is not certain whether or when white Americans are going to be able to eliminate their "race-color" consciousness. If they do not, the visibly colored groups will probably in some degree be treated as a minority, for an attitude of superiority is involved in this race consciousness.

Complete assimilation assumes likewise the disappearance of the minority as a distinct group. It is theoretically possible for groups differentiated on ethnic lines to be accorded equal status within a larger national society. We have in our previous discussions advanced the hypothesis that in the American scene this is not likely to happen, and have adduced the following points in its support: (1) Our largest minority, the Negro group, is not a distinctive cultural group; (2) both the European and Asiatic immigrant groups have already been so far acculturated that the time is now passed for the further development of a distinctive culture based upon their homeland tradition. Consequently the idea of cultural pluralism as concerns groups considered as minorities pertains only to Jews, Indians, possibly to Catholics as a whole, and to the Hawaiian situation. We have suggested that only where the plural groups are of somewhat comparable size, and where the conditions of original contact were such that coordinate status patterns were established at the start, are the prospects for cultural pluralism unaccompanied by dominant-minority relations favorable. Catholics, as such, fulfill the numerical condition although the original contact situation denoted inequality. The Jewish group meets neither of these conditions, nor do the Indians. In Hawaii, the original contact situation helped to develop a pattern of intergroup relations in which explicit forms of segregation were absent.

It is pertinent furthermore to consider the possible effect of the changing aspects of the social class situation in the United States upon the prospects for the assimilation of minorities. We have maintained that the class structure and the dominant-minority structure, although sometimes coinciding at points, are separate. The two structures, however, influence each other. In the past, the rapid expansion of population and flexible character of the class structure have made easier the eventual upward social mobility and assimilation of the noncolored minorities. In the future, the favorable prospects for the integration of remaining minorities into the larger society may be retarded by the growing rigidity of class lines. In a society in which the "rags to riches" dream has come true often enough to make it a widespread aspiration, the frustrations engendered by the tightening class lines may strengthen the will to display superiority over groups identifiable as minorities.

Viewing the dynamic situation in intergroup relations at the mid-century, however, the prospects for increasing movement of ethnic, racial, and religious minorities toward equality in status appears bright. Among the forces and influences operating in this direction, which we have discussed at recurring points, are: (1) the increasing improvement in the welfare of minorities and their increasing acculturation, (2) the continued vitality of the American Creed and of the democratic political institutions which give it expression, and (3) the increasing national self-consciousness of the inconsistency of discrimination in a fundamentally democratic society, stimulated by a realization of its significance in the conflict of ideologies in the international scene, and leading to a redefinition of the problem as vital to the broad national interest.

TOPICS FOR DISCUSSION AND PROJECTS

1. Discuss the thesis that dominant-minority relations are primarily a manifestation of capitalism.
2. If you belong to a dominant status group, analyze your own behavior toward minority people, and try as objectively as possible to explain why you act as you do.
3. If you belong to a minority status group, illustrate from your own experience how dominants discriminate often without apparently being conscious of the fact of their discrimination.
4. Do you think the general interpretation of dominant-minority relations presented in this chapter has assigned the proper weight to the behavior of minorities in the total picture? Expand your position.
5. Which, if any, of the propositions advanced under the heading, "characteristics of dominant-minority relations" in this chapter do you feel is least supported by the materials of the book itself or from any other sources?

SUGGESTED READING

Cox, Oliver C. *Caste, Class, and Race: a Study in Social Dynamics.* Garden City, L. I.: Doubleday & Company, Inc., 1948.
>   *Chapters 21, 22, 23 criticize other theories of race relations especially those of Park and of Myrdal from the viewpoint of the author that race relations are one phase of the capitalistic exploitation of labor.*

Himmelhoch, Jerome. "Tolerance and Personality Needs: A Study of the Liberalization of Ethnic Attitudes among Minority Group College Students," *American Sociological Review*, Vol. 15, No. 1, Jan. 1950, pp. 79-88.

> *A preliminary report on research on factors involved in the development and modification of ethnic attitudes using as subjects students of Jewish background in a metropolitan area.*

Myrdal, Gunnar. *An American Dilemma: The Negro Problem and Modern Democracy*. New York: Harper and Brothers, 1944.

> *In Chapter 3, "Facets of the Negro Problem," and in Appendix 3, "A Methodological Note on the Principle of Cumulation," the author sets forth the main bases of his interpretation of Negro-white relations in the United States.*

Park, Robert E. "The Nature of Race Relations," in *Race Relations and the Race Problem*, Edgar T. Thompson, ed. Durham: Duke University Press, 1939, pp. 3-35.

> *A theory of the race relations based upon the consciousness of difference arising between groups.*

Rose, Arnold, and Rose, Caroline. *America Divided*. New York: Alfred A. Knopf, 1948.

> *Chapter 10 contains a good summary of the various theories of prejudice.*

Schermerhorn, Robert S. *These Our People: Minorities in American Culture*. Boston: D. C. Heath & Company, 1949.

> *Chapter 18, "Minority Patterns of Adjustment," and Chapter 19, "Prejudice and Its Reduction," provide generalizations upon dominant-minority relations and present various theories of dominant prejudice.*

CHAPTER 17

Social Action and
the Minorities Problem

Definition of the problem. A current trend in social science holds that a social situation is not a social problem until a considerable number of people in a society regard it as such and believe that the situation should be changed.[1] We believe that the present minorities situation in the United States is viewed as a problem by wide segments of the American public. Among the groups who conceive a situation as a problem, however, there is usually no uniform opinion concerning the nature of the problem. The varying definitions of the problem reflect the varying value systems of the groups involved. Thus there are those who see the Negro problem as that of keeping the Negroes in their place; others view it as the full assimilation of Negroes into American society; and still others view it as keeping the tensions generated in intergroup antagonism from disturbing the peace of the community. When people think a social situation is a problem, they believe something ought to be done about it, and with varying degrees of intensity they want to do something themselves. Such people often form or join social action groups. We define social action as conscious organized effort by any group to change a present social situation in the direction of the value system of their group.

The social action undertaken by groups may be more or less effective in accomplishing their aims, depending in large measure upon

[1] John F. Cuber and Robert A. Harper, *Problem of American Society* (New York: Henry Holt & Company, Inc., 1948), pp. xii-xviii.

460

the amount of intelligence displayed and the understanding of the social processes involved. What knowledge has social science to contribute to such groups so that they may act with greater effectiveness? A recent survey of the existing knowledge in this respect states: "A dearth of appropriate research and consequent lack of a proved basis of action is one of the conspicuous features of existing intergroup programs." [2] Nevertheless, social science has far more to offer than is ordinarily used, and it is accumulating more knowledge in this field all the time. The purpose of this chapter is to suggest some of the principles of social science and some of the findings of empirical research which social action groups concerned with the problems of minorities can utilize.

Having indicated that groups define the problem in terms of their own value systems, it is difficult to pursue the topic of this chapter except in terms of some one value system. In Chapter 1 we defined our value system in terms of the democratic ideal. We shall presently restate our value frame of reference in more precise terms. There are, however, certain basic sociological principles, now well established, which any social action group, whatever its purpose, must take into account if it is actually to have any results.

Society is both a process of change and a process of order. That social structures once well established have a tendency to continue has been well understood. That social process is inevitably a changeful process has not been as generally recognized. Furthermore, the era in which we now live is extraordinarily dynamic. It is entirely safe to predict that dominant-minority relations 50 years from now will not be just as they are now, whatever social action is taken.

The second basic sociological principle pertinent to the discussion at hand is that the various separate social structures in a given society are interrelated and that changes in one have reactions upon the others. The relationship between these structures is not always harmonious. In fact, in modern societies some of these structures stand in considerable opposition to one another. In general, however, there is a strain toward consistency in the parts of a given culture. This means that each structure can change as a unit only within narrow limits, unless adaptive changes are made within other structures. For example, we have shown the sensitivity of dominant-minority relations to changes in the economic and political spheres. Social action directed at changing the dominant-minority structure in any direction can have

[2] Robin M. Williams, Jr., *Reducing Intergroup Tensions*, Social Science Research Council, New York, Bulletin 57, 1947, p. 8. This report is a summary of the significant research which up to 1947 had been undertaken in the field of ethnic, racial, and religious group relations. The findings are, of course, not definitive but stand as the best operational hypothesis which social science has to offer.

only a limited effect unless corresponding change in other structures is effected.

Four fairly distinct value frames of reference may be seen among the various social action groups in the United States concerned with the minorities problem. (1) The viewpoint of those who believe that the minorities should remain minorities, that the problem is one of keeping them in that status. The Ku Klux Klan is a group which illustrates this viewpoint. (2) The viewpoint of those who hold that the welfare of the depressed minorities should be improved within the framework of segregation, a philosophy followed by some liberal Southerners concerning the Negro problem. (3) A third attitude sees a problem only when tension and hostility between groups disturb the peace of the community through disorderly violence. This is sometimes reflected in the action of mayors' committees. (4) The fourth value frame of reference defines the problem in terms of the American Creed. This last value frame of reference will be adopted for the rest of our discussion.

Social action groups holding the value system of the American Creed believe that all members of the American national society should have equal opportunity. Since discrimination based upon ethnic, racial, or religious lines denies equality of opportunity, the central problem to this group is discrimination itself; and their objective is therefore to eliminate discrimination. Social action groups under the democratic value system stand in stark opposition to those primarily concerned with maintaining discrimination, i.e., holders of viewpoint (1). With the other two groups, the democratic social action group would logically cooperate at times but frequently differ. While the protagonists of the American Creed under certain circumstances support all-Negro housing projects, the kind of project logically favored by viewpoint (2) above, they would more properly sponsor an experimental project in mixed housing. Finally, the American Creed social action group might in periods of crisis and tension support viewpoint (3) above in establishing order through accommodative procedures, but it would maintain that the long range cure for such intermittent crises is to eliminate discrimination.

Planning in relation to crises. We have noted that tension in the relation between dominant and minority groups is characteristic of community life where the numbers of a minority are substantial. Minor incidents of overt interpersonal and reciprocal aggressiveness between individuals from the two groups are more or less daily occurrences. As has been seen, particularly in the dynamic Northern Negro-white situation, given the general tension, altercations between persons or small groups where the contestants are divided along ethnic or racial lines sporadically develop into widespread intergroup rioting. Thus whatever long range action a community may undertake toward the reduction of intergroup tensions, short range plans designed to nip potential riots in the bud are wise. Lee and Humphrey[3] have outlined programs for this purpose based on comparative study of riots in Detroit, Los Angeles, and New York City.

These writers present a detailed chart of community organization for this purpose which also suggests the functions which each group in the plan would perform. (See Chart 3, p. 465.) Their proposals in so far as they are designed primarily to prevent or alleviate crises may be summarized in three parts.

1. *A Constant Systematic Check on Intergroup Incidents.* Facts gathered after riots have occurred often reveal that there was an increased number of small incidents between the two groups before the riot occurred which went unnoticed by authorities. It is possible to devise an index of incidents which could serve as a sort of barometer of the degree of tension. Periodic checking of the items in the index would therefore serve to warn the responsible officials when the tension was rising.

2. *New Accommodative Measures to Reduce Tension.* Having a more specific and regular reading of the intergroup tension barometer affords the opportunity to attempt to reduce the degree of tension in its specific and localized manifestation through new accommodative procedures. For this purpose the auspices of a civic biracial committee, independent of the law-enforcing agencies would be appropriately enlisted. Such a committee should suggest some specific new accommodation and then enlist the support of responsible leaders of both groups in the area for their temporary solution. For example, fights between adolescent gangs of the two groups may be increasing. The biracial committee might propose some additional recreational facilities and the adding of a recreational supervisor who is interested in reducing prejudices.

3. *A Plan if Riot Occurs.* If in spite of all other efforts, a riot gets under way, the city authorities should have a systematic plan to curb it and reduce its spread and momentum. Lee and Humphrey suggest that the state militia or Federal troops should be called upon. This suggestion is based on the Detroit experience where it was clear that in employing force, the police manifested distinct anti-Negro bias and did not act impartially. In many communities, however, it might be possible to bring into police action, officers specially

[3] Alfred M. Lee and Norman D. Humphrey, *Race Riot* (New York: The Dryden Press, Inc., 1943). See particularly Part III, "A Program for Preventing Race Riots."

selected for lack of bias and trained to deal calmly with rioters. Of further usefulness in the riot plan is the employing of media of communication, such as the local radio, or patrol cars with loud speakers, which would provide all areas affected with objective information designed to offset rumors and to give official instruction to citizens. In the Harlem, New York City, riot in 1943, the use by the city's police of as many Negro policemen, military police, and air wardens as were available proved a measure of good judgment.

The plans just outlined comprise accommodative procedures designed to alleviate tension, not to "cure" it. "Cure" involves changes in the attitudes of dominant and minority people toward one another. Since, in Negro-white relations, for example, the antiwhite attitudes held by Negroes are in the nature of a response to the anti-Negro attitudes possessed by the dominating whites, the basic attack should be directed primarily at the dominants. As we turn to consider this more fundamental approach, it may be observed that the major effort of the Civic Biracial Committee in Chart 3 might be directed toward this end, although in order to make such a committee more inclusive, it might well be designated by some such title as "the committee for the improvement of intergroup relations."

Indirect attack upon discrimination. Discrimination may be attacked indirectly or directly. By the indirect attack is meant working to improve the general conditions in society known to breed prejudice and discrimination. Among the more important of these conditions, as seen in our general interpretation in Chapter 16, are: economic depressions and other economic conditions creating substantial downward social mobility; the ever-present efforts of special economic groups to cultivate discrimination for profit; and the failure of certain governmental officials to uphold vigorously and to implement the democratic institutions they are charged with administering. Social action groups interested primarily in reducing minority discrimination should properly support social action aimed at creating the general conditions favorable to nondiscrimination. It is entirely possible that this indirect line of attack accomplishes more than the direct attack.

Direct attack upon discrimination. The reduction of discrimination involves attack upon the two main sources of discrimination. One source is prejudice against the minorities, prompting discriminatory behavior. The other source is the established patterns of social organization which support discrimination, often in the absence of prejudice. The latter source of discrimination is not as well understood as the former. It can be illustrated as follows. Mr. A from Northtown

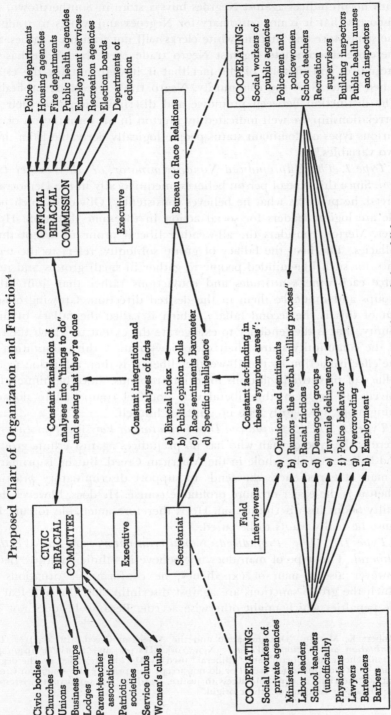

CHART 3

Proposed Chart of Organization and Function[4]

[4] *Ibid.*, p. 123. By permission of the senior author and the publishers.

with no prejudices against Negroes buys a store in Southerntown. He discovers that it is not customary for Negroes and whites to trade in the same store and that his white clerks will not wait on Negroes. He therefore discriminates against Negro trade even though he has no prejudice, and in spite of the fact that if it were not for the established patterns of the community, Negro trade would be profitable. The distinction between prejudice and discrimination and their interrelationship are well indicated by Merton in his formulation of the various types of dominant status people logically derivable from these two variables.[5]

Type I. The Unprejudiced Nondiscriminator, or All-Weather Liberal. Since this type of person believes unequivocally in the Democratic Creed, he practices what he believes consistently. Obviously such people are logical leaders for social action in the same direction. However, Merton considers the all-weather liberal prone to accept three fallacies. The first, the fallacy of group soliloquy, refers to the tendency for such like-minded people to gather in small groups and reinforce each other's attitudes and convictions rather than join other groups and influence them in the desired direction. Growing closely out of this is the second fallacy, which is called the fallacy of unanimity, that is the tendency to exaggerate the extent to which the rest of the community shares their own viewpoint. A third limitation to the effective action by the all-weather liberals is their addiction to the fallacy of privatized solutions to social problems. Since he himself has solved the problem, this liberal may not feel compelled to do anything more. He rightly feels no guilt for himself.

Type II. The Unprejudiced Discriminator, or Fair-Weather Liberal. Here is the type of man who has no prejudices against ethnic groups, and believes on the whole in the American Creed. But he is primarily a man of expediency who tends to support discriminatory practices when it is the easier or more profitable course. He does, however, feel guilty about his discrimination. He is therefore amenable to cure because he really wants to be cured.

Type III. The Prejudiced Nondiscriminator, or Fair-Weather Illiberal. This type of man does not believe in ethnic equality. Being however also a man of expediency, he conforms in situations in which the group sanctions are against discrimination through fear of the penalties which might otherwise accrue. Because he does not be-

[5] Robert K. Merton, "Discrimination and the American Creed," in MacIver, *Discrimination and National Welfare* (New York: Harper and Brothers, 1949), pp. 99-126. The terms "liberal" and "illiberal" used by Merton are based on the degree which the types illustrated accept or do not accept and practice the American Creed, that is, "the right of equitable access to justice, freedom, and opportunity, irrespective of race or religion, or ethnic origin."

lieve in ethnic equality, this illiberal person discriminates whenever the pressure against it is removed.

Type IV. The Prejudiced Discriminator, or the All-Weather Illiberal. This type is the true bigot. He believes firmly that certain minorities ought to be discriminated against and therefore can be counted on to discriminate as thoroughly as he is permitted by the customs and institutions of the community. This type is obviously hardest to change, although the situation varies in relation to the prevailing mores of the area where he lives. Where the mores support his position, he is a conformist, and change means making himself open to community criticism. Where the mores in general are against him, he is a social deviant and here change on his part would draw him closer into the general community structure.

Altering institutions and social organization. Where discrimination arises out of habit alone, in which case the prejudice existing may or may not be conscious, or where as in the Merton analysis cited, it arises out of expediency, it is clear that the alteration of the institutions and prevalent group practices in the community will reduce discrimination. Two of the basic motivations of expedient discrimination are the desire to conform generally to the prevalent norms of group behavior, an aspect of the desire to belong, to be accepted oneself; and the desire for personal economic gain. To the extent that the norms of community group life can be made nondiscriminatory, the individual strongly motivated to social conformity will find it expedient also not to discriminate. To the extent that law can be brought to define discrimination against minorities in the economic field as illegal with penalties imposed upon the violator, it no longer becomes profitable for the person whose primary drive is to make money to discriminate against the minority. The considerable success already achieved by laws against occupational discrimination and new judicial decisions in the cases involving restrictive covenants and educational opportunities well illustrate the value of altering the rules of the game for everybody so that nondiscrimination becomes expedient, does, in fact, pay.

Reducing prejudice. In actual practice, a program to reduce discrimination may well affect both the reduction of prejudice and the alteration of institutions or established patterns of intergroup behavior through which discrimination flourishes. Before taking up the various lines of approach to or attacks upon discrimination, we wish to present some general considerations concerning prejudice.

Prejudices have their genesis in two quite different psychological experiences. They may be acquired early in life through indoctrination from the social surroundings. It is generally held as a result of a number of studies of intergroup situations among young children that they do not manifest prejudice unless they have been taught to do so.[6] The most economical method of reducing prejudice is not to condition one generation of children to it. Realistically we know this cannot be done in any such wholesale fashion since the people who indoctrinate social attitudes in children are in considerable measure prejudiced themselves. This does, however, suggest that insofar as action groups can influence the original conditioning favorable to their purpose it should be a prime consideration. Obviously the public school system is the most strategic place to make large inroads in this connection because it reaches nearly all children and because as a public institution in a democratic society it cannot, in principle, oppose the American Creed.

The other main source of prejudice lies in the needs of the personality. The true bigot, or the all-weather illiberal is a frustrated, insecure person. The nature of his psychological problem and the connection it has with his behavior toward minorities has been elaborated in other contexts. At this point our interest centers upon what can be done about him. For those who are already bigots, it is doubtful if there is much which can be done to change their attitudes. However, the expression of their fanatical prejudices in overt forms of discrimination can be curbed in considerable measure by the firm and alert practice of legal restraints. This will occur, of course, only if the community in general insists upon such action. Outside of certain localized areas, as in the Deep South in relation to Negroes, it is probable that this all-weather illiberal group comprises a numerical minority of all the dominants. Here the legal institutions and the nominal acceptance of the American Creed provide powerful weapons for a persistent social action group to utilize to their advantage.

From a long range point of view, the problem arising from this type of prejudice can be attacked from a preventive viewpoint, through the creation of a generally more stable and secure and less competitive society. At this point, efforts to curb discrimination become linked with the broader efforts to remake society in general.

The lines of activity. There are many lines of activity open to reduce discrimination. Those engaged in social action desire to know what kinds of activities will be the most fruitful. Shall they attack on the educational, legal, or the economic front, or where else? Both Williams and MacIver agree that no single line of approach yields the greatest results at all times. Strategy seems to lie in attacking at all fronts, not

[6] See MacIver, *The More Perfect Union* (New York: The Macmillan Company, 1948), pp. 195 ff.

simultaneously, but in terms of the opportunities and circumstances of the given situation.[7] In the selection of the area to attack, care should be taken to evaluate the reaction which the project will produce in a given time and place. Gains at a certain point may appear less likely to arouse antagonism than at others. The probable antagonisms should be weighed against the importance of gaining the particular point at the particular time. We shall therefore give these lines of activity separate consideration.

Educational approach. The purpose of the educational approach is to prevent the formation of prejudices against minorities, to persuade people not to discriminate, and to gain the support of as wide a public as possible for policies designed to alter the established community patterns of discrimination. As mentioned above, the most useful institution to prevent prejudice is through positive programs in public schools. Since, however, the adult public influences what the schools can do and is most responsible for the existing patterns which now exist, adult education must be part of the program. The content of such a program should aim to educate the public concerning the modern views on race, such as described in Chapter 3, and to bring to the attention of the citizenry the actual situation of minorities in their own community. The latter may well involve a special survey by the group of its community since, outside of such areas as the South where caste has been institutionalized, much of the dominant population does not realize how much it actually discriminates nor has it given thoughtful attention to the consequences. To conduct a really useful survey, the social action group needs the technical assistance of the social scientist, of which we shall speak later.

Groups, however, who carry on educational programs do so with little real knowledge concerning the actual effects of their program. Research in this field has yielded a number of findings which stand today as the best available contributions of social science to guide educational programs. We shall present a number of these findings as illustrations.

It is recommended that propaganda in behalf of minorities should aim to identify the latter's cause with the common welfare.

An effective propaganda approach in intergroup relations is that which emphasizes national symbols and common American achievements, sacrifices, destinies, etc., while unobtrusively indicating the common participation of minority group members.[8]

[7] *Ibid.*, p. 247.
[8] Robin Williams, *op. cit.*, p. 67.

Concerning the effectiveness of various methods of presenting the educational material, a number of pertinent propositions are the following:

. . . straight lectures on the interests, rights, and virtues of the minority groups accomplish very little.[9]

Educational programs will have maximum effects, all other things being equal, when information is presented as part of the ordinary action of a group in carrying out its usual social function (e.g., as part of general teacher training, job training for public officials, conferences of industrialists, labor leaders, merchants, real estate dealers, etc.).[10]

Changing the attitudes of *groups* rather than individuals is the more effective approach for breaking up group stereotypes.[11]

In intergroup relations, as in many others, word of mouth propaganda, especially that which appears spontaneous and informal is more effective than visual or formal propaganda in influencing attitudes and behavior.[12]

Concerning the value of ethical appeals, the following should be noted particularly by those inclined to make idealistic approaches to social problems.

Appeals to conscience or ethics must be carefully handled, if they are to diminish rather than intensify hostility; for example, where individuals are utilizing prejudice to satisfy strong emotional urges, such appeals may heighten psychological conflict and thus result in increasing irrational hostilities.[13]

Finally, the achievements of the minorities should not be overdone.

Propaganda which appeals for minority rights on the basis of the group's achievements tend beyond a certain point to arouse insecurity-hostility in the dominant group by stressing group differences and competitive success.[14]

The legal approach. Concerning the use of law as a means of prohibiting discrimination, there is considerable difference of opinion. It has often been held that the phenomena like that with which we are concerned fall into the class of behavior which is least amenable to control by legal fiat. With respect to law and the minority problem in the United States the first significant point is that the Federal Constitution itself, in general, defines discrimination on the basis of minority background as illegal. However the actual forms of discrimination

[9] *Ibid.*, p. 65. Quoted from Gordon W. Allport, "Catharsis and the Reduction of Prejudice," *Journal of Social Issues*, Vol. 1, No. 3, 1945, p. 6.
[10] *Ibid.*, p. 65.
[11] *Ibid.*, p. 66.
[12] *Ibid.*, p. 66.
[13] *Ibid.*, p. 67.
[14] *Ibid.*, p. 67.

which are illegal are determined only when the court makes its interpretation of each specific form. As we have seen, court rulings have upheld many forms of segregation but have insisted that the facilities should be equal wherever segregation is enforced. In recent decisions, the United States Supreme Court has shown a trend toward narrowing the field of segregation which it will approve as constitutional. Specific interpretations by the court wait upon a complaint. The social action group has here a most concrete mode of action at hand, to see that such complaints are raised and carried through for an ultimate decision. This has been, as previously noted, one of the main functions of the National Association for the Advancement of Colored People.

Local law has at times been at variance with Federal law. Such statutes may stay in force until challenged and carried to higher courts. We have seen also that even where law is specific and consistent and where a general pattern of minority discrimination prevails, the administration of the law tends to be unequal. The social actions group is on firm ground when it challenges the legality of local law and publicizes possible miscarriage of justice through efforts to get legal review of such cases.

With reference to new laws designed to prohibit present forms of discrimination not hitherto prohibited by statute or interpretation of general law, social scientists are in considerable disagreement. It has long been held in principle that where a law is opposed to the prevailing mores of a community, it cannot be enforced. One of the most instructive developments concerning this point has been the experience with new legislation specifically prohibiting discrimination in employment. Without doubt, the states where such legislation has been passed and agencies have been established to enforce it have found law highly useful in widening the area of occupational opportunity for minorities. On the other hand, it is important to note that the states where such legal machinery has been put in motion are those where thus far the patterns of discrimination are relatively weak. As Williams concludes, "Whenever there is sufficient flexibility in public attitudes, the abolition of legal discriminations and disabilities in the long run will reduce hostility and conflict." [15] Thus the usefulness of law depends upon the exercise of judgment in deciding what next move forward can be made without incurring intense reaction to its enforcement which may set back any gains. This is the error which the extreme idealist often makes. The logical next legal move in New England would be quite different from that in Mississippi. The usefulness of new laws against discrimination depends likewise upon the manner in which they are administered. In the state

[15] *Ibid.*, p. 74.

of New Jersey, the Antidiscrimination Division has the power to investigate complaints of discrimination in employment or in the use
of public facilities. If it finds discrimination with respect to employment, it confers with the employer and endeavors to persuade him
to employ the person concerned, if it is still feasible to do so; should it
fail to reach an agreement, it takes the case to court. In actual practice, the agency has been successful in adjudicating most complaints
without recourse to court procedure (see Ch. 11).

Promoting integration. Another avenue of activity for the social
action group is to bring about the association of minority people
with dominant people on a plane of equality in situations where it
has not occurred before or has occurred only occasionally, e.g., on a
job, in a neighborhood, or in a club. If and when a project of this
sort is successful, the results are highly satisfying, for in themselves
they represent a direct reduction in discrimination. The belief is
widely held that desegregation increases friction between the two
groups involved. Increased antagonism does sometimes arise in the
beginning phase of a new integration situation, particularly when the
process is initiated without planning. A number of studies, however,
indicate that once the association of minority persons with dominants
on an equal basis becomes an accomplished circumstance, integration reduces rather than increases intergroup tension. In the Detroit
race riot of 1943, Lee and Humphrey found that "No Negroes and
whites who lived close together as neighbors showed any tendency
to fight each other" and that whites and blacks worked together in war
plants during the height of the rioting without disorders.[16] Deutsch
and Collins studied the changes in white attitudes effected by whites
living with Negroes in an interracial housing project in comparison
with changes in the attitudes of whites living close to a new segregated Negro housing project. Their main conclusion was that in the
interracial project "more frequent and more extensive favorable attitudinal change toward the Negro people" resulted, in comparison
with only slightly favorable change in the attitudes of whites neighboring the all Negro project.[17] However, among those who have had
experience in this type of activity, opinions concerning the best techniques to employ for satisfactory results are far from unanimous. Some
of the difficulties involved can be seen by taking a problem where
considerable experience has been acquired, in the occupational field.

In this field, the integration program aims to place minority people,

[16] Lee and Humphrey, *op. cit.*, p. 17.
[17] Morton Deutsch and Mary Evans Collins, "Intergroup Relations in Interracial
Public Housing; Occupancy Patterns and Racial Attitudes," *Journal of Housing*,
Vol. 7, April, 1950, pp. 127-134. Reprinted in part in *Race Prejudice and Discrimination*, Arnold Rose, ed. (New York: Alfred A. Knopf, Inc., 1951), pp. 555-564.

Negroes, for example, into occupations where they will work alongside of white people in similar functional capacities with the cooperation of management and also of the unions. Shall the company go ahead and gradually place a few individuals in the positions without any discussion or announcement? Or shall a statement be issued announcing that Negroes are going to be so placed, and their prospective co-workers urged to cooperate? Or shall the white workers be polled as to their wishes on the subject, and the decision to go ahead or not be determined by their majority vote? According to Williams, the results thus far indicate that the last of these alternatives is likely to be the least effective. The first can be accomplished if there are relatively tolerant attitudes among the white workers; the second is most effective when the initial attitudes of the whites are strongly prejudiced. Furthermore, if the initiative for the integration of Negroes comes from the management of the company, the workers in the lower ranking levels will accept the new situation better if a top ranking official employs a Negro man or woman in his own department.[18]

Our discussion of the trends in the decade 1940–1950 would lead us to agree with MacIver that the attack upon economic discrimination promises the most immediate and effective results. While suggesting that the placing of Negroes, for example, at the present time in high executive position would meet with great resistance, nevertheless MacIver writes:

. . . But the way from semiskilled labor to skilled labor, from skilled jobs to the responsibility of foremanship, from foremanship to lower executive functions, and so forth, is a gradient that is nowhere too steep to be climbed by successive well-directed advances. Each advance provides an habituation on the part of the dominant group and an experience on the part of the advancing forces that together make the next advance no more or little more difficult than was the one before.[19]

Whether it be in the occupational field, or in the more difficult field of housing and "sociability" situations, projects to integrate minority members into dominant groups require careful planning.

Kinds of social action groups. The groups promoting social action in the field of intergroup relations fall into two general classes: those organized exclusively for this purpose and groups with other primary purposes who undertake action in this field. Both types have a place to fill in the whole program. Because it is their major interest, the intergroup relations organization plays a larger role in the determina-

[18] See Williams, *op. cit.*, p. 73, for a summary of the conclusions on work integration of minorities.
[19] MacIver, *The More Perfect Union*, p. 254. By permission of the publishers, The Macmillan Company.

tion of programs of action and of keeping the interest of the public alive. There may be in fact several groups of this type in the same area, each pursuing somewhat different interests. Some groups are especially interested in the problems of a particular minority. Others are primarily concerned with some phase of the problem. Harold A. Lett, out of his broad experience, comes to the conclusion that the "omnibus" type of organization has relatively little chance to succeed in race relations any more than in other problem areas.[20] The value of several organizations lies in the fact that people like to work in certain areas and will thus join an organization working along lines of their interest. Likewise, people vary in how far they are ready at the moment to go in a given direction. The disadvantages of several organizations lie in the possibility of duplication of function and in the possibility of opposition concerning a specific objective. These disadvantages can be partially offset by coordinating councils or agencies at the national or state level, organized to minimize these possibilities.

It is generally agreed from experience that the action group which is composed of both dominant and minority members has values greater than those composed of one element alone. Dominant status members can usually work more effectively in persuading the dominant community to support the group's program and furthermore, their participation indicates that they consider the problem a general community problem. The minority status members are needed to interpret realistically to the dominant members the actual situation and attitudes of the minority group as a whole. Likewise, the minority status members can interpret to the minority people in general the purposes of the group and promote confidence in the sincerity of the dominant status members. One of the greatest difficulties in this connection is to secure minority status members who adequately represent the minority as a whole. The minority group is frequently divided into factions and often divided into socioeconomic groups whose interests are by no means identical. The action group frequently finds that it is opposed, or only nominally supported, if it permits its membership to be unrealistically representative of the minority community.

Psychological Barriers in Intergroup Work. New recruits among the dominant status group who enter the field of intergroup activity will not find it as easy as they supposed to work with minorities. They will be surprised to discover that there are all kinds of people among the minority group as there are among the dominant group. They will

[20] Harold A. Lett, "Techniques for Achieving Interracial Cooperation," *Proceedings of the Institute on Race Relations and Community Organization*, June 1945, University of Chicago and American Council on Race Relations, p. 38.

be perplexed at the apathy and indifference to their efforts in the minority. They will be hurt when they find that their friendly overtures are often met with rebuffs and suspicion. It takes the novice some time to appreciate the extent to which long experience in encountering discrimination has created a deep-seated resentment in the minority person toward dominant people as a category.

For the beginner in the field of intergroup relations, Margaret Halsey has some practical advice growing out of her rich experience in operating a servicemen's canteen where a strictly nondiscrimination policy was followed.[21]

1. Don't overdo. When you start in to work for improved race relations, pick some goal that you have a reasonable chance of achieving. The integration of the Negro into American society is a job for the long pull. It is foolish to knock yourself out right in the beginning.
2. Don't be surprised when you find jealousy, backbiting, rivalry, and pettiness among your Negro compatriots. These qualities exist among Negroes in about the same degree that they exist among Caucasians.
3. Don't expect to find that all Negroes think alike and agree among themselves as to the best means for their advancement. White people do not think uniformly and in a mass, and neither do Negroes. There are great differences of opinion among Negroes as to what are the most judicious courses for them to pursue, and these differences are sometimes argued hotly.
4. When you first start meeting and working with your Negro fellow citizens, you will probably feel both noble and nervous, in about equal parts. This is uncomfortable, but it wears off.
5. Be prepared to recognize overstrain among your Negro friends or co-workers, if evidences of it should appear. . . .

    Don't however, adopt a Florence Nightingale or Nurse's Aid attitude toward all Negroes. Some Negroes are extremely well balanced and well integrated and show fewer signs of strain than you do.
6. Sooner or later, in every interracial venture, the issue comes up of the Negro who has been rejected for some position or other, because he is not qualified, and who then makes the welkin ring with cries that he has been discriminated against solely for reasons of color. Just as some white people are guiltily benevolent toward the Negro, so some Negroes try to trade on the white man's sense of guilt.

    If, in these cases, it is possible to train or educate or condition the Negro so that he will be suitable for whatever the position is, that should be done. But if there is no way of making him the right person for the place, it is better to stick to your guns, even though the outcry is likely to be terrific. Intelligent and responsible Negroes will respect you for maintaining

[21] Copyright, 1946, by Margaret Halsey. Reprinted by permission of Simon and Schuster, Publishers, pp. 156-159.

standards and not letting yourself be bullied into what, after all, only amounts to empty and unconstructive charity.

7. Don't force equality on Negroes who are frightened by it. Sometimes elderly Negroes, or Negroes just up from the deep South, are more alarmed than gratified by gestures of equality. In these cases don't press the matter. You have fulfilled your obligation by offering equality. If the Negro is too apprehensive to accept it, that is his business. The main job is to see that young Negroes now growing up are not conditioned to be afraid of white people.

Minority cooperation in intergroup activity. We referred above to the functional role of minority membership in the interracial social action group. Here we are concerned in a broader sense with what minority people in general can do to help these efforts succeed. Or perhaps, in view of our discussions above of the impact of minority status upon minority behavior, the question should more properly read, what things can be done by minorities to help their cause?

Dispersion of minorities has been shown to reduce group hostility. In a free society, such dispersion must be voluntary and therefore requiring initiative and cooperation from the minority. There are many practical problems in moving. In the case of a minority there are additional problems of a psychological nature. Like all people, minority people find life quite barren without sociability. They cannot be sure that they will find this if they move as an individual family or in numbers too small to establish a separate communal life if not accepted into the dominant community life. Theoretically, minorities should disperse, but they will not do so in any rapid fashion without more positive assurance that the new communities want them.

Concerning other ways in which minorities can help in the attack upon discrimination, the Social Science Research Council Survey concludes as follows:[22]

A vulnerable minority can itself help to reduce hostility and conflict insofar as there is group control over individual members, by:
  a) educating its members to an understanding of the dominant group's reaction to the minority's values and behavior
  b) careful study of the behaviors of its own members which are regarded as objectionable by other groups
  c) minimizing conspicuous display of traits of marked negative-symbol value
  d) participation *as individuals* in wider community activities which are widely regarded as necessary in the common welfare

Point (a) above is difficult to get over to minority people, especially the less erudite members of the group. We have stressed before that

[22] Williams, *op. cit.*, p. 77.

much of dominant discrimination is the result of habit acquired innocently in childhood. Tolerant understanding of this point is a mark of maturity for the minority individual.

The significance of the italicized words *as individuals* in point (*d*) above is this. In many community enterprises, it is recognized that much good can be accomplished if cooperation from the minority can be improved by having a member of their group on the committee. But as long as such a person merely represents the group, it does little to redefine the status of the group or to break down the stereotype of the group. When a minority person is selected for a community service because of his individual talents for the task, integration has been advanced.

Some steps in local social action work through groups. Persons living in communities where there are no minorities can cultivate and sustain their interest in reducing discrimination by joining and supporting any one of a number of the many national organizations engaged in social action of this kind. Like-minded people in a community where there are minorities can work more effectively by forming a group.

Explore and Define the Local Situation. Unless some other group has surveyed the community fairly recently, it is safe to assume that there does not exist a realistic evaluation of the extent of discrimination. While in fact it would be reasonable to assume that the situation in a given community is characteristic of that of many others with similar minority groups, there is a tendency for each community to feel that it is somehow different. Therefore, the local group needs to prove to the less interested part of the community that a problem exists.

If at all possible, a social action group should procure the technical assistance of professional social scientists before undertaking a survey. Such technicians can aid the group in defining what they want to find out; in planning the procedures to follow in ascertaining the facts; and in tabulating and analyzing the data. Without such assistance, local surveys frequently become a hodgepodge of assorted information, not of great use as a guide for action. But for two matters, a social action group might well have the survey conducted by expert technicians. One is that the local group usually lacks the financial resources to employ such technical assistance; and another, that the interest of local people in the problem of discrimination is increased if they have the opportunity to participate in such a survey, or "audit." Through this process they see for themselves more clearly what the situation is. The values of the self-survey are aptly summarized by Harding in these terms:

A basic assumption of the self-survey method is that many of the people who participate in a survey have a strong belief in the "American Creed" but have not previously done anything about discrimination because either (1) they didn't really believe that discrimination existed, or (2) they felt no sense of personal responsibility for taking action against discrimination, or (3) they saw no effective action which they could take. The self-survey process is designed to make the facts about discrimination seem "real" to the individual survey participant. He feels personally involved with these facts, since he helped to discover them, and this leads to a sense of personal responsibility for doing something about them. This sense of personal responsibility is likely to be reinforced when he starts explaining the survey findings to other people; their usual reaction will be: "Well, now you've found out these things, what do you propose to do about them?" [23]

The survey should be designed with the view to determining the present attitudes of the community toward its various minorities for the purpose of locating the most vulnerable points in the wall of discrimination. Employers often say, "My workers won't work with Negroes"; or restaurant owners repeat, "My customers will desert me if I serve Japanese"—simply because this was rather generally true in the past. Recent experience has shown that in many carefully planned desegregation projects—in schools, in shops and stores, and even in housing projects—the reactions of the dominant people involved are either more neutral or more positively favorable than had been anticipated by the authorities concerned. Defining what are at the present time the most strategically vulnerable points to attack first is a major objective of a community survey.

Action in the Local Community. In a large number of instances, local groups of like-minded individuals who gather to promote better relations between ethnic and racial groups hardly qualify for the label *action* groups. As Merton suggests, often such groups simply meet, discuss their interest, and further educate and inspire one another. The action of other groups is frequently confined to a general education program, including holding of open public meetings, distributing literature, and sending speakers to other community groups to talk on their cause. Commendable as such activities may be as an earnest of the groups' zeal and enthusiasm, there is little evidence to indicate what such activity accomplishes. The trend of events in their community may move in the direction congenial to the group's interests. This circumstance, however, does not prove that their educational activities influenced the trend.

While we consider that the local group which operates on the basis of a recent self-survey of their community is a step ahead of the kinds of groups just discussed, even such a group often confines its action to

[23] John Harding, "Some Basic Principles of Self-surveys", *The Journal of Social Issues*, Vol. 5, No. 2, Spring, 1949, p. 28. By permission.

publicizing its findings to the community in the hope that the story the survey tells will prompt specific changes in the discrimination pattern. In Northtown (the anonymous name of a medium-sized Eastern community where Jews and Negroes are the main minorities) the members of a committee sponsoring a self-survey consider an important change in the employment practices of Northtown's retail stores to have resulted from the survey, although the precise connection between the change and the survey is not clear. At the time the survey was getting under way, the largest department store in the city for the first time hired a Negro salesclerk and two other stores shortly followed suit.[24]

A further step forward in the effectiveness of local human relations groups is indicated when the group proceeds to undertake projects, one at a time, directed at reducing specific discriminations revealed in their survey. The Northtown Committee on Human Relations was headed in that direction two months after their findings had been publicized to their fellow citizens, as the following summary of their plans at that point indicates:

> The Committee on Human Relations started its program with a two-page story in the local newspaper summarizing the findings of the survey and announcing the formation of the action committee. Several months were devoted to planning the activities which were to be undertaken in the effort to end existing discriminatory practices. As the guest of the chairman, I attended the meeting at which the committee decided on its first two projects. One was to break down the barrier against Negro teachers in the public schools. The survey had revealed that only two Negroes were teaching in Northtown. Both were in one school, which had an almost exclusively Negro student body. The committee planned to concentrate on securing the appointment of Negro teachers in schools which were not predominantly Negro. The other project was to be concerned with discrimination against Negroes in the area of public accommodations. The two projects which were to be undertaken initially were purposely limited in scope. The committee expressed the hope of working on one problem after another, always making its objectives as realistic as possible.[25]

Research and Social Action. The discussion in this chapter clearly indicates that activity by social action groups aiming to effect change in dominant-minority relations is a difficult undertaking. As with all social action, people do not participate unless they are motivated with a strong social conscience. But effective action in the field of dominant-minority relations, certainly no less and perhaps even more than in other human relations, requires the professional knowledge and the technical skills which the specialist will have to provide. In

[24] Margot Haas Wormser, "The Northtown Self-survey: A Case Study," *The Journal of Social Issues, loc. cit.,* pp. 19-20.
[25] *Ibid.,* p. 19.

this chapter something of the scope of the insights already acquired by social science pertinent to this field has been indicated. Social scientists are well aware of the need for continuing research to expand the horizon of knowledge in this exceedingly complicated area of human relations. In general, it may be said that research thus far has brought us closer toward the understanding of the conditions which create and sustain prejudices and discriminatory practices. The focus of research interest now deserving encouragement is in the designing of carefully planned experiments in altering these attitudes and practices, and in painstaking evaluation of the results.

Two national organizations serve as coordinating agencies in the field of intergroup relations. The Committee on Education, Training, and Research in Race Relations is under the direction of Louis Wirth at the Universtiy of Chicago.[26] A major activity of this committee is to publish, at intervals, an *Inventory of Research in Racial and Cultural Relations.* The National Association of Intergroup Relations Officials[27] was formed in 1950 replacing the American Council on Race Relations. Its purpose is to provide an informal clearing house for all the activities being carried on in the field of ethnic intergroup relations, particularly those of an official character. The monthly bulletin of this organization, *The Reporter,* affords the opportunity to keep abreast of important developments throughout the nation.

TOPICS FOR DISCUSSION AND PROJECTS

1. If you have ever participated as a member of a social action group interested in any social reform or improvement, describe the activities and program of such a group during the time you were identified with it. How would you evaluate the effectiveness of the group's activity? Advance any judgments you have concerning why it did not accomplish more.

2. Select some delimited local minority situation with which you are familiar. Through interviews with people whom you feel are in a position to know the current situation, try to size up the present situation. Now consider yourself a member of a social action group interested in reducing discrimination. What would you suggest as the first specific project for the group to undertake? Defend your choice of project.

3. What are the limitations of a social action group composed entirely of members of a minority group? likewise, of a group composed entirely of "dominants"?

4. Explain as fully as you can why it is that minority persons do not always participate actively in social action groups and programs aimed at improving their own situation.

[26] Committee on Education, Training, and Research in Race Relations, 4901 Ellis Ave., Chicago 15, Illinois.
[27] Office of President, Maurice B. Fagen, National Association of Intergroup Relations Officials, 260 S 15th St., Philadelphia 2, Pa.

5. Make a list of research projects in the field of dominant-minority relations, the findings of which you feel would be valuable to social action groups interested in reducing discrimination. Draw up a plan for conducting one of these research projects.

SUGGESTED READING

Allport, Gordon W., ed. "Controlling Group Prejudices," *Annals of the American Academy of Political and Social Science*, Vol. 244, March 1946.

Papers on the problem involved and the various agencies and institutions working to reduce prejudice.

Brameld, Theodore. *Minority Problems in the Public Schools.* New York: Harper and Brothers, 1946.

A study of school programs in particular communities designed to improve intergroup relations.

Johnson, Charles S. *Into the Main Stream.* Chapel Hill: University of North Carolina Press, 1947.

A survey of the practices in race relations in the South aimed at adjusting race relations on a basis more consistent with the American Creed and the Christian ethic.

Journal of Social Issues, "Community Self-surveys: An Approach to Social Change," Vol. 5, No. 2, Spring, 1949.

Claire Sellitz and Margot Haas Wormser edit this issue, which is completely devoted to the subject of community self-surveys, citing examples of surveys made, examining the principles involved in the process, and evaluating their effects.

Lett, Harold A. *Techniques for Achieving Interracial Cooperation.*

Proceedings of the Institute on Race Relations and Community Organization, University of Chicago and American Council on Race Relations, June, 1945.

MacIver, Robert M. *The More Perfect Union.* New York: The Macmillan Company, 1948.

Systematic analysis of the problem of reducing discrimination and discussion of the strategy of social action to that end. Analyzes various patterns of techniques for working in the field of dominant-minority relations.

President's Committee on Civil Rights. *To Secure These Rights.* Washington: Government Printing Office, 1947.

Summary findings of an official survey of the extent of discrimination in the United States at the close of World War II, and recommendations for Government action to cope with the problem.

Vickery, William E., and Cole, Stewart G. *Intercultural Education in American Schools.* New York: Harper and Brothers, 1943.

A summary of the posed objectives in this field of education and of the methods by which schools may proceed to achieve them.

Watson, Goodwin. *Action for Unity.* New York: Harper and Brothers, 1947.

Classifies various methods of reducing discrimination and discusses their merits and demerits.

Index of Authors

Index of Subjects

M